AF519699

TEA INDUSTRY
A Road Map Ahead

TEA INDUSTRY
A Road Map Ahead

G.D. Banerjee
Srijeet Banerji

ABHIJEET PUBLICATIONS
DELHI 110094

ABHIJEET PUBLICATIONS
2/46 Tukhmeerpur Extension
Delhi 110094
Phones: 011-22960492, 65698474
e-mail: abhijeetpublication@gmail.com
abhijeet_singh1@indiatimes.com

TEA INDUSTRY: A ROAD MAP AHEAD

First Published 2008

ISBN 978-81-89886-47-9

PRINTED IN INDIA

Published by J.K. Singh fo Abhijeet Publications, Delhi 110094, Lasertypeset by Gaurav Graphics, Delhi and Printed as Himanshu Printers, Delhi.

Dedicated to

Guru Maharaj Revered Swami Bhutesananda,

the 12th World President, Ramakrishna Math and Ramakrishna Mission of Ramakrishna Order, Belur Moth, Hoogly, West Bengal. His continuous inspiration, encouragement etc. have piloted the authors to make this journey possible. Let Guru Maharaj's blessings shower on us.

Dedicated to

The Loving Memory of
Our Father/Grand Father
Dr. Indra Narayan Banerjee
and
Mother/Grand Mother
Chhayarani Banerjee
Both of them left for their Heavenly Abode few months back
Let their Blessings shower on us

Foreword

Tea is an everyday drink for many. Many are enamoured of its taste. However, all may not be familiar with all the aspects of this many splendoured drink. Here is a book that will come handy to all—the connoisseur and the layman alike. The book *Tea Industry—A Road Map Ahead* consists of five parts. Part I classifies the botany of tea, traces the origin of tea leaf, beginning and birth of Indian tea industry, tea trade, formation of tea associations/research institutes and Tea Board etc. Development of tea industry during 1950 to 2007 has been discussed with reference to growth variables. This part has effectively captured the important features of tea industry, primary marketing, development of auction system, auction rules, the qualities that make tea a healthy drinks, rationale of product diversification, switch over from primary to processed goods, value added products (packet tea, tea bags, instant tea), long term strategy for value added items, potential and scope for instant teas, tea powder etc,. Chinese Pu'er tea with its striking qualities, manufacturing black tea, green tea, oolong tea and other teas together with constraints facing the tea industry and possible remedial measure to combat them in the light of cost of production, exports, competition with other countries, supply and demand, quality up gradation etc. Part II confines basically to soil, fertilizers, farming practices, bio-dynamic composting and plant protection of tea. It also covers integrated management of nutrients in soil, bio-organic farming and sustainable tea cultivation along with the harnessing of important elements of nature, like soil, water, air, solar energy in raising tea plantation and utilization of various measures to protect tea crop from pest and diseases. Farming strategies in organic management of tea cultivation, composting in tea plantations, vermi composting in promoting plant growth hormones are some of the aspects that have also been incorporated in this part. Policy liberalization by the government, structural changes of Tea Companies and there impact on rising cost of production and a fall in demand, tuning production system to chaning demand and devising appropriate market strategies are some of the other areas covered in this part. Part III covers taste of various organic products and pruning in tea science (lung pruning, cut-across pruning etc.), use of pruning machine in mature tea field, prevention of environmental pollution, conservation of eco system, managing tea imports, shift from "chemical intensive pest control" to "bio-intensive pest management", prudent labour utilization plan, supervision and tips on efficient management of tea gardens, development initiatives/major highlights etc. Part IV presents major issues addressed by the various tea associations through their annual general meetings or conferences held from time to time, areas of concern to the industry with reference to international and national perspectives with a view to: *(i)* keeping the reader abreast of the latest developments that have been taking place, *(ii)* taking stock of the situation of tea industry in domestic and world markets, *(iii)* suggesting policy prescriptions. Recommendations of Madhukar Committee Report on problems of tea industry with remedial measures have also found place in this part. Part V concentrates on economics of tea cultivation in Kangra Valley, its revival strategy, problems and prospects of small tea growers in Assam and North Bengal with policy prescriptions.

Dr Banerjee is scholar in his field and gained experience both as an academician and a practioner. He served as a lecturer both in college and university levels; worked in UNDP, Global Project; Agro-Economic Research Centre, Visva Bharati, Santiniketan; Rice Research institute, Chunchura, Hooghly, Government of West Bengal; Sundarban Development Board, Development and Planning Department, Government of West Bengal; Tea Board, Kolkata; Uttar Pradesh Development System

Corporation under State Planning Board, Lucknow; National Council of Applied Economic Research, New Delhi etc. At present he is serving as Deputy General Manager (Officer in Charge), NABARD, Nagaland, Regional Office, Dimapur. He was awarded Ph.D. degree from the Jadavpur University, Kolkata; and published six books namely, *(i) Tea Plantation Industry in India between 1850 and 1992—Structural Changes,* 1996; *(ii) Challenges before Small Scale Industries,* 1997; *(iii) The Tea Industry Survey,* 2005; *(iv) Agricultural and Rural Development Policy Agendas in the New Millennium,* 2008; *(v) Sustainable Tea Plantation Management in India,* 2008 and *(vi) Darjeeling Tea—The Golden Brew,* 2008. He also contributed more than 200 papers in reputed journals/national dailies like *Yojana, Kurukshetra, Indian Journal of Agricultural Economics, Indian Journal of Agricultural Marketing, Man and Development, Afro-Asian Journal, Financing Agriculture, Indian Association of Social Science Institutes (IASSI) Journal, Agriculture Today, Waste Land Development News, National Bank News Review, NAB Law, Technical Digest, Suvikalpa, NABCON, NABARD, TAI News Letter, The Assam Review and Tea News, Chai ki Bat, Financial Express, Economic Times, Eastern Mirror, Nagaland Post, North–East Times, India Today* etc. I am sure, the present publication will be useful to not only the academicians and researchers but also to the students, tea companies, tea associations and those involved in tea trade etc. in various capacities.

Srijeet Banerjee, a post-gaduate student in computer science, Mumbai University is associated with the monumental task and helped in many ways for completing this work. His knowledge in computer science has facilitated to get momentum to give proper shape to the book.

With these few words, over to the readers, for the rest, let the book speak (or whisper into their ears) for itself.

Krishanjit Basu

Former Member, the Reserve Bank of India Service Board
Former Director, Bankers Institute of Rural Development and
Former Executive Director
National Bank for Agriculture and Rural Development.

Preface

The book *Tea Industry—A Road Map Ahead* consists of five parts. Part I defines the nomenclature, classification and botany of tea and the processing technology. It traces the origin of tea leaf, beginning of tea in India, birth of Indian tea industry, tea trade, formation of tea associations and research institutes, implementation of internation tea regulation scheme and tea agreement, enactment of tea control acts, its amendment and establishment of Tea Board etc. Further, role of plantation industry, placement of tea in India and World with reference to area, production and export, value of exports to total value of exports, ratio of tea labour to total labour employment, share of tea revenue to total revenue and tea as a supporter to allied activities have been discussed. Features of tea industry—farming & manufacturing, geographical location, primary marketing, exports, taxes and duties on tea in India, average daily labour employed, labour per hectare, production per labour have been deliberated. Growth of tea industry during 1950 to 2007 and factors responsible for such development, tea marketing, modes of disposal, development of auction system, auction rules, Ahuja Committee report, tea market trends (production, domestic and export), import of tea, healthfulness of tea, marketing of Indian tea—domestic versus export have been outlined. Interestingly, the rationale of product diversification, switch over from primary to processed goods, value added products, direction of packet tea export regionwise, export of tea bags, direction of tea bag regionwise, value added concept, forms of value addition, sharing of value added teas, instant tea and its development, incentives of value added teas, problem of value added instant tea, long term strategy of value added items, potential and scope for instant teas, tea powder etc. have been analysed with reference to data and relevant perspectives. Agro-technology, health aspects of tea, Chinese pu'er tea with miraculous functions, manufacturing black tea, green tea, oolong tea and other teas, world production, export and imports of green tea and importers of green tea have been incorporated. Besides current tea trends, (which include growth rates of area, production, yield and export of tea during 1950–1960 to 2000-2005), present status on research and development of tea, approach to tenth five year plan, new proposal for research during tenth five year plan, export market and competitiveness have been thoroughly examined. Constraints and remedial measure for tea in the light of cost of production, exports, competition with other countries, supply and demand, quality upgradation and product diversification schemes, market promotion, research and development, mothers club, demonstration plot & trial plantation, quality awareness, welfare measures, progress of recent technique of tea cultivation, production target in tenth plan period, FAO's projection for import of black tea, strategies of the tenth five year plan. This part includes six chapters (Ist to 6th).

Part II deals with Soil, fertilizers, farmings, bio-dynamic composting and plant protection of tea. In this part six chapters (7th to 12th) have been covered. Efforts have been made to focus on the Integrated Management of Nutrient of Tea Soil, which envisages three dimentional approaches like human, natural and cosmetic resources. Similarly, bio-organic farming in tea and principles of bio-organic fertilizers in tea state cold coverage in the area of tea, jumping the boundary—tea in its new avatar, sustainable tea farming and production of a prime quality of tea, soaring cost of inputs of tea, philosophy of revival of bio-organic tea, objective of bio-organic farming of tea, the transition to bio-organic farming, organic tea to boost exports, principles of bio-organic farming in tea, elemental energies of natural soil, water, air, solar energy and other in tea farming. Integrated management of plant protection in tea farming referes to utilization of various measures to protect tea crop from pest and diseases, inherent control by nature and applied control, classification of insects in three groups mainly harmless insects, beneficial insects and injurious insects. Further, attempt has been made to elaborate the area of pests, class of pests, behavious of pests and natural control measures. Physical, cultural, biological and herbal control measures have been properly dwelt upon. Farming strategies in organic management of tea cultivation, input-process-output, organic farm design and management, principle of organic/sustainable vs conventional approach, biodynamic composting in tea cultivation, digested biomas and organic matter—the composting process, composting in tea plantaions, vermi composting in plant growth harmones are some of the aspects that have been incorporated in this part. Liberalization policy of Indian tea company and international matchmaking business partnering elaborate actual liberalizing measures of government, structural changes of tea company and its impact on rising cost of production and a fall in demand, tuning production system to world demand, setting up of production and market activities etc. In recent decades, industrialized countries have developed a number of direct instruments to help their national companies to become active in the developing world. In matchmaking and similar business partnering programme, the sponsoring organization generally provides technical and financial assistancde to private sector finance in order to foster cooperation and help the companies to develop a profitable relationship. This aspect has been documented with reference to programme for cooperation with emerging markets (PSOM), Public Private Partnership (PPP) run by German Technical Agency, GTZ (Gesellschaft for Technische Zusammananbeit), Norwegian Aid Agency, NORAD and DANIDA Private Sector Development (PSD). This part illustrates Darjeeling Tea—some uniqueness and aspects of orthodox manufacture. It showcases the arts of plucking, manufacturing, tasting, tasting procecdure, tea glossary, definition of Darjeeling Tea, different flavours associated with Darjeeling tea etc. Manufacture of good orthodox tea and factors responsible for such tea like quality of raw materials, good plucking, pruning percentage; transportation of green leaf, withering (uniform and slow), rolling, fermenting, humidification, bacterial growth, drying, sorting, stalk picking and bulking of tea have been placed in this chapter.

Part III takes into account three chapters (13th to 15th). Taste for organic products and pruning in Tea Science have been slated in Chapter 13. In this chapter efforts have been endeavoured to ink the picture of international trade in organic products, strong growth potentials, consumer awareness of health and environmental issues, introduction of new standard of agricultural production, risk factors, opportunities for developing countries—products of tropical, off season, in season and novelty/speciality in nature, trade with certified partnor, market entry, tips for developing countries. Pruning is most important agricultural practices. It governs frame development and sanitation, controls plucking table height and rejuvenates or stimulates vegetative growth etc. A detailed discussions on lung pruning replaced by cut-across pruning, use of pruning machine in mature tea field have been made. Tea being eco-friendly industrty contributes to promote and sustain tea industry. In recent past, agreement regarding coal briquette as alternative fuel in place of fire wood is a land mark in preventing environmental pollution. Environmental law, conservation of eco system in tea industry and managing tea imports have also been documented in Chapter 14. Of late tea gardens are required to obtain letter from pollution Board for operating strictly as per provision of section 25 and 26 Prevention and Control of Pollution Act, 1974 and Section 21 of Air (Prevention and Control of Pollution) Act provision. Further, change over from "Chemical Intensive Pest Control" to "Bio-intensive Pest Management" has taken place in tea gardens as per guidance and specification of Tea Research Institute. The issues in relation to conservation of eco-system in hill areas, prevention of tillage farming on the slopping farm lands, desirability of sustainable farming of slopping land are identified with remedial measures in this Chapter. Managing tea import has squarely been debated in this chapter. It suggests prudent labour utilization plan, supervisory management of tea gardens, development initiatives, major highlights and tips on efficient management of tea gardens.

Part IV envelopes four chapters (16th to 19th). Chapter 16 presents major issues, which have been addressed by the various tea associations through their annual general meetings or conferences from time to time. Here agenda items of United Planters' Association of Southern India; Calcutta Tea Traders Association; Tea Association of India etc. together with probable strategies have been documented. Chapters 17 and 18 devote to major areas of concern with reference to International and national perspectives. These have been collected from various reputed international and national journals, magazines like *India Today, Business World, Agricultural Today,* periodicals and national dailies. All these have been updated and placed. The basic objectives of introducing these two chapters are to: *(i)* make the reader abreast of the latest developments that have been taking place, *(ii)* suggest policy prescriptions, and *(iii)* take stock of the situation of tea industry in domestic and world markets. Chapter 19 draws attention on the rationale of setting up of Madhukar Committee for addressing the problems of tea industry with remedial measures. The salient features of the committee report have also been penned in this chapter.

Part V concentrates on three chapters (20th to 22nd). Chapter 20 aims at working out economics of tea cultivation in Kangra Valley with primary data. Endeavours have been exercised to: *(i)* outline the back ground of the valley, *(ii)* trace the research efforts, *(iii)* estimate cost, gross income and returns per farm and per hectare, and *(iv)* calculate break even analysis. The marketing of Kangra tea is beset with problems like absence of product diversification, fall in tea output, poor quality of green leaf. Attention has been drawn on the weakness of the industry with probable opportunities like use of tea waste and development of product from such waste, eco-friendly or organic tea, health aspects of tea. Chapter 21 evolves the revival strategy of Himachal Pradesh Tea Industry. While mapping such strategy all probable aspects have been dwelt upon. These are replacement planting, filling up of vacancy, cultural practices, development initiatives like launching of business development cells, formation of farmers' club, commencement of rural entrepreneurship programme (REDP), establishment of self help groups (SHGs). Further, future policies of state government such as introduction of latest technologies, optimum utilization of land resources to encourage value addition, increase in employment opportunities in tea through further commissioning of processing units, and extending green cover of barren or fallow lands. Management of tea gardens, quality upgradation, weeding out substandard tea, shortening of pruning cycle, are some of the policy prescription suggested in this chapter. Chapter 22 intends to mention problems and prospects of small tea growers in Assam and North Bengal. Concept of small tea cultivation, socio-economic profile of selected borrowers of Assam, field practices and cultural operations of sample tea estates like variety, land preparation, manuring, fertilizing, pruning, weed and pest control, irrigation, drainage, harvesting and post harvesting have been discussed. Infrastructure support, credit flow, inputs, cost of cultivation, marketing, role of tea planters in development of Assam tea, rationale for bitter taste of Assam tea are some of the aspects which have been mentioned in this chapter. Besides, some of weaknesses of the industry have been analysed with reference to sample study. Based on the findings of these primary data recommendations and policy prescriptions have been suggested.

We are grateful to Professor Emeritus, Dr Ashok Rudra, who left for heavenly abode, for his continuous guidance. We could have given the best tribute to him, if the publication could have been brought out in his life time. We are indebted to our father/grand father, Dr Indra Narayan Banerji, and our mother/grand mother, Smt Chhaya Rani Banerji, both of them expired few months back, for their inspiration. Thanks are due to Smt Sikha Banerjee and Smt Sarda Banerjee MA (Eco), B.Ed. wife/mother and dauguther and sister, free lance writer and teacher, respectively for rendering help in many ways. We are obliged to Abhijeet Publications for bringing out such a treatise. We are confident that the book will be immensely useful to students, academicians, policy makers, tea practitioners, tea companies, research institutes, universities, tea auctioneers, and others involved in tea cultivation, processing, value addition, trade etc..

G.D. Banerjee
Srijeet Banerji

Contents

PART II
SOIL FERTILISER, BIO-DYNAMICS, COMPOSTING AND PLANT PROTECTION OF TEA

PART III
ORGANIC PRODUCTS, PRUNING TEA SCIENCE, LITTLE-KNOWN FACTS OF TEA, ENVIRONMENTAL LAW, CONSERVATION OF ECO-SYSTEM, EFFICINT MANAGEMENT PRACTICES ETC.

PART IV

REDRESSAL ISSUES OF TEA INDUSTRIES, ISSUES OF TEA INDUSTRY IN NATIONAL AND INTERNATIONAL PERSPECTIVES, REPORT OF WORKING GROUP OF TEA INDUSTRY

PART V

CASE STUDIES ON TEA INDUSTRY

PART 1
AN OVERVIEW OF TEA INDUSTRY

Nomenclature, Classification, Botany and Processing Technology of Tea; Origin of Tea Leaf and Role of Tea in Indian and World Economy; Facets of Tea Industry; Growth of Tea Industry during 1950 to 2007 and Factors Responsible for such Growth; Tea Marketing, Modes of Disposal, Development of Auction System, Auction Rules, Ahuja Committee; Product Diversification and Value Addition; Agro-Technology and Health Aspect; Chinese Pue'r Tea—Tea with Miraculous Functions; Chinese Method of Manufacturing Black Tea, Green Tea, Oolong Tea and Other Teas, World Production, Exports and Imports; Current Tea Trends, Export Markets and Competitiveness; Constraints, Remedial Measures and Approach to Tenth Five Year Plan etc.

This part covers six Chapters. Endeavours have been made in this part to deal with the nomenclature, classification, botany and processing technology of tea. Tracing the history of tea industry by covering evolution of tea leaf, beginning of tea in India, birth of Indian tea industry, tea trade, formation of tea associations and tea research associations, implementation of international tea regulation scheme, imposition of tea control act and its amendments, establishment of tea board, the role of plantation industry, tea in agriculture and industry have been analysed. India's place in world of tea in terms of area, production, exports, foreign exchange, employment, revenue etc. have been discussed in detail. Aspects like facets of tea industry, which cover farming and manufacturing, geographical locations, primary marketing, exports, internal consumption, taxes and levies both central and state governments, imports, labour (average daily number of labour, labour per hectare, out put per labour) etc. have been included in this part. Efforts have been attempted to analyse the growth of the industry with reference to various parameters during pre and post plan period (1850 to 2007) together with factors responsible for such growth. Primary marketing of tea, modes of disposal, development of auction system, auction rules, rational of product diversification, forms of value addition, value added teas, price differentials, black teas, green teas, Oolong teas, and other teas have been incorporated in this part. Current tea trends, which take into account rate major growth variables, present status on research and development of tea, approach to tenth five year plan, new proposals in the tenth five year plan, have been outlined. Constraints and remedial measures for tea in the light of cost of production,exports, competition with other countries, supply and demands, quality upgradation, product diversification scheme, market promotion, mothers clubs have been analysed with relevant perspectives and data base.

1

Nomenclature, Classification, Botany and Processing Technology of Tea; Origin of Tea Leaf and Role of Tea in India and World

Nomenclature, Classification, Botany

Tea (*Camellia sinensis* (L). O. Kuntze) is a highly heterozygous and outbreeding crop, exhibiting great diversity with form and shape. The scientific description as well as nomenclature dates back to the early part of the eighteenth century. Tea plant is broadly classified as Assam, China and Cambodia types. The scientific nomenclature is as follows:

A. The China Plant	:	*Camellia sinensis* (L),
B. The Assam Plant	:	*Camellia assamica* (Maston)
C. The Cambodia plant	:	*Camellia assamica sul* sp. lasiocalyx (Planch. M.S.)

Flora Biology and Embryology

The morphological vegetative organs of tea plant are affected by the parent plants and environmental conditions but flora characteristics are relatively stable and provide reliable basis for specific identification. There is significant difference in flora characteristics between Chinese and Assam tea varieties.

For example, in length of style and style arm; the number and length of outer stamens; size of inter petals etc.

Pollination—Artificial/Hand Cross

Tea plants show an appreciable degree of self sterility and invariably set a better crop of seeds with pollen from another bush nearly four times that of self-fed seeds. With efficient cross transfer of pollen, more than 3 per cent of total seeds formed will be self fertilized Healthy flowering branches are chosen for artificial pollination. To avoid contamination, open flowers and immature fruits are removed.

Genetics

Cytology: Chromosome number is the basic criterion for differentiation between species. Cytological investigation on tea studies the somatic chromosome of different species and varieties which show a constant number (2n = 30).

Inbreeding: Continuous inbreeding of a cross pollinated crop species increases homozygosity. Homozygous diploids are of immense importance in plant improvement particularly in crops like tea where genetic study is scanty.

Compatibility: A study conducted by TRA, Tocklai revealed that the degree of self-incompatibility was generally prominent in China and Assam varieties than in Cambodia. The inbred progenies in all the varieties also showed segregation of characters with loss of vigour which was maximum for China plants.

Inheritance: Because of non-availability of homogenous lines, most of the characteristics of tea are polygenic in nature. The pattern of inheritance is quantitative. Observations on the inheritance of yield in biclonal crosses showed that positive correlation existed between mean yield of parents and progenies in crosses involving widely different clones. But the relationship broke down when morphologically similar clones are used.

Development in Plant Improvement

Mass Selection: Seeds were the only source of propagating

tea during the early years of tea cultivation. The first scientific attempt to select inputs in North East India was made in 1860 by establishing standard sources of tea seeds. The seeds from the particular seed garden were known by the name of that garden or locality and was called JAT.

Selection Criteria for Yield and Quality: Initial selection was done based on visual characteristics of a plant like leaf and branching pattern. The size of leaf is directly proportional to its weight. The yield of a tea bush is the product of the number of shoots multiplied by weight of individual shoots. Further, area of plucking surface, density of plucking points and weight of prunings are responsible for yield.

The following morphological characters related to quality are used for selections:

(a) Pubescence: It is the amount of hair on the under surface of a young leaf. It has been found to have a significant relation with quality of black orthodox tea in various parts of the world. However, no correlation could be observed between pubescence and CTC.

(b) Colour of Leaf: A better tea quality was produced by light green leaved type. For liquor, colour and strength, over quality and flavour, light-leaf sections were better than dark leaf ones.

(c) Anatomical Character: Three factors which have an influence on quality and strength are pubescence, phloem index and vascular index. In general, only high values of vascular index are associated with the desirable combinations of big bushes with high yield per unit of bush surface and better response to fertilizers.

(d) Clonal Vs. Seed Propagation: The seed grown plants are not uniform as their characteristics were governed by genotypes of their parents and soil conditions. In some cases, yield and quality were unpredictable. But, as the planters want a uniform plantation both for morphological features and quality, tea plants were propagated vegetatively. These were propagated by means of layering, budding or grafting on root stocks to obtain seed gardens on selected bushes. The standardization of the technique of single leaf

internode cuttings, practiced today, took a long time to be successful.

(e) Selection Procedures/Criteria: In view of the commercialization of tea, planting materials have been developed and selected from the desired plant material. In recent years the extent of improvement has been slowed down due to lack of reliable selection criteria. Various morphophysiological markets have already marginally improved for desired agronomic trades as they are greatly influenced by environmental factors. Selection may be improved to a large extent using cytological, biochemical and/or molecular markets linked to various desirable agronomic characters. The factors which contribute to the quality are improved controllable practices like field, cultural and factory operations, the genetic input, non-controllable environmental factors and their interactions with genetic factors.

Agroclimatic Conditions of Tea Growing Regions

In India tea is concentrated in two widely separated regions in the North East and South India. In addition, tea is grown in a limited area in Kangra (Himachal Pradesh), Tripura and Dehradun Valleys (Uttaranchal). In recent years tea has also been introduced in some non-traditional areas like Arunachal Pradesh, Meghalaya, Nagaland, Mizoram, Manipur, Sikkim, Orissa and Bihar.

North East: Tea growing areas in this region lie between 24 and 27 latitude and 88 and 95 longitude. Tea growing areas can be divided among several distinct regions viz. Brahmaputra and Barak Valley in Assam, North Bengal Plains of Dooars and Terai as well as Darjeeling Hills. In the Brahmaputra valley, tea is grown on both the banks of the river on flat land between 50 and 120 m (160-400 ft) above Mean Sea Level (MSL). In South India, tea area lies between 8°C and 13°C on the slopes of Western Ghat mountains and adjoining plateaus at elevations ranging from 800 to 2000 MSL. Some tea areas are, however, situated above or below this. Climatic conditions of different tea districts are given below:

Table 1: Climatic Conditions of Tea Growing Districts of India

Tea districts	*Location of Meteorological Stations*	*Average Rainfall (mm)*	**Wet Months (Nos.)*	*Range of mean monthly temp. Max (°C)*	*(°C)*
North East India Including North of West Bengal					
Assam Valley	Jorhat	2642.10	8	32.60	8.30
Cachar	Silcoorie	2994.60	8	32.20	10.60
Dooaras	Nagarkata	3956.70	7	31.00	10.40
Terai	Gunagaram	3178.00	7	32.20	8.90
Darjeeling	Nagri Farm	2371.70	7	24.90	7.70
Kangra (Himachal)	Palampur	2667.40	8	29.40	4.90
South India					
Annamalai	Cinchona	3686.30	8	29.30	11.50
C. Travancore	Vandiperiyar	1145.00	5	31.60	13.40
High Ranges	Munnar	3843.00	7	25.00	5.90
Karnataka	Durgabetta	2914.00	6	33.90	11.10
Nilgiris	Coonoor	1452.00	6	25.40	9.50
Nilgiri Wyanaad	Gudalur	1782.00	6	40.00	7.00
Wyanaad	Meppadi	22.30.7	5	32.90	148.00

Source: Global advances of Tea Science 96,* wet months: rainfall > 90mm per month.

Field and Processing Technology-The Changing Trends Over The Years

Field Technology: From the beginning, improvements in field cultivation practices and processing technology have been a direct result of research activities of the Tocklai Experimental Station, Jorhat, Assam and United Planters' Association of South India (UPASI), Tea Research Institute, Tamil Nadu. Subsequently, the Council of Scientific and Industrial Research (CSIR) Institute of Himalayan Bioresource Technology in Palampur, Kangra, Himachal Krishi Vishwa Vidyalaya, Assam Agriculture University, Jorhat, Tea Board's Darjeeling Research Centre at Kurseong and Tea Husbandry Department at North Bengal University played important roles in this regard. Further, Research Centres were also started by Tata, Goodricke Tea Company etc. Various important agro-techniques developed in plucking, pruning, shade, soil management with emphasis on drainage and conservation have indeed made a tremendous impact on increase in tea crop production and yield.

Manuring: To begin with, nitrogen alone was used as fertilizer in tea in the form of ammonium sulphate which turns soil highly acidic in due course. Urea was later introduced. The importance of potassium as a key element was recognized when widespread potassium deficiency caused defoliation on a large scale. Liberal application of NPK fertilizer has increased the uptake of other essential micro-nutrients from the soil. The concept of balanced nutrients to counteract deficiency of micro nutrients was introduced in tea cultivation. Foliar application of micro nutrients such as zinc, manganese is presently done on a regular basis under specific conditions. The prolonged application of urea is likely to exacerbate 'sulphur deficiency' in tea plants. Sulphur is likely to become a major nutrient in fertilizer schedule. The application of SOA for long term has turned the soil over acidic and this is being rectified by the application of lime or dolomitic lime.

Research and Development: Research on tea has contributed very significantly towards the scientific development of the tea industry. Major R&D breakthroughs provided by Tocklai Experimental Station during different periods are summarized below:

1950's : Shade, N-fertilizers, McTear's Rotorvane;

1960's : Longer pruning cycles, chemical weed control, use of organophosphates, Continuous Tray Drier, Barbora's Fifties. Continuous Leaf Conditioner, catchment planning;

1970's : Drainage, K-manuring, herbicides, infilling and consolidation, plant population, Barua Continuous Roller, high-yielding clones and hybrid biclonal seeds;

1980's : Balanced NPK manuring, synthetic pyrethroids, high-yielding clones and new hybrid seeds, optimum plant population, young tea management package, Tea Breaker cum Separator, Green Leaf Storage System.

In recent times, Tocklai Experimental Station at UPASI (Tea Research Foundation) TRF has been concentrating on the following research areas:

(a) Breeding & selection	: Development of superior clones and seed stocks;
(b) Tissue culture	: Micropropagation and genetic engineering;
(c) Pruning	: Rejuvenation and consolidation, bush architecture;
(d) Plucking	: Mechanical aids;
(e) Tea physiology	: Photosynthesis, respiratory loss, growth promoters and biogenetic pathways;
(f) Microbiology	: Identification of microbes and role of nutrient metabolism, bio-fertilisers;
(g) Nutrition	: Need-based study of macro and micronutrients;
(h) Pests and diseases	: Bio-control and integrated pest management systems;
(i) Tea chemistry	: Quality parameters, increased cuppage and pharmacokinetics; and
(j) Tea manufacture	: Microprocessor based electronic monitoring and process control system.
(k) Health aspects of tea	: Helps in arresting cardio attack, skin diseases etc.
(l) Manufacturing of Tea	: Network programming on automatic and integration in manufacture of tea starting from withering to sorting of dried tea.

(m) Irrigation	: Studies of different irrigation systems and critical evaluation of secondary and micro nutrient status of tea soils in South India.
(n) Studies	: Studies on residues of insecticides, fungicides, weedicides and heavy metals in South India.
(o) Bio-technology	: Bio-technological and bio-control studies on tea blister and pathogen.
(p) Processing	: Optimisation of processing parameters to maximize the quality of South Indian Tea.
(q) Quality Testing	: Establishment of chain of quality testing laboratories and strengthening of existing analytical facilities of Regional Centres.
(r) Product Diversification and Value added items	: Development of technologies for product diversification and value additional.

Development of South Indian Tea has been possible due to R&D breakthroughs and adoption of new technologies at UPASI Tea Research Institute. Nutrition of potassium and zinc, control of blister blight by specific fungicide, control of short-hole-borer, rejuvenation pruning and no tillage replantation etc. are some of the time tested practices developed by the Institute. Amongst the more important recommendations of recent origin are routine hormone formulations and nursery grafting of fresh cuttings, biclonal seed stock, partial mechanization of harvesting, leaf expansion concept in programming, plucking intervals, organic systematic fungicides etc. The use of ultra violet rays to improve processing quality is a major break through.

Thrust Area in Tea Research: The tea industry in India needs an integrated research strategy. The thrust of future research should be on specific technical needs which include: *(i)* Plant improvement, *(ii)* Plant nutrients, *(iii)* Water management, *(iv)* Applied physiology, *(v)* Improvement of tea quality and flavour, *(vi)* Biological control of pest diseases, *(vii)* Modernization and automation of tea factories, and *(viii)* Alternative uses of tea.

Origin of Tea Leaf and Role of Tea—India and World

History of Tea Leaf

The origin of the tea bush has been contested by scholars. It is native to certain areas ranging from the interior of Southern China to the border of Assam. Tea has only one species which is called *Camellia sinensis* ((L.)O. Kuntze). It came to the light in fourth century. By about 650 A.D. during the Ts'ang dynasty the growing popularity of tea induced farmers in most provinces in China to cultivate Tea and subsequently it became an article of commerce. In the early years of 780 A.D., Lu Yu commissioned the first book on tea entitled "*Chaching*" a tea classic. The first printed reference by a European writer about the mysterious Chinese drink was dated to 1559 A.D. The knowledge of tea travelled slowly from East to West. The Dutch Merchants established a trading base at Benton by 1596. The first consignment of tea from China was transported to Benton in 1606 and from there it was shipped to non-tea-conscious Europe. By the mid-1650s, a quick brisk trade in tea was made with Holland. In France, the future of tea was linked with the Sterling Company.

Beginning of Tea in India: The discovery of indigenous tea in Assam in 1823 led to the origin of the tea industry in India. However, the Kolkata Agricultural Society differs from the above opinion. It has consistently held that in the early 1700's, the ships of the East India Company frequently brought the tea plants in the country by way of curiosity. Col. Kyd, a resident of Kolkata and a famous botanist, saw tea plants growing in his garden in 1780. This information was sent to Sir Joseph Bank and in 1782 his garden was handed over to Botanical Garden of Kolkata. In 1788, Sir Joseph Bank recorded the existence of indigenous tea growing wild in Coochbehar and Rangpur districts of Bengal and suggested the cultivation of this plant. The wild teas of Coochbehar confirmed the first discovery of indigenous tea in India.

Birth of Indian Tea Industry: The birth of Indian tea industry was marked by the discovery of indigenous tea plant in Assam in 1823 by Robert Bush. This received momentum when the East India Company in 1833 lost the tea trading monopoly in China. In 1835, a scientific deputation was sent to Assam to report on prospects of the tea industry and the team saw tea plants in many parts in the hills between Assam and Burma. In 1836, C.A. Bruce was made the Superintendent of Tea Forests. Among others, he formed the Bengal Tea Company at Kolkata with the objective of purchasing the produce from the East India Company's tea plantations in India. A similar Company was also established in the same year in London with the same objectives.

In 1839 the first consignment of tea from India (eight chests) was shipped to London and it was auctioned at a price ranging from six to thirty four shillings per pound. In 1840, two thirds of experimental teas were handed over to new company. In 1852, the first tea company in India paid its final dividends. The second limited company in 1859 was formed in Assam called Jorhat Company. During 1862-67, tea cultivation started in Chittagong and Chotta Nagpur. Ultimately tea cultivation was commissioned in many districts in India wherever there was some hope of a success. Within a few months, India along with Sri Lanka dominated the world tea trade/market.

Tea Trade: In 1874 the land located in the east of Teesta river was explored with the foreign liability of growing tea plants. By 1876 as many as 13 gardens had started cultivating tea. In 1878 the first two Indian tea gardens by name Megalkat Tea Estate and Indian Tea Company Ltd. were established though the Company actually received a grant of 741 acres on 19 March 1981. The first tea auction started on May 26, 1841 in London under the pioneering leadership of Lyal & Co., Mincing Lane, London was the centre of World Tea activities prior to World War II. The first tea auction in Kolkata in December 27, 1861 and the second in

Cochin in 1947 for South Indian teas were held. Subsequently, many tea auction centres were opened in Coonoor, Guwahati, Amritsar, Siliguri etc.

Formation of Tea Association and Tea Research Association: The Tea planters formed an association named Indian Tea Association (ITA) in 18 May 1881, with its headquarters at Kolkata for promoting their common interest and objectives. Subsequently many associations were formed in various tea regions of North and South India. For greater interest of the industry, the Tea Research Association was established in 1964 at Tocklai, Assam and was funded jointly by Council of Scientific and Industrial Research (CSIR) and Tea Board of India. Subscriptions of member tea estates and other associate members were called for to carry out the research work. United Planters Association of South India (UPASI) Tea Research Institute had its origin in the year 1926 at Coimbatore District, Tamil Nadu.

International Tea Regulation Scheme and Tea Agreement: During the second half of the 19th century and first half of the 20th century, four major slumps (1866,1879, 1896-1904, and 1920) took place. To counteract the situation India, Sri Lanka, Netherlands and East Indies reached an agreement on voluntary basis to curtail tea production. The world economic depression resulted in decline in tea consumption and stocks continued to pile up till 1932. Producing countries like India, Indonesia and Sri Lanka entered into an agreement on April 1, 1933 for a period of five years to bring about balance between supply and demand for tea in the world market. A second agreement was signed and came into force for a further period of five years i.e. 1st April, 1938 to 31 st March, 1943. The agreement was extended upto 31st March, 1948. Further an interim agreement was signed in April, 1948 and continued till 31st March, 1950.

Tea Control Act, its Amendment and formation of Tea Board: The Indian Tea Control Act 1933 was amended in 1938 and 1943, and subsequently in 1950. The administration of the Act in 1938 was vested in a Committee called "Tea Licensing Committee" which consisted of a Chairman appointed by the Central Govt. and 14 other members of which 10 were nominated by the Industry and 04 elected from the constituencies embodied in the Act. The Committee continued upto 31st December 1949. Both the Central Tea Board Act 1949 and Indian Tea Control Act 1938 were replaced by the Tea Act 1953, which came into effect from 01st April 1954. The functioning of the Central Tea Board and Indian Tea licensing committee were entrusted with the Tea Board, which was responsible for promoting development of tea industry under the control of Central Govt.

Tea in India and World

The '*Plantation Industry*', which was developed over 150 years, has a colonial origin. It is now a valuable asset to the nation. Plantation industry is a branch of agriculture in the broader sense. The organization of modern plantation relates more to the factory than to the farm. Generally, there is a specialization in one crop, which is produced on a large scale for export and for maintenance work. The output is continuous through out the year. The major plantation crops like tea, coffee, rubber and cardamom have now developed to a large extent.

Plantation Industry

In India, plantations account for 0.8 per cent of the total cultivable land. They also contribute 5 per cent to the national income in agriculture. Besides they provide more employment per rupee of investment in the country than either agriculture or in industry. Plantation industry employs a large amount of labour force especially women workers which are highest compared to any industry. Moreover, this industry helps in the development of other industries.

Among the different plantation crops, tea is considered to be the most important crop in our country. It is the second biggest foreign exchange earner and is exported to about 85 countries. It also contributes a sizeable amount to the national income. Moreover, it provides direct gainful employment to a large number of people and helps in providing indirect employment in various sectors like road construction, transportation, building of warehouses, manufacture of plywood tea chest, aluminium foil, tin-plate, metal fittings, paper, card board, fertilizers, insecticides, pesticides, coal, iron, steel, etc. Apart from its contribution to the economy of India, tea today provides to the common man a pleasant and stimulating non-alcoholic beverage.

Tea: Agriculture as well as Industry

Tea can be placed both under agriculture and industry. It is industry in the sense that tea is a processed and manufactured commodity, which is subject to excise duty and cess. It is also an agricultural crop because it is grown on land and thus agricultural income tax is also levied on it. Moreover, tea plantation is governed by both agricultural and industrial rules and regulations. The tea crop involves both agricultural and industrial operations. Agricultural operations like cultivation, plucking, manuring, irrigation, weed control, disease and pest attack, transportation of green leaf and uprooting are undertaken for growing tea. The final product of tea comes through various processing and manufacturing stages like withering, rolling, fermenting, drying. weighing, sorting, cutting that place it under industry. Thus the tea plantation, though a big agricultural enterprise, has also some characteristics of industry. The establishments and operations of such industry require massive investment of capital. Modern technical equipment is also necessary for processing the product. An outstanding feature of the plantation economy is that a large portion of tea has been sold in the internal markets from the very inception of this industry. This has, therefore, made it necessary to have well-organised marketing services. The requirement of capital, technical know-how and organized marketing services explain why, the unit of production of tea has taken the shape of a large industrial establishment.

India's Place in the World of Tea

(a) Area under Tea—India and the World: The number of tea producing countries in the world has been increasing since 1950 and at present there are more than 85 such countries. Among the principal tea producing countries in the world, India occupies the first place in terms of area. India's area under tea presents appreciable increase during the period from 1961 to 2005 and the world's tea area exhibited a significant

rise. While the world tea area increased by 194 per cent, India's rose by just 56 per cent. India's tea area as per centage to world tea area has declined over the years from 34.33 per cent to 18.28 per cent. In absolute terms, India's total area in 1961 was 331 thousand ha., which increased to 518 thousand ha. in 2005. Similarly, the world's area under tea was 964 thousand ha. in 1961 and 2833 thousand ha. in 2005. Comparative picture is shown in Table 1.

Table 1: India's Share in World Tea Area during 1961-2005

(Area in thousand hectares)

Year	*World*		*India*		
	Area	*Absolute increase/ decrease*	*Area*	*Absolute increase/ decrease*	*India's share as per centage to world area*
1961	964	—	331	—	34.33
1971	1386	(+)422	357	(+) 26	25.75
1981	2358	(+)972	384	(+) 27	16.28
1991	2569	(+)211	420	(+) 36	16.35
1997	2572	(+) 3	434	(+) 14	16.87
1998	2597	(+) 25	474	(+) 40	18.25
1999	2692	(+) 95	490	(+) 16	18.20
2000	2668	(-) 24	507	(+) 17	19.00
2001	2735	(+) 67	510	(+) 3	18.65
2002	2756	(+) 21	511	(+) 1	18.54
2003	2780	(+) 24	513	(+) 2	19.38
2004	2807	(+) 27	515	(+) 2	18.34
2005*	2833	(+) 26	518	(+) 3	18.28

Source: Tea Statistics, Tea Board, Kolkata, various issues.

Note: (+) indicates increase and (-) indicates decrease in absolute amount.

* Estimated.

(b) *Production of Tea—India and World:* World production increased by 275 per cent during the period, while India's production enhanced by 140 per cent. India's production to world production has substantially reduced from 41.60 per cent to 26.60 per cent. Average annual rate of growth of tea production in India stood at 3.18 per cent while it was 6.24 per cent for the World. India's share in the world tea production is given in Table 2.

Table 2: India's Share in World Tea Production during 1961-2005

(Production in million kgs.)

Year	*World*	*Increase/ Decrease*	*India*	*Absolute increase/ decrease*	*India's share as per centage of world production*
1961	851	-	354	-	41.60
1971	1348	(+) 497	435	(+) 81	32.27
1981	1884	(+) 536	560	(+) 125	29.72
1991	2639	(+)755	754	(+) 194	28.57
1997	2799	(+)160	810	(+) 56	28.94
1998	3058	(+) 250	874	(+ 64	28.58
1999	2971	(-) 87	826	(-) 48	27.80
2000	2989	(-) 18	846	(+) 20	28.30
2001	3091	(+) 102	854	(+) 9	27.62
2002	3099	(+) 8	838	(-) 16	26.65
2003	3138	(+) 39	857	(+)19	27.30
2004	3151	(+) 13	820	(-) 37	26.03
2005*	3195	(+) 44	850	(+) 30	26.60

Source: Tea Statistics, Tea Board, Kolkata, various issues.

Note: (+) indicates increase and (-) indicates decrease in absolute amount.

* Estimated

(c) Export of Tea—India and the World: India is the largest exporter of tea in the world. However, Sri Lanka has been closely following India's footsteps. India's share in world export expressed in terms of per centage has declined between 1961 and 2005, but there is only marginal decline in absolute quantum of exports. Tea has remained, on an average, at 200 million kgs. during the period. The main reason for fall of India's share for the last 44 years is that a large quantum of tea has been retained for domestic consumption. World exports increased by 180 per cent and India's exports reduced

by 5.33 per cent during the period from 1961 to 2005. India's share in the world exports declined from 37.18 to 12.58 per cent during the same period (Table 3).

Table 3: India's Share in World Tea Exports during 1961-2005

(Exports in million kgs.)

Year	*World*	*Absolute increase/ decrease*	*India*	*Absolute increase/ decrease*	*India's share as per centage of world export*
1961	554	-	206	-	37.18
1971	667	(+)113	202	(-4)	30.28
1981	818	(+)115	241	(+)39	29.46
1991	1079	(+)261	212	(-29)	19.65
1997	1207	(+)128	203	(-)9	16.82
1998	1308	(+)101	210	(+)7	16.06
1999	1265	(-)43	192	(-)18	15.18
2000	1334	(+)69	207	(+)15	15.52
2001	1394	(+)60	183	(-)24	13.13
2002	1432	(+)38	201	(+)18	14.04
2003	1388	(-) 44	173	(-) 28	12.46
2004	1501	(+)113	163	(+) 10	12.19
2005*	1550	(+) 49	195	(+) 12	12.58

Source: Tea Statistics, Tea Board, Kolkata, various issues.

Note: (+) indicates increase and (-) indicates decrease in absolute amount. * Estimated.

Tea Industry—Earner of Foreign Exchange: A considerable volume of tea is being exported from India and this has given the tea industry a place of importance in the national economy of India as an earner of foreign exchange. Table 4 shows the value of exports of tea as compared to total value of exports of all commodities.

Table 4: Value of Exports of Tea to Total Value of Exports of All Commodities During 1961-62 to 2004-05

(Rs. in crores)

Year	*Total Value of exports of all commodities@*	*Absolute incr./decr. of total value of exports*	*Value of exports of tea @@*	*Absolute incr./decr. of tea exports*	*Share of tea to total value of exports*
1961-62	661	—	122	—	18.46
1971-72	1608	(+) 947	184	(+) 62	11.44
1981-82	7808	(+) 6200	406	(+) 222	5.20
1991-92	33452	(+) 25644	1194	(+) 788	3.57
1997-98	38752	(+) 5300	1945	(+) 751	5.01
1998-99	39892	(+) 1140	2129	(+) 184	5.33
1999-00	41285	(+) 1393	1867	(+) 262	4.52
2000-01	41875	(+) 590	1890	(+) 23	4.45
2001-02	42453	(+) 578	1696	(-) 194	4.00
2002-03	43450	(+) 997	1665	(-) 31	3.83
2003-04	44040	(+) 590	1637	(-) 28	3.71
2004-05	44640	(+) 600	1688	(+) 51	3.78

Source: @ Director General of Commercial Intelligence and Statistics (DGCIS), GOI. @@Tea Statistics, Tea Board, Kolkata, various issues.

Tea Industry as a Source of Employment: Tea plantation industry not only occupies a very important role in the national economy as an earner of foreign exchange but it also provides gainful employment to a large number of people. This industry, which is largely labour intensive provides employment to a large number of female workers. The industry accounted for 20 per cent and 10 per cent of the total labour force employed in the private sector in 1961 and in 2005 respectively. The ratio of tea labour to total labour employed in the private sector has registered a declining trend in recent years.

Table 5: Ratio of Tea Labour to Total Labour Employed During 1961 to 2005

(Number in lakhs)

Year	*Total number of labour employed in private sector@*	*Number of labour employed in tea @@*	*Share of tea labour to total labour employed*
1961	50	10	19.8
1971	67	8	11.3
1981	73	8	11.0
1991	76	8	10.5
1997	79	8	10.1
1998	80	8	10.0
1999	79	8	10.1
2000	80	8	10.0
2001	81	8	10.0
2002	82	8	10.0
2003	83	9	10.8
2004	83	9	10.8
2005*	84	8	9.5

Source: @ Economic Survey, GoI, @@ Tea Statistics, Tea Board, Kolkata * Estimated

Contribution of Tea Industry to Total Revenue: Tea is a commodity which is subject to direct taxation in the form of excise duty, export duty, and cess. under Tea Act 1951. In addition to these, various state levies are also imposed on the tea industry and these varied from State to State. Revenue earned by way of export duty, excise duty and cess is presented in Table 6.

Tea as a Supporter of Allied Activities: Tea is the mainstay of plywood industry in our country. Tea produced in different regions is mostly packed in plywood chests for sale at the auctions and for exports. However, recently various other alternatives have been evolved in place of plywood chests. Tea helped the coal industry. Huge amount of coal is required

Table 6: Share of Tea Revenue to Total Revenue

(Rs. in crores)

Year	*Total revenue*	*Revenue earned through Tea*				*Tea revenue in per centage to total revenue*
		Export duty	*Central excise duty*	*Cess*	*Total*	
1961-62	1037	9.83	10.78	0	20.61	1.98
1971-72	4027	4.00	37.16	0	41.16	0.35
1981-82	11573	-	63.51	4.45	67.96	0.50
1991-92	35960	-	75.08	10.88	85.96	0.19
1997-98	40857	-	95.05	26.26	121.31	0.06
1998-99	42015	-	115.98	26.07	142.04	0.33
1999-00	43765	-	128.84	25.17	154.01	0.35
2000-01	44978	-	141.27	25.06	166.33	0.36
2001-02	46123	-	145.06	25.34	170.40	0.78
2002-03	47241	-	152.01	25.05	177.06	0.37
2003-04	48256	-	160.06	25.15	185.21	0.38
2004-05*	49570	-	165.20	25.45	190.65	0.38

**Source:* Director General of Commercial Intelligence and Statistics, GoI.

@ Tea Statistics, Various issues, Tea Board, Kolkata. * Estimated.

for running the factories. Of course, in recent times, instead of coal, gas is being used. Further, tea industry facilitates the fertilizer industry and forest industry. It supports the industries engaged in the manufacture of pesticides, insecticides and weedicides. It also adds to the development of various industries like iron, steel, cement, aluminium foils, tin plates, metal fittings, paper, card boards, transport and warehousing.

2

Facets and Growth of Tea Industry During 1850 to 2007

The facets of the tea industry include: *(i)* Farming and Manufacturing, *(ii)* Geographical Locations, *(iii)* Marketing, *(iv)* Exports, *(v)* Internal Consumption, *(vi)* Imposts, *(vii)* Labour, and *(viii)* Development initiatives.

i. Farming and Manufacturing

It starts from preparation of *"seedbed"* and goes on to the packing of tea. Seedlings are grown in the nursery generally for one or two years and are transplanted in the fields. The transplanted young tea plants require levelling and deep hoeing under shade trees. Proper growth of tea plants demand planting of shade trees, timely application of manure and fertilizers, maintenance of good drainage, control of pest attacks and plant diseases. Besides, pruning and plucking are essential operations for inducing vegetative growth and ensuring continuous supply of green flushes as well as improving quality of manufactured tea.

(a) Withering: The plucked green leaves are spread out in racks made of wiremesh or hessian cloth arranged in withered shades. They are kept for a period of 18 hours for a good wither. During this period they loose a good deal of moisture and become placid for rolling which breaks down the leaf cells and release the juice, and enzymes

contained in them. The withered leaf is fed in to the rolling machine which twists the leaf and breaks the leaf cells. The leaf juice oozes out and becomes exposed to the atmosphere. A process of oxidation (called fermentation) begins with change in colour and release of its characteristic aroma.

(b) Rolling and Fermenting: The rolled leaf leaves the roller in the shape of twisted balls and are placed under roll breakers. The leaf is taken to the fermenting room, the atmosphere of which is kept cool or humid. Sometimes this is done with the help of wet screens or suitable water spheres. The time taken for fermentation which depends on various factors, may vary from 20 minutes to 60 minutes. Having received desired degree of fermentation, the fermented leaves are removed to driers which consist of large enclosed chambers having trays inside where fermented leaves are put. The nature of drying and intensity of heat affects the quality of tea.

(c) Grading and Packing: The manufactured tea which comes out of the dryers is then sorted and graded with the help of sorting machinery which consists of mechanically vibrated sieves or tables. The larger particles are often cut into smaller bits with the help of cutting machine before grading. The grading of tea only refers to size of process leaf not to quality or flavour. The two main classifications in the main grade are leaf grade and broken grade. Broken grades include small particles resulting from the shifting and sorting of tea and leaf grades consist of large particles left after broken grades are removed.

ii. Geographical Locations, etc.

In India, tea growing regions are located in the monsoon belt comprising Assam, West Bengal and the foot hills of the Himalayas in the North and moist slopes and the plateaus of the Western Ghats in the South. The climate and the soil of these widely separated locations exhibit wide variations, the impact of which is naturally noticed in wide difference in productivity and cultural practices.

(a) Area, Production and Yield of Tea: Tea is mainly

produced in Assam, West Bengal, Tamil Nadu and Kerala and also produced to a small extent in Tripura, Karnataka, Himachal Pradesh and Uttar Pradesh. Total area under tea stood at 331 thousand hectares of which North East and Eastern India contribute 77.6 per cent and South India 22.4 per cent in 1961. It however increased to 518 thousand hectares in 2005. Similarly, production improved from 354 m.kg to 850 m.kg during 1961 to 2005. Besides, tea is also cultivated in Mizoram, Manipur, Orissa, Arunachal Pradesh, Meghalaya, Uttaranchal etc. Number of tea estates, area, production and yield of tea according to states/districts are given in Annexure I.

(b) Zonewise Classification of Tea etc.: Tea units and tea growing regions are classified into revenue units and zones. At present there are two zones. Zone I includes Dibrugarh, Lakhimpur, Shibsagar, and Darrang (excluding Barsola circle in North India) while Zone II includes all other North Indian districts excluding Barsola circle of Darrang and also South Indian districts.

(c) Area-wise Distribution: Tea estates are distributed according to the various size groups. Ninety eight per cent of the total tea estates belong to the size group of upto 10.12 hectares and the remaining 2 per cent falls in the size group of above 10.12 hectares. Out of this size group, as many as 200 tea estates have average size holdings between 50 to 100 hectares while about 300 tea estates have holding between 100 to 200 hectares and 400 tea estates are in the size group of above 200 to 400 hectares. Moreover, a little less than 400 tea estates have size holding above 400 hectares.

(d) Agewise Classification of Assets: Bushes are the assets of the tea estate-owners as they provide green leaves which are the basic raw material for made/green tea. The composition of assets i.e. bushes are classified into three age groups viz. tender (below 5 years), economic (5-50 years) and old (above 50 years). On an average, 30 per cent of the total area under tea contain bushes which have attained the economic age group while 65 per cent are old age bushes and only 5 per cent are tender bushes. As about two-thirds of the total area is covered by overage bushes,

there is a need for rehabilitation programmes in the form of new planting (extension/replanting) etc.

iii. Primary Marketing

Tea being a perishable commodity should be disposed off quickly and the economic viability of the tea industry depends crucially on profitable disposal of products. There are various modes of disposal of tea viz. i.e. auction, exfactory and forward contract. About 76 per cent of total tea is disposed off through auctions while forward contract and exgarden sales constitute 3 per cent and 20 per cent respectively. Details of Primary Marketing of Indian Tea is given in Table 1.

Table 1: Primary Marketing of Indian Tea

	1999		*2000*		*2005*	
Year	*Qty. in Th. kgs*	*Per cent to total sales*	*Qty. in Th. kgs*	*Per cent to total sales*	*Qty. in th. kgs.*	*Per cent to total sales*
NORTH INDIA						
Kolkata Auction	87801	14.09	95926	14.97	98482	14.82
Guwahati Auction	145072	23.28	159427	24.88	144794	21.80
Siliguri Auction	86789	13.93	79145	12.36	75791	11.43
Amritsar Auction	556	0.09	388	0.06	350	0.06
Teaauction.com	—	—	80	0.01	450	0.06
Sub-total North India	320218	51.39	334966	52.28	319867	48.17
London Auction	—	—	—	—	—	—
Total Auction	320218	51.38	334966	52.28	319867	48.17
Export under FC	32886	5.28	36032	5.62	35843	5.40
Ex-Garden Sale	270155	43.34	269758	42.1	308360	46.43
Total Sale	623259	100.00	640756	100.00	664070	100.00
SOUTH INDIA						
Cochin Auction	59632	29.42	66132	32.08	60995	28.25
Coonoor Auction	79285	39.12	70967	34.42	78555	36.35
Coimbatore Auction	20262	10	33274	16.14	26118	12.09
Kolkata Auction	1371	0.68	2188	1.06	494	0.15
Sub-total South India	160550	79.22	172561	83.70	166162	76.84
London Auction	—	—	—	—	—	—
Total Auction	160550	79.22	172561	83.7	166162	76.84

Export under FC	5543	2.73	6995	3.39	5050	2.35
Ex-Garden Sale	36583	18.05	26610	12.91	44863	20.81
Total Sale	202676	100.00	206166	100.00	216075	100.00
ALL INDIA						
Indian Auction	480768	58.32	507527	59.93	470688	53.48
London Auction	—	—	—	—	—	—
Total Auction	480768	58.21	507527	59.93	470688	53.48
Export under FC	38429	4.65	43027	5.08	53217	6.04
Ex-Garden Sale	306738	37.14	296368	34.99	356240	40.48
Total Sale	825935	100.00	846922	100.00	880145	100.00

Source: Tea Statistics, Tea Board of India, Kolkata, various issues.

iv. Exports

India's exports of tea during the last 5 decades have shown a fluctuating trend. It is interesting to note that India's exports of tea has been hovering around 200 million kg.s and is exported to about 35 countries in the world. The quantity exported from India was reduced to 201 million kgs in 2005, but value realisation has not been reduced to that extent. Details of quantity and value of tea exports from India during 1954-55 to 2005-06 is given below:

Table 2

Quantity and Value of Tea Exports from India

(Excluding Instant Tea)

Year	*Quantity Th. Kgs*	*Value Th. Rs*	*Unit Price Rs./Kg*	*Year*	*Quantity Th. Kgs*	*Value Th. Rs*	*Unit Price Rs./Kg*
1954-55	208462	1482316	7.11	1954	203195	1307523	6.43
1955-56	183769	1096448	5.97	1955	166708	1136132	6.82
1956-57	233088	1451344	6.23	1956	237484	1428249	6.01
1957-58	191755	1436435	7.49	1957	200786	1233859	6.15
1958-59	217322	1296953	5.97	1958	229503	1365859	5.95
1959-60	215459	1290846	5.99	1959	213680	1260135	5.9
1960-61	196473	1222549	6.22	1960	193063	1199883	6.21
1961-62	205329	1221680	5.95	1961	206292	1242513	6.02
1962-63	220800	1296000	5.87	1962	211826	1235339	5.83
1963-64	209328	1231885	5.88	1963	223542	1323710	5.92

1964-65	212325	1246657	5.87	1964	210523	1249012	5.93
1965-66	197385	1148374	5.82	1965	199365	1149747	5.77
1966-67	190383	1562189	8.21	1966	179205	1565921	8.74
1967-68	203333	1801974	8.86	1967	213676	1890384	8.85
1968-69	200824	1565092	7.79	1968	208440	1664825	7.99
1969-70	174112	1245029	7.15	1969	168709	1205371	7.14
1970-71	199139	1842470	9.25	1970	202016	1487533	7.36
1971-72	214317	1609204	7.51	1971	202052	1536678	7.61
1972-73	193228	1472935	7.62	1972	198195	1511439	7.63
1973-74	190268	1448490	7.61	1973	188192	1427072	7.58
1974-75	225057	2235355	9.93	1974	210583	1927972	9.16
1975-76	211409	2382948	11.27	1975	218128	2446592	11.22
1976-77	242418	2954777	12.19	1976	233611	2731364	11.69
1977-78	221522	5637117	25.45	1977	229637	5416157	23.59
1978-79	177327	3591193	20.25	1978	176051	3628916	20.61
1979-80	208448	3768961	18.08	1979	199639	3618401	18.12
1980-81	231736	4352730	18.78	1980	224026	4290277	19.15
1981-82	224200	4068252	18.15	1981	241246	4342541	18
1982-83	194090	3694482	19.03	1982	189933	3555525	18.72
1983-84	202312	5575549	27.56	1983	208476	5168145	24.79
1984-85	217401	7713889	35.48	1984	217040	7404551	34.12
1985-86	214234	6479796	30.25	1985	214021	6952966	32.49
1986-87	196232	5794783	29.53	1986	203149	5808510	28.59
1987-88	201830	6277688	31.1	1987	201891	6392466	31.66
1988-89	204075	6352799	31.13	1988	200956	6126937	30.49
1989-90	210615	9047231	42.96	1989	211622	8400923	39.7
1990-91	198240	10620939	53.58	1990	209085	11041507	52.81
1991-92	215166	11964625	55.61	1991	201720	11203136	55.54
1992-93	178950	10316425	57.65	1992	173358	9717402	56.05
1993-94	153427	10398935	67.78	1993	173726	11325271	65.19
1994-95	150836	9635458	63.88	1994	149317	9652334	64.64
1995-96	166239	12184298	73.3	1995	167143	11908077	71.24
1996-97	167172	12568167	75.18	1996	160004	12070978	75.44
1997-98	208773	19453207	93.18	1997	200713	17218472	85.79
1998-99	203431	21288720	104.65	1998	207640	22383087	107.8
1999-00	189837	18672822	98.36	1999	189092	19024369	100.61
2000-01	203550	1889770	92.80	2000	206820	1898610	91.80
2001-02	190000	16957907	89.25	2001	182590	1682110	92.13
2002-03	184390	1664920	90.29	2002	173680	1590216	91.56
2003-04	183070	1636990	89.42	2003	183640	1673520	91.13

2004-05	185830	1688440	90.86	2004	193540	1783471	92.15
2005-06	191450	1770913	92.50	2005	201000	1753390	87.23

Source: Tea Statistics, Tea Board of India, Kolkata, various issues

v. Internal Consumption—Factors Determining Demand For Tea

Internal consumption of tea grew appreciably. It was 31 per cent of total production in 1947 which went up to 78 per cent of the total production in 2005. *Thus the task before the government is to fix up trade priorities. If the priority is to make available tea in the domestic market, the export front is neglected. On the other hand, if the priority is to ensure maximization of export earnings, the tea may not be available in the internal market at reasonable prices.*

There are various demographic, economic, social and psychological factors that determine demand for a commodity like tea in a developing economy like India. Income, prices of tea and its substitutes and complements, change in consumer taste, preferences, population, social satisfaction, and health aspects are some of the important factors in this regard. Another factor is urbanization, the pace of which in the developing countries is very rapid. The details of internal consumption are given below.

Table 3

Estimates of Internal Consumption of Tea in India

Year	*Internal Consumption (in million kgs)*	*Actual increase or decrease (in million kgs)*	*Per centage increase or decrease*
1971	221	-	-
1980	340	119	56.56
1981	360	20	4.04
1982	372	12	3.33
1983	386	14	3.76
1984	400	14	3.62
1985	415	15	3.75
1986	431	16	3.85

1987	446	15	3.85
1988	462	16	3.42
1989	480	18	3.58
1990	500	20	5.65
1991	511	11	4.1
1992	524	13	2.54
1993	537	13	2.48
1994	550	13	2.42
1995	562	12	2.18
1996	580	18	3.2
1997	597	17	2.93
1998	615	18	3.01
1999	633	18	2.92
2000	653	20	3.14
2001	673	20	3.06
2002	693	20	2.97
2003	705	21	2.97
2004	715	20	2.80
2005	720	19	2.63

Source: Various issues of Tea Statistics, Tea Board, Kolkata.

vi. Taxes and Duties on Tea in India

Tea is a major source of revenue to the National Exchequer. The major imposts are excise duty, cess on tea as well as various Central and State taxes like sales tax, entry tax, agriculture income tax etc. Present taxes and duties (Central Levy and State Levy) on Tea in India are given below.

Central Levy

1. Tea Cess

(a) 30 paisa/kg on tea produced except in Darjeeling Plantation Dist.

(b) 12 paise per kg on tea produced in Darjeeling Plantation district.

2. Excise Duty

(a) Re.1 per kg on tea imposed on 01.03.2002 has been

abolished w.e.f 01.03.2003. However, an additional excise duty of Re. 1.00 per kg has been introduced w.e.f.01.03.2003 for development purposes.

(b) 16 per cent ad valorem on Instant Tea falling under heading 2101.20

3. *Export Duty —NIL—*

4. *Import Duty*

(a) 100 per cent ad valorem on teas falling under heading 09.02

(b) 30 per cent on Instant Tea falling under heading 2101.20

(c) 7.5 per cent on teas imported under Indo Sri Lanka FTA

(d) NIL-when imported for re-export under Duty Exemption Scheme and/or by EOU/EPZ/SEZ units

5. *Corporation Tax*

35 per cent plus 25 per cent surcharge

6. *Education cess on all Duties and Taxes:* 2 per cent of the levy amount.

7. *Service Tax:* 10 per cent on taxable service.

8. *Central Sales Tax*

(a) 2 per cent on teas sold at Kolkata/Siliguri/Coonoor and Coimbatore Auctions.

(b) NIL on teas sold at Guwahati Auction.

(c) 4 per cent on ex-garden sale against Form - C

(d) 8 per cent on teas sold to unregistered dealers.

State Levy

(A) Assam

1. *Assam Sales Tax*

(a) 1 per cent on all teas sold through Guwahati Auction (including private sales through GTAC). Orthodox teas purchased for export are exempted.

(b) 8 per cent on sales outside auction but within Assam.

2. Green Leaf Cess Payable under Assam Taxation on Specified Land (Amendment) Act, 1994

(a) 20 paisa per Kg on green leaf produced by producers having tea area above 4 hectares but within 40 hectares.

(b) 32 paisa per Kg on green lean produced by producers having tea area above 40 hectares in Brahmaputra Valley (Upper Assam).

(c) 29 paisa per Kg on green leaf produced by producers having tea area above 40 hectares in Cachar/Barak valley.

(d) Producers having tea area upto 4 hectares exempted.

3. Land Revenue Under Assam Land Revenue Reassessment Amendment Act

(a) Rs. 12 per bigha for tea estates in Brahmaputra Valley.

(b) Rs. 9 per bigha for tea estates in Barak Valeey plus local tax on land revenue @ 25 per cent and surcharge on land revenue @ 30 per cent.

4. Entry Tax under Assam Entry Tax Act, 2001 on several inputs (both Revenue and Capital Items) by the tea industry 8 per cent.

5. Agricultural Income Tax

Upto income of Rs. 1 lakh-30 per cent and above Rs. 1 lakh

- 35 per cent with effect from 1.4.04. For teas routed through ICD Amingaon on admissible deduction @ Rs. 50 paise per kg.

(B) West Bengal

1) Sales Tax (w.e.f. 01.01.2000)

a) Tea sold in Kolkata or Siliguri Auction

i) Tea sold to registered dealer for exports : Nil

ii) Tea sold to registered dealer for re-sale in original form : 1 per cent

iii) Tea sold to an unregistered dealer : 8 per cent

b) Tea sold other than in Kolkata or Siliguri Auction

i) Tea sold to registered dealer for exports : Nil

ii) Tea sold to registered dealer for re-sale in original form : 1 per cent (Form 13 required)

iii) Tea sold to an unregistered dealer : 8 per cent

2) Inter-State Sale

i) Tea purchased in Kolkata or Siliguri auctions in course of Inter-State trade CST : 2 per cent

ii) Tea sold ex-garden in the course of Inter-State trade CST : 4 per cent

3) Agricultural Produce Marketing Fees

1 per cent under West Bengal Agricultural Produce Marketing Regulation Act, 1972

4) Green leaf payble under West Bengal Rural Employment and Production Cess. (w.e.f. 01.04.1981) : 8 paise per kg of green leaf.

5) Green leaf cess payable under West Bengal Primary Education Cess (w.e.f. 01.04.1981) : 4 paise per kg of green leaf

6) Agriculture Income Tax (levied on 60 % of the total income) - 45 per cent brought down to 30 per cent w.e.f 01.04.2003.

C) Tamil Nadu

1. Sales Tax

(a) 4 per cent on tea sale through tea serve (Auction)

(b) 8 per cent on tea sale through Auction and other than Auction

(c) Infrastructure Surcharge, 5 per cent on Sales Tax

(d) Resale i.e. on second and subsequent sale on dealers above Rs. 1 lakh 1 per cent

2. Inter-State Sale : (a) 2 per cent on teas sold in Auction; (b) 4 per cent of tea sold through Tea Serve (Auction)

3. Agricultural Income Tax levied on 60 percent of total income. Exempted, Tamil Nadu Government has passed a Bill in the Assembly to repeat the Tamil Nadu Agricultural Income Tax, 1955 w.e.f. 1.4.1955.

4. Land Tax (Land Assessment) including local cess and local sales surcharge payable to panchayat: Rs. 51.87 per hectare.

5. Factory Licence Fee: Ranging from Rs. 6400 to Rs. 54000 per factory.

6. Pollution Control Consent Fee Under Water and Air Pollution Acts: Ranging from Rs. 5000 to Rs. 25000 per factory.

7. Salami (Payable on transfer of properties other than by way of inheritance at the time of renewal) Rs. 15000 per hectare.

8. Land Revenue: (i) @ Rs. 30 per acre under West Bengal Land Revenue Amendment Act, 1955;

(ii) plus Road Cess @ 6 per cent of land rent;

(iii) PWD Cess @ 25 per cent of land rent;

(iv) Rural Employment Surcharge @ 15 per cent of land rent

D) Kerala

1. Sales Tax (i) Tea sold through auctions: 8 per cent
   (ii) Tea sold through other than Auction: 8 per cent
   (iii) Additional sales tax... 15 per cent

2. Inter-State Sale : (i) 4 per cent on teas sold in Auction for inter-state sale; (ii) other than auction: 4 per cent

3. Agricultural Income Tax (levied on 60% of the total income)
   (a) Upto Rs.25,000—45 per cent
   (b) Above Rs. 25,000 to Rs.1 Lakh—50 per cent
   (c) Above Rs.1 Lakh to Rs. 3 Lakhs—55 per cent

(d) Above Rs.3 Lakhs to Rs.10 Lakhs—60 per cent

(e) Above Rs.10 Lakhs—65 per cent

4. Agricultural Tax has been exempted for holding 50 acres and below during the year 2000-01 to 2003-04.

5. Plantation Tax (under Kerala Plantation Act, 1960): Plantation tax on tea has been exempted for the financial years 2003-04 and 2004-05.

6. Land Tax Under Kerala Land Tax Act, 1961: (i) Panchayat tax Rs. 50 per has per annum. (ii) Corporation Area Rs. 200 ha per annum. (iii) Township orn Municipal Area: Rs. 200 per ha per annum. (iv) For Registered Dealers, sale of unbranded tea grown by him in the state is 9 per cent.

E) Karnataka

1. Sales Tax - (i) Unbranded 8 – 12 per cent

(ii) Branded .... 15 per cent

(iii) Central tax = 4 per cent.

2. Turn Over Tax 4 per cent: (a) Above Rs. 5 lakhs but less than Rs. 5 Crs - 1 per cent

(b) Above Rs. 5 Crs but less than Rs.10 Crs - 2 per cent

(c) Above Rs. 10 Crs - 3 per cent

3. Infrastructure Development Tax—5 per cent on Tax payable

4. Agricultural Income Tax (levied on 60 % of the total income)	(a) Upto Rs.1 lakh—30 per cent
	(b) Above Rs. 1 lakh to Rs. 5 lakh - Rs.30,000 plus 40 per cent of the amount by which total income exceeds Rs. 1 lakh
	(c) Above Rs 5 lakh – Rs.190,00 plus 50 per cent of the amount by which total income exceeds Rs. 5 lakhs.

Source: Various issues of Tea Statistics.

vii. Labour

Tea plantation in the country provides employment opportunities to the rural poor living in the remotest areas. It is a highly labour intensive industry and engages maximum employment per household. Labourers are

Taxes levied in other producing States, non-tea producing States/Union Territories

(in percent)

State	*Central Sales Tax (in per cent)*	*State Sales Tax (in per cent)*	*Other Taxes*
Andhra Pradesh	4	10	CST without Form 'C' 10 per cent
Bihar	N.A.	10	Additional tax 1 per cent. CST without Form 'C' 10 per cent
Delhi	2	5.5	—
Goa, Daman, Diu	N.A.	4 (w.e.f.30.5.95)	—
Gujarat	4	8	12 per cent packages below 20 kgs, 8 per cent for packages above 20 kgs + Surcharge 10 per cent, Octroi 1 per cent
Haryana	4	8	CST without Form 'C 10 per cent
Himachal Pradesh	4	7	—
Madhya Pradesh	N.A.	8	On loose tea and 10 per cent on tea in Packets
Maharashtra	4	8	Surcharge 10 per cent
Meghalaya	4	7	Surcharge 1 per cent
Mizoram	NIL	NIL	—
Nagaland	4	6	—
Orissa	4	12	Entry tax 1 per cent, CST without Form 'C' 12 per cent
Pondichery	3	3	—
Punjab	2	4	—
Rajasthan	4	4	—
Tripura	4	8	—
Uttar Pradesh	4	6	Single point and additional tax 2 per cent
Sikkim	4	8	

Source: Various issues of tea Statistics, Tea Board, Kolkata.

Table 4: Productivity and Labour per Hectare during 2005

(a) North India

State	*District*	*No. of Estates*	*Area in ha.*	*Prod. in Th. Kg*	*Est. Avg Daily Labour*	*Lab. per ha.*	*Prodn. per ha.*	*prodn. per lab (kg)*
Assam	Darrang	829	41037	77030	114629	2.79	1877	672
	Goalpara	249	3460	6297	9508	2.75	1820	662
	Kamrup	54	3442	4302	8918	2.59	1250	482
	Dibrugarh	21388	93076	163426	197145	2.12	1756	829
	Lakhimpur	326	4815	9068	14056	2.92	1883	645
	Nowgong	213	7994	11788	18910	2.37	1475	623
	Sibsagar (a)	15735	74807	119978	156825	2.1	1604	765
	Karbi Anglong	143	1869	1945	4512	2.41	1041	431
	N.Cachar	8	4004	6179	10320	2.58	1543	599
	Cachar	206	32008	49206	67708	2.12	1537	727
	Total Assam	39151	26652	449219	602531	2.26	1686	746

(Contd.)

Table 4: *(Contd...)*

State	*District*	*No. of Estates*	*Area in ha.*	*Prod. in Th. Kg*	*Est. Avg. Daily Labour*	*Lab. per ha.*	*Prodn. per ha.*	*Prodn. per lab (kg)*
West Bengal	Darjeeling	85	17228	9281	51515	2.99	539	180
	Terai(b)	910	20548	43291	38420	1.87	2107	1127
	Dooars(c)	545	69703	128964	163524	2.35	1850	789
	Total West Bengal	1540	107479	181536	253459	2.36	1689	716
Others	Tripura	292	6623	6431	12105	1.83	971	531
	Bihar	244	1350	538	50	0.04	399	10760
	Uttar Pradesh	11	1068	264	387	0.36	247	682
	Manipur	39	907	96	504	0.56	106	190
	Sikkim	74	296	105	392	1.32	355	268
	Arunachal Pradesh	50	2176	993	2086	0.96	456	476
	Nagaland	94	1214	43	228	0.19	35	189
	Orissa	1	214	105	279	1.3	491	376
	Himachal Pradesh	3679	2325	1247	1033	0.44	536	1207
	Meghalaya	15	351	140	239	0.68	399	586
	Mizoram	12	391	39	107	0.27	100	364
	Others Total	4511	16915	10001	17410	1.03	591	574
North India Total		45202	401097	642510	873400	2.23	1639	734

(b) South India

State	District	No. of Estates	Area in ha.	Prod. in Th. Kg	Est. Avg Daily Labour	Lab. per ha.	Prodn. per ha.	Prodn. per lab (kg)
Tamil Nadu	Coimbatore	52	11764	32831	25281	2.15	2791	1299
	Kanyakumari	7	434	137	167	0.38	316	820
	Madurai	6	973	2660	3078	3.16	2734	864
	Nilgiris	60549	60427	95194	225440	3.73	1575	422
	Tirunelveli	4	800	990	1814	2.27	1238	546
	Tamil Nadu	60618	74398	131812	255780	3.44	1772	515
Kerala	Wynaad	86	5657	12307	12706	2.25	2176	969
	Idukki(d)	4969	26750	51406	58399	2.18	1922	880
	Kottaym	954	840	308	1109	1.32	367	278
	Palghat	33	850	2267	1958	2.3	2667	1158
	Quilon	104	1348	364	546	0.41	270	667
	Trichur	1	530	1896	1539	2.9	3577	1232
	Trivandrum	6	965	399	829	0.86	413	481
	Kerala	6153	36940	68947	77086	2.09	1866	894
Karnataka	Coorg	7	299	687	647	2.16	2298	1062
	Chickmangalur	29	1428	3521	2531	1.77	2466	1391
	Hassan	1	395	1199	611	1.55	3035	1962
	Karnataka	37	2122	5407	3789	1.79	2548	1427
South India	66808	116417	206735	336655	2.97	1817	612	
Total All India		112010	517514	849245	1210055	2.4	1679	700

Source: Various issues of Tea Statistics, Tea Board, Kolkata. (a)Including Mikir Hills & North Cachar upto 1989, (b) Including West Dinajpur, (c) Including Cooch Behar, (d) Including Ernakulam.

employed in the tea industry both in fields and factory operations. They are mainly resident and also outside workers. Resident workers are the permanent labourers of the estate whereas outside workers are temporary and casual labourers. Both resident and outside workers are again divided into male, female, children and adolescent depending upon the nature of the work involved. Productivity and labour per hectare is given in table 4.

Growth of Tea Industry During 1850–2007 and Factors Responsible for Such Progress

Growth of tea industry in India can be grouped under two major periods. (1) Pre-Five Year Plan period (1850-1950) and (2) Five Year plans (1952-2007).

Pre-Five Year Plan Period (1850-1950)

The pre-Five Year Plan period may again be sub-divided into four periods like: (a) period of rapid growth 1850-1890, (b) period of stability 1890-1918 (c) inter war period 1918-1939 and (d) period of prosperity 1939-1950.

(a) The Period of Rapid Growth (1850 to 1890)

The growth of the industry was remarkable during this period. Area under tea was only 750 hectares in 1852 while it was 1,52,000 hectares in 1890 showing an annual average growth rate of 504 per cent. Similarly, production was 97,000 kgs in 1850 and 57 million kgs in 1890 accounting for an average annual growth rate of 1466 per cent. Yield was 138 kgs per hectare which increased to 373 kgs per hectare. The details are given below:

Particulars	*Year growth rate*		*Avg. annual (per centage)*
	1850	*1890*	
Area under cultivation (in th. ha.)	0.75	152	504
Production (in million kgs)	0.97	57	1466
Average yield (kg/ha.)	130	373	5

Source: Various issues of Tea Statistics, Tea Board, Kolkata.

The various factors responsible for such progress were:

- Govt. grants on easy terms and conditions to the planters,
- leasing of land to the planters at a nominal rent,
- low investment cost per acre of land varying between Rs.40 and Rs. 70,
- emergence of private entrepreneurs in cultivation of tea,
- availability of labour in the early years,
- formation of Indian Tea Association on May 18, 1881,
- spread of tea cultivation in Govt. plantation,
- introduction of improved method of manufacture in 1870 (Mechanical Roller in 1870, Dryer in 1877 and mechanical packaging)
- formation of Kolkata Tea Brokers Association in 1879,
- operation of a daily paddle steamer service between Kolkata and Guwahati in 1883,
- opening of the first railway line in Assam (Jorhat Provincial and Dibursadia) in 1885 and
- establishment of the Kolkata Tea Traders Association.

(b) The Period of Stability (1890 to 1918)

The tea industry witnessed all round development between 1890 and 1918. Area increased from 152 thousand hectares to 275 thousand hectares (average annual growth rate 2.9 per cent) while production enhanced from 57 m. kgs to 173 m. kgs (average annual growth rate 7.3 per cent) and yields was enhanced from 373 kgs per hectare to 692 kgs per hectare showing average annual growth rate of 2.5 per cent.

Details of area, production, yield during periods of stability are shown below:

Particulars	*Year*		*Percentage increase/ decrease over*	*Av. Annual growth rate (in per centage*
	1890	*1918*		
Area under cultivation (in th. ha.)	152	275	2.90	2.90
Production (in million kgs)	57	173	7.30	7.30
Average yield (kg/ha.)	373	692	2.50	2.50

Source: Various issues of Tea Statistics, Tea Board, Kolkata

The factors which accelerated the growth of the industry during the period were mainly:

- development of tea into an industry in South India towards the end of 1895, formation of United Planters Associations of South India (UPASI) at Coonnoor in 1894 and other Associations in Assam and Bengal;
- appointment of Dr. Mann as the Scientific Officer in the laboratory of the Indian Museum in Kolkata to carry out Scientific Research enactment of Tea Cess Act in 1903 by the Govt. of India to raise funds for tea propaganda abroad,
- imposition of a levy of 28 paise per 100 kg of tea construction of Assam-Bengal metregauge railway line in 1910, setting up of Scientific Department in 1909 by UPASI undertaking tea research exclusively in 1924,
- shifting of research station from Assam to Tocklai in 1911 importance of developing domestic market for tea in 1918,
- direction of making provision in the India Tea Cess Act for propaganda in India and formation of Indian Tea Planters Association in Jalpaiguri in 1918.

(c) Inter War Period (1918-1939)

The tea industry during the inter war period experienced many ups and down in its growth. Area increased from 275 thousand hectares (th. ha.) to 337 th. ha. and production from 173 million Kgs (m. kgs.) to 205 m. kgs during the period. Increase in production was mainly due to expansion of area. Average annual rate of growth of area was 1.1 per cent and production was 0.9 per cent. There was a decline in yield rate by 0.1 per cent. The average annual rate of growth of tea exports was 0.5 per cent, while it was 2.9 per cent for internal consumption and 1.2 per cent per head annual consumption.

Particulars	*Year*		*Per centage increase/ decrease over 1918*	*Avg. annual growth rate (in per centage)*
	1918	*1939*		
Area under cultivation (in th. ha.)	275	337	22.50	1.10
Production (in million kgs)	173	205	18.10	0.90
Average yield (kg/ha.)	629	610	-3.00	-0.10
Export (in million kgs)	148	165	11.50	0.50
InternalConsumption (in million Kgs)	25	40	60.00	2.90
Per head consumption (in kg)	0.1	0.13	25.00	1.20

Source: Various issues of Tea Statistics, Tea Board, Kolkata.

The worldwide depression of 1929 had its impact on tea. Tea market was so depressed that it was unremunerative to go in for tea cultivation. To sort out the problems the first International Tea Agreement (ITA) was signed in 1933 and the Tea Control Act 1933 was introduced. The International Tea Committee (ITC), Tea Cess Committee 1937, India Tea Market Expansion Board were also constituted

(d) Period of Prosperity (1939-1950)

The outbreak of the Second World war, introduction of bulk purchase scheme, end of British Rule in India, further extension of Tea Agreement, creation of Central Tea Board and establishment of new auction centre at Cochin were the major events that led to the prosperity of the tea industry. Although there was a decline in area by 6.2 per cent, production increased by 36 per cent and yield by 44 per cent. Similarly, Internal consumption increased by 92 per cent, exports by 22 per cent and per head consumption by 64 per cent. The position during the period of prosperity is given below:

Particulars	*Year 1939*	*1950*	*Per centage increase/ decrease over 1939 centage)*	*Avg. annual growth rate (in per*
Area under cultivation (in th. ha.)	337	316	-6.20	-0.58
Production (in million kgs.)	205	278	36.00	3.20
Average yield (kg/ha.)	610	881	44.00	4.00
Export of tea (in million kgs.)	165	201	22.00	2.00
Internal Consumption (in million kgs.)	40	77	92.00	8.30
Per head consumption (in kgs.)	0.13	0.2	64.00	5.80

Source: Various issues of Tea Statistics, Tea Board, Kolkata.

Post Five Year Plan

(a) First Five Year Plan (1951-52 to 1955-56)

During the First Plan period, the industry developed mainly due to participation of private entrepreneurs. Average annual rate of growth of area was 0.3 per cent, production by 1.7 per cent and yield by 1.4 per cent. The average annual growth of export was 3.9 per cent, unit value by 5.5 per cent and revenue from central excise by 14.3 per cent and internal tea consumption by 1.6 per cent.

Particulars	*Position as at the*		*percentage*	*Avg. an-*
	comme-ncement of plan on 1.4.1951	*end of plan on 31.3.1956*	*increase/ decrease over 1951*	*nual growth rate (in percentage)*
Area under cultivation (in th. ha.)	317	321	1.30	0.30
Production (in million kgs)	285	309	8.40	1.70
Average yield (kg/ha.)	901	963	6.90	1.40
Export of tea (in million kgs.)	195	233	19.50	3.90

Value of export of tea (in. crore Rs)	91	141	54.90	11.00
Unit value (Rs. per kg)	4.7	6	27.70	5.50
Internal consumption (in million kgs.)	73	97	8.20	1.60
Revenue from central excise (in crore Rs)	1.4	2.4	71.40	14.30

Source: Various issues of Tea Statistics, Tea Board, Kolkata.

(b) Second Five Year Plan (1956-57 to 1960-61)

Although average annual rate of growth of area declined by 1.7 per cent, production and yield were enhanced by 2.9 per cent and 2.2 per cent respectively, export of tea declined by 2.4 per cent and revenue from central excise by 4.8 per cent but internal tea consumption increased by 8.9 per cent.

Particulars	*Position as at the*		*Percentage*	*Avg. annual growth*
	commencement of plan on 1.4.1956	*end of plan on 31.3.1956*	*increase/ decrease over 1951*	*rate (in %age)*
Area under cultivation (in th. ha.)	361	331	-8.30	-1.70
Production (in million kgs)	309	355	14.90	2.90
Average yield (kg/ha.)	963	1070	11.11	2.20
Export of tea (in million kgs)	233	205	-12.00	-2.40
Value of export of tea (in crore Rs)	143	124	-5.30	-3.10
Unit value (Rs. per kg)	6	6	1.50	0.30
Per centage of foreign exchange earnings	24.5	18.5	-23.80	-4.80
Internal consumption (in million kgs)	97	140	44.30	8.90
Central excise revenue from tea (in crore Rs)	3.2	10.8	237.50	47.50

Source: Various issues of Tea Statistics, Tea Board India, Kolkata.

The major factors affected the growth of tea industry during the period were:

(i) prevalence of long lasting Suez Canal crisis in 1956

(ii) submission of Report on Plantation Inquiry Commission (PIC) to the Govt. of India

(iii) Issuance of Tea Distribution and Export Control order (TDECR), 1957

(iv) Tea Waste Control Order (TWCR), 1959 and

(v) Formation of Tea Association of India in 1956.

The long pending Suez Canal crisis had an adverse effect on tea industry causing hardship in transporting tea to U K i.e. the highest buyer of Indian tea and this resulted in considerable suffering to the interest of the tea manufacturers.

The submission of the Plantation Inquiry Commission report had a positive impact on the tea industry. The Commission made valuable recommendations like: *(a)* reduction in the cost of production, *(b)* breaking up of concentration of tea trade, *(c)* grant of financial assistance to tea industry, *(d)* emphasizing the need for extension, replacement and replanting in a phased manner, *(e)* improvement in transportation, and *(f)* promotion of tea exports.

The issuance of TDECR had a positive impact on tea industry. It sought to regulate the activities of exporters and distributors of tea through a system of licencing. It also imposed some restrictions on the quality of tea to be observed, by exporters and distributors. The purpose of introduction of TWCR was to control and regulate Buying, Selling, Stocking etc. of tea waste so that it may not reach the hands of adulterators to be used by them for adulterating tea for human consumption. The Tea Association of India which was set up in 1956 aimed at protecting the interest of Indian tea growers in North East India.

(c) Third Five Year Plan (1961-62 to 1965-66)

Average annual rate of growth of area stood at 0.80 per cent while it was 1.20 per cent for production and 0.4 per cent for yield. Exports of tea declined by 0.8 per cent and foreign exchange earnings by 1.1 per cent. However, internal tea consumption increased by 6.3 per cent and central excise by 8.9 per cent

Particulars	Position as at the Commencement of plan on 1.4.1966	End of plan on 31.3.1966	Percentage increase/ decrease over 1961	Avg. annual growth rate (in %age)
Area under cultivation (in th. ha.)	331	345	4.20	0.80
Production (in million kgs)	355	376	5.90	1.20
Average yield (kg/ha.)	1070	1089	1.80	0.40
Export of tea (in million kgs)	205	197	-3.90	-0.80
Value of export of tea (in. crore Rs.)	124	157	26.60	5.30
Unit value (Rs. per kg)	6	8.7	45.00	9.00
Per centage of foreign exchange earnings from tea	18.5	13.5	-5.50	-1.10
Internal consumption (in million kgs)	140	184	31.40	6.30
Central excise revenue from tea (in crore Rs)	10.8	15.6	44.40	8.90

Source: Various issues of Tea Statistics, Tea Board, Kolkata.

The aggression of China in October 1962 and subsequent aggression of Pakistan in 1965 on India created problems for the tea industry. The Chinese aggression delayed the export of tea due to heavy war supplies to North East Regions to repel Chinese aggression. The war created major problems one relating to the transportation of tea from Assam valley and Cachar to Kolkata and the other regarding supply of essential raw materials to tea gardens of these regions. The second note worthy event which had a positive effect on the tea industry was the establishment of auction centres at Coonoor in 1963 for South Indian tea and Amritsar in Punjab for North Indian tea in 1964. The persistent decline in tea prices has been a matter of serious concern for the tea exporting countries. During 1964 and thereafter, Food and Agricultural Organisation (FAO) introduced certain informal regulatory schemes for tea exports.

(d) Annual Plans (1966-67 to 1968-69)

Average annual growth rate was 2.3 per cent in area, 4.8 per cent in production, 2.9 per cent in yield and 10 per cent in internal consumption. In June 1966, the Govt. of India devalued the Indian Rupee for the second time since

Independence and imposed a heavy duty of Rs. 2.00 per kg on export of tea. As the impact of devaluation on the tea industry was not encouraging, the Govt. had to reduce the rate of export duty in November 1966.

(e) Fourth Five Year Plan (1969-70 to 1973-74)

The average annual rates of growth of area, production, yield, export, internal consumption, central excise, were 0.5 per cent, 4.8 per cent, 4.2 per cent, 4.2 per cent, 5.6 per cent, 40.6 per cent respectively.

Particulars	*Position as at the*		*Percentage*	*Avg. an-*
	comme-ncement of plan on 1.4.1969	*end of plan on 31.3.1974*	*increase/ decrease over 1969*	*nual growth rate (in %age)*
Area under cultivation (in th. ha.)	353	362	2.70	0.50
Production (in million kgs)	394	489	24.00	4.80
Average yield (kg/ha.)	1114	1353	21.80	4.20
Export of tea (in million kgs)	174	211	21.80	4.20
Value of export of tea (in. crore Rs)	121	193	59.50	11.90
Unit value (Rs. per kg)	7.1	9.2	26.00	5.60
Per centage of foreign exchange earnings from tea	8.8	6.7	-5.00	-0.50
Internal consumption (in million kgs)	203	260	26.00	5.60
Central excise revenue from tea (in crore Rs)	13.2	40	203.00	40.60

Source: Various issues of Tea Statistics, Tea Board, Kolkata.

In 1973 the Govt. of India passed the Foreign Exchange Regulation Act (FERA) which provided for diluting the foreign equity capital and quickening the process of Indianisation of tea industry.

(f) Fifth Five Year Plan (1974-75 to 1978-79)

Except for revenue from central excise and export, (decline of 0.5 per cent and 1.8 per cent), there was appreciable increase by 0.6 per cent for area, 2.2 per cent for production, 1.5 per cent for yield, 5.7 per cent for internal consumption and 9.4 per cent for central excise revenue.

Particulars	*Position as at the* commencement of plan on 1.4.1974	end of plan on 31.3.1979	*Percentage* increase/ decrease over 1974	*Avg. annual growth* rate (in %age)
Area under cultivation (in th. ha.)	362	374	3.30	0.60
Production (in million kgs)	489	544	11.00	2.20
Average yield (kg/ha.)	1353	1455	2.00	1.50
Export of tea (in million kgs)	211	200	5.00	-1.80
Value of export of tea (in. crore Rs)	193	362	87.00	17.40
Unit value (Rs. per kg)	9.16	18.12	97.00	19.40
Per centage of foreign exchange earnings from tea	6.7	5.9	-0.86	-0.20
Central excise revenue from tea (in crore Rs)	40	58.9	47.80	9.40

Source: Various issues of Tea Statistics, Tea Board, Kolkata.

The overall development of the tea industry was the combined effect of various strategies adopted by Govt. of India during the Plan period. These are as follows:

- Setting up of Indian Tea Industry Development Association in 1974 with a seed capital of Rs.25.00 lakh acquired by way of voluntary subscription.
- Opening of new tea auction centre at Siliguri in 1976 helped the producers in the locality in reducing the cost of marketing and also saving time and avoiding risks.
- The Committee on Tea Marketing under the chairmanship of Mr. Prakash Tandon the then Director General of National Council of Applied Economic Research, Govt. of India in its report had made numerous valuable suggestions for marketing of tea in India and abroad. The Committee for the first time cautioned that India should not go for

export only but also make efforts for import of tea to keep India's position in the world market.

- A meeting was held on 18 February 1980 with the officials of Tea Board, State Trading Corporation, Tea Trading Corporation of India, Mr Pranab Mukherjee, the then Commerce Minister, Govt. of India stressed the need for increasing country's export of traditional and non traditional goods. Mr Pranab Mukherjee requested the Tea Board to take steps to increase production of tea so that there was a considerable surplus after meeting internal consumption needs.
- Decision was taken for revival of the Darjeeling tea industry as it was potentially viable to produce 22 m kg of tea annually.
- Amendment of Import policy of tea bagging machine. However Govt. of India amended the import policy governing import of tea bagging machine from February 1980. Import of tea bagging machine is allowed under 'Open General Licence'.

(g) Sixth Five Year Plan (1980-81 to 1984-85)

There was overall increase in area (1.8 per cent), production (2.8 per cent), productivity (0.9 per cent), exports (1.7 per cent), foreign exchange earnings (2.4 per cent) and internal consumption (5.6 per cent) except for decline in central excise revenue from tea by -0.8 per cent.

Particulars	*Position as at the commencement of plan on 1.4.1980*	*Position as at the end of plan on 31.3.1985*	*Percentage increase/ decrease over 1980*	*Avg. annual growth rate (in %age)*
Area under cultivation (in th. ha.)	374	408	9.1	1.8
Production (in million kgs)	544	620	14	2.8
Average yield (kg/ha.)	1,455	1,523	407	0.9
Export of tea (in million kgs)	200	217	8.5	1.7

Value of export of tea (in. crore Rs)	36.2	771	113	22.6
Unit value (Rs. per kg)	18.1	35.5	96.1	19.2
Average per centage of foreign exchange earnings from tea	5.9	6.6	11.9	2.4
Internal consumption (in million kgs)	337	431	27.9	5.6
Central excise revenue from tea (in crore Rs)	58.9	56.7	-3.9	-0.8

Source: Various issues of Tea Statistics, Tea Board, Kolkata.

During the Sixth Plan period, there was overall growth of the Tea Industry, which was the cumulative effect on various policies or strategies implemented by the Govt. Some of which are as follows:

- A National Level meet was held on 3rd August 1981 under the chairmanship of Mr P. K. Kaul, the then Secretary, Ministry of Commerce, Govt. of India, and was also attended by the representatives of Govt. of Assam, West Bengal, Tripura, Kerala, Tamil Nadu, Karnataka, Himachal Pradesh and the Association of Tea Producers including small tea growers. Discussions were held on the present and future prospects of the Tea Industry and recommendations made for substantial reduction in excise duty rates on both bulk and packet tea, reduction in agricultural income tax rates, exemption from rural employment cess, suspension of sales tax on auctions, full credit requirements at concessional rates of interest to the Govt. of India, State Govt. and tea producers.
- The RBI had constituted a Committee under the chairmanship of Mr K. B. Chore, Chief Officer, RBI in October 1980 to examine the problems relating to the financing of tea industry. The Committee had given a recommended that the tea industry would provide from its own funds and long term resources, fund equal to at least 25 per cent amount of peak deficit. Besides, the cash credit limit is to be fixed on the detailed monthly cash budget for the entire

season. The Committee had also recommended for prompt liquidation of accumulated deficit from the past, within 2 to 3 years. Further, the Chore Committee recommendations had dealt a serious blow to the working of tea industry. In a meeting with Dr Manmohan Singh, the then Governor of RBI, the tea industry representatives had pointed out the adverse effect of Chore Committee recommendations. The Governor assured that nothing would be done to harm the industry.

- Three main tea producing countries i.e., India, Sri Lanka and Kenya hold informal consultations at Geneva in an effort to sort out their differences on international tea agreement. Mr V. P. Singh, the then Union Commerce Minister, GoI, directed the Tea Board to gear up its export promotion efforts so that it can contribute a lion's share to the country's foreign exchange earnings. He also advised the Tea Board to derive maximum possible benefit from participation in any generic promotion by the existing Tea Council by suitable modifications in the pattern of contribution and unilateral promotion of Indian Tea through the role of Tea Board.
- R & D areas for Tea were identified by the producers and exporters of tea all over the world including India. The main thrust areas for carrying out R&D work to boost output and sustain production increase, are:
  - creation of central information services for tea industries for the world
  - analysis of bio-chemistry of tea during and after its manufacture
  - Evolving packaging technology.
- The Tea Marketing Control Act, 1984 stipulated that producers were to sell a minimum of 70 per cent of tea through public auction.

The Crash Programme for 1987 formulated by the Consultative Committee of the Plantation Association envisaged the utilisation of internal resources for augmenting tea production in the short term.

- In the 25th Annual General Meeting of Indian Tea Association held on November 1982, it was urged upon by the Govt. to include tea under priority sector to enable it to obtain financial facilities as extended to other agricultural commodities.

(h) Seventh Five Year Plan (1985-86 to 1989-90)

Except for decline in export of tea by -0.5 per cent and foreign exchange by-10.0 per cent there was improvement in area by 0.5 per cent, production by 3.1 per cent, yield by 2.5 per cent, internal consumption by 4.1. per cent and central excise by 7.8 per cent.

Particulars	*Position as at the*		*Percentage*	*Avg. an-*
	comme- ncement of plan on 1.4.1985	*end of plan on 31.3.1990*	*increase/ decrease over 1985*	*nual growth rate (in %age)*
Area under cultivation (in th. ha.)	408	417	2.20	0.50
Production (in million kgs)	620	720	16.30	3.10
Average yield (kg/ha.)	1523	1729	13.50	2.50
Export of tea (in million kgs)	217	209	-3.60	-0.50
Value of export of tea (in. crore Rs)	771	1104	43.20	3.50
Unit value (Rs.per kg)	35.5	52.8	48.70	4.20
Average per centage of foreign exchange earnings from tea	6.6	3.4	-50.00	-10.00
Internal consumption (in million kgs)	431	500	16.00	4.10
Central excise revenue from tea (in crore Rs)	56.7	78.9	38.80	7.80

Source: Various issues of Tea Statistics, Tea Board, Kolkata.

The industry made progress during the Plan period except quantum of tea exports and per centage of foreign exchange earnings. The progress was the cumulative effects of various strategies, policies, programmes, etc., adopted during the Plan period. These are as follows:

- identification of new areas to be brought under planting of tea/coffee rubber and cardamom of about 1.7 lac hectare besides the planting of 85000 hect. and rejuvenation and infilling of 1.3 lakh hect. by UPASI.
- initiation of join efforts of West Bengal and Assam to bring more areas under Tea.
- appointment of Venkatachalam Committee of Tea Auction, suggesting modification of stipulation of selling 70 per cent of total production through auction.
- announcement of new marketing policy by Union Govt. regarding adequate supply of tea at reasonable prices for domestic market and maximization of export earnings from tea.
- launching of modernization plan for West Bengal Tea Development Corporation.
- implementation of major development programme for Assam Tea Corporation
- convening of Tea Scientists Meet from all over the World at Coonoor under the aegis of UPASI to study the impact of plant density & manuring of soil groups in tea gardens.
- familiarization of tea planting method which includes chopping of the old bushes at the ground level and applying chemicals to kill them.
- holding of Tea Finance Meet.
- Launching of export campaign for Darjeeling tea.
- formulation of a comprehensive credit plan to revitalise the ailing tea industry in Kangra valley by State Bank of India, Kangra.

- setting up of new projects worth Rs.7.55 crore covering an area of 8000 hectares in Western Ghats in joint sector by Govt. of Karnataka.
- establishment of a permanent centre for development of plantation in Kerala.
- constitution of a Ramakrishnayya Committee to review the working of Tea Board.
- organising National Conference on Tea Productivity.
- reconstitution of Tea Board.
- launching of Darjeeling logo.
- opening of mini auction centres by TATA.
- setting up of a committee on a long term strategy and plan for development of tea industry. The viability of cheaper packing material and bringing Orissa, Meghalaya, Arunachal Pradesh etc. in the tea map.

During the Plan period, the tea industry had undertaken various development activities which enabled step up of production. The strategy of raising tea production includes, short, medium and long term measures. Short term measures included cultural and cultivation practices, medium measures incorporated new planting, rejuvenation, pruning, replanting, infilling etc., while long term measures includes attainment of 1100 m. kgs of tea in 2000 and extension of planted area by another 53600 hectares, carrying out infilling of about 38,500 hectares and 44600 hectares.

(i) Eighth Five Year Plan (1991-92 to 1995-96)

Average annual rate of growth of production was 1.1 per cent due to increase in area by 0.6 per cent and yield by 0.5 per cent. Export was marginally increased by 0.5 per cent and internal consumption by 2.3 per cent and central revenue by 1.0 per cent.

Particulars	*Position as at the*		*Percentage*	*Avg. an-*
	comme-ncement of plan on 1.4.1991	*end of plan on 31.3.1996*	*increase/ decrease over 1991*	*nual growth rate (in %age)*
Area under cultivation (in th. ha.)	420	433	3.00	0.60
Production (in million kgs)	754	795	5.50	1.10
Average yield (kg/ha.)	1794	1839	2.50	0.50
Export of tea (in million kgs)	201	205	2.40	0.50
Value of export of tea (in. crore Rs)	1120	1165	0.40	1.80
Unit value (Rs.per kg)	55.15	58.7	6.50	1.30
Average per centage of foreign exchange earnings from tea	3.8	3.6	-5.30	-1.00
Internal consumption (in million kgs)	520	560	11.50	2.30
Central excise revenue from tea (in crore Rs)	75.5	79.4	5.20	1.00

Source: Various issues of Tea Statistics, Tea Board, Kolkata.

(j) Ninth Five Year Plan (1997-98 to 2001-2002)

Although area under tea increased over the years by 17.97 per cent, but production improved marginal (less than 0.4 per cent per annum) mainly on account of fall in productivity. Export was more or less equal over the years but value of exports went up because of improvement in unit value (Rs 85.79 to Rs 87.13 per kg). Internal consumption was hiked @ 3.24 per cent annually. Details are given below:

Particulars	*Position as at the*		*Percentage*	*Avg. an-*
	comme-ncement of plan on 1.4.1997	*end of plan on 31.3.2002*	*increase/ decrease over 1997*	*nual growth rate (in %age)*
Area under cultivation (in th. ha.)	434	512	17.97	3.59
Production (in million kgs)	810	826	1.97	0.40
Average yield (kg/ha.)	1865	1620	-13.14	-2.62

Export of tea (in million kgs)	203	201	-0.98	-0.19
Value of export of tea (in. crore Rs)	1721	1753	1.86	0.37
Unit value (Rs. per kg)	86	87	1.56	0.31
Average per centage of foreign exchange earnings from tea	4	3	-2.85	-0.57
Internal consumption (in million kgs)	597	693	16.20	3.24
Central excise revenue from tea (in crore Rs)	95.05	152.01	58.26	11.65

Source: Various issues of Tea Statistics, Tea Board, Kolkata.

(k) Tenth Five Year Plans (2002-03 to 2006-2007)

Annual production in 2007 was estimated at 860 million Kgs compared to 855 million kgs in the previous year. Export was expected to increase to declined to 200 million Kgs. The detail of various parameters are given below:

Particulars	*Position as at the*		*Percentage*	*Avg. annual growth*
	commencement of plan on 1.4.2002	*end of plan on 31.3.2007*	*increase/ decrease over 2002*	*rate (in %age)*
Area under cultivation (in th. ha.)	512	522	1.95	0.39
Production (in million kgs)	838	860	2.62	0.52
Average yield (kg/ha.)	1620	1647	1.66	0.33
Export of tea (in million kgs)	201	200	Negl.	Negl
Value of export of tea (in crore Rs)	1753	1870	8.09	1.62
Unit value (Rs. per kg)	87	94	8.05	1.60
Average per centage of foreign exchange earnings from tea	3	NA	-	-
Internal consumption (in million kgs)	693	750	8.22	1.64
Central excise revenue from tea (in crore Rs)	152	171	1.25	2.5

Source: Various issues of Tea Statistics, Tea Board, Kolkata.

The industry made progress during this plan period on account of various strategies adopted. Some of these are listed below:

- Tea Board together with the Ministry of Commerce organized a stake-holders conference on 16 and 17 September 2004 at New Delhi, which enumerated recommendations of various issues affecting the Indian Tea Industry and submitted the same to the Ministry of Commerce for consideration.
- Ministry of Commerce formed a National Tea Advisory Committee to look into the recommendations that emerged in the State holders conference.
- Tea Board started a generic promotion campaign propagating the health aspect of tea.
- Tea Board has been participating in the fairs and exhibitions within the country to increase the domestic demand.
- Excise duty @ Rs. 1 per kg of teas falling under heading 09.2 has been abolished w.e.f. 01.03.2003. Additional excise duty @ Rs. 1 per kg has been introduced for development purpose w.e.f. 01.03.2003 which was subsequently withdrawn in 2005-06 budget.
- Sixteen (16) per cent ad valorem of instant tea falling usual heading of 2101.02
- Export duty has been withdrawn at present.
- Rate of cess has been enhanced w.e.f. 01.04.1997. It is 12 paise and 30 paise per kg for Darjeeling and non-Darjeeling teas
- Policy decisions taken by the Tea Board with regard to operational aspects of the loan schemes
- The existing guideline with regard to time of pruning in South India (April to October) under the Board's Rejuvenation Pruning and Consolidation Scheme were revised.
- Approval was accorded to TRA for setting up a separate advisory cell to render extension services to small growers. The cell started functioning w.e.f. 01.04.2004.

- The cell has been advised to help the growers to set up Self Help Groups (SHGs)
- Modified the eligibility criteria for grant of subsidy to SHGs
- Accorded approval for inclusion of soil testing laboratory of M/S Hindustan Bio-Fertilizer and Soil Testing Services as one of the approved laboratories for issuing soil suitability certificate for the purpose of claiming subsidy.
- Launching of Tea Quality Up-gradation and Product Diversification Subsidy Scheme
- Made one time grant amounting to Rs. 12.00 lakh to Palampur Cooperative Tea Factory for procuring direct fire heater required for withering of green leaf.
- Implemented Human Resource Development Scheme to induct professionalisation in plantation management, improve labour productivity, skill improvements at all levels from workers to management through extensive training and carrying out plantation labour welfare measures.
- Introduced Research and Development scheme focusing development needs of small growers like extension of advisory services, setting up of nurseries for supply of good quality planting materials, organizing study tours.
- The Board, in order to establish closer interface with the small growers, recommended for opening new field offices in the N.E states, viz – Arunachal, Nagaland, Meghalaya, Mizoram, Manipur, Dibrugarh and Jalpaiguri in a phased manner.
- Commissioned Price Subsidy Scheme and Price Stabilization Fund Scheme.
- Tea Board continued to maintain four tea bar/buffers in Parliament House, Yojana, Bharam, Udyog Bhawan and North Block in New Delhi.
- Introduced price stabilization formula for small tea growers.

- Monitored the status of closed and sick units
- Undertook various research activities by TRA, UPASI-TRF, Darjeeling Tea Research Centre, National Tea Research Foundation.
- Focused on quality of tea on a sustained manner
- Projecting tea as a life style beverage to youth and propagating health aspects of tea to young house wife.
- A promotional support scheme for providing promotional assistance for various activities to exporters/associations introduced in 2001-02, continued to be implemented.
- Implemented medium term export strategy and targets (2002-07)
- Launched Export Rating System (ERS)
- Set up India Tea Portral for information dissemination system.
- Market consolidation and diversification of export market portfolio
- Participated in international fairs and exhibitions.

(l) Area, Production, Yield, Export, Value of Export, Quantity Sold, etc. during the Period from 1950 to 2007

It is observed from the data Table 1 that production had increased over the years expect 1999, 2002 and 2005. This was mainly on account of improvement in yield rate. Of course, there was marginal increase in area. Yield was improved by 88 per cent over the year whereas area by 65 per cent. The average annual rate of growth of yield was 1.54 per cent while it was 1.14 per cent in case of area.

Development Initiatives

To increase production and improve quality of tea, there is a need to adopt various short term and medium term measures. Further, tea cultivation has to be further extended on a wider scale to non-traditional areas keeping in view the climate suitability. The existing manufacturing capacity has to be again augmented for scientific processing in large

Table 1 : Area, Production, Yield, Exports and Prices of Tea during 1950 to 2007

Year	Area	Production	Yield	Export		Unit Price	Auction		Labour
				Qty.	Value		Qty.	Sale Price	No.
1950	316	278.21	881	200.70	80.42	4.10	113.64	4.23	94859
1960	331	312.07	971	193.00	119.99	6.21	173.79	5.28	84516
1970	354	418.51	1182	202.00	148.75	7.36	241.31	6.47	75964
1980	381	589.17	1494	224.00	429.03	19.15	306.95	13.60	84665
1990	416	720.33	1731	209.10	1104.15	52.81	482.25	43.23	98678
1991	420	754.19	1794	201.70	1120.31	55.54	501.58	40.31	99673
1995	427	756.01	1770	167.10	1190.87	71.24	428.36	47.99	1028785
1997	434	810.03	1865	202.90	1721.84	85.79	459.02	66.89	1032267
1998	474	870.40	1844	210.30	2238.31	107.80	442.35	76.43	1035050
1999	490	826.00	1685	191.70	1902.44	100.61	480.71	72.80	1036070
2000	504	847.00	1679	206.90	1898.62	91.80	507.53	84.50	1037006
2001	510	854.00	1675	182.60	1682.11	92.13	463.69	86.70	1039452
2002	511	838.00	1620	201.00	1753.39	87.13	456.54	88.15	1039560
2003	513	857.00	1670	173.00	1534.50	88.76	473.49	89.14	1039750
2004	515	820.00	1592	183.00	1658.15	90.56	454.20	90.15	1039950
2005	518	850.00	1640	195.00	1783.25	91.45	470.15	90.75	1040160
2006	520	855.00	1644	198.00	1813.68	91.60	473.45	91.45	1040250
2007*	522	860.00	1647	200.00	1870.03	93.50	475.20	92.45	1040345

Area in th.ha., Production and Export in m.Kgs., Value of export in crore Rs., Yield kg per ha, Sale in m.kgs, Sale price Rs per kg, labour in number.

Source: Tea Statistics, Tea Board, Kolkata @ estimated.

estates. Additional provisions may be made for innovation and modernization of tea factories and for construction of new labour houses and ancillary buildings.

Though the major part of the increase in output of tea comes from the largest estates, socio-economic considerations necessitate special efforts to improve productivity and income of the existing large number of small garden units which are commonly called family gardens. The entrepreneurs of the family gardens are required to be provided with further technical and financial supports on a cluster approach basis. Besides, construction of modern tea factories in the cooperative sectors, establishment of clonal multiplication centre, supply of improved planting materials, setting up demonstration plots, are some of the activities which require to be strengthened in the interests of small tea planters For effective application of findings of tea research, it would be necessary to organise additional suitable course in technical training very frequently for persons employed in the tea industry as well as for those who opt for a career in tea particularly in non-traditional areas.

3

Primary Marketing and Product Diversification of Tea

SECTION I
Primary Marketing of Tea

Signs of maturity were observed in the tea-marketing scene, which was, perhaps, partly due to the effects of disintegration of the former USSR and partly to the economic liberalization move stoutly pursued by the then Finance Minister, Dr. Manmohan Singh. Early glorious period of Indian tea marketing was restricted to production of teas on Indian soil to suit the needs of British Blenders. Indian tea-sahibs were happy to satisfy the visiting agents, pack the produce in plywood chests and put them on to the holds of vessels sailing for London Port. The estates were largely owned by the Britishers (at least the rich ones) and the accountants in London determined prices. It was happy time. But, frankly, no marketing was involved. It merely served as commodity suppliers for big business. This situation continued for a long time through independence. First shock came from Foreign Exchange Regulation Act (FERA), which was renamed as Foreign Exchange Management Act (FEMA). A great deal of hesitation regarding permissible share of foreign holdings, lack of decisions usually with Govt. of India, led to shifting of ownership of gardens. British planters were losing interest and started developing an alternative source of supply for which Kenya was found to be suitable location. That is, however, another story.

Loss of London Market

With the loss of London market, former USSR and East European countries appeared on the scene, strengthened by a long-term friendship treaty involving rupee trade agreement. Tea became an important item in this pact. Within a short time, the share of former USSR and East European countries surpassed 50 per cent of Indian.export quantum. So the need for exporting more than what India could conveniently do was not strong. However, an ambitious projection of 370 m. kg export by 2000, kept the tea industry busy all the while. The slogan of need for exporting more value added products like packet tea, tea bag and instant tea was heard from all corners. It was all for increasing the foreign exchange earnings. Some meek attempts were made to popularize Indian tea in foreign markets by way of subsiding advertising expenditure on India exporters for their packs with the mention of Indian tea on it. Foreign packers would also receive subsidy if they used a certain per centage of Indian tea in their blends and advertised that point. Funds for such activity were small and mechanism of payment was complicated. As a result, real big tea marketers hardly cared for such schemes. But year after year some money,.which appeared large in Indian context, but chicken feed in the context of global operation, used to be dissipated. After the loss of USSR market when exports fell sharply, there was hardly any scope for toying with such experiments. Collaboration with global operators, attempts to establish brand image, realizing need for consumer research, production of bio-tea and specialities etc. gave Indian tea industry a smart appearance. Convertibility of rupee as a part of liberalization plan provided necessary support for taking right steps. Devalued rupees had positively encouraged larger interest from general currency areas. Indian tea was found more competitive in the world markets. Breakdown of the buying system in CIS countries created such an impact in the international trade that the normal rules of demand and supply did not work. Export projection called for substantial efforts in the field of marketing.

Attempt

Attempt has been made to deal with marketing system of tea, modes of disposal of tea, seven marketing modes, primary marketing, development of auction centres, tea auction facilities, tea auction systems, advantage of auction sale, Tandon Committee on Tea Marketing, ex-garden sales, mini-auction, auction for blended and packet teas. Besides, efforts have been made to devote critical analysis on new auction rules-Ahuja committee 1981, marketing of Indian tea —domestic v/s exports, unrestricted import of tea to allow or not etc. Tea is the most popular of all the beverages in the world. As the largest organized sector, tea is one of the oldest industries in India and holds a considerable potential for the economic development of the country. India has the largest area under tea and is also the largest producer, consumer and exporter of tea in the world. In 2007 India's production was estimated at 850 m. kgs accounting for 29 per cent of world production. Tea export from India was about 210 m. kgs, which represents 18 per cent of world exports. In addition to contributing substantially to national and state ex-chequers directly and indirectly, it is the largest single export commodity earning foreign exchange.

Marketing System of Tea

Tea being a perishable product should be disposed of as quickly as possible. The economic viability of tea industry depends crucially on profitable disposal of its products. The marketing system of India tea deals with marketing channels and Govt. regulations on tea disposal. It refers to the complex system of institutions and operations, which intervene between the producer of tea on one hand and ultimate consumer who drinks his cup of tea, on the other hand. Among the alternative means of disposal, the producer chooses the channel, which brings the best price to him within the purview of Govt. regulations. The marketing channel in tea is the pathway of movement of teas through intermediaries from production in the garden to the hands of the ultimate consumers within or outside the country. Das committee in its study early in 1974 found that marketing of Indian tea was done by a two stage process in which the first stage was the passage of Indian tea as a primary product via the various channels to (i) Indian blender packers (ii) Indian loose tea wholesalers (iii) U.K. importers, (iv) rupee country importers, and (v) non- rupee- non -U.K. importers overseas. In the domestic market, the second stage of tea marketing was two compartment affairs, one of which was the marketing of packets in India by Indian blender packers and the other was the loose tea marketing system.

Modes of Disposal

Tea is marketed and made available to the consumers in two different forms viz. loose and packaged. Loose tea is not subjected to any further major processing after it is purchased at auction. It is sold to the consumer rather in the same condition or in blended form. It is generally not packed in convenient sizes before it is sold. In packet tea trade, on the other hand, tea undergoes further processing and different types of tea are blended and sold to the consumers in packets of conventional sizes. There are mainly three modes of disposal of tea viz. auction, ex-factory or ex-garden and forward contract. Among these the public auction system plays the most important role as Tea (Marketing) Control Order (1984) specifies that 75 per cent of the total output of tea estates should be sold through it. The interlinked modes of disposal of Indian tea are as follows (a) Direct consignment to London auction, (b) Direct sale by forward contract to overseas buyers, (c) Consignment to Indian auctions, (d) Direct ex-factory sale to Indian buyers, (e) Direct sale by forward contract to Indian buyers, (e) Direct Marketing (loose tea) in wholesale markets and. (g) Self-packeting and exports of packets overseas. Over and above, there are some sales of Indian packaged tea abroad and small scale attempts to sell packaged tea in home market by Indian producers.

Marketing Modes of Tea

The seven marketing modes are discussed below:

Direct Consignment to London Auction: London auction is the oldest and pioneer of institutional marketing of tea in the world. Though over the years, the quantity of Indian tea sent directly for auction to London is coming down, still a good quantity of quality Indian tea is shipped directly to London for sale.

Direct Sale by Forward Contract to Overseas Buyers: This practice was very common in the first quarter of the present century. Large buyers in the United Kingdom or the East negotiated forward for the purchase of the whole output of an estate, or for a part there of, over a period of one year or more. The eventual disposal might take many forms. It might be shipped direct to the buyers for general trade distribution; it might be transported in varying quantities to different parts of the world, some of it might find its way to London auction; it might be retained at the port of shipment to be blended and possible packeted there and reshipped to various consuming countries.

Consignment to Indian Auctions: Most of the tea produced in India is sold through the seven auction centres situated in different parts of the country. Here tea is sold to the buyers through brokers, a middleman, who sells tea on behalf of the growers. The tea is sold to highest bidder under the usual rules of sale governing such auction. The seven auction centres of the country are Guwahati, Kolkata, Siliguri, Cochin, Coonoor, Coimbatore, and Amritsar.

Direct Ex-factory Sale to Indian Buyer: By this system tea is sold in the garden itself. This applies to sales from bought leaf factory. Tea produced in such factories is more regularly sold ex-factory to local collectors or dealers through whom it passes to merchants, from whom it may be sold in auction or by private treaty or be shipped. Some estates located on the main road sell tea rather loose or in packets to retail buyers at the factory door, although the amount is less. This gives a quick return to the garden.

Direct Sale by Forward Contract to Indian Buyers: Buyers

Table 1: Primary Marketing of Indian Tea During 1980-2007

Particulars	*1980*		*1990*		*1995*		*2005*		*2007**	
	Qty (1)	*Pc (2)*	*Qty. (1)*	*Pc (2)*	*Qty. (1)*	*Pc (2)*	*Qty. (1)*	*Pc (2)*	*Qty. (1)*	*Pc (2)*
Indian Auction	306.96	53.89	482.25	66.95	428.36	56.66	433.00	52.79	454.00	52.79
London Auction	31.73	5.57	8.13	1.13	3.31	0.44	2.95	0.36	3.00	0.35
Singapore Auction	-	-	-	-	-	-	-	-	-	
Total Auction	338.69	59.46	490.38	68.08	431.66	57.10	435.95	53.15	457.00	53.14
Export under forward contract	22.29	3.92	25.61	3.55	30.02	3.97	38.95	4.75	41.00	4.76
Ex-garden sale	208.56	36.62	204.35	28.37	294.33	38.93	345.32	42.10	362.00	4.77
Total Production	569.54	100.0	702.34	100.0	756.01	100.0	820.22	100.0	860.00	100.0

Source: Various issues of Tea Statistics, Tea Board, India, * provisional, Note –Quantity in million kgs. (1), Per centage to total production (2).

and sellers make a contract even before tea is produced to sell it at a fixed price later. This producer has to sell the teas to the buyers at the agreed price, irrespective of the price of tea later.

Direct Marketing (loose tea) in Wholesale Markets: Growers are selling tea directly in wholesale outlet in the market.

Self-packeting and Export of Packets Overseas: Tea is exported in packet forms from the garden to different countries of the world in company's name.

Primary Marketing

A detail of primary marketing of tea during 1980 to 2005 is given below:

The buyers at the other end of each of these channels are not distinct groups. There is considerable overlap and inter mixture among them. To describe this inter linkage the buyers are categorized into several main types viz. (i) Indian packeters (ii) Indian (loose tea) whole sellers, (iii) rupee country buyers (iv) U.K. importers/ buyers and (v) non- rupee overseas importers. Out of India's total production of 860.00 m. kgs in 2007, quantity sold through auction was 457.95 m. kgs (53.14 per cent), export under forward contract 41 m. kgs (4.76 per cent), and ex-garden sale 362 m.kgs representing 42.10 per cent.

Development of Auction Market in the World

The first organized sale of tea through auction took place at Mincing Lane in London. The East India Company sold its tea in India House, privately till 1838 but after it lost its monopoly of the Indian trade, all tea was sold in the commercial sale- room at Mincing Lane. For the first five years after 1834 tea sold at Mincing Lane was exclusively from China. On 10th January 1839 the first commercial consignment of Indian Tea was sold in the commercial sale –room by the east India Company, which was an event of great importance in the history of Indian tea. As Sir Percival Griffiths in "The History of the Indian Tea Industry" said, "The first importance of tea from the British territories in Assam, consisting of eight chests, containing about 350 pounds, was put up by the East Indian Company in public sale in the commercial sale rooms, Mincing Lane, on the 10th January, 1839 and excited much curiosity". This was the first auction of Indian Tea. The first Indian Tea Auction Centre was established in Kolkata on 27th December 1861. Kolkata Tea Broker's association at first conducted the auction. Since 1947, auctions have been held in Kolkata under the auspices at the Kolkata Tea Traders Association (CTTA). There are 13 auction centres in the world at present out of which seven are in India. Table - 2 shows the dates of establishment of the tea auction centres of India

Table 2: Tea Auction Centres of India

Sl. No.	*Name of the auction centre*	*Date of establishment*
1	Amritsar	30th April, 1964
2	Kolkata	27th December, 1861
3	Cochin	4th July, 1947
4	Coimbatore	22nd November, 1980
5	Coonoor	23rd March, 1963
6	Guwahati	25th September, 1970
7	Siliguri	26th October, 1976

Adapted from G.D. Banerjee's paper on Marketing of Tea is no longer a fashionable slogan, published in IASSI Journal, 2000.

Auction Centres of Abroad

Auction market in Colombo started on 30th July 1883 for Sri Lanka tea. Chittagong auction centre was established on 16 July 1949 to deal in teas of then East Pakistan, now Bangladesh. Nairobi auction market began sale on 7 November 1956 for the sale of African teas. Nairobi auction market has since moved to Mombasa on 14 July 1959. Before the War, Amsterdam was an important auction centre for Indonesian tea. Sale ceased in that auction centre in April 1940 but was resumed in January 1949 and then again suspended in July 1958. Auction sale was inaugurated in Antwerp in 1959 and later suspended in 1966. In 1960 auction started in Hamburg and suspended in 1965. These two auction centres handled Indonesian tea. Limbo auction market started operation in February 1970 and Djakarta auction on 11 December 1972. Thus while London auction market is "*cosmopolitan*" in nature, other markets handle tea of the local producers.

Tea Auction Facilities

The auction facilitates distribution of the largest quantities of the product in the shortest possible time, increases competition among buyers and sellers because of the concentration of the factors of supply and demand under one roof, improves grading and packing, offers advantages to the buyers in finding quickly the type and quantity he wants and extension of credit to buyers by financial institutions. The auction serves, the buyers by enabling them to purchase tea of a much broader variety than they would otherwise be able to, moving from garden to garden individually. The consumer demands certain standardization in tea blends. This is an extremely delicate operation as the quality of tea manufactured day to day of different tea estates very greatly. To achieve this standardization the auctions allow the blenders to match teas from all over India with their blends. Buyers are afforded the widest choice to fulfil their particular requirements, be they for exports, wholesale, retail or blending, while the sellers are provided a platform for attracting the widest range of market through numerous buyers, both internal and export. No other commodity of such a varied quality can be disposed of in so short a time.

Tea Auction System

It has often been claimed that the tea auction system has withstood the test of time. The auctions have been found acceptable by both sellers and buyers and have the approval of the government as well. The auctions provide the producers a ready and reliable means of selling their produce. A new entrant, thanks to the auction system, does not have to necessarily worry about marketing his production. This is not the case with other products where marketing is an essential input. The tea industry has attracted many investors because it is in business straight away, without searching for markets. The producers receive the sale proceeds timely, 14 days after the sale, through a well established, system of *'prompts'*. The buyers have found the auctions beneficial as they cannot only buy at a central point but can watch the operation of their competitors. They do not have to go from door to door for their requirements. Even for private transactions auctions are the barometer. The brokers have been able to evolve an effective system whereby services are efficiently provided to both buyers and sellers. They have been providing market intelligence, manufacturing and agricultural advice to the producers and have regularly compiled useful data for the tea industry, including statistical information. However, as the countdown to the 21st century begins, there appear to be some cracks in the system. More and more producers are going in for direct marketing, by passing the auction system. This trend is likely to continue, as producers would like to exercise personal control over their production. The major buyers have supported the auction system in past. The former USSR bought the bulk of its quantity through the auctions but the disintegration of the former Russia has meant a change in their buying policies and purchases for the Russian Federation and CIS countries today are being done substantially through private sales. Similarly other buyers, to secure quantities, are buying teas privately. In fact, the main supporters of Darjeeling tea have shown a clear preference for private sales during quality periods. The Tea Marketing Control Order of 1984 prescribes that the producers must sell 75 per cent of their production through seven recognized auction centres of India-Guwahati, Siliguri, Cochin, Coonoor, Coimbatore and Amritsar. This order, however, has no teeth and, in any case, it is withdrawn as India moved towards a free economy.

Advantage of Auction Sale

Tea auction centre collects supplies of teas from a large number of go-downs and canalizes them into many areas of the highest demand spread all over the world. As a mechanism of sale, the outstanding virtue of the auction is integrity—the selling and buying are done publicly. The auction is economic gaps of money to the seller. As Goradia observes, the auction centre is a meeting place, where up to 1000 gardens meet some 1000 buyers to trade 3000 to 5000 lots of tea every week, in the course of only 20 hours. The present system of selling tea in auctions through brokers, are selling samples to buyers and printing information catalogue originated in London. The same system, therefore, have been adopted in other tea auction centres also. The auction mechanism has some definite advantages. These are as follows:

- The producers is assured of the fair price on the prevailing market,
- Assurance of continual flow of sale to the producers without fear of a buildup in unsold stocks which may happen in case of other selling modes in times of recession
- No problem of bid collection as payment is automatically collected on the 14th day
- The pushing nature of bidding in tea auction improves price and helps in maintaining a similar price level for comparable lots of tea
- Free sampling, which costs less than 2 per cent, is a vehicle of sales promotion ideal for a commodity of such variety
- As the auction takes place publicity, the integrity of sale in implicit to a producer regardless of his situation from the auction centre or unfamiliarity with mechanics of trading.

Tandon Committee on Marketing

Thus the system of tea auctions, which is more than a century old. Inspite of views occasionally expressed to the contrary, all committees and commissions set up in India and abroad have recommended the continuation of the auction system as the most efficient method of disposal of bulk commodity like tea. The last committee to examine the auction system in India was the Tandon committee, which submitted its report in November 1978. After very careful examination of all aspects of the matter the committee confirmed the need to allow auctions to progress freely.

Recommendations

The committee also recommended that efforts should be made to introduce in different auction centres useful practices followed in other auction centres and to achieve uniformity in rules in different auction centres as far as possible.

Ex-garden Sale

The Tea Board constituted a committee to examine the role of mini auction and recommended that experiments to be watched and modus operandi and their impact on tea trade should be carefully examined to decide the advantages and disadvantages. The committee clearly envisaged the possibility of Mini Auction assuming bigger role in coming years. What is more remarkable is the committee did not decry ex-garden sale and took a certain portion of teas produced being sold at ex-garden as a fait accompli and indispensable from the point of view of products, particularly the weaker section. The need for ex-garden sale arose from the common wisdom of not putting all the eggs in the same basket, which inevitably reduce price. Moreover, having some volume of ex-garden sale is also important for maintaining a satisfactory cash flow position since the sale through auctions it takes 3 to 6 months for the sellers to receive the sale proceeds. In this background the stipulation under the Tea Marketing Control order 1984 that 70 per cent of crop in 1984 and 75 per cent of crop in 1985 onwards should be sold through public auctions in India has been causing serious financial problems for the products apart from reducing the prices realized at auctions.

Recommendations

Stipulation of minimum of crop for sale through auctions in India was held good for two years i.e., 1985 and 1986 but form 1987 on wards, the proportion started declining. This was due to considerable delay in sale through auctions on the one hand and reduction in prices as a result of too much tea being available at auctions, on the other. The existing auctions will also find it extremely difficult to handle the largely increased volume of tea smoothly and promptly unless their facilities are augmented. It is, therefore, proved that other method of disposal of tea should be allowed to play a growing role.

Mini Auction

Tata, which organized mini auction, filled the gap to some extent. It should be encouraged. Simultaneously ex-garden sale, which in 1995 and 2007 accounted for 38.93 per cent and 42.10 per cent to total production, should be allowed to continue and if necessary to increase depending on circumstances so that producers may receive the best possible prices for their produce and sale proceeds may also be received as early as possible which is essential in view of their tight cash-flow position. The quantity sold through auction in 2007 constituted 53.14 per cent of total crop. Over the years, the sale through public auction in per centage terms started fluctuating and it could be able to handle 45 per cent of the crop in immediate future and still lower proportion in the following years. As a result, a bigger role will be played by mini-auctions, London auctions, ex-garden sales as well as C and F Export.

Recommendation

Any dogmatic insistence on increasing sales through public auctions in India without considering the capacity of the auction centres on the one hand and effects of such a policy on tea prices and financial position of tea producers, on the other hand, will only create utter confusion in the tea industry and trade and an inevitable slump in tea prices. Mini auctions in particular have a big role to play as a method, which lies in between public auction and ex-garden sale. Tea Board had drawn up a set of model rules to govern, these mini- auction so as to remove the scope for under invoicing and evils associated with public auctions.

Auction for Blended and Packet Teas

There is a need for other innovative approaches. Auctioning of blended teas and packeted teas would be one such approach. It should cover not only teas blended and or packeted by tea producers but also teas blended and or packeted by buyers of loose tea. In fact traders rather than producers may take the lead in organizing auctions of blended and packeted teas, which may be purchased by second stage traders for either domestic consumption or export. On immediate beneficiary effect of this approach would be elimination of the oligopolistic hold on the matter for packer teas enjoyed by few packers with consequent reduction in prices for the ultimately consumers who have to pay exorbitant prices for the teas purchased by them because of high profit margin enjoyed by traders at different levels of distribution channels and do not get any relief even when auction prices decline. Table 3 indicates the per centage of offerings through auctions since 1990.

Table 3: Production and Sales of Tea During 1900 to 2007

(Quantity in million kgs)

Year	*Production auctions*	*Sold through auctions*	*Percent sold in*
1900	89.60	24.60	27.45
1910	119.60	34.50	28.85
1920	156.60	37.50	23.96
1930	177.40	42.00	23.67
1940	210.40	45.20	21.48
1950	275.50	113.60	41.23
1960	321.10	173.80	54.13
1970	418.50	241.30	57.66
1980	569.20	307.00	53.93
1985	656.20	505.30	77.00
1986	620.80	468.40	75.45
1987	674.30	472.50	70.07
1988	701.10	504.40	71.96
1989	684.10	477.40	69.78
1990	702.34	474.00	65.80
1991	754.20	501.20	66.45

1992	732.30	448.00	61.18
1993	760.80	441.70	58.06
1994	752.90	428.30	56.89
1995	756.90	428.40	56.66
1996	780.00	427.30	56.52
1997	810.60	442.20	56.99
1998	870.40	454.70	52.24
1999	880.20	464.70	52.79
2000	846.92	447.93	52.89
2001	853.92	460.60	52.95
2002	838.47	457.22	54.20
2003	857.06	472.47	55.25
2004	820.22	435.95	53.13
2007	860.00	457.00	53.14

Source: Various issues of Tea Statistics, Tea Board, India.

The tea market control order came into force from 19th April 1984. It will be seen from the data that quantity of offerings went up to 1991. It however, showed steady decline, except 2004. With the ever-expanding middle class in India, packets and branded goods are becoming more and more popular. The number of producer packet, the sale of which privately permitted under the tea marketing control order, has increased. The poly pouch with the "garden fresh" slogan is popularizing packet teas in India. The consumer packets, packed at the gardens, are sold directly and do not go through the auctions. Improved communications have also helped expanding the private sale market.

New Tea Auctions Rules—Ahuja Committee, 1985

The tea (marketing) control order 1984 was promulgated by the government of India in April, 984. This order made it obligatory for the organizers of public tea auctions and brokers to obtain a license from the Tea Board. Furthermore, all tea manufacturers in India had to register themselves with Tea Board and sell 75 per cent of their annual production through the medium of public auctions. The Chairman, Tea Board being the Licensing/Registering Authority was empowered to oversee the functioning of the tea auction centres and to issue directives whenever necessary to ensure that the public auctions run smoothly, efficiently and in the best interests of all concerned. The Tea Board, thus, became directly involved in the tea auction system. The public tea auction system plays a vital role in the tea trade and industry. There are seven recognized auction centres in India at Kolkata, Siliguri, Guwahati, Cochin, Coonoor, Coimbatore and Amritsar. Out of the total Indian production of 820 million kgs in 2004, 435.95 million kgs of tea was sold through the auctions (details in Table 3).

The tea auction committees at various centres have been reviewing the rules governing their respective auction centres from time to time and have been updating them in line with the changing times, conditions and need. Despite this, the tea board received grievances and requests from all sections of the trade to look into certain areas, which needed further improvement. The *"Out lot"* sales and distribution of free trade samples were the first amongst the issues raised with the Tea Board. In August 1985, by an administrative order, the Chairman, tea board formed a committee headed by Sri S.S. Ahuja, the then Deputy Chairman, tea board *"to study the existing rules of all the public tea auction centres in India and to suggest changes wherever necessary to bring improvement in the auction system"*. This committee on auction rules also known as the *"Ahuja Committee"* submitted its final report.

Recommendations

The committee submitted its recommendations in the third week of April 1990. As its first task, the Committee identified eleven areas. These are: *(a)* auction day, *(b)* catalogues, *(c)* prompt date, *(d)* broker's commission, *(e)* size of lots, *(f)* brokers commissions, *(g)* division of lots, *(h)* withdrawal of lots, *(i)* sale of outlets, *(j)* warehouse rent and insurance, *(k)* closing of catalogues, and *(l)* distribution of samples, for details examination. The Ahuja Committee submitted four interim reports and a final report, the recommendations of which were accepted by the Chairman, tea board. The main features of this report were as appended below:

i. *Auction Day*—The committee had examined the

possibility of conducting auctions at all the centres on the same day instead of separate days as is the current practice to avoid speculative tendencies, if any. The committee, however, recommended that the present system of holding auctions on different days at different places should continue as it is running satisfactorily. The auctions at each centre have to be completed in two days and no more. For this, the auction committees have been asked to look into their infrastructure and make additional alternative auction rooms, if required. The brokers must be given fixed timings and must strictly adhere to them.

ii. Catalogue—The committee recommended that CTC leaf, orthodox leaf. Darjeeling leaf, green tea, all dusts and the supplemented teas be printed separately. This was because of sampling norms and proper maintenance of category wise statistical data. The brokers have been asked to deliver samples, catalogues etc. strictly within the specified time limits so that the buyers are not inconvenienced.

iii. Prompt Data—The committee suggested no major change in the present system of payment of prompts at the various auction centres. The buyers and sellers prompt falls due on different days after the date of the sale at various centres. For example, in Coonoor the buyers prompt, is on the 12th day after the date of the sale and for the sellers it is the 13th day after the sale. In Siliguri prompt is payable by the buyers on the 13th day which is paid to the sellers on the 14th day. In Kolkata, the buyer prompt is on the 14th day for leaf and 15th day for dust. Although there is no specification on sellers prompt in Kolkata, the brokers disburse to the producers' prompt on the same day it is received from the buyers. The committee recommended that the payment of the prompt to the seller by the broker should be the next working day immediately after the stipulated prompt date of the buyer. The committee has also recommended that the auction committee should not extend prompts unless the circumstances are exceptional.

iv. Brokerage—The sellers pay 1 per cent of the selling price to the brokers as commission. However, in South India, the brokerage is calculated on the selling price minus excise duty. Furthermore, buyers pay to the brokers, for various services rendered at the rate of Rs 5 per 100 kg in Siliguri and Guwahati. In the South there is no commission payable by the buyers to the brokers but there is a system of "lot money" According to this report, henceforth, brokerage paid by the seller will be calculated on the "knocked down" price, thus changing the current practice in the South.

v. Size of Lots—In the North, tea estates (except Darjeeling) producing two lakh kg or more will have to pack in lots not less than 30 packages during manufacturing periods between 1st July to 30th November. The only exceptions will be BPS, small Dusts and Secondary in the CTC category and tippy teas like BPS, Fannings, Dusts and Secondary in the orthodox category.

vi. Division of Lots—In order to expedite the speed of sale in the North Indian auction centres, the committee has recommended that brokers should not issue more than two contracts for 30 packages for under and more than three contracts for 31 packages and above. No buyer should get less than five packages in a division. However, for Darjeeling teas there is no change recommended and therefore up to 15 chests one buyer, 16 to 30 chests two buyers and above 30 chests three buyers will continue.

vii. Withdrawal of Lots—In Kolkata, where auctions normally take place on Mondays and Tuesdays every week, sellers will have to give advance intimation to the brokers about withdrawal of any teas included in the catalogue for sale at the latest by 1.00 p.m on Wednesday of the week immediately proceeding the week prior to the sale in question. This principle will apply to all other North Indian centres. In the South this problem is not so visible and therefore no change has been suggested.

Viii. Sale Lot Outlets—The Tea Board had earlier directed that teas remaining unsold in the auction room should *not be sold as outlets*. The Auction Committees have the option either to supplement the unsold teas in the following week's auction without re-sampling or reprinting them in subsequent auctions with fresh sampling. This practice is to continue. The quantity of Indian tea sold through different auction centres in India are presented below:

Table 4: Disposal of North and South Indian Tea Through Various Auctions During 1984-2004

(Quantity in million kgs)

Particular/year	*1984*	*1887*	*1990*	*1993*	*1997*	*1999*	*2004*	*2007*
Total production	639.90	674.30	720.30	760.80	810.60	880.20	820.22	860.00
Quantity sold through								
Kolkata	114.70	132.60	129.20	102.30	89.00	95.10	86.31	90.28
Siliguri	72.20	80.60	90.00	75.80	80.00	85.30	85.20	89.12
Guwahati	89.00	147.70	140.90	151.30	150.20	151.30	138.30	144.66
Amritsar	0.30	0.40	0.40	0.10	0.80	0.90	0.90	0.94
Total North Indian Auction Sale	276.20	361.30	360.50	329.50	320.10	332.60	310.70	325.00
Quantity sold through								
Cochin	64.00	52.30	52.30	52.00	56.10	58.50	54.60	57.20
Coonoor	23.00	27.40	36.90	41.00	44.80	57.30	54.95	57.70
Coimbatore	27.50	31.50	24.30	19.00	21.20	16.30	15.70	17.10
Total South Indian Auction Sale	114.50	111.20	113.50	112.20	122.10	132.10	125.25	132.00
Total All India Auction Sale	390.70	472.50	474.00	441.70	442.20	464.70	435.95	457.00

Source: Same as Table 1.

ix. Warehouse Rent and Insurance—In Siliguri and Guwahati the sellers' liability for rent and insurance is up to a specified time on the prompt date. Thereafter, the liability, passes on to the buyers. In Cochin, Coonoor and Coimbatore, the goods are at sellers risk to the extent of sale price only until a specified time on the second working day after the prompt date. However, in Kolkata the sellers bear additional 14 days rent beyond the prompt date. The Committee recommended that the system in Kolkata should be urgently reviewed so that the system prevalent in Siliguri and Guwahati finds acceptance in due course and progressively.

x. Closing Catalogue—The committee felt that the availability of teas for the domestic market, despite seasonality of tea production in the North, should be regular and adequate all through. Therefore, regular consultations were suggested to achieve this objective.

xi. Distribution of Samples—This has been a major area of debate and the committee's recommendations were elaborate. The committee felt that issuance of free trade samples to the trade could not be claimed as a matter of right. Free trade samples should be worked out and supplied in a manner that encourages genuine, regular and energetic buyers but at the same time discourages frivolous and/or casual buying. The committee, therefore, specified qualifications for small, medium and large buyers for each category of tea and for each auction centre. The committee further recommended that over and above the minimum per centage purchase qualification, each buyer shall have to operate in at least 25 per cent of the sales held for the category concerned for the purchase year to be eligible for free trade samples in the immediate succeeding sampling year. The committee further dealt with matters like purchase of trade samples, restricted sampling of expensive teas, defined powers of the sampling committee and status of 'on account of concerned' teas.

x. Quantum of Samples—The brokers ensure delivery of proper quantum of samples to the buyers in order to streamline the system. Further, it is recommended that brokers while sending trade samples must clearly indicate in the challans the number of large, medium and small samples-category- wise sent in a consignment with its total net weight. The quantity of purchase samples has been increased to 300 gm.

xi. Bidding Rates—With a view to improving auctioning efficiency the following scales of bidding should be introduced in Kolkata, Siliguri and Guwahati:

Up to Rs. 26.99	20 paise/kg
Rs. 27.00 to 49.99	50 paise/kg
Rs. 50.00 to 99.00	1 Re./kg
Rs. 100 & above	5 Rs/kg

xii. Claims for Shortages, Non-Delivery, Damaged Teas—The Committee has recommended that no claim for short weight will be admissible unless the shortage exceeds 0.1 per cent of the declared weight per lot purchased by any buyer. The Committee recommends that where lots purchased by the buyers are not to be found at the ware house at all either wholly or in part, a compensation amounting to 30 per cent of value of such teas should be payable to the buyer.

xiii. Supervision—The Committee considered that way back in 1978, the P.L. Tandon Committee strongly favoured the public auction of teas as the best means of bulk marketing and also desired that infrastructure of the tea board should be strengthened for the proper supervision and co-ordination of the public auction system. Owing to various financial and other aspects, this has possibly not been given effect to so far. Tea (Marketing) control order, 1984 issued by the government under the tea act, 1953, provides that 75 per cent of the tea production is to be routed through the public auctions thereby clearly indicating the mind of the government of India in this respect. The committee, therefore, after carefully reviewing the situation recommended that the tea board should devise ways and means of strengthening the infrastructure for proper supervision and co-ordination of the public auction system in North and South India to sub-serve the Government policy and the larger public interest.

The Ahuja committee comprised of members, from all sections of the Indian tea trade and its, recommendations have been sent by the chairman, tea board to the auction committees. Tea Board accepted some of the recommendations made by the Ahuja committee report and therefore it becomes a directive under the tea (Marketing) control order 1984. The Auction committees can, however, approach the authorities on specific issues with their problems and suggestions to ensure easier implementation of the Ahuja Committee report. The 'Report of the Committee on auction rules' is a major report on the auction system and is a valuable document produced after a great deal of effort and toil. It is a work of dedication and shows genuine interest in the working of the tea industry. The Report will go a long way in further strengthening the bonds between the trinity of the tea trade, namely, buyers, sellers and brokers.

Collaborations Such as Tata-Telly, Maceil Magor, Nestle are valid international tickets for global market destinations. Big contract by Iran did help to push up export but such sales cannot be depended upon until demand for a particular brand arises from consumer level, going alone in the world market to establish a blend is a tough job. Indian big business houses are glancing at tea for diversification for example ITC-who can use their overseas connections not only for bulk exports but marketing a brand as well. Internally most of the big tea companies are buying for better share of their brands at the consumer level. As a result number of packs have appeared in the domestic market leading a healthy competition. A commendable step was taken by Bombay Burmah group by creating production facilities for ecologically cultivated tea at Singampatti—southern tip of India. There is a wide- open area in the speciality market, taping of which calls for marketing skill. There is no more a fashionable slogan shouting and bureautic luxuries. It is hopeful sign that mature marketing activity is seen today in Indian tea scene. Hopefully 2010 would begin with a boom of innovative marketing process.

Tea Market Trend

Tea is a tradition bound industry. The changing world order in the last three years, however, has left its own impact on tea. The coming down of the Berlin wall and the disintegration of the former USSR have led to many changes and opened up several opportunities for the tea world. The first, second and the third world are moving more and more towards freer economy, freer trade and freer investment. Consumerism has taken the front seat even in the developing and poor countries. Further more, the developed countries are moving towards healthier products and quality assurances. Environmentally friendly bulk packaging is being encouraged and to put pressure on the exporters, the disposal or "unfriendly" packaging material is being made the responsibility of the exporter. In addition, many new trends have emerged, particularly for Indian tea, some of which are discussed below.

Production: In 2007, the Indian production should reach 880 million kgs, which will be second highest ever. Quality consciousness and the widening price concerting have put brakes on rapid growth of production. In 2007, if the weather is right, India should harvest a crop of 900 million kgs. It is also clear that unless new areas are brought under tea cultivation, tea production will grow at a small rate of around 3 per cent per annum. Again, it is necessary to renovate tea areas, which are more than sixty years of age. A replanting programme of two per cent per annum will ensure a rotation over fifty years. An attempt was made in Union Budget of 2005 to go for Special Purpose Vehicle for replantation/rejuvenation of tea areas by Tea Board. The Board is looking into this aspect and several meetings with Ministry, GoI, stakeholders etc. were convened. It is expected to have a concrete shape.

Domestic Market: India's per capita consumption of tea is amongst the lowest. Yet in volume terms India is the largest consumer. With the population having reached more than 100 crore in 2007 even if an Indian were to drink one extra cup a year, the additional requirement of tea for domestic consumption would be 2.55 million kgs. If ten cups extra were to be drunk every day by every Indian, then the requirement would be 25.5 million kgs. Taken into account one cup extra to be drunk every day by every Indian, the additional requirement works out to 931 million kg per annum. Indian is indeed a very powerful market. Another important factor to note is that the Indians drink the very best of CTCs and are prepared to pay a premium for quality. Because of the strong domestic base, Indian tea prices are generally higher than the world prices. The superior quality of Indian tea and its vast variety has also helped in maintaining higher price levels.

Export: It has now become clear that the government of India will not hinder, in any way, exports of Indian tea. Procedures are being simplified and restrictions have been eased or fully removed. The Government of India and the tea industry have been working towards improving per unit returns from exports and value added products have been gaining ground. Whilst it is unlikely that the government will impose any restrictions on exports in the foreseeable future, the pressure from the domestic market will limit the quantum of Indian tea exports in the years to come. A strategy, therefore, has to be evolved so that even through the export quantities remain around 200 million kg, the value will go on increasing. Barter deals and government-to-government buying appear to be thing of the past and trading, in future will be done in hard currency. The former USSR is today an open market and although there is a preference for Indian teas in the Russian Federation and CIS countries, other producers especially China, which has a vast common border, would exploit the large potential of this market. The producer exporters are already playing a major role in certain importing countries and this trend is likely to spread further.

The Auction System

The major tea groups, today, are increasingly marketing their own teas either through domestic packers or direct exports. Whilst the auctions will continue to be the barometer for price levels, more and more producers are likely to go in for direct marketing. The smaller producers who have gone in for direct marketing through soft packs may find the going rough unless they start putting in the essential marketing inputs like advertising etc. as well. Their present method of sale is virtually bulk-marketing through a third party. The quantity from these producers is likely to revert back to the auctions.

Import of Tea

From time to time idea of importing tea into India has been mooted. Importing cheap teas for domestic consumption will not solve the problem. Indians drink good quality tea and the imported varieties will not suit their taste. Furthermore, if 40 to 50 million kg of tea were to be imported, there would be a phenomenal price increase in the world markets. India has to be very careful so as not to upset the apple cart.

Promotion-Healthfulness

As consumption of tea in certain developed countries is not increasing, the time has come to give a new *"position"* to tea. The world is today more health conscious than ever before and *"healthfulness"* could be the new slogan for tea. The *"cheapness" slogan has to be discarded.*

Quality: One way of increasing tea consumption, in the world market, is to ensure that the consumer is served good quality teas. Producers and importers of tea will have to make sure that sub-standard teas are neither produced nor imported. Universal acceptance of international standard ISO 3720 will help in lifting quality standards of all growths. India is perhaps the only country today, which strictly follows rigid quality standards.

Culture Products: All the tea bagging machines in India is busy fulfilling export- orders and some domestic needs. But the product of the future is instant tea. Time is not far when a "drinkable" pure instant tea, which is both hot and cold water soluble, will be on the shelves.

Bulk Packaging: While bulk packaging is still searching for an alternative to the tea chest, paper sacks are being used more and more. The real answer lies in convincing the tea importers to accept gunny bags, which are already popular in the domestic market. In the overall, the future prospects of tea appear to be bright and the tea industry in India is ready to face the challenges of the 21st century.

Table 5: Country Wise Exports from India During 1947 to 2004

(In million kgs)

Country/year	*1947*	*1957*	*1967*	*1977*	*1987*	*1991*	*1997*	*1999*	*2004*
United Kingdom	127.20	135.40	117.20	74.30	22.40	22.50	25.40	25.00	25.10
Per cent of export	66.30	68.00	53.80	32.40	11.09	11.09	12.70	12.10	12.11
Ireland	9.00	8.30	6.20	6.40	2.10	2.50	2.60	2.50	2.50
Per cent of export	4.70	4.20	2.80	2.80	1.04	1.23	1.28	1.20	1.19
Netherlands	1.50	0.90	3.70	3.40	1.60	1.90	2.70	2.60	2.60
Per cent of export	0.80	0.50	1.70	1.50	0.79	0.90	1.33	1.27	1.26
West Germany	NII	1.90	2.20	5.80	4.70	4.70	6.90	6.60	6.65
Per cent of export	Nil	0.90	1.00	2.50	2.33	2.30	3.40	3.20	3.21
Rest of West Europe	0.60	0.10	0.50	0.90	0.50	0.60	0.80	0.80	0.80
Per cent of export	0.30	0.05	0.20	0.40	0.20	0.30	0.40	0.40	0.40
Poland	NIL	NIL	1.80	5.30	10.70	11.90	14.00	14.70	14.75
Per cent of export	NIL	NIL	0.80	2.80	5.30	5.90	6.90	7.10	7.11
Yugoslavia	NIL	NII	0.50	4.70	1.40	0.20	0.30	0.40	0.40
Per cent of export	NIL	NIL	0.20	2.00	0.70	0.10	0.15	0.17	0.16
Rest of East Europe	NIL	0.10	1.70	1.40	3.30	1.00	1.60	1.40	1.40
Per cent of export	NIL	0.05	0.80	0.60	1.60	0.50	0.80	0.70	0.70
USSR	4.00	7.30	20.70	47.70	96.60	104.50	90.70	92.80	94.10
Per cent of export	2.10	3.60	9.50	20.80	47.80	51.50	44.70	44.90	44.95
Afghanistan	NIL	NIL	5.70	8.60	3.60	1.60	0.80	1.20	1.20
Per cent of export	NIL	NIL	2.60	3.70	1.80	0.80	0.40	0.60	0.60
Iran	3.90	5.60	1.80	6.60	18.90	14.80	11.70	12.80	12.80
Per cent of export	2.00	2.80	1.10	2.90	9.40	7.30	5.80	6.20	6.15
Iraq	1.40	0.02	2.50	4.60	8.80	—	0.10	0.04	0.40
Per cent of export	0.70	0.00	1.10	2.00	4.30	—	0.01	0.02	0.02
Persian Gulf Ports	4.40	2.60	3.00	6.20	7.00	5.20	6.80	7.02	7.02

per cent of export	2.30	1.30	1.40	2.70	3.50	2.60	3.35	3.40	3.40
Jordan	NIL	NIL	1.40	0.60	—	0.50	0.10	0.60	0.60
Per cent of export	—	—	0.60	0.30	0.05	0.20	0.20	0.30	0.36
Rest of Middle East	0.60	0.30	0.05	0.07	0.30	—	0.20	0.20	0.20
Per cent of export	0.30	0.10	0.02	0.03	0.10	—	0.10	0.10	0.10
Pakistan	NIL	NIL	NIL	4.60	0.60	0.30	0.40	O.4	0.40
Per cent of export	—	—	—	2.00	0.30	0.15	0.20	0.20	0.26
Japan	NIL	NIL	0.30	0.80	1.40	2.00	1.90	2.30	2.30
Per cent of export	—	—	0.10	0.30	0.30	1.00	0.90	1.10	1.10
Arab Rep. of Egypt	1.80	7.30	16.60	14.10	7.80	7.90	7.20	7.60	7.60
Per cent of export	0.90	3.70	7.60	6.10	3.90	3.90	3.50	3.70	3.76
Sudan	0.70	2.00	10.00	13.60	0.10	—	0.10	0.10	0.10
Per cent of export	0.40	1.00	4.60	5.70	0.05	—	0.05	0.06	0.06
Tunisia	NIL	NIL	3.80	1.20	1.00	1.70	1.50	1.90	1.90
Per cent of export	—	—	1.70	0.50	0.50	0.80	0.70	0.90	0.90
Rest of Africa	NIL	NIL	—	0.40	3.70	7.00	9.80	9.50	9.50
Per cent of export	—	—	—	0.20	1.80	3.40	4.80	4.60	4.60
Canada	8.20	7.70	3.90	2.50	0.80	0.60	0.10	0.15	0.15
Per cent of export	4.30	3.90	1.80	1.10	0.40	0.30	0.05	0.07	0.07
USA	17.30	10.60	8.40	10.00	1.80	2.50	2.90	3.30	3.30
Per cent of export	9.00	5.30	3.90	4.40	0.90	1.20	1.40	1.60	1.60
Australia	7.00	3.40	5.40	4.60	0.70	0.80	0.50	0.60	0.60
Per cent of export	3.70	1.70	2.50	2.00	0.30	0.40	0.25	0.30	0.30
New Zealand	0.50	0.70	0.40	1.30	—	—	—	—	—
Per cent of export	0.30	0.40	0.20	0.60	—	—	—	—	—
All other countries	3.60	5.00	0.10	0.50	4.30	8.10	13.40	11.95	11.95
Per cent of export	1.90	2.50	0.05	0.20	2.10	4.00	6.63	5.81	5.81
Total	191.70	199.20	217.80	229.60	201.90	201.72	200.71	189.02	183.64

Source: Same as Table 1.

Marketing of Indian Tea—Domestic Verses Export

Indian tea's popular slogan since Independence has been "world's largest producer, consumer and exporter of Tea". In 2004, however, Sri Lanka forged ahead and exported 238 million kg against Indian exports of 184 million kg. Again, in 1991 and 2003 Sri Lanka exported more than India. Sri Lankan exports for these years were 212 million kg and 235 million kg respectively, against Indian exports of 201 million kg and 202 million kg. Another feature of Indian exports has been the sea change in its profile between 1947 and 2004. In 1947 U.K.'s share of Indian exports was 66 per cent and in 2004 it has declined to 12 per cent. On the other hand, the former Soviet Union, which bought no Indian teas till the 60's became the major importer of Indian tea, it accounted for 44.9 per cent of Indian tea exports in 2004.

Countries like Poland, Yugoslavia, Afghanistan, Japan, Tunisia and even Germany bought no teas from India in 1947 but today are strong supporters of the Indian produce. Iraq, Iran, Gulf, ARE have been buying more but Canada, USA, Australia, New Zealand and the UK, have reduced their purchased from India substantially. In the 57 years period since 1947, African Countries, particularly Kenya, have been giving stiff competition to Indian CTC teas and have gained popularity in the hard currency areas. Sri Lanka, on the other hand, a major producer of orthodox, has been stepping into the Indian orthodox exports and took credit for catering to the entire expansion and demand in the orthodox segment. The only exception has been the former USSR who has supported Indian orthodox varieties strongly. Sri Lanka has been catering to the growing markets of ARE, Iran, USA, and Pakistan.

An encouraging feature of Indian tea exports has been a rise in value added goods and instant Tea. Packet exports in a 24 years span between 1981 and 2004 went up from 32 million kgs to 125 million kgs, thus showing and increase of about 400 per cent. The instant tea exports in the same 24 years period nearly doubled raising, from 0.78 million kgs to 117.68 million kgs Exports of value added teas have

Table 6 : India's Share in World Exports During 1947-2004

(In million kg)

Country/year	*1947*	*1957*	*1967*	*1977*	*1987*	*1991*	*1997*	*1999*	*2004*
India	191.70	199.20	217.80	229.60	201.90	201.72	200.71	189.02	183.64
Per cent Share	53.30	39.90	35.60	28.20	20.70	17.90	13.20	18.50	18.25
Sri Lanka	130.30	166.80	216.50	185.50	201.20	212.40	234.85	238.05	291.01
Per cent Share	36.30	33.40	35.40	22.70	20.60	18.80	21.24	21.52	21.60
Indonesia	3.90	38.80	26.60	51.30	90.40	109.60	103.90	102.50	86.42
Per cent Share	1.10	7.80	4.30	6.30	9.20	9.70	9.40	9.60	9.70
Bangladesh	N.A	4.50	Negligible	26.00	21.60	25.30	24.30	25.40	12.45
Per cent Share	Negligible	0.90	Negligible	3.20	2.20	2.20	2.40	2.30	2.32
Kenya	4.40	8.20	19.70	70.20	135.00	191.60	245.50	251.10	326.20
Per centShare	1.20	1.60	3.20	8.60	13.80	16.90	22.20	22.70	22.73
Uganda	1.10	2.80	9.60	14.70	2.10	4.70	15.20	15.10	16.10
Per cent Share	0.30	0.60	1.60	1.80	0.20	0.40	1.40	1.40	1.42
Tanzania	0.50	2.40	6.20	12.00	11.40	15.00	18.80	19.90	24.95
Per cent Share	0.10	0.50	1.00	1.50	1.20	1.30	1.70	1.80	1.82
Malawi	5.90	8.80	16.80	29.90	33.40	41.20	36.50	35.40	47.20
Per cent Share	1.70	1.80	2.70	3.70	3.40	3.60	3.30	3.20	3.21
Mozambique	1.50	5.90	14.40	15.60	2.10	1.00	0.42	0.95	0.97
Per cent Share	0.40	1.20	2.40	1.90	0.20	0.09	0.04	0.05	0.08
Others	20.20	61.70	84.40	180.60	277.50	338.40	223.23	213.60	216.15
Per cent Share	5.60	12.30	13.80	22.10	28.40	29.90	25.12	18.93	19.25
Total	359.50	499.10	612.00	815.40	976.60	1132.10	1105.70	1106.20	1501.00

Source: Same as Table 1, Note—Exports in 2007 has been estimated at 200 m. kgs.

Table 7: Indian Consumption of Tea During 1947-2004

(In million kgs)

Particulars/Year	*1947*	*1957*	*1967*	*1977*	*1987*	*1991*	*1997*	*1999*	*2004*	*2007*
Consumption	98.5	112.9	180.7	302.0	446.0	520.0	635	670	740	785
Growth (per cent age)	—	14.6	60.1	67.1	47.6	16.6	22.1	5.5	10.5	6.1
Average annual rate of growth per cent age	—	1.46	6.01	6.7	4.76	4.2	3.7	2.3	2.8	2.0

Table 8: Indian Tea Consumption: As Per centage of Production

Particulars/Year	*1947*	*1957*	*1967*	*1977*	*1987*	*1991*	*1997*	*1999*	*2004*	*2007*
Consumption in m. kgs	98.5	112.9	180.7	302.0	446.0	520.0	635.0	670.0	740.00	785.00
Production in m kgs	254.8	310.8	384.8	556.3	674.3	741.7	810.6	880.2	820.00	86.00
Per cent of production	38.7	36.3	47.0	54.3	66.0	70.1	78.3	76.1	90.12	91.3

Source: same as Table 1.

gone up in 9 years from 33.85 million kgs to 116.68 million kgs. In value terms the earnings from Packets increased from Rs 69.98 crores to Rs 836.65 crores; in the case of tea bags the earnings raised from Rs 3.26 crores to Rs 13.58 crores. The total value of Indian exports in 2004 was Rs 990.50 crores as against Rs 55.38 crores in 1947 and Rs 76.90 crores in 1999. India's share in world exports is shown in table below:

In the domestic front also, the scene has changed. In 1947, Indian consumption was only 39 per cent of production and in 1999 this figure reached 76 per cent. In the past, the equation was "Indian consumption equals production minus exports". In the eighties, this equation was reversed and on several occasions, the government restricted export to conserve tea for the domestic market. The details of Indian consumption of tea in given below:

The break-up of the Soviet Union has therefore had a strong impact on the Indian tea market. However, it gained momentum over the years. Russia and other CIS members did not cross 45 million kgs. Total Indian exports estimated at 200 m. kgs at 2007. Indian domestic market continues to grow at around 2 per cent per annum. The 1999 domestic consumption was about 670 million kgs. By 2007 this figure went up to 7852 million kgs. If export of 200 million kgs is added, production in 2008 would be about 985 million kgs. The CTC element of Indian consumption is over 94 per cent. It is estimated that in 2010 the Indian requirement for CTC teas has been estimated at 1034 million kgs, which would go up to 1050 million kgs in 2012. State wise split of estimated consumption of tea is furnished below:

New strategies will have to be evolved for the Russian Federation, CIS and Pakistan. Above all, exports will have to be given a clear priority over domestic need. While future supply and demand, on the overall, appears *'hand to-mouth'* the future of speciality varieties, such as Darjeeling and Assam orthodox, would depend upon aggressive marketing.

Unrestricted Import of Tea: To Allow or Not

Proposal of ministry of commerce, Government of India,

modified the export-import policy (2002-07) with a view to facilitating the EOU/EPZ to freely import teas for bulk-re-exports generated unfathomable dissatisfaction among many Barons of the India's tea industry. Tea imports were allowed with the rider that they should be used only for re-export with a 20 per cent value addition. But the imports were insignificant because the facility was limited to re-export of packaged teas, tea bags and instant tea. The Commerce Ministry sought the industry's view on allowing bulk re-export of tea blended with the imported product. Barons of the Indian tea association asserted: (i) having an exportable surplus, India does not need to import teas; (ii) if the imported low grade teas are blended with better stuff of the country to export as tea bags, packets, instant tea, its image would be damaged at the international market and exports suffer in the long run; (iii) under the Exim policy (2002-2007) for tea, exporters were not allowed to sell any portion of the manufactured items in the domestic market.

Table 9: A State-wise Split of Estimated Consumption During 1991-2008

(Million kgs)

Particulars/Year	*1991*	*1995*	*1999*	*2004*	*2007*	*2008*
Uttar Pradesh	44	50	57	67	72	71
Bihar	18	23	25	25	28	27
Maharashtra	67	76	86	99	107	105
West Bengal	38	43	48	52	57	55
Andhra Pradesh	25	30	32	33	35	35
Madhya Pradesh	32	38	40	43	47	46
Tamil Nadu	21	23	26	28	30	30
Rajasthan	45	48	52	56	60	59
Gujarat	45	50	57	67	72	71
Orissa	10	12	18	20	21	21
Kerala	33	37	40	44	49	48
Assam	18	20	23	25	27	27
Punjab	40	45	50	55	59	57
Haryana	18	20	22	24	25	25
Jammu & Kashmir	10	15	20	22	25	24
Karnataka	26	30	34	36	39	38
Others	30	35	40	44	47	46
Total	520	595	670	740	850	785

Source: Same as Table 1.

But the leaders of the Indian tea industry feared that once bulk teas, allowed to be imported, there would also be an option for unloading these teas in the domestic market. And a few larger business houses, facing stiff competition in the domestic market, would practically use the cheap imported product to reduce their prices in a bid to earn and maintain substantial profit and hold the domestic share; (iv) import of teas by India would raise international prices of teas while depressing domestic markets, a situation, which would adversely effect the growth of tea industry that may eventually lead to recession. The aforesaid premises, as a corollary, led many barons of the industry to raise strong objection against the government's intention of further liberalizing the Exim policy, which may open the floodgates for import of teas. They felt that the policy, if implemented, would not, in anyway, help the growth of the country's tea industry. But, however, one should not be touchy and emotional while considering the policy of import. Rather, it was imperative to visualize the necessity of imports in the perspective of reality. And no denying the fact, that only such a study can help comment judiciously either in favour or against the proposed policy.

Production vis-à-vis Consumption

Whilst it was unlikely that the government would impose any restriction on exports in the foreseeable future, the pressure from the domestic market would limit the quantum of Indian tea exports in the years to come. As stated earlier that with the country's population touched more than 100 crore, ever if an Indian was to drink one extra cup a year, the additional requirement of tea would be 2.55 million kgs again, if ten cups extra were to be taken every day by every Indian, the additional requirement would be 931 million kgs per annum. But *how much the industry with its present capacity can produce at the maximum*? It may be mentioned, however, that tea production was achieved in 2007 at 860 million kgs. It was high in 1998 with the crop amounting to 874 million kgs, indicated by Mr. A.K. Bothra, Chairman, North Bengal branch of the India tea association at the 27th annual general meeting of the association. And this achievement is, of course, due to maximum favour of all inputs, practically the climatic condition. But he reiterated that the tea industry immediately requires more additional plantation area to meet the target of 1,000 million kgs by the end of the twenty first century. Otherwise, tea production will grow at a small rate of around 3 per cent per annum.

Nevertheless, it is necessary to renovate tea areas, which are more than sixty years of age. A replanting programme of 2 per cent per annum will ensure a rotation over 50 years. Obviously, the argument in favour of 'exportable surplus' needs be reconsidered. It is a plain truth that if not today, tomorrow India will have to import sizeable quantity of tea either, or to curtail its export for the sake of domestic consumer. Otherwise, where is the guarantee that, in the near future, domestic consumers will not be strangulated with severe pressure of demand-pull inflation? Where is the guarantee that the industry will be able to maintain exportable surplus, as expected? These matters are, indeed, related with the industry's social obligation to two segments-first, obligations to domestic consumers in terms of right price for the right product at the right time; second, obligation to the nation in terms of helping earn foreign exchange. Contextually, the observation of Mr Jimmy Hilditch may be referred to. In course of summing up the convention papers presented at the U.K. Tea convention held in May 1993, we observed during this period India's "production has increased remarkably. So, too, have their population and the per capita number for the same period. With these statistic it is difficult to assess how India can feed internal demand and increase exports without increasing production". The following table shows the future of India's exportable surplus of tea.

Imports for Re-Export

There are countries like U.K., U.S.A., importing huge quantity of teas, of course, high grade, to re-export them in the value added from. It should not go unnoticed that international buyers are fast leaning towards packet tea, instant tea and tea bags. So, it is high time to catch them young. Indian tea barons should realize this fact. They should

Table 10

Export, Production, Population and Per capita Consumption During 1950 to 2007 in India

Particulars/Year	*1950*	*1960*	*1970*	*1980*	*1992*	*1995*	*1997*	*1998*	*1999*	*2004*	*2007*
Exports (m/kg)	181	193	200	224	190	167	203	205	206	183.64	200.00
Production (m/kg)	278	321	419	570	704	756	810	870	880	820.22	860.00
Population (million)	354	429	539	675	869	915	935	937	952	1105.00	1180.00
Per Capita (kg)	0.21	0.29	0.39	0.57	0.61	0.68	0.74	0.79	0.87	0.95	0.99

further appreciate that endeavour to re-export value added teas will help to find new markets and to contribute more foreign exchange in the national exchequer through non-traditional way. This is likely to attract new investment also. This besides, two other significant matter should not go un-escaped from our view. First, India's overwhelming dependence on traditional buyers—Russia and CIS, who were the principal buyers of Indian tea? Although, at the moment, India enjoys comfortable position the possibility of creating discomfort by the infiltrated sellers in these markets should not be over-looked. The *'seller's market'* at that time was turned to *'buyer's market'*. Second, China is preparing vigorously to exert its pressure in the international market. Tea is listed as one of the key export commodities. Due to overwhelming importance of hard currency earnings it was very likely that the China government provided all sorts of incentive to the tea industry. It is worth noting that between 1950 and 2004 total tea area in that country increased by more than 7 times, 155,000 hectares to 1,115,300 hectares. Output increased by more than 3 times over the same period from 255 m kg to 820 m.kg. Export - increase accounted for 10 times from 18 m kgs. in 1950 to 182 m.kgs in 2004. Nevertheless, China has the greatest range of tea in different grades and varieties. China intends to be at the top of the list of tea traders in the world market. And no denying the fact, China may, at the earliest opportunity, penetrate in the Russian and CIS market. Keeping in view this possibility, the industry should right now find new market, which may easily be possible with selling value-added teas.

Standard of Quality

Of course, the standard of quality matters much at any export trade. It may be recollected that only a few years back the quality of tea sold to Russia was so bad that million kgs of tea were destroyed. Serious complaints were lodged to the tea board. Russian television cautioned the domestic consumers with the words: *"Don't sip Indian tea"*. No doubt, industry's goodwill has been severely damaged by this act of the exporters. The questions are obviously, who has *to be blamed for this event; what measures have been taken so far to prevent recurrences*. The Tea Board, being the appropriate authority, should devise full-proof measures to ensure quality. Tea Board should: *(i)* scrutinize every export order received; *(ii)* ensure the creditworthiness of the exporter; *(iii)* arrange intensive checking at the time of shipment; *(iv)* arrange random checking after unloading; *(v)* introduce mandatory use of the Tea Board's logo, subject to the fulfilment of stipulated conditions, for every export.

Conclusion

It is unlikely that with further liberalization of imports, the domestic market will be flooded with low-grade imported tea. For the Gresham's Law does not hold good in an open market. The law reacts in the opposite manner-good product drives away bad product. As far as India's domestic tea market is concerned, consumers here drink the best of CTCs. Not only that, they are prepared to pay a premium for quality. Because of the strong domestic demand Indian tea prices are generally higher than the world prices. And it is to be noted further that in volume terms India is the largest consumer. Evidently, in the perspective of the country's consumer behaviour it is doubtful that to what extent importers will be able to sell the low grade imported stuff to increase their profits and be able to exert dominant voice in the domestic market.

It was unwise to view that once India started buying of low priced tea, the price of its produce in the international market would have fallen. Some Asian sellers would have been benefited out of this transaction. From the viewpoint of open market economy, however, it was felt that the aforesaid promise was not correct. In an open market mechanism only the appropriate substitute and its price played a dominant role in determining the demand of the principal product the vice-versa. Since Indian importers intended to import only cheap variety of teas, the price of Indian tea was likely too remain unaffected until now suppliers entered the market. And in this matter the only threat was likely to come from China the Asian Dragon—having a large variety and quantity of tea at its disposal.

In the light of the above study it was viewed that there was no point of becoming shaky even though the Ministry of Commerce allowed free import of teas for re-exports in bulk as well. The only necessity is to remain alert against the unscrupulous traders who may take the advantage of import liberalization policy of the Government of India just to further their own interest.

SECTION II

Product Diversification and Value Addition of Tea

Rationale of Product Diversification

Even 50 years ago, tea drinkers abroad used to buy *'pure'* tea from the producing country of his choice from among the neighbouring grocers. The teas of different origins were being sold under well advertised brand names by trading companies located in the importing countries. These companies got their merchandise from a number of tea producing countries. In other words, there was a so-called international division of labour under which tea was grown by poor developing countries especially for the purpose of exports in bulk as raw materials to various developed countries. The imported tea was then sold by the developed countries through a network of large sized companies with substantial capital investment who were marketing the tea in attractive consumer packs under different brand names built up by intensive campaigns. This division of labour was not based on any natural advantage as understood in the theory of international trade. It was based on historical factors and on advantages artificially created for different companies by virtue of dominant position of their countries over the erstwhile colonies. The companies not only controlled over 40 or 50 per cent of the markets of developed countries but also controlled trade channels for marketing and distribution of tea. Moreover, there were some bigger companies which owned plantations and controlled a large part of retail marketing of packaged tea. Thus, it is of vital importance that an attitudinal change must precede our attempts towards boosting of tea exports by the developing countries. This would work as catalyst to mark a departure from the traditional position of tea producing countries being content with export of tea as a primary product to value added items. This change covers the diversification into blending of tea and its packaging would enable the tea producing countries to free themselves from the vagaries of the wholesale market of tea and enter the consumer markets directly where prices are more stable compared to wholesale markets. Packet tea can help the producing countries to earn added value on account of blending and packaging and thereby earn more foreign exchange. Similar is the case of instant tea and tea bags.

Switch Over from Primary to Processed Goods

It may, therefore, be the strategy of all the developing countries that they should bring in certain structural changes in the product they export. This will help them in improving their share in world trade and in earning more foreign exchange. Besides, this would enable the developing countries to be known not only as exporters of *'primary'* products but also as exporters of *'convenient'* products or manufactured goods which can directly find place in the display counters of the consumer stores in the developed countries. In other words, a switch over from *'primary' to 'processed'* goods might open up new vistas of economic growth for the developing countries through increased exports. India, which is one of the developing countries, has progressively ushered in diversification in many of its agricultural commodities in recent years. India started by exporting groundnut seeds and then moved to export of oilseeds and thereafter to products like meal. In case of leather products, India has moved from raw hides to tanned, semi-processed to processed and finished leather, and for over a decade, India has been developing markets for shoe uppers, shoes and leather as well as leather garments and goods. The same could happen in the case of tea. The question is what type of structural changes in tea exports i.e. product diversification has been achieved in India so far.

Export of Packet Tea

India is the largest producer and exporter of tea in the world and is expected to produce 820 million kgs in 2008 assuming an average annual growth rate in tea production to the extent of a little over 3 per cent, other things remaining constant. On an average, India produced about 840 million kgs annually during the last ten years. India produced 8 60 million kgs of tea in 2007 and her share in world production was 27 per cent. The volume of her tea exports was 200 m kgs in 2007 which accounted for 14 per cent of world exports and these are mostly in bulk form. India has been trying to maximise exports particularly in the form of processed tea such as packets, tea bags, and instant tea.

Value Added Products

In India, tea packets containing loose tea are still the normal form of packaging. India for the first time started the export of packet tea (in consumer pack upto a size of 1 kg) in 1965. Six years later she ventured into export of tea bags, instant tea, etc. Since then India has been making steady and consistent progress in the export of packet tea. In 1965, with only two firms in the field, she had exported 2 m. kgs of packet tea and at the end of five years, with entry of few more firms, her tea exports doubled to 4 m. kgs 1971-72 and in another 4 years, exports reached the level of about 11 m kgs (1975-76). The progress, since then, noteworthy with the entry of more than 200 firms in the field.

The year-wise growth of exports of packet tea in India for the last three and a half decades since 1973-74, is given below:

Table 11: Export of Packet Tea from India during 1973-74 to 2007-2008

Year	*Quantity (th. kg)*	*Value (th. Rs.)*	*Unit Value (Rs./kg)*
1973-74	4744	50216.00	10.58
1974-75	6095	83051.00	13.56
1975-76	10787	172457.00	15.99
1976-77	12612	193635.00	15.37
1977-78	25187	519834.00	20.64
1978-79	38599	787384.00	20.40
1979-80	30024	580703.00	19.34
1980-81	32322	699834.00	21.65
1981-82	20493	468216.00	22.85
1982-83	10101	263232.00	26.06
1983-84	17368	521288.00	30.01
1984-85	21841	930552.00	42.61
1985-86	25690	994063.00	38.69
1986-87	16847	595727.00	35.36
1987-88	21142	785994.00	37.18
1988-89	25541	879841.00	34.45
1989-90	75817	3548148.00	46.80
1990-91	71514	3908642.00	54.64
1991-92	78321	4520917.00	57.72
1992-93	65245	4040263.00	61.92
1993-94	64917	4685722.00	72.18
1994-95	52042	3577669.00	68.75
1995-96	83965	6162394.00	73.39
1996-97	81016	5714458.00	70.53
1997-98	78115	7490434.00	97.89
1998-99	82013	8904328.00	108.57
1999-00	63518	6743290.00	106.16
2000-01	69315	7195601.00	103.81
2001-02	42719	5211372.00	121.99
2002-03	33606	4084322.00	121.54
2003-04	34013	4057973.00	119.31
2004-05	34412	4068530.00	118.23
2005-06	34815	4166786.00	119.56
2006-07	35220	4242249.00	120.45
2007-08	35630	4332608.00	121.60

Sources: Various issues of Tea Statistics, Tea Board, Kolkata.

India's export of packet tea increased from 5 m. kgs in 1973-74 to 36 m. kgs in 2007-08. Yearwise data further revealed that on many occasions India could not retain the volume of her preceding years exports. Export of packet tea showed a record increase of 84 m. kgs in 1995-96 followed by 82 m. kgs in 1998-99 and 81 m. kgs in 1996-97. On an average India exported about 68 m. kgs fetching Rs. 712 crore with average unit price of Rs 105 per kg. India acquired an important position as the worlds largest direct exporter of packet tea surpassing the U K. She is the leading exporter of packet tea and accounts for 60 per cent of world trade in packet tea. It is interesting to note that packet tea imports constituted nearly 20 per cent of total world imports and India constitutes for nearly half of it by way of direct export of this item during the year.

Direction-Regionwise Packet Tea Export

During the last 4 decades major changes have already taken place in the tea market in the world. Countries like USA, UK, Canada and others have preference for packet tea, tea bags, instant tea in recent years. The countries in the region of West Asia and North Africa place their order mostly for these items. The exports of packet tea in the countries of West Europe (United Kingdom, Ireland, Netherlands, Germany, Austria, Finland etc.) are also gradually falling. On an average, about 4 m kgs are exported to West Europe, 21 m. kgs to East Europe, 1.5 m. kgs to America {North & Latin America) and 4 m. kgs to North Africa during the year 2004-05.

Export of Tea Bags

In order to cope up with changing consumer preferences, India started production and export of tea bags from 1971 onwards with three firms. Progress made since then has been considerable and at present there are many firms manufacturing tea bags. The progress relating to Export of tea bags in India is set out below:

Table 12: Export of Tea Bags during 1973-74 to 2007-08

Year	*Quantity(th. kg)*	*Value(th. Rs)*	*Unit Value (Rs/kg)*
1973-74	144	3571	24.80
1974-75	108	2752	25.48
1975-76	157	5914	37.67
1976-77	285	10560	37.05
1977-78	390	18522	47.49
1978-79	238	10570	44.41
1979-80	493	20275	41.13
1980-81	754	32591	43.22
1981-82	777	33531	43.15
1982-83	618	23172	37.50
1983-84	514	24259	47.20
1984-85	631	36551	57.93
1985-86	590	37839	64.13
1986-87	467	31845	68.19
1987-88	498	32424	65.11
1988-89	626	44409	70.94
1989-90	546	46875	85.85
1990-91	496	43715	89.20
1991-92	483	71408	147.84
1992-93	520	72536	139.49
1993-94	1007	101456	100.75
1994-95	1008	144180	143.04
1995-96	861	125811	146.15
1996-97	1716	252479	147.16
1997-98	2169	449957	207.45
1998-99	2415	498180	206.29
1999-00	2305	557207	241.74
2000-01	1917	385232	200.96
2001-02	2542	597103	234.89
2002-03	3180	668558	210.37
2003-04	4900	943075	192.46
2004-05	5865	1146783	195.53
2005-06	6575	1289686	196.15
2006-07	7238	1427334	197.20
2007-08	8015	1590577	198.45

Exports of tea bag in 1973-74 was 144 thousand kgs which went up to 8015 th. kgs in 2007-08 showing an increase of 34.52 times. There was an appreciable increase of this item from 1994-95 on wards. Except 1995-96, exports of tea boosted up from 1716 th. kg in 1996-97 to 2169 th kgs in 1997-98. It further improved from 2415 th. kgs. in 1998-99 to 2542 th. kgs. in 2001-02. The export started improving appreciably from 2002-03 to 2007-08. Average export of tea bag during last five years was to the level of 6518 th. kgs. fetching Rs 196 per kg.

Direction of Tea bag Exports—Region-wise

Tea bags are exported to mainly countries like United Kingdom, Irish Republic, Germany, France, Belgium & Luxembourg of West Europe. A substantial quantity is also exported to east Europe i.e., CIS countries (Russian Federation, Ukraine, Latvia, Kazakhastan, etc.) and Poland. Meagre quantities are exported to USA, Canada and Brazil of America as well as Iran, UAE, Kuwait, Bahrain, Muscat, Yemen of West Asia and North Africa. Further less quantity in the level of 20 thousand kgs is exported to Asia other than West (Japan), Africa other than North (Angola, South Africa) and Australia and Oceania (Australia). It is interesting to note that over the last three years quantities exported in East Europe has increased from 1816 th. kgs in 1999-00 to 3115 kgs in 2007-08, while it was 16 th. kgs 84 th. kgs during the period in America. There was fall in exports from 207 th. kgs to 106 th. kgs in West Asia and north Africa.

Value Added Concept

By introducing structural changes in tea exports India has been sharing the value added market. Before making any attempt to define *'value added'* concept it would be worthwhile to mention that despite over a century of India's entry in world tea export market Indian tea has been hardly known by name or origin except in the country like UK and Germany. In these countries there was good demand for fine Darjeeling Tea while Chinese and Sri Lankan Tea are well known in export markets abroad. Even the small amount of value that may be added on account of the consumer preference for a particular origin of tea has not reached us. The *first value added exercise started with Indian tea known for superior quality* and flavour to create among consumers a purchasing preference for Indian tea. The next stage was to create awareness among the consumers about the regional varieties such as Darjeeling tea, the Nilgiris tea, the Assam tea, Kangra tea etc..

Forms of Value Addition

There are three methods by which values are added to tea. These are: *(i)* Breaking bulk and blending involving no technology but require skills that we possess. *(ii)* Consumer packing in attractive packets, cans or bags using modern packing materials, if sold in other brand names (to devote attention towards marketing and promotional skills) and cost, if sold under own brand name. *(iii)* Product processing and qualitative improvement extracting tea solubles i.e., solids and flavour. The country which exports tea in bulk quantities without recourse to value added system is, therefore, not only deprived of legitimate share or value added but also fails to reach the consumer directly. The value added items of tea which are sold in the retail market, are in the forms of tea in consumer package and tea bags.

Sharing of Value Added Tea

The sharing of value added which could be seen from the price differentials in respect of packet teas and tea bags as compared to bulk teas is shown below:

Table 3: Price differentials during 1966-67 to 2007-08

(fob Rs./kg)

Year	*Packet tea*	*Tea bag*	*Bulk tea*	*Percentage of value addition in packet tea/tea bag to bulk tea*	
1966-67	9.88	—	8.21	20.34	—
1971-72	9.48	20.39	7.51	26.24	172
1973-74	10.58	24.80	7.61	27.90	225
1974-75	13.76	25.48	9.93	38.56	157
1975-76	15.99	37.67	11.27	41.88	234
1976-77	15.36	37.05	12.19	26.01	204
1977-78	20.64	47.49	25.45	18.90	86

1978-79	20.40	44.41	20.25	0.70	35
1979-80	19.34	41.13	18.08	6.70	77
1980-81	21.65	43.22	18.75	15.28	130
1981-82	22.85	43.15	18.15	25.90	138
1982-83	26.06	37.50	19.03	36.94	97
1983-84	30.01	47.20	27.56	8.88	71
1984-85	42.61	57.93	35.48	20.10	63
1985-86	38.69	64.13	30.25	27.70	112
1986-87	35.36	68.19	29.53	19.70	131
1987-88	37.18	65.11	31.10	19.50	109
1988-89	34.45	70.94	31.13	10.60	128
1989-90	46.80	85.85	42.97	8.90	100
1990-91	54.64	89.21	53.58	3.50	69
1991-92	57.72	147.84	55.61	3.80	62
1992-93	61.92	139.49	57.65	7.41	142
1993-94	72.18	100.75	67.78	6.50	33
1994-95	68.75	143.05	63.88	7.62	121
1995-96	73.39	146.15	73.30	0.12	99
1996-97	70.53	147.13	75.18	-6.18	97
1997-98	97.89	207.45	93.18	5.05	123
1998-99	108.57	206.29	104.64	3.76	97
1999-00	106.16	241.74	98.36	7.90	145
2000-01	103.81	200.96	89.99	15.35	106
2001-02	121.99	234.89	86.53	40.90	171
2002-03	121.54	210.37	86.95	39.78	142
2003-04	119.31	192.46	85.60	39.38	124
2004-05	118.23	195.53	85.90	37.63	127
2005-06	119.56	196.15	86.15	38.78	128
2006-07	120.45	197.20	87.25	38.05	126
2007-08	121.61	198.45	88.15	37.95	125

Source: Various issues of Tea Statistics, Tea Board, Kolkata.

The data presented in the above table showed that packet tea and tea bags added more value approximately 26 per cent and 173 per cent respectively than the bulk tea during 1971-72. Value addition in respect of packet tea and tea bags stood at 38 per cent and 125 per cent respectively in 2007-08. Value addition for packet tea ranged from 0.70 per cent to 42 per cent, while tea bag ranged from 35 per cent to 25 per cent during the period from 1966-67 to 2007-08. Value addition was reduced to minimum during 1990-91 and 1992-93 in respect of packet tea and tea bags as compared to bulk tea because of increase in the price per kg of bulk tea.

Packet tea can offer a dependable and standardised product to a consumer while tea bags standardisation simplifies the process of brewing. In the second stage, by marketing tea under a brand name, although being a costly process in terms of high costs of distribution and consumer promotion, the exporter gets an easy access to preferences and some command over the market, together with increase in profitability comparatively higher than the returns available from the export of loose tea.

Instant Tea—Its Development

As regards instant tea, India is still on the threshold of product development. With the gradual acceptance of instant tea by the consumer, its demand is bound to rise gradually in the near future. Instant tea is processed in two forms, the cold water solubles (CWS) and hot water solubles (HWS). These are manufactured both from the green leaf and from the black tea or from a combination of both types. HWS has limited market in the UK, Australia, etc. While CWS has markets in USA. Tata Finlay, is specialising in CWS and food specialities in HWS. Both the products are manufactured in South India. The data relating to export of instant tea from India is given in the table below:

Table 4: Export of Instant Tea from India: 1974-75 to 2004-05

Year	*Quantity(th. kg)*	*Value (th. Rs)*	*Unit Value (Rs/kg)*
1973-74	295	9217	31.24
1974-75	255	8563	33.58
1975-76	478	19162	40.09
1976-77	584	25066	42.92
1977-78	598	31533	52.73
1978-79	686	35500	51.75
1979-80	656	30509	46.51
1980-81	761	36608	48.11
1981-82	832	41712	50.13
1982-83	799	43185	54.05

1983-84	1049	66874	63.75
1984-85	1138	95538	83.95
1985-86	938	80428	85.74
1986-87	1134	94896	83.68
1987-88	861	66611	77.36
1988-89	733	66909	89.92
1989-90	1147	100986	88.05
1990-91	925	90068	97.37
1991-92	1283	158039	123.18
1992-93	1740	270592	155.51
1993-94	1121	221463	197.56
1994-95	1320	228667	173.23
1995-96	1230	260940	212.15
1996-97	1868	446403	238.97
1997-98	2483	578336	232.92
1998-99	2428	629703	259.35
1999-00	2602	653770	251.26
2000-01	2783	831013	298.60
2001-02	2594	741979	286.04
2002-03	3054	881347	288.66
2003-04	3463	995689	287.70
2004-05	3724	1119024	300.49
2005-06	4010	1224052	305.25
2006-07	4345	1348471	310.35
2007-08	4675	1476132	315.75

Source: Various issues of Tea Statistics, Tea Board, Kolkata.

It will be seen from the above table that the export of instant tea increased from 295 th. kgs in 1973-74 to 4675 th. kgs in 2007-08 showing an improvement of 13 times. Similarly, in value terms it was Rs. 92.17 lakh in 1973-74 and Rs. 114761.32 lakh in 2007-08.

Export Market for Indian Tea

Indian instant tea is exported to 23 countries. Among those countries USA accounts for about 71 per cent of the total followed by Switzerland 9 per cent, Canada 6 per cent, Italy 5 per cent, etc. It is interesting to note that instant tea is gaining popularity in United Kingdom, France, Austria, Netherlands, UAE, Japan etc.

Incentives to Value Added Teas

In order to encourage value added teas, the Central Government has been providing various incentives as under:

A. Package Tea Incentives

	Rate of duty Rs/Kg
(a) Tea packed in any kind of containers containing 25 grams or less net of tea.	Rs. 0.44 + duty for loose tea, if not already paid
(b) Tea packed in any kind of containers of containing more than 25 grams but not exceeding 20 kgs net tea.	Rs. 1.00 + duty for loose tea, if not already paid

a. Loose Tea Cess:

The rate of cess on teas produced in the country is 4 paise per kg.

Excise duty @ 10 paise per kg for Green tea, for Black tea 25 paise per kg, for black tea in Zone I, 50 paise for Zone II, Rs. 1.50 for Zone III, Rs. 1.00 for Zone IV, and Rs. 1.50 for Zone V.

Full rebate of excise duty has been granted on loose tea exported out of India w.e.f. 27.4.1988.

b. Package Tea (Rebate):

Export on Outright sale:

The additional excise duty of Rs. 0.40/1.00 is refundable on exports. In addition to this the following rebates are also allowed:

(i) Tea packed in metal containers containing not more than 1 kg net of tea.	30 per cent of f.a.s. price in excess of Rs. 9.75 per kg on the actual duty paid on loose tea whichever is less subject to the overall ceiling of 75 paise/kg
(ii) Tea packed in any other than metal container containing not more than 1 kg net of tea.	30 per cent of f.a.s. price in excess of Rs. 6.25 per kg on the actual excise duty paid on loose tea whichever is less subject to overall ceiling of 75 paise/kg.

Export on Consignment Account:

(i) 30 paise per cent of f.o.s. price in excess of Rs. 11.20 per kg on the actual excise duty paid on loose tea which ever is less subjct to the overall ceiling of 75 paise per kg.

(ii) 30 per cent of f.o.s. price in excess of Rs. 7.70 per kg on the actual excise duty paid on loose tea whichever is less subject to overall ceiling of 75 paise per kg.

(iii) All other types ot package tea: same rebate applicable in case of loose tea.

(B) Instant Tea (Duty Rs/kg) Incentives

10 per cent of ad valorem plus loose tea duty if not already paid and if such tea is used in the manufacture of such instant tea w.e.f. 1.3.1986.

Rebate: Instant tea if exported is exempted from excise duty.

(C) Loose Tea

Rebate of Excise Duty granted on exports of Bulk tea w.e.f. 23.7.1983 has been withdrawn w.e.f. 1.2.1985.

(D) Cash Compensatory support: W.e.f. 1.4.1989 the C.C. S. Has been granted at the following rates on f.o.b. Value of exports (valid upto 31.3.1992).

Description of the product	*Rates of C.C.S.*
(a) Tea Bags	8 per cent (Eight)
(b) Packet Tea caddies and Tea chestlets	18 per cent (Eighteen)
(c) Instant	8 per cent (Eight)
(d) Quick Brewing Black Tea	12 per cent (Twelve)

Problems of Value Added Instant Tea

For expansion of exports of value added items of Tea, India is facing various problems. These are: *(i)* Dearth of indigenous know how in international market, *(ii)* inadequate production capacity of tea bags, *(iii)* lack of investment for establishment of firm's brand name and entry into the super markets in foreign countries, *(iv)* imposition of various tariff as well as non-tariff barriers created by developed countries against the entry of Indian tea in consumer packs.

Long-term Strategy for Marketing of Value Added Items

For evolving a long-term strategy for marketing of value added items, the "Committee on Tea Marketing " set up by the GoI recommended in its report a three phased approach which is quoted below:

In the first phase packet tea export should be confined to our neighbouring countries through local collaboration particularly in those cases where there are no packeting facilities and tea is imported in packages especially in premium range. This would mean less investment, no clash of interest among own customers and a price advantage on account of lower freight. On both sides of India upto Africa and South East Asia, there is great demand for imported packet teas where our exported tea could successfully compete with others.

The second phase would be collaborating with existing packers in Europe and supplying the blends in bulk and sharing part of their profits.

The third phase could be independent marketing efforts in value added, medium priced tea in major markets of UK and Ireland. Over riding all these phases, there are at least two considerations to ponder over.

First, research into new tea products and tea entente. *Second,* to support export of value added tea abroad in the form of packets, bags and instant tea, we should first encourage and organise markets at home. It was noted by the Committee that exact strategy would depend on three factors like creating favourable market conditions, increasing investment on export promotion and building of organisational marketing strengths.

As regards tea bags, the Committee has recommended that the facilities for manufacturing units in India with tea bagging facilities should be carefully examined and maximum encouragements may be given. It has also been observed that to acquire market facilities and skills abroad, the cost will be high and will have to be standardised. The public sector agencies like Tea Trading Corporation and State Trading Corporation will be able to work on the problem of external marketing of value added items of tea. As regards instant tea, the Committee recommended that the existing companies in the field as well as new entrants should be encouraged. The company should invest capital in promoting technical and marketing skills by encouraging only or part acquisition of R&D equipments and sharing international promotion expenditure on time bounds which must be result oriented and monitored against expected returns.

Potential and Scope for Instant Teas

Tea is probably one of the most widely consumed beverage in the world and is accepted and acclaimed everywhere. The worldwide acceptance of tea is because of its zero alcohol content, stimulating effect and aroma etc. Many types like black, green, orange, flavoured, golden, pekoe, etc. grades of tea are available in the market. These types are mainly classified according to their manufacturing process, compiled with spices and other flavour rendering substances. Brewing of instant tea is a common and old practice. Black and green teas are only products obtained on a large scale from the tea bush and at present none of the other products mentioned above are being exploited on a commercial scale. Efforts will be made for developing and standardising suitable and effective technologies for tea industry to keep pace with other tea producing countries like China, Sri Lanka and Kenya who has already made their mark in the world export market for tea.

Tea Powder

Although commercial production of instant tea began in the 1940s, little information is available as to what sort of process is suitable, as these techniques have been kept a secret by patent rights over the manufactured products. Generally, tea powder, the basic material is derived from the fermented leaf. The usual steps adopted in the preparation of powder are extraction of tea solids followed by concentration of extracts and finally drying of these concentrates, to convert them into powder. Extraction is generally carried out by recovering the solids in water. Concentration of extracts is effected by evaporation of the water at low temperature and under reduced pressure. The final step of drying the concentrated leaf is achieved by subjecting the concentrate to either low temperature, spray, fridge or foam drying. The solid thus obtained is brown in colour and amorphous in nature but on breeding it turns into brown powder.

One such study was conducted in the tea research laboratory in Himachal Pradesh Krishi Vishwa Vidhyalaya, Palampur. The yield of powder from the fermented tea was generally better than that of made tea. At present a number of laboratories are set up which have invented the technologies for preparation of tea powder.

4

Agro-Technology, Health Aspects of Tea, and Chinese Pu'er Tea with Miraculous Functions

Chapter 4 confines to three sections. In section I important aspects of agro-technology focusing on adoption of South Indian Clones/minimum tillage in hills, application of caustic wash of medium pruned Darjeeling tea, tilling periodically the top soils, etc. and role of Darjeeling Tea Research Centre have been taken into consideration. Section II deliberates on tea, a health drink which contains inherently aroma oriented various medical herbs properties with preventive and curing qualities. Besides, an attempt has been made to know what brewing in the organic tea bushes? What is all about? Organic certification, the Long Life Herbal Tea Classics etc. Chinese Pu'er tea with miraculour properties searching historical records, characteristics of Pu'er tea with its processing technology, manufacture and sale of Pu'er tea, health properties of such teas, China's domestic sector, fall and rise of China's tea industry etc. have been outlined in Section III.

SECTION I
Agro-technology and Health Aspects of Tea

Introduction

'Darjeeling Tea' is the pride of India teas world over for its unique flavour. This charisma is also attached with the peculiarities of the place for its topographic and agroclimatic reasons. China (Camellia sinensis var, sinensis) tea is grown here. For a decade or so, production of Darjeeling tea is almost static and this has drawn attention of all. Area under tea cultivation is 17705 hectares in 2005, representing 5 per cent of tea area in India. Production is recorded at 11.20 million kgs accounting for 2 per cent of All India production. Yield of tea worked out to 645 kgs per hectare compared to All India average of 1650 kg per hectare. Further, are occupied by over-aged bushes (above 50 years of age) constituted 65 per cent against 35 per cent in Assam and 52 per cent in All India. Annual rate of replantation is less than 0.5 per cent against recommended 3 per cent. Application of inputs to tea bush is also done at a low profile rather too cautious in this respect. With all these odds, Darjeeling tea is still continuing to bloom, since charisma of flavour tea persists and unit value realization is going up constantly.

To address the identified issues, research and development efforts have been intensified both by Tea Research Association (TRA) and Tea Board instituting its Darjeeling Tea Research Centre (DTRC) at Kurseong with laboratory complex attached to an experimental tea area of 20 hectares. Although, various limitations have slowed down the process, research since 1980s in the Board's DTRC on common technological problems had generated some useful knowhow. The process of translation of technical knowhow into practice has been given a boost with the launching of crash development loan programme of Rs.43 crores. Based on continued experimentation at DTRC, a few important aspects of agrotechnology are highlighted here which might help to review the scientific management programmes for Darjeeling tea.

Important Aspects of Agro-Technology

(i) Introduction of South Indian Clones: With the objective to introduce some suitable popular South Indian clones in Darjeeling hills, 14 such clones namely Sundaram, Spring field, Arthrey, Brooklande, Evergreen, Pandian Jayaram, Swarna, Golkonda, Singara, Craigmore, Attikana, B(6/182 and B/7/372 were tried in DTRC since 1978. Initial evaluation on performance of young teas in the hills favoured introduction of Sundaram, Springfield and Arthrey. In the meantime, Sundaram a triploid variety, has already established itself in quite a good number of tea estates for its standard yield and average flavour. Spring field with its characteristic behaviour of developing laterals and quick frame formation during the initial years also with good yield and average flavour seems promising. Similarly, Arthrey has also established in the hills. Final recommendations are awaited:

(ii) Minimum Tillage Replantation: 'Minimum tillage' or popularly known *'Malwai type of replantation'* was worth tried in South India and now it was found suitable for Darjeeling hills. Detailed experimental findings, based on extensive researches at DTRC indicated that in hill tea estates this new method of replantation was less expensive. This endanger no soil erosion and preserves valuable top spoil unlike traditional method of uprooting and replanting.

A dilution of 1:75 2-4 D in water by volume. 500 to 750 ml of this solution per bush if applied after chopping at ground level during winter months, could completely exhaust the old root system and decay ultimately. Neither regeneration of shoots from the chopped bushes nor infection of root diseases from the decaying biomass to the young plants were observed. No residual toxicity could be traced in soil which hampered the growth of young plants.

In old tea sections in slopes having wide spacing (4′ X 4′ or 5′ X 5′), double hedge (3′ X 2′ X 2′) close planting could be suitably accommodated after chopping of old bushes and without much disturbing the top soil. If the soil is compact, poor in organic content and heavily infested with perennial weeds, top layer of soil (4"–5") may be tilted after 3 weeks of chemical treatment of chopped bushes and be kept for one year under rehabilitation programme followed by double hedge planting. The root system of chopped bushes will decompose *in situ* in 3 years time but this will not hamper in the establishment of young tea plants.

(iii) Old But Useful Recipe: Caustic wash of medium pruned Darjeeling teas is an old but not obsolete practice. To free stems of old bushes heavily infested with moss and in lichens, many other protective chemicals are readily available. In general, this 'practice if adopted, is still very much effective and it pays back especially in the sections which are having black rot history and hard stem barks, shy and delay in bud breaking.

The original formula was caustic soda: water: :1: 50 plus slaked time of appropriate quantity for colour. As caustic soda causes burn and is difficult to handle it is usually replaced by the new formula which is washing soda: quick lime: water: water: 3: 1: 50: or soda ash: quick lime: water: 075: 1: 50 plus slaked lime for colour in both the cases. About 700 litres of fluid is required per hectare and can be applied by brush or by a piece of jute sack tied to a stick. Spraying is difficult since the suspension frequently block the nozzle. The appropriate time of application is after pruning during sunny days of November and December.

Alkali wash also protects the pruned bushes from black rot thread blight, etc. beside lichens, mosses and creepers on old bush frame. It softens the bark and hastens bud breaking by causing initial injury to the old stems. It protects the frame and newly exposed barks from sun search also. This practice helps in generating new laterals comparatively from lower region of the frame and thus in developing a good canopy of maintenance foliage.

(iv) Tilling Top Soil: Tilling top soil periodically, especially in the year of light prune, around the tea bush is essential field operation which helps in root aeration, weeding, bush sanitation and for better bush health. This common garden practice include cheeling, hoeing, thulling, scraping and so on. Operation like thuling is done around the bush upto a radius of spread of the bush foliage which constantly erode

not only valuable fertile top soils from the base of the bush also expose the feeder roots. This improper and non methodical practice as practiced at large scale in hills, drag the bushes to ultimate death.

Thus, while adopting any tillage operation in slops, care should be taken in the lines as: soil should be placed back on and around the bush after breaking of clods without forming basin or thully removing all weeds. Soil should not be dug too deep to expose feeder root zone and finally loosen soils should be mulched properly to check erosion.

Preparation of Plan for Doubling Average Yield for Darjeeling Tea Industry

The availability of improved planting materials and a greater thrust in R & D efforts especially tailored to the needs of the Darjeeling tea industry. It was possible to prepare a plan which would double the present average yield of 700 kgs per hectare without in anyway sacrificing quality. Principally, when one talks of production increases in Darjeeling, one must ensure that the qualitative aspect is not lost sight of. To chase a high crop in the short run will be disastrous in the long term. Planning, therefore is to be done keeping in view the short, medium as well as the long term benefits. The economies of each operation will need grass-root level decision as the costs of production are already very high in the lower yielding estates. The task is by no means easy and it is not practical to achieve it until a joint effort is made by the management, employees, local state and Central Governments.

Darjeeling Tea—A National Symbol

Tracing the history of tea in Darjeeling it revealed the industry has been in existence since the 1840s when a few small gardens were set up. Commercial planting started on a large scale in 1853 and since then the industry had grown. Darjeeling tea is now renowned the world over for its unrivalled aroma and quality.

Darjeeling Tea was in fact a national symbol of supremacy in quality and was accepted as such throughout the world.

It is therefore in the national interest that supply of Darjeeling tea is improved both quantitatively and qualitatively. Apart from being the only industry in the hilly areas of Darjeeling and the major source of income and livelihood to the population of the area, Darjeeling commands the highest unit value export realization. The task of the Darjeeling planter is to bring out and enhance in the cup the qualities endowed due to unique environmental reasons. Whilst the tea industry had been described as India's finest agro asset, without doubt, Darjeeling had been the flag bearer of Indian tea companies in the markets overseas. In fact, Darjeeling had a very special significance not only for India but for the whole world due to its image of quality and exclusively.

Tea Industry Suffers From Marketing Inertia

It is, however, regretted that the industry suffered from a marketing inertia. It is a pity that an exclusive and unique product such as ours had been treated purely as a commodity. The long exploitation of the name Darjeeling by competitors is known to us all and it is only after the successful launch of the Darjeeling logo campaign that some checks were introduced on the growth of fake Darjeeling brands. We are proud of the fact that the Tea Association was the first to suggest a world wide patent for the use of the Darjeeling symbol and following its success the Nilgiris and Assam logs were introduced. But is this enough ? Reiterating that Darjeeling Tea was not a commodity. The earlier we get out of this commodity circle the better it will be for us. The concept of drinking Darjeeling Tea, its rare character and exclusivity must be turned into its primary 'U.S.P.' (Unique Selling Propositions).

Generic Promotion of Darjeeling Tea Urged

It is an established fact that approximately 80 per cent of Darjeeling tea was exported. To improve unit value export realization and also total quantum of exports, the Government should further strengthen in undertaking general promotion of Darjeeling tea through the following marketing efforts:

(*a*) A further promotional campaign in the foreign media

to educate tea lovers-current and prospective on the origins of Darjeeling tea and its special attributes;

(b) The habit of drinking Darjeeling tea should be marketed as a 'concept'.

(c) Extension of the logo campaign other than the U.K., West Germany, France, Japan and USA may be further strengthened to create awareness amongst the consumers and remind them regularly through mass media.

(d) Greater priority to the exports of tea in value added form for obtaining the best possible price for packeted tea. Here the producers are facing genuine problems, which need to be looked into. To start with, there is a difficulty in promoting individual brands when the finances of small individual units of Darjeeling do not permit diversion of funds for market promotion. Moreover, producers have always found it puzzling that the rate of Central excise duties varies according to the size of the package. The additional excise duty on small packs places an unnecessary burden on the packs since, as it is, the cost of packaging increases with reduction in the size of the packet. Moreover, garden packed teas are bearing a dual duty-packet excise duty over and above the basic exercise on Tea. This appears to be discriminatory and not in consonance with export encouragement policies.

(e) It is suggested that regular visits should be arranged to Darjeeling for important customers/buyers of our teas. Although the International Tea & Tourism Festival held in Darjeeling in March, 1991 was first step, the Ministry of Tourism extended support, guidance and involvement in festival meets both objectives in equal measure, "Tea and Tourism".

(i) Consumers

Consumers are already conscious about the cost and quality and they will always regulate the above aspects and appreciate only the best one. We would like to add in the monitoring purview the following as their yardstick.

(a) That good looking–Bloomy & Black Crystal Tea may not be always of acceptable liquor quality.

(b) On the other Blackish Brown, open flaky tea contain the best preserved inherent aroma and liquoring quality with more cupages.

(c) Garden packed tea are more reliable and of value added quality.

(ii) Research and Development

Scientists have contributed a lot and now once again they are invited to come forward with latest technical inventions to meet the challenges of the hour with a view to providing:

(a) Further improved rich genetic planting materials

(b) Modern agro-cultural practices coupled with ideas of balanced application of various fertilizers and chemicals with organic and bio-chemical materials.

(c) Modified manufacturing techniques to produce better value added blended tea, i.e. a combination of Orthodox & CTC in one operation, with limited grading system

(iii) Production

Planters are always, trying their best to deliver the goods to consumers to their satisfaction and now the effort should be more to lean on quality with the introduction of effective controlling measures and directing attention to aroma-based cupages and keep the cost within reasonable limit.

(iv) Global Marketing

Strategies to promote Indian Tea in foreign market by various publicity campaign, including *Tea Festivals*, should be initiated to provide additional breakthrough.

A Consortium of Tea Trade

With a view to enjoying the latest development of modern manufacturing and marketing technology, a *consortium of tea trade* i.e. *all under one umbrella–Producer, Scientists, Brokers, Traders and Exporters* may be further strengthened. Such a consortium may render valuable services in reviewing the existing nature of production, standard of quality and the price at present on the one hand, the trend of the market demand, the nature of product and the price behaviour on the other, with a view to providing the industry a total backing to hold the global market firmly.

SECTION III
Tea—A Health Drink

This section outlines tea as health and delicious drinks, avenues and dimensions in manufacturing and marketing, drinking tea and attaining fitness, growth of organic tea business, aspects of organically growing tea practices and organic tea a vote for change towards a more gentle way of existing with nature. In the ptorcess the issues relating to increase in productivity of tea have been addressed.

Introduction

Tea, an unique gift of nature to mankind has multipurpose inherent properties. Tea has its own culture. None except tea can provide us such aroma-oriented pleasant chevalier satisfaction. The scientists all over the world accepted the proven fact that tea is a *'Health Drink'* which inherently contains aroma oriented various medico-herbal properties with preventive and curing qualities.

Tea Passing Through Turning Points: As a natural process of gravitation each one has to come out with its own perception and this is applicable to tea also. Tea is now passing through such a turning point, when avenues of various dimensions in manufacturing and marketing are looking for a felicitous gateway. During the past century, there were series of modification in tea manufacturing processes to cater to the need of quality oriented production to satisfy the consumers and now it requires total evolution to attain the next high.

Delicious Drink: The tea manufacturing process is in fact highly technical method of preserving the inherent quality of tea in totality. The preservation process of tea is very important in the sense of its multipurpose responsibilities to preserve the perishable green leaf tea into value added concentration to deliver aroma-based delicious drink in due course. Existence of tea industry and its health is closely connected with its quantum and value of export. As per latest data available, Indian tea's share has come down sharply to 18 per cent from 58 per cent during the last two decades.

Global Market—Hygienic Status and Quality of Tea: Since global market is very much cautious and careful about the hygienic status and quality of tea, industry has to have a complete and comprehensive control on manufacturing and marketing concepts to keep its stake in the global market. To meet the challenge we have to review all aspects of tea and the trade from a common platform and in depth.

Drink Tea and Keep Fit: A noted Chinese Doctor, Prof. Lon Fuqing advised: "Keep drinking tea and you may avoid some of the worst heart diseases". Dr. Fuquing has developed a powder from tea pigments which has had 80 per cent success on patients suffering from hardening of the arteries. "The life saving pigments are abundant in both green and black tea. They contain an anti coagulant enzyme which keeps the blood flowing smoothly", according to the doctor.

Organic Tea Business: Retailers of tea would be wise to take notice of the growing sales of certified, organically grown black, green and herbal teas. Four of the leading US organic tea manufacturers all reported steady upward sales figures of at least 15 per cent per year. In 2004, total sales of organic food was estimated at 6.4 billion and 7.4 billion in 2005. The organic market has grown at an average rate of 25 per cent each year, according to the Organic Food Production Association of North America (OFPANA), leading national trade association which represents the organic food industry. Many in the organic industry attribute these higher sales to better flavours and increased consumer awareness concerning a healthier diet and a cleaner environment. Currently, these certified organic teas are mainly sold in natural food stores, though organic tea manufacturers describe how mainstream grocery chains are now finding shelf space to include certified organic tea. Organic tea is also selling profitably in Europe, Australia and Japan.

Organically Grown Tea: One may be wondering just what organically grown tea is all about. All of us have had the experience of stepping into a lush natural forest. It thrives without human intervention. Plant material falls to the forest floor, decomposes and becomes a nutrient rich bed of soil to feed the forest plants and trees. Organic growing practices imitate this natural cycle to produce abundant health in the plants. Composting is one such agricultural practice. Layers of leaves, plant materials, and manure are piled together and regularly turned to facilitate decay, creating fertile soil filled with nutrients and microbial life for the plants to consume. Conventional growing methods, which use chemical fertilizer, pesticides, and herbicides, disrupt the ecological balance of the plant and soils. For example, chemical fertilizers are like growth stimulants. They are made to speed up the growing process of plants, while organic cultivation allows plants to grow and mature as nature intended. This natural process gives the necessary time for development of the natural essential oils and a full spectrum of flavours. For the gourmet tea consumer, these subtleties of flavour are especially important.

Organic Tea is a Vote for Change Towards a More Gentle ways of Existing with Nature: The concern people share about protecting tea 'environment is universal and the purchase of certified organic products help to further this goal. Organic teas are making their entrance into the wider market. Now is the time to position the companies to ride this wave into the future. The consumer can purchase this organic tea knowing that it has been cared for from beginning to end in a conscientious way, thus adding to the enjoyment of tea time. What could be a more refined tea to present than one which is so carefully tended?

From its beginning, the soils where the tea is grown must be chemical-free for a minimum of three years and a farm plan developed to continually enrich the soil fertility. The tea bush is then nurtured in a way that is good for the earth and for the workers. When ready this tea is plucked and processed with documented care to assure that it is kept from contaminants it is shipped, stored and sent to manufacturers and buyers in a similar careful fashion. Knowing that this cup of tea is a way to support the cleaning up of the environment and is helping to halt the exposure of indigenous peoples to unnecessary chemicals is giving many consumers that added extra which comes from participating in something larger than a cup of tea. It is truly a vote for change toward a more gentle way of existing with nature and our fellow human beings.

The Organic Certification

Organic certification means that an independent organic certifier guarantees that the tea is handled in a regulated, consistent way through all steps involved in getting the product to the consumer. A system of detailed record keeping is set in place for the grower with yearly inspections and periodic testing of soil and water. Any and all applications to the plants and soils must comply with the accepted list of material. Organic certification is vital in the US for a product labelled as organic to be accepted as credible. Worldwide, there are more than 50 independent certification agencies. In the US, some states offer their own certification programmes. There are also private certifying agencies. Among those well known in the US are Farm Verified Organic (FVO), Oregon Tilth Organic Crop Improvement Association (OCIA) and Organic Growers and Buyers Association (OGBA). Presently, 30 states in the US have laws which regulate the sale of organic products. The US federal government is setting standards for the production processing and certification of organic foods authorized by the Organic Food Production Act of 1990. The act was implemented in the early 1995, at which time all foods sold as organic will be required to be certified. The US Department of Agriculture is in charge of this programme.

Celestial Seasonings, the herbal tea giant, has successfully ventured into the organic market with their first certified organic product—a black tea Granum, a Seattle-based company introduced their organic teas in 1990. Their tea sales have grown 30-40 per cent each year, offering certified orga-teas in 20 varieties including black, green and flavoured black teas. Great Eastern Sun, an 25 year old company in Asheville, North Carolina, added a line of seven organic black, green, flavoured black teas in 1992. The company has experienced significant and consistent growth, calling their endeavour a huge success. Long Life Herbal Tea Classics, a 25-year-old company with a commitment to using organic ingredients whenever possible, has grown on the average of 15–30 per cent each year. They comment that organic spices and herbs used in their herbal tea blends are often better tasting and more potent than the same ingredients purchased that were not organic A Boulder based company; Uni Tea Herbs has focused on organic herbal tea blends for seven years with great success 10–20 per cent in sales increases yearly. One of the first companies to supply bulk and green tea to the U.S is Hony Creek Organics in Lawrence, Kansas. They specialize gourmet Ceylon teas and spices and have a long term personal interest in helping Sri Lanka restore its ecology.

Productivity be Raised

The creation of demand for a high value product is one thing and gearing up to meet the demand is another. It is a fact that the tea industry in Darjeeling has been languishing for a long time. It is after Darjeeling logo was launched that prices have improved and the gardens which had turned sick are seeing better days. The per hectare yield is lowest in Darjeeling tea growing areas. The bushes have aged, productivity has declined and hardly anything has been done by way of replantation. When one mentions the question of raising the productivity one means the productivity of land as well as of the workers. Management must also take its share of blame, as in the difficult period, which we are not likely to forget in a hurry, there was hardly any plough back. The Darjeeling Interest Subsidy Scheme announced with great fanfare took over 2 years to take off, and when it did, unfortunately, the political situation took a turn for the worse. It is for these reasons that Darjeeling production has been stagnating between 11 to 11.5 million kgs. Now that the political situation appears to be stable, the industry is reasonably optimistic that the gardens will turn round to show a better performance. To start with, it is essential that a forward looking attitude is necessary if progress is to be made.

Available of More Land

Apart from increasing productivity of existing land and human resources, it was obvious that more land must be made available by whatever methods possible for increasing tea acreage. It was urged the State Government to see its way to giving lands suitable for tea cultivation which were contiguous to tea gardens and returning back the surplus land already acquired by the Government. Unfortunately, the detailed exercise on land carried out in 1984-85 has borne little results. An interesting situation in this context is the contention of the Forest Department, that the Forest Conservation Act, does not allow the use of land marked as 'forest' for any other purpose. Meanwhile, the areas mentioned above are getting steadily degraded and in many cases, this has resulted in encroachment and land slides."

New Planting and Replanting—Low Subsidy

The other inhibiting factor for new planting and replanting is the low subsidy offered by the Tea Board. While development finance was made available to estates under the Darjeeling Interest Subsidy Scheme, the level of finance provided in many cases was inadequate. The quantum of finance fixed for extension/replanting for tea areas in Darjeeling by NABARD at Rs.80,000 is only about 70 per cent of the actual cost, which is in the region of Rs. 1,10,000 per hectare during the period. It was important that the costs of development be revalued every 2 years to ensure that adequate finance is made available. It cannot be over-emphasized that in more cases than one lack of timely and adequate finance had resulted in either deferment of development activities or implementation of the programme in a phased manner. Thereby the desired results was not achieved. In this connection, one may remind that with the introduction of the Interest Subsidy Scheme, the Darjeeling tea industry was deprived of the benefits of all other schemes of subsidy and development currently in operation by the Tea Board. Many of smaller members had found NABARD schemes far too cumbersome and complicated and shied away from them. Consequently, they have also been denied the benefits in force under the Tea Board Schemes. This is an extremely unsatisfactory situation and highly discriminatory towards Darjeeling. The tea industry in all other areas can avail of assistance under the Tea Board's development schemes and still remain eligible to obtain refinance facilities offered by NABARD's long term schemes. It is the ailing Darjeeling industry alone for which all other avenues of financial assistance from the Tea Board have been provided except the NABARD scheme.

In conclusion, it is pointed out the tea gardens are a unique combination of fertile land, agricultural expertise, trained labour, processing factories and above all managerial skills. Nowhere else except in the realm of tea would one find such a wealth of agricultural infrastructure. One must remember that by far the most important part of this infrastructure is the body of managers and planters. The body of tea planters are, in fact, an outstanding jewel in the treasure of India's agriculture.

SECTION III

China's Pu'er Tea—Tea with Miraculous Functions

This section traces the origin of Pu'er tea based on historical records. Its processing technology, commodity variety and quality, development of manufacture and sale, nutritive and health functions, pharmacological and health giving properties have been discussed. Further attempts have been made to analyse area, production, yield, exports etc. Factors responsible for growth of such tea have found place in this chapter. A detail outline has been presented on China's Pu'er tea by 21st century. This covers shape of China tea, division of processing (crude and refined) standard of tea, categories of tea (black, green, yellow, white, dark green and gray). Besides future of China tea, untapped potentials in international markets, low profile and absence of powerful and influential national lobby to oversee the China industry etc. are some of the areas, which are reflected in this chapter.

Introduction

Since 1978, state control of production and marketing of tea in China have been considerably reduced. The bulk of tea produced, green or scented, is now freely grown, processed and marketed. This does not mean, however, that tea industry in China is now completely outside the purview of government regulation and control. Still the government plays a crucial role in terms of provision of inputs, supply of funds, purchase and sale of exports. Tea still requires a government export licence and is listed as one of the key export commodities. The notable feature of China's tea production today is its growing leaning towards specialized and green tea. Since it is no longer possible on the part of the Chinese Export Corporation to dump in the world market inferior quality subsidized black tea. This has resulted in a drop in output of over 20 per cent on an average. During the last five years production of green tea increased by 15 per cent. With the openness of economy, the purchase and sale of tea for both domestic and export markets have also been liberalized. A wholesale tea market was inaugurated in the South-eastern port city of Fuzhou, attracting two hundred operators from State, collective and private entrepreneurs. Despite these changes, the quality of Chinese tea is reported to have declined significantly comparing 1960's standard.

Area, Production and Yield by Province

China's production according to province has not been easily available. *The Tea and Coffee Trade Journal* of USA had published a report in 1993. It was stated in the report that production of tea in 1976 was 786 million kgs of made tea, giving an average yield of 2620 kgs per hectare. In 1986, output was 461 million kgs while it was 450 million kgs in 1988. This implies yield of 573 kgs/ha and 565 kgs/ha respectively. Of the total production of 450 million kgs in 1988, as much as 312 million kgs was steamed green tea, 10 m.kgs scented (jasmine) teas and the rest 128 million kgs standard roasted (chummei) green tea. In 1986, four per cent of production of green tea was of top quality fetching a price of US $ 2/kg which was low by Hangzhou standards and 35 per cent was lowest in 3 grades with a price of about 25 cent per kg. In 1988 an additional 250 million kgs of crude tea was brought from other grown for refining.

State and National tea area, production by province of China in 1986 are as below:

Table 1: State and National Tea Area and Production by Province of China in 1986

Province	*State*	*Total*	*State*	*Total*	*State*	*Total*
	('000 ha)		*(m.kgs)*		*(Kgs/ha)*	
National	31.9	803.8	35.0	460.5	1,096	573
Zhejiang	1.9	150.5	4.2	104.3	2,269	693
Anhul	2.4	96.8	5.2	47.0	2,183	485
Fujian	5.6	94.5	4.3	44.2	776	468
Jiangxi	5.0	43.7	2.1	15.8	422	360
Hunan	1.6	96.1	2.0	73.1	1,254	761
Guangdong	6.3	36.4	6.9	26.1	1,089	717
Guangxi	2.1	15.4	3.4	11.6	1,635	752
Sichuan	1.0	79.8	1.1	52.2	1,051	655
Guizhou	2.1	22.0	2.1	12.1	1,016	552
Yunnan	3.1	80.3	2.9	34.1	914	425
"Others"	0.9	88.4	0.8	40.0	872	452
Top 4	20.0	254.9	16.5	120.1	809	471
Top 10	31.0	715.4	34.2	420.5	1,102	588

Source: Tea and Coffee Trade Journal (Assam Review and *Tea News).*

Pu'er Tea Special in Many Respects

Pu'er tea is special in many respects viz., processing

technology, product assortment, quality characteristics etc. It is the most sought after tea world over. Searching historical records of the Pu'er Tea, Mr. Ding Junzhi, who was a force to reckon with China's tea trade and industry, narrated the Pu'er Tea's many facets. This investigation into the 1700-year old history of utilization of China Pu'er unfolds tea culture. The mild and invigorating nature of Pu'er Tea is the main reason why inhabitants of Hong Kong and Macao prefer it. The factor underlying its wide appeal for the consumer as well as its marketing vitality is the increasing evidence of its overall beneficial effect on the immunocompetence of the human body. It is projected that by the end of 2015, the export of Pu'er Tea will attain 1500 m. kgs and domestic consumption in provinces such as Guangdong will show great increase. Two major aspects for expanding the sale of Pu'er Tea were: *(i)* adherence to the strategies of "quality competition" and *(ii)* market diversification". It advocated upgrading of product structure and development of "Pu'er Tea" commodity series. All these directed towards the augmentation of economic benefit.

Origin of Pu'er Tea—Searching Historical Records

At what time did Pu'er Tea first appear? The historical record "Tancui Dianhai Wuheng Annals" states that Zhu Geliang, a famous statesman of the Minor Han Dynastry reknown for his extraordinary wisdom, himself did the breeding and selection. Thus, the utilization of Pu'er Tea has a long history dating 1720 years from today. Li Shi of the Southern Soong Dynasty recorded in his book, "*Sequel to the Encyclopedia of Natural Science*", that "people living in the area bordering Tibet, Yunan and Sichuan drank Pu'er Tea as early as the Tang Dynasty (618-907 AD). Thus, it can be seen that trade in Pu'er Tea already existed at that time. In the past, Pu'er Tea was classified into Tips Tea, Tender tips Tea and Daughter Tea. "A Brief History of Yunnan", of the Ming Dynasty and "On Pu'er Tea" of the Qing (Manchu) Dynasty also contained unmistakable records of this. Fang Yizhi of Lter Ming Dynasty in his book "Commonplace Knowledge" recorded "Pu'er tea forms clumps when steamed and is sold to western tribes". Zhao Yuemin (circa 1719-1805 AD) a famous pharmacist of the Qing Dynasty, in his *"Supplement to the Compedium of Materia Medica"* wrote: "Pu'er Tea is a produce of Pu'er Town, Yunnan, and is grown in Youle, Gedeng, Yibang, ... Liuchashan". During the Qing Dynasty, Pu'er Tea was processed into tea balls weighing 5 catties, 3 catties, 1 catty, 4 ounces, 1 ounce and ½ ounce, as well as in the form of tea paste and bulk tea. It was a favourite drink of the Imperial Palace. As early as during the reign of Emperor Qianlong, Pu'er Tea packaged in bottles, tin cylinders and wooden boxes was offered every year as tribute to the palace. Even today in the Imperial Palace at Beijing it is still preserved an exquisite sample of tribute Pu'er Tea of those days, namely, one "human head tea" weighing about 5 catties, in perfect form and vivid colour.

In the classical novel *"Dreams of the Red Mansion"* (1756-1763) allusion was made to Jia Baoyu's drinking of Pu'er Tea, attesting to the fact that Pu'er Tea was at that time already well-known. However, at that time the Pu'er Town of Yunnan (the Pu'er City of today) had not yet started cultivating tea, and the major Pu'er Tea producing areas were in Yiwu, Yibang, Youle, Mansha Manzhuang, and Gedeng, the "six major tea mountains" of Xishuangbana, whereas Pu'er was merely a place where sellers and buyers gathered for trading, a trading centre in modern terminology.

Pu'er Tea Characterised by its Processing Technology

The name Pu'er Tea was a specialized term used to describe a kind of tea characterized by its processing technology, commodity variety and quality all which evolved under certain circumstances: political, economical, production, consumption, communication and transportation. Thus, the so-called Pu'er Tea was a kind of post fermented tea, produced in the Xishuangbana and the Simao localities of Yunnan Province, and which was transported to markets in Pu'er Town, the then political and economic centre of (Xizhuangbana) Simao. It is recorded in the "Dianhai Wuheng Annals" (vol. 11) that "Pu'er Tea enjoys fame all over the world, this being the reason why Yunnan produce it to generate income..... thousands of people cultivate tea on the mountains, buyers collect the tea and transport it to other places for sale. Huge profits are reaped when business is good". Since the early periods of the Qing Dynasty, Pu'er Tea has been sold plentifully all over China. It could contest with other kinds of tea such as Mengding, Wuyi, Liuan and Longjing and was sold in distant lands such as Thailand, Laos, the South Pacific countries, Hong Kong, and Macao.

In 1729 (7th year in the reign of the Qing Dynasty Emperor Yongzheng) the Pu'er Tea trade was concentrated in Pu'er Town, where during 1911 to 1919 after the founding of the Chinese Republic, 30-40 companies were still dealing in tea business. At that time green tea was sun-dried to yield a heart-shaped product called "Tight Tea" or "Ball Tea". Pu'er "Square Tea Cakes" and "QuizBing Tea Cake" (so named from its disc shape and the fact that 7 were packaged in one cylinder), the last being the Pu'er Tea Cakes of today. Towards the end of the Qing Dynasty "Tuo Cha Tea" started to be made in Xiaguan (bowl shaped, the Pu'er Tuo-Cha of today). These belonged to natural Post-fermented tea. After the liberation, artificial post-fermentation started to replace the previous natural post-fermentation (done mainly by sprinkling water).

Manufacture and Sale of Pu'er Tea

As mentioned above, China Pu'er Tea was originally produced in the Xishuangbana area Pu'er and Xiaguan localities and concomitant with the popularization of the large-leaf varieties. Guangdong and Guangxi Provinces also commenced to cultivate this kind of tea and, especially in Guangdong, great increase in production and sale occurred. Other provinces like Hunan, Sichuan and Guizhou also produced this kind of tea utilizing small and medium sized leaf varieties. On the domestic market, Pu'er Tea is available in Yunna, Sichuan, and Xizang (Tibet) and sale in recent years has shown continued increase in Guangdong Province. On the international market, sales to Hon Kong and Macao predominate, but sales to Japan, Singapore, Malaysia and Western European counties are on the increase. Pu'er Tea is the primary tea variety on the Hong Kong market, almost one-half of the tea sold there belonging to this variety. According to the Hong Kong 27 April, 1987 cumulative No. 2016 issue of the *"Economic Guide"* journal, a total of 11,480 thousand kgs of tea was sold in Hong Kong. Out of which over 4,000 thousand Kgs was Pu'er Tea, Oolong Tea running second with 1,000 thousand kgs, while Scented Tea and White Tea together accounted for only about 500 thousand kgs. At present, the sale of Pu'er Tea on the Hong Kong market is about 6,000 th. kgs. Hong Kong's recent reselling of tea to Taiwan and Japan involves mainly Pu'er Tea also.

Japan's yearly consumption of Pu'er Tea increased from 100 to 2,000 thousand kgs. Ever since the Yunnan Tu-Cha (a variety of Pu'er Tea) won in 1986 and 1987 twice the white marble World gold cup, its production has been increased 5-6 times, but still not enough to meet the demand. In retrospect, of all the special varieties of tea exported by China over recent 20 years, the volume of Pu'er Tea showed the greatest increase.

Table 2: Export Volume of Special Teas in China, 1965-2005

(Qty. in m. kgs)

Year/Tea Brand	*1965*	*1975*	*1983*	*1988*	*1992*	*2001*	*2005*
Pu'er Tea	23.57	36.0	51.5	78.4	62	79.0	86.90
Oolong Tea	57.8	47.3	43.1	48.3	93.0	114.7	126.3
Scented Tea	19.3	20.3	30.2	31.3	35.0	44.5	48.9
Whito Tea	5.2	11.2	6.3	-	Negl	79.	8.7
Libdio Tea	14.0	23.8	13.9	-	-	-	-
Louging Tea	2.2	1.4	1.0	7.0	-	3.9	4.2
Total Tea	122.0	140.0	146.0	165.0	190.0	250.0	275.0

NB–1965 to 1985 figures for Oolong tea, Scented tea and Whito tea represent export by Fujian Province.

Source: International Tea Committee.

Analysis of data in the above table shows that the export volume of total special teas for the year 2005 increased by 2.25 times compared to 1965. The increase of Pu'er Tea was 3.70 times, Oolong Tea 2.19 times, Scented Tea 2.53 times, Whito Tea 1.53 times. Thus, it can be seen that the export volume of Pu'er Tea not only was higher than that the average figure for other teas, but also its increase was greater than other kinds of special teas. Guangdong Province has put great efforts into the development of Pu'er Tea production and can compare with Yunnan Province in export volume and product quality. Moreover, Guangdong has exceeded Yunnan on the Japan market. About 23 m. kgs of Pu'er Tea was imported by Japan, of which 18 m. kgs were produced in Guangdong comprising 78 per cent Yunnan Province that contributed 1.70 m. kgs (7.4 per cent); the remaining 22 per cent consisted of products from Sichuan Province, Hunan Province and competitive products from Vietnam and other foreign countries.

Pure Tea Sold in Japan Market

Originally, Pu'er Tea products made from the large-leaf varieties but the kind actually sold on the Japan market belongs mostly to the small-leaf varieties. This reflects the peculiarity of the Japan market. Japanese tea plants are of the small-leaf varieties. The Japanese are accustomed to take small-sized and entire-leaf tea. They believe that small leaves mean tender and good quality tea. Thus, Japanese firms prefer to import the small-leaf kind of Pu'er tea. Factor acting in this direction is that Guangdong was the first to export Pu'er Tea to Japan. It was mainly of the small-leaf varieties. Thus, the Japanese importers, wholesalers, retailers, and consumers have the impression that small-leaf was an attribute of Pu'er Tea. Consequently, the large-leaf Pu'er Tea was the orthodox kind and its export to Japan started later. Sale of the product from Yunnan has been restricted to a certain extent. The sale of Pu'er Tea in Guangdong is also on the increase. Black tea accounts 50 per cent of tea area tea followed by Pu'er Tea (15 per cent).

Projection of Pu'er Tea in 2015

Looking towards the end of the century, it is projected that in the year 2015 the export of Pu'er Tea can attain 1,500 m.

kgs, being one-third the total quantity of special teas (4,500 million kgs) for consumption abroad. As to domestic consumption, Provinces like Guangdong will show relatively great increase.

Pu'er Tea—What Makes it Special

The Nutritive and Health Functions: In modern times people by and large have three attitudes towards goods: namely, commodities should provide novelty, beauty or health. Of these requirements, health is the major one that is also the basic factor for any commodity to excel on the market. *"High mountains shrouded with clouds and mist yield famous tea"* is an old saying. Such places in Yunnan are cloud-clad mountains and plateaus in unparalleled geographical surroundings with picturesque mountains and ravines, moderate climate, non-frost winters and springs, abundant rainfall, winding clouds and mist, and fertile soil. They are the cradle of the world's tea culture and sometimes referred to as the homeland of tea. According to an ancient *Dai document* of the Xishuangbana Dai Nationality Autonomous District, tea cultivation in Yunnan Province existed as early as 1700 years ago. In the primeval forests of Mount Dahei Menghai county, a giant wild-growing tea tree was discovered and given the name *"King of all tea trees in the world"*. The excellent natural conditions of Yunnan allowed the large-leaf tea grown there to become one for the best tea varieties of the world. This together with the unique processing technology adopted which permits full oxidation of the polyphenol and caffeine, substances beneficial to the human body, yielded a product of unique flavour and quality.

Pharmacological and Health Giving Properties: In ancient times many books such as "Diannan Record" and "Supplements to the Compendium of Materia Medica" recorded the pharmacological and health giving of Pu'er Tea. In the chapter on trees of *"Supplement to the Compendium of Materia Medica"* volume 6, which was edited by Prof. Zhao Xuemin during the reign of Emperor Qian Long of the Qing Dynasty was stated : "Pu'er Tea is a panacea for all illness. For example, when ginger tea is given in tympany and colds, healing occurs immediately after sweating; in oral ulcers and sore throat, or fever and pain, one need only to hold 0.05 ounce of the tea in the mouth overnight to achieve cure...". These are early description of the medical efficacy of Pu'er Tea. Sorting out the clinical evidence provided by China's medical profession, it can be seen that Pu'er Tea has shown significant effect in reducing cholesterol level. It can be taken for long periods of time without any side-effects, and also has bacteriostatic effects, being able to prevent and cure dysentery and enteritis. Since 1978, Dr. Emile Karoubi, Head of the Clinical Instruction Department of the Saint Antolne Medical College, Paris, has subjected the Pu'er Tea (Tuo-Cha) of Yunnan to tests, focusing on the weight-reducing and anti-steroid actions of Pu'er Tea in human beings. The study demonstrated that 40 per cent of the people who took part in the test showed weight-reduction, and the results were especially notable in those over the age of 50. The anti-steroid efficiency attained 67 per cent, and the effect on the tricarboxylic glycerides of the human body more marked, with 30 per cent of the under test exhibiting reduction of cholesterol. When the results of the tests were published in France, it made an impact not only on France but also some other European countries. Consequently, the little known Tuo-Cha suddenly loomed to prominence in Western Europe.

Clinical Trials by NRIHM : Clinical trials conducted by the National Research Institute for Health and Medicine (NRIHM) in France since the eighties have demonstrated that Pu'er Tea (Tuo Cha) can lower the blood fat level. The patients with very high blood fat level, 20 per cent showed a reduction of 22 per cent within two months. Professor Lu Tong of the Laboratory of Nutrition, Orson, also performed similar tests and concluded that "This kind of tea apparently contains one or more constituents which can influence the metabolism of lipids" The book *"Pu'er Tea—The Tea with Miraculous Function"* written by Nu Setsuo and Soyama Ichiro created a Pu'er Tea fad in Japan. Clinical trials undertaken by the Kunming Medical College has shown that when 55 high blood-fat cases were treated with Pu'er Tea and the results compared with those obtained by treating

31 cases with the well-recognized anti-lipemia drug Clofibrate, the therapeutic effect of Pu'er Tea was better than that of Clofibrate in regards to the lowering of blood fat levels. Similar efficacies were seen in reducing blood cholesterol levels.

Helping the Digestion, Appetizing, etc.: Some of our researchers in China doing in vitro experiments with sections of excised rat intestine, have found that pu'er Tea possesses functions such as helping digestion, appetizing, relieving over stuffiness and weight-reducing functions. On the "Tea and Health International Symposium" held in Shizuoka, Japan, on 26-29 August, 1991, the participants evinced great interest in the paper "Tetramethoxybenzene in Genuine Black Tea and the Antioxidant Activity Induced by it" presented by Chinese and Japanese scholars. This created a sensation. Compatriots in Hong Kong and Macao believe that Pu'er Tea can generate body fluid and relieve thirst. It invigorates the digestive functions, alleviates drunkenness, increases appetite and relieves overstuffness. It is bacteriostatic and weight reducing. It values a marvellous item for maintaining health, a healthy beverage that one must take every day. They think that Green Tea is cold in nature, Black Tea hot in nature, whereas Pu'er Tea is neither cold nor hot, easy to afford and worth one's money, and so is a popular drink given the name "Baoli Tea". Pu'er Tea is moderate and mild in nature, can strengthen the body's defence mechanisms, and is suited to the digestive system of the people in Hong Kong. This may be the main reason why the Hong Kong people prefer to drink Pu'er Tea. Since so many people like to take it, others are influenced to follow suit. Recently, the chairperson of the Hong Kong and Kowloon Tea Business Association gave five reasons why the Hong Kong people like to drink Pu'er Tea. These are strong flavour, better reusability, moderate nature, health-giving properties and affordability. Pu'er Tea imported by Japan is often further processed into exquisite small packages, which after given attractive names like Royal Concubine Tea, Beauty Tea, Health Tea, Seclusion Tea and Longevity Tea are put on the market with good sales value. Pu'er Tea has been entitled "The Unimaginable Precious Tea".

Sale of Tuo Cha in Drug Stores or Departmental Stores: At present quite a few West European countries put Tuo Cha on sale in drug stores or in the cosmetics showcases of department stores. Some set them up in home as curios. It is said that in France there exists even the saying: "Do you want a beautiful body? Well, you should drink Tuo-Cha". From ancient recordings of the pharmacological action of Pu'er Tea to research utilizing improved physical and chemical means, reliable results have been coming not only from empirical prescriptions and clinical observations, but also from in depth studies using bio-chemistry, biophysics, molecular biology and genetics as well as in vivo experiments on animals. In recent years Ina Kazuo and Liu Qinjin, using biological and physical methods have conducted studies on the profound changes occurring in the characteristic aromatic constituents and flavour-producing substances during manufacture. These studies have great significance in studying the development of the characteristic flavour and pharmacological action of Pu'er Tea. Further, research to elucidate the overall effect of Pu'er Tea on the immunocompetence of the human body is of great significance. The head, Itamoto Keishiro, of the Japanese Oriental and Western Produce Co said : "The marvellous thing about Yunnan Pu'er Tea is that despite its thousand-odd years history, it is still full of vitality today. As long as you regularly drink it, you will enjoy innumerable health-preserving effects. For the benefit of more people in the world, it should be popularized".

China's Struggle for Tea Economy

There have been persistent requests for an estimate of Chinese economy, China, as is well known, has given tea its scientific name *Camellia sinesis L.* to the world and still holds a position of prestige, though India tops the list now. It is, however, difficult to get a proper account of the China's tea economy. Attempt has, therefore, been made to give an account from *The Tea & Coffee Trade Journal.*

While China's economy continued to experience rapid growth over the years, the same could not be said for the country's tea industry. The agricultural sector in China is threatened by a combination of unfavourable trends. If it is not corrected in time, it could undermine the whole base of its economy. Arbitrary taxes and charges levied by local authorities, declining investment in infrastructure, an alarming amount of farmland being diverted to other uses, are some of the factors responsible for poor performance of the tea Economy. Widening income differentials between the urban and rural sectors and between agricultural and non-agricultural pursuits and the mass exodus of peasants to cities in search of better-paid jobs have all combined to paint a bleak picture of China's agricultural economy. The tea industry is no exception. Just as the outlook remains uncertain for the Chinese economy overall, with a volatile mix of economic, political and social factors threatening to undo some of the impressive gains of the past fifteen years, so too the tea industry seems to be heading into unchartered waters. The Chinese tea press carried a series of articles pointing to the problems facing the industry on all fronts. According to these sources, China's tea industry experienced four principal problems since nineties. First tea producers met with an unprecedented difficulty in selling tea, resulting in tea fields begin abandoned and leaves being left unplucked. Second, there was a rise in production costs and a fall in tea farmers' income. Third, processing enterprises suffered from an increase in the scope of their losses. Finally, the domestic trading system found great difficulty in conducting business, with competition in sales districts being extremely fierce.

Plucking and Processing

As the plucking and processing of the spring season's teas got underway, several alarmist articles appeared concerning the state of the industry. From the south-eastern Fujian province there were reports of farmers cutting down tea bushes. From southern Hunan, headlines reported the outlook is bleak in meteorological terms as changing from cloudy to the prospect of rain. From Jiangxi, it was reported that while output had increased, selling the tea was going to be difficult. News from China's leading tea producing province, Zhejiang, was dismal. Spring tea output was down an unprecedented 24 per cent, on an average, annually. This decline was attributed to three principal factors. First, prices of the international and domestic markets were soft, with output exceeding demand. This results an abnormally large build-up of stocks leading to heavy losses being sustained by tea companies. It was estimated that stocks in the export sector alone totalled 30 million kgs and that total provincial tea stocks were at 80 million kgs—equal to one year's total sales. Second, the new tax rate levied on tea producers at 16 per cent was considered to be a deterrent to tea farmers. The fluctuating procurement prices had sapped their enthusiasm. Third, the export revenue quota set for Zhejiang by the general tea export company in Beijing was lowered from $90 million in 1993 to $ 55 million leaving the provincial company with a major problem in deciding which customers it would be unable to supply. With the accompanying reduction in tea procurements for export, overall procurements and sales in the province were deleteriously affected. The procurement price of spring tea plummeted as a result.

In contrast, to this widespread dismal picture, the outlook in Jiangsu continued to improve. Tea area in this province had increased 20 times over that of the mid-1950's while, over the same period, output had increased a remarkable 50 times. The area, production, yield and exports during 1989 to 2005 are shown below:

Table 3: Area, Production, Yield and Exports during 1989 to 2007

(Area in th. ha, Production and Exports in m. kgs, Yield in Kgs/ha)

Year	*Area*	*Production*	*Yield*	*Export*
1989	1065	535	502	204
1990	1061	540	509	195
1991	1061	542	511	184
1999	1130	675	598	200
2000	1090	683	627	227
2001	1141	702	615	250
2002	1134	745	657	252
2003	1207	768	635	260
2004	1262	835	662	280
2005	1310	870	665	285
2006	1325	880	664	295
2007	1345	890	661	312

Source: Tea Statistics, Tea Board, Kolkata, India.

Performance of China's Tea Industry

The Chinese press summed up the performance of China's tea industry. It was reported that there was a fall in output, a drop in procurement prices, a rise in quality, a contraction in exports, an increase in domestic sales, a fall in year-end stocks and a decline in enterprise profits. In 1989 China's total field area was 1065 thousand hectares (ha), which was reduced to 1000 ha in 1994 and perhaps the smallest area under tea. This meagre contraction in area was attributed to tea fields falling into disuse or even being abandoned. Plucked area was estimated to be about 9,89,000 ha. Further, most of China's tea fields having reached maturity, continuing large gap between total and plucked area. This is an indication of tea farmers' reluctance to pick leaves on the fields which they manage. Initial reports put national output for 1994 at 527 million kgs, which was lower than output of 565 million kgs of 1993. The situation started improving from 2000 onwards. Area under tea in 2000 was 1090 thousand ha which enhanced to 1345 thousand ha in 2007.

Production enhanced from 683 million kgs to 890 million kgs during the same period. Increase in production was mainly attributed to increase in area and partial improvement in yield from 627 kgs/ha to 661 kgs/ha. It was observed that area increased by 25 per cent and production by 65 per cent during 1989 to 2007. In 2008, output was estimated around 905 million kgs a rise of over 15 million kgs the figure for the previous year. However, it is highly likely that the final output figure will be higher than this.

Two points can be made about these domestic sales figure. First they reflect in their proportion the Chinese people's preferences in tea varieties. Of an estimated total black tea output of 905 million kgs in 2008 only about 15 per cent was sold on the domestic market. Likewise only a small per centage of the country's Oolong tea is consumed in China. Among the Han Chinese green and scented tea remains by far the most popular varieties. Second there is a crisis emerging in the border system. With production at 895 million kgs and sales of 1005 million kgs the Chinese authorities have to draw down stocks to satisfy demand for this variety which is consumed almost exclusively by minority nationalities in sensitive border regions. Although, this tea can be stored for a considerable period there must be a limit to stocks. Output of border tea fell by 15 per cent in 2005 before. Stocks in 2004 fell a further 20 per cent. The low procurement price of the raw material means that peasants are unwilling to produce this tea. Thus, it is likely that output will continue to slide. The widening imbalance between demand and supply will become even more acute.

Speciality and Famous Teas

The increased output of speciality and famous teas is one bright sport on the horizon for the Chinese tea industry. While these teas only comprise about 8 per cent of national output, their contribution in value terms is enormous. For example, in Zhejiang province, the 2004 spring season famous teas comprised 16 per cent of provincial output but in value terms these teas contributed over half of provincial tea output value. This was the first time that the value of famous teas had surpassed that of ordinary teas. Tea procurements through the state and cooperative system were estimated to 362 million kgs down 15 per cent on the previous year. The procurements by variety of tea were in the order of green 153 million kgs (down 19 per cent), black tee 110 million kgs (down 12 per cent), scented tea 30 million kgs (down 9 per cent), Oolong tea 42 million kgs (up 22 per cent) and raw materials for the processing of border tea 28 million kgs (down 21 per cent). In 2005, procurement prices for most tea categorise fell with the price of crude green down 16 per cent, crude black down 18 per cent, the price of compressed tea remained about the same and that of famous teas rose slightly.

These figures were up 6 per cent and 8 per cent, respectively, on sales figures for 2007. Sales through the state and cooperative system totalled 125 million kgs, an increase of 4 per cent over 2004 and allegedly comprised 51 per cent of sales. Domestic sales of black tea remained static at 14 million kgs Sales of green tea totalled 55 million kgs (up 6 per cent in 2003), sales of scented tea were 53 million kgs (up 7 per cent) Oolong 7 million kgs (up 4 per cent) and border tea sales at 41 million kgs remained the same. The increase in sales of green tea was attributed mainly to the sales of famous and quality teas. Sales of standard and low grade teas were not brisk and it was predicted that this situation would remain the same in 2008. With a fall in stocks in sales districts in 2007 it was predicted that in 2008 there would be a demand for this tea so long as output is not raised to unrealistic levels.

Government's Efforts/Incentives

In an effort to stem the time in late 2005 the Ministry of Finance announced a reduction of 10 per cent in the agricultural special products tax on the raw materials which go into the making of border tea. This favourable treatment will be extended only to those 16 designated tea factories which procure and process the tea. The Ministry of Finance and the Bureau of Taxation announced further that the value added tax will not be levied on those units designated by the state to sell border tea to minority nationalities. Whether these steps on the fiscal front will do anything to stimulate production remains to be seen. The anomaly of tight state control over the production, sales and price of border tea while other sectors of the tea industry have been opened to market forces can only be resolved by the continuing and counter productive use of administrative edicts or the completion of the opening of all sectors of the tea industry.

China's Tea Auction Centre—A Look

Following the accepted international practices approved by the Ministry of Commerce of the People's Republic of China and Shanghai Municipal People's Government, the tea auction centre in China, known as the Shanghai International Tea Commodity Auction Centre (SITAC), was established in the form of a limited liability company. It was with registered capital RMB 20 million (US$ 2.5 million). Its major business is although tea auction, spot and forward contracts of domestic and foreign commodities are dealt in. The members may make the dealings either on their own accounts or on a commission basis through the open competitive prices in the Centre. Current objective of the SITAC is to shape itself into a perfectly legal international tea and other commodities auction market. It further aims at transforming the internal market system to meet the requirements of GATT.

China exports tea to 16 countries. During 1972, she exported 50.15 m. kgs, which enhanced to 284.57 million kgs in 2005. This shows an increase of 440 per cent i.e., an average annual growth rate of 13.32 per cent. Out of total of 50.15 million kgs, black tea constitutes 40 per cent while green and other tea 60 per cent in 1972. The trend was totally reversed in 2005. Black tea accounted for 16 per cent and green and other tea 84 per cent. Among the 16 countries, share of USA to total tea production ranged from 7.7 million kgs to 12.74 million kgs during the period under review. Most interestingly, China exports to USSR/CIS in 1974 to the extent of 1.10 million kgs, which was hiked to 8.42 million kgs in 2005. Exports of tea from China to

Netherlands started declining from 1981 except 1997. During 1999 to 2005, export was less than a million kg. The countries like New Zealand, Tunisia, Sudan, etc. are buying China tea from 1974 onwards.

Fall and Rise of China's Tea Industry

The decline of the Chinese tea industry in the late 19th Century may be ascribed to both domestic and internal factors. Backward technology, ignorance of marketing and consumption trends, poor extension services, exploitation of small farmers by the these rural landlords and urban merchants, the burden of excessive charges and taxes levied by governments contributed to the rapid fall of tea industry in China. And the Britishers, taking advantage of this situation, established large-scale plantations with latest processing equipments in India and Sri Lanka where only black tea was produced. Borrowing Chinese tea production techniques, Japan devoted to the production of green tea. And China had practically lost its predominance in the international tea trade by the beginning of twentieth century. What is more significant to note that just in a span of fifty years since then China's tea production had fallen to a fraction of what it had once been. But China was unprepared to accept this disgraceful situation for long. Rather it started the struggle for reviving the tea industry with vigorous effort. Between 1949 and 2004 the total tea area increased by 8 times, 11,70,000 ha. Output increased from 410 m.kgs to 725 million kgs i.e., more than 20 times over the same period. Export increase accounted for 4 times from 101 m.kgs m. kgs in 1950 to 270 million kgs in 2004 (Table 3).

Modelled along Soviet lines, China was a planned economy between 1950 and 1980s. During the period, prices and standards for the wide range of teas produced in the country were specified. These were supervised by state agencies like the Ministry of Commerce and the All China Supply and Marketing Cooperative and their local branches. Nevertheless, this was not easy task for the bureaucracy. The situation has considerably changed with the leaning towards liberalization of the economy. Tea marketing has

Table 4: Exports from China during 1997 to 2005

(Qty. in thousand.kgs)

Destination	*1972*	*1973*	*1974*	*1981*	*1991*	*1997*	*1998*	*1999*	*2000*	*2001*	*2005*
United Kingdom	–	–	7454	8366	5835	8032	6742	4806	3721	4743	4824
Germany Fed. Republic	–	–	2593	3617	1894	4224	3491	2405	1963	2668	2695
German Dem. Republic	–	–	–	–	–	–	–	–	–	–	–
Netherlands	–	–	2827	2059	1217	2324	1869	571	550	462	472
USSR/CIS	–	–	1110	50	21560	7080	7406	5814	2077	7265	8421
Poland	–	–	3643	1620	326	2710	3020	2808	2935	4481	4710
USA	–	–	7709	7318	15442	12747	12111	7875	7214	7300	8310
Iraq	–	–	1445	400	–	5138	9816	1999	–	–	–
Pakistan	–	–	3943	4536	1488	1996	1290	135	1772	3873	3970
Yen Arab Republic	–	–	1573	315	2451	847	664	256	–	–	–
Yen Dem. Republic	–	–	1035	159	–	–	–	–	–	–	–
ARE	–	–	2000	–	311	8	128	22	–	–	–
Libya	–	–	1100	–	3150	1000	550	–	–	–	–
Sudan	–	–	4676	2916	28	57	–	–	–	–	–
Tunisia	–	–	2057	2500	5500	3334	4217	1700	2000	1097	1192
New Zealand	–	–	2041	1561	1891	356	422	53	96	71	75
Other Countries	–	–	7002	9041	137226	37291	17785	5150	7121	8987	10017
Total Black	20881	29053	52210	44458	74829	87144	69591	33594	29449	40947	44631
Green and Other Tea	29873	34510	54620	47510	110043	115320	147843	166014	198212	208731	239935
Total All Tea	50153	63564	106830	91968	184872	202464	217434	199608	227661	249678	284566

Source: International Tea Committee.

been partially deregulated. And the country intends to be at the top of the list of tea traders in the world market. China possesses the largest tea growing area in the world. Total area in 2004 equalled 23 per cent of the world's tea growing area. The country is also the world's greatest producer and exporter of green tea. In 2004, it produced 66 per cent of world output and contributed 72 per cent of world trade in the commodity. China has greater expertise in green tea. These besides China has the greatest range of tea in different grades and varieties. The country cultivates tea in a wide range of climate and topographical environments—from the moist of temperate Yunnan province to the more severe climates in the north.

Tea Processing Machinery in China

It has been reported that by the mid-1980s there were over 4,00,000 pieces of tea machinery installed in Chinese tea factories. Most of the China's tea processing machinery is produced in Zhejiang province in East China. In 1978, as many as 39,100 pieces of machinery were produced for the tea processing industry which increased to 63,300 units in 1990. However, a Sino-Japanese joint venture was set up in Hangzhou in 1990 to produce tea plantation machinery. The aim is to harvest 330 thousand hectares of tea fields by the year 2015. One million US $ was invested to produce bush trimmers and pluckers. The venture attained the set output target of 10,000 units by 1995, increasing to 70,000 units in 2015. Since 1974, a total of 1,550 items of tea machinery have been imported into China, the opening of this joint venture was partly as an import replacement exercise. It is expected that machine harvesting will reduce the cost of plucking by 50 per cent.

Taiwan Tea Cultivators' Interest in China

China Times reported that tea cultivators of Taipei's suburban areas are, of late, seriously contemplating of making new investment in tea industry in mainland China. Comparing fruits and vegetables as tea is less perishable due to its inherent quality, some traders of Taiwan were weighing the benefits of importing tea from established growers in China. But, of course another section of growers preferred tc make direct investment in the mainland industry. The finished crops would be sold to Taiwan. Growers in Mucha and Yangmingshan are the pioneer to consider such investment projects, observed the China Times.

China's Export to America

Chinese tea was virtually unknown in America two decades ago and attributed to just one percent share of the market. It has successfully captured the American market in recent years. During that period Sri Lanka teas have been their favourite and responsible for a market share of 24 per cent with Indonesia coming a close second securing 16 per cent share of the market. But over the past 20 years the entire tea import scenario of the country has changed. During this period, America imported a fair quantity from non-producing countries such as the UK, Hongkong, Netherlands and Canada. Their reliance on this market has been greatly reduced now. However, about 5 per cent is still obtained from Germany in the form of decaffeinated tea. China has taken the top berth with a 24 per cent market share. America's imports have increased from 88 million kgs in 1974 to 211 million kgs in 2004, which has mostly benefited other producers. China commands a market share of about a quarter of America's total imports and enjoy dollar earning of 18 per cent of the total expenditure on the import of tea. China's exports to America are not only confined to Black Tea but the country enjoys a significant market for Green Tea, Oolong Tea and Jasmine Tea.

China and Vietnam in Global Tea Market

It has been noted that China and Vietnam have emerged as major players in the global tea arena. Cost of production in these two countries is much low comparing that of India and Sri Lanka. Production cost of tea is also low in Kenya. In essence world's two major tea producers India and Sri Lanka are likely to face steep competition in near future.

Strategy to Take China's Tea Industry by 21st Century

Shape of China Tea: China, unlike other major tea-producing countries such as India, Sri Lanka or Kenya, produces an extensive range of teas. The shape of the leaf, initial method of manufacturing (withering or fixation) and extent of processing (crude, refined or reprocessed) may classify tea in China. The time of plucking (spring, summer or autumn), the region of production, scale of production (state farm, agricultural collective or smallholder), final market (domestic or foreign), counter-trade or cash and colour, aroma and taste are some of the aspects for classification of tea. The connoisseur has, therefore, ample scope to judge varieties and quality. Crude green consumed by peasant households is quite a different beverage to the refined gunpowder green tea exported to Morocco or the reprocessed jasmine scented tea, which uses green tea as its base.

Crude and Refined Processing: The division of processing into two distinct stages of crude and refined processing is a function of China's backward transport system and the miniature scale of the industry. Apart from the state farms run by the government, tea gardens in the country are small, dispersed and subject to vastly different levels of management expertise. Individual tea farmers in their homes, or in factories, which are very small, carry out crude processing by international standards. Unrefined or crude teas are subject to refining before being exported. Some domestically consumed tea is also refined. Tea refiners are usually large state-run factories in provincial cities and towns. In recent years smaller factories, many of them contracted to individuals and using old and inferior equipment and backward technology, have mushroomed in tea-producing areas, outbidding the state sector for raw material. The object of refining is to improve the product's external appearance, grade it, eliminate foreign bodies and raise its purity. The tea is also further dried to lower its moisture content, increase its aroma and then prepare it for storage and transportation. Final blending quality adjustment and unification of standards then takes place.

Standards of Tea: Two standards of tea are now ready for the market. The first is called "trade standard". Large state refineries at major ports of export, such as Shanghai or Canton (Guangzhou), are authorized to designate export code numbers to their teas and to stipulate variety and grade. If, on the other hand, the tea is processed, packed, inspected and exported directly by a local factory, its water and dust content must be 0.5 per cent below the criteria set for the above refineries. The second standard is called "processing standard" in which water content must be one per cent below the standard set for export quality and where the dust content is subject to inspection at the port of export after blending is completed.

In relation to method of manufacture, teas pass through the initial process of withering—including Wulong (Oolong), black (Chinese red) and white tea—in increasing intensity of withering so that processed leaf for white tea bears least resemblance to the freshly-plucked buds and tips. Other teas pass through an initial stage of fixation to prevent fermentation, including green, yellow and dark-green (Chinese black), in increasing degree of oxidation so that dark-green tea least resembles the fresh leaf. Chinese teas may also be grouped into six major categories such as: *(i)* green, *(ii)* black, *(iii)* yellow, *(iv)* white, *(v)* dark green and *(vi)* grey. It should be noted that the Chinese name their teas according to the colour the liquid whereas in English the colour is given to the dried leaf. Hence, the Chinese word for what in the English-speaking world is called black tea is red.

Six Tea Categories: Green and black tea is familiar to most tea consumer's. In China they make up the bulk of national output. In 2006, green tea comprised 60 per cent of China's output of 725 m.kgs, black tea 25 per cent, grey 5.6 per cent, compressed (essentially dark-green) 3.9 per cent, with unspecified "Other" teas making up the total. In 2005, green tea made up 65 per cent of total production of 720 m.kgs, a significant increase due to the higher prices it could fetch on the domestic market. By volume, China exports more black tea than green, but because it is generally of a low grade, black tea brings less revenue than green.

For example, in 2005 just over 50 per cent of China's tea exports of 260 million kgs were black with green making up 38 per cent. However, black tea comprised only 40 per cent of tea export earnings.

Green Tea with Three Stages in Processing: Green tea, the most popular hot beverage in China, passes through three stages in processing: fixation either by steam (preferred by the Japanese), or roasted (favored by the Chinese). Implements used for fixation include copper bowls, troughs or rollers. The next processing stage is kneading and twisting followed by drying—in copper works, by curing or sun-drying.

Roasted and Cured Green: The most common green tea in China is called chaoqing (roasted green) and is differentiated from hongqing (cured green) by two factors. First, in the kneading and twisting stage the process is lighter for the latter because most of this tea is sold on the domestic market, it must be able to withstand water of a high temperature and retain its original shape. Additionally, in the kneading and rolling stage, hongqing green is sifted and twisted a second time. Second, in the drying stage, hongqing green passes through a two-stage curing process of high-temperature curing as well as low-temperature drying. Hongqing is the base green for jasmine and other scented teas.

Division of Chaoqing Green Tea: Chaoquing green is in turn divided into two principal types according to the shape of the leaf-oval, known as mei, and pearl-shaped, known as gunpowder. There are also needle shaped and flat-leaf chaoqing greens. The famous Longjing (dragon well) green tea from Hangzhou is a well-known example of a flat leaf. Complications arise from the fact that because mei has traditionally been dried in a work and because of its shape it commonly called chaoqing or long chaoqing and thus confused with the generic term.

Black Tea with Four Stages in Processing: Black (Chinese red) passes through the four stages of withering, kneading and twisting, fermentation and drying. Black tea is divided into three principal varieties : *(i)* small-leaf black, *(ii)* gongfu (gongou) or traditional Chinese black and *(iii)* broken black (CTC), the tea most widely consumed in the West. Small leaf black is a traditional tea produced in a very small quantities in Fujian province in South East China. The leaves are plucked relatively late in spring. After fermentation the leaf is work-fired at 200 degrees centigrade to halt fermentation by destroying the active enzymes and to increase its aroma. It is then rolled a second time for 8 to 10 minutes and smoke-cured. The finished product carries a faint pine aroma which is its mark of identification. The most famous of all gongfu tea is produced in Qimen county, anhui province. One bud and two or three leaves are plucked to produce this tea. After refining the tea is divided into: *(a)* graded tea, *(b)* ungraded tea, and *(c)* leftovers.

China began producing broken black in the 50's for the Eastern European market. Most broken black is produced on state farms in the southern province of Guangdong, Guanxi, Guizhou and Jiangxi. Because a large leaf bush is more suitable for the processing of this variety, production has been concentrated in the southeastern province of Yunnan in recent years. Since 1964, production has increased rapidly to the point where, today, 80 per cent of China's black tea exports are of broken black. However, only on-third is processed from the large-leaf bush. Sales are directed almost entirely toward the international market as very little of this is consumed domestically.

Four Categories of Tea

Yellow Tea: The remaining four categories of yellow, white, gray and dark-green, because of their unfamiliarity to Western consumers, merit more detailed discussion. Yellow and white teas are traditional products which command a specialized and shrinking market. Very little is produced and even then output is intermittent. In fact Chinese statistics group both under the category of "other teas". In 2006, Huoshan country in Anhui province, with an output of 1.5 million kgs was the highest producer of yellow tea in the country. Yellow tea in the cup is characterized by its colour, clear and pleasant fragrance and rich flavor. Processing is similar to that for green tea except that after three processing stages a process of covering is added to impart extra colour to the tea.

White Tea: White tea is a specially product from Fujian province in east China and a small amount is also produced in Taiwan. It was discovered in 1885 in Fujian's Fuding county. Production is minuscule and in 1976 only 500 thousand Kgs were produced, equal to four per cent of tea output in the province. It's production increased to 1.5 million kgs in 2006. Most of the tea is exported to Chinese communities in Hong Kong and Macau. In 2006, China exported 800 thousand Kgs of this tea. White tea passes through two stages of withering and drying with the withering being of two kinds, complete withering or partial withering.

Dark Green Tea: Dark green tea (Chinese black) goes through four processing stages: *(i)* fixation, *(ii)* kneading and twisting, *(iii)* stacking and moistening, and *(iv)* drying. The stacking and moistening, performed in order to promote fermentation, is carried out in three ways: when the semi-finished product is wet, when it is dry, or to the finished product as repeated fermentation. This tea is normally reprocessed into compressed tea which is consumed in large quantities by China's minority nationalities, the Tibetans, Mongolians, and Uighurs of Xinjiang in particular.

Gray/Wulong Green Tea: Gray or Wulong (black dragon) tea is the most difficult of all teas to process. It is a semi-fermented tea combining the rich and sweet flavour of black and the freshness and fragrance of green. Wulong tea is an acquired taste, but one well worth acquiring. Its production is confined to the southeastern coastal province of Fujian and Guangdong and the island of Taiwan. Processing skills are jealously guarded and it is difficult to inspect a factory producing Wulong. There are five processing stages: *(i)* withering, *(ii)* semi-fermentation (according to the degree of which and the area grown the tea is known as north Fujian grey, south Fujian gray, Guangdong gray or Taiwan grey), *(iii)* roasting, *(iv)* kneading & twisting, and *(v)* drying.

Consumption of Gray /Wulong Tea

The consumption of Wulong tea is highest in the three producing provinces of Fujian, Guangdong and Taiwan. It also finds appeal in Hong Kong and Macau. In recent years, Chinese Wulong has found niche in Japan where it commands good prices. This is a good example of how new markets can be sought out and consumers, who have traditionally favoured steamed green, can be attracted to a different product if quality is consistently high.

Scented and Compressed Tea

Two others types of tea do not belong to separate categories, but, because they are made with different base teas, belong to one of the six categories above. The first is scented tea and the second compressed. Both are teas, which are reprocessed from either crude or refined tea. Fragrances have been added to tea in China since the Song dynasty (960 AD). In the late 19th century, production of scented tea was centered in Fujian province. Processing of the tea is now concentrated in two large factories in Suzhou (Jiangsu province) and Fuzhou (Fujian province). In the processing of scented tea, fragrant flowers are added to the semi-finished tea-base. The resultant tea retains the characteristics of the base tea whether it be cured green (hongqing) with jasmine flowers (jasmine tea), grey tea with osmanthus (osmanthus tea) or black tea with roses (rose tea).

Production of Scented and Compressed Tea: The main difficulty in producing scented tea is to synchronize the flowering of the jasmines or roses with the plucking of the leaf. Good-quality scented tea contains no flowers, only the fragrance resulting from the pressing of flowers between layers of tea. The northern cities of Beijing and Tianjin, Shandong province and Guangdong and Fujian province in the south of China are the leading domestic consumers. When tea is served in Chinese restaurants in the West it is most likely to be jasmine tea, and not always of a very good quality. Compressed tea in the form of bricks or cakes is so made for the convenience of shipment to outlying areas and, depending on the base tea used, it comes under the category of black tea (millet brick) or dark-green tea, (Sichuan fu brick, Hubei green brick, Sichuan gold tip and west Sichuan brick), which are all steamed, or Anhuafu brick and Sichuan fangbao tea, which are roasted, and scented brick. If the tea-base is green and it is then steam compressed and piled up to ferment, it comes under the category and dark-green and not green tea.

Instant Tea, Tea Bags, Tea Cola, Tea Orange, Lemon Tea, etc.: Finally there are instant teas, most of which are made from black tea and some from green tea. China first produced experimental batches of instant tea in 1972. She in 1974 has sold the tea at the Canton Trade Fair. Instant tea in teabags now commands a growing share of the tea market. Soft drinks, such as tea cola made with green tea, are now available in limited supplies in China. Canned lemon tea manufactured in Hong King is sold in joint-venture hotels. While it appeals to younger Chinese, traditional tea drinkers of an older generation find it to sweet.

Future of China's Tea Industry

The tea industry in China must continue to attract domestic consumers against increasing competition from imported drinks such as coffee and Coca Cola, which have become very fashionable in recent years despite their high prices. In 1988 a new teahouse was opened in Hangzhou. It was elaborately decorated in the traditional style of the Song dynasty (960-1127 AD), and situated in a street specializing in restaurants and designated a *tourist* attraction up the city government. It failed to attract customers and closed its door within six months—a warning sign that the local consumers cannot be taken for granted even in a city where the citizens are as addicted to green as Hangzhou.

Untapped Potential in the International Market

On the international market there is untapped potential for China's great variety of exotic teas. Over the past few years there has been a lot of writing in the Chinese press on the subject but apparently little action to match the rhetoric. Penetration of the Western market will require levels of skill, determination and flair which to date have been noticeably absent from Chinese marketing techniques.

Marketing of Green Tea: With clever marketing green tea could become a trendy drink in the high-income countries of the West. It has an appealing appearance and a refreshing taste. Chinese writers on the subject argue that the tea suffers from the disadvantage of the size of the leaf, which swells and returns to its original shape when hot water is added. They believe that a way must be found to process it into the desiccated size and shape of dried black tea.

Presence of Green Tea in the West: The fact that Chinese green has not yet established a strong presence in the West is due more to poor promotion by the Chinese than to the product itself. If, for example, a decent grade of green tea was placed in Chinese hotel rooms for foreign tourists, satisfied consumers might take their discovery back home and create a strong demand for what is both a satisfying and safe drink in this age of obsession for healthy foodstuffs. In this respect, China has gone backwards over the last decade. In 1977, the Longjing (green) tea supplied to guests of the Hanzhou Hotel was excellent quality. Prof. Keith Forster, Contemporary China Centre Research Scholar of Pacific Studies, Australian National University, and his wife drank green tea regularly during their stay in the hotel for three years. The hotel people supplied with good quality tea. Sadly, the same cannot be said now a days for the tea in that hotel. This issue was raised with various people connected with the tea industry in Hangzhou but no positive response was forthcoming.

Low Profile and Absence of Powerful and Influential National Lobby: The Chinese tea industry suffers from a low profile, which is surprising. It has cultural significance and contributes to the earning of foreign currency. Perhaps its inferior status to other agricultural crops is due partly to the fact that within most parts of the country tea is regarded as a luxury consumer item for which demand is highly price inelastic. Another important factor is the absence of a powerful and influential national body to oversee the industry. The recent articles in China have pointed out that there is no Tea Board in the lines of India to represent growers, producers and exporters. On the contrary, the industry is subject to the competing and conflicting bureaucratic interests of the Departments of Agriculture (production), Commerce (marketing) and Foreign External Relations and Trade (Exports), as well as involving the Ministry of State Farms (amalgamated with the Ministry of Agriculture in 1982), the Ministry of Public Security (which runs tea farms for offenders) and the Ministry of Agricultural Machinery (1979-82).

Difference in Opinion on the Development of China Tea: Regular reading of the Chinese press confirms the view that each department holds its own view of how the industry should develop. For example, ideas differ as to whether China should increase its export of black teas or concentrate on green tea. This has resulted in the constant switching of production from one variety to another, especially during the past decade. In 1984, a rise in the international price of black tea induced Chinese producers to process this tea. In 1985 Wulong tea attracted producers and in 1987-88 green tea became the rage. At present, the emphasis is on reducing production of green tea and switching over to black.

Price Reforms

The thorny and politically–sensitive question as to how far China should go in price reform and allow the market to determine prices has obvious and pressing relevance for the tea industry. The state-fixed export price is well below the domestic market price, resulting in shortages of supplies for export. Even the favourable exchange rate granted to exporters does not compensate for the losses incurred in placing the commodity on the international market. At present, China has back away from the limited deregulation of marketing and price instituted in 1984 and return to mandatory procurements and state-fixed prices. The calls form various commentators to establish domestic auctions are unlikely to be heeded in the present political climate.

Agreed Strategy of 21st Century

Overall, there is hardly any stated and agreed strategy to take China's tea-industry into the 21st century. If the growth rates of the past 50 years are to be maintained it is essential that a feasible plan be mapped out and put into place. Only in this way will China have any hope of overtaking India and resume its position as the world's number one producer of tea—a product identified so closely with Chinese culture and almost synonymous with the name China itself.

China's Share of World Area, Production and Exports of Tea

World area under the 2450 th. Ha in 1992 whereas China owns an area of 1084 th. ha constituting 44.24 per cent of total. In 2004, world area increased to 2775 th. ha compared to 1262 th. Ha of China tea accounting for 45.50 per cent. Thus, the growth rates of area under tea of world and china increased by 13.22 per cent and 16.42 per cent respectively. Table on next page shows the details.

It is observed from the above table that China occupies an important role in world tea economy. In 2004, she covers a little less than 50 per cent of total world area, one fourth of world production and one fifth of world exports. Year-wise share of area to world area ranged from 42.86 per cent tot 46.32 per cent, production from 22.96 per cent and export 17.26 to 18.56 per cent.

Looking Ahead

Sources in the Chinese tea industry predict that 2006 should witness further a recovery from the depths of 2005. It is anticipated that output should increase with continuing volume rise of famous teas and an increase in the processing of scented tea. However, it is likely that there will be a recovery in tea prices and business in the state and cooperative system may remain difficult. In 2004, China produced 25 per cent of the worlds tea output which was second only to India's 26 per cent. One problem for China is that only 25 per cent of the world's tea output is green

Table 5: Chinas Share of World Area, Production and Export during 1992—2008*

Year	*Area (th. ha)*			*Production (th. kgs)*			*Exports (m. kgs)*		
	World	*China*	*% Share*	*World*	*China*	*% Share*	*World*	*China*	*% Share*
1992	2450	1084	44.24	2438	560	22.96	1017	175	17.26
1993	2533	1171	46.22	2553	600	23.50	1156	201	17.43
1994	2448	1134	46.32	2523	588	23.32	1036	180	17.34
2001	2638	1141	43.25	3035	702	23.12	1391	250	17.94
2002	2646	1134	42.86	3055	745	24.40	1440	252	17.51
2003	2713	1207	44.49	3174	768	24.20	1401	260	18.56
2004	2775	1262	45.48	3306	835	25.26	1540	280	18.19
2005	2853	1312	46.28	3299	902	27.34	1620	295	18.20
2006	2893	1367	47.29	3419	962	28.13	1730	300	17.45
2007	2958	1412	48.03	3534	1017	28.77	1810	322	17.67
2008	3013	1478	49.05	3659	1082	29.57	1920	340	17.70

Source-Tea Statics, Tea Board,India, Kolkata, *Provisional.

tea of which China produced 71 per cent, Japan 15 per cent and Indonesia 7 per cent. Vietnam is the other significant producer. In the same year China supplied 15 per cent of the world's tea trade second only to Sri Lanka's 18 per cent. Almost 33 per cent of China's exports were black tea with the rest being green Oolong compressed and specialist teas.

Chinese authorities believe that the green tea market has limited growth potential and that the future lies in the black tea market. However China's black teas are generally of poor quality and fetch low prices. Authorities must decide whether to concentrate on volumes which seem to have been their strategy to date or to switch their emphasis to quality and price where the non-black tea varieties perform significantly better. With alarm bells now ringing in the industry as tea area declines, prices fall, output follows a roller-coaster ride and young consumer shift away from tea it is time for the Chinese government to introduce a coherent and viable package of reforms to sustain the industry into the next century.

One final point is that in 1994, the Sri Lankan authorities suggested the leading tea producing countries including Sri Lanka, Indonesia and Kenya, to establish a producers association along the lines OPEC in order to stabilize tea prices which have fallen to 1984 levels. A Chinese newspaper reported the proposal without comment. To give itself any clout at all such an association would have to enforce production constraints on member countries. In the past China has shown little interest in joining international producer cartels. Interestingly, China did attend the first meeting of tea producing countries but if the major threat to the international price of black tea is the over supply of low quality teas, as recent reports presented to the Food and Agricultural Organization suggest, then the responsibility was vested with China. The question is whether China is now ready to address this issue.

5

Black Tea, Green Tea, Oolong Tea and Other Teas; Green Tea—World Production, Export, Consumption, Import etc.

SECTION I
Black Tea

Introduction

Tea cultivation and manufacture in China has changed over the centuries. Even to day tea is cultivated almost all Chinese provinces mainly in the central and southern areas. Unlike India, Sri Lanka and other modern tea producing countries, there are no large estates. It is still grown along with other crops by peasant proprietors in small patches, from a few bushes to quarter of an acre, on hill slopes. Methods of cultivation and preparation are, therefore, still primitive, and vary widely from one village to the next, and between one district and another. Hobert Fortune brought some Chinese tea makers to India in 1848. They were sent to Assam and the Kumaon hills to manufacture tea according to their own methods. There were, however, quite a number of Chinamen already in India, as traders, sailors, artisans and collies. Most of them knew some thing about the rudiments of tea. They soon became aware of the demand for Chinese teamakers in the potential tea districts of North-East·India. Prospects of a settled home and good pay encouraged many to offer their services to the planters, and in the 1850's some of them were employed by the early Darjeeling pioneers, by Captain Masson at Tukvar, Mr. Stolke at Steinthal, etc. The descendants of these Chinese teamakers are still to be found in the Darjeeling District, though none carry on the trade of tea-maker. Some married hill women, became absorbed into the hill races. A. H. Singh who said his father came to Darjeeling in the middle of 1800's to work in the tea garden had married a hill woman. During World War II, whenever he was paid for a completed contract he always insisted upon 10 per cent being deducted from his account for the Fight Fund, his contribution to the war effort. Another of the original Chinese tea makers became an important Cooly Sircar at the ill-fated Rhoni Tea Estate. He married a Bhutia girl and became an inspector of Police. There are various accounts still in existence of the earliest manufacturing methods in the Darjeeling District. But accounts of any process or operation in tea planting are apt to become out of focus in inexperienced hands.

Preparation of Black Tea: In making black teas, the plucked leaves were spread out on shallow bamboo trays and allowed to remain for several hours some times in the sun. They were then gathered up, tossed, and gently beaten by the workers until they became flaccid when they were allowed to stand in collected heap for two hours. This was perhaps equivalent to the withering of Indian practice and doing it some fermentation occurred. The leaf was then heated in thin iron pans fixed in earth or brick fireplaces and was vigorously stirred to prevent any possibility of scorching. Rolling on bamboo tables was then carried out very thoroughly by hand. After it the leaf was exposed to the air in trays for about three hours being constantly turned over. The roasting and rolling were repeated until the leaf had all turned red and acquired the desired aroma. The roastings were never more than a few minutes. Finally, further fermentation was stopped by heating the leaf in the well known hour-glass baskets placed over clear charcoal fires and a second and more prolonged heating was carried out to complete the drying. The Darjeeling system, is roughly based on the above. As the leaf was brought in from the various sections in the field during the day, it was placed in shallow bamboo trays in the sun or if there was no sun, in the open verandah of the factory. After sunset, the leaf was roasted in shallow iron pans for a few minutes at the end of which it had become moist. The leaf was then put back in the bamboo trays which were stacked in the verandah or factory till the following day when proper manufacture commenced.

Primitive System: The drying pans or furnaces used for the first heating were of very primitive construction, but their arrangement bears some resemblance to the modern tea dryer. The shallow, circular pans were about 12 inches in diameter and made of thin iron known as our Indian 'Karahi' or cooking pan used for cooking vegetables or rice. They were built in a mud or brickwork furnace, so constructed that the sloping sides of the pan were continued up for three quarters of its circumference. It left an opening or feeding lip, rather like a board, shallow brick or mud basin. The actual bottom consisted of the iron pan. Running beneath the row of pans or basins was a flue, the fireplace being at one end, and a rough chimney at the other. When the wood fire started in the furnace, the flames, smoke and heat carried through the flue, heating the pans, and up the chimney. The next morning, the leaf was again sunned for a few hours or if it was considered to be withered sufficiently. It was next subjected to a series of roastings over charcoal in hour-glass bamboo frames and rolled and pulverised by hand on tables covered with bamboo matting. In some cases, the pulverising was done with the bare feet on wooden floors or on bamboo matting lying on the factory floor. This method was only adopted when dealing with any large quantity of leaf, or with coarse leaf. In later years, charcoal replaced the hour-glass bamboo frames. These box-like structures were of thick about 25 inches in height, with a 22 feet 8 inches square opening at the top, and a hole at the bottom for tending or drawing the charcoal fire. They look a tray of 2 feet 10 inches by 2 feet 9 inches by 3 inches deep, made of thin sheet iron punched with holes like a sieve (bamboo).

The leaf was next given what was called a deep fermentation by piling it in deep bamboo baskets. It was kept for few hours or until it had all turned red and was highly odoriferous. Finally, it was dried in pans over charcoal or in choolas, men stirring it constantly with sticks until it was black. Further, rolling was practiced if it was considered necessary during the final firing, which continued for several hours. How the delicate China leaf shoots of Darjeeling withstood all this bashing about is a mystery. Without present knowledge of the handling of green leaf one can only assume that the standard of plucking then was not the regulation 2 leaves and a bud. It was more like 4 or 5 leaves and a bud. In short, tea flushes were allowed to go rank before plucking, as only coarse rank leaf could take such treatment and at the end of it bear any resemblance to black tea as we know it today.

Chinese Way: In China, the peasants only got four or five full pluckings of leaf their bushes in a season. These points to the method of plucking adopted, that is, plucking rank flushes and taking a bud and four or five leaves. The early pioneers, in particular the Wernickes and Christison (the pioneers of Darjeeling Tea Industry), soon found that they made more and better tea by a regular system of weekly pluckings on younger flushes. They plucked fine two leaves and a bud. The amount of labour required to turn out a pound of tea by this primitive method of manufacture must have been considerable. During the manufacturing season, almost as much labour must have been required in the factory as in the field. Labour cost, even inspite of the cheapness of labour, must have been high in relation to the total cost of producing a pound of made black tea. One can well imagine that the earliest Darjeeling pioneers lost heart by watching the complicated and arduous treatment the tea leaf was given to produce a pound of very poor looking tea. The cost of production was calculated against the possible price, and an assessment of the very meagre profit was made. It hardly seemed worth taking risks and trouble of growing the tea bush. Many of them decided that tea could only be made to pay as a cottage industry. They packed their bags, left the district to try their hands elsewhere at something, which offered a quicker and easier return for the time, trouble, and money spent on it. Many of them had thrown up good jobs in Government service or in private business to become tea planters. They had put their last penny or price into the new venture and lost all. They either went back to their original jobs or tried in finding similar jobs.

Simplification and Standardization of Manufacture: Wernicke brothers and G.W. Christison solved the problems of the manufacture, simplified, and standardized them. They soon discovered three things. Firstly, sundrying during the humid, misty months of the Indian monsoon was a most haphazard process that held up plucking. Unless the leaf was very wet, sun drying seemed to produce loss of flavour and quality. Secondly, a runaway flush exhausted the tea bush and reduced the size of subsequent flushes. The very limited equipment and accommodation available with factories were better suited to regular daily pluckings of smaller quantities of green leaf than spasmodic plucking and great quantities of green leaf. Thirdly, with large quantities of leaf, Chinese methods were cumbersome, unhygienic, and the better quality tea shoots deteriorated in manufacture. They began to realize that the leaf grown in Darjeeling possessed something it lacked elsewhere. It has some intrinsic quality or flavour which increased its value if it could be preserved.

Assam Follows: Similar discoveries were also made in Assam. In regard to plucking, the following note by a Mr. J.F.W. Watson published in 1871, records: "I consider, therefore, that a complete circuit of the garden should be made by the pluckers once a week, if possible, and not later once in nine days, if quality and quantity are to be as nearly as possible combined. Great care must be taken by the Manager not to let the pluckers take shoots which are younger than he intends they should be. Each shoot plucked comprises two leaves and a bud, and not less. When then leaf is got in at its correct stage of growth its manufacture is very easily managed". Darjeeling manufacture began to be standardized to simple routine of withering, rolling, fermenting, firing and sieving. Experiments were made with artificial withering, and simple systems of factory ventilation, air current. Draughts were devised and tried out. Factories were planned so that manufacture could be conducted regardless of weather. The departmental arrangement or factory accommodation on ground floor with extensive withering lofts above took shape. In the field, they started a system of weekly plucking to ensure regular cropping and the right size and quality of leaf. Factories were built as near streams as possible, or stone water flumes were made from nearby springs or steams to factories. This is essential to allow plenty of water for keeping factory equipment, such as it was, as clean as possible.

The original Lingia factory, and later the Tumsong factory, were built on these lines. Other factories in the district followed the same pattern. The withering loft floor consisted of wooden slabs, 2.5" by 1.5", spaced about an inch apart. It was covered with bamboo matting, and flat racks of bamboo were constructed in the room in tiers one above the other. About 18 inches apart; not unlike the chung factories of the plains nowadays. Windows were well spaced throughout the length of the loft on both sides. Immediately below the centre of the withering loft floor was the oven room where firing and final drying was done. The heated air from this room percolated through the withering loft floor to the fresh green leaf spread upon it and the racks and withered it, the moisture-laden air then passed out of the windows. Withers were controlled by the simple expedient of increasing or decreasing the thickness of leaf spread on floor and racks. Withering loft floors were still in existence in a number of factories in Darjeeling in the 1920's. In course of time the racks changed from bamboo to wire mesh or Hessian were spaced much closer together and sloped with the object of facilitating the removal of leaf after withering.

Careful Step: When newly plucked leaf was brought to the factory in the coolies' baskets, the manager and his assistants very carefully examined it. This was a most solemn ritual. Each basket in turn received a thorough examination to see that the 'pluck' was the strict two leaves and a bud with no immature buds or coarse leaf. After weightment, the leaf was taken to the withering loft, where the teamakers spread it on the floor and racks for withering. The following morning leaf was taken in manageable quantities to the rolling room. Alternatively, it dropped through holes or shutes in the loft floor on to the rolling tables, (which were covered with bamboo matting or canvas). It was rolled by hand into tight balls, which were left on the table to cool off and ferment, that is, to change colour from green to copper. There was no fixed time for this colouring or oxidation which might go on for six to eight hours. During the period the leaf balls might be repeatedly broken and re-rolled to speed up fermentation. As soon as the fermenting leaf had developed the right degree of copper colour and the required aroma, it was taken to the drying room. Here the glass baskets and basket frames had been dispensed with and instead there were charcoal which were arranged in batteries of six choolas. One teamaker was in charge of each battery. He was skilled in these operation, especially in the maintenance of the charcoal fires at the right temperature. The charcoal fires were never allowed to get red-hot. Frequently ashes were sprinkled over them to prevent this. In order to get even drying, the leaf with his hand, and changed the position of the tray on the choola. It was generally impracticable to dry the tea off thoroughly at one firing. As the leaf in the trays was spread about 2 inches thick and the choola temperatures varied between 140^0F and 160^0F, the first firing was down to about 10 or 12 annas. After this firing the leaf was spread out on canvas or cloth tarpaulins on the floor about 4 to 6 inches thick, perhaps a good deal thicker if there was a lot of leaf, and left for the night.

Firing Rooms: The firing rooms were small compared with drying rooms nowadays. During the night doors and windows were closed so that the rooms remained warm and some evaporation of moisture from the leaf took place at night. The following morning the drying process was completed in 4 to 6 hours. Tea then had a moisture content of about 10 per cent. So teas were finally fired or "pucka battied" before packing. This "pucka battying" was a most important operation and was done on very slow charcoal fires with the object of developing a 'nose' or aroma. The sorting or sieving of the tea was done entirely by hand and with bamboo sieves. Later, when China sieves made of cane became available these were used in preferences to the bamboo. Bamboo scoops and circular trays, 20 inches in diameter, were used for winnowing the fannings and broken tea from the whole leaf grades. It was soon discovered that the best people for sorting and sieving were the women. Cutter and breakers were unknown. After separating out the finer leaf tea from the coarser, the latter was pounded with wooden mallets to break it up. Five grades of tea were produced, viz., Orange Pekoe, Souchong, Broken Tea and Fannings. After sieving the different grades were stored in large baskets until it was convenient to pack. The teas were packed in locally made wooden boxes lined with paper.

Dispatch of Tea to Kolkata—No Records: There are no records of how the teas were sent to Kolkata. One can make a pretty shrewd guess. Before the railways, all goods in India were dispatched from one place to another in convoys of bullock carts. The custom was for planters and businessmen to form syndicates to facilitate transport. One can, therefore, assume that Darjeeling teas were manhandled as far as Pankhabari, and thence transported to Kolkata by relays of bullock cart convoys. As brigandage and dacoity were common practice in the plains of India in those days, all convoys travelled under military escort or with some armed chowkidars. An interesting commentary on the Darjeeling teas of the period 1870 to 1886, as given by Lt. Col. Hannagan in 1886, follows: "I am not aware that there really is any deterioration in the quality of Indian teas, at least as far as Darjeeling is concerned. For the last five seasons (including this), I am certain that Darjeeling district, taken all round, has turned out a finer quality that it did during the five previous seasons, 1871 to 1875. Prior to 1871, I believe the flavour of Darjeeling tea was fine, owing to the gardens being young, very small outturn per acre being the rule, and pungency not being required by the broker, etc. This demand for pungency has been against the quality of Darjeeling teas in my opinion, as they ought to rely on flavour. As regards the keeping quality of teas, as well as flavour, I consider this has been injuriously affected by the giving up of 'panning'. But this only amount to an opinion, of course, and must be taken for what it is worth."

SECTION II
Green Tea—Various Aspects

The origin of green tea dates back to 1611 when the East India's Company established a factory for manufacturing green tea in Hirado Island in Japan. Until about a decade ago, green tea was mostly consumed in the producing countries in Asia and North Africa. China is the main producer and consumer of green tea. Green tea is getting increasingly more attention in the world markets because of its health benefits. It contains more vitamins and minerals than black tea and produces many effects that can fight infection and disease in human bodies. World green tea production, consumption and exports are mainly dominated by China followed by Japan, Indonesia, Vietnam, India, Bangladesh, Sri Lanka etc.

i. Distinct Quality Green tea is distinct from black tea in as much as the brew from it on infusion of water is nearly similar to the brew from fresh green tea leaves. This characteristic is maintained because of killing of enzymes which cause oxidisation of phenolic components. As a result of action of bacteria and other microorganisms, the green tea leaf as also the black tea leaf, spoils easily. Therefore, it has to be preserved for use during off-season and transportation to distant markets. The most primitive, and by far the cheapest, method of preservation is sun drying which removes moisture from tea leaves thereby preventing spoilage. Unlike black tea, green tea is not fermented during its manufacture and the green colour and the chemical composition is maintained to retain the original characteristics. Green teas rich in caffeine and tannins are quite distinct because of their bitter or astringent taste due to polyphenolics.

ii. Manufacturing Processes: There are two distinct and

prominent methods of making green tea. De-enzyming is typical of green tea processing which can be done through either steaming or pan-heating. Rolling and twisting can be done either through baking or roasting. The Japanese method uses the steaming process to deactivate the enzymes whereas the Chinese follow the pan heating method. In both cases, raw materials used are high quality leaves and buds, freshly harvested from green bushes.

iii. Conservation Ratio: On an average 4.2 to 4.8 kg of green tea leaves are required to manufacture 1 kg of manufactured black tea, whereas 4.6 kg to 6.1 kg of leaf are required for making 1 kg of made green tea. Green tea is more vulnerable to spoilage under adverse keeping conditions than black tea and it has to be stored under controlled atmospheric conditions.

World Production of Green Tea

World production of green tea has been growing consistently and increased from 167.06 million kg in 1978 to 667.61 million kg in 1999. It is estimated that total production of world green leaf is around 771 million kgs in 2005. During the year 2006, it would be in the range of 790 million kgs. The share of green tea in total tea produced has been consistently increasing and Japan dominated with more than 60 per cent share. From September 1980 onwards, China started having a much larger share. However, Japanese production of green tea has declined so much so that it has only 12.81 per cent share in comparison with China which produces nearly 75 per cent of the world production of green tea. Vietnam has been also increasing production of green tea and of late it has a stable 5 per cent share.

The share of green tea produced in total tea has been consistently increasing from 9.35 per cent in 1978 to 23.45 per cent in 1999. (Tables 1 and 2). However, green tea has less than 10 per cent share in world exports of tea and that share has been fluctuating. More and more green tea production is retained in producing countries for domestic consumption.

Table 1: Per centage of Green Tea Production

Destination	*1978*	*1979*	*1980*	*1981*	*1982*	*1983*	*1984*	*1985*	*1986*	*1987*	*1988*
India	4.72	3.73	2.40	1.96	1.97	1.66	1.86	1.96	1.80	2.13	1.55
Bangladesh	0.31	0.12	0.12	0.11	0.11	0.09	0.06	0.22	0.23	0.19	0.20
Srilanka (Med)	0.00	0.00	0.00	0.00	0.19	0.16	0.27	0.28	0.32	0.26	0.24
Indonesia	10.43	11.75	5.82	7.89	5.29	6.78	6.85	7.93	7.34	6.38	5.97
China	0.00	0.00	50.70	52.11	58.26	56.12	57.04	55.18	57.71	61.89	65.76
Japan	62.69	60.38	29.06	26.46	23.22	23.81	21.76	22.10	21.02	19.79	17.45
Vietnam	8.56	9.55	4.52	4.40	4.36	4.64	5.06	5.30	5.01	4.42	4.27
Georgia	0.00	0.00	0.00	0.00	0.00	0.00	0.00	0.00	0.00	0.00	0.00
Russian Fed	0.00	0.00	0.00	0.00	0.00	0.00	0.00	0.00	0.00	0.00	0.00
USSR/CIS	13.29	14.48	7.39	7.06	6.60	6.75	7.10	7.03	6.58	4.93	4.55
Total Green Tea production (m kgs)	167.06	162.32	352.00	386.65	424.21	431.26	425.15	432.17	445.32	486.50	514.72
per cent share of Green Tea in total tea produced	9.35	8.93	19.05	20.53	21.79	21.00	19.39	18.88	19.56	20.78	20.79

Destination	*1989*	*1990*	*1991*	*1992*	*1993*	*1994*	*1995*	*1996*	*1997*	*1998*	*1999*
India	1.62	1.59	1.82	1.67	1.27	1.25	1.43	1.41	1.35	1.34	1.23
Bangladesh	0.19	0.27	0.24	0.20	0.16	0.19	0.09	0.02	0.02	0.03	0.04
Srilanka (Med)	0.19	0.18	0.15	0.07	0.24	0.24	0.08	0.09	0.09	0.10	0.06
Indonesia	6.57	6.58	6.13	6.22	5.62	5.66	5.76	6.13	5.88	5.90	5.54
China	63.51	64.32	66.46	69.04	71.61	71.67	72.28	71.89	72.41	74.61	74.44
Japan	18.29	17.39	16.35	16.36	15.68	15.35	14.81	15.10	14.90	12.83	13.26
Vietnam	4.51	4.60	4.54	4.48	4.41	5.00	5.17	5.04	5.07	4.82	5.09
Georgia	0.00	0.00	0.00	0.00	0.00	0.00	0.33	0.29	0.26	0.36	0.33
Russian Fed	0.00	0.00	0.00	0.00	0.00	0.00	0.04	0.02	0.01	0.01	0.01
USSR/CIS	5.13	5.07	4.31	1.96	1.02	0.64	0.00	0.00	0.00	0.00	0.00
Total Green Tea Production (mkgs)	494.91	516.91	537.73	562.46	587.54	562.10	572.44	587.32	612.02	643.62	667.61
per cent share of Green Tea in total tea produced	20.24	20.36	20.84	23.09	23.04	22.32	22.70	22.23	22.53	21.73	23.45

Source: various issues of ITC Bulletin, London.

Note: Estimated production of green leaf during 2000, 2001, 2002, 2003, 2004 and 2005 are 687.76 m.kgs, 708.28 m.kgs, 729.45 m.kgs, 750.25 m.kgs, 765.25 m.kgs and 774.55 m.kgs respectively.

Table 2: Per centage share of Green Tea Exporting countries

Destination	*1978*	*1979*	*1980*	*1981*	*1982*	*1983*	*1984*	*1985*	*1986*	*1987*	*1988*
China	0.00	0.00	50.70	52.11	58.26	56.12	57.04	55.18	57.71	61.89	65.76
India(e)	3.77	3.27	1.44	4.58	4.32	4.93	1.58	2.23	2.59	5.72	3.21
Srilanka	0.00	0.00	0.00	0.00	0.11	1.33	1.10	1.74	1.89	1.23	1.35
Indonesia	0.05	0.16	0.14	0.15	0.31	0.15	0.19	0.16	0.14	0.21	0.14
China (Mainland)	60.75	61.82	67.57	64.82	70.96	69.96	83.40	83.22	85.07	84.41	84.07
Taiwan	20.38	19.10	14.66	12.18	5.25	6.46	3.66	3.37	3.05	1.70	2.11
Japan	4.55	3.99	3.70	4.18	3.90	2.96	3.80	2.42	1.69	1.27	1.32
Vietnam	10.50	11.65	12.48	14.09	15.16	14.22	6.27	6.86	5.57	5.46	7.81
Total Green Tea Exports million kgs)	74.25	76.38	72.10	63.88	62.67	70.33	71.80	72.89	71.77	82.38	93.51
per cent of Green Tea	9.24	8.98	8.39	7.50	7.64	8.08	7.63	7.65	7.38	8.47	9.03
per cent of Green Tea Production exported	44.46	47.15	20.48	16.51	14.78	16.32	16.89	16.87	16.13	16.92	18.16
per cent of Green Tea Production retained	55.54	52.85	79.52	83.49	85.22	83.68	83.11	83.13	83.87	83.08	81.84

Destination	*1989*	*1990*	*1991*	*1992*	*1993*	*1994*	*1995*	*1996*	*1997*	*1998*	*1999*
India(e)	2.93	3.15	3.09	2.47	2.69	2.94	3.65	4.10	3.08	2.30	2.07
Srilanka	0.02	0.44	0.03	0.40	0.62	0.73	0.97	0.55	0.49	0.36	0.38
Indonesia	1.48	1.82	2.67	4.48	10.08	7.43	3.93	5.91	4.51	2.71	5.06
China (Mainland)	85.83	86.92	86.86	85.41	79.36	81.00	81.38	76.34	80.94	85.78	83.99
Taiwan	1.78	1.06	0.91	1.05	0.69	0.74	0.99	1.59	0.71	0.27	0.38
Japan	0.62	0.30	0.26	0.25	0.27	0.30	0.56	0.58	0.51	0.50	0.52
Vietnam	7.33	6.30	6.18	5.94	6.28	6.85	8.52	10.93	9.76	8.06	7.60
Total Green Tea Exports (million kgs)	74.25	76.38	72.10	63.88	62.67	70.33	71.80	72.89	71.77	82.38	93.51
Per cent of Green Tea	9.10	8.39	9.02	9.95	9.67	9.91	7.53	6.51	8.13	10.05	11.64
Per cent of Green Tea Production exported	20.66	18.41	18.05	17.98	18.95	18.17	14.37	12.47	15.90	20.22	21.68
Per cent of Green Tea Production retained	79.34	81.59	81.95	82.02	81.05	81.83	85.63	87.53	84.10	79.78	78.32

Source: Various issues of ITC Bulletin, London

Note: Green tea exports in 2000, 2001, 2002, 2003, 2004 and 2005 were 98.12 m.kgs, 102.15 m.kgs, 106.24 m.kgs, 110.24 m.kgs, 115.24 m.kgs and 119.63 m.kgs.

SECTION III
World Exports and Imports of Green Tea

World exports of green tea in 1999 totalled 93.51 m kg, 70 per cent more than what it was two decades ago. In 1978, China had 60.75 per cent share in production, consumption and export of green tea in the world and the same had increased to 84 per cent in 1999 (Table 2).

World Imports of Green Tea

Prior to 1990 Pakistan was a key importer of green tea but thereafter Morocco emerged as the most significant importer with over one-half of world imports (Table 3).

Table 3: Countries Importing Green Tea (per cent share)

	1993	*1994*	*1995*	*1996*	*1997*	*1998*	*1999*
Austria	0.04	0.06	0.3	0.17	0.28	0.36	0.48
UK	1.77	2.93	2	1.47	1.1	0.71	0.89
Belgium & Lux.	0.88	1.13	0.41	0.38	0.16	1.17	0
Denmark	0.01	0.01	0.02	0.01	0.02	0.06	0.03
Finland	0.01	0.02	0	0.08	0.14	0.04	0
Germany	0.58	0.51	0.88	2	3.27	7.15	9.74
Ireland (Rep.)	1.13	0.11	0.05	0.01	0.18	1.47	0.17
Italy	0.42	0.24	0	0.58	0.5	0.32	0
Netherlands	1.36	1.18	1.52	2.15	2.25	1.83	1.32
Switzerland	0.05	0.04	0.06	0.17	0.23	0.4	0.57
Total (mkg)	52.23	60.29	62.4	62.38	70.19	72.92	76.15
	1993	*1994*	*1995*	*1996*	*1997*	*1998*	*1999*
Japan	10.49	7.83	10.36	17.35	16.11	8.66	15.82
Pakistan	8.03	6.02	3.24	2.89	0.8	1.32	1.57
Egypt	0	1.97	0.29	0	0.25	0.03	0.21
Morocco	50.56	54.35	60.18	45.32	49.79	54.85	46.26
Australia	0.41	0.37	0.41	0.51	0.4	0.49	0.57
New Zealand	0.04	0.1	0.02	0.02	0.29	0.2	0.06
Tunisia	2.87	3.32	3.4	3.37	3.56	2.71	1.84
USA	9.39	9.66	8.51	9.26	5.9	8.62	10.1
Canada	1.7	2.04	2.13	2	2.26	2.31	3.39
France	10.25	8.11	6.21	12.26	12.5	7.3	6.97

Source: Various issues of ITC Bulletin, London.

Producers of Green Tea

i. China Nearly 75 per cent of all tea produced in China is green tea and China has 84 per cent share in world exports of green tea (Table-2). China also exports sizable quantity of other teas, which includes Oolong tea, Pouchong tea and speciality teas. Production of green tea in China includes several sequential processes. China produces several types of green tea, each with distinct flavour and taste (Box 1).

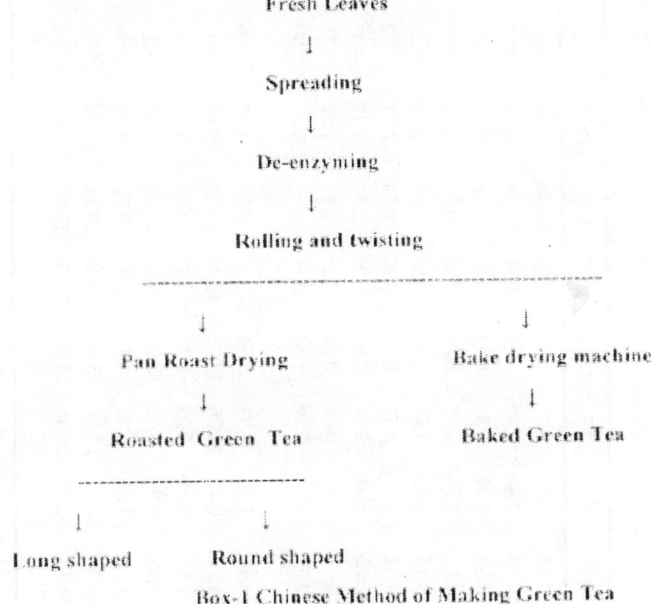

Box-1 Chinese Method of Making Green Tea

According to available statistics, China's exports of green tea have fluctuated between 55.87 million kg and 121.63 million kg during the period 1990-99 (Tables 4 & 5) On the whole, the export market for Chinese green tea is balanced and well distributed. The key destinations have been Morocco (23 per cent share) followed by CIS/USSR (13.86 per cent), Senegal (6.25 per cent), USA (5.70 per cent), and Afghanistan (5.19 per cent). Exports to Mali during 1990-99 have been only 2.96 per cent with a very high coefficient of variation indicating a very high fluctuation in per centage share that

Table 4: Analysis of Per Cent Share of Exports of Green Tea from China 82.80 Per Cent Share of World Exports of Green Tea

(1990-99 averages)

	1990	1991	1992	1993	1994	1995	1996	1997	1998	1999	Avg	COV	G. Rate	Min.	Max.
France	3.62	2.11	2.25	4.64	2.7	2.7	0.72	2.22	10.88	5.88	3.77	76.43	6.39	0.72	10.88
USSR/ CIS	12.09	16.41	6.26	17.53	22.86	1.99	11.67	22.57	13.16	14.04	13.86	47.13	1.56	1.99	22.86
USA	6.35	5.4	5.72	4.53	6.24	7.54	10.13	4.2	3.75	3.17	5.7	35.89	-4.59	3.17	10.13
Afghanistan	6.78	2.81	4.64	10.1	2.74	6.42	8.86	5.49	2.31	1.76	5.19	55.11	-7.13	1.76	10.1
Hongkong	5.94	5.46	10.01	8.43	9.62	4.17	2.47	3.94	2.94	0.58	5.36	59.05	-18.88	0.58	10.01
Japan	1.69	2.51	4.11	4.84	3	3.47	5.3	4.87	0.74	2.71	3.32	44.52	-1.82	0.74	5.3
Pakistan	3.03	1.07	4.37	2.92	6.04	5.51	7.8	5.98	2.88	4.42	4.4	45.09	9.35	1.07	7.8
Algeria	4.45	6.93	2.76	-	-	0.66	0.28	0.2	4.9	1.82	2.75	89.97	-	0.2	6.93
Libya	3.81	3.58	9.07	0.59	-	2.69	1.38	2.16	-	0.6	2.99	92	-	0.59	9.07
Mali	0.18	0.56	0.79	0.46	1.13	9.54	3.54	2.27	6.23	4.87	2.96	104.64	43.98	0.18	9.54
Morocco	30.8	33.61	30.12	24.22	20.47	22.76	14.73	13.46	13.18	25.68	22.9	32.38	-7.91	13.18	33.61
Nigeria		3.67	3.67	1.61	5.96	5.29	7.71	3.87	4.02	5.21	4.56	37.94		1.61	7.71
Senegal	3.37	3.78	3	3.96	4.99	7.65	10.24	9.04	10.45	6.05	6.25	46.19	13.69	3	10.45
Tango	2.7	1.87	2.47	1.95	1.36	2.46	1.71	3.36	3.75	3.33	2.49	31.75	5.27	1.36	3.75
Other countries	15.2	10.22	10.76	14.21	12.89	17.11	13.46	16.36	20.81	19.88	15.09	23.4	6	10.22	20.81
Total exports (mkg)	82.73	84.33	86.32	88.43	82.72	66.88	55.87	78.78	111.68	121.63	85.94	22.23	2.07	55.87	121.63

Source: Various issues of ITC Bulletin, London.

has ranged between 0.18 and 9.54 per cent. In 1999, Mali had 4.87 per cent share in the Chinese exports of 121.63 million kg of green tea. This was of course less than the share of Morocco and USSR/CIS. Pakistan with a 4.40 per cent share and a high rate of growth has been consistently importing green tea from China.

China also exports sizable quantity of other teas, which includes Oolong tea, Pouchong tea, and speciality teas (Tables 4 and 5). Quantities have ranged between 23.16 million kg in 1990 and 3.65 million kg in 1997. Japan had imported nearly half of these exports.

Table 5

Quantity-wise Analysis of Green Tea Exports from China 82.80 Per Cent Share of World Exports of Green Tea

(1990-99 mkg averages)

	Average	*CV*	*Growth Rate*	*Min.*	*Max.*
France	3.63	96.76	8.59	0.41	12.51
USSR/CIS	12.11	49.34	3.67	1.33	18.91
USA	4.6	16.11	-2.61	3.31	5.66
Afghanistan	4.15	50.11	-5.2	2.14	8.93
Hong Kong	4.48	61.54	-17.19	0.7	8.64
Japan	2.71	40.21	0.21	0.83	4.28
Pakistan	3.61	37.63	11.61	0.91	5.38
Algeria	2.54	90.05	-	0.16	5.85
Libya	2.44	98.19	-	0.53	7.83
Mali	2.57	106.37	46.96	0.15	6.96
Morocco	19.82	39.46	-6	8.23	31.23
Nigeria	3.82	36.62	-	1.42	6.33
Senegal	5.32	52.82	16.05	2.59	11.67
Tango	2.23	50.08	7.45	0.95	4.19
Other countries	13.3	43.44	8.2	7.52	24.18
Total Exports	85.94	22.23	-	55.87	121.63

Source: Various issues of ITC Bulletin, London.

Table 6: Per centage Share of Exports of Other Tea from China

(1990-99 averages)

	1990	*1991*	*1992*	*1993*	*1994*	*1995*	*1996*	*1997*	*1998*	*1999*	*Avg*	*CV*	*G. Rate*	*Min.*	*Max.*
USA	4.57	5.58	5.80	4.00	2.33	2.11	2.56	3.47	4.40	3.90	3.87	33.05	-4.21	2.11	5.80
Afghanistan	-	-	1.23	4.12	1.68	1.43	3.81	3.61	2.68	0.95	2.44	52.32		0.95	4.12
Hongkong	32.45	30.95	27.11	22.41	18.61	17.08	15.48	18.54	16.23	17.60	21.65	29.10	-7.64	15.48	32.45
Japan	40.35	48.96	44.10	36.12	44.64	57.47	57.67	49.95	49.94	55.37	48.46	14.91	3.24	36.12	57.67
Malaysia	3.36	3.37	1.91	2.32	2.18	2.43	2.43	2.33	2.95	4.07	2.74	24.75	1.25	1.91	4.07
Mongolia	9.19	0.00	2.94	13.89	0.04	0.25	0.02		0.00	0.00	2.93	174.11		0.00	13.89
Singapore	2.30	3.19	4.03	4.19	6.44	6.48	3.46	4.07	3.42	1.42	3.90	40.85	-2.61	1.42	6.48
Other countries	7.79	7.87	12.88	12.95	24.07	12.74	14.57	18.03	20.38	16.69	14.80	34.87	9.46	7.79	24.07
Total expo-rts (mkg)	23.16	25.72	24.76	27.08	32.12	31.69	32.83	36.54	36.16	44.38	31.44	20.75	6.73	23.16	44.38

Source: Various issues of ITC Bulletin, London

Table 7 : Exports of "Other Teas" from China

(1990-99 averages)

	Quantity-wise (million kg)				
Country	*Average*	*CV*	*Growth Rate*	*Min.*	*Max.*
USA	1.19	30.7	2.24	0.67	1.73
Afghanistan	0.8	51.48		0.3	1.32
Hongkong	6.52	15.38	-1.43	5.08	7.96
Japan	15.5	31.68	10.19	9.35	24.57
Malaysia	0.87	41.5	8.06	0.47	1.81
Mongolia	0.96	151.45		0	3.76
Singapore	1.21	43.78	3.94	0.53	2.07
Other countries	4.84	47.03	16.83	1.8	7.73
Total	31.44	20.75	6.73	23.16	44.38

Source: Various issues of ITC Bulletin, London.

ii. JAPAN Black tea production has practically ceased after 1971 since it had become highly uncompetitive after trade liberalization. Production of green tea in Japan has been gradually decreasing since 1980. Japan is a mountainous country and about 60 per cent of tea plants are located on the hillsides and plateaus in Shizuoka, Kyoto, Mie and Kagoshima districts. The Japanese method of manufacturing green tea is a complex process involving several steps and several types of green tea are manufactured in Japan. Japan is a significant producer of green tea and most of it is consumed internally. The share of Japanese tea to total green tea export was only 4.55 per cent in 1978. However, it has reduced to 0.52 per cent in 1992. Japanese exports are mainly directed towards USA and Canada. The method of manufacturing green tea is a complex process involving several steps. Several types of green tea are manufactured in Japan with the details as under.

In addition to the domestically highly popular grade Sen Cha made of young tender leaves and well twisted, Japan produces several other grades of green tea, Gyokuro or Pearl Dew is the finest tea in Japan made from leaves grown under the shade which reduces the tannin content,

Table 8: Exports of Green Tea from Japan

(1990-99 averages)

	1984	*1985*	*1986*	*1987*	*1988*	*1989*	*1990*	*1991*	*1992*	*1993*	*1994*
Green Tea per cent	98.03	97.62	96.03	94.49	97.62	94.63	87.89	87.54	88.62	92.99	90.14
Green Tea (mkg)	2.73	1.76	1.21	1.05	1.23	0.64	0.28	0.25	0.26	0.31	0.31
Total (mkg)	2.79	1.81	1.26	1.11	1.26	0.67	0.32	0.29	0.29	0.33	0.35

	1995	*1996*	*1997*	*1998*	*1999*	*Avg.*	*CV*	*Growth Rate*	*Min.*	*Max.*
Green Tea per cent	93.7	86.21	86.03	86.47	91.18	89.08	3.14	-0.02	86.03	93.7
Green Tea (mkg)	0.46	0.43	0.5	0.65	0.76	0.42	41.41	5.45	0.25	0.76
Total (mkg)	0.49	0.49	0.58	0.75	0.83	0.47	41.46	5.48	0.29	0.83

Source: Various issues of ITC Bulletin, London.

Table 9: Percentage Share and Unit Value of Exports of Green tea from Indonesia 4.86 Percent Share of World Green Tea Exports

(1990-99 averages)

	1990	*1991*	*1992*	*1993*	*1994*	*1995*	*1996*	*1997*	*1998*	*1999*	*Avg*	*CV*	*G.Rate*	*Min*	*Max*
Green Tea per cent	1.56	2.35	3.72	9.06	8.94	4.08	4.26	6.56	5.26	7.56	5.34	49.1	12.62	1.56	9.06
Green tea mkg	1.73	2.6	4.53	11.23	7.59	3.23	4.33	4.39	3.54	7.33	5.05	56.67	7.06	1.73	11.23
All teas mkg	110.96	110.33	121.78	123.93	84.92	79.23	101.53	66.84	67.22	96.99	96.37	21.84	-4.93	66.84	123.93

Source: various issues of ITC Bulletin London.

Process chart of Indian Green Tea

Freshly plucked leaves

Steaming (upto 2 minutes)

Curling and drying (in hot air at 90 ° -100 ° C for 40-50 minutes the leaf moisture reduces from 76 per cent to about 50 per cent)

Rolling (without heat for 15 minutes)

Pressing and drying (hot air at 50 ° -60 ° C for 30-40 minutes, leaf moisture reduces to about 30 per cent)

Curling(Drying directly on a hot pan at 80 ° - 90 ° C

Twisting (for 40 minutes under pressing and rolling by a curling-hand mounted on a pan)

Drying (at 80 ° C until moisture content of 6 per cent is achieved)

Made Sin Cha

Storage

increases caffeine and amino acids, brightens the colour of the leaf and sweetens its flavour. Matcha or ceremonial tea is made of leaves from shaded bushes. The manufacturing process is similar to that for Gyokuro but without rolling. After drying, the product is pulverized, Kamairicha is made in Kyushu district. The raw material is the same as in Sen-cha, but the first process is parching in place of steaming. It has a curly appearance. Bancha is coarse tea, made of coarser leaves, or by separating from raw Sen-cha in the refining process.

Source: Kunio O, Tea Industry in Japan "Tea Science and Human Health", Proceedings of the International Symposium on Tea Technology, Kolkata.

iii. India India produces only a small quantity of green tea. Its share in green tea production has been declining from 4.72 per cent in 1978 to 1.23 per cent in 1999. During 1993-94 India exported 3.36 million kg (nearly 84 per cent of green tea production to Afghanistan and Russia. In 1999 India exported around 3 m kg having a 2.07 per cent share in world exports. Although India is not a large consumer of green tea, in the hilly regions of Kangra and Kashmir valleys, green tea goes well with low temperatures. In some Indian markets green tea is also sold as herbal tea usually mixed with aromatic condiments.

During 1993-94 India exported 3.36 m kg (nearly 84 per cent of green tea production) to Afghanistan. Thereafter exports to Afghanistan declined rapidly but exports to Russia picked up. Like black tea, Russia has been having a large share in Indian green tea exports. Per centage share of green tea export from India was 2.07 per cent in 1999. The procedure in India regarding green tea is as under:

Temperature below 100°C, moisture content below 6 per cent concentration of oxygen lower than 2 per cent and humidity controlled inert gas packaging.

iv. Indonesia Indonesia produces about 37 million kg of green tea with 5.54 per cent share in world production. Indonesia has a large demand for scented teas and a significant proportion of Indonesia green tea is scented using jasmine, red gambir and other types of flowers. Therefore Indonesia has only 5.06 per cent share in world exports of green tea. Since 1989, Indonesia has exported sizable quantity of green tea to the Middle East and Morocco.

Table 10: Exports of Green Tea from Indonesia

(1990-99 averages)

	Quantity-wise (million kg)				
	Avg	*CV*	*Growth Rate*	*Min.*	*Max.*
Green Tea	5.05	56.67	7.06	1.73	11.23
All Teas	96.37	21.84	-4.93	66.84	123.93

Source: Various issues of ITC Bulletin, London.

Importers of Green Tea

i. Consumer Preference

Major importers of green tea are Japan, USA, Indonesia, North African countries and Afghanistan. The consumers in these markets have different tastes and preferences. However, a common feature generally sought is that the dried green tea leaves should have bright olive green colour without any brown or red. The Chinese green tea is preferred in Japan and USA. Chinese green tea leaves are generally polished using French chalks or gypsum and coloured with indigo. Afghans prefer the green tea liquor similar to Chinese green tea and unlike the Moroccans, they are much less fussy about the appearance of the dry tea leaves.

ii. Morocco

Morocco has the largest market for green tea having imported as much as 35.23 million kg in 1999 and almost all of that came from mainland China. Imports of green tea in Morocco have been rising and so also its share in the world imports. During 1990-99, Morocco imported an average of 33.67 million kg having a 51.62 per cent share at a moderate unit import price of US $ 2.10. Imports from China have been consistently increasing (98.4 per cent share in 1999). Per head consumption of tea in Morocco is in excess of 1 kg.

iii. Japan

Japan has been a significant consumer of green tea but its imports have been less than one-fourth of the imports of Morocco. Of the total tea imported during 1993-99, black tea had taken an increasing share between 28 to 42 per cent. In terms of per unit import value in 1993, green tea was only 44 per cent of the black tea and 59 per cent of the other teas. While the volume and unit value of imports of other teas has been somewhat declining, the unit import value of green tea has increased slightly from US$ 2.20 in 1993 to US$ 2.45 per kg in 1999.

iv. France

Nearly 82 per cent of green tea imported in France is from China and 13 per cent is re-exports from Belgium. The French market had paid an average of US$ 3.71 per kg. The quantity imported has fluctuated and the average for 1990-99 was 5.36 m kg in 1997 as much as 8.78 m kg of green tea was imported.

v. USA

USA imported an average of 6.20 m kg of green tea during 1990-99 in which China had nearly 77.68 per cent share. The popularity of green tea in US is largely on account of its health benefits which has been receiving increasingly more and more media attention. Although imports from other countries are small, they receive higher unit import value when compared to China, which on average received just about US$ 1.11 per kg.

vi. Tunisia

Although in 1997 Tunisia imported 2.5 m kg of green tea imports, this was abruptly halved in 1999. A highly fluctuating pattern of imports of green tea in Tunisia from China existed during the years 1990-99 with the average of 82.46 per cent Further the quantity-wise (million kg) average imports of green tea in Tunisia from China for the period 1990-97 is 1.38.

vii. Canada

In 1999 Canada imported 2.58 m kg of green tea. Imports have been increasing consistently and exhibiting a good growth rate. China, Hong Kong, Japan and Taiwan are the main sources although US also had nearly 34 per cent share. Green tea from Taiwan fetched the highest price at US$ 4.49 per kg whereas China, Hong Kong and USA teas fetched under US$ 3.5 per kg.

Oolong Tea

i. China

Oolong tea is produced mainly in Fujian and Guangdong provinces of mainland China and Taiwan. Oolong tea is semi-fermented. In 1990, 90 million cases of Oolong tea and 70 million cases of black tea were produced in Japan. Oolong tea is more stable than other beverages and is therefore easier to pack in tins, cans or bottles. As black tea is milk or lemon flavoured, its storage in vending machines is somewhat difficult. For these reasons, Oolong tea has found favour with the food processors particularly in Japan.

ii. Taiwan

Tea production in Taiwan has been declining and production in 1999 at 3.07 million kg was less than one-third of the production in 1987. Production of green tea has been declining and reached a low of 0.55 m kg in 1999. However, Taiwan is a key producer of Oolong tea and almost all of its production in 1999 was of this type. During 1990-99, the share of green tea in tea exports has been between 14 and 33 per cent. Information on exports of green and other teas from Taiwan is not available.

6

Tea Trends, Export Markets and Competitiveness, Constraints, Remedial Measures, Research and Development, Tenth Five Year Plan and Development of Small Tea Growers

SECTION I

Current Tea Trends, Research and Development

Next to water, tea is the most widely consumed non-alchoholic beverage world over and it is grown in more than 32 countries. Amongst them, India is the largest producer (28% of the world production). World Tea Trade is going through a significant change. While developed markets stagnate, growth is expected in the developing countries. These markets have now been opened in the wake of WTO regime. This will facilitate increasing global competition in the areas of cost, price, quality, supply schedules, packaging, market focus and customer satisfaction.

In India, tea is grown in 13 States with diverse agro-climatic conditions. Tea production in India has been increasing and so also has domestic consumption. Increased production in tea was achieved by enhanced productivity through introduction of high-yielding clonal material, improved water management and transferring results of research to the field. Further, cultural practices such as pruning cycles, proper use of fertilizers and foliar applications of nutrients and plant protection measures using safe chemicals have increased yields. Production also increased on account of increased plant density and rehabilitation of old tea lands through replanting, using the best available planting materials and better husbandry. Vast resources of skilled and motivated workers, competent managerial manpower, strong research backing, modernized and upgraded manufacture etc., have all contributed to a sound base and progressive industry. The growth profile in terms of compound growth rate of area, production, productivity, yield and exports during the last five decades is given below:

Table 1: Growth rates of Area, Production, Yield and Export of Tea

Period	*Area*	*Production*	*Yield*	*Export*
1950-60	0.45	1.16	0.98	-0.39
1960-70	0.74	2.98	1.98	+0.47
1970-80	0.67	3.48	2.37	+1.06
1980-90	0.96	2.03	1.48	-0.68
1990-00	0.53	1.35	0.83	-0.34
2000-01	0.67	1.49	1.23	-0.03
2006-07	0.43	0.52	0.33	+0.10

Source: Xth Five Year Plan. Report on sub-group on Plantation Crops II, Ministry of Commerce.

Food and Agriculture Organisation (FAO) Projections for 2005

According to FAO, world black tea production is estimated to be in the region of 2700 million kg of which India's contribution is expected to be 1015 to 1018 million kg. World consumption by 2005 is estimated to go up to 2670 million kgs. and India's export is likely to rise to the level of 246 to 250 million kg. China, Indonesia and African countries are expected to increase production. There will be a production surplus of 24 million kg and possible imbalance and downward pressure on prices. Of course the emergence of that situation is contingent upon weather conditions in production areas.

IIMC Study on Domestic Consumption

The recent study conducted on behalf of Tea Board by the Indian Institute of Management, Calcutta (IIMC), reveals that tea consumption has not been of the order as seen in the past. Expected annual domestic demand for the next 5 years as estimated by IIMC is as follows:

Table 2: Demand projections for Tea

Year	*Rural*	*Urban*	*Total*
2000	388	265	653
2001	398	275	673
2002	408	285	693
2003	418	296	714
2004	428	307	735
2005	439	318	757
2006	450	330	780

Source: X Five Year Plan. Report on Sub-group on Plantation Crops II-Ministry of Commerce.

Imports

Imports touched around 14 million kgs in 2004 against average levels of 1 to 2 million kgs in the past. The unique CIF value of tea imported from a few countries was lower than the prices faced at Indian auctions. This has affected market sentiments. With the emerging trends in the globalised economy, markets can no longer be protected. Indian Tea Industry will have to compete in the domestic market. Protecting the home market is going to be a challenging task and the Tea Industry has to evolve some strategy to counter the new competing forces unleashed by globalization.

Continued supplies of tea at reasonable prices to the domestic market and to maintain and improve the export share in the global tea trade were the twin objectives of the previous plan period. These twin objectives hold good for the Xth Plan period and they could be fulfilled, only if the industry continues to grow with profit and remains healthy.

Present Status on Research and Development in Tea

(i) R&D Contributions on Tea

Tea Research Association and UPASI Tea Research Foundation have released 30 high-yielding vegetative clones each. This has enhanced productivity from 1416 kgs. per hectare in 1981 to 1850 kgs per hectare in 2000 in North India and 1645 kgs per hectare to 2300 kgs per hectare in 2000 in South India. UPASI-TRF-I recently released in South India has yield potential upto 11000 kgs per hectare.

Biotechnological approach in tea breeding has progressed towards protoplast fusion, haploid line and market developments in pruning, DNA, finger printing and patenting of elite clones. Nutrition in Tea is now based on computerised model and green leaf yield potential. Sulphur and zinc nutrients have been accommodated along with NPK requirements.

Cultivation aspects like pruning, shade management, organic nutrition in soil, soil amendment and application of weedicides and balanced application of fertilizers have been refined over the years to harvest increasing yield. Further, Irrigation Drainage Technologies in tea have been improved and their requirement in improving yields has been established.

Protection of crops is linked to minimum application of pesticides and its linkage to follow Integrated Pest Management (IPM) practice. Maintaining bio-diversity and minimum or no pesticide residue is the call of the day. Biocides and biocontrols have been developed. Chemistry of Tea manufacture and flavour chemistry of Tea have helped in refining manufacture of Tea on scientific basis and understanding the role of enzymes involved in it.

Quality improvement in Tea has been achieved through training, modernization of factory, upgrading of plucking standard and improving sanitation and hygienic situations. ISO-9000 and HACCP as a package for quality improvement, have been introduced.

Research on health benefit aspects has yielded positive results. Tea drinking is beneficial in the cure of Hypertensions, diabetes, cancer, kidney, malfunction, dental caries etc.Tea contains antioxidants which help human beings to avoid many health complications. Packaging of tea is now being done with recently developed packaging materials like jute, laminated bags, multi-wall paper sacks and use of flexible packaging substances.

ii. New Areas of Fundamental Research

Specific areas of research can be identified to launch new areas of fundamental research in different fields, like advance programmes in bio-technology, characterization of clones etc.Nutrition of Tea Plants is a grey area. Computer simulation models for balanced nutrition for Tea will be a step to apply non-contents of fertilizer to the Tea plant based on variable criteria like soil conditions, bush frame and age, environmental factors etc. This will help in scientific management of tea estates in accordance with the production need.

Computer aided database, if stored for future utilisation and guidance to the management and sectional information of tea gardens will help both the research institutes and tea estates to save time and initiate prompt action in taking corrective actions.Quality of Tea can be enhanced from the information on bio-chemical pathways, if these are identified and packages are developed.

Electronics can play a big role once the bio-chemical pathways are identified and these are linked to computer sensors By-products of Tea can be gainfully utilized for other industrial use. Similarly, value added items like RTD, flavoured tea are the areas on which new research could be thought of.

Sustainability is a major problem in Tea. It is observed that Tea productivity is not increasing in the replanted areas. This has been linked to soil sickness, reasons for which are not well established. Bio-agriculture is a new research area, which can give answers to the problems as indicated, in organic tea estates with stable yields.

Quality control is a major issue in Tea. The Quality Control Laboratory Chain in South India as well as in North India needs to be strengthened soon. Well developed field laboratories for quality testing of tea and monitoring of adversities with Tea Estate is essential. The conducive environment for trade has prompted such steps to ensure quality tea production. If needed, a phased programme can be developed and computer net work monitoring may be essential.

New Proposal for Research

Tenth five year plan conducted research relating to network programme for transfer of technology, computerisation and software development, data collection and strengthening of transfer of technology units in each zone (7 centres in North East, 7 centres in South India and connection with base laboratories). A chain of Quality Control Laboratories (4 in North East—Tocklai, Dibrugarh, Cachar, Nagrakata), upgradation of laboratories in South India (Valparai, Coonoor, Vandiperiyar, Gudalur) have been established. Proposals relating to (i) Integrated Nutrition Management and Computer Simulation of data in each of the Advisory Centres and connecting base laboratories including development of models, (ii) Irrigation and Drainage Research Project, (iii) Bio-chemical Analysis and Quality Upgradation Programme in North East and South India and (iv) Development of Forecasting Model for Pest Disease Control including Bio-control aspects are on the process of implementation. Soil management and Organic Cultivation of Tea, Tea and Human Health, Value Added items and Product Diversification in Tea, Packaging, Eco-friendliness and other related areas and Bio-technology in Tea are new proposals for research in the Tenth Five Year Plan.

SECTION II
Export Markets and Competitiveness

Keeping in view the global competition in black tea mainly among India, Sri Lanka and Kenya, there is need to assess their competitive positions. The World Bank study has done so in the context of Sri Lanka's tea industry. This analysis is based on recent theories of competitiveness as per Porters Framework. That framework is largely dependent on manufacturing industry while the agricultural scene is rather different. The framework with suitable modifications, would perhaps be suitable for application to the industrial part of agriculture but not quite so far to agricultural production and trade commodities which continues to be analyzed in traditional theories of comparative advantage. One takes a rather simple view of competitiveness in global trade in tea. The competitive positions in the market are a cumulative expression of interactive effects of all variables from production and processing to consumer markets.

The details of global players in tea industry [country position of competitive factors are given below] [Table 3]

Table 3: The Global players in the Tea Industry: Country Position on Competitive Factors

	India	*Sri Lanka*	*Kenya*
Natural Resources and Human Capital			
Land	Average	Weak	Strong
Water Resources	Average	Strong	Strong
Quality of tea bushes	Weak	Weak	Strong
Yields	Average	Weak	Strong
Availability and quality of workers	Average	Average	Weak
Literacy rate	Low	High	Average
Macro economic Environment			
Macro economic and sector policy	Weak	Average	Strong
Sector investment growth	Weak	Average	Strong
Exchange rate regime	Strong	Strong	Strong
Trade and tax regime	Weak	Strong	Average
Price regime	Weak	Strong	Strong
Labour regime	Weak	Weak	Strong
Infrastructure			
Transport and communications	Weak	Average	Weak
Marketing	Average	Weak	Strong
R & D	Average	Weak	Average
Extension	Average	Weak	Strong
Marketing Environment			
Key market's size and growth rate	Strong	Average	Average

Income and growth of income in key markets	Weak	Average	Strong
Price position in key markets	Weak	Strong	Strong
Competitive strength	Weak	Average	Average
Micro-marketing and co-ordination			
Production/Marketing co-ordination	Strong	Weak	Strong
Local Processing and linked industries	Strong	Strong	Average
Quality control	—	Strong	Strong
Risk sharing	—	Strong	Strong
Technical, financial and managerial skills	Weak	Average	Strong
Cost structure	Average	Weak	Strong
Marketing strength	Average	Average	Average
Product innovation	Strong	Average	Weak

Source: Reproduced from World Bank[1997], Sri Lanka's Tea Industry, Discussion Paper No.368 Washington D C. August p.86

Competitor Analysis of Sixteen specific Markets

An attempt has been made on the basis of data given in *Annexure II* to present competitor analysis for 16 specific markets, which together cover an average of over 70 per cent of world imports of tea. On the supply side, analysis have been made on 13 countries, commanding over 96 percent of the world exports. For illustration, consider the UK market. During 1990-99 it commanded an average 13.01 per cent share in the world imports in quantity 145.99 m kg and rate of growth@ 0.24 per cent and per head consumption 2.52 kg per annum. All in all, UK is a very large size market to which many countries supply. Sri Lanka, a key supplier to the UK market, has a 6.16 per cent share with a decline in rate of growth at—3.44 per cent with unit input value at US $ 2.01. As regards, Sri Lanka, 5.2 per cent of tea exports from Sri Lanka have gone to UK with growth rate at—6.15 per cent and an export unit value realisation at US $ 1.97. For each cell in the Annexure-II, interpretations are similar and provide the basis of comparison and assessing competitive position.

Comparing relative position in terms of market share rate of growth in market share and unit value realisation yields a good understanding of competitive position which are summarized in *Annexure-III.*

For illustration, Kenya is the market leader with 28 per cent of the total World Tea Market, comprising UK, Pakistan, Egypt and Ireland. In contrast, India is a market leader only in 16 per cent of World tea market which includes Russian Federation, Poland and Germany. For Sri Lanka leadership is of 2.5 per cent markets. China leads in 7.5 per cent for markets but a large share of that is in green tea. Argentina has a market leadership in USA, which commands a 7.53 per cent share in the world imports *(Annexure-III).*

Analyzing markets in this framework, an understanding of and evaluating the competitive position, would help the tea industry to develop competitive products and market strategy. After all, Paulskrugman puts it, "A country does not loose in the competitiveness game but performance of firms do. An individual firm is competitive and it can" sell its goods at the market price and make money". Otherwise the firm goes bust but the economy does not. However, in case of tea, economies of small nations would also falter if their firms fail to compete. Thus consequences of uncompetitiveness could be a disaster for both countries as well as firms depending upon how important tea imports are to their economies. To that extent, India, as a nation, has a large cushion and that is probably the reason for our complacency and lack of competitiveness in world markets.

Area, Production and Exports of Tea of Different Countries

Although as many as 34 countries are producing tea in the world, the major countries are India, China, SriLanka, Indonesia, Kenya, Uganda, Myanmar etc. On an average, India has an area of 498 thousand hectares with an average annual production of 830 million kgs showing an average yield of 1666 kgs per hectare. Sri Lanka, on an average, cultivates tea to the extent of 191 thousand hectares producing average an annual crop of 295 million kgs with the yield rate of 1545 kgs per hectare. In spite of the fact that China occupies more than twice the area [average of 1115 thousand hectares] held by India, the production was not significant it was only 689 million kgs on an average. This was due to low yield rate [618 kgs per hectare]. On the export front, Kenya exports 93 per cent of total production followed by SriLanka at 83 per cent, Indonesia 66 per cent, China 36 per cent, India 24 per cent etc. There are various reasons for low exports from India and these are discussed separately in Section III.

Table 4: Area, Production and Exports of Tea of Different Countries

a. Area Under Tea in Different Countries (Area in '000 hectares)

Year	*India*	*Sri Lanka*	*China*	*Indonesia*	*Kenya*	*Uganda @*	*Others*	*Total*
1989	415	221	0	129	87	21	613	2551
1990	416	221	1061	135	97	21	609	2560
1991	420	222	1061	137	100	21	609	2570
1997	434	194	1076	154	118	20	694	2690
1998	474	195	1056	157	118	20	672	2692
1999	490	195	1130	157	120	20	580	2692
2000	504	189	1089	157	122	21	583	2665
2001	509	189	1141	151	132	21	495	2638
2002	512	189	1155	151	132	21	500	2646
2003	513	188	1207	143	132	21	509	2713
2004	515	189	1263	142	132	21	512	2774
2005	518	195	1275	145	133	21	528	2815
2006	520	200	1290	147	133	21	554	2865
2007	522		1310	149	133	21	567	2905

b. Production of Tea in Different Countries (Qty in million kgs)

Year	*India*	*Sri Lanka*	*China*	*Indonesia*	*Kenya*	*Uganda*	*Others*	*Total*
1989	688	208	525	147	181	5	739	2503
1990	720	234	540	161	197	7	725	2584
1997	731	278	665	158	240	20	792	2883
1998	798	280	670	159	245	22	778	2952
1999	825	284	676	161	249	25	753	2973

2000	847	307	683	157	236	29	733	2992
2001	853	296	702	161	294	33	752	3035
2002	836	310	715	166	287	34	761	3055
2003	852	315	720	167	289	34	772	3174
2004	820	315	725	166	290	34	956	3306
2005	850	320	730	166	289	34	1042	3431
2006	855	325	720	167	291	34	1159	3551
2007	860	335	725	170	295	34	1243	3662

c. Exports of Tea from Different Countries

(Qty in million kgs)

Year	*India*	*Sri Lanka*	*China*	*Indonesia*	*Kenya*	*Uganda @*	*Others*	*Total*
1989	213	204	204	115	163	3	223	1125
1990	210	215	195	111	170	5	229	1135
1997	188	256	194	105	220	18	269	1250
1998	189	260	195	102	230	20	259	1255
1999	191	262	194	99	242	22	250	1265
2000	207	280	228	106	217	26	270	1334
2001	183	288	250	99	258	30	287	1391
2002	201	286	250	100	272	31	289	1441
2003	173	291	252	100	269	34	282	1401
2004	183	291	260	88	334	30	354	1540
2005	195	292	268	88	340	30	392	1605
2006	198	293	275	90	350	31	433	1670
2007	200	292	279	95	360	32	492	1750

Source: Tea statistics, Tea Board of India175

Note: @Others' include Bangladesh, Taiwan, Japan, Vietnam, Papua & New Guinea, USSR/CIS, Iran, Turkey, Tanzania, Malawi, Mozambique, Zaire, Mauritius, Rwanda, Burundi, Cameroon, Argentina Brazil, Peru, Ecuador, Zimbabwe, Thailand, Malaysia, South Africa, Australia, Ethiopia and Nepal.

* Others' include Bangladesh, Taiwan, Japan, Malaysia, Vietnam, Papua & New Guinea, Iran, Turkey, Malawi, Mozambique, Zaire, Mauritius, Rwanda, Brundi, Argentina, Brazil, Peru, Ecquador, Zimbabwe, Cameroon, Thailand, Nepal, Myanmar, Georgia, Ethiopia and South Africa.

SECTOR III

Constraints, Remedial Measures and Tenth Five Year Plan

Viewed from long-term perspectives, the Indian Tea Industry has several constraints that are directly affecting both production and productivity. The following are some of the important constraints.

- Old age of tea bushes - Nearly 40 per cent of present tea plants in India have exceeded the economic threshold age limit of 40 years. This has been affecting productivity.
- Limited availability of land for extension in traditional areas of tea cultivation.
- Slower pace of replantation, the rate of replantation is less than 0.4 per cent as against the desired level of 2 per cent
- Fluctuations in tea prices.
- Higher rate of taxation on income from tea.
- The dual structure (agriculture and industry) of Tea Industry has resulted in the incidence of high taxes, some of which are not applicable to non-plantation agriculture.

  *Stiff competition from soft drinks is needed to position tea as a health drink.
- Poor drainage and lack of irrigation when needed greatly reduces yield.
- There is considerable gap between potential and current tea yields.
- Low productivity and high cost of production on account of high input cost particularly wages and the social benefits that always with wages, reduce attractiveness of tea production.
- Untrammeled growth of small growers and poor adherence to quality production norms.

Cost of Production

Labour cost accounts for a major part of the total cost of production of tea which has been rising sharply. The stagnation in productivity levels is compounded by high land labour ratios. The productivity and cost of production matters the most in determining the profitability of tea estate. Considering the high cost and inadequate resources, the owners of tea gardens prefer to continue with the existing tea bushes for reasons of economy.

Production Base Getting Concentrated

India's Tea production is skewed towards black tea, especially the CTC variety which accounts for 98 per cent of production. Within black tea, CTC variety is dominant for reasons of strong flavour and higher cuppage and productivity. What counts in the Indian domestic market is strength, affordability, cuppage and availability. Orthodox tea constitutes a significant portion of the world tea trade and fetches higher price realisation than CTC variety. Sri Lanka dominates in supply of orthodox tea. Lower cost CTC tea producers like Kenya, etc. are competing against Indian tea for market share and has displaced Indian Tea in key export market cities like UK.

Domestic production of orthodox tea has dropped by 40 per cent during the nineties; however, orthodox tea has significance in the World trade. Indian Tea Industry lags behind Kenya, Malawi in terms of yield per hectare mainly due to old age of tea bushes. The aging bushes are pulling down gains from adoption of improved cultural practices and increase in areas under tea. Domestic production of green tea is marginal; China dominates the global market for green tea.

Issues Impacting India's Export Performance

There are various issues which have some impacts on the performance of Indian exports. If these issues are addressed squarely ,there are hopes of increasing India's exports. These are as follows

- Inadequate efforts made in respect of marketing and brand building of Indian tea in overseas market.
- Exposing India's tea exports to concentration of risk arising out of over-dependence on Commonwealth of Independant States (CIS), UK and UAE.
- For CIS and UK markets, growth rates have been slower as compared to other import destinations.
- Indian teas are getting edged out of emerging higher growth markets by competing produce from Sri Lanka, Kenya and China.

- A large market like Pakistan which accounts for 9% of world imports remains closed to India. Black CTC tea from Kenya dominates consumption in Pakistan. Though Indian Tea would work out cheaper on landed cost basis in Pakistan, trade in tea remains marginal because of political sensitivities.
- Stagnant export realisation.
- Limited presence in emerging markets.
- Market share depleting in matured markets.
- Tea exports constitute less than 2 per cent of India's export revenues and hence it has not been covered under the priority list.
- Given policies and regulations are oriented towards protection of domestic market; availability of tea in domestic market and price stability are the over riding concerns dictating policy formulation.

India's Competitive Position in the World Tea Trade

India's competitive position has weakened in the world tea trade due to various reasons which are discussed in various interaction meets/work shops/seminars etc of national and international nature. The following factors are held responsible for such weakness:

- India's tea exports are facing a double crunch with a production slow down and loss of share in major markets served and inability to make significant headway in potential/emerging markets.
- World export growth @ 5.3 per cent Compound Annual Growth Rate (CAGR) was higher than India's export growth @ 3.4 per cent - CAGR during the period 1995-99.
- Export realisations in dollar terms have been stagnant during the 1990's.
- Region-wise trends indicate that other than the CIS countries, India's share has been declining (in North America, India continues to be a marginal player).
- In UK, the second largest importer after the CIS

group, Indian tea has lost significant market share to Kenyan produce.

- In green tea China has registered a much higher growth rate (@15.3 per cent CAGR) than Indian tea exports (@3.4 per cent CAGR) during 1995-99.
- Even in India's traditional strongholds, CIS, Sri Lanka has made significant inroads since 1993 following the disbanding of the centralized marketing system. The main reasons attributed to Sri Lanka's success are better and more organised marketing efforts.

Indian Tea Industry—Supply Side Constraints

The Indian tea industry is facing various supply side constraints. The rate of growth of land under tea cultivation dropped from the level of 15 per cent + during the 1970's and the 1980's to about 6-7 per cent during the 1990's. Growth in land under tea cultivation was much higher in Kenya and Indonesia during the 1990's. India already has the second highest area under tea cultivation after China and further scope for expansion is limited.

India's cost of production is higher than that of Kenya and Sri Lanka essentially due to the higher production overheads, besides labour costs. Thus Indian CTC tea is less competitive than Kenyan produced tea on the issue of pricing alone. With the opening up of the Indian market post WTO, a possible scenario is that cheaper imports may cater to the domestic demand while finer quality tea could be diverted to export markets.

The inward-looking nature of the tea industry has resulted in a lack of innovation and genuine value creation efforts and the result is a rather diluted export focus due to lack of competitiveness in international markets. Consumer satisfaction more than production efficiency is the key to long-term survival and growth. The Indian tea industry thus has to move towards 'productising' Indian tea into a 'consumer product'. It needs to shift away from the commodities, nature of exports in order to move up the value-curve.

The industry needs to address the issue of value creation through a concerted effort that addresses the product form and the delivery system (with the accent on convenience and innovation in packaging).Focused brand building and a marketing campaign that positions tea as a 'healthy alternative to other beverages' and reinforces the superior value of Indian tea, are critical. The industry also needs to establish strategic alliances in its major markets.

Schemes during the Xth Five Year Plan

For effectively dealing with the constraints, the following five schemes have been taken up for the Xth Plan period [2002-07].

a) Plantation Development Scheme—Under this Scheme, extension of loans will be continued for undertaking extension planting, replanting/replacement planting and procuring irrigation equipments. Similarly, subsidy support for replanting/replacement planting, rejuvenation pruning and consolidation will also be continued. Renovation of the existing field assets rather than expansion would be the thrust area during the Xth Plan. Further, subsidy for irrigation and subsidy for new planting at different scales is possible under the scheme.

b) Quality Upgradation and Product Diversification Scheme—Under this scheme, loan will be advanced for procuring tea processing machinery, tractors, light commercial vehicles, packaging machinery and setting up of cooperative factories. During the Xth Plan period, thrust would be on more value realisation. For this purpose, the factories are required to be equipped with adequate machinery for undertaking dual manufacture of orthodox or CTC type as the market demands. Further, proper infrastructure needs to be created for improving the volume of value added teas and specialties such as green teas, flavoured teas, ready to drink teas, etc. In order to ensure quality of tea, the process of manufacture needs to undergo changes to suit the emerging new markets. To facilitate this tea growers and manufacturers may participate in the quality improvement programmes such as capital HACCP and ISO certification.

c) Market Promotion Scheme—The scheme would continue to support activities such as market research survey, uninational campaign for Indian tea in selected markets, brand promotion support to Indian companies for launching the brands in international markets, genetic campaign for tea in new markets and setting up of an umbrella unit in India to meet the requirements of product and packaging standards in international markets. There is an all round realisation that the growth rate of the domestic markets need a step up for sustainability of the tea industry. Towards this end, there is a need to make special provisions for launching domestic schemes under the scheme. The market for tea is changing. Tea is now facing increased competition from soft drinks. In view of this, tea needs to protect its carefully nurtured market. It also needs to make forays into soft drink markets with a view to creating competition rather than merely reacting to it. This can be done through further value addition and development of new productsThe system of auction will have to be strengthened and technologically improved by moving to appropriate electronic formats modifying the existing systems. Accordingly, it is proposed to extend financial support for creating suitable database/information collection/dissemination system and electronic auction system.

d) Research and Development Scheme—Research and development scheme may expand the extension services of the research institutes so that the gap between lab and land is narrowed down and all the growers are able to ensure interface with the research institutes through a network of advisory centres. Further, research institutes may be directed to focus attention on productivity improvement, cost reduction in field operations, quality manufacturing process, value addition, product diversification, etc. Greater awareness about environmental issues for emphasizing the ecofriendliness of tea has to be created. Organic tea is emerging as a special product and demand for it is likely to increase. Therefore, there is an urgent need for research intervention for developing appropriate package of practices. Health benefits of tea have been rediscovered recently through scientific research. Awareness campaigns will make tea "the new age drink" that is beneficial for physical health.

e) Human Resource Development Scheme—The scheme will aim at achieving overall improvement of the skills of persons associated with tea plantations at all levels (workers to managers) through extensive and intensive training. For this, the services of (i) Indian Institute of Plantation Management, (ii) Training Centre for Small Growers and Manufacturers (iii) Comprehensive labour welfare schemes implemented by Indian Tea Association (ITA) and United Planters Association of Southern India (UPASI) and (iv) Imparting technical training by Tea Research Association and UPASI may be availed of.

The innovative idea of a Mothers Club being tested in Dooars region provides a new model for improving workers' health at the estate level. This model needs to be extended to all other tea growing regions for which additional funds need to be earmarked under this scheme. A new approach is required to tap local talent and internal training in estate management. In addition, continuing development of the managerial skills of existing managers is also required. The existing status of small and marginal farmers and identifying their basic needs for development of these sub sectors and evolving strategies to make them more active participants in overall development may be given priority. Organizing training programmes on modern aspects of tea growing and manufacture, establishment of demonstration plots in the important areas of small growers concentration and supply of high yielding planting materials at subsidized rates.

Demonstration plots and trial plantations in important areas with concentration of small growers in collaboration with UPASI and CSIR in Himachal Pradesh may be explored Further training of small tea growers by UPASI, Assam Agricultural University, North Bengal University, etc.may be conducted. In addition, study tours to small tea farmers in North Eastern States, West Bengal, etc. to learn improved cultural practices being adopted by them are to be organized.Visit to Cooperative Tea Factories in Nilgiris to study their devotions, etc.is another area which requires to be looked into. Quality upgradation scheme which aims at creating an awareness among the small growers and manufacturers as to the importance of adopting finer plucking standards and improvement of manufacturing process of tea are to be launched.

Tea Board implemented the programmes like: *(a)* Quality awareness campaign in different villages, *(b)* Quality upgradation experiment cum demonstration in different regions, *(c)* publicity including advertisements, film/posters, notices, etc. *(d)* Quality awareness seminars/conferences/farmers' meets for growers as well as bought leaf and industrial cooperative tea factories in different talukas during the current financial year include.

While area for expansion of tea in the estate sector is getting exhausted, there is distinct scope for bringing additional area under tea in the small growers sector. The land policy of the Government is also conducive to this development. Growing of tea especially in the North Eastern region would help in generation of sufficient income to sustain rural households, creation of employment opportunities for unemployed youth and landless labourers, conservation of natural resources through control of shifting cultivation and degradation of forest areas, and providing a means of harmonious living by minimizing the social unrest in the rural areas

SECTION IV
Development of Small Tea Growers and Approach to the Xth Plan Period

The Tenth Plan has adopted multi-dimentional measures for the welfare of the small tea growers who are concentrated in some parts of Assam, TamilNadu, Karnataka etc. and constitute a major share in total tea estates of the country. Some of the measures are: *(i)* setting up of demonstration plots in each of the North East States for demonstrating all aspects of tea growing, in a more comprehensive manner, *(ii)* formation of central nurseries for supply of right kind of planting material to the small growers, *(iii)* arranging training programmes to all the participating farmers on all aspects of tea growing in collaboration with TRA, Assam Agricultural University and North Bengal University, *(iv)* launching of advisory services in each State for periodic field visits and advising on practical aspects of cultivation and providing soil analytical survey, *(v)* arranging study tours for the growers to visit the developed areas especially in south India as well as foreign countries such as Kenya and Indonesia where considerable work has been done for the benefit of small tea growers.

All activities will be carried out by the Tea Board through its regional offices and in collaboration with respective State Governments.

Progress in Recent Techniques in Cultivation of Tea

In recent times, micro-propagation, hybrid seed production and seedlings, hi-density planting, integrated nutrient management, use of bio-fertilizers, micro irrigation, fertigation, protected cultivation, organic farming, integrated pest management and use of bio-pesticides, mobecular diagnostics, pesticides residues, etc. are some of the techniques in tea cultivation. Propagation of tea includes release of high yielding clones, bi-clonal seed stock and grafted plants. These planting materials have shown extremely satisfactory results. However, existing materials and techniques need to be improved.Standardisation of package for cultivation of organic tea is yet to be made.High density planting is sufficient for obtaining higher yield from an unit area. Any further increase in the density would only lead to uneconomic production in the long run.With introduction of stringent Minimum Residual Limits (MRLs), integrated post harvest management, techniques required to be further researched. More research and development efforts are called for in the areas of micro-nutrient management.

Production Target for Xth Plan

Based on the projected domestic demand, as per studies conducted by Indian Institute of Management, Calcutta and World Export demand as estimated by Food and Agriculture Organisation and removal of quantity restrictions (QRs) under the Agreement of Agriculture of WTO, the estimated production and export targets during the Xth Plan period are shown below:

(in million kgs)

Targets	*2002-03*	*2003-04*	*2004-05*	*2005-06*	*2006-07*	*2006-07*
1. Domestic consumption*	693	714	735	757	770	780
2. Export ++	234	241	248	256	265	264
3. Total production	927	955	983	1013	1035	1044

* Based on IIMC study

++ According to FAO, export availabilities are projected to reach 1600 million kg in 2005, it is targeted to achieve a share of 16% of the total global exports

Source: Xth Five Year Plan, Report of Sub-group on Plantation Crops-II-Tea, Coffee and Rubber, Ministry of Commerce, GOI.

FAO Projections for Black Tea—2005

FAO made future projections taking into account the committed reduction in tariff rates for tea imports. This reduction was on account of trade liberalization after 1994. The FAO projections indicate that world black tea imports would increase by a further 2.9 per cent, from 1355 m.kg to 1394 m.kg by 2005 because of the impact of tariff reductions resulting from the URA.

Black Tea	*Country*	*Without tariff reduction*		*With tariff reduction*	
		m.kg	*% share*	*m.kg*	*% share*
Production	India	1015	36.11	1018	35.96
	Sri Lanka	285	10.14	287	10.12
	Kenya	278	9.80	280	9.94
	China	220	7.83	224	7.92
	Indonesia	210	7.47	213	7.51
	Turkey	215	7.65	215	7.60
Exports	India	245.8	17.12	249.8	172.20
	Sri Lanka	254.5	18.22	262.6	18.09

Kenya	254.0	17.69	256.8	17.68
China	192.0	13.37	201.2	13.85
Indonesia	200.0	13.93	214.0	7.51

Source: FAO, (1995), Impact of the URA on the World Tea Economy: Projections to 2005, Committee on Commodity Problems, IGG of Tea, Rome.

On the Production Front

On the production front, the strategies required to be adopted are:

(a) implementation of HACCP and ISO standard,

(b) launching of quality assurance scheme by Tea Board,

(c) undertaking a planned programme to encourage shift in production from CTC to orthodox,

(d) designing and launching of a separate scheme,

(e) focusing on increasing yield of area under tea in order to contribute a higher percentage to world production and also increase exportable surplus,

(f) reducing cost of production by educating workers at garden levels through workshops while maintaining targets for replanting, rejuvenation planting, etc.,

(g) narrowing down in number of grades produced which lead to confusion in importers' mind and

(h) exploring the possibility of providing zero interest/ low interest loans for purchase of rolling machines for orthodox, especially in the context of the crisis in South India.

On the Product Front

On the product front, continuous emphasis on value added forms of tea (tea bags followed by packet tea and instant tea) in order to maximize returns and foreign exchange earnings, may be made. For this, there is a need to undertake specific activities to promote these forms of tea. These are:

(i) exemption of import duty on tea bagging machinery and filter papers,

(ii) arranging of workshops to help promote packaging standards in association with Indian Institute of Plantation Management (IIPM),

(iii) on the bulk tea exports, focus on orthodox and Darjeeling as thrust areas while maintaining traditional markets,

(iv) improving packaging standards to meet world norms,

(v) encouraging export of green tea with focus on specific markets like Morocco. Marketing an Indian green tea that is unique and not necessarily a replica of Chinese green tea, and

(v) developing specific value added products i.e., flavoured tea and teas with herbal infusion while maintaining the brand equity of Indian tea.

On the Marketing Front

On the marketing front one must identify markets based on global predictions on demand and ability to pay premium demand by different types of Indian teas and develop specific strategies for focused markets and allocate funds in these markets coinciding with penetration strategies.

There is need to build on value perceptions around Indian tea with Darjeeling as flagship and launch promotional campaign in major markets and provide legislative protection for teas of Indian origin alongwith Indian geographical indications such as Darjeeling, Assam and Nilgiris.

Further attempts may be made to launch an Indian tea logo as a mark of quality and speciality tea register together with extensive promotion of speciality teas by way of using using website as a marketing tool to hasten the buying process.

Emphasis may be shiftted from product to quality based on appearance, cuppage, ecology, sensiiivity to bio chemicals, health benefits and lifestyle.

There is a need to project India as a stable, reliable producer and supplier which will honour commitments.

On the Infrastructure Front

Infrastructure is the key factor in sustaining development for any sector and tea is not an exception to this. Keeping this in view there is a need to:

(i) develop infrastructure for value addition,

(ii) provide duty free facility to exporters,

(iii) support the purchase of foreign brands/distribution arrangements/warehouses in foreign markets by Indian companies. Further traditional markets for primarily bulk tea must be retained. A drive to locate large growing segment of consumer markets across the globe has to be further launched and strengthened. We must promote our own global brands and secure a long term markets for Indian tea in origin.

On Government Front

Government may further consider the followings:

Duty free imports of capital equipments/machinery for packaging of tea bags,

Instant tea, ready to drink tea and canned tea machinery,

Duty free imports of filter papers for tea bags,

Remove infrastructure bottlenecks and improve infrastructure facilities (ports, customs, banking, insurance, etc.).

Provision of incentives for value added teas.

Launching promotional campaigns for Indian teas in thrust markets,

Conducting market service to assist Indian exporters in their marketing efforts,

Deputation of delegations to prospective countries to enhance contract for exports.

Study strategies followed by competing producer countries.

In order to increase India's export potential, there is need to relook on these aspects as given below:

The option of importing tea for re-export will have to be kept open, as world blends will require teas from other growing areas.

A separate focus on tea bags is essential.

One of the highest value added emerging markets is instant tea and ready to drink beverages.

With a view to making India to a globally competitive position in value added teas, there is need for setting up of the blending, packaging and processing facilities at internationally competitive levels.

Globally, competitive canning lines, processing equipment and branded/private level option needs to be organized.

This is a highly technical field and an early edge would open up sophisticated markets in future.

Investment Activities during Xth Plan Period 2002-07

A) Proposed Development Measures—The development measures contemplated for the Xth Plan period in terms of physical area and the anticipated contributions are presented below:

Activity	*Area to be developed (ha)*	*Contribution (m.kg.) (ha)*	
1 Extension/new planting	4,500	4	2
Replanting	20,000	14	
3 Rejuvenation/pruning	50,000	25	4
Irrigation	50,000	10	5
Improvement of drainage	100,000	10	6
Productivity improvement	120,000	12	
Total	344,500	75	

More thrust would be on renovation of field assets and improving productivity from the existing areas rather than expansion. It is proposed to integrate the above activities under one scheme viz., Plantation development Scheme during the Xth Plan period. The total requirement of funds for the Five Year period adds up to Rs. 939 crores. The sources of fund would be as under:

(Rs. in crore)

Sr. No.	Sources of Fund	Amount
1	Tea Board	
	Loan	29.00
	Subsidy	130.00
2	33 AB a/c. Under Tea Development Account Scheme	405.00
3	Tea Industry's own resources	81.00
4	Bank/Institutional loan	294.00
	Total	939.00

B) Quality Upgradation and Product Diversification: One of the main reasons attributed to the price slump in South India during 2000, was the poor quality image. It is, therefore, proposed to pay more attention towards quality improvement of the basic product and on value addition. All the process related activities and quality upgradation and product diversification programmes would be covered under a new scheme viz. Quality Upgradation and Product Diversification Scheme. The estimated requirement of funds adds up to Rs. 811 crores with the following sources of funds:

Sr. No.	Sources of Fund	Amount
1	Tea Board	
	Loan	24.00
	Subsidy	100.00
2	33 AB a/c. Under Tea Development Account scheme	250.00
3	Tea Industry's own resources	109.00
4	Bank/Institutional loan	328.00
	Total	811.00

c) Research and Development—Research areas to be covered during the Plan period are: *(i)* integrated nutrient management, *(ii)* forecasting model for pest incidence, *(iii)* energy conservation, *(iv)* product diversification and value addition, *(iv)* tea and human health, *(v)* transfer of technology, *(vi)* establishment of chain of quality laboratories in the important tea growing regions, (*vii*) irrigation and drainage, (*viii*) biochemical analysis and quality improvement, (*ix*) soil management and organic cultivation of tea, (*x*) packaging, eco-preservation and other related areas, (*xi*) biotechnological aspects and (*xii*) pesticide residues, metals, myco-toxic and connected research work.

Development areas include: *(a)* setting up of a training centre and advisory centres for the benefit of small tea growers in NE region, *(b)* opening of new Development offices of Tea Board for closer interface with the small growers in the non-traditional areas, *(c)* strengthening the existing field offices of the Board, *(d)* setting up of nurseries for supply of planting materials to the small growers, *(e)* setting up of demonstration plots, *(f)* organizing study tours, workshops, seminars etc. and *(g)* institution of productivity and quality awards.

The estimated requirement of funds for the above activities including service charges for implementing the schemes would be in the region of Rs. 225 crores with the following source of funds:

Tea Board: grant in aid	Rs. 125 crores
Tea Industry: contribution	Rs. 100 crores
Total	*Rs. 225 crores*

d) Market Development—As a result of changes in the market scenario, the marketing orientation demands a new approach. Towards that end, it is necessary to make a specific provision for launching generic promotion campaign in the domestic market in joint collaboration with the tea industry. Besides, the regular promotion measures such as market research survey, uni-national campaign, brand promotion support, participation in fairs and tea festivals, exchange trade delegations etc. would be continued. The estimated funds requirement for the above activities is in the region of Rs.300 crores to be equally shared by the Tea Board and the industry on 50:50 basis.

Financial assistance to be extended under this Scheme

would be in the form of subsidies for various market development and export promotional activities.

Summary of the Tenth Plan outlay

It is proposed to cover the above noted activities under the following schemes:

Sr. No.	*Sources of Fund*	*Amount*
1	Tea Board	
	Loan	53.00
	Subsidy	535.00
2	33 AB a/c. Under tea development Account scheme	655.00
3	Tea Industry's own resources	440.00
4	Bank/Institutional loan	622.00
	Total	2305.00

The estimated outlay and the sources of fund for each of the scheme is summarized in the table below :

Sl.	*Name of the*	*Estimated fund requirement*	*Tea Board*		*33 AB Deposits*	*Industry's resources*	*Bank/ Institutional finance*
			Loan	*Subsidy*			
1	Plantation development scheme	939	29	130	405	81	294
2	Quality upgradation and product diversification scheme	811	24	100	250	109	328
3	Market promotion scheme	300	-	150	-	150	-
4	Research and development	225	-	125	-	100	-
5	HRD	30	-	30	-		-
	Total	2305	53	535	655	440	622

Source: X Five Year Plan. Report on Sub-Group on Plantation Crops II - Ministry of Commerce.

Conclusion

Targets should no longer be production oriented, but shall aim at improving productivity, value addition and marketability. It further states that one must concentrate on increasing the productivity of existing gardens rather than establishing new plantations with huge investments. There should be continued efforts towards further increasing the profitability of tea gardens through replanting/ rejuvenation and mechanization of operations.

The main thrust would be on quality so as to make our teas competitive in the light of opening up of the economy under the WTO agreement on agriculture. Thrust is to be given on improving marketing capabilities as well as substantially improving packaging and value addition. Conversion to organic methods of tea growing to be encouraged.Information technology needs to be given due consideration for making available ready information to the tea industry and for promotion of our produce in other markets There must be continued efforts towards further increasing the profitability of tea gardens through replanting/ rejuvenation and mechanization of operations.

The strategies of the Tenth Five Year Plan are to: *(i)* enhance production through vertical development measures such as replantation, rejuvenation, pruning, infilling of vacancies with better varieties, etc. *(ii)* improve the productivity of small tea gardens, *(iii)* emphasize special attention on irrigation and drainage, *(iii)* manufacture additional crop; tea processing facilities are to be augmented by construction of new tea factories, *(iv)* modernize the existing tea factories for ensuring production of clean teas without any trace of foreign material in end products, *(v)* encourage product diversification and creation of facilities for dual manufacture of tea (orthodox and CTC), *(v)* encourage value addition and production of instant, ready-to-drink tea, decaffeinated tea and specialty teas, *(vi)* ensure adherence to the prescribed international and domestic SPS (Sanitary and Phyto-sanitary) standards for tea, *(vii)* make higher investment on R&D and transfer of technology, *(viii)* reach technological advances to smaller estates where potential for improvement is the best, *(ix)* reduce packaging costs and use alternative and inexpensive packaging materials, *(x)* explore the possibility of setting up of modern packaging and blending units within India with foreign collaboration, *(xi)* support for promotion of value added teas in overseas market by exporters, importers to take advantage of IT tools for promotion vigorously, *(xii)* encourage organic tea cultivation and production of green teas, *(xiii)* initiate special promotional programmes in thrust countries, *(xiv)* need to continue an intensive generic promotion campaign within the country so as to increase per capita consumption and to arrest declining trend in domestic demand. A strong and vibrant internal market will create the necessary synergy's for expanding the export market, *(xv)* reduce the cost of production by improving productivity and minimizing wasteful expenditure to increase profits from the existing plantation. The competitive advantage of tea industry depends primarily on quality of manpower. Therefore, HRD inputs are critical to future development of the tea industry.

PART II
SOIL, FERTILISER, BIO-DYNAMICS COMPOSTING AND PLANT PROTECTION OF TEA

Integrated Management Nutrient in Tea Soil, Bio-Organic Farming and Principles of Bio-organig Fertilizers in Tea; Integrated Management of Plant Protection in Tea Farming; Organic Tea Farming Practices and Biodynamic Composting of Teà Cultivation; and Aspects of Orthodox Darjeeling Tea—Some Uniqueness, Liberalisation policy of of the Indian Tea company, and Internal Matchmaking and Business partnering and taste of Organic Products.

Part II documents four chapters (7 to 12) and concentrates on soil, fertilizers, bio-dynamic farmin etc. These are very important in the era of liberalization and globalisation The integrated management of tea soils that envisages three dimensional approachs (human, natural, and cosmetic) have been dovetailed. Bio-organic farming in tea and principles of Bio-organic fertilizers in tea cultivation state cold beverage in the arena of tea, jumping the boundary—tea in its new avatar, sustainable tea farming and production of prime quality of tea, soaring cost of inputs, philosophy of revival of bioorganic tea, transition of bioorganic farming of tea, and boosting of organic tea, principles of bioorganic farming.

The integrated management of plant protection means utilization of various measures to protect the crop from pests and diseases. It helps in directing towards suppressing pests and diseases and keeping the loss within economically safe limits. The tea farming practices and bio-dynamics composting of tea cultivation evolve farming strategy in organic management of tea cultivation, input-process-output, organic farm design and management, priciples of organic or sustainable vs conventional approach,biodymanic composting in tea cultivation, digested biomass and organic matter, composting process,vermicompostingin plant growth hormones.

Trade remedies are exceptions to the World Trade Organisation (WTO) principles of free trade. The procedures are also unique in the WTO system in giving an active role to the business community. Governments seek trade remedies almost exclusively on the instigation of local business or because of business concerns. The WTO identifies three main types of import restraints as trade remedies like anti-dumping measures, countervailing duties anti-dumping measures and safeguard measures etc. Aspects and uniqueness of Darjeeling tea are also included in this chapter.

7

Integrated Management of Nutrients in Tea Soil

Introduction

Integrated management of nutrients in tea soil is a method of managing nutrition. It is based on organic products requiring proper composting (both vermin and vegetation). It is judiciously applied in the domain of soil and has an impact on the level of production. It also encompasses the balancing and rebalancing of nutrition level at a prescribed requirement, creating a congenial compatibility of development and activation of microbes to transform the product into a form acceptable to the soil and finally to plants. The whole system involves skill of human resources and cosmic power of nature. The system of organic tea farming aims at feeding the soil, the microbes and other fauna of soil and finally to plants. Once the soil is fed properly and microbes are activated, then chain system of serving food to tea plant is established. The system continues to function uninterrupted till the replenishment in the soil is continued in direct proportion of its utilization. The system of bioorganic conversion initially control damages inflicted by indiscriminate use of chemicals and fertilizer. The nature in her own wisdom discriminates and neutralizes the toxic effect present in the soil. The evolution process propagated by nature corrects the artificial intervention in action and revives the normal form. It is impertinent to evaluate the immediate gain, in view of its long-term prospects. Initially it helps in healing and nursing processes in tea soil. Then it goes to plants to attain a sustainable productivity. Bioorganic farming in tea does not depress the crop permanently unless a wide variation in the status of soil compared to its desired level goes unattended for long time. This leads to the blockade of natural inflow of nutrition to plants. Hence, production and application of compost must be proper to maintain the living soil vibrant.

Three Dimensional Approaches: The three-dimensional approaches are through: *(a)* human resource, *(b)* natural resource, and *(c)* cosmic resource. When all these resources interact in harmonious way, a fruitful result is achieved. Here attempt is made to dwell upon resources *(a)* and *(b)*.

(i) Human Resource

Human resource is the driving force to achieve a productive and profitable return from bioorganic farming. The practitioner in bioorganic farming in tea should have a few years of experience in the changed and diversified condition to practise in a rational way. Building of human resources through thought, concept, and ideas is no less important than financial resources for they ensure long-term return.

Cognition: Clear knowledge in the arena of soil and plant is required. One should know exactly the method of application, absorption and utilization of different inputs. It is also necessary to understand the nature, behaviour and requirement in dealing with lively nature of soil and plants.

Orientation: This reveals the multiple routes of functions on different pattern of soil, the systematic flow of nutrients in tea plants and its growth. This also indicates the activity of different channels spread over the domain of both soil and plant. The orientation reveals the clear understanding and determines the functional pattern and its origin by the help of human resources.

Dedication: After having conceived the concepts of functional and relational aspects of soil and plants, one has to devote to proper application of compost at an appropriate time.

(ii) Natural Resources

In the prescribed range of application, integrated use of all the natural resources are tapped for enrichment of soil such as bio-fertilizers, inorganic nutrients in its natural form, organic manure including compost and green manure. All these in combination comfortably meet in the soil, develop a compatible harmonious combination and create the condition to fulfill the entire requirement to enrich the soil.

Bio-fertilizer: Bio-fertilizer (microbial nutrients) contains various types of living cells of microorganisms with the ability to mobilize important nutritional elements from non-usable form through biological process. It may be termed as biological inoculants that activate the availability of nutrients to serve the plants. Bio-fertilization signifies using living organisms as fertilizer, either to fix atmospheric nitrogen or to solubilise the mineral nutrients by decomposing organic matter. Bio-fertilizer is apparently environment and farmer friendly renewable source of non-bulky and low cost organic agro-input. Their use has so far not received desired attention. This is mainly because of inadequate awareness to their utility in the tea plantation. Their short shelf life, lack of ready availability in time, in desired quantity, and inconsistency in results may be other factors to overlook it.

A bio-fertilizer is an organic product containing a specific microorganism (microbial inoculant) in concentrated form which is derived either from nodules of plant roots or from the soil of root zone (rhizosphere). It possess unique ability to fix atmospheric nitrogen either symbiotically or non-symbiotically or to transfer native soil nutrients such as phosphorous, zinc, copper, iron, sulphur etc. from the non-usable (fixed) to usable form through biological process. Bio-fertilising agents control the plant pathogenic fungi directly as well as indirectly. The application of bio-fertilizer in the soil stimulates and augments the activity of saprophytic microorganism. Legume inoculation protects plants from attack of insects. Although, these fixers are naturally present in the soil, it is necessary to increase their population, which would have a multiplier effect on the enhancement of crop productivity.

Soil harbours various range of microorganisms, which bring about a number of bio-chemical reaction in soil. The soil organisms are classified into two broad groups i.e. soil flora and soil fauna. These are again sub-divided depending upon their size such as micro and macro flora. Soil micro flora includes bacteria, fungi, actinomycetes, algae, etc. Of these groups, bacteria are abundant followed by actinomycetes and fungi, algae are found under specific situations. The presence of these microorganisms makes the soil living and active. It plays a significant role in the life cycle of plants and animals through decomposition, solubalisation, nutrient fixation and helps in supplementation to plants.

Organic Manure: The best organic manure is produced by using local resources in which available energy is used to its maximum. Commercial enterprises are also marketing organic product under different brands. In addition, these brands are used in absence of local products after due checking and verification.

- Neem and castor related products in different forms.
- Bio-soil conditioners in different forms.
- Products of aerobic decomposition of wastes of agricultural products.
- Vermi-compost, vegetation compost and other composts.
- Neem based micro-nutrients product made of different agricultural wastes.

Organic manure is important source of plant nutrients. It maintains and restores health and active soil life. The chemical composition of organic residues, which is a part of manure, influences the rate and extent of decomposition by the soil microflora and thus the potential for increasing the soil organic matter.

Carbon and Nitrogen Ratio: The carbon and nitrogen ratio (C:N) indicates the amount of organic matter and nitrogen in the soil. As carbon is the main constituent of organic matter, C:N ratio indicates the strength of the soil. If too little nitrogen is present, the compost is made slowly and the product will be of poor quality. Too much nitrogen will result in loss and create an unpleasant odor. The ideal C:N ratio for a good compost is in the range of 8-12. To maintain the proper C:N ratio, the compost must be made of proper mixture of nitrogen rich and carbon rich materials. A mixture of rich and poor substances, young and mature materials will always ferment better than a single and small number of materials. In order to avoid escape of nitrogen and carbon in gaseous form, soil is mixed with the heaps. The soil bacteria are hungry for humus; they work hard to avoid anything getting lost. They also interact with organic matter so that maximum plant food is stored in the humus.

Compost: The different types of compost are made out of organic wastes with the help of earthworms, bacteria and fungi. Composting is an easy method to replenish the soil what has been taken away from it by plants. Composts maintain continuity of fertility in the soil. The selection of compost is based upon the requirement of nutrition to soil and the availability of the required materials. The compost is easily made in the garden.

Vermi Compost: The method of producing compost, using earthworms is vermi composting. The earthworms feed on the organic matter and convert it into nutrients-rich humus. The nutrients are in a form that plants can easily absorb. Earthworms also plough and aerate the soil as they move from one soil layer to another. Vermi compost is an important aspect of bioorganic farming. It is easy to prepare and is harmless to plants. Vermi castings are the faecal casting released by the earthworms, while vermiculture is the culture of earthworms. Earthworms support soil for healthy population of bacteria, fungal, actinomycete, protozoa, spiders, millipedes etc. These are essential for sustaining healthy soil. The case of earthworms is five times richer in combined nitrogen, seven times richer in available phosphates and eleven times richer in potash in the upper six inches of the soil. The loss of such potent contributors through chemicals and fertilizers is never compensated.

There are three kinds of earthworms. These are: *(a)* Epigeics, which operate on the top layer of soil just below the leaves and litters. They are surface feeders, feeding on the organic matter present on the soil surface and convert it into humus. Generally, they are pale red in colour, *(b)* Anecics, which are seen just below the soil surface feeding both on soil and organic matter are called Anecics. They make vertical burrows as they move up and down in the soil. This movement helps to aerate the soil. *(c)* Eudogeics, these are seen deep in the soil and feed only on organically rich soil. They are usually colourless. These earthworms make horizontal burrows as they move around the soil. This also helps to aerate and improve the structure of soil. The earthworms while performing their job of soil enrichment, makes the soil porous for growth of healthy root system, retain moisture in the soil, make available to plants the essential minerals found in the lower strata of soil, invite predators to control pests etc. In the initial stage of conversion form conventional to bioorganic, they help to detoxify the soil.

Vegetation Compost: The general conception is associated with a heap of garbage infected with flies and pathogens, emitting bad smell are connected with compost. These unprocessed wastes carelessly dumped can create health hazard and cause more pollution than any good effect. This is applied in the field without passing through the process of composting. It contributes immediate good return. The process of making compost is an art, based on scientific techniques propagated by nature. Even farmyard manure is considered quite useful but is very much different from compost manure. Composting is a fermenting process and the principles of composting are the same but different methods are applied based on variety and availability of inputs in the area.

Organic Tea to Boost Exports

According to tea industry pundits and experts the demand

for organic tea has surged in the global market. In their opinion, the growing demand of organic tea in Europe, united States and Japan is not just a craze now but has really caught on with health-conscious consumers. In the near future, it will get good reception from Australia, New Zealand and other developing countries also where the demand of organic agricultural products is on the rise. This was confirmed from a report of the International Trade Centre, which indicated that the demand of organic products is fast expanding due to growing awareness of the people against harmful effect of fertilizer and chemicals. Naturally, it would not be misleading to infer that organic tea has also a bright market. Indian tea industry should capitalize this opportunity to boost its sluggish exports. In this context it may be mentioned that while in the last couple of years exports and prices of our conventional teas fell severely, organic tea commanded premium, demand in the market as well.

Currently, the world demand for organic tea is about 3 million kg a year. The growth rate is 10 per cent per annum. But with the consumers' growing preference for organic tea to conventional tea, it is likely to be increased phenomenally. So the industry should be wiser to avail the advantage of a market at its nascent stage. It will enable the industry to secure a strong foothold before competition intensifies, which will occur over the next few years. However, organic tea production on a large scale should be launched only after building up adequate knowledge on foreign market. The industry should not overlook the necessity of viability study, such as collecting sufficient information on potential demand, the strength of other suppliers and the prices offered future competitors, distribution channel available and the right importers of such product. The Tea Board and the tea associations should not target just for the export market and without formulating supportive marketing strategies one more point, production of organic tea. It has to be popularized in the domestic market also so that the producers do not depend on export market only. This will serve as a shield to the producers against possible catastrophe in export demand.

It should be mandatory, therefore, for the tea garden management to pay more attention in this matter, arrange thorough study of the health of workers to find out if any correlation existed between workers' health and pesticides. In case, the gardens are inadequately staffed with medical personnel and not equipped with laboratory to undertake various pathological tests, NGOs may be asked to conduct specific study in this regard. The Governments of tea producing countries should also take up this matter without further delay. For, it is the social responsibility of the Government and the producers as well to take care of the health and living conditions of the people and the posterity.

8

Bio-Organic Farming in Tea, Principles of Bio-Organic Fertiliser in Tea

SECTION I
Bio-Organic Farming in Tea

Prologue

The fortune of the Indian tea industry is further struck by the wave of globalization. The industry depends on the limited world market which prevented it from blooming to its elegance and arrested march of progress. The induced deviation did not pay any appreciable dividend. Finally the industry shattered due to poor promotion and absence of vigilance to excel over other competitors. The dwindling economy of such market first changed over to slow gear and looked for parallel avenues to cope with circumstances. The opening of import of tea has put the industry on the crest-fallen. The obvious fall in export will further desiccate the industry. The domestic consumption, however, traced the subdued line of progress, but that is not enough to spur the growth. The fabric of the industry is loosing its strength. It will be further worn out if economy continues to wilt and investment continues to wait. The exponents of the tea industry are exploring the various possibilities to tide over the critical crisis. They are realigning from present discontent to future eminence. Concurrently, there has been a tacit effort to conceive the reality of predicament, and opened a new avenue of the exalted product, made within the parameter of sustenance, and an ambience of bracing support to health. The consolidated efforts culminated in consistency and established the integrity of the end product in tea. It revived the principle of participation of living soil and tea plants with involvement of cosmic power of nature.

Cold Beverage in the Arena of Tea

The market experts observed the encroachment of 'Cold beverage' in the arena of tea. The humble tea remained helpless with drooping face. It was diagnosed the symptoms of internal causes and external lapses.

- More human effort is involved in making tea than serving cold drink in keeping pace with the time. Haste in hectic life and involvement of tropical environment attract cold beverage to keep cool. Hot tea cannot be taken in haste. It also needs thermal compatibility with the taste/tongue.
- The visual content of the colourful soft beverage is displayed with younger generation in action. They also maintain consistency in their product. The audio-visuals are produced, based on the choicest interest incorporating incentive based programmes by promoters to in-grace the younger generation. Whereas, the colourful container of tea is focused as prime object with more information of producer than product. Also, the consistency in tea is based upon many variable factors out of some are beyond the control of human efforts.
- It was not contemplated or ignored of growing upsurge for cola—a product would come forward in direct confrontation with tea.

Jumping the Boundary—Tea in its New Avatar

The matured thinkers suggested the tested dictum, "if you cannot fight them, then join them". There may be some cultural deviation from traditional practices. After all, whatever nomenclature is called in its new garments, the final judgement converges to the empirical wisdom of consumers. Some aggressive fighters tend to believe in converting the tea into semi-hard drink with association and affiliation to open a new front of crusade, deviating from the traditional and aging path of survival. By jumping the boundary, tea in its new-avatar may loose its charming behaviour. The tea unlike other agricultural products as jute, sugar, cotton etc., where growers and manufacturers are two different units of establishment. Their responsibility and burden are divided into two fractions, whereas tea carries the full burden of both growers and manufacturers. In view of the staggered situation, it seems imperative to share one more burden of marketing to complete the full cycle of investment, effort and achievement. The present scenario in the tea is dragged into internal confrontation instead of intrinsic persuation. Persuation and confrontation do not go side by side. The latter is born out of hatred, passionate and uncompromising attitude, coupled with a mistaken sense of choice. The refinement in planning and re-orientatation in promotion can cover the larger interest and satisfaction. It may be rejoicing in the aftermath but is simplistic to link cause and effect. It may be rarely ignored but it seems doubtful whether it provided anything other than apprehension. The missing link seems to be the deployment of skilled marketing personnel to overcome cold calculation.

Sustainable Farming and Production Of a Prime Quality Product

There has been a great resurgence of interest recently in search of a sustainable farming and production of a prime quality product. The growing awareness of the after-effect of indiscriminate use of fertilizers and chemicals is widely conceded now an essential factor in creating the unsustainable degree of yield and gradual drop in quality. The misuse of modern methods helped to destroy soil, eliminated bio-diversity and succeeded eventually in producing contaminated end product. These studies have become extremely important, in the light of the worldwide efforts to seek an alternate to modern agricultural practices and evolve a sustainable eco-friendly strategy for development. The framework of development must encompass the region of ecology.

Soaring Cost of Inputs

The soaring cost of inputs is gradually becoming handicap to run the tea industry smoothly. The economic strains and non availability of inputs in time have put a barrier on the growth and development of the industry. Under the circumstances, the final result turns out to be a sheer disappointment and mere frustration. In order to ease out of such major problems, the bio-organic farming in tea envisages the utilization of cheap local products in making compost for fertilization and botanical (herbal) concoctions to protect the plants from pests and diseases. The initial cost of such devices may be high due to teething problems faced in meticulous planning, lack of skills and coordination and channelisation and collection of local resources. The identified basal dose of fertilization should consummate with the requirement of soil in compliance to a fruitful and faster result. Thereafter, it becomes easier and cheaper to maintain sustainability after adding what is taken out from soil.

Philosophy of Revival

The philosophy of bio-organic is based upon desirable concepts of intelligent care and the sound principle of integration with nature. The nature is the first teacher and the next are those who interacted and followed closely on her steps. It is the revival of wisdom to understand those who gathered experience based on deep observation and clear understanding. The practice of classical farming does not mean rigidity in techniques; rather it is a process of thinking to maintain a dynamic balance, which can always be adjusted as the circumstances demand. The subject to bio-organic farming is a level of organic farming, which is followed by skills, determination and dedication. The various scattered practices based on morphological character have been filtered through the wisdom of experience to serve the bio-organic farming in tea. The various news and literatures gathered from different sources have been properly scanned and practised to produce a workable harmony in the revival of bio-organic farming in tea.

Objective of Bio-Organic Farming of Tea

The objective of bio-organic farming in tea is evolved towards the maintenance of production at a level necessary to meet the increasing demand of teeming world population without degrading the eco-system. It is also focused in relevance to a successful management of natural resources, available local inputs, intelligent skills, consistent efforts and a suitable outlet of value added product to a commercial benefit. The bio-organic farming while restores the optimum beneficial character of tea, it improves the balancing effect of socio-economic problems, maintains a healthy living, strengthens the eco-system and sustains the natural resources of nature. The gain gathered on conventional persuasion, whether it will be retained or not is not the pertinent question but it will ultimately succeed in inflicting a lot of damage before it is realized.

The Transition to Bio-Organic Farming in Tea

The economic studies of transition to bio-organic farming at tea garden level only took a static approach, ignoring the permeable performance and the difficulty associated with transition from one system to another. The realistic approach of transition from conventional to the bio-organic farming is like a drug addicted person who is transformed into the normal life of importance. As such a rational approach must be incorporated in the study and interpretation.

Factors during Transition Period

Many factors can influence the economic performance of garden during the transition period. The use of certain chemicals and fertilizers has disrupted natural predators and other biota. It all depends upon, how fast the soil is enriched by application of a judicious basal does of organic manure/compost/green manure to improve the Carbon and Nitrogen ratio of the soil by uniform application in the area under consideration. The proper feeding of soil is the primary criterion to achieve the result faster. It is then, followed by the integrated management of plant protection by natural, biological and botanical (herbal) methods of pest control to accelerate the result. Re-establishing the microbes' population by improving the fertility of soil, particularly by application of composts (both vermi and vegetative composts), will tend to restore the balance faster. The tea planters also need a few years of experience to acquire the additional knowledge and the management skills necessary for more diversified operations. The economic impact of management's decision to change from conventional to bio-organic methods on all or part of a garden operation will vary depending on the factors such as type of the soil (full analysis of soil is required), age of the bushes and state of their health, crop history, inputs available for making composts, the planter's skill of adoption and many other consideration.

SECTION II
Principles of Bio-Organic Fertilisers in Tea

It should always be remembered, the principle of bio-organic fertilization is first for the soil, second for the microbes and other fauna of the soil, and the last for the plants. Initially these microbes require themselves soluble Nitrogen as food for doing their job of decomposition. The soluble Nitrogen they absorb is later set free after completion of their work and they also become the part of decomposition. The starter dose of Nitrogen is must to start the function of micro organisms. In order to avoid the depressing effect of crop, due to decomposition of large quantity of organic matter in the soil, the system of composting is evolved. The sustainability of the soil and other related systems are maintained, only after replenishment of what has been taken out from soil. Although, the transition in the initial stage may be difficult, successful transition tend to produce value added and a better quality product to get more of returns. The consistency in the yield and return to the economic performance can change significantly after a period of evolution from conventional to bio-organic practices. Once the system is set, then it starts functioning smoothly. Thereafter, the pay back period starts and it becomes easier and cheaper to maintain sustainability and the yield touches the new height and the quality emerges to its optimum level. A potential benefit of bio-organic farming that deserves further study, persistent practices and a close observation and a clear understanding, as it is still in the inception of infancy in tea. An honest effort has been initiated to consolidate and explain the various aspects of cultural practices in bio-organic farming in tea, at the level of scientific approach, on the role of rational pursuit and on the design of commercial benefit, on one platform.

Classification of Organic Farming

The organic farming when viewed from different angle of perspective, have been leveled with different link of classifications:

- ✓ Natural Farming: The role of nature is the best model of farming. The nature's self-propelled methods activate production and distribution of nutrients to plants.
- ✓ Organic Farming: It is a soft agricultural system totally dependent on the soil's natural fertility enhanced by compost and vermi compost.
- ✓ Bio-Organic Farming: This farming is based upon the techniques of intimate understanding of natural resources and interaction with cosmic energies. It also encourages the sustainable use of land and protects it from degrading.
- ✓ Bio-Dynamic Farming: It exploits bio and cosmic rhythms of nature in farming.
- ✓ Micro-Biotic Farming: It is a low external input sustainable agriculture (LEISA) originated from Dutch farmers and scientists committed to soft agriculture.
- ✓ Eco-Farming: The soil's living population of microbes and other organisms are the significant contributor

in fertility and the system is well protected from pollution.

✓ Permaculture (permanent agriculture): It advocates the planting of perennial tree crops and employ the environment in planning farm activities.

Elemental Energies of Nature

The concept in each case of farming stands behind the spirit of organic relationship and dynamic interaction with components of five active elemental energies of the nature. The concerted efforts are put forward for enrichment of soil to perform as server to plants, by facilitating the multiplication of microbes and penetrating into nutrients to activate it. The five active elemental energies—

(i) Elements of Soil: The soil is a living organism, born put of a colloidal affair between clay and humus. They represent 2-5 per cent of plant's dry weight. It contains 12 vital elements and 18 trace elements. The plants feed on qualitatively from soil and quantitatively from atmosphere. The elements taken from soil are of two types—constitutive and non-constitutive of plant matter. The constitutive elements are absorbed by plants either in an oxidized or chelated form. These transformations are brought about by the micro organism of the soil. The non-constitutive elements are borrowed from the soil and simply provide the plants with electric charges needed for their various growth processes. These elements are returned to the soil at the maturity stage. Only certain portion of plants and seed retain minute quantity of these elements. It appears that all constitutive elements pass through the biological cycle and then enter the plants in an organic way. The elements that enter plants in an atomic way are not constitutive of plant matter. Plants have thus an organic diet. These facts and this knowledge set aside, once and for all, the notion that plants have mainly and purely a mineral diet.

(ii) Elements of Water: It can take all the three forms of matter viz. solid, liquid and gas (vapour). Water is a compromise between solid and gas and it manifests itself only in it is activated form when necessary conditions are

fulfilled in its molecular structure. Water as liquid is indispensable to sustain life in all biological systems for drinking, metabolic functions and cleansing of the body system. The plant contains 80 per cent water in its system. The important part of plants i.e. Carbon, Hydrogen and Oxygen are absorbed through photosynthesis via water. The drought effect is caused by dehydration in the plants and microbes are also affected by water.

(iii) Elements of Air: Plants virtually feed on the air. Even in the soil, air is an ingredient of major importance. The atmosphere of the earth is a layer of gases around it. The mixture of gases that make up the earth's atmosphere consist of nitrogen—78 per cent, oxygen 21 per cent and argon. There are also traces of carbon dioxide and other noble gases, together with variable amount of water vapour. The atmospheric air acts as a protective layer screening the harmful radiation of the sun and serve as insular against its excessive heat. It prevents the earth cooling too rapidly at night and is a life saving barrier that burns up meteors before they can hit the earth. The weather is governed by depression (cyclones) and anticyclones. Depression are areas of low pressure caused by warm air rising and expanding. Anticyclones are areas of high pressures caused by cooling air, sinking. The violent movement of air tends to cause storms, hurricanes, cyclones or typhoons. Another extremely dangerous disturbance of the atmosphere is the whirlwind or tornado due to imbalance in the various elemental energies.

(iv) Elements of Solar Energy: Solar energy in the form of light, heat, electricity, etc., is the energy of the whole universe that expresses and manifests itself in an unlimited number of ways. No life is possible without the blessings of solar energy. The plants mainly feed on the atmosphere but the nutrients are absorbed by photosynthesis with the help of solar energy. The importance of solar energy in regulation of weather and climatic system is well known.

(v) Elements of Ether: It contains different subtle power in fine and delicate forms and act in a latent fashion.

Epilogue

The current crisis is created by the urge of the reprisal mind, reigned by deflection in thinking. It engaged the global mobilization and deployment of elite forces to fight in repercussion. It has also blocked the free passage of international trade and a sense of uncertainty shadowed over the fate of export. Unless an amicable settlement is reached at the face of impending issue, either by design or by persuation, it is difficult to predict the chain of events and outcome.

9

Integrated Management of Plant Protection in Tea Farming, Pesticides in Tea Estate, Applied Measures to Control Tea Pests—Physical, Cultural, Biological, and Herbal

SECTION I
Type of Insects, Arena and Class of Pests, etc.

The integrated management of plant protection refers to utilization of various measures to protect the crop from pests and diseases. It is directed towards suppressing pests and diseases and keeping the loss within economically safe limits. The inherent control by nature and applied control by planters are integrated by realistic approach to attain a degree of consistency. It helps determining the activities of pests on crop and their mode of infestation followed by various methods of control.

Type of Insects

Considering the role of insects in tea farming, they can be classified into three groups: *(i)* Harmless insects. *(ii)* Beneficial insects, and *(iii)* Injurious Insects. The *(i)* & *(ii)* Insects mentioned above are considered productive. While *(i)* is harmless to tea but plays in important role in the production of other useful products viz. honey, silk, Lac, wax, medicines etc and the *(ii)* acts as predator and controls the injurious insects i.e. *(iii)*.

Food Chain of Insects

All living organisms are dependent directly or indirectly on plants for their survival. They are :

- *Producers:* Plants feed and take energy from soil, atmosphere, and sun to produce food. So they are producers.
- *Primary Consumers:* The herbivorous insects and animals feed on plants and depend directly on them for their existence and growth.
- *Secondary Consumers:* The carnivorous feed and depend on herbivores for their growth and survival.

In the system of food-chain each one is dependent on the other. Under the agro eco-system, the population of all organisms are kept under control ensuring a healthy system of competition. However, in our haste to increase yield, we are facing the consequences—decreased yield, pest resurgence, drop in quality, health hazards, besides pollution and contamination of natural resources.

Arena of Pests

Pests, which normally cause a loss of 5 to 10 per cent of the yield, are said to be "minor pests". These major and minor pests are differentiated by their nature of infestation.

- *Regular:* These pests occur most frequently and have close association with the tasted crop.
- *Occasional:* They rather occur infrequently. These pests visit in absence of their associated tasted crop.
- *Seasonal:* Insects, which occur during a particular period of the year that is most conducive for their growth.
- *Persistent:* the pests occur on the crop throughout the year with complicated cycle of growth and evade control measure.

- *Sporadic:* They occur in isolated locality whose infestation remains low and insignificant for long period of time.

Class of Pests

Again the pests are classified on the basis of their feeding habbits.

- *Monophagous:* They are confined to a single species of plants and feed on the group of closely related plants.
- *Oligophagous:* They characteristically feed on a group of botanically related plants usually within single plant family.
- *Polyphagous:* These pests feed on many plants from a diverse range of plant families.

Behaviour of Pests

Behaviour of pests is based upon their eating habit and the way they damage the plants. The details are given below :

- *Sucking pests:* These insects have hypodermic needle type of mouthy to insert inside the sp of cells and such the juice of the plants. While taking out they also inject toxin of their body. This creates disturbances in the functional system of plants. As a result of which spots appear on the leaves and the growth is retarded.
- *Chewing pests:* These insects possess sharp teeth to chew the leaves of plant. The chewed parts of leaves suffer from blights.

The above factors constitute their class, habit, behaviour and their place in insect kingdom. It is necessary that tea garden managers/planters have adequate knowledge about that, which would help them in exploring the possibilities to check the population of insects and pests, devising measures to completely eliminate the menace.

Natural Control Measures

In the chain of control by meteorological. Physical, and

biological factors, natural control plays a vital role and work independently. These factors are explained below:

(i) Meteorological Control: It is governed by meteorological behaviour activated by the elemental energies of nature. Climatic control is an important natural factor in keeping insects and pests population under control.

- *Temperature:* It controls the development of fertile, fruitful, feeding movement and disposal or distribution of both crops and insects. The body temperature of insects depends on the environment. A warm humid environment is most conducive for the development of insects. The extreme temperatures, both low and high, effect on heir gestation or hibernation.
- *Rainfall and humidity:* The body composition of all insects consists of high percentage of water. It is vital constituent of the cell protoplasm. The activity of some insects are enhanced on the advent of rain, some get wet and infected by viral/fungal diseases and some are washed out by rain from their infestation.
- *Light:* Sunlight is the only source of energy for almost all biological systems and its different cosmic rays (x-rays, Gamma rays, ultraviolet, and infra rays) effect directly on the development, reproduction and growth of insects. The photoperiod, which is the number of sunshine hours in a day, has considerable influence on the development of insects. In the absence of photoperiod the activity of the sexual instinct of insect is induced.
- *Atmospheric pressure:* The phototropic insects are more active and thrive well in high barometric pressure and particularly when it is rising. The activities of some insects are directly influenced by low pressure when possibilities of rain are high.
- *Air Current:* Air current plays an important role on flying insects. Some insects fly away along the current of wind and some habitually fly against it. The air current helps in widespreading the insect in bigger

area but some of them die by falling in rivers and jhoras.

(ii) Physical Control: Physical factors play an important role in distribution and dispersion of insects. Mountains, lakes, deserts etc. form physical barrier to insects.

- *Mountain:* Range of mountains form barrier for insects to cross and their spread is checked.
- *Sea, lakes and rivers:* Some flying insects do not possess the ability to flight, so either they do not venture to cross or fall in it. This way their population remains under control.
- *Deserts:* The insects who dare to cross the large desert but in absence of vegetation and soil texture they suffer, die or retreat and their spread is restricted.
- *Soil structure:* The type of soil and its fertility determines the plants and animal lives in the soil. This in turn tends to restrict the number of types of species. Similarly, physical and chemical composition of soil determines the presence fo soil inhibiting species in sandy and clay soil.

(iii) Biological Control: Every insect has natural enemies in the nature in the form of predators, parasites, cannibals and pathogens causing diseases.

- Insect predators: They feed on the living insects and inhibit their population. Some important predatory insects are:

  Wasps : Feed on small and big insects
  Soldier Beetles : Feed on bigger and hidden insects
  Praying Mantis : Feed on small insects
  Lady bird Beetle: Feed on mites and aphids
  Syrphid Fly : Feed on many insects
- *Parasitic insects:* Parasitic insects live on other insects and kill them.
- *Pathogens:* Insects also suffer from diseases in great numbers like any other animals and their population is checked by the nature. The important micro-organisms which cause disease are as follows:

(i) Protozoa, *(ii)* Bacteria, *(iii)* Fungi, *(iv)* Worms, and *(iv)* Nematodes.

SECTION II

Applied Measures to Control Tea Pests—Physical, Cultural, Biological, and Herbal

Applied measures to control tea pests include those methods, which are under the control of man. These are necessary when natural forces could not keep the pests under control. The following points will help in devising effective pest control measure.

- ✓ Exact taxonomy and morphology of the pests.
- ✓ Life cycle and seasonal history of the pests.

Physical Control Measures

The suppression of pest population in tea farming by designs or devices by physical factors of the environment is induced under this group of control.

- ✓ *Hand Collection of pests:* The bigger pests are collected by hand and then burnt or buried.
- ✓ *Hand nets:* Hand nets are useful to catch flying pests during their migration when they are in large number.
- ✓ *Barriers:* Barriers are used to check the movement of pests from one place to another place.
- ✓ *Tree banding:* Adhesive or sticky bands around the tree trunks are put to trap pests.
- ✓ *Fencing:* The migrating pests can be prevented from spreading out of infested areas by putting high fence of bamboo mat.
- ✓ *Trenching:* Migration of crawling pests can be stopped by cutting trenches around fields.
- ✓ *Light Trap:* It is generally used at night for the pests who are phototropic, i.e. attracted towards light.
- ✓ *Attractants:* Sometimes an attractant is also used to attract pests and then they are trapped.

Cultural Control Measures

Cultural practices followed in tea gardens create power of

internal resistance in plants against pests.

- ✓ *Cultivation of land:* Insects are largely affected by the texture of the soil, chemical composition, moisture content, temperature and other soil organisms. Hoeing and chilling, done in dry weather, cut down the capillary action of the soil and protect it from moisture evaporation. It also helps regenerate the root system in plants and supply bio-mass to soil. The pests, which are exposed on the surface, are picked up and become prey to predators.
- ✓ *Sanitation of soil:* Many pests hide and hibernate under loose bark or in deep and healthy branches of tea and shade trees. Removal of such shelters by scrapping, pruning and plastering prevents the multiplication of various pests.
- ✓ *Time of planting:* A careful selection of time for the planting of tea and shade trees may help avoid egg-laying period of pests and also their infestation.
- ✓ *Variation in green vegetation:* Tea being a perennial crop, varieties of shade trees, green crop in vacant places are quite useful in diverting the persisting pests as the availability of getting continuous supply of food of the tasted variety would be limited.
- ✓ *Mixed cropping:* In tea area mixed cropping means growing of different varieties of plants and shade trees apart from tea. Only healthy and non-infested seeds or cuttings of plants should be sown to check the carry-over of the pests. Sowing of trap crop is also a suitable method to destroy and check the infestation of pests.
- ✓ *Eco-System:* The wide variety of plants, trees, insects, birds and animals in the area provide stability and resilience to the system. Trees provide nesting areas for birds and other animals that play an important role in pest control. Introduction of multipurpose tree species into the agro ecosystem help removal of toxic effects created by the use of chemicals. Thus more predators come into the system and help re-establish the food chain thereby aiding in pest control.

Biological Control Measures

Functions of biological control mentioned under natural control is the same in applied control, but in the absence of adequate measures the help of outer agency is taken to support the functional activities in different forms. In a disturbed ecosystem, pests can be controlled by releasing predators and parasitic insects, mites, fungi etc. So biological control measure involves: *(i)* conservation of natural predators, *(ii)* release of parasites, *(iii)* use of microbial agents like bacteria, virus, fungi etc, and *(iv)* use of predators. Various ranges of biological control agents are under experimental stage but only a few are being tried in tea. As these agents are very selective, a long period is required to judge their efficacy. Sometime the introduced agents are also parasitised by parasites and some may have suitable environmental condition for its development. More time is required to study and judge the adaptability of the agent.

SECTION III
Application of Pheromones, Hormones, and Chemosterilants

It is the chemicals, which are released into the external environment by an animal. This causes a specific reaction in a receiving individual of the same species. These chemicals are also known as ectohormones and are used to control pest population. In recent years, hormones are also used successfully in minimizing the insect pest population. Hormones have been found to change the course of development in insects and to cut short their life span. They interfere the reproductive capacity of an insect in any way and are called chemosterilants. The basic concept behind its use is to minimize the reproductive potential of the insects.

Benefits of Biological Control

There are many benefits of biological control. They have no harmful residual effect. Effect of control is permanent type. They do not harm the beneficial organisms. Some agents can be mass-produced easily. It is free from resistant problem.

Botanical (Herbal) Control Measures

The bio-insecticides extracted from leaves, flowers, seeds, stems and roots of some plants are termed as botanical insecticides. The indiscriminate use of chemicals has taken its toll by creating problems like pesticide-resistant insects, contamination of product by toxic residue, resurgence of pests and effects on non-target organisms. The deterrent effect of chemicals has aroused interest in herbal method of plant protection.

✓ *Neem (Azadirachta indica):* It is a common and fast growing tree found in the tropical region. The leaves and its seeds have insecticidal properties and are effective against a whole range of pests. The seeds stored between 3 to 8 months are found to be more effective. It acts as an antifeedant, repellant, growth inhibitor, nematicide and in some cases also prevents egg laying. The *Neem* contains the following nutrients such as: Nitrogen: 3.56 per cent, Calcium: 0.77 per cent, Phosphorus: 0.83 per cent, Magnesium: 0.75 percent, Potassium: 1.67 per cent.

Neem leaves mixed with soil may be used as nematicide and bio-fertiliser. Neem seed cake applied to the soil/crop provides it with various nutrients required for growing plants. It also reduces pest, fungi, bacteria and nematodes and protects the crop from damage caused by these organisms. The neem cake applied to the soil produces organic acids, which help in neutralizing alkalinity. The kernels contain Oil – 30-40 per cent, Turpeniod – 2.5-3 per cent and Azadirachtin – 0.2-0. per cent 6 per cent. Besides, neem also contains more than 20 sulphurous compounds.

The products are highly photogdegradable ensuring

their nonresistance in the environment. If desired, the residual action of neem bio-insecticides in the field can be extended with addition of ultra-violet absorbants of sunscreens to the formulation. These also do no induce pest resurgence unlike other synthetic pesticides. Pests developing resistance to single active component may not be able to develop resistance to neem compounds as they contain numerous bioactive principles.

✓ *Tobacco (Nicotiana tacacum):* This is a small plant thrives well under tropical, sub-tropical and temperate climate. Tobacco powder and extracts are in use as agricultural insecticide. It works as stomach and respiratory poison, insecticide, repellant and fungicide.

Other botanical (herbal) extracts: It is the inclination of the nature to grow all the required herbs needed for the area. It is also a part of balancing effect of nature and a compliment to establish eco-friendly environment.

(i) *Leaf Extract*: Apart from the leaf extract mentioned earlier, the other leaf extracts have been tried and found useful. These are Tulsi *(Ocimum basilicum, Ocimum sanctum)*, Aloe *(Aloe vera)*, Papaya *(Carica papaya)*, Nirgundi *(Vitex nigundo)*, Dhatura *(Datura stramonium)*, Bhang *(Cannabis sativa)*, Sharifa *(Custard apple)*, Castor *(Ricinus communis)*, Nux-vomioca, Citronella, Lemon grass *(Cymbopogan citrates)*, *Tej-patta* (bay leaf), Basak *(Adathoda vasica)* Tagets (Mexican marigold), Eucalyptus, Lantana, Guma/ Thumbai *(Lucas aspera)*, *Ageratum conyzoides*, *Artemisia valgaris*, *Eupatorium glandulosum*, *Polygonum hydroppier*, *Cassia tora*, *Cassia occidentalis*, *Cassia fistula*, etc.

(ii) *Root extract*: The extract of root/rhizomes/bulbs of the botanical origin of the other families has been tried and noticed quite effective in the control of pests in tea farming. They include Sweet Flag *(Acorus calamus)*, Ginger *(Zingiber officinale)*, Onion *(Allium cepa)*, *Kala Haldi (Golchicum luteum)*, Garlic *(Allium sativum)*

(iii) *Seed extract*: The seed extracts of other platns are found useful to control pests in tea,. They cover Sharifa (Custard apple), Chillies (Capsicum frutescens), Dhatura (Datura sttramonium), Peppers (Piper longum, P. nigrum), Papaya (Carica papaya), Poison nut (Nux vomica) Citronella, Lemon grass, Menthol, Eucalyptus

(iv) *Oil Extract*: The oil extracts of the following herbs are mostly used as repellant to control pests:

Name of Plants	*Alkaloid Extract*
1. Chrysanthemum cinereriae folium	Pyrethrum
2. Chrysanthemum coccineum	Pyrethrum
3. Derris elliptica Derris malaccensis	Rotenon
4. Ryania speciosa	Ryania
5. Veratrum album/V. viride	Hellebore
6. Schoenocaulou officinale	Sabdilsa
7. Quassia amara	Quassia
8. Picrasma excelsa	Picrasmin
9. Heliopsis scabra/H. longipis	Scabrin

(v) *Extracts–commercial:* Some extracts based on the genetic character of plants have been found to contain alkaloids having insecticidal properties. They are also marketed by commercial organizations for use as bio-pesticides.

Conclusion

Since the early seventies of the last century, application of pesticide in tea gardens of the country is a regular event to prevent tea plants from the attack of various insects. Of course, its utility has always been welcomed as yield boosting agent despite its bad effects on the health of garden workers causing much anxiety. It has been reported, chronic ailments among the tea workers and their families are on the rise in the Darjeeling district of West Bengal. Research conducted by the Centre for Sustainable Living noticed that the toxic content of the insect repellants has led to many children being born with physical and mental deformities. A BBC survey on the effect of pesticide on the health of tea workers in this hill district indicated the impact more severe on the second generation. The revelations are alarming and should not go unheeded by the managements of tea gardens within and outside the country as simply isolated event restricted to one place. Although more extensive study is required to arrive at a conclusion, it may be said that careless handling of pesticide is likely to cause various ailment among the garden workers and their families. The researchers of the Centre for Sustainable Living emphasized that pesticide needs sometime to accumulate in the body, only then the effects could be noticeable. The ill-effects are more prominently manifested on the next generation.

10

Organic Management of Tea Gardens, Bio-Dynamics Composting of Tea Cultivation, and Trade Remedies to WTO Principles of Free Trade

SECTION I
Farming Strategies in Organic Management of Tea Gardens

Tea estates have traditionally been monocultures. Estate management systems, therefore, have been built around this convenient linear model of:

Input-Process–Output

This allowed for clinical management of the estates with monitoring parameters similar to those in an industrial factory such as production efficiency, productivity indices etc. This system lent itself to hands off remote management of estates. The objective of the conventional farming system is to minimize variables, while the proposed organic farming system deals with maximizing variables and maintaining dynamic and integral balance of various elements.

Organic Farm Design and Management

Organic farm management requires an entirely different approach to managing a conventional farm. While the focus of the latter was on maximizing output, the focus of management in an organic estate would be in terms of providing a dynamic self-sustaining system. The difference in farm management has implication on manpower organization on the estate and decentralization of operations into self-sustaining blocks within the estate itself. Certain principles apply to Designing Sustainable Agricultural System. A few of the elements are briefly detailed:

— *Relative Location:* No element of an estate exists in isolation. Functional relationships exist between plants, animals and structures, eg. Location of compost yard with reference to biomass sourcing, manure and plantation fields.

—

— *Multiple Functions for Single Element:* eg A wind break for cattle fodder, bee nectar, biomass for compost.

—

— *Multiple Elements supporting Single Function:* eg. Dependence of a tea grower on a single crop–tea Vs an organic farm where there are multiple source of income.

The above paragraph can be briefly explained considering a few elements and the corresponding "Organic/Sustainable Approach" Vs the "Conventional Approach".

While this part is not the core of this attempt, it has been dealt with to drive home the point that conversion to organic farming is not a mere shift of farming techniques but rather a shift to an entirely new dynamic and environmentally responsible farming system.

Table 1: Principle of Organic/Sustainable Approach Vs Conventional Approach

Principle	*Organic/Sustainable Approach*	*Conventional Approach*
Element Connection	Holistic: Agriculture, Forest, People	Reductionist: Agriculture separate from nature's diversity model
Cyclical Nature	Recycle Resources	Linear thinking: Fast in fast out, increase input-increase output
Soil	Feed & Protect Soil	Soil as a medium for plant nutrient feed (primarily chemicals)
Diversity	Increase diversity by crop rotation, mixed cultivation, alleys	High Yielding Varieties often the same crop with the inevitable pest build up

Source: The Assam Review and Tea News, November 2002.

SECTION II
Biodynamic Composting in Tea Cultivation

Why Compost?

The tragedy of modern agricultural science is its obsession with soil chemistry, chemical values in the soil to the exclusion of biological values. This has led to the depletion of the life element in soil, the humus. It is the humus in an organic system that provides the nourishment for the plant through its biological processes. Composting is our means of enriching soil with humus.

What is Compost?

It is particularly important to understand that all decayedbiomass and organic matter is not compost. Compost is defined as completely digested biomass and organic matter possessing the structure of humus.

What is Humus?

Humus is not a definite chemical substance but rather a

state of matter, an integration of mineral and organic matter. Humus activity in the soil provides the link between physical material and life as expressed in the plants cultivated. Soil then cannot be treated as a mere facilitator of chemical substances for plant growth – it is the foundation for biological processes from which the plant derives its health and well-being.

Digested Biomass and Organic Matter—The Composting Process

A good organic farming system will provide almost all the components necessary for composting within the farm itself. It is most important that we distinguish composting from rotting and putrefaction. Foul smelling biomass indicates the presence of unproductive micro-organisms. It can also indicate ammonia gas and thus the loss of precious nitrogen. A good compost should either smell sweet or hardly have any odour at all. There are three distinct phases that compost goes through and an organic farmer should meticulously observe these phases and be ready to intervene if the compost overheats or does not get hot enough.

- *Breakdown phase:* When the heap is completed, biodynamic preps are added to ensure a controlled composting process. This phase is characterized by heat ideally up to 50-65^0 C and a pH of around 5-6.5. Should the heap overheat it can be turned to avoid loss of biological value. In this stage biomass is broken down or disintegrated.
- *Stabilisation phase:* In this phase there is proliferation of micro-organisms as the temperature of the heap slowly drops to between 30-40^{0}C. This micro life is a vital addition to soil and is the core element of the humus that is forming. PH moves towards neutral and it is best to get the compost on the field at this point because it is at its maximum biological value. Ensure that compost is immediately spread into the soil and not left in heaps exposed to sun, light and drying.
- *Mineralisation phase:* The original biomass begins to

revent to soil and pH is 7+. Intrinsic biological value gets depleted even though chemical NPK values may be satisfactory (Table 2).

Table 2: Application of Compost to the Field

Criteria down	*State 1 Break- ation*	*Stage 2 Stabilis- ation*	*Stage 3 Mineralis-*
Temperature degree C	50-65 degree C perature 35-40	Decreased tem-	Ambient
PH	Acidic (5-6.5)	Towards Neutral	PH7+
Moisture per cent	Damp 50-60	40 per cent	Noticeable drop
Colour Yellow	Brown Green to Black Brown	Dark Brown to	Soil Colour
Aroma hint of ammonia	Musty-with a	Earthy to woody	Soil

Source: Assam Review and Tea News, November 2002.

What has been described is the classical Indore composting model developed and perfected in India decades ago. But with machinery like shredders and front-end loaders it is possible to make this activity for more cost effective. Shredders for example can break up biomass into 5 cm components and both proteinaceous and carbonaceious elements can be premixed before heaping. Composting can then be done in a fraction of the time. It is possible to do sheet composting on the field itself spraying the mulch with CPP to stimulate the breakdown process. All sorts of cost effective variations on the basic composting principle are possible as long as they adhere to the organic/biodynamic guidelines.

Composting in Tea Plantations

Is it practical to get compost out onto tea blocks? More difficult than in coffee plantations. But tea is pruned every 4-5 years and this is an opportunity to put out large amount of compost with a high C/N ratio so that it lasts in the soil. Nitrogenous additives can be given through foliar sprays to ensure satisfactory foliar growth. With a dynamic organic system in place it is not necessary that yields be compromised. It would seem that a conventional tea estate does not have enough biomass available to be converted into sufficient quantities of compost. Thus a major factor in the conversion process is making available land for this purpose. It should be along the edges of the garden. Especially using the sides of the roadways to this purpose. Practical considerations such as location of the composting yard, availability of water, loading and unloading facilities and convenience of transport are critical elements that can determine the viability of a farming system.

Vermi-composting Rich in Plant Growth Hormones etc.

Vermi-compost is rich in plant growth hormones, organic matter and is the perfect medium for the multiplication of beneficial micro-organisms. Vermi-compost or earthworm castings have been acknowledged by research world wise ad an excellent and a stimulating medium for plants to grow in. In addition to adding nutrients to the soil and enhancing bio-life, vermi-compost also improves the soil structure. Vermi-compost can play a very useful role in the nursery of a tea estate. However, practical considerations such as the cost of producing compost restricts its value in terms of application over a wider plantation area. Further, good compost has a C : N ratio of around 1 : 10. A compost of this C : N ratio has limited use in a long-term crop such as tea. The compost will break down quickly leaving very little organic matter and nutrient value even after a couple of months of application. Vermi wash on the other hand could b e used to great advantage as a foliar stimulant in a tea garden. Earthworms have been inoculated into another Biodynamic product called CPP with good result. Having said this, a well-managed compost yard done the Biodynamic way will draw in the earthworms into the compost heaps.

Conclusion

The motive and impetus to convert a conventional estate to an organic/biodynamic farming system must be more then just the fact that organic produce fetches up to double the market price. Such a motive will not sustain the operation for long. The commitment regarding understanding of organic farming principles must be deeper. Long term studies have shown that organic methods are far more energy efficient and self-sustaining than conventional chemical methods. And, the greatest benefit will be human health and a toxic free environment.

SECTION III

Trade Remedies to WTO Principles of Free Trade

Trade remedies are exceptions to the World Trade Organisation (WTO) principles of free trade. The procedures are also unique in the WTO system in giving an active role to the business community. Governments seek trade remedies almost exclusively on the instigation of local business or because of business concerns.

The WTO identifies three main types of import restraints as trade remedies.

- *Antidumping Measures:* The most commonly used are antidumping measures to counteract unfairly low prices. The WTO Agreement on Antidumping deems that goods are "dumped" when companies export them at prices lower than those at which they sell in their home market. Dumping is not illegal in itself; it becomes illegal as soon as it results in injury to local businesses in the importing country. Therefore, to initiate and antidumping investigation, local businesses must demonstrate evidence of dumping, injury to themselves and a causal link between the dumped prices and the injury to them. Generally, this takes the form of a written application to the relevant national authority (eg the Ministry of Trade). This authority will provide a notice a receipt of a "properly documented application" to the government of the exporting country. The national authority may, in "special circumstances", initiate an investigation without receiving an application from businesses. In any case, all interested parties receive a copy of a notice of initiation (which includes a copy of the application). The national authority also issues a notice and/or a report to the public.

Trade Remedies—The Fact

In 2001, WTO member States reported they had initiated 348 antidumping actions, imposed 27 countervailing duties and taken 19 safeguard measures. For the first time, developing countries in the majority in launching antidumping investigations.

In the second half of 2001, China headed the list of countries whose exports were being investigated (25 cases), a drop from 32, while Brazil, Chinese Taipei, Thailand and the United States were next. India initiated the most investigations (51, up from 21 in the second semester of 2000). The United States was second (35, down from 38) and Argentina third (16, a decrease from 34). Investigations into products from the iron, steel and aluminium sector were more numerous (60), accounting for 33 of the 35 US investigations. Chemicals (451) and plastics (34) were next. India initiated 28 of its 51 investigations on chemical products. Plastics accounted for 12 of Turkey's 13 investigations.

However, the 79 antidumping measures finally imposed against exports from 33 countries or customs territories represented a sharp drop from the 107 in the second semester of 2000. The United States imposed most of them (21), a significant increase from 8, while India was a close second (20). The European Union and Argentina each adopted 11 measures (down from 32 for EU). Of the total, 21 measures were imposed against China, and 6 were imposed on Chinese Taipei.

- *Countervailing Duties:* Countervailing duties counteract subsidies by national authorities that unfairly enable their companies to export at a lower price.
- *Safeguard Measures:* These measures do no counteract an unfair practice, but allow countries to suspend import surges temporarily in order to grant local

industries time to adjust to increased foreign competition on national markets.

However, if a country is thought to be breaking the rules by imposing limits for unjustified reasons, other WTO members can—and do—challenge them through the WTO's dispute settlement system.

Business Concerns

The business sector and legal experts in developing and transition economies report several difficulties in interpreting and applying trade remedy laws. To help national officials and business leaders in these countries to understand the workings of the trade remedies system. ITC's World Trade Net programme organized regional workshops in Asia and Eastern and Central Europe, focusing on national regulations and practice in the United States, the European Union (EU) and Canada, and their implications for business. Participants in these workshops cited these main business concerns:

— *Heavy Procedural Requirements:* During antidumping investigations, the EU gives exporters only 37 days to complete its questionnaire, which participants do no think is sufficient time to complete it in details. Also, accounting and yardsticks can differ significantly from their home countries. Participants requested more cooperation from EU representatives during their investigations.

— *Use of "Sampling":* When the EU investigates a group of companies, it may choose certain companies, it may choose certain companies as a sample group for indepth investigation. It uses findings from the sample as the basis to calculate whether or not the entire group has been dumping goods. Because this system lacks precision, exporters not included in the sample may consider that they are unduly penalized.

— *Simultaneous Actions:* Exporters from developing countries are sometimes subject to simultaneous antidumping actions and countervailing duties. Such practices are too burdensome for companies from developing countries. Participants suggested that developed countries should consider pursuing just one trade remedy action at a time against exporters from developing countries.

— *Rules not Transparent:* Certain national authorities have discretionary power in their operations. Participants called for more transparent rules regarding investigations.

— *Lack of Expertise and Resources:* Participants stressed the lack of expertise and resources of developing countries, which cannot afford to hire foreign law firms specialized in WTO law. They also expressed the need to strengthen the relationship between business and government in order to better cope with trade remedy proceedings initiated by other national authorities.

— *"Non-market Economies":* A common concern among transition economies—that is, former centrally-planned economies—is that the Agreement on Antidumping does not offer sufficient guidance on how it should be interpreted. So the treatment of "non-market economies" varies greatly, depending on how importing countries interpret the agreement. As a result, an exporting country may be given a different status in different market. If investigating authorities are unsure whether to consider a country a non-market economy, they may require exporters to fill in two questionnaires, one designed for market-economy countries and the other for non-market economy states. This represents a significant effort and financial cost. Also, being classified as a non-market economy leads to an almost automatic assumption of dumping against exporters.

Recommendations

Workshop participants reported practical difficulties encountered by exporters in preparing before, during and after a potential antidumping investigation. A number of suggestions to help overcome these difficulties are outlined below:

Trade Remedies in Major Markets

United States: US companies have been among the frequent users of trade remedy laws. In addition to anti-dumping measures, countervailing duties and safeguards, US trade remedies include legal action against imports that infringe intellectual property held by a US company (Section 337 of the Tariff Act of 1930) or market barriers limiting US exports to another country (Section 301 of the Trade Act of 1974).

Antidumping measures and countervailing duties are the most frequently used remedies. In 2001, the United States initiated 79 anti-dumping cases (it has initiated 910 cases since 1980) and 18 countervailing duties investigations (340 cases since 1980). The frequency of investigations increases when the economy weakens. The number of countervailing duties cases has dropped over time because US companies have realized that anti-dumping measures are more effective. Foreign companies involved in the steel industry are the most frequent targets (about half of recent cases).

European Union: Even though anti-dumping actions are the most frequent trade remedy used in the European Union (27 cases in 2001), countervailing duties investigations have increased in recent years, showing a greater willingness to oppose government subsidies that are deemed to be trade distorting. In several cases, European institutions have undertaken simultaneous antidumping and countervailing duties investigations. As a result, proceedings are very burdensome for exporters, who have to provide, within very short time periods, detailed information with regard to the alleged dumping and subsidies.

Before A Case is Filed

Companies vulnerable to action should have a good knowledge of their export trends and profit levels as well as those of their competitors. In a situation of loss or decline in profits, particularly in sensitive sectors such as steel or textiles, it may not be wise to try to compensate by increasing exports. A drop in profits that occurs simultaneously with an export boost can lead to an assumption of dumping. In such cases, companies should already have prepared coherent, verifiable arguments backed up with hard data to counter any charges. With regard to the United States, exporters need to be attentive to danger signals such as deterioration of competing US producers' financial performance as well as increases in market share, since US law makes it easy for US companies to press for action against foreign competition if they have financial problems. Again, an exporter must be well prepared to respond to dumping charges.

When A Case is Filed

Since businesses do not have the legal status to bring cases to the WTO Dispute Settlement Body, they have to request their national authority to initiate proceedings and it is by no means certain that requests will be successful. What is certain is that it will usually take some time to sort out. Therefore, in a dispute over trade remedies, it might be better to explore first the alternative solutions available under domestic laws. Exporters who are under investigation should gather data very quickly. They should collect detailed information (particularly when dealing with US authorities). Businesses need to ensure they submit complete, correct and verifiable data. They must also be well prepared during every stage of the verification visit by trade remedy planners. A country whose business is under investigation can request an extension of time to reply to the questionnaire. It can also require the full test of the written application for action, and thus build up a detailed rebuttal against charges. Parties may request protection of confidential information, obtain access to non-confidential information submitted by other parties and make submissions based on this information. Businesses are recommended to document verbal information they provide to authorities. Exporters should be informed if authorities are to make on-the-spot investigations.

For investigations under EU law, exporters should identify their best option at an early stage; whether to be included in the sample used to determine the duty, and, as a result, be subject to an individual margin; or not to be included and therefore benefit from the average duty that is imposed. Parties have the right to be informed of the essential facts that form the basis of any final decision in sufficient time to defend their interest. Business under investigation should use this right. Intergovermental negotiations can avert the need for action in WTO and expensive litigation, particularly if the case of the complaining party has weak points, which defending countries need to identify.

Beyond Antidumping

Even when an antidumping measure is imposed, this is not the end of the story. The exporting country can appeal to the WTO Dispute Settlement Body. But it should initiate the process immediately by requesting a consultation and deciding on panellists. To save time and resources, the exporting country should limit its attack to the weakest part of the decision rather than focusing on all its possible defects.

11

Liberalisation Policy of the Indian Tea Companies and International Matchmaking and Business Partnering; Taste of Organic Products

SECTION I
Liberalisation Policy of the Indian Tea Companies

Introduction

Liberalisation has been a common tool among politicians all over the world to restructure the economy in such a manner that functions more efficiently and generates economic growth. The greatest danger that lies in the implementation of this policy is a too one-sided approach. Liberalising, in other words moving away the government from the economy, also involves the removal of government protection, which can damage several vulnerable parts of the economy. This was about the general thought. Keeping this in view attempts have been made to assess the influence of the India's liberalization policy on the tea sector. The policy, started by the government on a large scale in the early 1990s, was initially focused on the industry and services. For agricultural branches like tea, government control largely remained.

Actual Liberalising Measures of Govt.

To start with the actual liberalizing measures of the government was viewed first. It turned out that several measures where taken, none with a major impact. The government still did not allow most imports and maintained many other laws to control the domestic tea trade. The limited number of liberalizing measures focused on looking at anticipating moves of the tea companies. The measures also dealt with the consequences of the policy. This required a more qualitative approach into the changes in the behaviour of the companies, either as a result of changes in the government policy or expected future changes. Several indicators were chosen to analyse changes in the behaviour of the tea companies. They were categorized in five groups viz., *(i)* market changes, *(ii)* product changes, *(iii)* company structure changes (involving merger and takeover), *(iv)* investment changes, and *(v)* trading changes.

Changes in Company's Structure—Impact of: Especially when company structure changes were concerned, the large tea companies turned out to have well defined strategies to deal with, the liberalizing of government activities. They mostly saw a further growth of competition in their advantage. This opposed the view of most small companies. They were happy with the current government protection and did not think they would or even could change their company strategies.

Small Companies—Rising Costs and A Fall in Demand: This was confirmed by an interview with the ITA, in which they said that many small companies are facing a hard time currently. Rising costs and a fall in demand are the main contributors to the problems of the companies. While changes in the demand can be regarded as an external process, changes in costs can be attributed to the liberalization policy, partly. Many costs have risen sharply since the government started to liberalise the economy, mostly because the goods that were kept for the Indian market in the past were increasingly exported. These exports led to scarcity on the domestic market.

Companies Turned their Production System to World Demand: This shows the new situation, where the Indian economy has to compete increasingly with the world market. In the case of tea, the companies have a number of disadvantages in this battle. Next to the high production costs there is a technological disadvantage. Companies from traditional (world) market-oriented countries have turned their production system to the world demand for centuries. Therefore, their tea is best fit for modern tea products like tea bags and flavoured tea. This requires low quality, cheaply produced tea. India on the other hand always set its priority on quality of the tea. On the domestic market the government maintained the protecting laws like the Tea Waste Act and the Market Control Order. Most companies claimed that these protecting laws should be abolished to face foreign competition.

Companies Hardly Set Out Production and Market Activities: In general the perception of the companies was that not much has changed so far as a consequence of the liberalistion policy. This was supported by the fact that most companies did not set out new production or market activities. While the rationalization of the licensing system was started successfully, this was not an incentive for the companies to export more, or to expand. Predominantly companies that already exported reduced profit. The companies experienced the removal of import restrictions as the main consequence of the liberalization policy for the Indian tea sector, although the influence of the current imports is negligible. None of the interviewed companies considered more imports to be beneficial. Many foresaw problems when imports would grow especially the small companies that are not into exports. For a large group there is strong confidence in the position of their tea on the domestic market, even when import restrictions are removed further. While on average the companies seem to have gained in international orientation, their view on the domestic market remained largely unchanged. Although many of the companies that participate in the research had invested significantly, the situation for India as a whole must be different, considering the large amount of large companies that joined the research. Currently, the average Indian tea company appears not able to withstand competition from imports.

SECTION II
International Matchmaking and Business Partnering

In recent decades, industrialized countries have developed a number of direct instruments to help their national companies to become active in the developing world. In matchmaking and similar business-partnering programmes, the sponsoring organization generally provides technical or financial assistance to private sector partners in order to foster cooperation and help the companies to develop a profitable relationship.

What kind of Matchmaking?: Many linkage programmes directly encourage European companies to invest in developing countries, including LDCs such as Bangladesh, Mozambique, United Republic of Tanzania and Uganda. Most of the matchmaking and partnering programmes are aimed at small and medium-sized enterprises (SMEs) in the industrialized and developing countries. Experience in rich as well as poor countries shows that the potential of SMEs to have a substantial impact on the development process in much greater than that of micro-enterprises.

Some Examples: Some of the more developed programmes sponsored by European countries include:

- the Programme for Cooperation with Emerging Markets (PSOM–Programma Samenwerking Opkomende Markten) run by Senter International, an independent agency of the Netherlands, Ministry of Economic Affairs under sponsorship of the Netherlands Aid Ministry;
- the Public-Private Partnership (PPP) project run by the German Technical Cooperation Agency, GTZ (Gesellschaft for Technische Zusammanarbeit);
- the Matchmaking Programme of the Norwegian Aid Agency, NORAD; and
- the DANIDA Private Sector Development (PSD) programme of the Danish Aid Agency.

All of these programmes are relatively new. PSOM started in 1997 in China, Egypt, India and South Africa, but activities in LDCs began only in 1999, though it has expanded rapidly, matching more than 100 projects to date. NORAD's

Matchmaking Programme, which started in 1995, has focused on only two countries until now, South Africa and Sri Lanka, though NORAD is considering expanding to others soon. The DANIDA programme has existed since 1995 and currently supports cooperation between Danish firms and companies on 11 countries, including Bangladesh, Mozambique, Nepal and Uganda.

NORAD—A Focused Approach: Norwegian companies which are looking for a partner in a developing country submit a profile to the coordinating center in Norway, which reviews it and sends it to a corresponding center in the host country. When a match is found, NORAD can back the Norwegian company with up to US$ 2290 as a grant for the first trip. If the parties agree to develop their relationship further, they can apply to NORAD for various types of industrial and commercial support. Developing country companies can also initiate the process.

In Sri Lanka, for example, the programmme has received 120 profiles from Norwegian companies since 1995. Of these, 104 matches were found, 78 of the companies made visits to Sri Lanka and 22 have carried out preliminary studies. In all, 16 companies have signed cooperative agreements and 12 joint ventures have been formed. NORAD has also been contacted directly by 96 Sri Lankan companies. The collaboration encompasses diverse branches including boat building, furniture and mattress production, fishing, data processing and environmental inspections.

GTZ—Rapid Expansion: The German Public-Private Partnership is aimed at companies that would not, on their own, have the resources to find appropriate partners abroad. The PPP steps in with support when their projects are considered worthwhile from a development perspective, and financial assistance can support the sustainability of the ventures. PPP projects are planned, financed and implemented jointly. There are no pre-qualifications by country or sector. The companies submit their proposals directly to GTZ and go though a six step feedback and approval process. Since PPP began in 1999, more than 100 projects have been implemented in many countries, including Bangladesh, Ethiopia, Mali, Senegal, United Republic of Tanzania and

Uganda. One example is the cooperation with the Association of German Flower Traders. Increasingly, German consumers want assurances that production follows international environmental and social norms. Flower farms are certified and receive the "Flower Label". LDC producers that join the Flower Label partnership agree to respect ecological standards, eliminate child labour, protect mothers and implement minimum wages. Producers in five African countries and 36 German importers have joined the programme.

Matchmaking Programmes—Common Fruits:

- Identification of target countries.
- Establishment of country-specific parameters.
- *Call for project proposals:* SMEs in the donor country are invited to make proposals for investment on the basis of the parameters decided. An announcement is also made in the recipient country(ies), generally through the local embassy. The call for proposals specifies the maximum assistance budget, partner contribution requirements, minimum scope of activities, etc.
- *The "matchmaking" stage:* This may be done in various ways. For example, a donor country enterprises may identify a potential developing country partner on its own; or, in the recipient country, an enterprise with a concrete idea may actively seek a partner in the donor country. The sponsoring institution generally arranges for matchmaking though its local embassy or implementing agent in the LDC, and thorugh its own contacts with the donor-country business community.
- *Project submission, evaluation and selection:* Projects are submitted to the sponsoring agency and then evaluated by country and sector experts. A contract is signed with the partners laying out the various responsibilities and setting time frames for implementation.
- Project implementation and performance reviews : The sponsoring agency supervises the implementation of the project and periodically reviews its performance.

The DANIDA Concept of Business Linkages: DANIDA's approach is similar to that of GTZ. Danish companies are invited to submit proposals for cooperation with a partner in one of 11 target countries, including Bangladesh. Mozambique, Nepal, Nicaragua, United Republic of Tanzania and Uganda. The LDC company can also submit a proposal and ask for help in finding a suitable Danish partner. The programme provides a combination of advisory services, grants and loans to the partners.

US Efforts: In the United States, the US Chamber of Commerce has begun a matchmaking operation with support from the United States Agency for International Development. The operation was initially oriented towards South East Asia, but the organization is considering expanding its activities to other regions, including LDCs. Its Strategic International Assistance and Matchmaking programme, for example, concerns Thai-US partnerships exclusively, with the objective of providing assistance in finding potential trade and investment partners for long-term relationships and laying out the institutional and financial framework so that the programme can be sustained independently.

Issue of Capital Supply: Since many of these linkage programmes are quite innovative, the instruments themselves are more or less pilot programmes. One of the issues on which the programmes differ is the need for inclusion of a capital component. Most of the bilateral programmes, such as DANIDA's or the German PPP, concentrate on the 'software', i.e. technical assistance and training, market and feasibility studies or project management. These elements are wholly or partially financed on a grant basis.

The Dutch programme, PSOM, provides a capital component for machinery, buildings and materials on a grant basis (up to two-thirds of the cost). This approach differs from that of other programmes, which leave this aspect to financial institutions. DANIDA also realized that an investment project might need a capital component and can provide loans within the framework of its programme, but the interest charged is close to market rates.

PSOM's experience shows that the combination of a capital and technical component within the same programme through a partial grant appeals to many companies. Even in an LDC like Mozambique, the threshold has proved low enough for companies to embark on an investment with local partners on a pilot basis.

It seems clear that private companies willing to invest in developing countries, where the market is considered highly volatile, are looking for support for the total investment. For SMEs that need only modest investment capital (between US$ 0.5 and US $ 2 million), there are few alternatives. Financial institutions such as the International Finance Corporation (IFC) or the European Investment Bank (EIB) are interested solely in big loans with a minimum of approximately US$ 5 million. They also usually charge market rates and, in addition, sometimes require payment of administrative fees. Private sector development schemes such as matchmaking fill that gap.

Conclusion

Liberalisation in the tea sector only took place to a small extent, because the companies have problems to survive with the high taxation and the increasing production costs. The interest of the government in the employment and the supply of cheap drinks on the domestic market are too strong to liberalise more. In general, the liberalization measures that turned out to have significant effect on the business of the tea companies all benefit the large or exporting companies this did not result in an increase of exports, the large companies have showed strong expansion movements; many mergers and large acquisitions took place by the large tea companies. Small companies did not show significant expansion activities. This concentration of power in the tea sector is the clearest result of the liberalization policy for the Indian tea companies so far.

12

Aspects of Orthodox Tea in Darjeeling: Some Uniqueness, Orthodox Tea Manufacture

SECTION I
Darjeeling Tea, Some Uniqueness

The Inception

The story of Darjeeling Tea started some 150 years ago, when a Dr. Campbell, a civil surgeon, planted tea seeds in his garden at Beechwood, Darjeeling, 7000 ft above sea level as an experiment. He was reasonably successful in raising the plant because the government, in 1847, elected to put out tea nurseries in this area.

According to records, the commercial tea gardens planted out by the British Tea interests were Tukvar, Steinthal, and Aloobari tea estates. This was in 1852 and all these plantations used seeds that were raised in the government nurseries.Darjeeling was then only a sparsely populated hamlet which was being used as a hill resort by the army and some affluent people. Tea, being labour intensive enterprise, required sufficient number of workers to plant, tend, pluck and finally manufacture the produce. For this, employment was offered to people from across the border of Nepal. It appears that in 1866, Darjeeling had 39 gardens producing a total crop of

21,000 kgs of tea. In 1870, the number of gardens increased to 56 to produce about 71,000 kgs of tea harvested from 4400 hectares. During 1860-64, the Darjeeling Company was established with 4 gardens while the Darjeeling Consolidated Tea Co. dates back to 1896. By 1874, tea in Darjeeling was found to be a profitable venture and there were 113 gardens with approximately 6000 hectares.

Present Scenario

Today there are 86 running gardens producing Darjeeling Tea on a total area of 19,000 hectares. The total production ranges from 10 to 11 million kgs annually. The tea industry in the Darjeeling at present employs over 52 thousand people on a permanent basis, while a further 15,000 persons are engaged during the plucking season which lasts from March to November. A unique feature of this work force is that more than 60 per cent are women and the employment is on a family basis. Income of a garden worker is half in the form of cash and other half by way of perquisites which have over the years effectively provided a cushion against the impact of inflation and scarcities, for example, the workers are provided with free accommodation, subsidized cereal ration and free medical benefits. Gardens used to run primary schools which have since been taken over by the government but the buildings continues to be maintained by the garden management. According to the Census carried out in the hills in 1971, the total population of three hill sub-divisions of district viz. Darjeeling, Kurseong and Kalimpong was approximately 600,000. From the records maintained by the tea gardens, the resident population is over 300,000. Apart from tourism, tea is the biggest industrial activity, offering the largest employment in the hills. The turnover of the Darjeeling tea industry is nearly USD 7.5 million, which is acknowledged to be more than the money generated by tourism in the Darjeeling hills.Besides, a large segment of the population earn their livelihood from the peripheral sector of the industry. This consists of transport, supplies, repair, establishment, forests, fertilizers, coal etc.

Processing of Tea—The Arts of Plucking and Stages of Manufacturing

Plucking—Proper plucking of Darjeeling tea leaves is as unique as its flavour. Great emphasis is given to plucking as true quality is inherent in a good raw material (tea leaf) and the special Darjeeling flavour is generated from the very fine plucking standard. He smallest shoots, comprising of two leaves and a bud are plucked. It requires 22,000 such shoots, all plucked by hand to produce 1 kg of tea. In attaining this high plucking standard, the hilly terrain makes the task even more difficult. Darjeeling tea pluckers have strived hard for years, battling against difficult terrain, cold, mist, rainfall etc. to maintain exacting standards. They begin early in the morning, when the overnight dew is still present. Only the tenderest leaves are finely plucked by gentle hands. Pluckers are so quick and skilful that it is often impossible to follow the motion of their hands and fingers as they pluck.

Processing—Darjeeling tea leaves are processed in the traditional Orthodox Form. Very careful and gentle treatment must be given to the finely plucked leaves so that the inherent quality is not lost. Although the stages of manufacturing are uniform, application is varied according to the leaf quality, climate etc.

Stages of Manufacture

(i) *Withering:* During this process, the green leaves are evenly spread on troughs through which hot and cold air are blown in a regulated manner. The object is to move moisture in the leaf slowly over a period of 14-16 hours.

(ii) *Rolling:* The withered leaves are loaded into rollers where they are twisted by a mechanical action. The process is carefully monitored so that the style of the leaf is maintained and overheating does not take place.

(iii) *Fermentation:* After Rolling, the leaf is spread in a cool and humid room in very thin layer. The process lasts between 2-4 hours, depending on temperature, humidity and leaf quality. During the process tea develops a

unique flavoru and aroma. The tea makers' sensory judgement is critical to quality of the liquor.

(iv) *Drying (Firing):* The fermented leaf is taken to a dryer where it is subjected to regulated varying temperature for a period of 20-30 minutes. The result is black tea whose moisture has been lost after natural fermentation is checked.

(v) *Sorting and Packing:* This is the final stage, where the tea is graded according to the size and packed in specially designed foil lined packages.

The Art of Testing (in Factory), Tasting Procedure and Selling

Testing—Darjeeling tea tasting is a refined art, which necessarily encompasses a large number of variables. A taster palate and factory senses are finely sensitive and highly discriminatory. An experienced taster can identify the garden, ambient conditions of the plucking day and can even suggest adjustments in the manufacturing process. A taster uses his sharp sense of sight, smell, touch and taste while judging the quality of tea. A taster must also have an in-depth knowledge about the prevailing market conditions, consumer preferences and manufacturing techniques while evaluating the tea. These are endowments of birth – it would be true to say that tasters are born and not made. These natural talents, however, have to be trained and developed through long years of practice before the palate is proficient enough to register the minute differences. This is particularly true for Darjeeling tea tasters as the quality of tea differs from invoice to invoice. It is an exclusive tea and has not yardstick to standardize.

Tasting in the Factory—It is only an excellent cup that truly cheers and taste is perceptible only by the human palate. No wonder that this craft is viewed with a tinge of awe and wonderment.

Tasting Procedure—In the tasting procedure, pots and cups made of the finest china, kept spotlessly clean, are used; 2.5 grms of each tea is weighed into pots and water which has just come to the boil is poured over it. The pots are then covered with a lid and the tea is infused for either 5 or 6 minutes, depending on the individual taster preference. The liquor is poured out into a cup and the tea is ready for tasting.

The colour and evenness of the infusion, as also its nose, are an index to the intrinsic value of the brew. This examination takes place in a well lit room away from direct sunlight, shade and shadow. Light from the north, which is steady and uniform, is ideal. The scrutiny of the leaf and infusion over, the taster turns his attention to the liquor and takes a sip from the cup, rolls it in his mouth and spits it out. In that split second, the palate registers the taste—flavour, briskness, strength and any faults and flaws are recorded and the taster is ready with his judgement.

The Art of Selling—Darjeeling tea like any world famous product, requires an efficient and reliable marketing network to promote and sell it world wide. The Auction system is a crucial channel in the sale of Darjeeling tea. Since more than 50 per cent of the produce is sold through the Kolkata Auction Centre, the role of the auction system can be viewed as a barometer to access the prevailing markets. The auctioneer plays an important role. Apart form personally tasting and evaluating each and every invoice, he has to use his knowledge of the world demand and marketing skill in judging the marketability of the tea. He has final jurisdiction and his judgement determines the selling price of the tea, to a certain extent.

The four registered Brokers, selling the maximum quantity of Darjeeling tea, are: (1) J Thomas & Co. Pvt. Ltd., (2) Carritt Moran & Co. Ltd. (3) Contemporary Targett Ltd., (4) Paramount Tea Marketing Pvt. Ltd.

Tea Glossary Different Grades and Varieties of Darjeeling Orthodox Tea

Kind of Tea	*Grade Name*	*Nomenclature*
Whole Leaf	FTGFOP	Fine Tippy Golden Flowery Orange Pekoe
	TGFOP	Tippy Golden Flowery Orange Pekoe
	TGFOP1	Tippy Golden Flowery Orange Pekoe One
	GFOP	Golden Flowery Orange Pekoe
	FOP	Flowery Orange Pekoe
	OP	Orange Pekoe

Broken	BOP1	Broken Orange Pekoe One
	GFBOP	Golden Flowery Broken Orange Pekoe
	BPS	Broken Pekoe Souchong
	GBOP	Golden Broken Orange Pekoe
	FBOP	Flowery Broken Orange Pekoe
	BOP	Broken Orange Pekoe
Fannings	TGOF	Tippy Golden Orange Fannings
	GOF	Golden Orange Fannings
	OG	Orange Fannings
GREEN TEA		
Whole Leaf	YH	Young Hyson
	FYH	Fine Young Hyson
Broken	GP	Gun Powder
	H	Hyson
	FH	Fine Hyson
Fannings	SOUMEE	Soumee
Dust	DUST	Dust

Different Seasons

(i) *Easter Flush:* These are springtime teas, harvested from late February to Mid-April. The young leaves yield a light tea with a flavour of green Muscat. Their arrival impatiently awaited by connoisseurs, and they are sometimes specially airlifted to the buyers around the world. A gentle, afternoon tea.

(ii) *Spring Flush:* Harvested in May and June, these teas are more fully constructed than First Flush varieties. The liquor is bright, the taste full and round with a fruity note. An afternoon tea.

(iii) *Summer Flush:* During this period the nature of the liquor changes, becoming stronger, yet retaining the brightness and character that Darjeeling is known for.

(iv) *Autumn Flush:* These autumn-harvest Darjeelings are characterized by large leaves that give a round taste and coppery liquor. They can be drunk in the morning with a bit of cold milk.

Taster's Language

Bloom: A sign of good manufacture and sorting (where reduction of leaf has taken place before firing) a sheen that has not been lost through over-handling or over-sorting.

Make: A term used to describe tea manufacture, in tea taster terms make means a well made tea or not true to its grade.

Well Twisted: Used to describe Whole-leaf Orthodox tea grades, often referred to as well made or rolled.

Wiry: Leaf appearance of a well-twisted, thin, long leaf.

Aroma: Smell or scent denoting inherent character usually in tea grown at high altitudes.

Bright: A lively bright appearance, which usually indicates that the tea will produce a bright liquor.

Brisk: The most live characteristic, results from good manufacture.

Character: An attractive taste, specific to growth origin describing teas grown at high altitudes.

Flat: Not fresh, usually due to age, the tea tends to lose its characteristics and taste, unlike some wine which mature with age.

Flavour: A most desirable extension of character caused by slow growth at high altitudes. Relatively rare.

Harsh: A taste generally due to the leaf being under withered during manufacture resulting in a very rough taste.

High-Fired: High-fired, over fired or dried, but not bakey or burnt.

Muscatel: Desirable character in Darjeeling teas. A grapey taste.

Soft: The opposite of briskness. Tea lacking live characteristics and is caused by inefficient fermentation and/ or dying.

Frequently Asked Questions

(i) What is Darjeeling Tea?

(ii) Where is Darjeeling Tea produced and what is its Annual Production?

(iii) What makes Darjeeling Tea so Exclusive?

(iv) What are Different Flavours associated with Darjeeling Tea?

(v) What is the importance of the Darjeeling Logo?

(vi) How to make a cup of Darjeeling Tea?

(vii) What should be checked before buying a packet of Darjeeling Tea?

What is Darjeeling Tea?: According to the Tea Board of India—"Darjeeling Tea" means tea which has been cultivated, grown, produced, manufactured and processed in tea gardens (current schedule whereof is attached hereto) in the hilly areas of Sadar Sub-Division, only hilly areas of Kalimpong Sub-Division comprising of Samabeong Tea Estate, Ambiok Tea Estate, Mission Hill Tea Estate and Kumai Tea Estate and Kurseong Sub-Division excluding the areas in jurisdiction list 20, 21, 23, 24, 29, 31 and 33 comprising Subtiguri Sub-ivision of New Chumta Tea Estate, Simulbari and Mariobari Tea Estate of Kurseong Policy Station in Kurseong Sub-Division of the District of Darjeeling in the State of West Bengal, India. Also, tea which has been processed and manufactured in a factory located in the aforesaid area and which, when brewed, has a distinctive, naturally occurring aroma and taste with light tea liquor and the infused leaf of which has a distinctive fragrance.

Where is Darjeeling Tea Produced and What its Annual Production?: Darjeeling Tea is grown and produced only in the hilly area of Darjeeling district. There are only 86 Tea Estates which produce Darjeeling tea. All of these are in Darjeeling District and only teas coming from these estates can be called Darjeeling tea. It cannot be produced anywhere else in the world. Annual Production of Darjeeling tea is approximately 10 million kgs.

What makes Darjeeling Tea so Exclusive?: Darjeeling tea widely and universally acknowledged to be the finest tea, because its flavour is so unique that it cannot be replicated anywhere else in the world. It has no equal. Grown in the romantic and mystical mountainous region of Darjeeling at an elevation of 750-2000 metre, the tea is imbued with an incomparable charisma and quality. Grown in century old tea gardens, these tea bushes are nurtured by intermittent rainfall, sunshine and moisture laden mellow mists. The soil is rich and the hilly terrain provides natural drainage for the generous rainfall the district receives.

Even the tea pluckers, well aware of the status their produce enjoys throughout the world, pick only the finest two leaf and the bud to enhance the unique flavour which has been described as Muscatelo. Gifted with these natural elements, the simple fact that only 10 million kgs of tea, produced annually by the Darjeeling district, has made it all more exclusive and desirable. Adherance to this high quality profile results in extremely low yields. The Darjeeling planters have never succumbed to the temptation of increasing yields at the expense of quality and make every effort to ensure the highest quality standard, inspite of the high costs involved.

What are the Different Flavours associated with Darjeeling Tea?

The flavours of Darjeeling Tea differs from season to season. According to the plucking period, the seasons can be categorized as under:

(i) *Easter Flush (March–April):* It arrives just after the dormant winter months. The leaves are tender and very light, green in appearance. The liquor too is light, clear, bright and imparts a pleasant brisk flavour.

(ii) *Spring Flush (May-June):* This flush is famed for its prominent quality. The leaf has a purplish bloom. The liquor is more round, mellow and with more colour (amber) and has a slightly fruity flavour. It is during this period that the famous Mucatelo flavour becomes pronounced.

(iii) *Summer Flush (July-September):* During this period the nature of the liquor changes, becoming stronger, yet retaining the brightness and character that Darjeeling is known for.

(iv) *Autumn Flush (October–November):* The tea during this period has a light coppery tinge and liquor ha a delicate character.

(v) *Winter Months (December–February):* Dormant period with no production.

What is the Importance of Darjeeling Logo?: The Darjeeling

Logo is a property of the Tea Board of India. It was launched in 1983. It is a symbol that verifies that the packet/caddy etc. contains 100 per cent pure Darjeeling, unblended with teas from any other growth. There are certain procedures prescribed by the Tea Board of India to be complied with to get permission for the printing of the logo on a product.

How to Make a cup of Darjeeling Tea?: The standard procedure, is, take 1 level tea-spoon of pure tea in each cup. Nothing for the Pot. Pour water, immediately after bringing it to a furious boil. Brew it for 3-4 minutes. If Broken/Fanning grades of tea is used, tea-spoon of tea would suffice. In case milk or sugar is to be added then brewing has to extended to about 5 minutes. The quantity of tea and brewing time can be altered according to personal preference. Iced tea is also popular, with a slice of lemon.

What should be Checked before Buying a packet of Darjeeling Tea?

The Packet must have a Darjeeling Tea Logo, "Darjeeling or Pure Darjeeling or 100 percent Darjeeling must be mentioned.

SECTION II
Orthodox Tea Manufacture

With the globalisation and free market economy the scope of exports and imports have been widened. This has resulted an increased awarness among the consumers and bulk buyers for quality and price.It is, therefore, imperative to produce valu added and quality products for survival of any units.Good orthodox tea production can can add value to teas provided standard is maintained at all stages of harvesting and manufacturing.

Factors Responsible for Good Orthodox Manufacture

There are various factors which are responsible for manufacture of good orthodox teas. These are quality of raw materials, good plucking, pruning percentage, transportation of green leaf, withering etc. Details are presented below:

Quality of Raw Material: Like any other product good raw material is required to produce a high class orthodox tea. This raw material includes selection of: *(a)* Green leaf from clonal sections which possesses high pubescent hairs on the leaf and tips like P126A, N436, TV 14, TV 17, S3A3 and seed jats like Betjan and Khorijan etc., and *(b)* fine plucking of Green leaf from such selection. The fine count should be between 70-75 per cent to make best possible tea during second flush and 65-70 per cent thereafter. Green leaf should contain maximum number of two and a bud and about 7-10 per cent one and a bud.

In orthodox production tips play a very important role to push the price of tea apart form other characteristics which will be discussed later. When the plucking standard is poor the tip content shows decline because three leaves and a bud and banji leaves etc. make much of the volume. As the size of the leaf grows larger due to opening of buds into leaves the size of the tip decreases and the bulk of the non-tippy material increases. It is, therefore, important to enforce 7 days plucking round, and to pluck in such a fashion that mostly 2 and a bud, are harvested. This way the tip content in tea will remain prominent. Moreover stalk content remains low with good plucking. The presence of tips increases the value of tea but the presence of stalks reduces it drastically. Orthodox can be produced from ordinary clones and seed jats too. Provided the above conditions are maintained, but the manufacture may not fetch the best price.

Good Plucking Gives Good Liquor: Good plucking also gives good liquor because the fine parts of the tea shoot contain higher percentage of tea tannin. Tocklai provides the following figures of tea tannin and caffeine (Tables 1 & 2) in different parts of the shoot:

Caffeine content in tea shoot also reduces as the shot gets older. Caffeine content is maximum in bud followed by 1st leaf, second leaf and third leaf in the order. Caffeine determines the creaming behaviour of tea. Tea cream is the material that settles down on cooling the tea infusion, is a complex of Tehaflovin, Thearubins, Caffeine and Polyphenolic material. Caffeine is an important constituent of the infused

Table 1: Leaf Size and Tanning

Leaf Size	Percentage of Tannin
Bud	26.5
1st Leaf	25.9
2nd Leaf	20.7
3rd Leaf	17.1
Upper Stem	11.5
Lower Stem	5.3

Source: The Assam Review and Tea News, November, 2002.

Table 2: Tea Shoot and Caffeine Tea Shoot

	Caffeine Content
1 + Bud	5.30
2 + Bud	4.20
3 + Bud	3.38
4 + Bud	3.20

Source: The Assam Review and Tea News, November 2002.

brew responsible for briskness of the liquor due to its association with Theaflovins and Thearubins.

Pruning Percentage: In case one likes to make 100 per cent or higher percentage of orthodox, it is important to adopt well balanced pruning style. Under-pruned garden hardly can help in producing good quality orthodox tea. Un-pruned pays handsomely in the first flush but as the season progresses the quality of leaf drops and poor tea is produced. Therefore, pruning is important. There is no doubt that if un-pruned is plucked well it will produce stylish tea, which is one of the major characteristics of good orthodox manufacture due to small size of the leaves. It is suggested to keep the un-pruned percentage between 25-30 per cent or even low. Good plucking is the main requirement to make good tea. Plucker should develop the habit of breaking back the larger leaf and the long stalk while plucking.

Transportation of Green leaf: In orthodox manufacture the degree of wither is more concerned to attain style and twisted tea. Therefore, green leaves need more time to wither. This can better be obtained if three weigthmetns are taken. It also becomes easy to transport the leaf to the factory within a minimum time after plucking. Green leaves should remain fresh, and not get damaged in the plucking basket or in nylon bag. Green leaf should be handled gently while filling in the basket and should not over load the basket. Over loading and forcible pushing may damage the leaves and inviting fermentation which will result in poor liquor and dull infusion. As soon as green leaves arrive in the factory it should be unloaded immediately on the withering troughs and compactness formed in the containers should be dispersed to eliminate the heat generated.

Withering: Withering is the next important stage of manufacturing. The size of the leaf varies with the type of prune. Light pruned leaf is larger than deep skiff and the deep skiff is again larger than unpruned. These different types of prune should be kept separately in the withering troughs to attain uniform wither as light pruned leaves and skiff leaves take more time to wither than un-pruned and light skiffed leaves.

Uniform Withering: Segregation of green leaves of different prunes is one step to achieve uniform withering. The next step is uniform spreading of leaf on the withering troughs. Always leave at least 4″–5″ area from the one end of the trough and then start spreading to fill up the space left. This method ensures that the leaf is fluffed and spread properly. If it is not spread properly air escapes from certain portion and blowing takes place resulting in damaging the leaves at blown out places and if the air is not fully distributed in the whole trough it gives uneven wither. When leaf is spread, fluffed and evenly distributed on the trough withering will be good. Orthodox producing gardens should have sufficient space for proper withering.

Slow Withering: Slow withering is better than fast withering by applying high heated air within a short time. Higher temperature only damages and dries the lower portion of the leaf bed and the tea produced will be open and leaving in more fanning and dust grades. The golden rule is to apply hot air when required at lower temperature for longer time. When ambient temperature is high one should avoid the use of hot air in the trough by a skillful use of reverse and forward air flow. On very hot days reverse flow may damage the upper layer of the leaf bed. It can be avoided by applying reverse air in the evening when the temperature drops. Aim green wither without causing any damage to the leaves. Sometimes damaged leaf with excessive handling is mistaken as high withered. Check the leaf stalk, if it breaks, it is a Kutcha wither. The second test is to take a handful of leaves and to make a ball and if the ball remains intact it is a good wither.

Wither and Type of Manufacture

The degrees of wither will depend upon the type of tea one likes to manufacture. For example, in the first flush general demand is clean stylish wiry tea. During second flush tea is preferred with good liquor and golden tips which can be achieved with lighter wither. Thereafter, there maybe demand for clean black and well twisted teas. Withering has to be adjusted depending upon the demand of the market. The ideal wither during second flush is between 67 per cent and 68 per cent for light pruned leaves. In case of unpruned leaves, it varies from 63 per cent to 65 per cent. Wither should be around 65 per cent in case of light prunes and deep skiffs. It ranges from 60 per cent to 62 per cent in case of light skiffs and Unpruned after second flush.

Rolling: Rolling plays a very important role to rapture the cells of leaf and to initiate fermentation. Apart from chemical changes it also physically manipulates the leaf to take the twist which is an important orthodox quality parameter. In the first roll the finer particles of the leaf receives the blow. At least 100-105 minutes of rolling is essential for making well twisted and stylish orthodox tea. It may be reduced if the leaves are super fine. Twist is an important characteristic which may be attained by applying devoted rolling and proper pressure. Devoted rolling means pre-determined rolling time should be followed with accurate pressure sequence. It is always better to break and size the tea in the rolling table than in the tea breaker during sorting since the latter method will make the tea grey. Motorized Pressure Caps will ensure proper pressure. Alarm watches should be made available to the rolling staff for monitoring pressure sequence so that it may be applied as desired. Practical pressure sequence should be applied. It is preferable to have only one time pressure of 35 to 40 minutes roll because too many ups and downs are not practically followed. Every year during over-hauling time the factory manager should check the wells of the rolling tables. In case these are worn out either should be replaced or be repaired. If the wells of the rolling tables are damaged rolling may not take place to the desired level. Wells may be sharpened when required. There should be full movement of the withered leaves in the rolling table. Sometimes it may happen that the leaves may get jammed in the rolling table and there is no movement. It may occur due to continuous long pressure in the rolling table. Withered leaves in the rolling table must rotate and move up and down freely. Long rolling as well as continuous pressure are detrimental to the liquor.

Thick juice of the leaves must appear during rolling. When tips of the leaf take bath in the thick juice, the desired golden tip colour is obtained. Excessive extraction of thin juice gives poor cup character and pale tips. Only proper withering, as explained above, can give golden tips and thick quality cup. Proper feeding in the rolling table is essential as over feeding will not allow full leaf movement and under feeding will spill the leaf on the edges of the rolling table. Ideally, 280-300 kg of withered leaves charged in 46 inches rolling table and 140-150 kg in 36 inches rolling table should be given.

RPM of the Rolling Table: A very high RPM of the Rolling Table will produce more broken and flaky grades whereas right RPM will produce desirable well twisted teas. An ideal RPM of the rolling table should be between 45 to 50. It is better to have rolling tables with variable pulley drive which may be adjusted according to the demand.

Extraction of Fine Particles: One should have three extractions after each roll. It is found that the extraction is better in wire mesh ghoghi. After the first roll one should aim to separate only the finer particles of the leaf which received proper roll due to tenderness of tips and soft leaves. The percentage of the fine leaves should not be more than 20 per cent to 25 per cent otherwise unrolled leaf will find way in the extraction. If the quality of leaf is super fine then the percentage of the first may be more. Extraction of the second roll should be more due to medium pressure. Try to take more extraction in the third roll which receives the hardest pressure. On the whole, an extraction between 65 per cent to 75 per cent is ideal.

Fermentation: Fermentation is a very important step in tea manufacture. During this process the rolled leaf undergoes many chemical changes which bring about briskness, brightness, strength and colour in the liquor. The vacuole in the leaf cell contains a solution of soluble substances like catechins, caffeine, amino acids, sugar etc. In the fluid of the cell there are plastids, containing oxidative enzymes and tea pigments, like chlorophyll and carotene. The object of the fermentation is to bring the above substances together so that the polyphenols can diffuse in the cytoplasm.

Polyphenolic compounds that undergo changes during fermentation are Epigallocatechine, Epigallocatechine gallate and Epicatechine. The above polypheronlic compounds are oxidized to form important group of colour substances that are Theaflavins (TF) and Thearubins (TR).

Caffeine and Pectin present in the leaf also undergo changes. Caffeine reacting with Thearubin forms an insoluble substance which is known as cream. It influences the thickness of the liquor. The chemical changes which takes place during fermentation are influenced by room temperature, humidity, degree of wither taken, leaf structure, severity of processing, in the rolling table and medium of fermentation used etc. Liquor characters which develop during fermentation are briskness, quality, colour and strength. It is quite a difficult task to achieve all the characteristics because, when strength is at its best, the briskness has already dropped. It is, therefore, advisable to have a compromise among all the liquor characters.

How to Determine the Fermentation

Fermentation for orthodox type of manufacture can be done on concrete floor painted with Epalic paint or on aluminium sheet spread on the concrete floor, aluminium sheet racks by spreading uniformly at ¾ inches thickness for fines and 1 inch for course mal or Fermenting Machine. Time of fermentation will vary on different mediums. In order to determine the time one can try the following methods:

- ✓ By conducting experiments of variable period or using nose and by observing colour of the fermenting leaf. When very hard wither is taken one can not determine fermentation time by the latter method because both nose and colour may deceive. There may be great variation in the fermenting time ranging from 1 hour 30 minutes to 3 hours for the same type of manufacture due to the use of different mediums. Therefore, one should determine the time by conducting experiments. Whatever time is decided should be followed strictly. The finer the leaf, the lesser the fermenting time. Less withered leaf also requires less fermenting time. Hard treatment to the leaf requires lesser fermenting time.

Of course, room temperature has also an important role to play.

- ✓ Correct fermentation will produce the best result.
- ✓ Under-fermentation has less TF and TR which results in less brightness and thin liquor.
- ✓ Proper fermentation produces balanced liquor with brightness, briskness and strength.
- ✓ Whereas over-fermentation produces dull, flat and heavy liquor due to less TF and more TR.

Humidification: Humidification is necessary in the rolling as well as in the fermenting room because as the oxidation proceeds, the mass has a tendency to become dry. Under this condition physical contact of enzymes and organic compounds is likely to suffer. Without humidification, it is noticed, that the upper layer of the fermenting bed gets dry and black. It is, therefore, necessary to provide humid air to the mass while rolling, shifting and in the fermenting room. TF formation is favoured at low temperature and peaks at about 28^{0}C to 30^{0}C. Therefore, low temperature leads to brisk tea because of more TF.

Bacteria: In the field the surface of the green leaf carries large number of naturally accruing bacteria. Nearly, 90 per cent of the leaf area is loaded with such bacteria. Bacteria, which develops during tea processing, belongs to the Saprophytes group and attacks only dead tissues or chemical compounds. The average size of the Bacteria is 1/25000 inch in length. It is so small that 3 millions of bacteria may lie on the head of a pin without over lapping. Under favourable conditions of temperature, moisture and food, bacteria cell can divide once in every thirty minutes or less. Accordingly, one bacterium cell produces 1.2 million of bacteria in 12 hours. Under favourable conditions the growth of bacteria can be very rapid especially when fresh food supply is constant. Such situation happen in the tea factory when there is juice in the succeeding roll of leaf.

Bacterial Growth: During rolling there is about 90 per cent drop in the bacterial growth due to the antiseptic properties of oxidized poly-phenols but the surviving bacteria population multiply rapidly during tea processing. This population and can spoil the tea quality which will result in dull infusion and liquor. Therefore, it should be fought at all stages starting from the plucking. Bacterial growth depends on three essentials; temperature, moisture and food. If one of the three can be eliminated, bacterial growth will cease. In order to achieve this, care should be taken to keep all the processing machines, rolling room, fermentation floor or machine cleaned after day's processing. Tea juice left on the machine or on the floor carries great number of bacteria which is carried over with daily processing. Suitable detergent maybe used to wash properly with clean water so that no residue is left. In orthodox manufacture wire mesh ghoghis are the main source of contamination. It should be flamed to kill the bacteria because the rolled leaf and the juice stick on the wire mesh. This gives rise of bacterial infection which is then carried on to the fermentation, and the resultant tea is of poor quality. In the rolling room, bacteria grow if the rolling tables are not cleaned properly and the leaf. The leaf the juice is left on the cap door, and battens.

If there are cracks and holes on the floor the bacteria thrive and mutiply. In the fermenting room bacteria can also spread if the tea juice is left on the floor or on the machine. It is, therefore, necessary to remove the juice deposits and maintain dry conditions which check the bacterial growth. Leaf trolleys should be of aluminium or stainless steel and there should be no crack or dent. When cleaned attention should be given to clean corners and joints. Fermenting floor and fermenting machine should be kept clean and there should not be any left over fermented leaves of the previous batch lying on the floor or machine.

Drying: Drying is very critical for orthodox manufacture. It arrests the fermentation, removes the moisture content from the fermented leaves and obtains a product which is stable for handling and transportation. Drying at a temperature between 195^0–200^0 fahrenheit for 26–28 minutes has shown good results. Exhaust temperature may be kept at 130^0 fahrenheit. It will be difficult to maintain 130 degree fahrenheit exhaust temperature while drying course tea. The exhaust air escapes freely from the top circuit because of large size of the tea. Do not try high temperature when wither is light. This may cause hardening.

It is important to monitor moisture content of tea regularly. Tea with heavy moisture content will produce dull infusion whereas dry tea will produce thin liquor. The ideal moisture content should be between 3 per cent and 3.5 percent. In orthodox drying more volume of air is needed. In the conventional dryer the damper of the inlet fan should be kept fully open.

Tips while Drying Tea

The following points must be remembered while drying tea:

- Check spreaders of the dryers so that tea is evenly fed in the dryer as well as spread also on the top tray.
- One must check the baffles fitted in the dryer to regulate the air supply by spreading all the circuits on the dryer.
- Test inlet and outlet temperature meters with boiling water so that correct temperature is applied.
- The drying chamber should be cleaned to avoid accumulation of leaves in it as that it may not get over-fired.
- The discharge valve of the dryer should be of proper size to facilitate easy way out. Narrow discharge may break the tea and also may cause more accumulation in the drying chamber resulting over drying.
- Perforated trays of the drier should be kept clean to have uniform air flow otherwise it will result in uneven drying.
- There should be sufficient openings over the drier so that there is no back pressure of air and the moist air can escape through the openings, freely.

Sorting of Orthodox Tea

The following points may be remembered while sorting orthodox tea:

- Never sort hot tea as there will be maximum loss of bloom.
- Avoid Repetitions: Orthodox tea is very sensitive and even one presses the tea in his hand it loses its bloom or glaze.

- Sort out tea in such a way to produce more remunerative grades.
- Try to sort out the entire day's bulk including course tea, daily, and do not keep any left over. Generally, the left over is of inferior grade which should be mixed with that day's production. When it is not done in time a large quantity of inferior tea is sorted out later which brings poor average price.
- One has to sort out dryer mouth tea to commercial grades. Orthodox tea is sorted out with the help of Middletons, Arnot sorter, Macintosh sorter, Hexagonal ghoghis, Andrew's Breakers, Tocklai Tea Breaker (TTB), etc.
- Run machines at recommended RPM.
- The sorters must have proper wire meshes fitted to them. It is better to use stainless steel wire mesh because this does less graying of tea than the ordinary steel wire mesh. The mesh when fitted on the sorter should be drum tight. Slack wire mesh will sort uneven grades and the teas will also loose its bloom due to more rubbing against the wire mesh.
- The primary teas should receive minimum handling. In orthodox sorting the tea has to receive several rounds of breaks in the Andrew's Breaker or TTB to achieve proper size of the commercial grades. Too much break may produce the most un-remunerative grades. This can be avoided by skillful use of the machines. For example, Andrew Breaker with 4 or 6 pitches should be used with very little pressure, every time. TTB has a few adjustments to suit one's requirements like number of rods. It contains 12 no. of rods which may be reduced. The machine also has variable speed pulleys to provide three different RPMs. Slow RPM and reduction in the rods will do less breaking.

Stalks Picking

Red stalks in orthodox tea are not desirable. The presence of red stalks indicates poor plucking standard and brings down the value of tea. It is, therefore, necessary to remove the stalks. In most of the factories stalks are picked manually by deploying women. It is a labour intensive operation, and the productivity varies from 6 to 10 kg per manday. A garden which produces 100 per cent orthodox has nearly 45 per cent for stalk picking. This is not possible on a daily basis. As a result, a huge stock is built up in the sorting room. So, dispatch is delayed and a valuable quantum could not reach the auction center on time and later on fetches poor price. In order to sort out this problem one should use available machines in the market for stalk cleaning. Manual stalk picking can not be completely eliminated but certainly it can be minimized to a great extent.

Bulking of Tea

Proper Bulking of sorted tea before packing is very important. There may be variance in day to day manufacturing due to difference in leaf type. Tip content in drier mouth also varies every day. It is, therefore, necessary to bulk or mix properly the graded tea sorted on different days before packing, so that, there is no difference in tea packed either in chests or in paper sacks. Any variation detected by buyers later on may even lead to rejection of consignment, causing great loss to the producer. Good orthodox tea can improve the average price provided high standard is maintained. The process is starting form selection of suitable raw material, maintaining good plucking standard, attaining uniform withering, following proper rolling sequence, and producing remunerative tea grades to suit the demand of the market.

Conclusion

In order to make Darjeeling tea much remunerative there is urgent need to have a holistic approach which will take care of all the operations undertaken in both field and factory levels. Further, the various stakeholders of the industry must make interface session to chalk out an effective plan which is based on SMART (specific, measureable, attainable, reasonable and time-bound) principle.

PART III
ORGANIC PRODUCTS, PRUNING TEA SCIENCE, LITTLE-KNOWN FACTS OF TEA, ENVIRONMENTAL LAW, CONSERVATION OF ECO-SYSTEM, EFFICIENT MANAGEMENT PRACTICES ETC.

This part outlines major aspects like Taste for Organic Products and Pruning in Tea Sciences; Environmental Law, Conservation of Eco System in Tea industry and Managing Tea Imports; Plant and Plantings, Supervisory Management at Tea Gardens, Cooperative/Bought Leaf Factory, Development Initiatives/Major Highlights, Present Tea Scenario, Tips on Efficient management Practices,and Scientific Problems of Tea Plantation.

Part III consists of three chapters (13th to 15th) and confines to issues like taste of organic products, pruning tea sciences, little known facts of tea, and management practices. In Chapter 13 efforts have been endeavoured to ink the picture of international trade in organic products, strong growth potentials, consumer awareness of health and environmental issues, introduction of new standard of agricultural production, risk factors, opportunities for developing countries—products of tropical, off season, in season and novelty/speciality in nature, trade with certified partnor, market entry, tips for developing countries. Pruning is one of the most important agricultural practices, govern frame development and sanitation, control plucking table height and rejuvenates or stimulate vegetative growth etc. A detailed discussions on lung pruning replaced by cut-across pruning, use of pruning machine in mature tea field little knwon facts of tea highlighting first recorded tea tax, tea as a medicine, spin-off effect of tea, a real tea break, tea as breakfast, afternoon tea, reading tea levaes etc. have been made. Tea being eco-friendly industry contributes to promote and sustain tea industry. In recent past, agreement regarding coal briquette as alternative fuel in place of fire wood is a land mark in preventing environmental pollution. Environmental law, conservation of eco system in tea industry and managing tea imports are also been documented in

Chapter 14. Of late tea gardens are required to obtain letter from pollution Board for operating strictly as per provision of section 25 and 26 (prevention and control of pollution) Act, 1974 and Section 21 of Air (Prevention and Control of Pollution) Act provision. Further, change over from "Chemical Intensive Pest Control" to "Bio-intensive Pest Management" has taken place in tea gardens as per guidance and specification of Tea Research Institute. The issues in relation to conservation of eco-system in hill areas, prevention of tillage farming on the slopping farm lands, desirability of sustainable farming of slopping land are identified with remedial measures in this Chapter. Managing tea import has squarly been debated in chapter 15 . It suggests prudent labour utilization plan, supervisory management of tea gardens, development initiatives, major highlights and tips on efficient management of tea gardens and little known facts.

13

Taste for Organic Products and Pruning Tea Sciences, Little Known Facts of Tea

SECTION I
Growing Taste for Organic Products

Picture of International Trade in Organic Products

Although the lack of specific trade statistics prevents a complete picture of international trade in organic products, retail sales figures provide some under standing of its magnitude. International Trade Centre (ITC) research suggests that retail sales in Europe, Japan and the United States—the major markets for these products—more than doubled between 1997 and 2001 (from an estimated US$ 10 billion to about US$21 billion). With retail sales of around US$9.5 billion in 2001 (or 1.5 per cent to 2 per cent of total food sales), the United States is the world's largest market for this product group.

Strong Growth Potential: Sales figures alone for the sector are impressive. It is also interesting to look at organic food sales in terms of percentage of total food sales (organic and non-organic). At present they are still quite small—varying between 1 per cent and 3 per cent of total food sales in the major world markets—and thus indicate a strong potential for growth.

Sustainability: Industry sources in the United States expect the strong growth of recent years to continue over the short to medium term. According, to the Organic Consumer Trends 2001, published by the Natural Marketing Institute in cooperation with the Organic Trade Association (OTA), retail sales could reach US$ 20 billion in 2005.

Consumers Want Organics: Confident growth expectations are based on a strong and increasing consumer awareness of health and environmental issues, including a growing resistance towards food products made with genetically modified organisms. Food and beverage suppliers are catching on to the trend towards healthier eating and drinking – in fact, their actions make it likely that they will fuel greater demand. Many retailers have embarked on increasingly aggressive and targeted marketing and promotion for organic products. The marketing is likely to intensify as more mainstream retailers move into the organic trade. Major food manufacturers are also taking an increasing interest in developing organic product lines.

New Standards: In the United States, recently introduced national standards on organic agricultural production and handling are likely to have a significant impact on the development of the industry. Throughout the value chain, from the farmer to the final consumer, the standards will increase the focus on organic products.

Some Risk: Although the overall picture looks very positive, suppliers should bear in mind potential risk factors. First, occasional or more regular oversupply of certain products or product groups may have immediate and longer-term negative effects. For example, prices of organic products could drop, leading to insufficient profitability for producers and traders. Second, other forms of environmentally friendly and sustainable agriculture may provide increased competition in the future. Integrated farming systems that combine the use of chemical and biological controls (for instance, for pest, nutrient or week management) provide some examples. Buyers might see these integrated systems, which reduce but do not eliminate the use of chemicals, as an acceptable compromise between organic farming and conventional intensive agriculture.

Niches for Developing Countries: Types of products needed aregiven below

(i) tropical (grown outside the United states);

(ii) Off-season (when demand is unmet outside the United States growing season);

(iii) In-season (when demand exceeds the United States supply); and

(iv) Novelty/speciality products.

Finally media reporting of fraud, in the form of unscrupulous traders selling non-organic products for a higher price a organic foodstuff, could make the market more skeptical of products labeled as organic. Even if time proves the forecast of market expansion to be accurate. Growth rates in the United States are bound to slow down or stagnate at some stage. This would be similar to the slow-down that took place in certain European markets after years of rapid growth. They are Denmark and Switzerland (although growth appears to be picking up again).

Opportunities for Developing Countries: On balance, there is little doubt that the United States market will continue to offer producers of organic products interesting business opportunities. The question is whether they are domestic players or foreign traders who are looking for new markets. As far as developing countries are concerned, the product categories below should prove the most important:

- *Products, mostly tropical, that are not produced in the United States* (or only in very small quantities). Examples include coffee, cocoa and tea, most tropical fruit and vegetables (both in fresh and processed form, eg. fruit juices, concentrates and pulp), various spices and herbs, and dried fruit and nuts. Suppliers will be producers in developing countries.
- *Off-season products* such as fresh fruit and vegetables that are produced in the United States, but for which there is an unmet demand during certain periods of the year (outside the growing season in the United

States). Potential suppliers will mainly be producers in the southern hemisphere.

- *In-season products* such as fruit and vegetables, for which there is a temporary or more regular shortage because of strong and increasing demand. Suppliers are likely to include producers in developed and developing countries.
- *Novelty or speciality products* like high-quality organic wines, certain ethnic food products or retail-packed food products. At present, European food exporters are the biggest foreign players in this segment, though some developing countries might also profit from such opportunities, eg, wine exporters in Argentina, Chile and South Africa.

What is Organic Farming?: Organic foodstuff is produced with a commitment to respect biological and ecological processes. Organic agriculture is based on a holistic viewpoint that perceives nature as m ore than just the separate, individual elements into which it may be split. The principles of organic farming are found in ecology, a science concerned with the inter-relationship of living organisms and their environments. The concept of organic farming also covers economic and social aspects of agricultural production, local as well as global.

The aim of organic farming is to support and strengthen biological processes without recourse to synthetic fertilisers and pesticides and the genetic modification of organisms. Hence, this method takes mainly a preventive approach to controlling weeds, pests and diseases

New Standards define "Organic: In order to ensure that organic products are indeed produced according to organic farming principles, they, or rather the whole production and handling process from the farmer to the consumer, must be certified "organic". By certification, a third party (an accredited body) gives written assurance that a product labeled as organic is produced according to recognized standards for organic farming.

Certification is a necessary condition for international trade in organic products. When entering a market, suppliers should ensure that their products are certified as meeting the standards applicable in that particular market. Producers who supply several different markets should be aware that organic standards may differ somewhat from market to market, although they are generally based on the same principles.

Most import demand in the foreseeable future is likely to be for organic fresh produce (fruit and vegetable); bulk-packed organic raw material for repacking; or ingredients for further processing/packaging. Suppliers of other organic products, including processed and/or packaged items may also find buyers in the United States.

Based on national standards for organic production and handling, the National Organic Programme (NOP) of the United States Department of Agriculture (USDA) determines four categories of organic product:

A. *100 percent organic:* products containing only organically-produced ingredients.

B. *Organic:* products containing 95 per cent organically produced ingredients by weights.

C. *Made with organic ingredients:* a product containing more than 70 per cent organic ingredients. A maximum of three of the organically-produced ingredients can be specified on the principal display panel of the packaging.

D. *Processed products containing less than 70 per cent organically-produced ingredients* cannot use the term "organic" in the principal display panel, but the ingredients statement on the product's information panel can specify those ingredients that are organically produced.

Trade with Certified Partners: Any producer considering exporting to the United States should work with a reputable importer or trader who is associated with one or more USDA-accredited certification bodies, as this will greatly facilitate the process. The certification body does not have to be based in the United States. The USDA NOP website (*http://www.ams.usa.gov/nop*) provides detailed information on the NOP. It also gives full regulations and an application form for accreditation of certification of bodies. Suppliers can also obtain information from the Independent Organic Inspector's Association (*http://www.ioia.net*).

Distribution Channels are Widening: Traditionally, organic food products have been sold outside the conventional distribution system through alternative channels such as farm-gate sales, open-air markets, specialized grocery shops and natural product retailers. Likewise, small and medium sized companies, rather than major food manufacturers, have carried out most processing and packaging. However, due to strong growth of the organic food market in recent years, sales have also moved into the mainstream retail trade, and the conventional food industry is becoming increasingly involved. The organic food sector is also undergoing a consolidation process through acquisitions, mergers and alliances.

Use specialized Importers: Specialized importers or ingredient suppliers who supply distributors and food manufacturers usually handle imported organic products. The final consumer obtains organic food and beverages mainly through natural food stores followed by conventional supermarkets and other food channels, including food service (restaurants, schools, hospitals etc.), street markets and Internet sales.

Market Entry Tips for Developing Countries: Get in early. It is easier to enter a new market during periods of strong growth, so potential exporters to the United States should move quickly to take advantage of the current market situation. This will enable them to secure a stronger foothold before competition intensifies, which is likely to happen over the next few years.

Develop a strong supply base. A considerable amount of work is necessary to build up an organic export trade in developing countries, whether on the production or the marketing side. At country level, a good agricultural supply base with appropriate national or international certification is absolutely necessary. For the producers/exports, it is equally important to offer a range of products that meet the requirements of the market.

Collaborate with peers. As far as possible, producers should work in collaboration with their counterparts in the export country, eg. through an association, a cooperative or another group relationship. Working together can mean producing a greater choice of products in marketable quantities and at better prices. It can also mean improved post-harvest treatment, processing, packaging, storage, transportation and administration and may help to cut the costs of certification and participation in events like foreign trade fairs.

Check and comply with technical requirements. Exporters must make sure that their organic certification will be recognized and accepted by the NOP and that export products meet all legal and market requirements (eg hygiene, weight, size, ripeness, colour, packing and other technical specifications) or the United States.

Choose the right distributor(s). Exporters will find that making a careful selection of market segments and distribution channels is of the utmost importance. A strong and reliable relationship with an importer or distributor is an absolute must in building up a profitable business. Depending on the product(s) in question, it may be necessary in the long run to choose more than one importer (from different geographical areas), although this would have to be justified by sufficient quantities of exportable products.

Stay up-to-date. Exporters must keep themselves informed of market developments through information-sharing, following trade journals, the internet, etc. They should also visit organic trade fairs regularly.

Develop the local market. While exporting can be a profitable business, developing countries should not ignore or neglect building up their national market. A sizeable domestic market will help to reduce over-dependency on one or more export markets and will also help to secure the necessary organic production base.

Partner with the export market. Developing countries should look at the Untied States not only as a potential export market for organic products but also consider it as a possible partner in various forms of cooperation in the farming, processing, certification and marketing of organic products.

There are a number of individuals, companies and other organizations (several of which are mentioned in ITC's new study. The United States Market of Organic Food and Beverage) that are interested in expanding export projects in partnership with developing countries. Other good sources of business contact include the Organic Trade Association and similar organizations, and visits to specialized trade fairs and shows.

SECTION II
Pruning in Tea Science is a Surgical Operation in Medical Science

Introduction

Pruning is one of the most important agricultural practices in tea cultivation, which has a great influence on productivity. It primarily governs frame development, ensures frame sanitation, controls plucking table height and rejuvenates or stimulates vegetative growth. Dr. Gadd emphasized the impact of pruning on the growth of tea bushy in 1931 as "Pruning in tea science resembles a surgical operation in medical science". The recovery after pruning depends on vigour of the bush, environmental factors, method or style of pruning including bush sanitation and other post pruning practices. Failure to do a proper pruning could lead to poor recovery, bush debilitation and death. It is, therefore, very important to adopt proper pruning practices at the correct time. Shortage of labour has become a constraint in tea cultivation. As a result, labour-intensive cultural practices such as plucking and pruning are being mechanized. Pruning with brush cutter type machines give a very high output with a significant saving on labour. This also helps to complete pruning in a short time. However, the 'benefits' of mechanical pruning can be simply masked by its 'evils' due to negligence.

Lung Pruning Replaced by Cut-across Pruning: With the use of motorized machines in place of knives, lung pruning has been replaced by cut-across pruning. Consequently, the sanitation aspect of pruning has been neglected. This has become a 'danger', particularly in formative (first) pruning. In some instances, very high rates of casualities (over 40 per cent) have been reported after mechanical pruning of young tea. This may not only be attributed to the use of machines, but also to the style of pruning (cut across) that may deprive the bush of its 'supplementary source' of food (lung branches) after pruning. Bushes at the age of formative pruning do not have a well-established rot system to support recovery after pruning in the absence of lung branches. Vibration of the turning blade could also damage young tea, especially when the blade is not adequately sharpened. Field observations have also shown that the casualities are high when the soil conditions are poor. At formative pruning, branches should be selectively removed at varying heights depending on the location of primary and secondary branches. Improper formative prune will lead to the development of an ill-shaped or unproductive frame. Knot formation, wood rot and other secondary infections could also begin at this stage due to inadequacies of pruning. Therefore, it is more appropriate to do the formative pruning manually leaving healthy lung branches.

Use of Pruning Machine in Mature Tea Fields: Pruning machines can be used in mature tea fields provided that manual cleaning of frame is done concurrently. However, lung branches should be left to support recovery after pruning. If cleaning is not done manually, dead wood, pest and disease infected areas will accumulate leading to spread of wood rot in the frame. Consequent debilitation and death of bushes will lead to large scale infilling or replanting. However, manual cleaning after pruning could take low priority in old and marginal tea fields, which might be out of production in a short period. Use of blunt blades or steel blades without tungsten tips results in splitting of cut ends and uneven cuts. Improper handling such as cutting branches by either side of the blade, cutting before the blade results in splitting of cut ends and uneven cuts, which in turn lead to increased dieback. In some instances due to the shortage of skilled pruners, they are given double payment each day for completing 'double tasks'. They are paid on contract basis, completely disregarding the quality of work. Under such circumstances, supervision is minimal and the objectives of pruning are not fully achieved. The consequences of such inadequacies make their appearance only after a few pruning cycles. Therefore, the pruning machines should be used with the objective of increasing labour productivity (i.e. at the expense of labour but not at the expense of bush health) and not merely to overcome the labour shortage.

SECTION III
Little Known Facts of Tea

Introduction

Tea is a versatile beverage. It gives pleasure, joy and hope. Besides its medicinal and health values, it is ceremony and business to many. It helps to progress and develop other trades. In this context, it is important to highlight some of the little known facts of tea. These are listed below:

Facts of Tea: Although tea and Europe (and in particular, Britain) are synonymous for many, tea originated in China, later supplanted by India, Sri Lanka and Java. Soon, adventures and traders discovered the beverage for themselves and sent the first consignment of tea to Europe in 1619. It was brought by the Dutch from China, then to Java, and then to Holland.

First Recorded Tea Tax: Throughout the centuries, taxes have been a good reason for much unrest, and tea has been one of the products often singled out for taxing. The world's first recorded tea tax was imposed in China during the 8th century.

Known References to the Sale of Tea: Error! Not a valid link. made first reference to the sale of tea in Britain.

Important Trading Commodity: The first tea to arrive in Canada was brought by the Hudson Bay Co., bringing it to its trading posts as early as 1716, and became one of the most important trading commodities.

Tea as Medicine: In 1600s teas were available in Britain in only i.e. the cup and in leaf form in coffee houses and the apothecary's shop. Many tea drinkers looked on tea as a medicine.

"Spin Off" Effect of Tea: "Spin Off" is a modern description when another creates one development or product. In Britain, tea's popularity led directly to the rapid development of that country's pottery and porcelain industry because of the manufacture of tea wares.

Two Famous Tea Parties: Although tea parties are enjoyable events, they don't usually capture people's imagination or alter the course of history. However, tea has two famous tea parties to its credit. The Mad Hatter's Tea Party (which has been replayed by the Tea Council of Canada and Bacchus). The other is the Boston Tea Party at which citizens protested against the tax on tea at the start of the American War of Independence.

Tea in Marks of a Patriot: During the American Revolution, tea fell out of favour because of the tea tax. People made a point of refusing to drink tea because that was one of the marks of a patriot.

A Real Tea Break: The Russian version of the teapot is called a samovar. It is a combination of a boiling water heater and a tea pot. It can serve up to 40 cups of tea at a time, offering tea lovers in Russia a real tea break.

The Clipper Ship: To speed the transportation of tea from producing countries to consuming nations, a new type of sailing vessel was developed, the Clipper Ship. Sleek and speedy, this ship ruled the waves for many years, setting many speed records, and later, was the stuff of novels and films. Clippers finally sailed into oblivion only when steam took over.

Tea as Breakfast Drink: In seventeenth century England, tea became almost an obsession. King Charles II collected finely crafted teacups, bowls, saucers, trays, and caddies in pewter, silver, and pottery. The queen introduced tea as a breakfast drink to replace ale. Some considered the idea that tea should be served with food, although certain tea drinkers added salt, spices, and even eggs. Those who did not bother to brew tea, chewed the leaves.

Afternoon Tea—A pleasant Custom: Taking afternoon tea is pleasant custom that is growing in Canada. Afternoon tea aficionados owe it all to a Duchess who was hungry. In the late 1800s Anna, the Duchess of Bedford, conceived of a ceremony of serving tea and food together that would become a British institution. One day at Belvoir Castle, Anna was entertaining and five o'clock came and went. The Duke was still-hunting. This meant dinner would be late. So Anna proceeded to entertain her friends with cakes, pastries and a pot of the best tea. Thus, she began the custom that helps bridge the gap between lunch and the late evening meal.

Australians and Tea: Australians are known for their colourful language, and the word billy adds to their reputation. A billy is the can in which Australians living the bush boil their tea, as recorded in the Aussie song, *Waltzing Matilda.*

Tea Handling: In the early 18th century, tea was always sold in loose form. Then, there was a change in tea handling. In 1926, the first package of tea was introduced, designed to eliminate short weight at the scale by some unscrupulous merchants.

Birth of Tea Bag: At the turn of the 19th century, another type of packaging appeared–the tea bag. This is an American invention and it evolved like so many other ideas that have caught on–by chance. One inventive merchant sent samples of his tea wrapped in a piece of Indian silk to his prospective customers. Many of his customers endorsed the idea by reordering these "tea bags". The silk bags soon proved too costly and a less expensive porous material was found. Thus, the tea bag was born.

Iced Tea—A Refreshing One: The millions of people who enjoy a refreshing glass of iced tea can thank an ingenious merchant at the 1904, St. Louis World's Fair. The popular drink was "discovered" when a tea promoter at the fair, having difficulty selling hot tea in the good old summertime heat, added ice and reintroduced the beverage as "iced tea". It was a sellout and a new beverage treat was launched.

Tea Pot: As old as tea is as a beverage, so must be the pots it was brewed in. The first teapots on record are those found near Shanghai about 1500 AD. The pots were small which suggested that each person had his own pot. Perhaps this archeological find might have been a teahouse. One may wonder if its patrons had to endure a leaky teapot while pouring their tea.

Chinese Tea Brick: A Chinese tea brick had another important use besides making tea. These compressed bricks of black tea were also used as a type of currency. Later, the use of tea bricks was discarded and, instead the tea was ground to a fine powder.

World's Champion Tea Drinking Nation: The world's champion tea drinking nation is a tiny country called Qatar, part of the Arab Emirates. People there consume approximately 12 pounds of tea per year. That translates into 3000 cups of tea a year or 58 cups a week or 8 cups a day. By comparison, Canadians drink 1.6 pounds (400 cups) or 7 cups per week or 1 cup a day.

Varieties and Blends of Tea

Many types, varieties and blends of tea are enjoyed daily in Canada and Canadians have shown a preference. Over 90 per cent is black tea. Black tea is also known as Orange Pekoe and the term classically refers to "the youngest leaf that has opened next to the leaf bud on the tea bush". Now it is used to describe domestic blends marketed by leading tea packers.

Victoria Leads the Tea Drinking Parade: In Canada, Newfoundland is out front as the province drinking the most tea. Quebec consumes the least tea. Among Canadian cities, Victoria leads the tea drinking parade.

World of Tea

Reading Tea Leaves: Tea is a versatile beverage. It is a beverage of pleasure, joy and hope; it has medicinal and health values; it is a ceremony—a ritual and, it has international acceptability. Tea is business to many; it is a partner in progress and development and a major item of trade. It is also revolutionary and a part and parcel of literature.

Tea in Literature: In the words of William E Gladstone: "If you are cold, tea will warm you, If you are heated, it will cool you—If you are depressed, it will cheer you—If you are excited, it will clean you". Wrote Samuel Johnson: "I am a hardened and shameless tea drinker, who has for twenty years diluted his meals with only the infusion of this fascinating plant, whose kettle has scarcely time to cook, who with tea amuses the evening, with tea solaces the midnight, and with tea welcomes the morning." In the words of Sir Arthur Pinero, "While there is tea, there's hope". An unknown Chinese Poet wrote: "The first cup moistens my lips, the second cup breaks my loneliness, the third cup searches my barren eternal, the fourth cup raises a slight perspiration, the fifth cup purifies me, the sixth cup calls me to the realm of the immortals and the seventh reminds I can take no more". "There is a great deal of poetry". Said Ralph Waldo Emerson, "and fine sentiment in a chest of tea". According to Lu Yu, "Tea gives one vigour of body, contentment of mind, and determination of purpose, when taken over a long period of time." Rabindranath Tagore wrote, "Come oh come ye tea thirsty restless ones—the kettle boils, bubbles and sings, musically". "Love and scandal are the best sweeteners of tea", wrote Henry Fielding. In the words of Samuel Johnson, "Tea's proper use is to amuse the idle, relax the studious and dilute the full needs of those who cannot exercise and will not use abstinence". Henry James writes in *The Portrait of a Lady,* "There are few hours in life more agreeable than the hours dedicated to the ceremony known as afternoon tea".

Tea Ceremony: Talking of the ceremony, one cannot forget the Japanese Tea Ceremony. The Japanese Tea Ceremony requires years of training and practice of graduate in the art; yet, the whole of this art, signifies no more than the making and serving of a cup of tea. However, it is, a real art–a most exquisite art.

But more than the art, the Japanese tea ceremony reflects the Japanese culture and values. All aspects of the Ta Ceremony, amongst other things, are meant to help the participants surrender their attachments to the outside and material world and to concentrate on the Zen ideals of self-knowledge, harmony and balance. Sydney Smith praised tea by saying, "Thank God for tea! What would the world do without Tea?—how did it exist? I am glad I was not born before tea".

"Catch them young" is not a modern concept for tea. For tea featured in the nursery rhymes ago, "Polly put the kettle on, we'll all have tea," is a popular rhyme, which all kids chant. Who can forget Lewis Carroll's *Alice in Wonderland*? "Take some more tea," the March Hare said to Alice very earnestly. "I have had nothing yet", Alice replied in an offended tone, "so I can't take more". "You mean you can't take less", said the Hatter. "It's very easy to take more than nothing".

Tea Parties

Tea is a party maker and there is a tea party that has a special place in history—yes, the Boston tea party! The English brought tea to America and soon the beverage was as popular in the new World as in the Old. The British Parliament imposed taxes on commodities, including tea, without the approval of America's elected assemblies. In 1773, all taxes were repealed, save the one on tea. The tax on tea was retained as a symbol of the British government's right to tax. But when three ships laden with tea arrived in the Boston harbour and were not allowed to be unloaded without the payment of tax, a group of angry Americans threw overboard into the Boston harbour large bales of tea. Thus began America's most famous tea party. Angry at the events, the authorities closed Boston harbour and in turn set in motion the events that led to the American Revolution. The diary of John Adams, who led the Ameicans on this fateful night, has an entry dated December 17, 1773 following the night of the Boston tea party, which states:

> "This is the most magnificent movement of all! There is dignity, a majesty, and sublimity, in this last effort of the patriots that I greatly admire. The people should never rise without doing something to be remembered—something notable and striking. This destruction of tea is so bold, so daring, so firm, and inflexible, and it must have so important consequences, and so lasting, that I can't but consider it as an epoch in history!"

Tea Panacea for Many Ills: The health giving properties of tea, in this age of health consciousness is well known. Tea is the panacea for many ills. It prevents tooth decay and help to thwart caner. Tea contains various substances, which lower blood pressure and blood cholesterol, stabilize blood sugar, kill decaying bacteria and block the action of many carcinogens. A scientist, Dr. Harold N. Graham, predicts, "Once we determine which components of tea are most useful pharmaceutically, it should be possible to produce teas that are highly beneficial and still pleasing to people".

Tea in Beautification: Beauticians use tealeaves for hair dyeing. Tea liquor of thick consistency mixed with henna, egg, lime, oil will colour the hair dark, and bright—the luster comes from tea. Tea is also a good conditioner for hair after shampoo. It imparts a healthy sheen along with body.

Tea in Refreshment of Eyes: A used tea bags, well chilled, relax tired eyes. Leave them on for just ten minutes and your eyes will be refreshed.

Tea in Faded Clothes: For faded clothes and discoloured whites tea has an answer. Dip the garments for dyeing in a bucketful of tea liquor. After three to four hours of immersion, you would have turned old into new. The size of the garment and the depth of colour required will determine the strength of tea decoction and quantum of water.

Tea—A Myriad of Shapes: The 5th century Chinese poet Lu Yu wrote: "Tea has a myriad of shapes. If I make speak vulgarly and rashly, tea may shrink and crumble likes a Mongol's boots. It may look like the dewlap of a wild ox, some sharp, some curling as the caves of a house still others will twist and turn like rivulets carved out by a violent rain on newly tilled fields. Those are the very finest teas".

Tea in Fortune telling: Tea has been used for fortune telling as well. There are many who predict the future by reading the shapes formed by tea leaves left at the bottom of a cup. If you would like to look into your future, the next time you drink tea, do not use a strainer while pouring tea from the pot. Drink your tea but leave a teaspoonful of liquid and tealeaves at the bottom of your cup.

Here is what a skilled interpreter recommends:

Swirl the tea around three times counter clockwise. Concentrate on a question or issue confronting you in your life. Then turn the cup slowly back over and look at the patterns from different angles. Leaves at the bottom of the cup speak of the distant future; those near the top concern the near future. Leaves on the handle side of the cup relate to family matters. Images formed by the leaves should be taken in the context of other symbols nearby. An egg-shaped pattern is good luck; however, a cross that means bad luck or suffering, near the eff may mean that the good luck will be delayed. Sometimes, the leaves seem to be cloudy, forming no specific images. This implies a vague or confused state of mind, which makes an interpretation difficult.

There are some explanations for just a few traditional symbols to help you read your future in the wet leaves of your tea. These are: *(i)* Airplane—promotion, *(ii)* Anchor—success or voyage, *(iii)* Bird—good luck, *(iv)* Book—revelation, *(v)* Cat—treachery, *(vi)* Cow—prosperity, *(vii)* Cross—trouble, *(viii)* Dog—a good friend, *(ix)* Egg—increase, good luck, *(x)* Face—change, *(xi)* Flower—love and honour, *(xii)* Ladder—promotion, *(xiii)* Letters—initials of important people, *(xiv)*, Tree—success, happiness, *(xv)* Ring—marriage, *(xvi)* Star—good luck, *(xvii)* Umbrella—shelter, *(xviii)* Triangle—inheritance, *(xix)* Wings—messages coming, and *(xx)* Windmill—success through hardwork.

14

Environmental Law, Conservation of Eco-System in Tea Industry, Managing Tea Imports and Tea a Treasure in India etc.

SECTION I
Environmental Law Law and Tea Industry

Introduction

Tea is an eco-friendly industry. It has major contribution in promoting and sustaining environment. Tea planting is nearly 2000 years old spreading over widely in the world. It has been systematically cultivated in Assam, Bengal, Tamilnadu, Karnataka, Kerala and some parts of Himachal-Pradesh and undivided UP. At present tea cultivation has started in non-traditional areas like Mizoram, Manipur, Meghalaya, Nagaland, Arunachal Pradesh and Sikkim. It has been playing a positive role in promoting favourable environmental conditions starting from Soil Conservation Management to Energy Plantation etc. Above all, plant is making available made tea to a large number of consumers. It is not only fit for human consumption but has medicinal values.

Tea Industry Voluntarily Practising Eco-friendly Activities

Nature is a gift of God. Every one of us must make constant efforts to preserve it. Tea industry, of course, has been practising voluntarily eco-friendly activities for nearly a century in different forms. Even in recent past, agreement regarding Coal Briquette as alternative fuel in place of firewood is a landmark in preventing environmental pollution. Of late, tea gardens are also required to obtain letter from Pollution Control Board for operating strictly as per provisions of Sec. 25 & 26 of Water (Prevention and Control of Pollution) Act, 1974 and Sec. 21 of the Air (Prevention and Control of Pollution) Act, provisions of which are given hereunder:

(a) Tea Gardens of West Bengal are to submit to the Board the return of water consumption in prescribed form and to pay cess as specified under Sec.3 of the said Act. It is also obligatory to submit Test Report of Ambient Air, Fugitive Air, Stalk Emission & Water Analysis to the Board.

(b) "Consent to Operate" that the applicant shall have to make Registration for the use of Ground Water, if any, with the Central Ground Water Authority. The provisions to manufacture, store and import of Hazardous Chemicals and Hazardous Wastes (Management and Handling) Rules, 1989 are also applicable.

Change over from 'Chemical Intensive Pest Control' to 'Bio-Intensive Pest Management'

Though chemicals and fertilizers are applied in tea gardens as per guidance and specifications of Tea Research Institute, it is not out of environmentalists' ire. Infestations caused by pests and diseases affect the productivity in general from 5 per cent to 10 per cent and hence the need of using pesticides judiciously in controlling pests is necessary. The change over from "Chemical Intensive Pest Control" to "Bio Intensive Pest Management" using mainly safer pesticides has already been started in addition to promotion of predators, parasites and pathogens to develop a natural enemy complex to foster tea eco-system and highlight their role in regulatory system of pests dynamics in tea. It is also given condition that tea industry has to survive satisfying the importing countries' prescribed MRL Value (Maximum Residual Level ppn/EC).

Self-Regulated Environment Friendly Activities

One can not deny that tea gardens are practicing different self-regulated environment friendly activities which are unique in nature. Despite this, the tea industry cannot be above the Environmental Law. Hence, there is a need to have an introduction. Right to carry on business and the freedom of trade and commerce is limited. In M/s Indian Wood Products Co. Ltd. vs State of UP (AIR 1999), the Allahabad High Court had to examine whether compulsion in the State Rules framed under the Forest Law to obtain pass for transit of forest produce violated freedom to carry on business and freedom of trade and commerce. It was held that the rules were valid as they were enacted to prevent illegal exploitation to maintain ecological balance.

In other case Baleswar Singh vs State of UP (AIR 1999) a few owners of saw mills challenged the UP State Rule prohibiting presence of Saw Mills within 80 kms of any reserved or protected forest as violative of Article 19(a) (g) of Indian Constitution. Dismissing the challenge the Court held that the existence of Saw Mill in or around any forest is prohibited for the maintenance of forest wealth and ecological balance. It is also pertinent to refer the observation of Allahabad High Court in S K Garg vs State of UP (AIR 1999). The Hon'ble court observes that the right to get water is part of the right to life guaranteed by Article 21 of the Constitution and directed to form a committee to study the problem on war footing. The court also suggested evolving immediate and long-term measures along with amendment of follow-up action. It was also observed by the Court "In democracy, citizen should also be involved in solving their own problems". In Claridges Carbit Hindeaway vs. State of UP, the Allahabad High Court noted that the Articles 48A and 51A imparted on the State and on the citizens respectively duties to protect and improve the environment including Forest, Rivers and Wild Life (AIR 1999).

Environment Protection for Human Existence

Environment protection has become a great concern for human existence—trees and forest are necessities. This principle was accepted in Goa Foundation vs Conservator of Forest, Panaji

(AIR 1999) wherein the conversion of Agricultural and Orchard Zones and Agricultural and Natural Reserve Zones to Settlement Zones and Commercial Zones was held to be volatile of the provisions for prior sanction under Forest Conservation Act, 1980 . This was due to the fact the land in question is found to be forestland. As per the provisions of West Bengal Land Reform Act, 1955, changing the character of land without the permission of the Collector is prevented. It also restricts conversion of land for a purpose other than the one for which the land was settled or previously held.

The Kolkata High Court explained in Sri Ram Saha vs State of West Bengal (AIR 1999) that there is no bar for the legislature to enact a law in respect of felling trees in private lands. In fact, interesting questions arose in the above-referred case. Can anyone uproot tree in one's own land without permission? What about felling trees in a land classified as garden? The Court felt it desirable to enact a comprehensive law regarding felling of trees in non-forest area with a view to taking care of environmental necessities of the time. Hence, the matter of felling shade trees in West Bengal tea gardens required a new thought. Shade trees are an integral part of tea plantation. Uprooting of shade tree along with proposed uprooted tea area cannot be avoided. Moreover, the cycle of temporary and permanent shade trees planted has a specific guideline. Uprooting and replanting is controlled and regulated by the Tea Board.

Need to Amend Legislation for Felling of Shade Trees

However, there is a need to amend legislation to empower the Tea Board to issue necessary permission for felling of shade trees in tea areas. Felling of shade trees is largely a difficult process in tea gardens. At one stage it was decided that "Shade Trees over tea crop will not be regarded as trees within the meaning of West Bengal Private Forest Act", reference may be made to the Memo No. 8222 (11) 2M/203 Dated, Darjeeling 27.10.1955 issued by Mr. A.C. Gupta, Conservator of Forest, Northern Circle. The tea gardens are in the operational purview of such acts which include: *(i)* The Forest (Conservation) Act, 1980, *(ii)* The West Bengal Private Forest Act, *(iii)* The West Bengal Forest Produce and Transit Rule, 1953, *(iv)* The West

Bengal Estates Acquisition Act, 1953 and the Rules, 1954, *(v)* Environment Protection Act, 1986, *(vi)* Water (Prevention and Control of Pollution) Act, 1974, *(vii)* Air (Prevention and Control of Pollution) Act, 1981, *(viii)* Factories Act, and *(ix)* Motor Vehicles Act etc.

It is high time that the tea industry should practise its professional knowledge and practical experience in the areas pertaining to conservation of forest and environmental management. In conclusion, while referring to the Stockholm Declaration of 1972, it may be mentioned that the Basel Convention of 1989, Earth Summit, 1992 (UNCED), EPA, 1986 etc. have come to stay.

Moral Duty of Every Human Being to Maintain Conducive Environment

A panoramic view of Environmental Laws envisages the existence of the ancient Indian heritage in Upanishadas, Puranas and Arthasashtra, which prescribed it as a moral duty of every human being to maintain conducive environment in his habitat. Our ancient people learnt to live with 5 elements of nature—the earth, the water, the air, the light and the cosmos and they worshipped them in realities and/symbolically. Likewise, Christians are baptized in water as a sign of purification. The *Gurugrantha Saheb,* too, emphasized that human beings are composed of 5 basic elements of nature, i.e. earth, air, water, fire and sky. In *Holy Kuran,* there is a reference "Do not make mischief in the earth". The basic thrust of Jainism is on minimum destruction of living and non-living resources for the benefit of man. All the religions in India have environmental overtone for the observance of an ecological code of conduct and thus show reverence towards the nature and its creation. In this context, the observation made by Justice M.V. Rao in A P State Pollution Control Board vs Prof. M.V. Naidu (AIR 1999) is worth quoting: "Environmental concerns .... Are in our view of equal importance as Human Rights concerns. In fact, both are to be traced to Article 21, which deals with Fundamental Right to life and liberty. While environmental aspects concern Life, human right aspects concern Liberty".

SECTION II
Tea Cultivation Conserves Eco-System in Hill Areas

Introduction

Tea is an important cash crop of Himachal Pradesh, grown in an area of about 2300 hectares with a production of around 17 lakh kgs. Presently, about 7700 hectares of additional land, suitable for tea cultivations, have been identified in non-traditional areas. The policy to give it a proper shape is under consideration. Most of the area proposed to be taken under tea cultivation consists of marginal sloping land. Tea cultivation may be ecologically adapted on sloping lands and to maintain the forestry system. This would ensure ecological stability fo fragile mountain slopes as the necessity for maintaining a good forest cover of nitrogen fixing shade trees (Albizzia sp.) is met.

Tea is a Planter Domesticated High Value Crops

Tea is a planter domesticated perennial high value cash crop. It generates employment for minimum of 100-150 days per hectare per annum. As far as GDP of our country is concerned, contribution of tea is significant in terms of foreign exchange ranging from Rs.1600 crore to Rs.1800 crore annually. Tea is also an important health drink which is evident from its anticarcinogenic, antihypertensive and antiviral properties in its flavanoids. Apart that, doctors recommend the person recovering from long illness to stay around tea plantations area for 1 to 2 months.

Tea Plantation Prevents Tillage Farming on the Slopping Farm Lands

While tea plantation based production system would alleviate poverty from the mountain households, it will prevent, at the same time, tillage farming on the sloping farmland. Most tea gardens have a good bush cover on the floor, which supports soil conservation and provides firewood, taking pressure off from the forests. Tea cultivation on the marginal sloping lands would also improve direct and indirect employment opportunities for the landless and women. With improved economic condition, mountain households would enjoy better health care, housing and communication facilities. There will be increased consciousness of the need for family planning and better education to children. Improved earning would also encourage families to have improved breeds of livestock and arrange lesser number of stall feeding because fodder will be available from plantations/orchards. In this context it may be mentioned that the hilly areas which are considered unsuitable for cultivation of cereal and other food crops need not be left now as wasteland. Such areas may rather be used for tea cultivation with the assistance of the appropriate authorities of the government.

Sustainable Farming on Sloping Land Desirable

Sustainable farming on sloping land is becoming more desirable as a balance is sought between economic development and environmental protection. Sloping land of hills, mountains and highland areas are sensitive to rainfall and suffer from widespread soil erosion and land degradation. Small and marginal farmers in hilly areas have traditionally used sloping lands for subsistence farming despite poor yields and low farm productivity. In order to improve the quality of livelihood of farmland, they should be advised to grow fruit and cultivate tea. Fragile slope land may be sensitive to degradation under cultivation but may be sustainably for forestry and tea cultivation. Technologies may be known but the necessary incentives, institutions or inputs may be missing. The range of possible uses of sloping land are so wide and socio-economic conditions of upland/mountain/highland farmers so diverse that no definition can encompass all relevant factors. Marginality of sloping land may be the result of different combinations of constraints. For instance biophysically "good" land may be marginal on account of its isolation from markets, the availability of inputs, or the "small size of holdings", etc.

Four key factors make tea cultivation useful on marginal sloping lands:

1. It protects slope lands from fast degradation and soil erosion;
2. Tea cultivation ensures ecological stability of fragile mountain slopes as it provides a good forest cover of nitrogen fixing shade trees (Albizzia spp.);

3. Areas extremely uneconomic for cereal or other food crops production may be utilized for tea and thus improving the living standard of hill people;
4. It generates employment for minimum of 100-150 days per hectare per annum.

SECTION III
Managing Tea Imports

Backdrop

An issue of concern to the tea industry right now and the years to come is the permission granted to imports. On the one hand, the industry has been opposing the imports on the ground that there is no shortage—on the contrary, there is adequate volume to cater to both the home and export markets. On the other, the industry realizes that in the context of WTO and the globalization policy, it would be virtually impossible to get a blanket ban on imports for long.

Lack of Information of Import

Volume, Countries of Origin, Price, etc: The worst point about imports is that until now there is no authentic information. Neither the Tea Board nor the industry can say with authority the volume of imports, the countries of their origin, the price and the importers' details. There is hardly an authentic exposition on the resale of these imported teas. For all the organized nature of the tea industry, the fact is that the Tea Board governs the affairs of the industry. It is virtually unacceptable that the information on imports is lacking. Nevertheless, the hard reality is that the lack of information is causing more harm than the imports per se. With no authentic information, the market is driven by sentiments. Already, prices have fallen even as the production has reduced.

In 2007, for instance, the tea industry claims that the production slipped to around 900 million kgs against 900 million kgs in 2006. The total exports were put at 200 million kgs, against 210 million kgs of 2006. Therefore, this left some 740 million kg for domestic consumption in 2006 it was 775 million kgs. It is, therefore, inacceptable that the domestic consumption fell in 2007. The domestic consumption has been growing at an average of two per cent every year. Given the growth in population as well, it is expected that the overall consumption in the country grow annually, not falls. Hence, there is no way to accept a fall of 35 million kgs on the home consumption last year.

Imported Tea Filing up the Gap Caused by a fall in Production

It has happened that some imported teas had been filling up the gap caused by a fall in production. Whether such volume of imports is matched with these 30 million kgs or not is not officially declared yet. Nevertheless, the industry believes that the imports should be of this order. Usually, Indian exporters are allowed to import for value-added exports. This sort of imports totals around 10 million kgs. Therefore, in addition to this, more teas have entered the Indian Territory. Ordinarily, when the production falls 70 million kg, the price should shoot up. On the contrary, in 2007, teas on an average lost Rs.11 a kg. This is because of a low demand from the exporters, particularly for the Russian market. However, more importantly, even the domestic traders were not doing any panic buying. They knew that imported teas were available and that they need not bid at high prices at the auctions. Therefore, despite a production fall, prices fell because of imported teas taking care of the supply shortage. This is causing worry to the industry. If imports persist in times of good harvest, the industry feels that it would be doomed with a glut. So, it has asked for a total ban on imports.

Erstwhile Govt. Signed an Accord with Sri Lanka for Promotion of Free Trade among the SAARC Countries

Imports were facilitated particularly by the then Vajpayee Government signing an accord with Sri Lanka as part of its commitment to promote free trade among the SAARC countries. Sri Lanka is keen to export its teas to India. As such she is resisting any measure to impose a higher duty on its sales to India. More importantly, many traders are equally keen to import the Lanka teas. Traders, in Kochi were able to procure the Lankan teas for Rs. 50 a kg even as the auction average was Rs.70. Some traders in Coonoor said that they were scouting for the Lanka teas because it would work out cheaper to import these teas and sell them in upcountry markets. They said that it would be impossible to get Indian teas for Rs. 50 a kg.

Many Traders of Nilgiris Import Sri Lankan Tea

The Nilgiri teas are of matching grade to the Lankan teas and hence, many traders in the Nilgiris are keen to import the Lankan teas at a cheaper price. Many of these traders are commission agents in law. They just buy the teas on behalf of their customers in different parts of the country and sell the same as they are. They do not blend or re-pack these teas. To them, the only concern is to procure the teas at the cheapest possible price and sell at the maximum price. That way, they are happy to import matching grades of Lankan teas at a cheaper price and sell to their customers in the north. The demand for the Niligiri teas increases. If the price gap between the Assam and Nilgiri teas is more, then, these teas are bought for fillers. Otherwise, if the gap is less, the buyers prefer to pay a little more and go for the quality Assam teas. Therefore, except those producers in the Nilgiris who concentrate on quality production, others will have a tough time if imports continue. Meanwhile, reports suggest that the traders have committed with the Sri Lankan exporters to import 15 million kgs in the coming months for which the Government is prepared to allow a 50 per cent concession in import duty under the SAARC pact. This has upset the producers, particularly in the south, who feel that there is no need for either the import or the duty concession.

Industry's Urge to Finance Minister

The industry has urged the then Finance Minister, Mr. Yashwant Sinha, to increase the duty on imports to the maximum of 40 per cent prescribed by the WTO. Presently, the duty is at the minimum of 15 per cent. It has told the Finance Minister that the WTO does no insist on lowering the import duty as of now. The industry is obviously adopting this measure because it feels that it would be difficult for it to win its case for a total ban on imports. Sri Lanka itself is careful to protect its producers.

She levies a duty of 35 per cent on imports. Egypt levies a duty of 30 per cent on tea imports from India but it admits Kenyan teas for just 3 per cent. The logic is that it could help the nations forming parts of the Common Market for East and South Africa (COMESA). So, it is only India which has not taken adequate care to protect the indigenous industry. Also under the SAARC pact, India is unable to export its teas to Pakistan, another SAARC country, and a major importer. Hence, India is the loser on both sides–imports from Sri Lanka and inability to export to Pakistan.

Conclusion: The fact is that India has not been successful in grabbing new markets. It is not that the duty structure that has affected it. The fact is that there has been no sincere effort for an aggressive marketing in both the domestic and foreign markets for a commodity on whose production it ranks first.

SECTOR IV
Tea—A Treasure of India

Backdrop

India is a treasure land and has wealth of many facets. It has large tracts of rich soil, plenty of sunshine, readily available and well distributed water sources and a large population. Tea has been thriving on all these. In the words of Sir Francis Bacon: "of great riches there is no real use except it be in their distribution", and tea is a treasure which India shares with millions all over the world. The huge area of the country, with vastly different agro-climates through its length and breadth, coupled with degrees of latitude extending from the 8th to the 37th parallel, make Indian tea of the widest variety. There is no other tea producing country in the world which can offer to the discerning consumers, the world over, such variety in quality. Indian tea satiates every consumer taste within the country and outside. No wonder India is the unquestioned leader in the world of tea. The tea grown in different regions of India like Assam, Darjeeling, Dooars, Tripura, Tamil Nadu, Kerala, Karnataka, Orissa, Arunachal Pradesh, Himachal Pradesh and Uttaranchal have a distinct class. The main production of India is Black tea–both Orthodox and CTC. Green teas of different types are also manufactured in North as well as South India. In South India, teas are produced all through the year. In North India, tea production starts in late March and ends in early December, but the bulk of the Indian production comes from the North Eastern region.

Variety of India Tea

(a) North Indian Tea–Full, Gutty, Bright, Golden and Chunky Tip

Assam is the largest tea producing state in India. This region is sub-divided into the Brahmaputra Valley and the Surma Valley. Assams are famous for their full, gutty, bright and pungent/brisk liquors with unusual 'creaming down' quality. The peak in quality is reached during the 'second flush'. The Orthodox variety from this State has abundant bright, golden and chunky tip. West Bengal offers teas from Darjeeling, Dooars and Terai. The Darjeelings are known as "The Champagne of Teas", cultivated on the slopes of the mighty Himalayas, the Darjeelings have unique, delicate flavour and character. No one has been able to match "the Darjeeling flavour". No wonder the world record of Rs.5001/- per kg. is held by Darjeeling's Castleton tea : The teas from Dooars and Terai are well made, neat in appearance and have strong brisk liquors. They are immensely popular in the internal market. The state of Tripura is also a traditional producer of Orthodox and CTC teas. A small but quite different variety of tea comes from small growers of Kangra Valley in the picturesque Himachal Pradesh. The valley has been famous for its speciality green teas. Recently, four cooperative factories have been established which mainly produce flavoury Orthodox teas. The first flush of this region is particularly noteworthy. Dehradun in Uttaranchal contributes its own variety to India quality.

(b) South Indian Tea–Strong, Bright and Brisk Liquors

The 'first flush', the 'second flush' and autumnal teas from the North are indeed unique–each has its own distinctive taste. The special quality of these periods draws special attention of the connoisseurs. The quality of South Indian teas has its own distinctive characteristics. The Nilgiris are a gift from the Blue Mountains' and possess delicate flavour along with strength and brightness. In water from certain areas, they brew better than any other tea. The produce of high range has its own speciality. The CTC production from all the southern states is tuned to producing a large per centage of fine grades. The popularity of South Indian CTCs is attributed to good leaf appearance and strong, bright and brisk liquors. Amongst the fine variety of teas produced in India, the South Indians enjoy a place of pride. Today, many non-traditional areas in India are going in for tea cultivation in a big way. For example, Orissa, Meghalaya and Arunachal Pradesh are some regions which produce teas of flavoury Orthodox variety. They will further add to the vast variety of Indian tea in the years to come. Tea is synonymous with India and India's greatest agro-asset is Tea. Indian Teas' two great strengths are its vast variety and superb quality. But the greatest strength of 'the treasureland of tea' is that it shares the joys of drinking Indian Tea with the rest of the world!

How to buy Good Tea:

"We do not get good tea in India, does it all get exported?"
"Where can one buy good tea?"
"Which restaurant or coffee shop serves good tea?"
"Are Dusts also tea?"

These are some of the many questions which are asked of a tea man. The majority of Indians drink tea, less or more, but are at their wits end when it comes to selecting tea. With some of them dissatisfaction on this score lasts their entire life time.

With Tea Standardisation Difficult

The other beverages are different. A greater standardization is possible with them. With tea, things are different. Tea comes in infinite variety. There is Orthodox tea, CTC tea, Green Tea, Oolong tea, instant tea, flavoured tea and several other types available in the world markets. Furthermore, there are Orthodox teas from Darjeeling, Assam, South India and other growths. CTC teas in India alone, come from many districts. Green teas from the Kangra Valley are quite different to those from West Bengal or South India. Manufacturing techniques and equipment leave their own imprint on tea. Different varieties have their own distinctive characteristic. Then again, the seasons impart their own flavour and character on each variety. The problem is further complicated as it is possible to produce a different tea on the same estate on the same day at morning, noon, afternoon and evening. The following night, a weather change could produce yet another variety. This is a common happening in high elevation gardens, particularly Darjeeling.

Taste of Tea—Purifying Agents, etc.

Water used for brewing makes a big difference. Tea which tastes good in Mumbai water, may not do so well in Kolkata; in Hamburg or London it may brew quite differently. Purifying agents—like chlorine and boiled water also affect the taste of tea. In India, 70 per cent of the tea consumed is in loose form; only 30 per cent is in packets. In the developed countries, tea bags and packets claim the major share of the market. All packets are different. Their blends contain teas from different areas and tea growing regions. Loose tea, of course, can be different each time. To compound the problem further, every tea drinker is his own tea taster and expert. Some tea lovers like their brew light while others prefer it strong. Some drink it for flavour, while others need "a wake me up" strong drink. There are many who add tea leaves to boiling milk, and then drink it. Others brew it in water but here again there are several different methods—adding tea leaves to a pot full of water or pouring boiling water over tea leaves or boiling tea leaves with water are common brewing methods. It is not uncommon that spices, ginger and herbs are added to tea before it is consumed. Again, some drink tea with sugar, others without it; some drink it with a dash of lime. The sweetness requirement of the cup also varies with each tea drinker. For each taste and different brewing the tea has to be different.

A tea drinker must, first of all, decide what he expects from his cup of tea—whether he wants a strong cup or a light cup or a tea with pronounced flavour. The brewing method of his home must also be checked. CTC teas produce a strong cup; CTC Dusts even stronger. The larger the leaf, the lighter will be the cup and the smaller the grain of tea, the stronger will be the brew. For those who like light liquoring teas or drink tea with lime, Orthodox teas are best suited. Here again, larger leaf (whole leaf i.e. FOOP types) are lighter than broken

(BOPs). For those who drink tea for flavour, Darjeeling or high grown teas from the South provide the answer'. However, Darjeeling and high growns cannot be boiled in water and milk as the brew turns bitter. Furthermore, teas from high altitudes have to be drunk soon after brewing and cannot be re-heated or kept in the pot for long. If this is done, flavour will be masked by strength and bitterness.

SECTION V
Crisis of the Industry, Resultant Effect and Hope for Future

Crisis in Tea Industry

In any industry, critical situation develops when production exceeds the demand. Presently such is the case in Indian tea industry. Huge stocks piled up in warehouses, during the recent years, due to loss of export market of tea as would be evident from the following statistics.

Particulars/Year	*1970*	*1980*	*1985*	*1990*	*1995*	*2000*	*2005*
Production (million Kg)	418.5	569.2	656.2	714.7	756.0	847.0	900.0
Export (million Kg)	200.0	224.0	214.0	210.0	167.1	204.3	200.0
Intra Demand & carry over (million Kg)	218.5	365.2	442.2	504.7	588.9	602.7	700.0

The development of the critical situation may be ascribed to the following factors:

- Downfall of the Soviet Union;
- Gulf.War in the recent years;
- Detection of adulteration in tea supplied to Russia;
- Finding of Pesticide Residue in tea exceeding German Standard.

Resultant Effect

The resultant effect of the aforesaid factors is significant indeed. It may be emphasized that the Indian tea Industry has been passing through many critical periods, particularly due to the fall in exports to Russia, the major importer of India's 'common' and 'filler' tea since long years. The trade was handicapped due to political turmoil within that country, causing disintegration of the union of States and economic downfall etc.

- Efforts have already been made to ensure trade volume with the Russia. The problem lies in the absence of any other export buyer for the class of tea and the huge quantity Russia used to buy.
- The Middle-east Asian countries had been existing as a sizable export market of 'quality' tea. This has also suffered badly due to the effect of war in that areas, in the recent past. After the war has been over, and before India could regain its footing there, other more enterprising tea producing countries have entered the valuable market. India has, however, re-entered and success was noticed so far.
- When there was full fledged business with Russia for 'common' and 'filler' tea, some unscrupulous export trading organizations of India had dispatched consignments of adulterated tea to that country which was detected and massively publicized over the television with the caution—'Not to Sip Indian Tea'. This spread suspicion in the export market about the dependability on Indian supplies which caused a considerable damage to the already crippled export market. Of course, the Government took serious exception to that unethical business practices to regain the lost position.
- Germany, the largest buyer of valuable and prestigious Darjeeling tea, found Pesticide Residue in that tea in excess of the 'Permissible Limit' as specified by that country. On this issue, other export buyers have also been skeptical to some extent. As a measure against the damaging remark, the Indian garden managers have already been alert and have implemented more strict and judicious use of toxic chemicals, until the scientists invent alternatives to chemical pesticides from herbal product or anything else. A few have stopped application of chemical pesticides totally.

Hopes for Future

In spite of the above set backs, disappointments and disgrace, the Indian marketing experts proclaim that the Indian tea is still reckoned to be superior in the world of tea market and 'Darjeeling produce' have the laurel of 'Champagne of Tea'. They add that there is no dearth of demand in the market for 'quality tea' at a remunerative price. However, it is felt that over 150 years old tea industry of India, supported by the best scientific knowledge acquired through early 100 years old tea research and agricultural activities, would certainly be able to overcome the present difficult situation with the concerted effort of all pioneering tea marketing and controlling organizations in the country.

Quality tea production calls for adoption of improved plucking standard at the first instance. The whole of the processing stages thereafter need be channelised in the long established conditions of quality manufacture. Of course, over the past few years the machineries and techniques had undergone several changes to help handle over grown tea twigs along with coarser leaves, harder stalks and stems with fibrous growth, which had to be crushed by very severe mechanical actions and reduced to minute particles to get mixed thoroughly with the tender portions of the leaf shoots during the cell distortion stage. Under this severe processing operations the properties naturally grown in the tender portion of the leaf shoots, the constituents of 'quality' in the made tea, do get distributed over the coarser portions of the coarse plucked shoots and thus overall product is turned in poor quality. Nevertheless, the nature gifted good quality, inherent in the tender portion of the leaf shorts, do get lost due to abnormal severity of mechanical actions.

All those who are connected with the manufacture of tea should not forget that the practice, scientific theories and appliances developed through long years of experience and scientific research on tea manufacture are based upon a specific standard of plucking. Essentially, the theories and practice etc. fail to produce the desired result on the finished product when the raw material deviates from the set standard. It is a fact, inferior plucking can never produce superior quality tea, irrespective of the development attained in the mechanical appliances.

Factors generally responsible for deterioration of quality in tea may be outlined as:

- Poor plucking standard;
- Withering not effected in accordance with the method of manufacture;
- Extremely severe mechanical actions applied during cell distortion stage of manufacture;
- Lack of proper care and attention during fermentation stage;
- Violation of time and temperature sequences at drying stage;
- Recycling of tea waste and off-graded tea;
- Faulty and poorly maintained processing machinery and incorrect settings and adjustments;
- Disregard for cleanliness of machinery and factory area.

The tea garden managers and factory managers are fully aware of the fact. But they, in many instances, are not in a position to adhere to the norms prescribed for quality tea manufacture, due to pressure from higher authorities for quantity.

Conclusion

India has been the pioneer in systematic, organized tea plantation and mechanized tea producing industry in the world. It would undoubtedly be a great pity to see the Indian tea industry falling behind others in the international market, particularly in respect of quality. Indian tea would again have to establish her prominence in the international tea market, facing strong competition from East Africa and Sri Lanka, on the strength of her superior quality and confidence and full reliance over the standard of supply. This would require shaking of the easiness enjoyed over the recent past.

15

Plants and Planting, Co-operative and Bought Leaf Factory, Supervisory Management in Tea Gardens, Development Initiatives and Major Highlights, Present Tea Scenario and Tips of Efficient Management Practices, and Scientific Problems of Tea Industry

SECTION I

Plants and Planting—Prudent Labour Utilisation Plan

The Tea Industry of our country is passing through a difficult phase. Tea prices are very low, exports declined and the quality is not to the mark. Forty-five per cent of the bushes are more than 50 years old. What quality of teas can be expected therefore? Although the Tea Industry in North East India stopped 'Plucking' leaves for four months from December 1, 2001 as a market strategy, many tea units normally suspended their production during winter. Because quality of tea deteriorated with the approach of winter, so, suspension of production is a blessing in disguise. The labour force remains free from plucking and manufacturing tea for almost four months. But the permanent labour on 'Books' has to be given some work and paid 'wages'. Then, why not utilize them for raising 'Tea Plants' and plants for 'Fuel Bari' as well as eco-friendly plants. Thus, hundreds of thousands of tea plants will be available at no additional 'labour cost'. The 'material cost' of each plant is hardly 20 per cent to 25 per cent of the total cost. Here prudent 'Labour Utilisation Plan' comes in the picture. And the managements of tea units should be serious in this matter. A Labour Utilisation Budget has to be drawn up on the 'Priority of Job' basis. Essential jobs will have the top priority during the slack season. Sense of 'priority' (which job first) and sense of 'proportion' (to what extent) should be the guiding factor.

After 12 to 15 months 'lakhs' of tea plants will be available which may be planted in the field for infilling, Block Infilling, Rejuvenation, Interlining, Extension Planting, Replacement Planting and Replanting. They could be planted in the field at convenience, any time from April to the end of the season. But tea sections, more than 40 years old, should not be infilled. The old bushes will be obsolete and extinct by the time the young ones would come to peak maturity. It is suggested, however, that tea plants not immediately necessary to any estate may be sold out to other estates who need them to complete their planting programme. But it should always be kept in view that the tea estates, which do not have a plant to raise plants during the cold weather, employ their labour force on unproductive jobs. It is sheer waste of money and manpower. It would be judicious to utilize them raise new tea plants fuel tree, medicinal plants and to cultivate vegetable and spices. This endeavour would add to the income, though insignificant of the tea units.

SECTION II

Supervisory Management at Tea Gardens

Techno-economical Guidelines/Procedure for achieving the desired performance at tea units are given below:

1) Advance note on location, specification and standard of work schedule be prepared;

2) Different time schedules to have proper coverage and attention to specific kamjaries. One/Two plot/ Kamjari at random should be taken for thorough verification, by rotation;
3) Direct attention to 2/3 Sections/Departments regularly to have complete analytical ideas and make note of the same for future references;
4) Advance planning and allotment of required/specific kamjaries and labour deployment schedule will automatically yield better working result;
5) Cross verification of the attendance of workers should be made and kept note of such record for future references;
6) Regular verification and deployment of store items as per specific need should be taken care of and directly supervised;
7) Labour deployment and reporting system, particularly at starting and closing points should be monitored along with the standard of performances;
8) Combined approach of motivation and manpower management should be introduced for better working environment.
9) Techno-administrative methods, feedback system linked with sense of responsibility and accountability shall be suitably adapted;
10) Tea garden being a labour oriented industry dealing with various genetic characters of human behaviour, effective MIS Network is a must to have better co-ordination and control.

SECTION III

Co-op and Bought Leaf Tea Factories

Co-operative tea factories and the Bought Leaf Units (BLU) have been temporarily relieved of the Central Excise Duty of Rs. 2.00 per kgss on bulk tea, introduced by the 1999 budget on all teas, processed by these two sectors. According to a Notification, the duty will not be levied "on and from December 10, 1999 to March 31, 2000". These two sectors buy tea from gardens to process it. The co-operative societies processed 17.16 million kgs of tea annually. Of the 29 factories run by co-operative societies, 15 were located in Tamil Nadu, 9 in Tripura, 4 in Himachal Pradesh, and 1 in Kerala.

Bought Leaf Factories Be Monitored

Although in the last couple of years there has been massive growth of bought leaf factories in South India, North Bengal and Assam, their contribution to the making of quality tea has invited bitter criticism from the tea circle. The tea associations have expressed concern for the uncertain standard of the produce of bought leaf factories. This is one of the causative factors to depressed prices of other teas offered in the market. The growth of the nuisance of green leaf theft led by the bought leaf factories and making of dubious tea by them has worried the tea associations. It has been reported in the recent past that in South India and Upper Assam many such factories were engaged to reprocess worst quality tea dust with some fresh tea. In North Bengal, the Jalpaiguri police raided some factories that were making adulterated tea. This clearly indicates that most of these factories are least interested to make quality tea in keeping with the image of tea as a healthy drink. Ill-gotten fast buck is their primary objective while quality is not the matter of concern at all. Such trade practices are highly undesirable. Except the Prevention of Food Adulteration Act there is no other law and regulatory measure by which the conduct of the bought leaf factories can be monitored now. The Tea Board, now, has no jurisdiction to control their activities, as these factories need not be registered with the Tea Board. The tea associations are nonentity to them as well. Nevertheless, the bought leaf factories should not be allowed to operate on their own wishes. A comprehensive measure for guidance, supervision and control over the activities of the bought leaf factories is required to be introduced by the Tea Board and other competent authorities. Only then, these factories may be made to follow under compulsion a set of norms and behaviour necessary for the welfare of the tea industry. It is now the high time to be alarmed!

SECTION IV
Development Initiatives and Major Highlights

Some of the major events, which took place over the years, are discussed as they have major impacts on the Indian economy.

- Future Trading in tea was approved by the Union Ministry of Commerce as part of plans to further liberalise commodities business. The Government said that the players in the market would be able to take advantage of the facilities of hedging and hence could manage their price risk.
- Mr. Deepak Khaitan, Executive Vice-Chairman and Managing Director of Eveready Industries India Limited, announced the company's plan to expand its packet tea business.
- At a press conference in Siliguri, West Bengal, Naxalite leader Mr. Kanu Sanyal alleged police atrocities on labourers working in tea gardens close to Indo-Nepal border in Darjeeling district on the pretext of detaining Maoist infiltration from Nepal.
- After a decade, Indian tea was again on display in popular departmental stores like Harrods, Selfridges, Fortnum and Masons in the UK.
- The Union Minister of Commerce and Industry, Mr. Murasoli Maran, at a meeting of the Consultative Committee of Plantation Associations (CCPA) and the Tea Board, released Accenture's Report on medium term tea export strategy for the country.
- Hindustan Lever Limited closed down its tea packaging facility at Kanhan near Nagpur due to unviability.
- The Chairman of the Federation of All India Tea Traders' Association (FAITTA), Mr. P O Desai, strongly criticized the 'Dandi Namak' campaign which was discouraging tea consumption.
- Warren Tea Limited, a tea giant, and J Thomas & Co., the largest tea broking firm in the country, experimented tea promotion campaign through New Year Greetings Card.

- The Darjeeling tea planters requested the Tea Board to introduce a 'Scheme of Loan and Subsidy' for improving the soil structure of tea gardens in the hill district.
- Tea planters in South India criticized the Tamil Nadu Tea Plantation Corporation's decision to allot its eight factories to only three auctioneers for selling tea. Earlier seven auctioneers were given the right to operate.
- Chairman of the Federation of All India Tea Traders' Association, Mr. P O Desai, vehemently criticized the trade practice of a section of tea planters who were retailing their unblended teas in sloppy packets under obscure brand names. These products were available in Uttar Pradesh, Maharashtra, Madhya Pradesh, Rajasthan, Punjab and in some other markets.
- Concerned over the low price of tea, Mr. Hemanta Kumar Gohain, Secretary of the All Assam Small Tea Growers' Association (AASTGA) requested the bought leaf factories and the organized sector to buy only quality green leaf from the small growers on an area to area basis.
- A 6-day "Supervisory Development Programme for Plantation Supervisors" was organized by the National Productivity Council on request of the Tea Association of India (TAI), Barak Valley branch. A total of 70 supervisors participated.
- Tea plantation companies in the Nilgiris, South India slashed the wage rate of workers by nearly 11 per cent, besides getting them to sign a productivity agreement along with a penal clause. The daily wage rate was brought down from Rs. 78.40 to Rs. 70.
- Mr. B C Aiyamma, Chairman of the Kanan Devan Planters' Association asked the Government to take some measures to curb tea imports in the country. He said, imported teas of poor quality were affecting the market sentiments and, hence, free import be checked.

- Employees of the Assam Tea Corporation met the Chief Minister of the State, Mr. Tarun Gogoi, to apprise him of the plight of the employees of five tea gardens under the Corporation. They also threatened an indefinite strike.
- The Chairman of the Surma Valley Branch, Indian Tea Association advised the planters of Cachar to make substantial improvement of their produce for long term revival of the Cachar tea industry.
- The Government of West Bengal announced its decision to defer the setting up of a tea auction center at Jalpaiguri, West Bengal.
- The Assam Assembly raised a motion to relocate the headquarters of companies having tea gardens in the State, from Kolkata to Guwahati.
- Extremists fired a rocket-propelled grenade and followed it up with gunfire at the residence of the manager of the Majuli Tea Estate of Tata Tea Limited in Darrang district, Assam.
- An all party delegation from Assam met the Union Commerce Minister, Mr. Murasoli Maran, to convey its concern over the fall in export of tea and increased competition from smaller parties.
- Kolkata-based Duncans Industries Limited entered the retail tea market. The Company opened its first outlet for premium quality tea at Lalbazar, Kolkata.
- The planters of South India reported the availability of China's CTC grades in Russia at 50 cents per kg.
- Dr. P.R. Krishnaswamy, Director, Manipal Hospital said media persons that experiments on animals at the L.V. Prasad Eye Institute showed antioxidants in tea may help fight cataract.
- The General Manager of the National Bank for Agriculture and Rural Development stated in Kolkata the bank's plan to provide financial support to the ailing tea industry of West Bengal.
- Mr. V. Venkiteswaran was appointed Executive Director of Tata Tea Limited who was given the

charge of South India Plantation Division including Instant Tea Division.

- The Chief Minister of Assam, Mr. Tarun Gogoi, reported at Nagaon, Assam, that no private organization was interested to take over the financially-bankrupt tea gardens under Assam Tea Corporation Ltd.
- Ten (10) small tea growers of Assam visited Kangra valley to acquire knowledge on mechanized cultivation of tea, financial aspects concerned with it and also on the method of fixing price of green leaf.
- The Government of India approved 100 per cent Foreign Direct Investment (FDI) in tea plantation and industry.
- Tata Tea announced its plan to set up 200 vending machines across the country in order to boost sales of the company in the domestic market.
- Mr. D.M. Jain, Managing Director of Jayshree Tea and Industries Ltd. informed the press and the shareholders at the 56th AGM about the company's effort to sell tea directly through the selling agents.
- Setting up of a tea cell in the Department of Commerce and Industry, Government of West Bengal, was announced.
- The Standing Committee on Labour presented its second report in the West Bengal, was announced.
- The Standing Committee on Labour presented its second report in the West Bengal Assembly, which pinpointed flouting of labour laws by tea gardens in the State. The report suggested the Government to take stern action against the errant tea garden owners.
- The Tamil Nadu Government expressed willingness to set up a tea auction center in Chennai.
- The Trade Association in Coimbatore announced its plan to experiment on electronic bidding at the tea auction center.

- Mr. N. Dharmarajan, Chairman of the UPASI Tea Committee, said that Kochi was selected for tea futures trade.
- Goodricke Group decided to take over the 'Nargis' brand of tea managed by a consortium of five tea companies called Project India Blend Ltd.
- The Chairman of the Kolkata Tea Traders Association, Mr. Arun Grover, said that salvation package to help the tea industry overcome present crisis should be based on redefining bulk marketing of tea, generic promotion, building 'India' brand.
- Managing Director of Eveready Industries, Mr. Deepak Khaitan, announced the company's plan to sell Bhatpara, Central Dooars, Chuapara, Jyanti and Mathura tea gardens in Dooars since these gardens no longer produce quality tea.
- Duncans Industries informed its decision to retail Green Tea called 'Duncans Green' from the company's outlets in Kolkata.
- The Congress members in the Lok Sabha called for the attention of Central Government on the ongoing depression in tea industry of the country.
- The Rajya Sabha Standing Committee on Commerce asked the Tea Board to explain the causes of decline in country's tea exports and the initiative taken to check price fall in the market and upgrading quality of tea.
- The Deputy Chairman of the Tea Board, Mr. Basudeb Banerjee, informed the media of the Government's decision to introduce export rating system for both producer exporters and merchant exporters of tea by a third party.
- Some tea planters criticized Government's plan to reintroduce mandatory sales of tea through the auction system.
- The Chairman of the Tea Board, Mr. N K Das, indicted the Board's plan of launching a Rs.50 crore tea promotional campaign in Russia, spread over three years, to revive exports in that region.

- Flood washed away around 100 sprawling tea gardens mostly in parts of the northern and eastern districts in Assam.
- Unilever, the world's largest packet tea producer, reported the company's plan to centralize its global tea procuring activities and make Kolkata as the major center for this purpose.
- Rossell Tea intended to increase its private sales and exports to 20-25 per cent of production.
- The Assam Chah Mazdoor Sangha, representing 3.25 lakhs of tea garden workers, threatened to launch an agitation if their demands placed before the State Government were not met immediately.
- Under a project promoted by the Union Ministry of Science and Technology in cooperation with the West Bengal Government, the Indian Institute of Technology, Kharagpur, converted 10 acres of wasteland in Gopali, Midnapore, West Bengal into a 'tea orchard'.
- The Chairman of Tata Tea expressed the hope to increase company's exports by 15 per cent more this year compared to last year.
- The Union Minister of State for Commerce and Industry informed the Lok Sabha members of allowing two more ports—Mumbai and Vishakhapatnam—for importing tea from Sri Lanka.
- Duncans Industries Ltd. introduced 'Marybong Mystique', a value added tea freshly packed in wooden chestlets to preserve the aroma and flavour.
- Drought severely affected the tea plantations in the Nilgiris, Planters' Association of Tamil Nadu stated in a press release.
- The past President of the Indian Tea Association, Mr. Bharat Bajoria, urged the Assam Government to register bought-leaf factories in the State under the Factories Act.
- Following gross indiscipline of a large section of workmen, Warren Tea declared lock-out of its Duamara Tea Estate in Doom Dooma, Assam.

- A week-long international Organic Food Festival was held in New Delhi where India's organic teas were exhibited.
- The Tea Board decided to launch a web site which will store information relating to production capacity of gardens, market prices, quality of Indian teas and also techniques of preparing good tea.
- The Consumer Affairs Minister of the Ministry of Commerce, Government of India, Mr. Sharad Yadav, reported the Government's plan on introducing ISI certification for tea to help improve realization for tea growers and companies.
- Leading tea manufacturers in the country urged the Indian Tea Association to persuade the Government for allowing the use of natural identical flavours in black tea.
- The Executive Director of the Tea Board, Mr. Vikram Kapoor, suggested the tea growers in South India to switch over to Orthodox manufacture from CTC, which only could salvage them from the continuing dull situation.
- West Bengal Government decided to conduct a survey of the tea industry in the State.
- Representatives of Workers' Unions in North Bengal gardens met the Governor of West Bengal to apprise him of the workers' plight due to closure of many gardens and default of garden managements to provide statutory facilities.
- Tata Tea set to launch organic tea, said Senior Manager, Mr. P Mohan Kumar, in-charge of the Research and Development Centre at the company's Teok Tea Estate at Jorhat, Assam.
- Coca-Cola started selling tea through vending machines installed at different locations in New Delhi and Kolkata.
- Re-opening of 13 locked-out tea gardens in North Bengal was uncertain as the managements boycotted the meeting convened by the Labour Minister, Government of West Bengal.

- The Tea Board released the 'Defaulter List' which includes the name of several companies and some leading tea organizations, took loan and advances under various schemes of the Board.
- The Godrej Group entered the tea business through its recently launched company, Godrej Tea Ltd.

Major Highlights

✓ Due to obstruction created by a section of labourers and non-labourers against the effort to grow new plantation I the unused areas of the garden, the management of the Bandapani Tea Estate in the Dooars, West Bengal, declared a lock out of the unit.

✓ The World Bank informed that the tea estates in the country interested to change over from conventional to unconventional energy sources for their power requirement will be assisted financially.

✓ Dooars Branch Indian Tea Planters Association, started at Banarhat in the Dooars and later shifted to Birpara in the Dooars, West Bengal, celebrated its Golden Jubilee.

✓ The North Bengal national Chamber of Commerce initiated a signature campaign for a tea auction center at Jalpaiguri, West Bengal.

✓ In a press meet held at Nagon, Assam, the President and the General Secretary of All Assam Tea Tribe Students' Association alleged that the tea industry in Assam did not take up any constructive work for the economic development in the State other than providing arms and ammunition to the militant outfits active here, and air ticket for the leaders of some organizations.

✓ The Arunachal Finance Minister, Mr. L Wanglet announced on Febraury 23, a Rs.500 crore scheme for tea cultivation by small and medium growers to better the lot of the poor, particularly in insurgency-affected Tirap, Lohit, and Changlang districts.

✓ Hijacking of trucks with goods on the way destined to North-East India increased substantially.

- ✓ Demanding the cancellation of the proposed housing project by winding up an existing tea estate, the Chandmoni Tea Estate Anti-Eviction Joint Action Committee observed a three-day hunger strike.
- ✓ The Sang Martam Tea Growers' Cooperative Society, Sikkim, had initiated the cultivation of tea in a virgin land measures 1000 acres. The land is located at the height of 3500 feet and 30 km away from the state capital.
- ✓ The Makaibari Tea Estate in Darjeeling signed MoU with the society to set up a tea processing plant with 50 per cent equity participation.
- ✓ The Proposal to develop infrastructure and peripheral areas of tea estates was submitted to the World Bank, seeking financial aid amounting to Rs. 40 crore.
- ✓ Dry spell and little rainfall affected all tea-growing areas in North Bengal. This weather condition seriously damaged the first flush in Darjeeling, which generally produces better quality tea for the overseas market.
- ✓ The noted Assamese writer, Mr. Mahim Bora, was conferred the Assam Valley Literary Award for 1998, instituted by Magor Educational Trust.
- ✓ The Minister for Municipal Affairs, Government of West Bengal, Mr. Ashoke Bhattacharya, ruled out the possibility of setting up another auction center in Jalpaiguri.
- ✓ The Manipur Government launched a campaign to popularize tea as a horticultural product.
- ✓ Under an arrangement with RPG Group Company Spencers Ltd., Harrisons Malayalam got the right to use Spencers name to its latest brand of tea that was launched in Chennai.
- ✓ The Tea Board sanctioned Rs. 32.47 lakh for the development of Tripura Tea Industry.
- ✓ The Tea Association of India reported Tripura's Tea Industry in great distress due to unprecedented drought combined with kidnapping of garden

personnel and extortion by some extremist organizations.

- ✓ Abrupt change of course by the river Dima was threatening the existence of Atiabari Tea Estate at Kalchine in the Dooars region of North Bengal. According to a report the river had already swallowed a vast tract of land of the garden.
- ✓ With the signing of an agreement by the Coordination Committee of Tea Plantation Workers and the tea garden owners before the West Bengal Labour Minister, Mr. Shanti Ranjan Ghatak, 3 lakh workers of 276 tea gardens in North Bengal called off the strike on 21st July which had begun on 12th July. The garden owners agreed to absorb 10,000 casual workers on permanent basis and to supply potable water, electricity and firewood.
- ✓ The promoters of Project India Blend, comprising Tata Tea, Williamson Magor, Rossell Industries Ltd., Warren Tea, and Goodricke Group, sat up their packaging unit in Russia.The Bureau of Indian Standards brought a good number of tea companies under the Hazard Analysis Critical Control Point Certification. Accordingly, an apex Committee under the Secretary, Ministry of Food Processing, Government of India, was set up to implement this measure.
- ✓ At the Annual General Meeting, Tata Tea's plant to acquire major shareholding and management control in the UK based Tetley Limited, a global player in the tea industry, was approved. The meeting also approved Tata's plan to float a 'Special Purpose Vehicle' for funding controlling stakes in the UK based company.
- ✓ In order to massively campaign for the tea brand "Taj Mahal", Hindustan Lever Ltd. brought out a commercial feature wherein Ustad Zakir Hussain, the renowned Tabla maestro, and TV personality Ruby Bhatia shown associated with Taj Mahal tea.
- ✓ On being disturbed by the insurgents frequently,

tea companies located in Assam's Cachar Valley sat up a "private army" on the lines of Assam Tea Special Police Force operating in Bramhaputra Valley to provide security to tea garden personnel working in this area.

- ✓ Allaying the fears of the Russian buyers on the quality front, the Tea Board Chairman, Mr. S.S. Ahuja assured that competent authorities would inspect consignments marked for Russia.
- ✓ Huge quantities of tea in 14 Kolkata warehouses were damaged owing to heavy rain during the last week of September 17,000 tea packets were soaked with water, a first-hand inspection revealed.
- ✓ The Darjeeling planters initiated plans for marketing and promotion of Darjeeling tea for arousing consciousness of the consumers in both domestic and overseas market.
- ✓ According to Horticulture Station, Udhagemandalam, Tamil Nadu, spraying of Bordeax mixture (1%) or Copper Oxychloride (0.25%) at 7-10 days interval prevents Blister Blight. Nickel Chloride and Biteranol also contain the preventive properties against this disease.
- ✓ Hindustan Lever Ltd., re-launched Lipton's 'Taaza' brand tea, largest brand in India, to reach to 50,000 villages across the country.
- ✓ The National Dairy Development Board sold both tea and coffee as Amul product to be marketed by the Gujarat Cooperative Milk Marketing Federation of India.
- ✓ The new tea gardens, particularly in Raiganj, Sadar Kotawali, and Maynaguri, complained to the local police station of uprooting and cutting of tea bushes.
- ✓ The India International Millennium Tea Convention will be held from 22nd to 24th March 2000 in New Delhi. The Convention is a joint effort by the Consultative Committee of Plantation Associations and the Tea Board.
- ✓ Tea export from India to Russia is likely to drop

this year by 10 per cent to 15 per cent, The low purchasing power of the consumers in that country which compelled them to cut back on the quality and quantity of tea they drank.

- ✓ The Rossell Tea acquired the Nagrijuli Tea Estate in Nalbari, Assam, from Derby Tea & Industrial Ltd.
- ✓ The members of Dibrugarh, Moran, and Naharkatia circles under Zone-I, Assam Branch Indian Tea Association donated a sum of Rs.1,00,000 to the Assam Chief Minister's Army Welfare Fund in aid of the Kargil martyrs.
- ✓ The Teesta Tea and Tourism Festival, inaugurated by the West Bengal Tourism Development Minister, was held at Kanchenjhanga Stadium, Siliguri, West Bengal.
- ✓ Warren Tea Ltd's associate, the Darjeeling Plantation Industries Ltd. acquired the controlling stake of the Kathalguri Tea Estate in Dooars, West Bengal.
- ✓ Terai Branch Indian Tea Association on behalf of member tea gardens in Terai, West Bengal contributed Rs.2,02,251 towards Central Army Welfare Fund.
- ✓ At the initiative of the National Bank for Agriculture and Rural Development, various banks agreed to finance the small tea growers in West Bengal.
- ✓ There are about 600 small tea growers in the region and a potential 24,000 hectares of land under small scale tea plantation.
- ✓ The country's tea production has recorded shortfall of 61 million kgs till October, and according to industry estimates it could reach 75-80 million kgs by the turn of the year.
- ✓ The Expert Group, constituted by the Tea Board, comprising representatives of the Indian Tea Association, Consultative Committee of Plantation Associations and others concerned, to review the existing bulk packaging norms and to forward its recommendation for an alternative and effective system has examined the plus and minus points of Jute Bag-laminated with LDPE, Multi-wall paper

sacks, HDPE-woven bags. The Report of the group was discussed.

- ✓ Hindustan Lever Limited introducing tea containing Vitamin A, Niacin, and Vitamin B2 with the object of giving 10 per cent of the recommended dietary allowance in each cup of tea.
- ✓ Hindustan Lever, the first company in the country, opened the market for micronutrient fortified tea.
- ✓ According to a recent notification of the Union Ministry of Agriculture, tea plantation units in West Bengal and Assam came under respective state's agricultural sector for the allocation of Urea, a government-controlled input for which this sector was previously enjoying a separate quota.
- ✓ The Manipur Plantation Corporation, a Manipur Government Undertaking established in 1981, is set to manufacture tea at its own factory.
- ✓ The Asom Yuba Parishad, youth wing of the Asom Gana Parishad, took it upon itself the matter of collecting 'Dues' from the major tea companies. Parishad members picketed before some offices and submitted the Parishad's Charter of Demand.
- ✓ The Indian Tea Association advocated the repeal of the Tea Marketing Control Order 1984, since the tea industry, on one hand, is being asked to gear up for free trade and imports while, on the other, the industry is being fettered with internal control.

SECTION V
Present Tea Scenario and Tips on Efficient Management Practices

Tea Industries in both South and North India are facing the threat of extinction for the last couple of years. Sharp fall in ex-factory and auction prices lead the tea planters to sell tea below cost of production in many places. However, it has been noticed that there is still a demand for good quality tea. Gardens manufacturing high quality tea are fetching higher prices. Hence, the time is ripe when there is a need to nurture tea gardens in a highly professional manner employing latest management practices with the twin objective of attaining higher yield and ensuring quality upgradation. Let us first throw our search light towards the present scenario of tea industry. Data published by J Thomas & Co. Pvt. Ltd. presented in Table 1 can be useful in understanding present status of tea in the major tea producing countries.

Table 1: Tea Scenario during 1999 to 2004

	1999	2000	2001	2002	2003	2004
Crop Position (in million kgs)						
North India	604.3	641.9	650.8	631.7	648.3	662.1
South India	201.3	204.5	202.9	206.7	229.9	230.8
Sri Lanka	280.1	305.8	295.1	310.6	303.2	300.1
Kenya	248.8	236.2	294.6	287.1	293.7	324.6
Malawi	38.5	42.1	36.8	39.2	41.7	50.1
Bangladesh	46.2	52.6	56.8	53.6	58.2	55.6
Indonesia	118.7	62.66	166.8	162.2	169.8	164.8
Auction Averages						
North India (Rs./kg)	80.58	70.35	69.83	165.9	61.37	71.62
South India (Rs/kg.)	57.10	44.64	46.02	41.62	39.35	47.16
Colombo (Rs/kg.)	114.96	135.06	143.66	148.66	148.32	180.18
Jakarta (Us Cents)	105.27	119.53	97.39	110.11	95.49	102.22
Mombasa (US Cents)	178	202.00	153.00	149.00	154.00	155.00
Limbe (US Cents)	93.74	102.01	87.45	91.47	93.39	100.27
Chittagong (Rs./kg)	58.78	58.16	58.88	59.78	67.00	63.72
All India Exports (m. kgs)	191.72	206.82	179.79	198.09	170.27	193.9
All India Sale Quantity (million kgs)						
North India	336.4	336.4	304.4	310.9	359.8	337.2
South India	170.4	170.4	158.7	146.0	118.1	137.2
All India Category–wise Crop (m.kgs)						
CTC	726.4	758.6	758.0	568.4	667.8	626.1
Orthodox	79.2	87.8	95.7	42.1	40.7	39.61

If we look at above tea statistics for the year 2004, following features emerge:

Compared to 2003, production of tea increased in 2004 except Bangladesh and Indonesia Auction sale was reduced in while it went up in South. Export from India was low and much below the projected target. Average price fetched per kg in all the auction centers expect Chittagaon. South India, Sri Lanka and Bangladesh saw a gain in Auction averages while North India was marginally behind. Jakarta, Mombasa and Limbe auction centers saw a huge downfall. One interesting feature is there was high-rise in the production of Orthodox tea during 1999 to 2004. It , however, declined in 2001 onwards. The above features reveal that the crisis in tea is not restricted to India alone; other major tea growing countries are also in trouble making it a global phenomenon. In 2004, India produced about 892 m .kgs of tea of which 699 m. kgs was retained and only 194 m. kgs was exported.

The major reason towards fall in price is attributed to low export and high rate of domestic requirement as can be seen in the table 2.

Table 2: Major Parameters of Tea Industry During 1905 to 2004

Particulars	*1905*	*1950*	*1971*	*1991*	*2000*	*2004*	*Growth rate*
No. of Tea Estates	5696	6731	12015	13873	38707	129027	21.6
Area Under Tea (th.ha)	213	315	357	420	438	521	1.5
Production (m.kgs)	100	278	435	560	823	892	7.8
Yield (kg/ha)	471	881	1221	1794	1880	1713	2.63
Export							
Quantity (m. kgs)	98	201	202	292	207	194	1.0
Value (m. Rs.)	89	804	1534	11203	18270	17281	193
Unit price (Rs/kg)	1	4	8	56	89	89	99
Export (%)	98	72	46	36	25	22	-0.8
Retention							
Quantity (m. kgs) times	2	77	233	268	619	698	350
Retention (%.)	2	28	54	48	75	78	40 times

Tea is the most popular drink in the world, so is the condition in India. All know pharmacological value of tea. Tea has answer to any major diseases of human beings. A few aspects are presented below:

(i) Small amount of caffeine ingested per cup (40 mg) could only be beneficial as a stimulant.

(ii) Green tea liquor is rich in vitamins—Vitamin C & K and micro-nutrients required by the body.

(iii) Certain phenolic compounds in liquor were claimed to be an anti-carcinogenic because it is thought, they scavenge free radicals (in cell cultures & the body) and because they are good anti-oxidants. In Sri Lanka a signle dose of black tea extract (content: 21.5 mg EGCG [epigallo catechin–3–gallate) and 22.7 mg of TF (theaflavine)) elevated serum antioxidantactivity (Modder, 2001).

(iv) Tea phenolics counteracting hypertension (blood glucose levels are depressed).

(v) Cardiovascular disease could be prevented through lowering of free cholesterol, total lipid and triglyceride levels in plasma & liver.

(vi) Alleviate allergies by inhibiting histamine release.

(vii) Tea extracts have also shown to be bacteriocidal eg against dysentery and in addition extracts can also inhibit some bacterial toxins such as cholera for instance.

(viii) Both Catechins and the theaflavins derived from tea can inhibit HIV—reverse transcriptase.

(ix) Black tea extract inhibits the oral fungus Candida albicans by 30 per cent (Modder, 2001).

SECTION VI
Scientific Problems in the Tea Plantations

Tea industry is beset with many problems. These are typical in nature. However some of them e are summarized below:

(i) Poor establishment in the nursery;

(ii) Old and unproductive plantation; apathy towards replantation;

(*iii*) Improper selection of land;
(*iv*) Non adhrerence of scientific planting methods: shallows pits, inappropriate size of plants;
(*v*) Low organic inputs;
(*vi*) Absence of quality planting materials: Tea & Shade Trees;
(*vii*) Less attention towards mulching;
(*viii*) Improper Drainage;
(*ix*) Problems in pest management practices; to much dependence on synthetic chemicals;
(*x*) Dearth of sufficient knowledge of proper spray techniques;
(*xi*) Less awareness about organic farming;
(*xii*) Inappropriate manuring;
(*xiii*) Less knowledge about pluckers' productivity;
(*xiv*) Inadequate education and training of workers;
(*xv*) Apathy towards quality upgradation.

Poor Establishment in the Nursery and Tips on Nursery

Very often, tea nursery fails to maintain health due to lack of proper scientific management. Very much like human world if a 'baby tea plant' is produced in the nursery with physiological impediments, the future of this tea is ought to be problematic. Correcting only a few irregularities, healthy tea plants can be produced in a nursery. A few points are discussed here.

Tips on Nursery

(*a*) Condition inside the nursery should not be too humid. Put on appropriate shade to allow about 33 per cent to 50 per cent sunlight. Netlon shade could be useful.
(*b*) Waterlogged condition in the nursery tantamount to the infection of Fusarium, Pythium, Phomopsis etc.

(c) During winter, it would be advisable to raise arched transparent polythene tent over the beds so that correct humidity and temperature be maintained.

(d) Prepare appropriate soil media for proper growth of the plants.

(e) Go for composite plants in the nursery stage. This is a method of grafting in the cutting stage, so that a mechanical association of two different clones having characters be established. For example, the stock portion may be from a plant having good rooting system, which may be helpful in droughty condition, while the scion may be from a high yielding or high quality clone. Scion maker & graft maker are available in the market, which makes the process quite cost effective.

PART IV
REDRESSAL ISSUES OF TEA INDUSTRIES, ISSUES OF TEA INDUSTRY IN NATIONAL AND INTERNATIONAL PERSPECTIVES, REPORT OF WORKING GROUP OF TEA INDUSTRY

Part IV envelops four chapters (16th to 19th). Chapter 16 presents major issues, which have been addressed by the various tea associations through their annual general meetings or conferences from time to time. Here agenda items of United Planters' Association of Southern India; Calcutta Tea Traders Associations; Tea Association of India etc. together with probable strategies have been inked. Chapters 17 and 18 devote to major areas of concern with reference to International and national perspectives. These have been collected from various reputed international and national journals, magazines like India-today, business world, agricultural today, periodicals and national dailies. All these have been updated and placed. The basis objectives of introducing these two chapters are to: *(i)* make the reader abreast of the latest developments that have been taking place, *(ii)* suggest policy prescriptions and *(iii)* take stock of the situation of tea industry in domestic and world markets. Chapter 19 draws attention on the rationale of setting up of Madhukar Committee for addressing the problems of tea industry with remedial measures. The salient features of the committee report of working group on tea industry have also been penned in this chapter.

These issues are very critical and require policy decisions or interventions by the appropriate authorities like government of India, state government, tea board, tea research institutes, agricultural universities having tea husbandry as one of the disciplines, united planter's association of southern India etc. They pertain to abolition of excise duty, productivity linked wages, shift to value added products, tea has health properties, manufacturing practices to market requirements, review of excise duty and tea control order, over-obsessed with short term price fluctuations, poor demand and declining prices of tea, availability of domestic surplus of tea, conversion of tea factories for manufacture of orthodox tea, government support, harmonisation of sales tax and VAT scheme, crystal images of ball in the next century, steady remunerative prices, working environment, welfare measures, socio-economic development, use of latest technology in both field and factory operations, communication facilities etc.

16

Redressal Issues of Tea Associations

1. The 109th UPASI Annual General Conference

He came, he spoke and he conquered the hearts of the planters, but at the end of the day, their problems remain unabated. This would, perhaps, be the apt way of describing the participation of the then Union Minister of State for Commerce, Mr. Rajiv Pratap Rudy at the 109th UPASI Annual Conference in Coonoor in 2003. Impressed by the tone and tenor of his address, the outgoing UPASI President, Mr. IJJ Rebello, risked observing, "Never ever was the Annual Conference of the UPASI so lively as today". The incoming President, Mr. P S Walia, went a step ahead. In his vote of thanks, he said that after Mr. Nani Palkhivala and Mr. P Chidambaram, the UPASI did not have a speaker of such an eminence at its Annual meets. The following issues were discussed:

Issues

Abolition of Excise Duty: The planters themselves wondered what the Minister had promised for them to get over the present crisis and to merit such encomium. Mr. Rudy neither assured to the tea planters to support their plea for the abolition of the excise duty nor reacted to their plea for pressing the Reserve Bank of India to extend to tea the five per cent interest subsidy given to the small growers of coffee. He did not refer to the plea for funding a study to chalk out a road map on the strategic and structural issues. These will help the industry to face the global competition which arises from the Government throwing open imports of plantation products for domestic consumption. He did not commit himself to bring in market-oriented rather than production-oriented approach in the Tenth Five-Year Plan as sought by the industry. There was hardly any assurance that the listed obstacles in the auction procedures would be removed. He did not promise to leave the Tea Marketing Control Order untouched, which would help the producers market their teas, as they liked. The then Finance Minister did not care to speak about the removal of the duty free imports enjoyed by the export-oriented units as they brought in no mentionable increase in foreign exchange earnings. There was no mention about the plea for revising the EXIM policy.

Productivity Linked Wages: On the industry associations signing agreements with unions for low wages and productivity linked wages, the Minister mentioned Government's total inability to amend any of the outlived labour laws. Thus, there was no promise to help the planters come out of the statutory burden to provide housing, water and sanitation facilities, schools and crèches, etc. to their labour. He did not say about treating plantations as an agricultural enterprise for purposes of agricultural income tax or to move the state governments to get the rates lowered to the central income tax levels. He assured the planters that their future was safe and that the Government had confidence in them which they should also reciprocate. If these words could fill the hearts of the planters, at least in the coming year, the industry should post profits against Mr Rebello's complaint this year "the industry is losing heavily" .But, how does he propose to please the planters?. "The officers in my ministry are receptive to suggestions. So, we will find answers", he told this Correspondent.

Stop Expansion of Production: The then Commerce Secretary, Mr. Dipak Chatterjee in his address squarely dismissed the industry's plea to stop expansion of plantations in the North Eastern states to avoid glut. "The Government will push through the scheme of expansion because North-eastern states are, indeed, backward", he asserted. The Rubber Board in particular is promoting the extension of plantations in the North-eastern states. The then Minister told this Correspondent that the Government had drafted a scheme to increase the share of India in global exports to one per cent in 2007 from the present 0.67 per cent. One proposal was to launch agri export centres at an outlay of Rs.550 crore. "Would there be one for tea at Coimbatore as the exporters are asking for it?" Mr Rudy replied : "No. The proposal has to come from the State Government. Mr. Rudy also said that the Government was now focusing on Africa and Latin America. "These countries have shown encouraging response to our promotion", he said. But, would that also mean our import of teas from Africa? A spokesman of the Kenyan Tea Development Authority, for instance, recently told this Correspondent, "In five years from now, we see India as a net importer of tea. We would like to play a major role given the vast consumption here".

2. 106th UPASI Annual General Meeting

At the 106th Annual General Meting of United Planters Association of Southern India, Mr. R.S. Jhawar, the then Chairman, Consultative Committee of Plantation Associations (CCPA) was the Guest of Honour. The gist of the Speech on that occasion by Mr. R.S. Jhawar is presented here.

Issues

Role of Plantation Industry—Plantations play a very important role in the economic development of India. They are basically agriculture in nature, but also encompass an element of industry. They are highly labour oriented. Plantations directly employ 2 million labour, supporting a family of 8 million persons and if both direct and indirect employment is taken into account, plantations support about 15 million people throughout the country. Women constitute a significant portion of the employment. Plantation products are eco-friendly and earn substantial foreign exchange apart from contributing to the revenue of the Central and State

Governments by various taxes and duties. Thousands of small growers are engaged in its cultivation.

Shift to Value Added Products—India still continues to be the exporter of bulk commodities and there is considerable potential to shift to value-added products, which will substantially increase our foreign exchange earning. Unfortunately, as for other agricultural produces, the prices of plantation commodities have remained stagnant during the last twenty years in terms of US $. The yields of our plantation crops are, no doubt, satisfactory, but we should strive to further improve it. There is also scope for improving production through irrigation. A strategy for phased replanting needs also to be worked out. For this purpose, it is essential that the rates of agricultural income taxation, which are very high, are brought down to be on par with the Central rates, so that the plantations could use the available surplus for long term development. It should be realized, in this context, that plantations are different from ordinary agriculture and their growing involve a long gestation period before the crops start coming in.

Tea as Health Drink—It is rather unfortunate that we tend to depend on merely global demand-supply position for our prices. This scenario should change. There is ample scope for increasing the consumption of both coffee and tea in India, as the per capita consumption is very low. The position is the same in respect of natural rubber. There is enough research evidence that tea has several health beneficial aspects. It could, therefore, be promoted as a health drink. The Government should not take any hasty decisions based on temporary price phenomenon. It may be recalled that measures in the past like imposition of export duty, fixation of minimum export prices, ban on export of CTC teas etc. had considerably damaged the export position of Indian tea.

Review of Excise Duty and Tea Control Order—There is a case to review the levy of Excise Duty of Rs. 2 per kg on tea. The tea industry should also be enabled to get 100 per cent tax exemption for export profits. The Tea (Marketing) Control Order, which was issued in 1984, has no relevance in today's liberalized scenario.

The International tea Convention held jointly by UPASI and Tea Board earlier in September 1999 was a grand success. The CCPA has hold an International Tea Convention in Delhi in March 2000.

Gist of the Speech by Mr. S.S. Ahuja Chairman, Tea Board, India

India has been doing very well on the tea production front. Output of tea went up from 620 m. kgs in 1986 to a record 870 m. kgs in 1998. This increase of about 250 m. kgs is nearly what Kenya producers today. In the case of South India, the crop went up from 140 m. kgs in 1986 to 201 m kg by 1998 and the productivity reached the record level of 2290 kg per hectare; this is no doubt a remarkable achievement. In the past, South India had an average share of 34 per cent in India's total tea exports but today it is about 54 per cent. South India has also the unique phenomenon of small grower concentration in tea. There are over 50,000 small growers in the region. About 140 bought leaf factories and 17 cooperative factories cater to the need of the small growers.

The year 1999, however, has seen a downward trend. Bulk of the decline in production has been in the orthodox segment. Similarly, exports declined. The following issues have been dwelt upon:

Issues

Exports of Value Added Teas—Between 1986 and 1998 exports of tea bags went up from 0.5 m kgs to 2 m kg. Instant tea exports more than doubled from 1.1 m kg to 2.7 m kg. Similar figures for packet teas were 15.7 m kg and 81.4 m kg. There are, however, several other new products of tea that we need to explore. For instance, flavoured teas and iced teas have good potential. Another are is green tea. Global exports of green tea had jumped from 72 m kgs in 1986 to 126 m kg in 1998, but India's share is just about 2 m kg. Our markets also need to be diversified. There are several global markets like Syria, Tunisia, Pakistan etc. which are still to be explored by India.

Manufacturing Practices to Market Requirements—We need also to reorient and dovetail our manufacturing practices to market requirements. Unfortunately, for example, reconditioned teas go to certain overseas markets where these are not really in demand or the supplies are excessive. This is one of the reasons why South India teas are yet to make a breakthrough in the up-county markets even within India. We need, therefore, to undertake a study of the consumption pattern in different states and then manufacture the kind of teas that are required by the consumers in the respective regions. In fact, if we look back, in 1951 the average price of North India tea was Rs. 3.27 per kg and that of South India in the same year was Rs. 4.70 per kg. But in 1998, the average for North India was Rs. 80.22 per kg and for South India it was Rs. 68.78 per kg. This position surely requires serious consideration. While we have been doing very well on the field, I feel much more is needed on the factory side. For instance. The award for the highest productivity went to the South India garden with more than 5000 m kgs per hectare.

Should Not Get Over-obsessed with Short Term Price Fluctuations—It is also suggested that we should not get over-obsessed with the short-term fluctuations in prices while working out our long-term production strategies. On the price front, Tea Board has decided to commission a study by the Indian Institute of Plantation Management on the Introduction of futures. That is the only way to make sure that the violent fluctuations in tea prices are evened out to some extent and the growers are assured of a steady return. Future trading in tea, should be successful in India because of the large number of buyers and large number of growers.

Tea Research—As far as the future is concerned, Tea Board's priority is on sustainable development, research, quality improvement, productivity enhancement and cost effectiveness. Tea Board intends giving substantial fillip to tea research and the Tea Board has funded 49 per cent of the budget to UPASI TRI. Internationally, the Tea Board is involved along with other countries in the expansion of world tea markets. It is in this context that India is a contributory to the FAO Project on health benefits of tea.

In recent years, there is positive response from other tea producing countries like Sri Lanka, Bangladesh, Kenya, etc. towards cooperation on the tea promotion. After the new Government takes over, the Tea Board will launch a new initiative towards bringing the tea producers under a common umbrella. The Board established electronic auctioning of tea. Alongside some of the issues relating to the auction system are being studied by Indian Institute of Management, Kolkata.

3. 38th Annual General Meeting Tea Association of India

The 38th Annual General Meeting (AGM) of the Tea Association of India was held on January 25, 2002 in Kolkata. The then President of the Association, Mr. Umang Kanoria addressed the meeting. The major issues discussed in the AGM are given below:

Major Issues

Poor Demand and Declining Prices of Tea : The Tea Industry today is passing through a grave crisis and faced with a scenario of very poor demand and declining prices of all varieties of tea, more so in the common medium categories. While prices have dropped in the auctions significantly in the last two years there has been substantial increase in costs on account of steep increase in labour wages. As a result, most of the estates in Dooars and Cachar and a number of estates in Assam are facing severe hardship.

Domestic Surplus of Tea: The surplus of domestic availability of tea is the main cause of the crisis. It is the common medium category of tea that has been mostly affected. Prices of quality tea has declined but not to the same extent. Large-scale proliferation of small growers and Bought Leaf Factories have also contributed significantly to the surplus in the non-quality segment. Since they have developed without sufficient guidance, quality of their produce has been of uncertain standards, causing depressing effect on the prices offered for other teas also.

Unfavourable CTC-Orthodox Mix: One main contributing factor towards the poor export performance for the year

2001 and the sharp decline in prices for common CTC teas is the unfavourable CTC-Orthodox mix produced by the industry. The ratio in favour of CTC teas has resulted in surplus availability of CTC tea domestically and at the same time has resulted in a number of export enquiries for Orthodox teas being refused for want of availability. So, to increase our exports in the coming years it is imperative that we increase production of Orthodox tea. The demand of Orthodox in the global tea market is around 40 per cent at present but India accounts for a mere 10 per cent of this market.

Conversion of Tea Factories for Manufacture of Orthodox Tea: To enable estates increase production of Orthodox tea a scheme has been notified by the Government which will subsidise 25 per cent of the capital investment made on conversion of tea factories for manufacture of Orthodox and non-reconditioned CTC teas. The ups and down in our export performance is largely tied down to a single market–Russian Federation–which accounts for almost 50 per cent of our exports. Meanwhile Sri Lanka has entered the Russian tea market. With a free market in full swing in Russian Federation, tea importers have started redirecting their purchases to other sources thereby seriously affecting our exports.

Diversification of Tea Exports: We need to diversify our tea exports to a larger number of markets. Sri Lanka has done this and are highly successful in improving their export position as number one. The industry has identified some key markets as Russia, Pakistan, Iran, Saudi Arabia, UAE and Egypt, where Indian teas need to be pushed more aggressively. Strategies have been worked out to improve performance.

Government Suppcrt: Among various governmental measures taken in the recent past, some stand out. Restrictive practice like compulsory offerings of tea in auctions by the producers has been removed leaving the tea producers free to find their own marketing channels. Then, there is enhancement in deduction allowed under Section 33 AB from 20 per cent to 40 per cent for ploughing into development purposes. Enhancement of Import Duty rate on tea imports to 70 per cent is another welcome measure. It may be mentioned that there is an urgent need for higher rate of replanting, rejuvenation and modernization for quality tea production. Tea Board's loan and subsidy schemes have been of great help. But now a revision is required in the subsidy rate.

Imports: Tea imports into India, on an average, for the last three years is about 15 m kg. Most of this import goes into EPZ and EOU areas where it is blended with Indian teas and re-exported. Complaints of inferior quality admixture were received from abroad about such blended Indian tea exports. This tarnished the quality image of our tea exports without bringing in additional revenues from abroad. Although the import duty has been raised from 30 per cent to 70 per cent this Duty should be raised to 150 per cent, the Bound Rate as permitted under WTO, to ensure that this Duty this industry remains healthy enabling it to continue the good work being done in backward areas.

Per Capita Consumption: Per capita consumption of tea in the country is stagnating at about 660 gms as against over 1000 gms in Pakistan. To provide a boost to the consumption of tea in the country the industry has launched generic promotion of tea within the country and increase the Indian citizens' awareness of the natural therapeutic qualities of tea and its beneficial effects on consumers' health. This has now been followed up by large and regular promotional measures like Advertorials, Doctors' Mailers, Consumer Leaflets, Posters, TV, Media and other activities like essay competition, seminars and conferences.

Other Issues

Since this industry has no control over the tea market which operates solely on the demand and supply position at anytime it has to take measures which would trim its expenses, improve its productivity and quality, and seeks such fiscal and other measures which will help it in fast recovering from the present plight.

Labour Productivity: With the advent of WTO regime the industry is now faced with competition from other tea producing countries both in the domestic market and in the overseas market. Indian teas have turned costliest due to rising input cost including cost of labour. Steady rise in labour wages and cost of other labour welfare measures without matching growth in labour productivity over the long years have put Indian teas to a serious disadvantage in domestic as well as in overseas markets. Such labour phenomena as large-scale absenteeism and non-fulfilment of task are adding heavily to costs. Time has come to link labour productivity with wage increases. Productivity improvement must come along with quality improvement through fine plucking and improved processing methods.

Central Excise Duty: Tea is basically an agricultural produce and common man's beverage. It is an essential commodity under the law. For this reason, tea was completely exempted from Central Excise Duty payment in 1993. The re-imposition of Excise Duty @ Rs. 2/- per kg. since 1999 is not only highest ever on tea but the producers are also unable to pass on the incidence of duty to buyers under the present system of marketing of tea. In the present circumstances when the tea industry is reeling under the burden of high costs and abysmally low price realization, the tea industry certainly needs to be totally exempted from the payment of Excise Duty.

Harmonisation of Sales Tax and VAT Scheme: The troubles o the industry have been further compounded by raising of Sales Tax rate on tea under the Harmonisation Scheme of Sales Tax among all the states. The Sales Tax rate on tea has been doubled from 4 per cent to 8 per cent all over the country, which has added substantially to the price of made tea making it costly to the consumers and consequently leading to curtailment in its consumption within the country. Moreover, introduction of VAT in place of Sales Tax in all States from 1st April, 2002 envisages 4 slab rates enjoying nil, 4 per cent, 10 per cent and 12 per cent. Today the need is to promote domestic consumption of Indian teas. In the context of severe competition developing in the export and domestic markets and decline in domestic consumption growth and prices since 1999, it is necessary that the Central and State Governments should shift tea from the General Goods category to the Essential Goods category to save tea from punitive rate of taxes.

Social Welfare: The industry have provided financial assistance from time to time on various social development projects as education, agriculture, sports, games, etc. and also to medical centres.

4. The 122nd Annual General Meeting Dooars Branch Indian Tea Association

The above meeting (DBITA) was held on 15th January, 2000 at Binnaguri of Jalpaiguri district, West Bengal while addressing the AGM, Mr C P Kapur, the then Chairman, DBITA deliberated on the following issues.

Important Issues

Crystal Images of Ball in the Next Century: It would be interesting to attempt crystal gazing into tea's future. Tea being an organized industry data are available for such a study. Some of the images shown by Crystal Ball for the next century are as follows:

1. India is likely to remain major producer;
2. Per capita consumption is likely to go up in countries where it is low;
3. The current major suppliers may change;
4. Some exporting producers may become next importers'.
5. Production pattern may change dramatically – Instant tea, Bottle/aerated tea, Flavoured tea, Decaffeinated tea; health stores will demand teas grown with biological control;
6. New method of manufacture to increase cuppage;
7. Orthodox teas are likely to be phased out;
8. High yielding clones are expected to be developed with yields upto 10000 kg/ha.
9. Auction system will continue to play a significant role;
10. Tea industry is intended to pay greater attention to advertisement and promotion;
11. Modernisation of factory, use of solar energy, gas; and
12. Minimize seasonal quality fluctuations.

In Dooars, however, crop shortfall was due to severe drought, 10 days' strike during peak production month of July 2006 just when bushes were beginning to recover from the severest drought of the century. There was shortfall in back end crop due to lower temperatures. Despite shortfall in production, prices have remained lower than last year. Some of the reasons could be due to imports together with fall in exports. One cannot take for granted that prices would rise in case of shortfall in crop. Production cost has gone up by nearly 20 per cent due to fall in production, increase in labour wages, rise in cost of other inputs like HSD, Fertilisers, Pesticides, Power. There has been no relief from Excise Duty of Rs. 2/- per kg imposed few years back.

Steady Remunerative Prices: Steady remunerative prices are necessary to ensure future development of tea industry which requires large investments to uproot ageing low-yielding old tea and replanting these areas with new clones for enhancing land productivity. Even factory machinery needs be modernized. While replanting cost/ha is over Re.1 lakh, Tea Board Subsidy is too meagre to meet 50 per cent of cost. Replanting Subsidy must cover at least 75 per cent of cost for Small tea planters. Payback period can be reduced provided industry supplies with higher yielding clones.

Agro-based Industry: Tea is agro-based industry and production is adversely effected due to vagaries of weather. It is therefore necessary to improve technology application so that fluctuations in crop can be minimized. Steady production would also stabilize price fluctuation. This would help management to execute long term plans for development of the property. There is need to set up R & D activities in the Research Stations in our region to overcome specific problems. The Association needs to find further higher yielding clones to increase bush productivity.

Increase in Consumption (Internal & External): There is need to increase consumption both internal and external by finding new consumers and increasing per capita consumption which is low even in our country. Tea is natural and healthy drink and this should be conveyed to the public, especially the youth.

Sustained Efforts to Increase Exports: Sustained efforts are required to increase exports. It is to be noted that the production costs in some other major tea producing countries are lower than India. Ways and means have to be found to curtail production costs by increasing bush and labour productivity, improving operational efficiency, optimizing utilization of all resources/inputs, conserving energy, maintaining machinery, reducing wastages/losses, damage/wilful degradation. Last but not the least HRD Training and Development of staff and workers.

Working Environment: To achieve all that the need is proper working environment created by close co-ordination between Government/Administration, Labour and Management. Tea would possibly be the only industry which has withstood the threats faced from time to time due to its strength. It has received the least amount of subsidies and support from any quarter even under adversity. If the prices go up, serious effort is made by some quarters to force/demand reversal of this trend but when the prices go down, it is left upto the producer to protect the bottom line. Tea is the single largest labour intensive industry. Tea is the only industry where even in the year 1999, management agreed to increase another 10,000 workers to its permanent strength. By increasing labour force without ensuring optimum productivity from existing labour force would make the industry unviable. The 21st Century ushers in a new era of liberalization under the aegis of the WTO with a free global market place. Standards of quality would have to match global standards even when the Indian consumer no longer having to accept shoddy goods or surly services.

Land/Labour Productivity Modern Techniques of Cultivation etc.: Increase in production is also dependent upon the productivity of the workers. Land productivity has increased in the Dooars but labour productivity has remained relatively stagnant. Modern techniques of cultivation accord all opportunities to the pluckers to pluck more, yet by a factual study it can be ascertained that majority of the workers are unable to reach achievable levels. The workers cannot shy away from fulfilling their prime responsibility. The commitment and involvement of the workers is most essential in the present age of competition. At the same time, management of tea units needs to attach more importance to improve the quality of life of the workers within the parameter of their obligations so that workers are motivated to play their role in the manner it is required. In this connection, advice of the CCPA in respect of the medical facilities at our gardens needs be attended. Providing potable drinking water and construction of pucca quarters are some of the other welfare obligations of the management, progress of which would need to be accelerated.

Welfare Measures: The management of many tea gardens have initiated many measures on their own for the welfare of their workers and their families. In addition, to such welfare activities The India Tea Association through its Dooar's Branch with the help of the Project Office on Family Welfare Programme is continuing to assist garden managements to make sure that Mothers' Club continue to perform their role. It has been regretted that the 10 days of strike in July 2006 could not be averted despite all efforts. Interests of neither the workers nor the management are served by strikes or unrests. The Central Leadership of Trade Unions should, therefore, assess the capacity and capability of the industry before placing industry-wise demands.

Growth of Tea Industry—Govts. Interest: The Government of West Bengal is also keen to encourage growth of tea industry vis-à-vis the production. In a situation of less land being available with the District Administration, a move was initiated for re-settlement of resumed lands in favour of the applicant tea garden. However, the same is pending. It will not be out of place to mention that at the initiation of our Divisional Commissioner a Committee was formed to set guidelines in remodelling the Lease Agreement within the acceptable parameters. The recommendation of the Committee was submitted before the Commissioner. The proposed Lease Format be duly approved for the convenience of the Government as well as the lessee Tea Gardens.

Floods: Floods have been causing huge financial losses to the tea gardens year after year. Large tea areas are washed away together with damage to infrastructure. Metamorphological changes in the rivers flowing through many parts of the Dooars have resulted in a situation, in which flooding of tea gardens is almost a routine problem with the onset of rains. The problem of flooding is gradually becoming grave. The District Magistrate, of Jalpaiguri, apprehending darker days ahead, has submitted a comprehensive Report to the Tea Board for financial assistance in building up the protective measures.

Communication Facilities: Communication facilities need be improved, also the law and order situation. Garden property is subjected to damage and depredate due to trespass problems. To meet fuel requirements, shade trees are felled, tea bushes are hacked, pruning litter is stolen. Incidents of theft of green leaf have also increased. Thefts of V P cuttings, scions and plants have increased as a number of nurseries have mushroomed without having any source of procuring these materials. In the same connection another unnerving situation is gradually developing in the area in which anonymous letters of threat have been sent to many managerial personnel and others. This development is a new phenomena in the Dooars. Local Administration should take immediate action to control this situation.

5. The 75th Annual General Meeting—Terai Indian Planters' Association

The 75th Annual General Meeting of Terai Indian Planters' Association was held on 31st March, 2002 at Matigara of Darjeeling District, West Bengal. While addressing, Mr. R K Sengupta, the then Chairman of the Association presented the following issues:

Identified Issues

Decline in Price Realisation Affecting Cash Flow: The Tea Industry in North Bengal has been passing through five successive years of price decline. Such sharp decline in price had adversely effected cash flow of the companies. The price situation indicated that there was an over-supply of plainer quality CTC tea which the market has found difficult to absorb. The position was worsened by the increasing output from Small Growers and Bought Leaf Factories of West Bengal. According to estimates, the total number of units belonging to Small Growers segment in West Bengal was 809 in 1998 with a production of about 8 million kgs. In the year 2000, the number of small growers in West Bengal increased to 1250 units with estimated production of 18 million kgs. It is estimated that the number of small growers during 2006 would be 2100 with a production of 23 million kgs. This indicates that over the period 1998 to 2006 output from this sector was tripled.

Quality of Tea and Method of Private Disposal of Produce by Bought Leaf Factory: Forty one Bought Leaf Factories as enumerated by Tea Board have a declared installed capacity of around 26 million kgs. There is a serious concern over the quality of tea being produced at these factories and the method of private disposal of produce. Low price levels at which this produce is being sold is exerting a downward push on auction prices. Bought Leaf Factories are able to sell at low prices because of significantly lower production cost, as they do not have to bear many statutory liabilities.

Selling Teas below the Cost of Production: Along with the decline in prices, there has been a surge in costs. Large segments of the industry in North Bengal are selling teas below the cost of production. The sharp increase in the cost of production coupled with price decline is threatening the viability of tea gardens and has also affected the competitiveness of Indian teas in the global market.

Wage and Wage Related Benefits: Wages and wage related benefits account for around 40–45 per cent of overall cost of production. Another 10 per cent is accounted for statutory and non-statutory welfare facilities provided to workers. This means that for every Re 1 increase in wage, the impact on cost of production works out to almost 56 paise per kgs of made tea. Between 1997-2001, the total wage increase for Daily Rated Workers in West Bengal tea industry has been Rs.15.50, resulting addition of Rs. 9 per kg on overall cost of production.

Procurement Price of Food grain: Procurement prices of foodgrains for supplying concessional foodstuff to tea garden workers has also been skyrocketing. In the year 2000-01 the prices of foodgrains registered an increase by over 35 per cent as against the previous year. There are other significant costs comprising green leaf cess, land revenue, electricity charges and high interest. The Report by Accenture has made an important recommendation for the industry to reduce landed cost of tea which would be necessary to boost exports through enhanced competitiveness, to combat rising cost of production to achieve cost competitiveness internally against Small Growers and Bought Leaf Factories segments. This indicates the necessity to reduce labour cost which is the most significant component of the cost of production. It is felt that reduction in labour cost could be achieved with increase in the productivity level of workers. In case of tea workers, this will basically mean increasing the minimum basis task set for a worker for the day. But it is a matter of concern that tea workers in West Bengal are not fulfilling even their basic task.

Need Based Employment: It is necessary for the industry to have need-based employment. Automatic filling up of vacancies has to be done with. The problem of employment of temporary workers has to be reviewed seriously. Deployment of temporary workers in batches by rotation, depending on the requirement, should be considered to reduce the burden of cost.

Selective Mechanisation: Other competing tea producing countries have adopted selective mechanization, such as, shear plucking and mechanical harvester which has significantly increased output per man-day thereby reducing cost of production. To improve competitiveness, the necessity of introducing mechanization would have to be seriously considered.

Land for New Plantation: The biggest incentive to production is land. It is heartening that the State Government of West Bengal has cleared cases of new plantations that came into existence upto 30th June, 2001. However, in an extraordinary move to slap a hefty Salami, the Government imposed a Salami of Rs.15000 per hectare in case of transfer of lease, and also a Salami equivalent to 40 per cent of the market value of land where fresh tracts of land were brought under tea cultivation. It is felt such a decision did not provide the required impetus to the new entrepreneurs.

Enhancement of Land Revenue by Five Times: Tea gardens, which had been paying land rent so far under the West Bengal Estates Acquisition Act, 1953 have now been asked to pay land revenue at the rate of Rs. 30 per acre. As a result, the rate of land revenue stands enhanced from the pre-existing rate of Rs. 6.50 per acre by almost five times. Apart from the basic land rent, tea gardens have also been subjected to levies such as: *(i)* Road Cess—at the rate of 5 per cent, *(ii)* Public Works Cess at the rate of 25 per cent, *(iii)* Rural Employment Surcharge—at the rate of 15 per cent.

Rural Employment and Production Cess: It may be mentioned that the Cess at the rate of 8 paise per kgs of Green Leaf is already being collected on Rural Employment & Production Cess under the West Bengal Rural Employment and Production Act, 1976. Hence there is no justification for a double charge on Rural Employment & Production Cess.

Road Cess and Public Work Cess: With the Road Cess and Public Works Cess, the additional burden is 3.1 per cent which amounts to an additional liability of Rs. 9.30 per acre. The Government should review the impact of land rent and levies on tea estates and reduce the same, wherever possible, to retrieve the industry from the present crisis.

The Move of the Union Government: The move of the Union Government for imposing 100 per cent import duty on the tea imported from abroad and also the measure of reducing the Central Excise Duty by Re. 1 per kg of the made tea on the existing rate is appreciable. Also appreciable is the decision of the State Government to lower, although marginally, the rate of Agricultural income Tax on tea. The rate of Land Revenue needs be minimized and at the same time the Salami on transfer of tea land area be totally withdrawn by the State Government. The Cess on Green Leaf Collected under the Rural Employment and Production Act, 1976 and the Primary Education Act, 1973 at the rate of 12 Paise per kgs of Green Leaf finally works out to about 54 paise per kgs of made tea. This directly adds to the cost of production. In this critical period of the industry, the State Government should make substantial reduction, if not total waiver, of the Cess on Green

Leaf, at least for a temporary period, which will give respite to the industry to tide over the present crisis.

6. 110th CTTA Annual General Meeting

The 110th Annual General Meeting of Calcutta Tea Traders Association (CTTA) was held in Kolkata on November 12, 1999. The issues discussed by Miss Afroze Randerian, Chairperson of the Association are presented here:

Salient Issues

Impact of Drought—The year 1999 has thrown many challenges before the nation as well as the economy at large arising from the conflict in the Kargil sector and the cyclone in Orissa. We condole the tragic loss of life in Kargil and in Orissa. The effect of drought conditions in the beginning of the year in many tea growing districts has resulted in a sharp decline in tea production. It is estimated that as against the total tea production of 870 million kg in 1998, the tea crop in 1999 would be in the region of 810 million kg, registering a decline of 60 million kgs. Inspite of the drop in tea production, there has been no shortage in the availability of tea both for the export market as well as for the domestic market. This is primarily due to the carry over stocks of nearly 30 million kgs of 1998. Moreover, enquiries from Russian importers have been subdued and this has had a bearing on the availability of tea.

Significant Rise in Tea Prices—There has been a significant rise in tea prices at the retail level. While prices are influenced by supply and demand and quality it must be ensured that rising prices do not lead to a reduction I the quantity purchased by the customer. It is essential for the tea trade to ensure that there is no erosion in the per capita consumption of tea due to price factor as this would be detrimental to the long term interests of tea. In the long run, it is higher volumes which will ensure the continued prosperity of the tea trade. A strong domestic market will also help members market will also help members to promote Indian tea in overseas markets.

Reaching Consensus on the Service Charge—Over the last one year, the CTTA General Committee has tried very hard to reach a consensus on the service charges payable by buyers to brokers. Since 1982, the buyers pay a Service Charge of Rs.5 per 100 kgs to brokers. The brokers have sought an upward revision of the service charges to Rs.45 per 100 kgs, which the buyers feel is on the high side. It is important that the issue of service charges payable by buyers to brokers is resolved expeditiously as it would have a significant impact on the brokers' ability to render the services desired by buyers.

The distribution of free trade samples in recent years has become a contentious issue. In the engineering and electronics sector, the customer can assess the product on the basis of the specifications provided by the manufacturers. However, tea is an agricultural commodity, whose quality is determined by soil conditions and the climate. Trade samples are, therefore, essential to make an accurate assessment of the quality. While the proliferation of free trade sample holders is not in the interests of the trade, we must bear in mind the usefulness of the samples to genuine buyers. In 1988, over 16 million packets of trade samples were distributed by the brokers to eligible buyers in Kolkata or on an average of over 3 lakh packets of samples per week. This is a huge workload on the broker members and effort should be made to rationalize this load. The norms for free trade samples are receiving the attention of the Tea Board, and this matter should be finalized after taking into account the requirements of the buyers, brokers and sellers.

Granting of Credit to Buyers—A major area of concern to the tea trade in North India is the granting of credit to buyers by brokers. Over the years, the granting of credit has become an integral part of the tea trade. The credit is granted by broker members at their sole discretion and the auction committees have no role to play in the selection of buyers eligible for credit. Earlier this year, a member failed to pay for teas amounting to Rs.50 lakh. This is an example of deliberate exploitation of the auction system. The granting of credit has a significant influence on the buyer's ability to participate at the auctions. For several decades, many buyers have enjoyed credit facilities an the trade has benefited from this arrangement. There has been some debate in the trade on the practice of granting credit and buyers as well as brokers have strong views on this subject. It is felt that a mechanism for assessing the credit-worthiness of buyers has to be established and, if required help of professionals in the banking and financial institutions may be taken.

Improvement of Storage Conditions—In September 1999, about 17,000 packages in 14 warehouses were affected due to torrential rain. The CTTA General Committee regrets the loss of tea. The Association has received several suggestions to improve the storage conditions and it intends to take certain steps to prevent such incidents in future. The type of packaging has shifted from plywood chests to jute bags and paper sacks. The Association proposes to make it mandatory for the warehouses which were affected in the recent rain to store all teas on wooden pallets instead of battens. Although this will entail substantial investment on the part of the warehouse-keepers, this proposal should be supported by them.

In June this year, the Central Government introduced an All Industry rate of duty drawback on tea at the rate of Rs. 2 per kg of indigenous content. This was welcomed by tea exporters as the incentive of drawback could be passed on to overseas customers and thereby make exports of Indian tea more competitive. However, since September 1999 the Customs authorities have denied drawback claims on the ground that the exporters have not furnished certificates regarding non-availment of MODVAT credit by producers. Furthermore, some exporters whose drawback claims had been settled by the Customs authorities have now received notices to refund the amount received as drawback. This issue needs be resolved as quickly as possible so that tea exporters can avail the facility of duty drawback of Rs. 2 per kg.

17

Issues of Tea in International Perspective

Tea And Wine as Healthy Alliance

Identification of the same healthy chemicals in wine and tea has forged an unlikely alliance between the national drinks of Britain and France. Flavonoid, the most powerful antioxidant in nature, is found in higher concentration in red wine and green and black tea than in any other product. Officials from Brooke Bond met representatives of Bordeaux Wine Council to launch a joint public education programme on the benefits of the two drinks.

Courtesy: Energy Era

Tea Exports to Egypt Require Certificate of Origin

The Ministry of Economy and Foreign Trade in Egypt is learnt to have issued a directive revising the decree No. 619 of 1998, which made the Certificate of Origin mandatory for all imports into Egypt. As per the directive, exports of tea to Egypt should indicate the country of origin only on the invoice, which should be certified by the Egyptian Embassy/Trade Office in the supplying country free of charge. The new regulation allows manufacturers to ship tea to Egypt either from the country of production or their branches and distribution centres in other countries. It is reported that the new decree has come into effect from November 7, 1999.

Sri Lanka Tea Exports

On the basis of quantity bought by the major importers of Sri Lanka teas for the period from January to December 2006, the CIS still remains as the single largest importer although year to year figures show a marginal decline. Other notable declines have been from Turkey, UAR and Jordan. On the other hand, the UAE continues to rank as the second large importer of Sri Lanka tea and has shown a growth rate of around 16.6 per cent compared to the same period last year. Other significant gains in imports have been from Tunisia, Syria, Iran, UK, Saudi Arabia and Germany. However, the notable feature of Sri Lanka tea exports for the period January to December 2006 was: *(i)* marginal decline in tea exports, *(ii)* fall in value added tea exports, and *(iii)* short fall of Imported/re-exported tea.

London Paper Blackens Indian Tea Industry

The Sunday Mirror of London recently published a report alleging the use of child labour in Indian tea plantation. The paper claimed its reporters visited tea estates in Assam and found evidence of child labour in the plantations. The newspaper report has named England-based George Williamson Ltd. as one of the users of child labour in the plantations under its Indian subsidiary controlled by Mr. B.M. Khaitan. However, George Williamson has categorically denied the allegations made in the report.

Drought Severely Affected Bangladesh Tea

There has been a severe drought in Bangladesh this year, causing a sharp fall in production. It started to rain only at the beginning of May in the main tea growing area in Sylhet, but his was not enough, according to planters. They apprehended that the crop this year may be well below 2005's record of 55 million kg provided weather conditions remain favourable throughout the rest of the year. Owing to drought, there has been hardly any production worth mentioning in March, April, and May, resulting in meagre sales in this new season's Sales. The Chairman of Tea Producers Association of Bangladesh held a press conference in Dhaka recently with a view to drawing the attention of the government to the seriousness of this year's drought which caused severe damage to almost half of the tea bushes. Major producers of tea pointed out that they are likely to face problems in repayment of crop loans taken from the Bangladesh Krishi Bank.

World's Largest Tea Party

With a view to setting a record and finding place in the Guinness Book of Records, Hong Kong threw the world's largest tea party on the last Saturday of November, 1999 which was attended by 4,950 guests to brew pale green Chinese tea. Thousands of Hong Kongers gathered in small groups with colleagues, friends or family to sit cross-legged around tea pots and thimble cups on mats spread across a fair ground by the harbour. The Teaism Alliance Hong Kong, a charity organization founded by tea expert Yip Wai-Man, put together the events and auditor Price Waterhouse authenticated the number of participants.

US Tea Association Celebrating Centenary

The USA Tea Association is now more than one hundred year old. Born as the Tea Association of New York on January 5, 1899; it was rechristened as the Tea Association of the USA in 1912.

Training Workshops in Kenya

Mr. Surajit Ghose, Engineering Consultant, had just returned from Kenya having successfully conducted fifteen (15) days' of Training Workshops, between 7.12.1999 and 23.12.1999 "On The Theories & Practices of Maintenance Engineering and Management in Tea Factories" at all the twelve zones of the Kenya Tea Development Authority (KTDA) covering all their forty-five (45) tea factories. The Training Workshop was requested for by M/s KTDA to be organized by M/s Vikram Forging & Allied Industries Ltd., Kolkata the most leading developer and manufacturer of Tea Processing Machineries & Equipment since several decades in the world and a leading supplier of tea machines and spares in Kenya. The participants were all the Technicians and the Management personnel of each of the factories. The course materials for the Training package covered the following areas and were mainly prepared from the book "Guide to Maintenance Engineering & Management Practices in Tea" written by Mr. S. Ghose.

General	*Tea Processing M/Cs*	*Management*
1. Machines	1. Withering Trough	1. Maintenance Management
2. Lubrication	2. Rotorvane	2. Energy Management
3. Bearings	3. CTC	
4. Drives	4. CTC Roller Sharpening	
	5. Fermenting M/c	
	6. Drier M/c	

A one day Training Workshop was also conducted at the Changwi Tea Factory of M/s George Williamson, Kenya, for the Technicians and Management personnel of four of their tea factories at the Kericho area.

First World Tea Festival In Russia

The First World Tea Festival which was organized in Moscow continued upto May 2003. Mr Vladimir Volkov, the Festival's Director of International Programme said : "We believe that a global event connected with tea and the cultural tradition of various nations will draw worldwide attention to the cultural, historical, health-improving, aesthetic and economic value of tea". A number of tea related events were arranged. Pavillions for main tea producing and consuming countries, namely China, Japan, India, Sri Lanka, Kenya, England, Russia were set up.

Pakistan Allows Duty Free Tea Imports

The Government of Pakistan allowed duty free import of tea from Bangladesh and Nepal, the two countries being least developed among SAARC countries. The quantity of import was to the level of 10000 metric tonnes annually.

Pakistan Trade Delegation in Sri Lanka

Sometime in the first week of October, 2002 a trade delegation led by the then Pakistan's Minister of Commerce, Industries and Production, Mr. Abdul Razak Dawood, visited Sri Lanka to finalise the Free Trade Agreement (FTA) between the two countries. The Pakistani Minister visited the country earlier for bilateral trade discussion when the two countries signed the framework agreement of free trade. Pakistan is the second large trading partner of Sri Lanka in the SAARC region. The Sri Lanka Government expects to increase exports to Pakistan and thereby to reduce its existing trade deficit. The agreement includes the free movement of goods between the two countries through the elimination of tariffs.

Publicity of Indian Tea in Russia

In a bid to regain the lost market in Russia, the Tea Board of India publicized Indian Tea through TV channels and popular dailies of that country. The campaign programme, at a cost of Rs. 6 crore, started on October 24, 2002. India's export to Russia has sharply declined in the last couple of years due to Russia's leaning on Sri Lanka. This situation has prompted India to launch massive campaign.

Iran Temporarily Bans Tea Import

Iran imposed ban on tea import to support the country's tea producers. Nemat Yavarzadeh, who heads the tea producers' association in northern Iran, said the embargo was meant to boost production of local producers and to help disposing of stock of tea. In the past also Iran imposed temporary ban on tea import as locally produced tea was lying unsold and cornered by the imported teas. However, the embargo could not alleviate the sufferings of the local producers, as smuggling of tea in the country was rampant. Iran produces around half of its domestic annual consumption leveling 100 million kgs of tea. Iran has gradually relaxed state control over tea trading in recent years as part of reforms to liberalise the industry.

Tea Becoming Favourite Beverage in China

Liu Qinjin, a prominent Chinese expert on tea and Professor with the Food Science Institute of South-West China Agricultural University, said that tea drinks are poised to become the new favourite type of beverage in China, and will compete with the dominant carbonated drinks in taking the lion's share of beverage market. Over the past few years, the growth of tea drinks market has exceeded 300 per cent, making it the third favourite beverage in the country, after carbonated drinks and bottled drinking water. The consumption of tea as a drink is developing fast in China.

Chinese to Buy Tea from Sri Lanka

A Chinese delegation which visited Sri Lanka recently expressed to the then Minister of Commerce and Consumer Affairs, Ravi Karunanayake, willingness to buy tea from Sri Lanka. Initial steps were taken to export 90 metric tones of tea and rubber by the end of February 2002 and the quality is expected increase up to 3000 metric tones in near future, a ministry representative said. The Chinese delegation, in turn, requested the Sri Lanka minister to buy their products.

Tetley to Sell Private Label to US Company

The Tetley group sold its private label tea business in the US to Harris Tea, an American company, for a consideration of $ 15 million. The proceeds of the sale were used to bring down Tata Tea's (Great Britain) debt-equity ratio, which stood at 1.8:1. Tetley has firmed up distribution arrangements in Pakistan and Bangladesh. Though the global tea market was under pressure, during the 10-month period ended December 2001, Tetley's sale raised to 3 per cent. In the UK, though the tea market has grown by less than 1 per cent, Tetley has managed to increase its market share to 25 per cent, higher by 4 per cent over the last year. Its closest competitor in the UK, PG Tipps, has 23.5 per cent share of the market. Tetley has a 41 per cent share of the Canadian tea market, 11 per cent share of the US market and 16.2 per cent share of the Australian tea market.

ISO 9002 for Glasgow Estate

Glasgow Estate (selling mark Agra Ouvah), Sri Lanka, after pursuing Quality Management Systems Programme, has received the ISO 9002 certification from the Bureau Veritas Quality International (BVQI). The certification from BVQI qualified Glasgow Tea Processing Centre to be included in the Department of Trade and Industry—Q.A. Register in London, which is the foremost Directory of Companies both in the UK and abroad. This inclusion allowed for Glasgow teas to be available throughout the world as a product which is processed to the highest possible quality standards of a "Food Factory". Establishing quality circles involving the active participation of staff along with the repair and replacement of machinery and upgrading of the factory brought about a tremendous change in the productivity and hygienic conditions of the factory. Glasgow estate is a property of Agrapatana Plantations Ltd for whom the Managing Agent is Lankan Tea and Rubber Plantations (Pvt) Ltd.

Tea in Italy Gaining Popularity

Tea is becoming more and more popular in Italy. Italians tend to prefer light tea drunk with or without lemon, either hot or cold in the summer. All year round, supermarkets now sell ready-to-drink tea in bottles and cans as well as traditional packets of loose tea or tea bags. Compito tea, which has flavour somewhere between Indian Darjeeling and Chinese Keemun, will soon be available on the shelves of the local stores in Italy.

Eteatrade Launched Internet Auction

Eteatrade is a subsidiary of Plantation and General Investments Plc. Located in London, UK, which launched its first Internet auction recently. "A sizeable proportion of the industry does not need a complex network of representatives in every tea growing region. For them it is far more efficient and effective to log on to www.eteatrade.com from their office and buy tea directly from producers around the world", said Nick Hedges, eteatrade's Marketing Director. He further added that "From producers' perspective eteatrade is a first opportunity to expose their produce directly to a global market place. This will give many producers access to buyers that they have never been able to deal with directly before." Initially eteatrade is auctioning African tea, which accounts for nearly 14 per cent of the world's tea exports. Support from African producers is strong; the companies who have registered their intention to sell their tea through eteatrade account for around two-third of Africa's total tea production. Eteatrade has also received considerable response for their service from producers in China,

India, and Sri Lanka. To meet the demand eteatrade will have logistic capabilities in Northern India and Colombo by the end of the year.

Tea in Italy

Attempts to grow tea in Italy go back almost two centuries to 1810 when some English residents tried to grow the herb in Sicily. There were further attempts in 1973 and 1981, but it is only recently that tea plants have actually managed to grow and survive in Italian soil. The quality of tea now being produced in Italy is far better than even before. One of the novelties is the production of a black tea named "Te delle Tre Tigri" (Tea of the three tigers). This tea has a delicate and slightly aromatic flavour, judged by connoisseurs as really excellent. Its flavour is somewhere between Indian Darjeeling and Chinese Keemum.

Sri Lanka Tea Exports (January, 2002)

Total exports inclusive of imports/re-exported for the period January, 2002 shows an increase of 1.19 million kgs or 5.41 per cent when compared with the same period last year. Bulk exports show a growth of 1.4 million kgs or 10.9 per cent. Instant tea exports show a growth of 22.7 per cent. Total export earnings of Rs.5.1 billion indicate a growth of 6.7 per cent, compared with the Rs.4.8 billion earned in 2001. CIS continued to be the Number One market for Sri Lanka teas. Compared with the same period last year, exports to Syria, Iraq, Iran, Japan, UK, Saudi Arabia and Tunisia increased.

Mombasa Tea Auctions, 2006: Quality

Dry weather during the first three months of the year adversely effected quality. In the second and third quarters, low temperatures and somewhat mixed weather resulted in improved but variable quality. Thereafter, unseasonably cold temperatures produced some attractive quality. With progressively drier weather and reports of lower crop in North-east India, the market was expected to be more buoyant. The average price for all growths opened the year at US $ 1.79 and by the end of the first quarter was US $ 1.80, dropping to US $ 1.76 at the end of June; the third quarter saw an average of US $ 1.75 and closed the year at US $ 1.78 – disappointing when compared to the 2005 closing average of US $ 1.89. A feature of the year was the increasing dominance of Pakistan Blenders over the Bazaar and Afghan markets. Egypt, the Yemen and other Middle Eastern countries lent consistently good support and were often surprisingly quality conscious. The UK was active but generally selective. The Sudan bought with varying strength. Somalia purchased traditional cheaper Fannings types. There were line orders from South Africa and other markets.

In contrast to the excellent growing conditions of 2005 which created a record crop of 294 million kg, the weather in 2006 was mixed with extended periods of dry weather; low temperatures also inhibited growth. The 2006 crop figure is now estimated to be 248 million kg–approximately 16 per cent below the previous year. During the year, the Kenya Shilling weakened against the US Dollar opening the year at a rate of KShs 60.01 to a dollar and this rate increased to KS hs 62.77 in March with a further rise to KShs 70.57 in June; September averaged KShs 73.33, only strengthening slightly to close the year at KShs 71.68. Although volumes in auction were lower, there was no corresponding correction in prices and 1999 could be considered only a satisfactory year for the Mombasa Auctions.

Chinese Tea Export Not Flourishing

Though Chinese authorities believe there is great potential for increased exports, large number of small scale factories springing up across the country with poor equipment and low quality control mechanisms have been inhibiting the realization of this potential. The quality of the product from such enterprises affects the reputation of the country's teas on world markets, and makes the market chaotic by the introduction of cutthroat competition. Improper management of tea fields deteriorates the environment and stands in the way of producing quality tea and hence increased exports.

Vietnam Planning to Increase Export

Vietnam, the competitor of China in World Green Tea Market, whose tea output in 1997 came to 45 million kg and exports to 31 million kg has planned to export between 120 million kg to 150 million kg of tea by the year 2010. The country has enlarged national tea area to 100000 hectares.

Tea Trade in Egypt

Egypt was predominantly a Sri Lankan Tea market until the early 1990s. Since then the preference for Kenyan teas has grown steadily. Currently, Kenya is the main supplier, with almost 76 per cent of the total imports to Egypt, followed by Sri Lanka with 13 per cent, India with 5 per cent, Indonesia with 4 per cent and other African countries with 2 per cent. The Kenyan dominance could increase further consequent to the recent treaty establishing the Common Market for Eastern and Southern Africa (COMESA), whereby the Import Duty was reduced from 30 per cent to 3 per cent. The consumption of tea is approximately four times that of coffee (tea's closest competitor) followed by carbonated and fresh fruit drinks. Egypt's population presently grows by a little over a million a year. Since the majority of this growth is in the poorer segment of society, there will always be a large market for tea because it is the cheapest beverage and it has favourable health aspects.

Sri Lanka's National Safety Award

The following Estates managed by Maskeliya Plantations Limited won the Safety Awards in 1999 Forbes & Walker Tea Brokers (Pvt. Ltd), reported.

All Island Merit Award	: Medium Scale	: Poonagalla Tea Factory
Provincial Winners	: Uva Province	: Poonagalla Tea Factory
Provincial Winners up	: Central Province	: Strathspey Tea Factory
Provincial Merit Award	: Central Province	: Brunswick Tea Factory

Maskeliya Plantations Limited was also adjudged the First Runner Up in the National Productivity Award in 1998 and is the sole award winner in the National Quality Award contest in 1999. This Company was also selected as the "Top 10" best-managed companies in Sri Lanka this year.

Tea Auctions on the Internet

According to Tea & Coffee Asia, the oldest tea broking firms in London, Thomson Lloyd & Ewart Ltd., hold tea auctions on the Internet. It may be mentioned that tea auctions in

London was closed in 1998. Thomson Lloyd & Ewart introduced "Automated Tea Marketing On Line System". The website is www.atmostea com. Mr.Robin Harrison, Director of the company said, "it will mirror the traditional tea auction but on an electronic tea platform". In his opinion, the system will massively reduce the costs for a lot of producers.

HACCP Certification to Great Western Estate

Great Western Estate, Sri Lanka, a property of Talawakelle Plantations Limited, managed by Hayles Plantation Services Limited noted for its commitment to quality has been certified as an Estate that conforms to "Hazard Analysis and Critical Control Points System (HACCP) as set out by the Sri Lanka Standards Institution.

O-Cha Festival in Japan

The World O-Cha Festival, 2001 was held at Shizuoka, Japan between October 5 and 8 2001. The festival was organized to provide the people of Japan and the world with latest information on tea. Tea festival included fairs, exhibition, seminars and international conference. Teas from 12 countries and 13 districts in Japan were displayed, which facilitated the visitors to taste and buy teas. About 31 rare variety of teas had also been exhibited in the Tea Fair. Besides, manufacturing machinery, tea producing machines, mechanical harvesters, sprayers and fertilizer applying equipment, packing machines, etc. were displayed. As the part of festival, around 350 products using tea were exhibited in "Aru-Aru" O-Cha Plaza. Tea candles, tea soba noodles, cosmetics made with Green Tea ingredients, bath salt, skin cream, T-shirts dyed with tea and bed sheets with antibacterial treatment were exhibited which indicated a broad scope in product diversification using tea.

First World Tea Festival in Russia

The First World Tea Festival which was organized in Moscow continued upto May, 2003. Mr. Vladimir Volkov, the Festival's Director of International Programme said: "We believe that a global event connected with tea and the cultural tradition of various nations will draw worldwide attention to the cultural, historical, health-improving, aesthetic and economic value of tea". A number of tea related events were arranged. Pavilions for main tea producing and consuming countries, namely China, Japan, India, Sri Lanka, Kenya, England, Russia were set up.

Pakistan Allows Duty Free Tea Imports

The Government of Pakistan allowed duty free import of tea from Bangladesh and Nepal, the two countries being least developed among SAARC countries. The quantity of import was to the level of 10000 metric tons annually.

Pakistan Trade Delegation in Sri Lanka

Sometime in the first week of October, 2002 a trade delegation led by the then Pakistan's Minister of Commerce, Industries and Production, Mr. Abdul Razak Dawood, visited Sri Lanka to finalise the Free Trade Agreement (FTA) between the two countries. The Pakistani Minister visited the country earlier by bilateral trade discussion when the two countries signed the framework agreement of free trade. Pakistan is the second large trading partner of Sri Lanka in the SAARC region. The Sri Lanka Government expects to increase exports to Pakistan and thereby to reduce its existing trade deficit. The agreement includes the free movement of goods between the two countries through the elimination of tariffs.

Publicity of Indian Tea in Russia

In a bid to regain the lost market in Russia, the Tea Board of India to publicized Indian Tea through TV channels and popular dailies of that country. The campaign programme, at a cost of Rs.6 crore, started on October 24, 2002. India's export to Russia has sharply declined in the last couple of years due to Russia's leaning on Sri Lanka. This situation has prompted India to launch massive campaign.

Pakistan Preparing for Tea Production

Pakistan is getting prepared to produce tea. It has 500 acres under tea production, and in the next five years the tea-area is likely to be increased to 1500 acres. North Western Province of the country has been selected for tea cultivation. The Managing Director cum owner of UK based Teacraft., Mr. Nigel

Melican, is implementing the current project. Tea craft manufacturers various processing machinery for the Tea industry. It has purchased the rights for selling automated withering machined developed by the Tea Research Association at Tocklai in Assam.

15th Session of IGG on Tea

The Food and Agriculture Organisation (FAO) of the United Nations Organisation (UNO) has informed that the 15th Session of the Inter Governmental Group (IGG) on Tea was held in Sri Lanka from August 19 to 20, 2003.

Trade Fair in Germany

For the third time, Anuga FoodTec brought Food Processing and Packaging Industry at a Trade Fair in Cologne, Germany. The Fair was held from April 8 to 11, 2003 and covered the sectors like: *(i)* Process Technology, *(ii)* Packaging Technology, *(iii)* Food Safety and Quality Management, *(iv)* Environmental Technology, *(v)* Bio-engineering, *(vi)* Informational Technology, *(vii)* Technological Process Materials & Ingredients, and *(viii)* Services.

Libya Lifted Ban On Indian Tea

At the 8th Session of the Indo-Libyan Joint Commission, Libya lifted the ban on Indian tea. The minutes of the session indicates that NASCO, the buying Agency for Libya is now registering Indian companies which have applied for enlistment as a supplier of various commodities, including tea. According to an official release, both the countries agreed to increase the volume of bilateral trade. An exhaustive list of tradable goods was exchanged to enhance the two-way trade.

Indian Chai Achieves Major Success in UK Market

After stagnating for over a decade, Indian tea has achieved a major breakthrough in the UK market with the introduction of 100 per cent Indian tea product with Indian spices—Chai—by the leading British tea company Twinings. The success is the outcome of a series of campaigns launched by the London office of the Tea Board to popularize Indian Tea. The Twinings 'Chai' package mentions India as the origin of the tea and Nilgiri tea as th core of the blend. The Indian teas were displayed in popular departmental stores like the Harrods, Selfridges, Fortnum and Masons.

India is the largest tea producing country in the world but its share in the global market and particularly in the UK market is not commensurate with its potential. Although India exports 200 million kg of tea annually, exports to UK stand about 20 million kg with an earnings of about 33 million pounds (Rs.230 crore) per annum. India's exports to the UK have been stagnant for over a decade now. According to market sources, Indian tea had a very dominant share in the UK market till the 1980s. Since then, India lost the market share to African teas primarily due to inconsistent export policy of the country and lack of long-term vision. During 1980-90, the share of India's exports to the UK declined from 20 per cent to 14 per cent. But in the same period exports to Russia increased form 28 per cent to over 60 per cent. It was at this time the UK companies made good investment in African teas—changing the blend to substitute Indian tea with African tea. As a result, the sophisticated tea consumers of the UK got accustomed to Kenyan blend. In this situation, introduction of Indian Chai in the UK market is a grand success.

George Promoted Indian Tea in USA

Indian tea was an unlikely promoter in the country's, the then Defence Minister, Mr. George Fernandes, who impressed upon the US importers of the product as adroitly as he sold his views to America's political bosses. Mr. George Fernandes, who came to New York after his discussion in Washington in January, 2002 had visited and acted as a campaigner for Indian tea. The Indian Deputy High Commission had arranged a meeting with the US tea importers for Mr. Fernandes, who formally presided over the gathering. But to every one's surprise, he turned out to be a connoisseur of tea.

Emergence of Other Countries as Major Suppliers and Improper Use of Funds for Development of Tea Industry

The emergence of Sri Lanka as a major supplier of tea (with lower cost of production) to the global market in 1965 found India's share of world consumption declining from 45 per cent in 1958 to 18 per cent. In subsequent period, Kenya became a sizeable exporter followed by other East African and Asian countries including China. This situation limited prospects of common tea from India which account for over 60 per cent of country's production. The situation was compounded in 1990s by the uncertainty of the Indian tea's over-dependent Russian market following disintegration of the USSR. What went wrong on the Indian scene? Various reasons are cited and it would be prudent to highlight one of the aspects. A spokesman of the Kolkata-based United Bank of India which has fairly large accounts of tea producers in North-East India indicated that the funds allotted to the borrowers against hypothecation of tea crop were not being properly utilized towards development (not applicable to all) of the respective tea estates. In course of time, the lended sum turned out to be unproductive or became non-performing assets, as known in banking parlance. When the cumulative liabilities of the producers mounted, the banks exerted pressure on the former to sell the properties to clear the dues which ran into crores of rupees.

Sri Lankan Tea Import Permitted

Sometime in February, 2000 India and Sri Lanka agreed to operationalise the free trade pact that provides for removing duty and providing preferential access on a range of items before March, 2000. Among the items tea is also included. India permits import of Sri Lankan tea to the extent of 15 m. kgs per annum with a fixed tariff preference of 50 per cent.

Tata Tea Plans Retail Outlets

Tata Tea opened retail outlets for the promotion of Tetley in the premium category with the expertise of Barista outlets. While iced tea is another product rolled out by Tata Tea variants rolled under Tetley were flavoured tea and ready-to-drink mixes. Tata Tea launched Tetley in India to take on brands such as Taj Mahal Tea, Society Tea and Wagh Bakri. "There has been tightened advertising activity in anticipation of the launch of Tetley. You are about to witness a very exciting combat in the tea industry. We are launching at a time when the industry is under severe pressure," said Mr. Krishna Kumar, the Vice-Chairman of Tata Tea.

Tea Board Office at London

The Tea Board has been contending for some time that it did a good job in promoting the sale of Indian Tea at the Harrods exhibition in London. But, a programme on tea management sponsored by the London-based Commonwealth Secretariat in 2001 observed that Harrods hardly represented the buying place for the common British. Teas went up for sale at Harrods for any price equivalent of Rs. 1,000 a kg and most Indian teas could not qualify for a sale through the Harrods departmental stores. The worst point was that Harrdos fair etc. exhausted almost half the total budget of the London office of the Tea Board. Therefore, practically, nothing was left for the office to promote the Indian tea in the UK or the other centres coming under its jurisdiction. That is why, it become difficult to see a good advertisement on Indian tea anywhere in the UK. Nor, was it possible to see the Indian teas figuring prominently in the various fairs around the region. The Tea Board, for instance, was a conspicuous absentee at the world's largest food ingredient exhibition, FI Europe 2001, held in London, even as Sri Lanka promoted its various forms of teas including organic teas. That is why, Indian tea and the London Tea Board were not seen at the right places like the Wimbledon tennis or the Lords cricket tourney. So, it is a case of Indian Tea Board having a Director of Tea Promotion (DTP) in London and still not seen at the right places to promote the Indian tea. The Government of India, particularly the Commerce Minister, should realize that tying up the hands of the DTP helps none, least of the Indian tea industry.

Director's of Tea Promotion Office, London, located at High Rising "Indian House"

The indifference shown by the Government to put the Tea Board Office in London in the right perspective is already costing heavily. For instance, none of the dozen long time residents of London whom Shri P.S. Sundar, the Special Correspondent asked to guide him to the Tea Board Office, could, by themselves, locate the office. They referred to the Telephone Directory and asked the Indian High Commissioner's Office etc. The truth was that this office is located on one of the floors of the high rising "India House" which houses the office of the High Commissioner. So, all the formalities for entry to the High Commissioner's office are followed leaving an impression that one is entering the department of yet another Indian bureaucracy, not a commodity promotion office. Besides, there is no name Board for the Tea Board Office.

DTP's Office has Contingency Staff

Although the DTP is an IAS officer, he is not adequately staffed. He has only contingency staff paid a low salary with a mandatory technical break in service every three months. Therefore, there is neither loyalty nor continuity in the staff strength. Moreover, the DTP has no place to hold public relations meet. Nor are there good materials to highlight Indian teas or tea packets. Many a time, the guests are not even provided with a cup of tea as a matter of hospitality in the Tea Board Office. After all, the DTP has power to spend only 74 pound and for expense above this, he has to seek specific permission taking almost a month. Therefore, with half the budget going in for the in-store promotion at Harrods, the London office does not spend any money for media publicity, product or logo promotion or the development of market intelligence. It is spending less than one per cent of its total budget on buyer-seller meets and tea events.

UK Market is too Important to India

For all this, the UK market is too important to India to be ignored. For one, it is the world's second largest tea importer with a high per capita consumption of 2.7 kg, the consumption growing at 1 per cent per annum. For another, there has been some increase in the demand for the Indian teas of late, despite the Tea Board office's inability to promote the teas adequately, which should enable the country to find a good berth for some varieties of its teas. Now the UK imports around 150 million kg annually, but India supplies only 20 million kg fetching foreign exchange of around 33 million pound, Kenya is the largest supplier with a share of around 43 per cent and the British look to the Indian teas only when the Kenyan supplies dry up. On the other hand, the UK has a specific market for the PF/PD CTC grades for which India is looking for buyers. Again, while Indian teas are sold for an average price of 1.5 pound a kg, Sri Lankan teas fetch 1.6 pounds and Kenya 1.65

pounds. So, India should know to encash on this price advantage.

UK Imports and Exports after Value Addition

Another sphere for entry is the re-export segment. The UK imports teas, on an average, price of 1.3 pound a kg, but exports them after value addition, at 5 pounds a kg. These tea, branded and attractively packed, are sold to France, Canada, Ireland and the UAE. Presently, people drink tea in the UK thinking it from India. Some 10 brands are popular, but six of them are well known. Tetley and VDB brands account for 25 per cent of the UK market each, Premier 8 per cent, Taylors 5 per cent and Twinning 3 per cent. However, they do not disclose the country of origin for the teas. Thus, there is a definite need to promote the Indian tea highlighting its strengths, but for this, the London office of the Tea Board should be upgraded. It should be adequately staffed, duly empowered to carry a corporate identity and build brand equity for the Indian teas. It should become the hub of information on Indian teas. As of now, it is grossly under-equipped to face the challenge.

Generic Promotion within the Country and Outside Well

It is not only the generic promotion within the country, but outside as well that there is a lot of lacuna. As the Food Ingredients Europe 2001 exhibition held in London, for instance, while Sri Lanka displayed its teas, the Indian Tea Board did not show any interest despite it holding a Tea Promotion Office in London. Sri Lanka even displayed its organic teas and started attracting importers from Germany and parts of Europe at the fair. It will do a lot good to the Indian tea to utilize all possible channel like the Food Ingredient Fairs to put up whatever role as deemed fit and possible. On the campaign itself, the impact has been highly negligible. A sporadic full page ad on a particular week day in some select newspapers alone cannot help much. A lot of professional work has to go into this campaign programme so that the consumers are made to drink the Indian tea for its health benefits.

18

Issues of Tea in National Perspective

Organic Tea to Boost Exports: According to tea industry pundits and experts the demand for organic tea has surged in the global market. In their opinion, the growing demand of organic tea in Europe, united States and Japan is not just a craze now but has really caught on with health-conscious consumers. In the near future, it will get good reception from Australia, New Zealand and other developing countries also where the demand of organic agricultural products is on the rise. This was confirmed from a report of the International Trade Centre, which indicated that the demand of organic products is fast expanding due to growing awareness of the people against harmful effect of fertilizer and chemicals. Naturally, it would not be misleading to infer that organic tea has also a bright market. Indian tea industry should capitalize this opportunity to boost its sluggish exports. In this context it may be mentioned that while in the last couple of years exports and prices of our conventional teas fell severely, organic tea commanded premium, demand in the market as well.

Currently, the world demand for organic tea is about 3 million kg a year. The growth rate is 10 per cent per annum. But with the consumers' growing preference for organic tea to conventional tea, it is likely to be increased phenomenally. So the industry should be wiser to avail the advantage of a market at its nascent stage. It will enable the industry to secure a strong foothold before competition intensifies, which will occur over the next few years. However, organic tea production on a large scale should be launched only after building up adequate knowledge on foreign market. The industry should not overlook the necessity of viability study, such as collecting sufficient information on potential demand, the strength of other suppliers and the prices offered future competitors, distribution channel available and the right importers of such product. The Tea Board and the tea associations should not target just for the export market and without formulating supportive marketing strategies one more point, production of organic tea. It has to be popularized in the domestic market also so that the producers do not depend on export market only. This will serve as a shield to the producers against possible catastrophe in export demand

Report on Bulk Packaging

The Report of the Expert Group, comprising representatives of the Indian Tea Association, Consultative Committee of Plantation Associations and others concerned, on the existing bulk packaging norms with recommendation for an alternative and effective system is ready to reach to the Tea Board. After examining various alternatives such as Jute Bag-laminated with LDPE, Multi-wall paper sacks, HDPE-woven bags, the expert group recommended Polythene-lined jute bags as suitable for bulk packaging in North India. This Expert Group was set up by the Tea Board.

Little Cheer for Tata Tea

The general oversupply situation in the domestic tea industry has not spared the Rs.815 crore Tata Tea Ltd., as was evident from the financial result of the company for the year 2001-02. It is a lacklustre performance for the third year in a row. The total income of Rs.815 crore in 2001-02 was much lower than that of last year's figure of Rs.890 crore. Profit figure has also registered a sharp decline from Rs. 100 core to Rs.72 crore, in 2001-02. The total income of Rs. 392.74

crore and net profit of Rs.50.13 crore earned for the half-yearly period closing on 30.09.02 was also lower in comparison to that of the same in last year.

Tea from Coca–Cola

In the hot beverage market of the country, Coca-Cola presented soon with tea. Coke's hot beverage is available through vending machines in Delhi and Kolkata. Announcing this, Mr. Sanjiv Gupta, the then Deputy President of the Coca Cola India said, "Indians do not drink any one kind of tea. We have kept regional tastes in mind while developing the products." The company, however, declined to mention the launch site in Kolkata but said that for opening of retail spots this town was chosen next to Delhi on the basis of a study carried by the company. "Kolkata has a strong tea culture," the study reported.

IAF Plane Crashed in Tea Garden

On 14th November 2002 an IAF MIG 21 crashed at Bhoj Narayan Tea Garden near Siliguri, West Bengal. It was a sound of huge magnitude that rocked the local people and tea garden workers at around 6-45 am. Braving the fog, people swarmed the garden only to have a view of the burning wreckage of an aircraft. But the most alarming sight was the mutilated bodies of the two pilots, succumbed to injury. In July 2002, also a plane of the IAF had crashed near Rabavitta in Phansidewa, North Bengal. But at that time, the crew of ill-fated fighter could save their lives.

Re-opening of Locked-out North Bengal Gardens Uncertain: The meeting of tea garden managements and union representatives with Mr. Mohammed Amin, Labour Minister of the Government of West Bengal, held in Siliguri on November 25, 2002 failed to reach a consensus in lifting the lock-out of 13 tea gardens in North Bengal. Earlier attempts of the State Labour Department to solve the disputes failed as the managements of gardens boycotted the meetings. However, Mr. Amin said that the Government would take necessary administrative measures to reopen all tea gardens at the earliest. The management of the locked-out gardens have been asked to restore supply of water, electricity, rations and other statutory facilities within 10 days. The West Bengal Cha Mazdoor Sabha and Defence Committee for Plantation Workers' Rights (DCPWR) said, the Government had recognized only 13 gardens as closed, leaving 22 more closed gardens out of the talks.

Tea Board Defaulters: The 'Defaulter List' in November 2002 released by the Tea Board of India included the name of several companies besides Tea Trading Corporation of India which was then under liquidation, Andrew Yule, Duncans Industries Ltd. and McLeod Russell. The Tea Board of India gives loans and advances to tea companies for development and upgradation of the tea gardens. The list indicated that tea companies in the eastern region alone owe over Rs.14.36 crore to the Board by way of principal, interest and penal interest. The bulk of the bad debts are under Tea Machinery and Irrigation Equipment Loan Scheme and Tea Plantation Finance Scheme.

UBKV Introduces Diploma Course on Tea: The Centre for Advanced Studies under the Uttar Banga Krishi Vishwavidyalaya (UBKV) introduces a Post-Graduate Diploma Course on Tea Science and Technology. This is a 18-month course which would cost Rs.30,000. The curriculum was drawn up after taking into consideration the suggestion of the professors from Jorhat University – the only varsity in the country that offers tea science at the post-graduate level. UBKV was accorded the status of a separate university in May 2002 earlier it was the North Bengal campus of the Bidhan Chandra Krishi Viswavidyalaya.

Let the Gloomy Days Over: Yet another year is coming to an end. And when we look back, the passing year appears as a bad phase to every segment of the tea industry in the country. In fact the whole year was very much disappointing and disturbing. Tea production in 2005 had been severely affected by unfavourable weather—drought during the early part of the year followed by excessive rainfall. Till October, production shortfall stood at 61 m kgs, cumulative effect of the production fall in all tea growing areas, namely Tripura, Assam Valley and Cachar, West Bengal, and South India. It is estimated that the shortfall will be not less than 70 m kgs by the turn of the year. Prices of tea were also disappointing. The euphoria on prices that prevailed in 2003 and 2004 was short-lived and the prices continued to decline from the outset of this year. The All India Average Price up to October was lower by Rs. 5 per kg. In November last week, tea prices in South India reached to as low as Rs.37 per kg which is below the cost of production. Prices in North India also declined irregularly and erratically. Certainly the decline in prices is a serious concern to the tea industry since the lower crop has had significant impact on unit cost of production byway of labour wages, higher foodgrains subsidy and major import costs on account of fertilizers, fuel and transport. The situation has come to such a pass that tea production by the medium and small units is at stake thought the biggies have somehow managed to stay afloat.

Record of Tea Export is Disheartening Also. Throughout the year, the CIS operated selectively and the East European exporters were mostly quiet. As a result, quantum of tea export up to October 2005 had declined by 26 m kgs. This lower export has been ascribed as one of the prime reasons for the present state of affairs in the tea industry. Also, the domestic consumption growth has slowed in comparison to traditional assumption of around three per cent annually. While the situation in general is so dispiriting it has been made unbearable, more particularly in Tripura, Assam and Cachar, by various militant groups with their regular activities of extortion, abduction and killing of innocent tea personnel for ransom. We wish, however, the spell of gloom in the tea sector be over with the new sun of the year 2006, the mood of joviality and enthusiasm will come back.

New Highlights

The areas which got prominence over the year have been outlined as follows:

- ✓ Mr. Nirod Baran Das, General Secretary of the Tripura Tea Labourers Union alleged that the workers were "starving for the indifferent and apathetic attitude of the Tripura Tea Development Corporation". The corporation failed to provide work to workers in Kalacherra and Mohanpur Tea Estate for several months.

- ✓ The Union alleged that half of the state's 54 gardens, including the 7 owned by the TTDC and 8 by the workers' cooperative fighting for survival.
- ✓ Due to obstruction created by a section of labourers and non-labourers against the effort to grow new plantation I the unused areas of the garden, the management of the Bandapani Tea Estate in the Dooars, West Bengal, declared a lock out of the unit.
- ✓ The World Bank informed that the tea estates in the country interested to change over from conventional to unconventional energy sources for their power requirement will be assisted financially.
- ✓ Dooars Branch Indian Tea Planters Association, started at Banarhat in the Dooars and later shifted to Birpara in the Dooars, West Bengal, celebrated its Golden Jubilee.
- ✓ The North Bengal national Chamber of Commerce initiated a signature campaign for a tea auction centre at Jalpaiguri, West Bengal.
- ✓ The Assistant Manager of Bhatpara Tea Estate, Jalpaiguri district was killed by five unidentified persons while he was on his way to the office to pay workers.
- ✓ In a press meet held at Nagon, Assam, the President and the General Secretary of All Assam Tea Tribe Students' Association alleged that the tea industry in Assam did not take up any constructive work for the economic development in the State other than providing arms and ammunition to the militant outfits active here, and air ticket for the leaders of some organizations.
- ✓ The Arunachal Finance Minister, Mr. L Wanglet announced on February 23, a Rs.500 crore scheme for tea cultivation by small and medium growers to better the lot of the poor, particularly in insurgency-affected Tirap, Lohit, and Changlang districts.

- ✓ Hijacking of trucks with goods on the way destined to North-East India increased substantially in the earlier part of the year.
- ✓ Demanding the cancellation of the proposed housing project by winding up an existing tea estate, the Chandmoni Tea Estate Anti-Eviction Joint Action Committee observed a three-day hunger strike from 27th February.
- ✓ The Sang Martam Tea Growers' Cooperative Society, Sikkim, had initiated the cultivation of tea in a virgin land measures 1000 acres. The land is located at the height of 3500 feet and 30 km away from the state capital.
- ✓ The Makaibari Tea Estate in Darjeeling signed MoU with the society to set up a tea processing plant with 50 per cent equity participation.
- ✓ The first proposal of the Indian tea industry fro financial assistance being turned down, a second proposal to develop infrastructure and peripheral areas of tea estates was submitted to the World Bank, seeking financial aid amounting to Rs.40 crore.
- ✓ Dry spell and little rainfall affected all tea growing areas in North Bengal. This weather condition seriously damaged the first flush in Darjeeling, which generally produces better quality tea for the overseas market.
- ✓ Three plantation workers of Gopalpur Tea Estate, Jalpaiguri, West Bengal, were murdered by a group of unidentified persons.
- ✓ The noted Assamese writer, Mr. Mahim Bora, was conferred the Assam Valley Literary Award for 1998, instituted by Magor Educational Trust.
- ✓ The Minister for Municipal Affairs, Government of West Bengal, Mr. Ashoke Bhattacharya, ruled out the possibility of setting up another auction centre in Jalpaiguri.
- ✓ The Manipur Government launched a campaign to popularize tea as a horticultural product.

- ✓ Under an arrangement with RPG Group Company Spencers Ltd., Harrisons Malayalam got the right to use Spencers name to its latest brand of tea that was launched in Chennai.
- ✓ Mr. Abhijit Borgohain, Manager, Medalajan Tea Estate was killed by unidentified gunmen. The incident occurred near Jorhat, Upper Assam, at his residence.
- ✓ The Assam unit of the Bhartiya Janata Party appealed the Central Government for granting 'Scheduled Tribe Status' to the tea garden workers in Assam. The party also demanded a minimum daily wage of Rs. 50 for the workers and paid holiday every week.
- ✓ The Tea Board sanctioned Rs.32.47 lakh for the development of Tripura Tea Industry.
- ✓ The Tea Association of India reported Tripura's Tea Industry in great distress due to unprecedented drought combined with kidnapping of garden personnel and extortion by some extremist organizations.
- ✓ Darjeeling Planters Association urged the Tea Board to expedite the process of registration of 'Darjeeling' Trademark at London. The Association stated that as the first flush crop in Darjeeling was badly effected due to adverse climatic condition, the overseas market may be flooded by spurious tea marked 'Darjeeling' which will blacken the image of Darjeeling tea.
- ✓ The owner of Malirampur Tea Estate, Mr. Madhukar Premka, was kidnapped by some unidentified men at Doom Dooma in Tinsukia district, Assam. He was returning from the garden to his residence.
- ✓ Abrupt change of course by the river Dima was threatening the existence of Atiabari Tea Estate at Kalchine in the Dooars region of North Bengal. According to a report the river had already swallowed a vast tract of land of the garden.
- ✓ With the signing of an agreement by the Coordination Committee of Tea Plantation Workers and the tea garden owners before the West Bengal Labour Minister, Mr. Shanti Ranjan Ghatak, 3 lakh workers

of 276 tea gardens in North Bengal called off the strike on 21st July which had begun on 12th July. The garden owners agreed to absorb 10,000 casual workers on permanent basis and to supply potable water, electricity and fire-wood.

- ✓ National Commission on Labour Rights, a fact-finding team of various trade and labour organizations, published a report on the conditions of tea plantation labour titled "Brewed in the Sweat of Forced Labour" which alleged that "in the tea estates of Assam and West Bengal labourers are attached to the gardens from birth to death for generations or so". Apart that the report raised many other issues.
- ✓ But however, the Consultative Committee of Planters' Association rejected the allegations of the National Commission on Labour as preposterous and forwarded the association's say' against each issue raised in the report.
- ✓ The promoters of Project India Blend, comprising Tata Tea, Williamson Magor, Rossell Industries Ltd., Warren Tea, and Goodricke Group, decided at a meeting to set up their packaging unit in Russia in view of the hurdles against export to that country. The Bureau of Indian Standards decided to bring a good number of tea companies under the Hazard Analysis Critical Control Point Certification. Accordingly, an apex Committee under the Secretary, Ministry of Food Processing, Government of India, was set up to implement this measure.
- ✓ At the Annual General Meeting, Tata Tea's plant o acquire major shareholding and management control in the UK based Tetley Limited, a global player in the tea industry, was approved. The meeting also approved Tata's plan to float a 'Special Purpose Vehicle' for funding controlling stakes in the UK based company.
- ✓ In order to massively campaign for the tea brand "Taj Mahal", Hindustan Level Ltd. brought out a commercial feature wherein Ustad Zakir Hussain,

the renowned Tabla maestro, and TV personality Ruby Bhatia shown associated with Taj Mahal tea.

- ✓ Mr. Roshanlal Garg, a tea garden owner in Jalpaiguri, was kidnapped at gunpoint from his garden.
- ✓ The Indian Tea Association, Tea Association of India, and various other associations of the planters in Assam expressed their grave anxiety since extortion, kidnapping, killing of tea units, executives became a daily affair of the operations of extremist groups in Assam.
- ✓ On being disturbed by the insurgents frequently, tea companies located in Assam's Cachar Valley decided to set up a "private army" on the lines of Assam Tea Special Police Force operating in Brahmaputra Valley to provide security to tea garden personnel working in this area.
- ✓ Allaying the fears of the Russian buyers on the quality front, the Tea Board Chairman, Mr. S S Ahuja assured that consignments marked for Russia would be inspected by competent authorities.
- ✓ Huge quantities of tea in 14 Kolkata warehouses were damaged owing to heavy rain during the last week of September 17,000 tea packets were soaked with water, a first-hand inspection revealed.
- ✓ The Darjeeling planters decided to initiate plans for marketing and promotion of Darjeeling tea for arousing consciousness of the consumers in both domestic and overseas market.
- ✓ According to Horticulture Station, Udhagamandalam, Tamil Nadu, spraying of Bordeax mixture (1%) or Copper Oxychloride (0.25%) at 7-10 days interval prevents Blister Blight. Nickel Chloride and Biteranol also contain the preventive properties against this disease.
- ✓ Hindustan Level Ltd., formulated a plan to relaunch Lipton's 'Taaza' brand tea, largest brand in India, to reach to 50,000 villages across the country.
- ✓ The National Dairy Development Board has decided to sell both tea and coffee as Amul product to be

marketed by the Gujarat Cooperative Milk Marketing Federation of India.

- ✓ The new tea gardens, particularly in Raiganj, Sadar Kotawali, and Maynaguri, complained to the local police station of uprooting and cutting of tea bushes.
- ✓ Four armed men looted Rs.1,50,000 at gunpoint from the Manager of Debakipore Tea Estate, on the highway in the Dooars, West Bengal, while he was carrying the money for distribution of labour wages.
- ✓ A group of regional parties, comprising Jharkhandi Sangharsh Samity, the Uttarbanga Tafashili Jati-O-Adivasi Sangathan, the Transferred Area Suryapuri Organisation, and the SJP, demanded the Redbank Tea Estate and its two divisions – Dharanipur and Surendranagar in the Dooars region, West Bengal – be taken over by the West Bengal Government.
- ✓ A clerk being injured seriously on the head, the Manager and the Assistant Manger harassed by the workers, Terai region's Taipoo Tea Estate management declared lockout of the unit on 23rd October.
- ✓ Militants kidnapped three employees of the Dilkhusa Tea Estate, Cachar district, Assam.
- ✓ Tea Research Association, the research and development outfit sponsored jointly by the Central Government and the tea plantation industry again in fresh trouble. The Tocklai Employees Union demanded nationalization of the association because of mismanagement of the unit.
- ✓ The Chairman of the Tea Research Association refuted all the allegations of the union, however.
- ✓ The India International Millennium Tea Convention will be held from 22nd to 24th March 2000 in New Delhi. The inaugural Session at Vigyan Bhawan and other functions at the Taj Palace Hotel, New Delhi. The Convention is a joint effort by the Consultative Committee of Plantation Associations and the Tea Board.
- ✓ Tea export from India to Russia is likely to drop this year by 10 per cent to 15 per cent, to between

80,000 and 90,000 tonnes from 1,03,000 tonnes in 1998, owing to low purchasing power of the consumers in that country which compelled them to cut back on the quality and quantity of tea they drank.

- ✓ While coming to pay the salary of office employees, the Assistant Manager of Biloni Tea Estate, Cachar, Assam, was abducted by the NSCN militants at gunpoint.
- ✓ The Rossell Tea acquired the Nagrijuli Tea Estate in Nalbari, Assam, from Derby Tea & Industrial Ltd.
- ✓ The members of Dibrugarh, Moran, and Naharkatia circles under Zone-I, Assam Branch Indian Tea Association donated a sum of Rs.1,00,000 to the Assam Chief Minister's Army Welfare Fund in aid of the Kargil martyrs.
- ✓ The Teesta Tea and Tourism Festival, inaugurated by the West Bengal Tourism Development Minister, was held at Kanchenjhanga Stadium, Siliguri, West Bengal.
- ✓ Warren Tea Ltd's associate, the Darjeeling Plantation Industries Ltd. acquired the controlling stake of the Kathalguri Tea Estate in Dooars, West Bengal.
- ✓ Terai Branch Indian Tea Association on behalf of member tea gardens in Terai, West Bengal contributed Rs.2,02,251 towards Central Army Welfare Fund.
- ✓ At the initiative of the National Bank for Agriculture and Rural Development, various banks agreed to finance the small tea growers in West Bengal.
- ✓ There are about 600 small tea growers in the region and a potential 24,000 hectares of land under small scale tea plantation.
- ✓ The country's tea production has recorded shortfall of 61 million kgs till October, and according to industry estimates it could reach 75-80 million kgs by the turn of the year.
- ✓ The Expert Group, constituted by the Tea Board, comprising representatives of the Indian Tea Association, Consultative Committee of Plantation

Associations and others concerned, to review the existing bulk packaging norms and to forward its recommendation for an alternative and effective system has examined the plus and minus points of Jute Bag-laminated with LDPE, Multi-wall paper sacks, HDPE-woven bags. The Report of the group awaiting discussion.

- ✓ Hindustan Level Limited introducing tea containing Vitamin A, Niacin, and Vitamin B2 with the object of giving 10 per cent of the recommended dietary allowance in each cup of tea.
- ✓ Hindustan Lever will be the first company in the country to open the market for micronutrient fortified tea.
- ✓ According to a recent notification of the Union Ministry of Agriculture, tea plantation units in West Bengal and Assam came under respective state's agricultural sector for the allocation of Urea, a government-controlled input for which this sector was previously enjoying a separate quota.
- ✓ The Central Excise Duty levied in this year's budget at Rs. 2 a kg on bulk tea likely to be considered for reduction before finalizing the budget for the next financial year, said V Dhananjay Kumar, Union Minister of State for Finance.
- ✓ The Manipur Plantation Corporation, a Manipur Government Undertaking established in 1981, is set to manufacture tea at its own factory.
- ✓ The Asom Yuba Parishad, youth wing of the Asom Gana Parishad, took it upon itself the matter of collecting 'Dues' from the major tea companies. Parishad members picketed before some offices and submitted the Parishad's Charter of Demand.
- ✓ The Indian Tea Association advocated the repeal of the Tea Marketing Control Order 1984, since the tea industry, on one hand, is being asked to gear up for free trade and imports while, on the other, the industry is being fettered with internal control.

Micronutrients Fortified Tea by HLL: The Hindustan Level Limited (HLL) introduced tea containing Vitamin A, Niacin and Vitamin B2 with the object of giving 10 per cent of the recommended dietary allowance (RDA) in each cup. Hindustan Level was the first to open the market for micronutrient fortified tea. Tea will be the third move of the company towards capitalization of the market for fortified goods and commodities after salt and atta (flour).

Urea Allocation to Tea Gardens: A recent notification of the Union Ministry of Agriculture says that tea plantation units in West Bengal and Assam will henceforth come under respective state's agricultural sector for the allocation of Urea, a government-controlled input for which this sector used to enjoy a separate quota. Now, with this notification the tea plantation units in West Bengal and Assam will have to depend solely on their respective state government.

Revision of Central Excise on Bulk Tea Likely: At the 41st Annual Conference of the Karnataka Planters' Association the then Union Minister of State for Finance, Mr. V Dhananjay Kumar, had said that the then government reviewed the Central Excise Duty on bulk tea imposed in this 2000-01 budget. The realization from the levy was marginal in terms of the overall excise collection, he added. However, during the course of discussions to finalise the Budget for the next financial year, the matter of reducing the duty on bulk tea from Rs. 2 a kg to Re. 1 could also be considered, Mr. Kumar said to the reporters.

Tea from Manipur Plantation Corporation: According to an official report, the Manipur Plantation Corporation, a State Government undertaking established in 1981, produced tea during 2000 with the commissioning of its own factory. The corporation constructed tea factory at Jiribam based Manipur Tea Estate on a turn-key basis in three phases to produce around 3 lakh kg of tea at the first phase, 6 lakh kg at the second phase, and 10 lakh kg at the last phase. In 1982, the corporation took up tea cultivation on commercial basis. The garden started selling of green leaves to Jhirighat Tea Estate in Assam from 1985.

DBITA's Health and Safety Programme: Dooars Branch Indian Tea Association (DBITA), in collaboration with the

West Bengal Chapter of the National Safety Council and Directorate of Factories, Government of West Bengal, organized one-day Seminar on the "Executive Development Programme on Health and Safety" on September 1, 1999. It was attended by 40 participants from neighbouring member tea estates. Issues connected with health and safety were discussed.

Small Tea Gardens Growing Fast in North Bengal: On the strength of 'No Objection Certificate" (NOC) issued liberally by the Land and Land Revenue Department Government of West Bengal, small tea gardens have flourished in North Bengal. The District Magistrate of Cooch Behar said recently that the State Government had asked the Land and Land Revenue department to issue NOCs to small land holders without delay. However, the detail survey of land schedule submitted by the big tea cultivators is yet to be completed, the official source added.

Darjeeling Planters Unhappy in 1999: The Darjeeling tea output was projected to fall to 7.5 million kg in 1999 from 9.6 million kg in 1998. Darjeeling tea, known for its distinctive flavour fetches the highest price for its output in March and April. Some export consignments fetching more than Rs. 3000/- ($60) a kg, twenty times the prices of good quality tea grown in other regions of the country. Tea leaves plucked in March and April produce the best flavour and get the best price from buyers in Germany and Japan. However, the average price of Darjeeling tea sold in the period from January to July 1999 was Rs. 192.81 ($4.44) marginally highly than the average of Rs. 191.17 in the same period last year. According to Darjeeling Planters' Association, hardly anybody is making profit this year. And the fall in output has not helped boost prices of the Darjeeling tea. About 70 to 80 per cent of Darjeeling tea produced in the country is exported.

AYP Picketed for the Dues: On December 9, 1999 the Asom Yuba Parishad (AYP), the Asom Gana Parisad's (AGP) youth wing, took it upon itself the issue of collecting 'Dues' from the major tea companies on behalf of the people of Assam. It is learnt, parishad members picketed before the offices of Tata Tea and Williamson Magor demanding them pay up. A team led by two parishad conveners, Mr Jagdish Bhuyan (State Tourism Minister) and Mr. Kartik Hazarika, submitted a memorandum to the two companies which states: "Assam has given her everything *(sic)* to you during the last 200 years. Your moral obligation to reciprocate is long overdue". The memorandum added: "We sincerely hope that you don't allow to grow the resentment any further and come forward with concrete and positive approach". In the eyes of parishad, set up recently, the "concrete and positive approach" constitutes, among other things, shifting the companies' head offices to Assam. Some other demands listed in the memorandum are:

(i) All jobs in the industry must go to local youths; *(ii)* The industry must make all its purchases locally, preferably from local businessmen; *(iii)* Tea grown in the state must be auctioned within the state; *(iv)* All profits must be invested in the state to promote industrial and economic growth; and *(v)* The industry must undertake Community development projects, such as setting up of schools, hospitals, etc. and building roads and bridges. Magor officials told the team, "it may not be possible to fulfil" their demand that the state's entire tea crop be auctioned within the state. "We do carry out a lot of development work, but the people don't get to know about them because we don't publicise the projects. We are with the people of Assam", an official said.

Single Yardstick Needed to Define Small Growers in Assam: There is no agreed yardstick in Assam to define 'small tea growers'. While according to the Tea Board a small tea grower is he whose land under tea cultivation does not exceed 75 bighas (10 hectares), the State Government recognizes those as small tea growers whose area under tea cultivation does not exceed 30 bighas. However, the All Assam Tea Growers' Association has demanded that the area under cultivation for recognition as small tea growers be increased from 30 and 75 bighas to 250 bighas.

New Periodical from North-East: Assam Tea Planters' Cooperative Society is bringing out a new periodical, North East Tea News. It will be a quarterly and will aim at covering various issues connected with tea plantation, cultivation, marketing and futures.

Tea Control Order be Revoked, ITA: Recently the Indian Tea Association (ITA) has strongly asserted that the Tea Marketing Control Order 1984 (TMCO) be scrapped. The ITA said the TMCO is an "anachronism" since the tea industry, on one hand, is being asked to gear up for free trade and imports while, on the other, the industry is being fettered with internal control. ITA felt it was imperative for the tea industry to have the flexibility to determine the method of sale of its own product. Expressing concern over the decline in tea prices ITA said that the All India Average Price up to October 1999 remained lower by Rs. 5/- per kg and in South India the price were down by Rs. 12/- per kg. "The decline in prices is of serious concern to the tea industry. The lower crop has had a serious impact on unit cost of production by way of labour wages, higher foodgrains subsidy and major export costs on account of fertilizer, fuel and transportation."

Good Days Ahead in 2007: Although various internal and international constraints slowed down the pace of economic activity, the country is expected to achieve 9 to 9.5 per cent rate of annual economic growth in 2007. Leading economists of the country recently said that the bad days were over, the economy would be buoyant in 2007 onwards. On the basis of random survey it was emphasized that earlier constraints would not reappear and cripple the movement of economic enterprises. The national economy was slowly moving towards the better. The Secretary of the Union Commerce Ministry expressed hope that exports of the country in the year 2007 will be higher. The sign of improvement was already evident from exports in November 2006. In fact, economists painted 2007 as a better year, expected the upswing of economic activities to continue. It was stated that achieving of 9 to 9.5 per cent annual growth rate for the economy would not be difficult this year if our various industrial sectors take the advantage of large internal market and growing opportunities of export. The tea sector should take note of the fact and endeavour to contribute more to the higher economic growth expected in 2007. The tea units, individually and jointly, should take all possible steps to make the existing large internal market larger. The health message from tea drinking has to reach at every corner in the country and touch all age-groups. Exports could also be increased substantially in the face of keen competition from other tea producing and exporting countries. The International Consultant, Accenture, in its mid-term report presented before the Union Commerce Minister in December, 2006 also envisaged the possibility of increasing exports up to a maximum of 290 million kgs by 2007. Though, of course, opinion may vary on this matter, captains of tea industry are convinced that higher export target for tea could be achieved provided Orthodox tea production is enhanced by at least 100 million kgs in the wake of larger global demand and, moreover, the existing Orthodox tea drinking markets are re-energised. Production of Organic tea should be increased in view of growing demand in developed economies. Finally, clear-cut short and medium term export plan in place, say, for Chile, UAE, Iran, etc. has to be formulated. In matter of exports, all segments of the industry should be cohesive, seriously consider consumers' preference, competitors' role as well. Hope, the tea industry would consider the fact and draw up necessary action plan.

Mushrooming of Tea Factories: To combat the spiralling costs of production, a few tea estate owners and some newcomers set up bought leaf factories which mushroomed all over the tea producing regions in India. With lower overheads/expenses and little statutory commitments, owners of bought leaf factories were able to sell 'made tea' below Rs.40 per kg which is below cost of production of over 95 per cent of the established tea estates in India. These teas despite being devoid of quality attracted the price-conscious Indian consumer to the detriment of common and medium tea estates. Although official figures of production from bought tea leaf factories are not available, reliable sources indicate this to be in excess of 100 million kgs.

Equation of Supply and Demand of Tea: The equation of supply and demand plays a role in determination of prices but when a buyer gets tea @ Rs. 40 per kg., he would be wary of raising the value for a lot bereft of quality unless a state of urgency forces him to make purchases at higher prices. In the process, the established tea producer suffered—as the value of all categories of tea tumbled due to presence of sizeable quantity of common and medium varieties throughout the year.

Adulteration Racket: Although tea is known as a health drink, it could not escape the target of adulteration racket. Adulteration of tea had taken a new dimension from 2000 onwards. These unholy practices in the trade front not only rocked the growers' sentiments but also sent a shivering feeler to the consumers. The West Godavari Police unearthed a tea racket by seizing 59,950 kgs of fake tea made of cashew nut rind mixed with betonies powder and edible soda. The seizure of 54,000 kgs of spurious tea from four rice mills of Andhra Pradesh had revealed that it was difficult to differentiate spurious tea from genuine tea as both the colour, the smell and the granular finish were almost identical. Such fake tea could lead to health hazards including blindness and irrevocable damage to the digestive system. In North Bengal, consecutive raids in a few bought leaf factories confirmed that adulteration racket is active in this region too. Seizure of 200 gunny bags containing a non-tea, tea like material, from a factory of Jalpaiguri district was indeed shocking news.

No one can deny that tea is in a disastrous condition at the auction centres and ex-factory outlets. There is hardly any reflection of this gloom at the consumer outlet. It is difficult to buy an average quality tea below Rs.120 a kg. This riddle is a difficult to unfurl. There is hardly any answer to the question, why there is a gulf of difference between ex-factory and consumer retail outlets. This is the high time when all efforts to be made to improve both productivity and quality for the survival of Indian tea. Let us pin point a few scientific problems in the tea field and suggest measures to partially or fully overcome those problems:

Organic Food Festival in New Delhi: A week long International Organic Food Festival was held in New Delhi, starting from November 28, 2002. The festival has been arranged by the Biodynamic Association of India in collaboration with the Union Commerce Ministry. Jaswant

Purohit of the Tea Association said, "the festival will show-case India's organic teas and food grown the way nature intended. We are expecting a lot of foreign buyers."

Organic Tea to Increase Exports: In order to increase exports of tea from the country, the Indian tea industry is now giving more attention to organically grown teas. According to information available from the Ministry of Commerce, India exported 1.9 million kgs (4.1 million pounds) of organic tea in 1999-2000 fiscal and the plan was to double the export quantum in 2000-01. Fragrant organic tea from Darjeeling commands premium. During 2006-07, the annual export of organic tea would be around 12 million kgs. Growers believe, health-consciousness of consumers in Europe, USA and Japan has enhanced the demand of organic tea comparing to that of a decade ago. The industry is convinced that in coming years the demand will increase phenomenally in view of growing popularity of organic tea. And hence, the tea growers have been advised to take this opportunity to boost exports.

Tea Board to Launch Web Site: The Tea Board of India launched a web site as its strategy to boost the demand of Indian tea in international market. The site provides information relating to production capacity of gardens, market prices, quality of Indian teas and also techniques of preparing good tea. In this regard, however, Mr. Basudeb Banerjee, Chairman of the Tea Board said, "in any effort to boost demand of tea in the international market there is no alternative but utilizing information technology." In the setting up of the web site the Tea Board took help of IBM.

Government Considering ISI Mark for Tea: The Ministry of Commerce, Government of India introduced ISI certification for tea. Mr. Sharad Yadav, the then Consumer Affairs Minister, said, for this purpose "the Indian Standard for tea has been revised by the Bureau of India Standards (BIS) in consultation with the Ministry which will be published shortly". Ministry officials thought that the move helped improving realization for tea growers and companies as the consumers are provided with high quality certified produce.

ITA's Sales Promotion Campaign for Tea: In order to expand the domestic market of tea, the Indian Tea Association (ITA) has been advertising tea through TV and other publicity media. On the basis of the observation of the Director of American Health Foundation, the advertisement says that tea contains all the nutrients necessary for good health and regular drinking of tea reduces the risk of heart stroke, tumour, some types of cancer and many other diseases. Meanwhile, the impact of the advertisement on the viewers has been studied which indicated 70 per cent of them considers tea not only as a temporary stimulant but a beverage providing vigour and vitality.

Flavoured Tea Market in The Country: Tea majors namely Tata Tea and Hindustan Level Limited (HLL) have been exploring untapped flavoured tea market in the country. They wanted the Indian Tea Association to persuade the Government for allowing the use of natural identical flavours in black tea. Other leading tea manufacturers also supported this proposal.

Export of Tea Declined: At the 119th Annual General Meeting of the Indian Tea Association (ITA), held in first half of 2001, Mr. Bharat Bajoria, Chairman of the Association, expressed grave concern for the declining trend of exports in the last couple of years. Mr. Bajoria pointed out, the quantum of total export in 2001 was the minimum in the last five years. Russia's curtailment of tea imports from India, ban on Indian tea imports in Iran and Libya, lower prices of tea produced in Kenya, China, Indonesia and Vietnam have pulled down Indian exports, Mr. Bajoria added.

Orthodox Production Necessary in South India: At a seminar on Orthodox tea manufacture, organized by the Tea Board and the United Planters' Association of Southern India, Mr.Vikram Kapoor, Executive Director of the Tea Board suggested the tea growers in South India to switch over to Orthodox manufacture from CTC. In his opinion, this could salvage the southern tea growers from the continuing dull situation. The Tea Board had sanctioned Rs. 5 crore to 45 producers for the switchover to Orthodox tea production. He advised the planters to learn from Sri Lanka where 98 per cent of the produce was Orthodox and 68 per cent of the small growers engaged in the production of the same. Mr. Kapur said, the soil and weather in South India were ideally suited for the production of Orthodox tea.

Sanjiwani Rehabilitation Centre Inaugurated: In the third quarter of 2002, the permanent building of Sanjiwani Rehabilitation Centre for spastic children was inaugurated by Mr. Sanjoy Lohia, Deputy Commissioner, Sonitpur, Assam. Amongst others, the ABITA Chairman, Mr N.N. Sharma, ABITA Chairman (Zone 3), Mr. A. Singh, ABITA Secretary and offices of ABITA (Zone 3) attended the function. For the construction of the building the Assam Branch, Indian Tea Association (ABITA) Headquarters and the Zonal Office jointly contributed Rs. 2.5 lakh.

North Bengal University started Soil Testing Laboratory for Tea Gardens: The Department of Tea Management under the University of North Bengal has started a Soil Testing Laboratory for the benefit of the tea plantation units of North Bengal, Bihar and Sikkim. Estimation of Organic Carbon, pH, Nitrogen, available Potassium and Phosphorus, Electrical conductivity costs only Rs.50 per sample. That besides, estimation of Sulphur and soil texture is also undertaken at reasonable cost.

WB Government to Survey Tea Industry: On 23rd October, 2002, Mr. Nirupam Sen, Commerce and Industry Minister, Government of West Bengal, said in Kolkata that the government alongwith the Tea Board had conducted a survey and prepared a situation report on tea industry in the state. The survey covered and recorded the number of tea gardens, area of the gardens, and so on. The report was submitted in December 31, 2002.

Domestic Tea Consumption Down: Tea Consumption in India has declined by about 7 per cent during the last one-and-a-half year, said Mr. A Borgohain, the then Chairman of the Assam Sub-Committee of the Indian Tea Association, quoting survey reports. He said, recent survey reports by reputed market agencies have focused this aspect of tea consumption in the country since mid-1998. Mr. Borgohain felt, unless the issue was addressed immediately, near future of the industry would be unbeaming. There is already severe competition from other beverage sectors.

Tea Board to Monitor Organic Tea Production: Following the commerce ministry's decision to appoint the Tea Board of India as a 'National Accreditation Agency' for the national programme on organic tea production the Board has formed a sub-committee and fixed the terms and conditions for detailing the rules on organic tea production, accreditation and certification. The commerce ministry assigned the Tea Board four major tasks—prescribing the package of practices for organic production of the product; undertaking inspection and certifying product as having been produced in accordance with national standard for organic product; monitor inspection by the accredited inspection agencies; and laying down of the inspection procedures.

Study of Benchmarking by Tea Board: Tea Board of India conducted a study on benchmarking for the Indian tea industry by the Indian Instituted of Plantation Management (IIPM) at an estimated cost of Rs.6.00 lakh. The objectives of the study were: *(i)* to suggest ways to strengthen the tea industry at the enterprise level, and *(ii)* to develop data for enabling benchmarking at the operating unit level i.e. the estate level so as to have improved performance vis-à-vis other estates in the district and region.

Tripura Tea Strike: The insurgents have stepped up the activities of the tea industry in and around the tea plantation areas in Tripura. There were attacks on the management, officials and workers by militants in recent times, besides large scale extortions. The state's tea gardens observed a strike on 20th February 2000 in protest against the killing of Mr. D.K. Nath, Manager of the Ganganagar Tea Estate, North Tripura, on 18th February, 2000. Members of the state unit of the Tea Association of India (TAI) met the Chief Minister and demanded that all state tea gardens be brought under the disturbed area regulation.

Employment of Additional Workers in Gardens: The Consultative Committee of Planters' Association (CCPA) recruited 10,000 additional workers to the tea industry. The distribution of the new workforce currently remained confined in the 194 tea plantations of the Dooars and the Terai though it is uncertain whether the West Bengal Tea Development Corporation or the Tea Trading Corporation of India Plantations will absorb new workers. According to CCPA sources, however, Darjeeling tea estates might be excluded for the moment. The employment issue is an overriding one in the tea industry since July 21, 1999. This could not be solved due to Coordination and Defense Committees charge in on the one hand, and on the other tea associations' failure to establish a distribution formula of new workforce acceptable to the gardens. The employment issue was virtually settled.

Certification of Darjeeling Tea: The advent of 'Certification' pursuant to the Geographical Indication of Goods (Registration and Protection) Act, 1999 and the post WTO scenario will ensure that only 100 per cent Darjeeling will get certification and no tea without certification can be sold as Darjeeling. According to industry sources, the volume of teas sold annually in the name of Darjeeling is about five times the actual production in 80 gardens that produce champagne teas in the hills of North Bengal. Thus, while an often fake or adulterated Darjeeling tea commands a fabulous price at domestic and international outlets, Darjeeling gardens are in a state of perpetual penury. The industry circle feels, however, certification of Darjeeling tea is a welcome move to protect Darjeeling teas.

Despite Unsatisfactory Tea Business HLL Dividend Up: Although the tea business did not do well as anticipated because of weather conditions and "discriminatory tax on packaged, branded tea", the net Profit of the Hindustan Level Limited (HLL) for the year ending December, 1999 had shown improvement. "The audited results for the year ending December show the Net Profit has gone up from Rs.806 crore in 1998 to Rs. 1070 crore in 1999. The net Turnover has gone up from Rs.9482 crore to Rs.10142 crore". The consumer goods major, HLL has recommended a Dividend of Rs.17 per share and an Interim Dividend of Rs.12 per share, amounting to Rs. 29 per share, which is 31.8 per cent over last year's Dividend of Rs. 22.

Warren Acquires Eariabarie Tea: The Warren Group, a leader in the Indian Tea industry, has expanded its presence in Assam by acquiring the Eariabarie Tea Company producing a million kilogram of tea annually. This acquisition will be brought under Darjeeling Plantations and Industries Ltd (DPIL), a closely-held subsidiary of the Group flagship, Warren Tea Ltd. With the acquisition of Katalguri Tea Estate in the Dooars a few months ago and now the Eariabarie in Assam, the horizon of the DPIL will widen in virtually the entire tea belt in North India.

Tata Tea Extends Mr Kidwai's Term as Managing Director: At a meeting of the Board of Directors of Tata Tea Limited held on 24th January 2000, the contract of Mr. S M Kidwai as Managing Director of the Company ending on 31st January 2000 was extended upto 30th September 2000, with the approval of shareholders at the Annual General Meeting. All other terms and conditions of Mr Kidwai's appointment as Managing Director of the Company as prevailed on 31st January 2000 and approved by the shareholders remained unchanged.

Laudable Accomplishment: Zenith Machinery Co., known for the committed services to tea processing industries within and outside the country, has received the prestigious ISO 9001 Certification on 3rd April, 2002, a rare honour for a Tea Machinery Manufacturing Unit. The International Certification Services (Asia) Ltd., rigorously examined the extent Zenith could comply with various requirements of International Quality Standard for obtaining this certificate. The scope of study of the International Agency was wide enough, covering from Basic Layout Design to Manufacturing and Supplying of Tea Processing Machinery as per customers' requirements. Zenith services in all such matter highly satisfied the International Certification Authority and as a obvious outcome Zenith has been honoured with the ISO 901 award. It is a great achievement indeed. Despite the extreme adverse conditions, in the market, Zenith Machinery Co is surging ahead. During period 2001-2002 it has been able to sell 254 Cutting Units of "Samurai" CTC Machines, added Mr. P. Kejriwal, Executive Director of the company.

Indian Tea Exports Down in January, 2001: Indian tea exports, which fell over 13 per cent in 2001 compared to the year ago, continued the downward trend in January 2002, with a 23 percent fall over the same month last year. "Exports in January 2002 amounted to 10.88 million kg compared to 14.15 million kg in the same month in 2001", a Tea Board official said. Tea exports from India have suffered due to fierce competition from Indonesia, Bangladesh and Sri Lanka, and lower demand from traditional buyers like Russia and Britain. Indian Tea Association, the country's largest body of the tea producers, said recently that it was eyeing the market in war-torn Afghanistan to increase tea exports.

Tea and A Trust: Charles Wallace, an accountant, who came to India from UK in 1870 to look after a tea plantation in North India, found the tea estate and its surroundings in a mess and expressed desired to change things around. Under Wallace, the tea company did well and even diversified into timber. Wallace made a fortune, and thought it was his responsibility to give something to the country. And so, he wrote in his will that an educational trust will be formed for the benefit of scholars in the UK and India. Thus the Charles Wallace India Trust was born. Wallace died in Kolkata in 1916. But according to his will, only after the death of his youngest son in 1967, the trust was finally formed.

Move to Bring Tea Headquarters in Assam: The Assam Assemble moves to relocate the headquarters of companies having tea gardens in the State, from Kolkata to Guwahati. The tea industry, however, considers the move impractical and unacceptable. "Kolkata, as a distribution center of teas across the country as well as a hub of export, has locational advantages over Guwahati. Since the focal issue of the industry is marketing, and not growing, the companies are better placed in having their headquarters in Kolkata", said Mr C K Dhanuka of Dhunseri Tea. Though most of the industry representatives agreed that the law and order situation in the State has improved, they felt the existing infrastructure not conducive to attract executives. Apart from inadequate banking and communication facilities, the social infrastructure also needs be revamped. The Managing Director of Warren Tea said, there is no law that can impose on the companies to shift their headquarters to Assam, the decision must be taken by the management of respective companies. The major tea companies having bases in Assam are Tata Tea, Rossell Industries, Eveready Industries India, George Williamson (Assam), Warren Tea, Assam Company, Goodricke Group Ltd and Dhunseri Tea. This was the third attempt on the part of the Assam Government to move headquarters from Kolkata to Guwahati, though this was the first time that the legislative assembly had taken an initiative, said the Director of a leading tea company.

Rocket Attack on Tea Estate: According to a report received here, extremists fired a rocket-propelled grenade and followed it up with gunfire at the residence of the Manager of the Majuli Tea Estate of Tata Tea Limited in Darrng district, Assam, on the night of April 17, 2002. A part of the wall of the house was damaged. The incident could mark the beginning of yet another phase of intimidation to the tea industry. The Darrang Superintendent of Police, Mr M P Gupta, said that more that 20 jawans of the Assam Tea Plantation Protection Force are deployed in the garden. "The extremists fired the grenade probably because they could not dare to raid the bungalow with rifles given the presence of the ATPPF jawans". Asked if the attack on the garden was carried out because monetary demand of the ultras might not have been met, the S P said: "Neither the manager nor the company's officials in Guwahati mentioned receiving any extortion notice". The extremists could have carried out the attack to "show their strength" and intimidate the tea industry, he added. Majuli Tea Estate is located within 3 k.m. of the Indo-Bhutanese border under Paneri police station.

Orthodox Tea Manufacture: With the globalisation and free market economy the scope of export and import has been widened. This has resulted in increase awareness among the consumers and bulk buyers for quality and price. It is, therefore, imperative to produce value added and quality products for the survival of any unit. Good orthodox tea production can add value to teas provided standard is maintained at all stages of harvesting and manufacturing.

Indian Tea Industry under Threat: Kenya and China are emerging as a threat to the Indian tea industry and these countries are capturing more and more of the export market at the cost of India. Unless Indian exporters gear up to face the challenge, there will be surplus in the domestic market, said analysts.

Push for Tea Exports: A 19-member Committee comprising representatives of the government and the tea industry has suggested that Indian tea exports could be increased provided the industry adopts a strategic perspective of efforts rather than viewing it as a domestic surplus. It targets export volume of 240 million kgs by the year 2006. The Committee's Report is an outcome of four months of rigorous assessment of the country's relative competitiveness in the world trade, according to Mr. Anup K Matilal, Secretary, Tea Board of India. It calls for a differential approach to various markets, based on a specific assessment of the overall market attractiveness.

Tea Planters Retailing Unblended Teas: A section of tea planters in the country, not getting attractive prices at the traditional auction centers, have started retailing their unblended teas in sloppy packets under obscure brand names. These products have been launched in Uttar Pradesh, Gujarat, Maharashtra, Madhya Pradesh, Rajasthan, Punjab and other markets. As a result, the markets are flooded with various types of teas and at all sorts of prices. This has only resulted in a further decline in tea prices. Industry source said, "this move by the section of the planters can be called suicidal and it has in no way improved the prices of tea of average quality". Mr. P O Desai, President of the Federation of All India Tea Traders Association (FAITTA), has severely criticized the trade practice and said that it would not serve anybody's interest. "There is another negative aspect to the whole issue. More than enough tea is now lined up at the retail level, making the market over-saturated with all sorts of packet tea", Desai added. A producer of a leading packet tea brand said the planters concerned were attracted by the selling prices of the leading brand in the market. "However, they had no information that even these brands are selling their products at a lower price", the packeteer said.

"The planters have introduced their packets at random without any proper blending to suit the tastes of regional consumers. As a result, this is certain to make a negative impact on the future of the packet tea industry", the packeteer added.

ITA Plans for Afghan Exports: Indian Tea Association (ITA) sent a delegation to Afghanistan to revive India's export to that country. "Apart from a tea delegation comprising the Union Commerce Ministry, Tea Board officials and industry people, permission to export tea to Afghanistan as part of credit to that country helped the industry". The ITA Chairman, Mr Bharat Bajoria said. He told to the press that the association impressed upon the Commerce Ministry for sending a delegation to Afghanistan.

Duncan Establishing Tea Boutique Chain: Duncans Industries Ltd (DIL) sat up a chain of tea boutiques in select areas. The stores were established under the Duncans brand name and logo. "After extensive research into tea purchase habits and sales pattern, we have identified 10 locations where outlets will come up in four months", said Mr Gauri Prasad Goenka. The group collected data from actual visits to markets and buyers feedback from popular tea selling shops in the unorganized sector. The boutiques firmly focused on tea because "that is the business we understand the best", said Mr. Goenka. He added, "I am convinced that retail will be a good experience for us, given the strong data-based approach that we have taken and the direct retail model we have adopted". The first shop came up in B B D Bag. This is the central business area in Kolkata, where several popular tea retailers already were located.

Khaitans Exit from India Foils: The B.M. Khaitan Group has severed its last ties with India Foils Ltd (IFL) by transferring its entire 20 per cent stake in the aluminium foils market to ICICI. The transfer of India Foils Ltd. shares was a part of the group's strategy to hand over its long term equity investments in some companies to ICICI inlieu of the fees due to the financial institution for restructuring of the debts of Eveready Industries, the tea and battery maker from the Khaitan group.

AASTGA Steps to Check Price Fall: The All Assam Small Tea Growers' Association (AASTGA) took steps to ensure reasonable return for the small growers. Accordingly,

Mr. Hemanta Kumar Gohain, Secretary of the AASTGA requested the bought leaf factories and the organized sector to buy quality green leaf from the small growers on an area to area basis. The association also wants to get rid of the intermediaries, who were eating away into the profits of the tea growers. Mr Gohain remarked that these intermediaries are a major cause of concern to the association. They are making money while the growers are left with almost no return on their investment. He said, the mushroom growth of brought leaf factories in upper Assam has not contributed to the making of quality tea, and that these have led to the growth of the nuisance of green leaf theft and dubious tea making processes. He named a factory, which "does nothing but reprocess worst quality tea dust with some fresh made tea". For such unscrupulous tea makers, quality is the last concern and ill-gotten profit s the primary concern, Mr. Gohain said.

TAI's Supervisory Development Programme: National Productivity Council (NPC) arranged a 6-day "Supervisory Development Programme for Plantation Supervisors" on request of the Tea Association of India (TAI), Barak Valley branch sometimes in February 2002. The main objective of the programme was to sensitise the sardars regarding various aspects of tea manufacturing and processing, basic productivity concept, supervisory skills, teamwork and kaizen activities, discipline and motivation. The experts suggested the supervisors to keep a check on alcholism and absenteeism as the habits are barrier to quality tea production. 70 supervisors participated and exchanged opinion. 5 supervisors were selected for further training under the 'Training for Trainers' scheme.

TBITA on Tea Industry Crisis: Admittedly "pushed to the wall", the tea industry is considering to take up drastic measures. While addressing the 40th Annual General Meeting of the Terai Branch Indian Tea Association (TBITA), Mr A Bhagat, Chairman, said: "It's time we discard our grandmother's regulation. Children must be introduced to tea at an early age. He proposed a turn-around measure for the crisis–ridden tea industry by "repositioning" tea as a "health drink". The health properties of tea, backed by scientific evidence, can be a powerful platform for this campaign", he said. Mr A.K. Matilal, Secretary, Tea Board of India asked the tea industry to be "competitive" and emphasized for improvement quality.

Tea Plantation Companies Cut Wages by 11 percent: Tea plantation companies in the Nilgiris, South India, have managed to lower the wage rate of workers by nearly 11 per cent in end of 2002 besides getting them to sign a productivity agreement along with a penal clause. This is something unique in matter of wage settlement in tea industry. The daily wage rate was brought down from Rs. 78.40 to Rs. 70. The variable Dearness Allowance was frozen at the existing levels while the fixed DA was fixed at 0.25 paise per quarter, denoting wage increase of each worker by a sum of Rs.2.00 only in the next two years. The Nilgiri Plantation Workers' Union, whose members exceed 2 lakh signed the agreement.

However, while the workers accepted this wage cut, the plantation companies were somewhat fair also. Incentive rates were raised for various tasks that were performed in a tea estate. For instance, workers, whose plucking rate is higher, were given special incentives. Of course, the plucking job was determined by parameters like quality control, weather conditions, etc. The agreement, at the same time, took into account productivity increase in all tasks including weeding, drain cleaning, spraying of chemicals etc. by a hefty 20 per cent which meant workers coming down by the same percentage. This was obviously a cost reduction measure. The agreement was a historic one and paved the way for similar agreement in rest of the South India and more importantly, Assam and North Bengal.

Tea Imports be Drastically Cut: At the Annual General Meeting of Kanan Devan Planters' Association, Mr B C Aiyamma, Chairman of the association expressed grave fro allowing free tea imports in the country which had adverse effect on market sentiments. Mr. Aiyamma said that most of the tea imported was of very poor quality for countries from like Vietnam and Indonesia. Some quantity was imported from Sri Lanka at concessional rate of duty as per the SAARC agreement. This import of tea has serious implications for the industry in both the long and the short term and calls for some serious measures by the Government and the Tea Board. He wanted the Government to: *(a)* levy Bound Rate of Duty at 150 per cent on all tea imports; *(b)* withdraw duty concession of Sri Lanka tea; *(c)* strictly apply our quality standard norm i.e. IS 3720 on all tea imports; *(d)* stop free imports into EOUs and EPZs, as sufficient tea is available.

Assam Tea Corporation (ATC) Gardens in Dire Straits: According to employees of the Assam Tea Corporation (ATC), the tea gardens Katanibari, Dhekiajuloi, Naginijan, Sotai, and Saikata of the Corporation are in a crisis due to the indifferent attitude of the State Government. The employees demanded immediate action to revitalize the gardens. Employees of the gardens did not get their salaries for the last couple for months. It was reported. "We met the Chief Minister, Mr. Tarun Gogoi, recently for appris8ing of the prevailing condition of the gardens, but his attitude towards tea garden employees appears to be negative", the employees unequivocally said. They also threatened an indefinite strike in five gardens if the government fails to take an action immediately. The employees submitted a memorandum to the Chief Minister through a magistrate.

Cachar to Improve Quality of Tea: At the 101 Annual General Meeting of the Surma Valley Branch, Indian Tea Association, the Chairman of the Association in his written address laid overwhelming emphasis on the need to bring about substantial improvement in the quality of tea for the long term revival of the Cachar tea industry. He said that the time has come for Cachar to explore all avenues of marketing its tea and one such is to search overseas markets. Cachar producers can directly target markets such as Pakistan, which is an exclusive CTC market.

ASPEE's Farmer of the Year Award: At a function held on 23rd March, 2002 in Mumbai the "ASPEE L M Patel Farmer of the Year Award 2001" was given. The awardees were Mr Chandrashekar Haribhau Bhadsavle for Rainfed Farming Category—Rice Cfrop, Mr Subhash Dattatraya Arve for Horticulture Category—Grape Cultivation, Smt Maltiben

Joitaram Chaudhary for Women Farmer Category—Dairy Farming and Smt Padmaja Parshuram Chitala for Horticulture Category—Grape Cultivation.

Government Assistance for Tea Exports: To make Indian tea more competitive in the global market, the Government has prepared a plan for meeting miscellaneous expenditure of tea exporters. "A Rs.5.25 crore package has been finalized for reimbursing the expenditure tea exporters incur in value addition, handling, packaging, transport and freight to boost the sagging exports of the commodity", official sources said. "Basically, the idea is to encourage exporters to move from bulk trade to value—added segments without totally neglecting the former", the official added it. Exporters of tea bags, packet tea, orthodox, bulk tea and tea directly purchased from the bought leaf factories could now take the benefit of the assistance package. The break up is in favour of value-added product. The reimbursement rates are—Rs.10 per kg for tea bag; Rs. 2.5 per kg for packet tea; Ra. 2 per kg for Orthodox and bulk tea; and Rs. 2 per kg for Orthodox and CTC tea from bought leaf factories.

Diatea for Diabetics: The Boulevard Agro Services of Guwahati, Assam, has recently launched a new tea "Diatea", exclusively for the diabetic patients. This tea is a blend of pure Darjeeling tea and three Himalayan herbs. The tea was originally manufactured by Makaibari Tea & Trading Co(P) Ltd., of Kolkata, the expertise came from Mr P.N. Banerjee, a renowned tea planter of West Bengal. However, the entire bulk of this herbal tea was exported to Japan, said Mr. Raj Kamal Choudhury, Director of Boulevard Agro Services. According to Mr Choudhury, a diabetic patient can take diatea without sugar and milk three to four times a day along with antidiabetic regimen. This tea stimulates insulin secretion by pancreas, stimulates heart and circulatory system, increases the volume of urine and activates uterus in case of women, without influencing the carbohydrate metabolism. The diatea not only controls blood sugar but also obesity. Diatea is a pure herbal tea that has no side effect. Evidences reveal that sugar problem is under control who takes diatea regularly, added Mr. Choudhury. It has tremendous prospects, he said.

Tata Tea Relaunched Kanan Devan: On 17th March, 2002 Tata Tea relaunched its popular South India-based tea brand Kanan Devan in a new package. Commencing on the launch Mr P Siganporia, Deputy Managing Director of Tata Tea said, "the new packaging has been developed after intensive consumer research and embodies Kanan Devan's attributes of being a tea blended by nature. The company's investments in Kanan Devan's new packaging and production processes are in keeping with our commitment to bringing the best cup of tea to consumers". Kanan Devan derives its taste from combination of natural elements present in the Kanan Devan hills in Kerala. The forthcoming advertising campaign of Kanan Devan aims to capture the essence of the brans in its strap line, "blended by nature for that unique taste". Apart from Kanan Devan, Tata Tea's portfolio of brands include Tata Tea, Tetley, Agni, Chakra Gold and Gemini, With 55 tea estates across India and an area of 26,500 hectares under cultivation, Tata Tea produces over 60 million kgs of tea accounting for 21 percent share (in volume terms) of the Indian packet tea market.

ICICI Picks More in George Williamson: ICICI has picked up a further 1.54 per cent stake in George Williamson (Assam) taking the total of its holding in the company to 7.27 per cent. Confirming the development, Mr S K Mitra, Chairman and Managing Director of George Williamson (Assam), said the Williamson Magor Group has offloaded shares at market rate. According to market sources, the financial institution has acquired 2,17,950 shares of the tea company which together with its previous holding of 8,12,749 amounts to 10,30,699 shares, representing 7.27 per cent of the company's Paid-up Equity. The financial institution's picking stake in the company follows preparation between the Khaitan and Magor families last year around this time. Prior to this change, the Khaitans held 10.6 per cent in the company.

Decision on Tea Auction Unit Deferred: The Government of West Bengal has decided to sit on the proposal of setting up a tea auction center at Jalpaiguri for the moment. The matter was discussed at a meeting the State Indsutry Minister, Mr. Nirupam Sen, the tea lobby and Jalpaiguri district officials in Kolkata on March 56, 2002. Representatives of the Tea Board, Land and Land Reforms Department and Commercial Taxes were present. The Government will act on the matter after it receives a study report on the subject being prepared by a Kolkata based organization M/s A F Ferguson. The Tea Board engaged the firm for a study on "Primary marketing of Tea in India". Experts from Ferguson visited the Siliguri Tea Auction Centre on November 20, 2001 and had discussions with buyer groups, brokers, planters and bought leaf unit owners. They collected statistics related to sale figures, sampling norms, auction rules, volume and price trends, and evolution and growth of the Siliguri Tea Auction Centre.

Goodricke Launching Sub-economy Brand: In May 2002, Goodricke Group Ltd. has launched a sub-economy tea brand in the face of increasing competition from unorganized regional packeters. The brand will be sold at the same price as the regional brands.

At the Annual General meeting of the company held in Kolkata, Mr P A Leggatt, Chairman, said: "The recently launched economy brand, Zabardast was well received and the current year should see a substantial increase in sales. There are plans to give packet tea sales a further boost by introducing new brands and other campaigns to increase sales." Mr. K S David, Managing Director said that the company's gardens in Darjeeling is facing competition from highgrown teas from Nepal. Over the years, tea growing areas in Nepal, adjacent to Darjeeling, have been steadily improving their production using clones brought over from Darjeeling. With lower production costs and negligible statutory overheads, ssuch teas produced by Nepal are being sold to overseas buyers, especially Japan and Germany at one-third of the sale price.

DIPS School of Tea Introduces Advanced Training Programme: The School of Tea of the Dipras Institute of Professional Studies (DIPS) was established in Kolkata in February 2000. The school provides qualified and trained personnel to the tea industry. The first session of the school commenced in July 2000 and the course has been recently revamped according to the needs of the tea industry. The 10-month course has now been made a one-year course. The West Bengal State Council of Technical Education has recognized the 'Tea Management' course. The Post Graduate Course in Tea Management is for the fresh graduates without any exposure to tea industry.

Seminars and Advanced Training Programme: The school of tea is also conducting need based Seminar and Advanced Training Programme. These programmes are meant for upgrading and improving upon the technical skills and competence of the tea executives enabling them to take on the contingencies and deliver the best to the industry. DIPS conducted a seminar for three days from 3rd April to 5th April at Doom Dooma Planters Club on Tea Manufacturing, Tea Machinery & Tea Tasting. There were about 25 participants. The Institute is going to conduct another such advanced training programme in North Bank at Tezpur in Assam in 3rd week of May. The seminar will be on Tea Manufacturing, Tea Machinery, Energy Management and Tea Tasting. The details of contact person are as follows:

Ranjana Dutta, Secretary, Dipras Institute of Professional Studies, FE 477, Sector 3, Salt Lake City, Kolkata 700 106. Phone: 033-3593717, Telefax: 033 3212081, email: dipskol@vsnl.in

Institutions Offloaded 3 percent in Tata Tea: Institutional investors have offloaded nearly 3 per cent in Tata Tea during June-December, 2001. These investors include mutual funds (MFs), UTI, banks, financial institutions (FIs), insurance companies and foreign institutional investors (FIIs), who have reduced their holding by 2.92 per cent from 32.11 per cent in June to 29.19 per cent as on December 31,2001. FIIs offloaded the maximum from 4.97 per cent to 2.13 per cent followed by mutual funds (MFs) and UTI at 1.44 per cent.

However, banks, FIs and insurance companies rose their holding marginally. Public holding in the company has also come down by 3.02 per cent to 29.54 per cent. Simultaneously, private corporate bodies (PCBs) have increased their stake by 6.15 per cent to 9.77 per cent. Analysts, tracking the company, said the tea industry's woes would continue. "Globally tea prices crashed last year due to oversupply. However, the global output is understood to have come down, but, prices are yet to pick up in India and the situation is no different in the export market. Institutions may have opted for more attractive scripts during the period," said sources.

CAG Disapproved Rungmook Estate Roll: The Comptroller and Auditor General (CAG) has reprimanded the West Bengal Tea Development Corporation (WBTDC) for retaining 101 superannuated employees at its Rungmook Cedars Tea Estate due to its inability to pay their gratuity on retirement. Of them, 31 retired on May, 2000, and the rest were in service till March 31, 2001, the CAG report said. Some, in fact, served for 13 years after their date of superannuation. It has been pointed out by the report, their retention has cost the Corporation an additional amount of Rs.34 lakh. The Corporation paid out an additional Rs.1.72 crore for salaries, wages and other benefits to 690 excess staff. The estate retained 101 employees—in addition to the excess staff—for periods ranging from 1 years to 12 years after their dates of superannuation. The Corporation has also been pulled up for spending Rs.1.36 crore on a 0.5 MW Hydel Project at the same tea estate in 194.

Futures Trading in Tea Beginning Shortly: Futures Trading in Tea will start in India by the end of 2002. "This will break new ground in tea trading. For the first time, all Indian teas, irrespective of their origin, will be traded under one roof", said Mr. Karan Paul, Director of AFT Industries. He said that "Ideally the catalogue of the futures exchange should include teas of foreign origin. But Kenyan and Sri Lankan producers and foreign trading houses will watch the progress of the exchange for the time before they join it". The likely locations for the exchange are Kolkata and Cochin, which boast good infrastructure and very old auction centres. The Indian Forward Markets Commission (IFMC) insists that futures trading in tea will have to be screen-based from the beginning.

An official of the Indian Tea Association said, "the

government would do well to allow dollar-dominated trading, which will facilitate participation by other producing countries and major tea importers. Auction centres all over the world deal only with locally grown teas. But tea of all origins can feature in the proposed futures exchange provided quotes are accepted in dollars". It is not clear how many contracts the futures exchange will offer. But the trade analysts say since teas are grown throughout the year in South India, Sri Lanka and Kenya the exchange should offer 12 contracts in a year. According to trade circle, futures trading will lend stability to tea prices and will give producers and buyers access to more reliable and transparent price information.

UPASI Seeks Import Duty Hike on Tea and Coffee: United Planters' Association of Southern India (UPASI) has urged the Union finance minister to increase the basic import duty on tea and coffee to 35 per cent from the current 15 per cent to ensure adequate tariff protection, as provided in the WTO stipulations. The apex association has also demanded a retrospective amendment of Sub-Section 4(B), incorporated in the last Budget, by virtue of which a tea producer-exporter was made eligible to get export profit exemptions to the extent of 40 per cent only. In a representation made to the finance minister, UPASI said several hundred items likely to be placed on the free list of imports, effective April 1, 2000, had been pegged at the peak rate of 35 per cent plus surcharge. But the basic import duty for tea and coffee remained unchanged at 15 per cent.

Such low levels of import duties would, the association said, lead to the import of cheap tea from various other countries and ring the death knell of both the tea and coffee industries in India. With the progressive dismantling of QRs in regard to imports, it was becoming essential that tea and coffee be given adequate tariff protection (like other agricultural commodities) by increasing the basic import duty to 35 per cent, UPASI said. The association added : "If the import duty (in the light of QR removals) is a new problem for the plantation industry, excise duties in the case of the tea industry is an old issue that needs to be sorted out. The revenue implication of the total withdrawal of excise duty on bulk tea would not be significant if one were to take into account factors like excise exemptions already granted to cooperatives and bought-leaf tea factories, the refund on exports, the revenue loss to central and state governments by way of lower income tax and no agricultural income tax and the infrastructural costs of collecting all these taxes".

Distressed Small Tea Growers: Due to severe fall of the prices in the last two years the small growers in the country suffered most. The misery of small growers in both south and north India was of same magnitude. According to available reports, their produce could not be sold to the bought leaf factories and to other regular buyers even at a price of Rs. 6 per kg throughout the last year. This low price, in turn, crippled the normal functioning of many business units. And finding hardly any possibility to get remunerative price the small growers became frustrated and restive. They demanded the government of respective tea growing states to share their pains. The governments should come forward immediately with a package of relief to rescue them from the strangulating market condition. Hence, they urged to set a floor price of their produce, a subsidy as well. And to make their demand forceful the small growers frequently resorted to road blockade, various forms of movement in front of assembly house of the tea growing states. But fulfilment of their demand is in no way the remedy of present maladies. Relief package would not prevent recurrence of the situation. Rather the small growers would be judicious if they remember that those remained consistent in quality and supply did not suffer much due to price fall. The low price in the market was not too low to shake the confidence of quality tea producers in their business. It is imperative for the small tea growers to put their home in order. For higher price realization all they have to do is to see across the fence to realize that quality tea producers get better return in terms of prices. World's demand is now only for quality tea. In coming years the survival of tea units will virtually depend on this slogan– quality first, quality second, quality last. This is the only "mantra" for their survival. Small tea growers alongwith their different associations shall have to take do or die resolution for achieving this "mantra and should leave no stone unturned to upgrade the quality of teas.

Dandi Salt and Tea: The Board after long duration was able to stop the negative publicity the manufacturer of a table salt which is giving in TV commercials in Hindi and regional languages. This advertisement from the manufacturer of Dandi triple refined salt was telecast over Doordarshan and private channels. In the course of the commercial, a doctor was shown to be advising the people to stop drinking tea and save Rs.2 a cup which could be spent on consuming the Dandi salt. The stress was that Dandi salt helps people gain mental and physical health. It was not for any one in the tea industry to waste time, effort, money and other resources to test the veracity of this claim by the Dandi salt manufacturer about the product. But, a question that remains unanswered is: why should the tea industry allow a negative publicity of tea by a salt manufacturer just to promote his brand?

Positive Health Effects of Tea—Research: More so, now that researchers from all over the world have proved the positive health effects of tea. They have repeatedly stressed that tea drinking can help fight cancer, common cold, flu, cholesterol and heart ailments. This is in addition to stimulating mental ability. On the contrary, the general feeling is that the intake of salt leads to blood pressure, heart ailments and even obesity. So, many a doctor for many a patient advises less salt intake. Whether the Dandi brand is above such ill effects of salt consumption in general is a different question. But, in promoting this brand what is the sanctity for lowering the health effects of tea ? In fact, it is only recently that the Government, through the Tea Board, has shown interest to promote tea consumption based on the positive health effects proved by the scientific community at large. On a day in September 2001, the Government released an advertisement through the Tea Board covering full pages in some select newspapers with the title: "Live life healthy way—Piyo more chai every day".

Research Findings—Role of CCPA: The advertisement highlighted the research findings in support of tea consumption and said that for more details, one could contact the Kolkata-based Consultative Committee of Plantation Associations (CCPA). If so, why is the CCPA keeping mum over the current adverse publicity launched on tea by Dandi brand? Why is it not releasing advertisements and press releases to keep the media and the general public informed of the action it has taken to stop the advertisement from getting telecast in its present format? Why is it not giving a counter to the ad by disputing the ill-health link implied in the salt ad against tea? Likewise, why is it that the other producer organizations are not keeping the media informed of their action to stop the advertisement including the pressure they lay on their apex body viz. the CCPA ? Some of these bodies are known to be issuing press releases on what they want the CCPA to do for them. For instance, on November 20, 2001 the UPASI President, Mr. I.J.J. Rebello, issued a press statement wherein, inter alia, he said: "The domestic promotion campaign on tea emphasizing the health benefits initiated by the CCPA and Tea Board needs to be strengthened". Definitely, one way of strengthening the campaign is to weaken the adverse publicity accorded for tea by the producers of other commodities. In this it is stated that Shri Prabal Basu Roy, Welfare Officer, Nagaisuree Tea Garden, Jalpaiguri, West Bengal wrote a letter to the Editor, The Assam Review and Tea News, protesting the anti-tea publicity strongly. This is reproduced below :

Letter to the Editor

Date: 02/01/2002

To
The Editor
The Assam Review & Tea News
Kolkata

Sir,

Save Tea from Anti-Tea Publicity: This is to inform you that an advertisement is being often shown in SAB TV/B 4 U/SAHARA regarding the product 'Triple Refined Dandi Namak'.

The advertisement states in part that "Do Rupaiya Ka Cha Kam Pee Lena Lakin Triple Refined Dandi Namak Hee Khana".

I believe it's an insult not only to the Tea as a product (which earns foreign exchange, maintains ecological balance, bears medicinal values, and in which India is the largest producer and consumer) but to the person drinking tea and to the tea industry as a whole.

The advertisement by comparing Tea with Salt directly intends to defame the unique product Tea. It also wants to convey the message that eating of triple refined dandi namak is better than drinking tea. The advertisement directly intends to reduce consumption of tea when the Tea Board, Tea Industry and its associations are struggling hard by trying all round efforts:

(i) to increase per capita consumption of tea;

(ii) to promote tea as a health drink through generic promotion of tea and public relations campaign to communicate positive health aspects of tea.

The advertisement is totally anti-India, anti-Tea Industry and anti-people. It directly points towards destruction of Tea Industry and playing with future of millions (executives/workmen/brokers/suppliers/consumers/shareholders/retailers/exporters/importers and bankers).

I will request you to take immediate legal steps against the producer or manufacture/the advertiser and also against the writer or composer of the campaign/advertisement 'Do Rupaiya Kya Cha Kam Pee Lena Lekin Triple Refined Dandi Namak Hee Khana' and stop the advertisement immediately from being aired—to save the Tea Industry.

Prabal Basu Ray, Welfare Officer
Nagaisuree Tea Garden, Jalpaiguri

Observations: Surprisingly, even the companies dealing with tea help the promotion of soft drinks. Take Brooke Bond, for instance. Its Bru Instant Coffee of 200 gms priced Rs. 122 comes with a free gift—not tea, another compliment beverage of the HLL group to which Brooke Bond belongs—

but with 500 ml Pepsi pet jar worth Rs. 18! Those engaged in tea promotion have to consider all these minus factors.

Murasoli Maran Released Accenture's Report on Tea Export Strategy: The then Union Minister of Commerce and Industry, Mr. Murasoli Maran, was in Kolkata on January 21, 2002 to formally release Accenture's Report on medium term tea export strategy for the country in a meeting held with members of the Consultative Committee of Plantation Associations (CCPA) and Tea Board officials. Mr. Maran suggested the tea industry to submit proposals for stepping up exports immediately to countries like Afghanistan, Iraq and Iran. He urged the industry to chalk out a comprehensive action plan for quality upgradation and quality assurance particularly for the bought leaf sector. The key elements of the Accenture's recommendations revolve around market portfolio diversification, differentiated market development activities including a focused effort at developing and promoting the "India" brand, a comprehensive exporter rating system, export quality and reliability management programme, building up of a robust industry-wide information backbone for greater transparency and dissemination of price and market-related information, and value addition opportunities in specific market economies. The back-end recommendation included realignment of production in line with demand in key high value markets. This envisages a shift of part of the production base to quality Orthodox tea.

HLL Closed Tea Packaging Unit: Hindustan Lever Ltd. (HLL), the fast moving consumer goods major, closed down its tea packaging facility at Kanhan near Nagpur, due to unviability.

FAITTA against Dandi Campaign: The Chairman of the Federation of All India Tea Traders' Association (FAITTA), Mr. P.O. Desai, strongly criticized the 'Dandi Namak' campaign which discourages tea consumption. The campaign sends out the message that, if need be, a cup of tea can be sacrificed for the sake of iodised salt which is more expensive. Mr. Desai pointed out that the Tea Board has also raised the issue with the company.

FAITTA Pushes Sports Sponsorship for Tea Promotion: The Federation of All India Tea Traders' Association (FAITTA) suggested to push the idea of generic tea promotion through sports sponsorship. Mr. P.O. Desai, Chairman of FAITTA, said : "We will discuss the issue with Tea Board. Producers, packet tea companies and buyers' associations must come together and contribute towards this generic promotion. If all producers contribute around Re. 1 per kg of tea produced, then given the fact that total production is around 850 million kgs. the budget will be as good as that of the colas". Mr. Desai further pointed out that the exercise would lift the image of Indian tea in the global market. "Exports will increase by 20 per cent and prices fetched by producers at the auction will also increase substantially."

Export Increase in Afghanistan Likely: The fall of the Taliban brought a ray of hope for the crisis ridden Indian tea industry. Officials of tea associations hoped on a boost in exports of Afghanistan. The country used to import tea regularly before the Taliban took over, officials said. In 1998, Indian tea exported to Afghanistan amounted to 55 million kg. Afghans lost their interest in Indian tea under the Taliban regime and exported in 2001 came down to just 0.20 million kg. Traditionally, Afghanistan and other Central Asian countries imported Green Tea, most of it from India. Aerated drinks as alternatives to tea are yet to gain popularity in Afghanistan. Seniors in the industry believe that the demand for Indian tea in that country has not decreased. Now, with the defeat of the militia, the industry took all effort to regain its market in Afghanistan.

Krishna Kumar on Tata Sons Board: Mr. R.K. Krishna Kumar, Vice-Chairman of Tata Tea, has been appointed to the Board of group holding company—Tata Sons, Mr. Krishna kumar joined the Tata Sons Board on January 22, 2002. He will be joining as a non-executive director. Mr. Krishna Kumar, who has spent 38 years with the Tata group, was appointed the Managing Director of Tata Tea in 1991. His main achievement during his tenure at Tata Tea was the acquisition of the UK based tea major Tetley.

Tea Campaign through New Year Cards: As the tea industry has been trying to bolster generic promotion of tea within the country through different ways, a unique experiment was carried out this year by Warren Tea Limited, a tea giant, and J Thomas & Co., the country's largest tea broking firm. Warren Tea has come out with two types of cards. One wishes friends and associates and says : "This year drink four cups of tea everyday". The other hopes that "every cup of tea will bring cheer to those who drink tea". The cards also harp on the many health aspects of tea : "Tea refreshes and relieves tension" and "Tea reduces the risk of cancer, heart attacks and strokes", say the cards. J Thomas greeting cards have been highlighting the antioxidant qualities of the early morning beverage. What is more interesting that a New Year Greeting Card (2002) of the German company, Kloth and Kohnken Teehandel GmbH depicted the goodness of tea thus: "Tea for two-thousand two! One for me. One for you".

ICICI Picks 6 per cent in George Williamson: ICICI Ltd. has picked up 5.73 per cent in Magor–held George Williamson (Assam) at Rs.80 a share. Mr. S K Mitra, Chairman and Managing Director of George Williamson, said the B M Khaitan group has offloaded part of its holding to the term lending institution. Deepak Khaitan, Vice-Chairman and Managing Director of Eveready Industries India confirmed the development. The group had sold the shares in the open market and subsequently ICICI may have acquired the shares, he said.

Vikram's Products & Services Bulletin: Vikram India Limited, which has a track record of rendering services to the Tea Industry for over 27 years, has brought out a Bulletin. The newsletter presents a summary of the nature and development of activities of the company, Range of Products for Withering, Rolling, Fermenting, Drying, Sorting and Packing, Workshop equipment, etc. with a few colour photographs. Paper and printing of the Bulletin are of very good standards though, of course, a few mistakes cannot escape from the eyes of a meticulous reader. All said and done, it is a respectable publication.

Tea Traders Unhappy with HLL Campaign: The tea traders in the country expressed their unhappiness with Hindustan Lever Ltd's (HLL) Taj Mahal campaign branded

'Ustaad's Challenge'. It was alleged, though the closing the date of the contest was October 30, 2001, the company did not give details of the result even after second week of January, 2002. A company spokesperson of HLL, however, refuted that there had been any contest. "It was just a campaign with Zakir Hussain saying that if anyone finds a brand better than Taj Mahal then he would quit playing tabla. But it was not a contest," said the spokesperson.

Tata Tea's Net Profit UP: Tata Tea Ltd., India's second large tea company, reported its Profit After Tax (PAT) at Rs.20.67 crore in the October-December quarter of 2001, which indicates a rise of 26 per cent over the PAT in the corresponding period of the previous year. The boost in Profit has been attributed partly to the sale of shares in Tata NYK. The operating Profit after Tax was lower at Rs.13.66 crore. The income from operations for the quarter ending December 31, 2001 stood at Rs.198.9 crore while the Profit before Tax (PBT) fell to Rs.18.44 crore a drop of Rs.5.8 crore over the corresponding quarter. The Managing Director of Tata Tea, Mr. Homi Khusrokhan, said that the company continued with its strategy of introducing and building brands and variants. The company launched two new brands - Temptation and Agni Sholay–during the third quarter. To beat adverse conditions, the company focused on improving product mix.

Eveready's PBT Sharply Declined: In the three months ended December 31, 2001, the Tea division of Eveready Industries, engaged in cultivation, manufacture and sale of tea posted a Loss Before Tax and Interest amounting to Rs. 11.37 crore. In contrast, the FMCG division, operating in dry cell batteries, flashlights and packet tea, posted a Profit before Tax and Interest from the two divisions amounted to Rs.10.46 lakh. Sale/income from FMCG division stood at Rs.145.04 crore and that from the tea division at Rs.81.01 crore. Combined sales income from operation in the same period last year was Rs.263.38 crore.

Loan Sought to Improve Soil Structure: The Darjeeling tea planters have requested the Tea Board to introduce a 'Scheme of Loan and Subsidy' for improving the soil structure of tea gardens in the hill district. According to Mr. R.K.

Dixit, former Chairman of the Darjeeling Planters Association, the top soil of the Darjeeling tea gardens has been washed away during the last 150 years. As a result, carbon content in the top soil has fallen drastically. "Unless we improve, the soil structure and increase the carbon percentage to the required minimum level of four per cent, the desired result of uprooting and replanting will not be achieved which is evident from the existing yield of young tea areas," Mr. Dixit added.

Assam Trade Body Urges Lower Tax Rates: There is an urgent need for a better relationship between the trading community and the Government for a congenial business climate in Assam. This is the view of Kamrup Chamber of Commerce President, Mr. M.P. Jain. The Chamber is the premium body of traders in the state. Mr. Jain said, members of the Chamber feel that increasing tax rates in the State will not help the government improve its financial condition. Rather, what is required is a better monitoring and collection system to check leakages in tax collection which take place at various check gates.

Assam Agricultural University Tea Industrial Work Experience Programme: Since 1968 the Tea Husbandry & Technology Department of the Assam Agricultural University (AU) has been imparting education leading to graduate and post-graduate degree in Agriculture with specialization in Tea Husbandry and Technology (in undergraduate) and on single crop i.e. Tea on post-graduate curriculum. Each student taking up the discipline as elective in under-graduate course gets first hand knowledge of commercial tea estate where a student has to undergo practical garden training as a partial requirement for fulfilment of B.Sc. (Agri) degree. Rural Agricultural Work Experience Programme (RAWEP) now finds its place in the B.Sc. (Agri) degree programme of the AAU. Moreover, in view of the emergence of small tea cultivation in North East region, the department has decided to revamp the course curriculum of Practical Garden Training. A Memorandum of Understanding (MoU) between Assam Agricultural University and All Assam Small Tea Growers' Association was signed on January 9, 2002 to extend full co-operation in conducting intensive training, henceforth be termed as Tea Industrial Work Experience Programme. The Department has launched the programme and it is expected to take off with its first batch in February 2002.

Tantea's Auction Arrangement Criticised: Tea planters in South India criticized the Tamil Nadu Tea Plantation Corporation's (Tantea) decision to allot its eight factories to only three auctioneers for selling tea. It was alleged that norms were violated and hence investigation was demanded that why the selling arrangement of around 10 million kg of tea was changed when auction through seven brokers earlier had ensured all India sales of the Corporation's tea. The planters said, often seven at least four auctioneers operating in all six auction centres in the country, three each in north and south. This facilitated Tantea to sell its teas through any of the centres.

ITA's Tea Promotional Campaign: The tea industry of the country is under recessionary pressure even today. While production of tea has continued to increase regularly, exports from the country has fallen drastically in the last couple of years. Domestic demand of tea did not increase also. This situation has led to over-supply of tea in the market resulting in sagging prices at all the auction centres in the country. Obviously, to alleviate the suffering of the tea plantation units, the need is to increase demand commensurate with growing production. Although increasing the demand of our tea in the global market is an Herculean task, which, however, is not impossible. In this regard, the tea industry is required to identify the strategic and structural issues, immediate and remote, and then to formulate a comprehensive plan of action. For, the global market is now highly competitive with the presence of other tea exporting countries as Kenya, Sri Lanka, China, Indonesia and Vietnam. Prices of their teas are not only lower to that of ours, they are conscious of quality and the demand pattern of the buyers. Naturally, the expected result from an endeavour to boost exports is unlikely to come immediately. It is a must, therefore, to substantially improve the domestic demand of tea. Indian Tea Association (ITA) has realized it. The Association, besides taking up some other measures, already launched a tea promotional campaign through the TV and other media. The opinion of the viewers reported, 70 per cent of them favoured drinking of tea regularly. They were convinced that it should not only be considered as a temporary stimulant but a beverage that could keep a person energetic and healthy, far way from some deadly diseases. All said and done. It is point to ponder that ITA along with other promotional bodies have failed to facelift the reputation of the Indian Tea damaged by the unscrupulous exporters. They have not succeeded in moulding the importers to start buying the Indian Tea by assuring them that the unethical an irreligious doings of exporters would not occur again.

Organic Food Festival in New Delhi: A week-long International Organic Food Festival was held in New Delhi, starting from November 28,. 2002. The festival has been arranged by the Biodynamic Association of India in collaboration with the Union Commerce Ministry. Jaswant Purohit of the Tea Association said, "the festival will showcase India's organic teas and food grown the way nature intended. We are expecting a lot of foreign buyers".

Organic Tea to Increase Exports: In order to increase exports of tea from the country, the Indian tea industry is not giving more attention to organically grown teas. According to information available from the Ministry of Commerce, India exported 1.9 million kgs (4.1 million pounds) of organic tea ion 1999-2000 fiscal and the plan was to double the export quantum in 2006-07. Fragrant organic tea from Darjeeling commands premium. During 2006-07, the annual export of organic tea would be around 12 million kgs. Growers believe, health-consciousness of consumers in Europe, USA and Japan has enhanced the demand of organic tea comparing to that of a decade ago. The industry is convinced that in coming years the demand will increase phenomenally in view of growing popularity of organic tea. And hence, the tea growers have been advised to take this opportunity to boost exports.

Tea Board to Launch Web Site: The Tea Board of India launched a web site as its strategy to boost the demand of Indian tea in international market. The site provides information relating to production capacity of gardens, market prices, quality of Indian teas and also techniques of preparing good tea. In this regard, however, Mr. Basudeb Banerjee, Chairman of the Tea Board said, "in any effort to boost demand of tea in the international market there is no alternative but utilizing information technology". In the setting up of the web site the Tea Board took help of IBM.

Government Considering ISI Mark for Tea: The Ministry of Commerce, Government of India introduced ISI certification for tea. Mr. Sharad Yadav, the then Consumer Affairs Minister, said, for this purpose "the Indian Standard for tea has been revised by the Bureau of Indian Standards (BIS) in consultation with the Ministry which will be published shortly". Ministry officials thought that the move helped improving realization for tea growers and companies as the consumers are provided with high quality certified produce.

ITA's Sales Promotion Campaign for Tea: In order to expand the domestic market of tea, the Indian Tea Association (ITA) has been advertising tea through TV and other publicity media. On the basis of the observation of the Director of American Health Foundation, the advertisement says that tea contains all the nutrients necessary for good health and regular drinking of tea reduces the risk of heart stroke, tumour, some types of cancer and many other diseases. Meanwhile, the impact of the advertisement on the viewers has been studied which indicated 70 per cent of them considers tea not only as a temporary stimulant but a beverage providing vigour and vitality.

Flavoured Tea Market in The Country: Tea majors namely Tata Tea and Hindustan Lever Limited (HLL) have been exploring untapped flavoured tea market in the country. They wanted the Indian Tea Association to persuade the Government for allowing the use of natural identical flavours in black tea. Other leading tea manufacturers also supported this proposal.

Export of Tea Declined: At the 119th Annual General Meeting of the Indian Tea Association (ITA), held in first half of 2001, Mr. Bharat Bajoria, Chairman of the Association, expressed grave concern for the declining trend of exports in the last couple of years. Mr. Bajoria pointed out, the quantum of total export in 2001 was the minimum in the last five years. Russia's curtailment of tea imports from India, ban on Indian tea imports in Iran and Libya, lower prices of tea produced in Kenya, China, Indonesia and Vietnam have pulled down Indian exports, Mr. Bajoria added.

Orthodox Production Necessary in South India: At a seminar on Orthodox tea manufacture organized by the Tea Board and the United Planters' Association of Southern India, Mr. Vikram Kapoor, Executive Director of the Tea Board suggested the tea growers in South India to switch over to Orthodox manufacture from CTC. In his opinion, this could salvage the southern tea growers from the continuing dull situation. The Tea Board had sanctioned Rs.5 crore to 45 producers for the switchover to Orthodox tea production. He advised the planters to learn from Sri Lanka where 98 per cent of the produce was Orthodox and 68 per cent of the small growers engaged in the production of the same. Mr. Kapur said, the soil and weather in South India were ideally suited for the production of Orthodox tea.

Sanjiwani Rehabilitation Centre Inaugurated: In the third quarter of 2002, the permanent building of Sanjiwani Rehabilitation Centre for spastic children was inaugurated by Mr. Sanjoy Lohia, Deputy Commissioner, Sonitpur, Assam. Amongst others, the ABITA Chairman, Mr. N.N. Sharma, ABITA Chairman (Zone 3), Mr. A. Singh, ABITA Secretary and officers of ABITA (Zone 3) attended the function. For the construction of the building the Assam Branch, Indian Tea Association (ABITA) the headquarters and the Zonal Office jointly contributed Rs. 2.5 lakh.

North Bengal University Started Soil Testing Laboratory for Tea Gardens: The Department of Tea Management under the University of North Bengal has started a Soil Testing Laboratory for the benefit of the tea plantation units of North Bengal, Bihar and Sikkim. Estimation of Organic Carbon, pH, Nitrogen, available Potassium and Phosphorous, Electrical conductivity costs only Rs. 50 per sample. That besides, estimation of Sulphur and soil texture is also undertaken at reasonable cost.

WB Government to Survey Tea Industry: On 23rd October, 2002, Mr. Nirupam Sen, Commerce and Industry Minister, Government of West Bengal, said in Kolkata that the government along with the Tea Board had conducted a survey and prepared a situation report on tea industry in the State. The survey covered and recorded the number of tea gardens, area of the gardens, and so on. The report was submitted in December 31, 2002.

Godrej in Tea Business: Godrej Group recently entered in tea business through a new company, Godrej Tea Limited. This new company was established in September 2002 in which the Group have 65 per cent shares.

CCPA Chairman: Mr. Bharat Bajoria, Managing Director of the Bormajan Tea Co (1936) Ltd., has been re-elected Chairman of the Consultative Committee of Planters Association (CCPA).

Excise Duty on Tea Waste: Excise authorities in South India have been insisting that Excise Duty should be paid on 'tea waste', even if it is destroyed at the garden level. It is understood that there has been similar demand in North India. Since tea waste destroyed at the garden level does not have any commercial value, the United Planters' Association of Southern India (UPASI) has sought total exemption of Excise Duty on tea waste.

Missing Siliguri Tea Trader Returned: A Siliguri-based tea trader, Mr. Shyam Lal Bansal, missing from November 5, 2002 was found wandering in a remote railway station near Katihar, Bihar on December 14, 2002. According to a missing person diary with the Siliguri police, Mr. Bansal left home on November 5, for Jaintika Tea Garden in Chopra (North Dinajpur) but did not return. The Siliguri ASP said, no ransom was paid to Mr. Bansal's release. The Siliguri Tea Traders' Association, however, expressed grave concern over this event. The Association said, two tea traders of Siliguri were kidnapped last year and one of them was killed. Discontent is on the rise in tea gardens due to labour problems. Several unemployed workers are suspected to have turned to crime, it added.

Garden Managements Boycotted Meeting: At the initiative of the Deputy Labour Commissioner, West Bengal, a meeting of the Sepoydhoorah and Simulbari tea garden managements and the labour unions was convened in early December, 2002 to fix a date for the re-opening of the closed gardens. But the managements of the two gardens boycotted the meeting. The Sepoydhoorah Tea Estate in Tindharia was closed on August 1, 2002 while the management of Simulbari Tea Estate abandoned the garden on November 24, 2002 declaring suspension of work. Both managements blamed the employees for this situation. President of the Darjeeling unit of Chia Kaman Mazdoor Union, Mr. Ananda Pathak, alleged that remaining absent from the meeting was ploy of the two managements to foil the possibility of an amicable settlement of the disputes. Union representatives of the two gardens were present at the scheduled meeting, however.

Worry for Tea Workers: Revolutionary Socialist Party MLA, Govt. of West Bengal, Mr. Nirmal Das expressed concern over the plight of 40,000-odd tea workers in North Bengal. Mr. Das said, the workers have become jobless after 19 tea gardens in Jalpaiguri, Dooars and Darjeeling were closed down in the last few months.

NUPW on Crisis of Gardens: At a meeting of the Congress-affiliated National Union of Plantation Workers (NPUW) held in Darjeeling in 2003, 22 branches of the union attended. Most speakers highlighted the difficult phase tea gardens in North Bengal were passing through and accused the managements of exploiting the workers. NUPW Secretary, Mr. Dawa Norbula, who is also the President of Darjeeling Hill Congress Committee, said only a concerted effort by workers' unions and tea garden managements could provide relief from the present crisis.

Tea Auction Cancelled throughout India: Tea auctions, scheduled to be held on Monday, January 6, 2003, were cancelled throughout India when tea traders boycotted the auctions in protest against the Tea Marketing Control Order (TMCO) 2003 issued by the Ministry of Commerce, Government of India. Trade sources said, auctions were postponed in Kolkata, Coonoor, Guwahati and Siliguri. While

Mr. P.K. Sen of Carritt Moran, who is in the General Committee, had expressed hope that the auctions might resume within a week, the tea buyers appeared more aggressive and wanted the government to roll back some of the measures introduced.

Construction of Satellite Township Opposed: The Chandmuni Anti-Eviction Joint Action Committee has Vehemently opposed the construction of the proposed satellite township in Chandmuni Tea Estate in North Bengal. The Committee alleged that the promises made during the meetings held to reopen the tea estate have not been fulfilled. In this matter, the State Government was not at all serious. Both the management and the government played with the lives of the workers, it was said. On June 26, 2002 two tea workers were killed in police firing when they opposed the uprooting of tea bushes for setting up the proposed township. However, the Darjeeling district administration is determined now to start work on the already delayed project.

Pesticide Effect on Tea Workers' Health: With chronic ailments on the rise among tea workers and their families, especially children, a BBC team visited in second half of 2003, Kurseong, Darjeeling District, West Bengal, to conduct a survey on the effect of pesticides on the health of workers. The survey reported more severe impact on the second generation. Dr. Sujit Chakraborty, Director of the Centre for Sustainable Living (CSL) said, "most of the cases are found in the slums where tea garden workers live. The graph has become steeper since the mid Eighties. Uncontrolled use of pesticides started in the country in the early Seventies. Pesticides need some time to accumulate in the body, only then we see how it affect. The disorders are carried on to the next generation."

North Bengal Tea Workers in Distress: The then Naxalite and trade union leader, Mr. Kanu Sanyal alleged, 68 workers have died of starvation, malnutrition or waterborne diseases. This was due to lockout of Kanthalguri tea garden in Jalpaiguri, North Bengal, in October 2002. The combined death toll of 23 tea gardens in North Bengal increased to more than 600 over the past few months, he added.

Gujarat Violence Affected Assam Tea Trade: Assam's tea trade was badly damaged by the violence in Gujarat in 2001. According to industry circle in Assam, between 30 and 40 percent of the tea produced here goes to Gujarat and is then smuggled out to Pakistan for distribution among the West Asian countries. In "normal circumstances", buyers from Pakistan purchase truckloads of tea at auction centres in Gujarat and Punjab and smuggle these out through the "porous border". The Pakistani buyers even pay the transportation charges. "We have not had a single buyer from Gujarat since the beginning of March. If the trend continues for a few weeks more, the industry will be down in the dumps", an Upper-Assam-based planter, Mr K.K. Saikia said. With buyers from Gujarat conspicuous by their absence, prices of tea have slumped at the Guwahati Tea Auction Centre. "The average price now is between Rs.52 and Rs.54 a kg, which is much lower than what we used to get", Mr A.K. Baruah, a planter in Assam said.

Assam Delegation Met Murasoli Maran: An all-party delegation from Assam met the then Union Commerce Minister, Mr. Murasoli Maran, on April 29, 2002 to communicate its concern over the fall in export of tea and increased competition from smaller countries such as Kenya, reported PTI from New Delhi.

Lower-end Product from Tata Tea: In keeping with the strategy to offer packaged tea across all price points, Tata Tea has entered the fast growing lower-end economy segment with Agni Sholay. "Agni Sholay will be our vehicle to complete in the fast growing low-end category which has traditionally been dominated by regional players. Market size of this category is 80-90 million kg", said Mr P Siganporia, Managing Director of Tata Tea. Initially the product will be available in North and East India.

Duncans in Retail Tea Market: In a significant shift from its earlier policies, the Kolkata-based Duncans Industries Limited (DIL) has entered the retail tea market. On April 5, 2002 the company opened its first outlet for premium quality tea at Lalbazar, Kolkata. Mr. J.K. Mazumdar, Senior Vice-President, said the company will initially focus on West Bengal, a major tea consuming state. The company, however, intending to set up 30 outlets across the state in the next few months. DIL also plans a "Duncans self-dependence programme" whereby the company would sponsor retail centres by small entrepreneurs under the Duncans umbrella. The company has 13 tea estates, located in the Doors, Terai region and Darjeeling.

Eveready Promoters Raise Stake: The promoters of Eveready Industries India, the tea and battery maker of the Brij Mohan Khaitan Group, have enhanced their holding in the company to 61.1 per cent, an increase of 6.68 per cent in the last one year, from 54.42 per cent as on March 31, 2001. Eveready sources said, part of the increase is through the creeping acquisition route, while part is a reflection of the merger with Bishnauth Tea Company. "The shares acquired through creeping acquisition were bought at market rate", sources said. Bishnauth was merged into Eveready to ensure a better focus on the tea business and also rationalize and streamline the management of the company. The initial plan after the separation with Magors was to bring the tea business under the Eveready fold and then demerge the battery business.

Government Considering FDI in Tea Plantations: The government is planning to make an exception in its "Foreign Direct Investment (FDI) policy for the plantation sector, and allow fresh foreign investment in tea plantation companies. According to an official of the Union Commerce Ministry, "there is an increasing feeling today that if we do not allow foreign investment, the tea plantation companies will find it difficult to grow". This will not apply to other plantation sector, growing rubber and coffee as most of the companies are Indian owned and smaller in size. They could raise money from the domestic market to expand their business, the official added. The Commerce Ministry has recommended that FDI of up to 75 per cent be allowed in tea plantations. However, the final decision on the issue has not been taken over the government yet.

Southern Tea Planters Worried over China CTC Tea: While global tea experts advise the South Indian tea sector to focus on newer areas to establish comfortable market, majority of the tea plantation in the South India are yet to reorient their manufacturing practices to suit the market requirements. The South, in particular, has until recently been exporting a substantial chunk of the produce to Russia. The setting was perfect until other tea producing countries emerged and India lost its place in terms of export to Russia. China has entered the scene and has started to produce CTC grades similar to that of South India. These teas, according to market sources, are available in Russia at 50 cents per kg.

Sick Tea Estates—An Investigation

Generally sickness in tea estates stems initially from mismanagement, and a low non-viable yields, and usually a mis-guided, lazy indisciplined work force. This finally leads to annual losses and ever rising liabilities. Sufficient funds are therefore not available for upkeep and necessary development. Often these estates tend to be attracted to bank schemes in an effort to improve and develop, which is all well and good, if the managerial structure is capable of proper utilization of the loans sanctioned.

Factors Affecting Sickness

However, sickness is usually caused by mis-management over a long term and unless the entire managerial infrastructure is not first corrected, then the utilization of loan funds will prove to be of little value, and indeed the repayment of the principal with interest can lead the sick estates into further financial problems. At the risk of sparking off a controversy, one would caution, any board of directors of a sick estate from taking any loans for improvement unless the entire project has been studied by an expert, who would advise the estate management at every step regularly. The expert would see that sufficient planting materials, and all other aspects would also be available in time to effect proper utilisation of the loan funds to render the programmed scheme effective. For example, it is often the case that the planting schemes programmed under the loan cannot be properly implemented to cover the extension hectarage, or replanting schemes, envisaged under the project.

This then leads to areas planted out not being consolidated by infilling of mortalities, thereby rendering new young tea areas full of vacancies. Having worked in the industry for a longer period and gained some experience of the weaker tea sector, it is advised that one may avoid any loans of any kind, until and unless the estate viability creates the possibility for further development in field and factory.

Quite often sick estates have a permanent labour force too large for the small yield per hectare of tea to maintain effectively. This only aggravates the sickness, and coupled with unskilled managerial expertise, really renders the position bleak.

What is the Remedy?

The first step is to recruit better experienced experts in the managerial cadre, and believe in general that estates workers can be quite quickly trained in better all round practices. Sick estates usually have most of the following defects:

1. Absence of proper drainage over several years.
2. Existence of vacancies in the sections, along with sporadic lack of shade tree canopy.
3. Poor or inadequate fencing and large scale entry of cattle in the estate.
4. Prevalence of general water logging and local water logging in bush collars.
5. Dearth of proper phased prune cycle.
6. Negligence of medium and other height reduction prunes and necessary knife clean out of knots in the frame.
7. Persistence of general poor standard of pruning followed by poor plucking standard.
8. Insufficient crop protection and weed control spraying.
9. Poor weed control in general.
10. Non balanced managing and poor supervision of the same

Expert Management of the Available Workers

Assuming that most of these factors, do exist, can see no remedy in taking loans to rectify the situation. Rather, again assuming that permanent and casual workers are available, the situation can be vastly corrected in a span of about 6 years, by better expert management of the available workers, based mainly on the prune cycle adopted, and remember that the permanent workers have to be paid in any case. Thus, it is believed that the first thing is to fix a prune cycle either 3 or 4 years cycle, dependent on type of manufacture and availability of pluckers, viz. L.P. – UP-UP OR LP-UP-DS-UP. Normally sick estates neglect to provide proper tools and implements such as pruning knives, hoes etc., so that workers engaged can do a decent job. Height reduction prunes and knot clean out are usually neglected on poor estates. It is wise to check each section for height of the bushes at the last light prune (or cut across prune). Sections at or above 32" (or 82 cm) must be medium pruned or lowered as soon as possible. At the same time all knots in the bush frame should be removed. Therefore, to perform this proper implements are required. Initially during the cold weather the drains can be redug and repaired only over the light pruned sections as a start to reinvigoration of the sections, so that in 3 or 4 years, depending on the prune cycle selected, the entire estate drainage structure can be initially corrected.

Repaired/Deepened Drainage in Old Tea Section and Supervision of Fertilizer Application etc.: It should however be noted that repaired, deepened drainage does not give a quick and miraculous response in old tea sections if drainage has been neglected over a long period. The bushes tend to seek new root level of water availability. Therefore shoot growth is initially affected. The new rooting leads to better shooting only after a year or two. Fertilizers are expensive, and scarce. One can use Urea and Muriate of Potash only at rates selected according to standard. Yields of the sections of the estate becomes more viable. Strict supervision of fertilizer application is essential and where weed control is ot possible, a single dose on damp soil in April is the best bet.

Maintain Well Control Plucking Round: Having covered drainage, pruning and fertilizer application, one must ensure that plucking is well supervised, and if possible maintained on a well controlled plucking round. Although expensive, new planting and infilling can also be carried out with the estates' own labour force available with surpisingly little difficulty in actual practice. The Tea Board has some good schemes for replanting, extension and hire purchase, for irrigation and factory machinery etc. however, one would be inclined to avoid even these facilities until the estate becomes more viable and better organized, and one agrees and knows that one views on this aspect will not be supported my many, however one stick to his guns so to speak!

Tea Section be level Cheeled During Cold Weather: During the cold weather as many sections as possible should be level cheeled with filling of soil in bush collars to check local water logging, and in light pruned section where drains have been attended to, all drain soil must be levelled up. Crop protection can be handled with some economy if pests are controlled on appearance and not sprayed on a prophylactic or palliative basis. Of course a water tanker and some decent hand sprayers are a must and probably the hypothecating bank would probably offer a term loan for this purpose for this smaller capital outlay. This would obviate the usual sick estate from resorting to "more praying than real spraying"!

Having dealt with some of the problems usually faced by sick or semi-sick estates it is summarized as follows:

1. Properly teach and guide the work force.
2. Provide proper implements so that the workers can do a better job.
3. Estate workers do have an Inherent capacity to pick up better practices for the well-being of the estate and for themselves eventually, if properly taught and guided.
4. In a fairly short span of time, by utilization of the basic resources available at the estate level, the estate can be made more viable, and can earn a surplus of funds and a degree of availability.

19

Madhukar Committee Report on Problems in Tea Industry, Package of Relief Measures and Price Stabilization Funds

SECTION I
Madhukar Committee Report on Problems in Tea Industry

Background

A meeting on the problems of Tea Industry was convened at RBI, Mumbai under the chairmanship of Shri Vepa Kamesan, the then Deputy Governor, RBI. The meeting was attended by L.V. Saptarishi, Addl. Secretary, Ministry of Commerce, Chief Executives of various Banks, Chairman, Tea Board and representatives of Tea Associations. During the above meeting, a small Working Group was constituted to study the problems of tea industry in-depth and come out with acceptable solution. The Working Group was chaired by Shri Madhukar, Chairman and Managing Director, United Bank of India, and members were Chairman, Tea Board, representatives of Ministry of Commerce and Industry, Govt. of India, representatives from NABARD, Kolkata, State Bank of India, Tea Associations of North India and South India.

It was further decided that Working Group would submit the report to the RBI before 25 July 2002.

In the light of the above decision, a meeting of the Working Group was convened at United Bank of India, HQ, Kolkata on 22 and 23 July 2003 where 05 representatives from United Bank of India, 03 from State Bank of India, 02 from Tea Board, Kolkata, 02 from India Tea Association, 01 from NABARD RO, Kolkata, 01 from United Planters Association, South India,01 from Ministry of Commerce, and 01 from Nilgiri Boughtleaf Tea Manufacturing Association. Before convening this meeting, a questionnaire was circulated among the members of the Group and the data elicited by the questionnaire is given below.

Suggested Solutions Based on the Feed Backs

Based on the suggestions received from the various Members of the group and the replies to the aforesaid questionnaire, the current problems of tea industry vis-a-vis the suggested solutions were discussed at length in the above meeting of the Working Group. During the discussions, it was decided that for revival of the tea industry, all the agencies involved in the process viz. the Banks, NABARD, Tea Board, Govt. of India, Tea Associations and the borrowers have their respective roles to play. The deliberations were accordingly structured on the above basis and the decisions taken thereof are appended below:

For Banks

i) The major problems currently being faced by the tea industry are due to the high cost of production, and sharp decline in sale price as a result of which many tea borrowers are findings it difficult to maintain their cash budgets prepared by them at the beginning of the season. Since this projected cash budget is the basis of providing working capital limit to the tea borrowers, operations in their accounts become difficult because of low cash inflow resulting in irregularity in the accounts. Normally, the borrowers are required to liquidate their outstandings in their tea hypothecation account by the end of the season. But failure on the part of the borrowers to liquidate the hypothecation dues by the end of the season, results in further difficulty for the borrowers as they are not in a position to avail fresh working capital limit for the next season. In view of this, it was recommended that

> The seasonal deficit of tea borrowal accounts (classified as standard assets) may be converted to a term loan repayable within a period not exceeding 5 years subject to the conditions that at least 70 per cent of the peak hypothecation outstanding has been liquidated by the borrowers:

ii) In many tea accounts, it has been observed that though the borrower is not in a position to liquidate its seasonable dues by the end of the season, it is backed by adequate stock of tea which could not be sold due to lack of demand in the market. In such cases, there is no need of converting the dues to a term loan and instead, an extension of repayment period to liquidate the outstanding seasonal dues in hypothecation account to a maximum period of 6 months may be allowed without affecting its drawing in the tea hypothecation account of the current season,. Accordingly, the Working Group recommended that;

> Extension of period to liquidate the working capital dues of last season may be allowed to a maximum of six months in those cases where the entire outstanding is backed by a stock of tea or the prompt receivables without affecting the drawings and the working capital limit of current year, provided at least 60per cent of the tea hypothecation outstanding has been included and in this case there is no need of conversion of working capital limit to term loan as stated above.

iii) In order to enable the borrowers to operate the tea garden during the current season after aforesaid conversion /restructuring of the account, a fresh working capital may be extended and it was recommended that

> Release of needbased working capital finance for current season based on realistic position, keeping

in view the production track record, accepted price levels, market demand etc. may be allowed in accounts classified as standard assets.

iv) Many tea borrowers are enjoying term loan facilities from banks, which were taken earlier to meet various project costs undertaken for development and expansion of tea garden/processing units and they are not in a position to service their instalments of such loans as per the earlier terms stipulated at the time of sanctioning such loans. In view of genuine problems of tea industry, it is recommended that

> Reschedulement of existing term loans repayment schedule on the basis of borrowers' future position and repayment capacity, may be allowed.

v) As the banks are required to undertake the aforesaid conversion/restructuring/reschedulement in many tea accounts , such accounts should not be treated as NPA because the borrower could not service in time on instalments or liquidate tea hypothecation dues and the account was otherwise treated as standard asset. In the light of the above discussions, it is recommended that

> After the conversion/restructuring and rescheduling in tea accounts, the term loan as well as working capital limit shall be treated as current dues, and need not be classified as NPA provided that at the time of conversion/restructuring, rescheduling, the account was classified as standard assets as per the prudential norms issued by RBI from time to time. The asset classified thereafter would be governed by revised terms and conditions adopted at the time of restructuring of the account.

vi) The tea advances have since been categorized as agricultural advance as per the latest guidelines of RBI. The prudential norms in respect of agriculture advances, inter-alia, treat that in respect of advances granted for agriculture purpose, interest and/or instalment of principle remains unpaid for two harvest season but for a period not exceeding two and half years, such an advance will be treated as NPA. The crop cycle for tea plantation is one year and hence in terms of the above guidelines issued by the RBI, the tea accounts are not getting full benefits because of the existing ceiling period not exceeding two and half years, whereas for tea plantations crop cycles are equivalent to two years. In view of the above and considering the current crisis through which the tea industry currently passing, it is recommended that

> In respect of tea advances where interest and/or instalment of principle remains unpaid for two harvest seasons but for a period not exceeding two years, such an advance should be treated as NPA.

vii) In case of many tea accounts, the borrowers are in current capital expenditure towards development of tea gardens, expansion of tea processing units, without arranging the corresponding sources of long term finance, particularly, when the tea industry was doing well. Tea borrowers did not face much problems at that time, as they could finance such projects either out of cash generation or by utilizing a portion of their working capital advance. Assets were created out of such capital expenditure and such assets are also changed to the lending banks. However, due to the current problem of the tea industry, such borrowers are now finding it difficult to meet their working capital requirements as a portion of it is tied up with capital cost of the project. In such cases the banks, may allow working capital term loan to meet such mismatch in the asset liability position of the borrowers, provided that working capital facilities extended to such borrowers is not utilised for interunit investment to a company under the same group or for any other purpose outside the tea business of the unit and debt equity ratio in such cases is not worse than 3:1 This facility may be given to genuine and good borrowers having satisfactory track records, for capital expenditure incurred during the last 3 years and not supported by any long terms source. The Working Group accordingly recommended that

> Fresh working capital term loan in an account classified as standard asset may be allowed where

due to capital expenditure incurred by the borrower during the last three years for development/extension of tea estates processing units etc. without arranging corresponding long term funds resulting in asset liability mismatch, affecting the net working capital position of the borrowers. This facility would be granted to genuine, good borrowers with satisfactory track records having a minimum debt equity ratio of 3:1 and who have not diverted funds by way of investment in other companies , transferring fund to the subsidiaries group company or created assets other than for productive purposes.

viii) There is a continuous demand from the industry that the rate of interest being charged by the lending banks is required to be reduced at this hour of crisis, for enabling them to become more competitive. In this respect it was mentioned that all the individual banks have their own credit rating system which is linked with the prices i.e. credit of interest and does not justify to allow a rate of interest not commensurate with its credit rating. However, considering the difficult time through which industry passing, it is recommended

> Bank may allow a rate of interest upto two stages better than the rates as applicable to such borrowers according to its credit rating by the individual banks subject to the condition that after such reduction, such rate of interest should not be below prime lending rate (PLR)

For NABARD

Under refinancing scheme, NABARD is presently charging 10 per cent p.a. interest for various projects under tea finance. Considering the current crisis it is recommended that

> Under the refinancing schemes related to tea industry NABARD may charge an interest rate of 0.5 per cent below the rate applicable to a similar project to other industry.

For Tea Board

The Tea Board is at present providing 20 per cent capital subsidy in respect of certain capital cost projects, including development of tea plantations, it was fill that Tea Board may allow similar subsidy in respect of those capital expenditure which a tea borrower has incurred during the last 3 years arranging the corresponding long term funds and which has created productive assets towards such borrowers enhancing its production capacity and if such subsidy is allowed by the Tea Board, there will be corresponding reduction in the long term loan requirements from banks. It is recommended that

Tea Board may provide 20 per cent capital subsidy in respect of those capital expenditure incurred during the last three years in creating assets for enhancing the production capacity of the borrowers, where such borrowers could not arrange for the food tie-up of such capital costs provided the borrower is having satisfactory track record. Such release of subsidy should have linkages with the term loan from the bank for the same purpose, if availed, the subsidy should be released to the lending of such borrower.

For Central and State Governments

The representatives of Ministry of Commerce, Govt. of India mentioned that the Central Govt. is likely to set up a Price Stabilization Fund for plantation including tea industry, and its modalities of operation is now taking final shape. All members of the Group appreciated the efforts taken by the Government and requested for expanding the creation of the Fund because the benefit should accrue to the industry as soon as possible. It was further discussed that the respective State Govts. may avail the facility under Rural Infrastructure Development Fund being provided by NABARD for the purpose of development of infrastructure at the tea estates such as housing, irrigation, etc. which will ease the financial burden of the borrower who are at present supporting these expenses.

The State Govt. may also consider reimbursement (by availing RIDF) of the capital expenses incurred by tea borrowers during the last three years for meeting these requirements of infrastructure of tea estates. The Working Group therefore recommends.

(a) The formation of Price Stabilization Fund for plantation including tea industry is to be expedited.

(b) The State Govt. may avail the RIDF Fund from NABARD to meet the expenses towards development of infrastructure at tea estates and reimbursement of earlier expenditure incurred by the tea borrowers during last three years for the purpose of building up required infrastructure at tea estates.

For Tea Associations

At present the Associations do not communicate with the banks as a result of which their views on the latest development in the industry is not forthcoming. Many policy decisions in respect of efficacy of auction system, review of various benchmark parameters like average yield, coverage of tea cultivable land, replantation, conversion ratio of green leaves, wastages, etc. are not being regularly communicated by the Associations. It is expected that there should be continuous interface between the associations and the banks. Moreover, the Association shall bear the moral responsibility for fostering for improved performance among its members and assist them towards this objective in every possible way.

The Association has a greater role for better marketing efforts to improve the domestic demand for tea as well as developing new export markets for better price and for more export orders. Currently the tea market is under threat from contemporary beverages and the Association is required to immediately initiate image boosting exercises for tea.

In the light of the above discussions it is recommended that:

The Tea Associations should have regular interface with the tea lending Banks to appraise the bankers about the general health of the industry, major policy decisions, the status of the Industry and the needs of the industry. They will foster for the improved performance among its membership and assist the members towards this object in every possible way.

The Tea Associations will have to take a more active role for development for both domestic and global tea markets through publicity in different media and thwart the challenge posed by contemporary beverages. It should carry out continuous efforts to improve the tea price in the domestic as well as international market.

For Small Tea Growers and Bought Leaf Factories

The small tea growers and bought leaf factories are facing certain specific problems due to price differentiation, non-realisation of receivable in time, etc. As more in-depth study is required for these problems, separate working groups may be formed under the chairmanship of the convener bank of SLBCs of the respective States with members from SBI, Tea Board and the Industry to study the problem in-depth and come out with their recommendations within a month. In the light of these discussions it is recommended that:

> Separate Working Groups under the chairmanship of the Convener Bank of the SLBC of respective States along with the member from lead bank of the district, SBI, Tea Board and the Industry may be formed for an in-depth study of the problems of small tea growers and bought leaf factories and the report of the Group(s) may be submitted within a month.

For the Tea Borrowers

The Group's recommendations in this respect are:

> Every tea borrower should report its unaudited results at least each quarter.

The tea borrower should have better financial discipline. There should be no diversion of fund to any sister unit or outside the business without proper tie up of funds and consultation with its lending banker(s) prior to taking up any such commitments. There should be at least 1per cent replantation every year in each tea estate.

SECTION II
Price Stabilization Fund

Deeply concerned with the problems being faced by the growers of coffee, tea, rubber and tobacco due to continued low prices of these commodities (both domestic and export), for quite some time, Government of India (GOI) has taken a series of measures to ameliorate the hardships being faced by the growers of these crops. The Price Stabilization Fund Scheme (PSFS) is yet another step in the direction by GOI to safeguard the interests of the growers.

Objective

The PSFS aims at providing financial relief to the growers when prices of these commodities fall below specified levels, without resorting to the practice of procurement operations by the Government agencies.

Duration of the Scheme

The Scheme will be operational for a period of ten years, subject to a review after five years.

Mode of Intervention

Under the scheme, a fund called the Price Stabilization Fund will be established with contribution from the GOI and entry fee @ Rs 500 from each grower desirous of participating in the Scheme. The corpus of the fund shall remain undistributed and interest earnings alone will be utilized for operationalising the PSFS.

Who Can Participate in the Scheme? Initially, the Scheme will be open to growers of tea, coffee, rubber and tobacco having operational holdings of 4 hectare or less. Subsequently coverage of other growers could be considered.

How to Become a Member?

Growers of aforementioned commodities willing to participate shall apply to the respective commodity Board in the prescribed form within the date stipulated thereof. The

Commodity Boards will select the members on first come first serve basis with preference being given to the members with the least holding size. The Commodity Boards will thereafter enrol the eligible growers as member who will be required to deposit an amount of Rs 500 with the Commodity Board.

Opening and Maintenance of Bank Account

The member would be provided with an application form to enable him/her to open the 'PSF' account with the designated bank branch. The Commodity Board will also inform the concerned bank branch for opening the account in the name of the member. The account will be maintained as Savings Bank Account and would be entitled for payment of interest at rates applicable to Savings Bank Accounts. No service charges of any kind would be levied. Members have to deposit their annual contributions to the account by 31 March every year. Govt..of India contributions to the account would be made not later than 31 May every year. At the end of the duration of the Scheme, the entire balance in the account would be payable to the member.

Modus Operandi for Calculation of Contributions from Govt. of India and Members

Govt. of India will announce a price band for each commodity based on the seven year moving average of international prices as the mid point with the lower bound and upper bound as 20 per cent (-) and 20 per cent (+), respectively. When the average prices fall below the lower bound of the band in a particular year, Govt..of India will contribute upto Rs.1000 to the account of the member. In that year the member will not be required to contribute any amount to his/her account. In those years when the average price pierces the upper bound of the band, the member will have to contribute Rs.1000 to his/her account while the Govt..of India will not contribute any amount

In the normal years when the price remains within the price band, the member will be required to deposit Rs.500 each year to his/her account within a specified date. The

Govt. of India will also contribute upto Rs.500 to the member's account during the normal year. During years when the average market price falls below the lower bound of the price band, the member would be allowed to draw Rs. 1000 from the account. At the end of the ten year period, the balance outstanding can be withdrawn by the grower including the Govt. of India's contribution and the interest earnings. The initial contribution of Rs. 500 as an entry fee however, will not be refunded. The Scheme will be implemented through a Trust Fund to be set up jointly by Ministry of Commerce and NABARD and the operations will be monitored by a High Powered Committee set up by the Ministry of Commerce.

Defaulters

In case a member defaults in making his contribution within the stipulated date, he will be deemed as a defaulter. The PSF account maintained with the bank would be closed and no further deposits either from the Govt. of India or the member, would be credited to the account.

New Membership

New growers willing to subscribe to the Scheme during the period of operation of the Scheme may be admitted in place of dropouts; however, the benefits of the Scheme will be restricted to the remaining period of the Scheme.

Price of Commodity	*Contribution to the a/c*	*Withdrawal from a/c*
Price say Rs.31 per kg (below lower bound)	Rs.1000 by GOI . No contribution by member	Rs.1000 can be drawn by member
Rs.45 per kg (within the price band)	Rs.500 by GOI Rs.500 by member	No drawals
Rs.52 per kg (above upper bound by Govt.	Rs.1000 by member No. contribution	No drawals

Illustration

The operation of the Scheme is illustrated below. Let us presume that the 7 years moving average price of the commodity is Rs. 43.00. The lowers bound of the band would be Rs. 34.40 and the upper bound of the band would be Rs. 51.60. If the prevailing price of the commodity is Rs. 31.00 per kg the position will be as under.

Price Stabilization Fund Account

Guidelines for Opening and Maintenance of Account by Banks

- The account will be opened by designated bank branches based on a Certificate of Eligibility issued by the concerned Commodity Board.
- The banks would not insist on introduction of the account holder and would rely on the Certificate issued by the Commodity Board.
- The accounts would be opened with the deposit of Rs.100.00, which will be the minimum balance in respect of these accounts. The accounts would be designated as PSF Accounts.
- The account would be maintained as Savings Bank Account and would be entitled for payment of interest at the rates applicable for SB Account.
- No service charges of any kind would be leviable.
- In accordance with the terms and conditions of the scheme, deposits will be made by the account holders or by the Government of India through the concerned Commodity Board which would be credited to the account.
- Drawals would be allowed from the account only on receipt of specific advice from the concerned Commodity Board in any particular year. The advice would indicate the extent of drawal that could be allowed to the member.
- Members have to deposit their annual contributions to the account by a prescribed due date which is presently set as 31st March.

- The Government contributions would be made not later than 31 May every year.
- When the grower fails to contribute his share to the account by the due date, he will be deemed to be a defaulter.
- Once the account is in default i.e. if the contribution due from the member is not made by the prescribed due date, i.e. by 31 March, the account would be closed.
- No further deposits of the grower members should be accepted for credit to a defaulter's account.
- No Government contributions could be credited to the defaulter's account.
- At the request of the grower member, the balance in the defaulters account could be repaid to the extent of the member's contributions with interest thereon.
- No part of Government's contributions and interest thereon should be paid to the defaulter grower members.
- After payment of the dues to the defaulter, the balance representing Governments contributions and interest thereof in such accounts should be remitted back to the Price Stabilization Fund Trust through the concerned Commodity Board.
- Banks have to provide an annual return to the concerned Commodity Board indicating the number of accounts maintained, the balance therein and the list of accounts to which Government contributions were credited during the year and also a list of accounts which have turned into default with details of accounts closed on account of default. Further, details of payments made to the defaulting member as well as amount remitted to the Government from the defaulting account, on its closure should also be sent to the Commodity Board every year.
- At the end of 10 years, the entire balance in the account is payable to the grower members.

- In case of any doubt, clarification/s could be obtained from the Price Stabilisation Fund Trust Office, R No.133, C wing Nirman Bhawan, Maulana Azad Road, New Delhi 110 011 TeleFax 011- 2301 9891/ Commodity Board.

SECTION III
Package of Relief Measures for Tea Industry

The tea industry has been experiencing difficulties in their operations since 1998 on account of drastic fall in the prices of tea both in the domestic and international markets. The problems were triggered by a glut in production during 1998 and the depressed conditions continued unabated till the end of 2003. The prices are now looking up and the industry is seeing the trend as a turn around and they expect market conditions to remain favourable in the coming years. During 2002, the RBI had announced certain relief measures following studies conducted by an Expert Committee. While the financial assistance extended under the scheme benefited the industry to some extent, the Tea Associations had represented to the government for a fresh look at the package relief measure since market conditions continued to be unfavourable even during 2003.

Following a request received from the Chairman, Tea Board, IBA had arranged a meeting between senior bankers and representatives of Tea Board/Tea Association of Kolkata on January 12, 2004. At the meeting the Chairman, Tea Board and representatives of major Tea Associations presented difficulties faced by them both in the domestic and the export market, the current state of tea industry, the challenges and opportunities in the global market, efforts being made by the tea industry to overcome their weaknesses, and their expectations of relief measures from the banking industry. Based on the discussions in the meeting, this package of relief measures was prepared and was approved by the Managing Committee of the Association in its meeting held on 31 October 2004.

The Status of Tea Industry in India

India is the largest producer of tea in the world and the country has retained its leadership in production over the last 150 years. India is also the largest consumer of tea in the world. Tea has been an important foreign exchange earner contributing to about Rs.2000 crore to the export basket even though in terms of share in the world market, we lag behind Sri Lanka, Kenya and China. The fragmentation of USSR, strained relationship with Pakistan and the problems in Iraq had adversely affected Indian tea exports in the last decade. The relatively higher cost of production and poorer quality of our output has affected the competitiveness of our tea industry. High cost of labour coupled with low productivity has been the primary reason for the high cost of production. Productivity and quality of tea produced in the country is also affected due to existence of ageing plantations in the country. A significant portion of our tea plantations is aged beyond economic life of tea bushes. The tea gardens of Sri Lanka and Kenya are of relatively younger origins. It is therefore felt that the Indian tea industry needs to take drastic measures to improve productivity and also take up replantation/rejuvenation on a war footing, to improve competitiveness and long term viability.

The necessary conditions continuing since 1998 had resulted in many of the tea plantations incurring losses in the recent years. The strained cash flows has also affected much needed developmental activity in the plantations.

Outlook for the Future

There has been a pick up in the demand for tea and consequently prices since December 2003. The tea industry representatives view the developments as a turn around and expect the positive sentiments to continue over the next 4-5 years. The prospects of reviving business with Iraq and Pakistan, add to the optimism. The Government has also initiated promotional measures aimed at developing new export markets and encouraging consumption of tea in the country. The Government has also earmarked more funds for development of this sector in the Tenth Plan. This could encourage tea growers to take up replantation/

rejuvenation on a larger scale.

Approach to Restructuring of Borrowal Accounts

Borrowers under the tea sector could be divided into three segments: 1) Small tea growers with holdings not more than 10 hectares 2) Bought leaf factories which do not have own gardens and 3) Large tea growers and manufacturers. The bank lending to this sector consist of both term loans for development gardens, construction of factory sheds, processing facilities, etc. and working capital facilities for on-going production. Any restructuring exercise would involve segregation of overdues into a separate facility to be repaid over a period of time. The unit would need fresh working capital limit for operations and may also need term loans for replacement/balancing of facilities to achieve projected levels of production. As part of restructuring, the units may also like to carry out productivity improving measures like implementation of voluntary retirement schemes, etc. While in respect of small tea growers, a standardized approach could be taken, it is felt that decision on restructuring of larger units should be on the basis of case-by-case evaluation. In the prevailing market conditions and interest rates scenario, banks could consider converting existing rupee loans into foreign currency denominated funding. This would enable the units to enjoy the benefit of lower interest rates without the banking system having to make sacrifices.

While restructuring the borrowal accounts in the tea sector the regulatory requirements vide RBI's circular DBOD No.BP.BC.98/21.04.048/2000-2001 dated March 30, 2001 will have to be kept in mind. The industry had sought extension of delinquency period beyond 2 half years on the plea that the harvesting season for tea is 9-12 months. However, Reserve Bank of India had not acceded to this request.

Recommended Relief Measures for various segments of Tea Industry

i. Small Tea Growers

Banks may carve out irregular portion of outstanding in term/working capital loan accounts as on 31 December

2003, into a Special Tea Term Loan (STTL) repayable in 5 to 7 years with a moratorium of one year. Interest on STTL may be charged at the Benchmark Rate of the bank. Fresh working capital limit may be considered based on assessment of requirements. Working capital limits upto Rs.2 lakh may be sanctioned at a concessional rate of interest not exceeding 9 per cent p.m. For loans exceeding Rs.2.00 lakh, interest may be charged at the Benchmark Rate of the bank.

ii. Bought Leaf Factories

Banks may carve out irregular portion of outstanding in term/working capital loan accounts as on 31 December 2003 into a special tea term loan (STTL) repayable in five to seven years with a moratorium of one year. Fresh working capital limit may be considered based on assessment of requirements. Interest on STTL and fresh working capital may be considered at Benchmark Rate of the bank.

iii. Large Tea Growers and Manufacturers

It is suggested that restructuring options for the borrowers coming under this category may be considered on a case-to-case basis on merit. The position of accounts as on 31 December 2003 may be considered for restructuring. Irregular portion of outstanding in term/working capital loan accounts as on 31 December 2003 may be carved out into a Special Tea Term Loan (STTL). As part of the restructuring exercise, funding requirements for carrying out a VRS exercise or such other measures for improving productivity could also be considered depending on the viability of the proposal and suitable repayment fixed on the basis of cash flow projections. The repayment of STTL may be allowed over a period of 5 to 7 years including a moratorium of one year based on the cash flow projection. Interest on STTL may be charged at the Benchmark Rate of the bank. Banks may examine feasibility of converting Rupee Loans including restructured loans into Foreign Currency Loans to pass on the benefit of lower interest rates to the borrowers. Fresh working capital limit may be considered based on assessment of requirements. Interest on fresh working capital would be as per the pricing policy of the bank. In cases where the asset cover is insufficient, banks may seek additional collateral security from the borrowers.

Strategies

The following strategies may be evolved or implemented, as happened in some of the tea growing states, are given below:

- Tea growing regions, because of the use of shade trees in West Bengal and the Northeast, can be classed as forests.
- In Kerala, they are converting potato and other available land to tea and the findings of the experts are that tea areas carry out the same positive functions as forest land, so far as ecology and land erosion are concerned. Industry's plea is simple, tea areas with shade are almost as good as forests and certainly much better than the degraded forests. As such, degraded forests can be given to the industry for growing tea not only in the national interest but also in the ecological interest.
- It is the industry has formed partnership with the Government to extend its wings and gives effective support to the industry by allotting land, a big portion of which can be degraded forests.
- Pragmatism is called for not legalism or bureaucratism. As these forests 'on paper' cannot claim any standing trees, it would be better to plant these areas with tea and shade trees! We may classify shaded tea areas as forests and the ratios laid down for forest -land, will be effectively maintained.
- One may have to only amend the definition of a forest! Taking about the Government, as an active partner, the first partnership contribution industry seeks from the Government is maintenance of law and order and rationalization of taxation.

? The industry and Government have gone into a genuine partnership where it is in the interest of both parties to see that the industry keeps on growing and generates increasingly more wealth, so that the

Government can partake of it and get bigger revenue amounts in coming years. As a good partner, it is industry's duty to see that both the Centre and the State earn increasingly more revenue from the tea industry.

- Government should consider by taking a smaller per centage of a big and growing cake, rather than a big per centage of a stagnating and slowly diminishing smaller cake. Hence there is a necessity for continuous growth of production through increased productivity of both land and labour and increased production with more land coming under tea.

Conclusion

While the industry understands that the Government has certain basic fiscal needs, and is willing to do its best, the Government also has to appreciate that if the industry is to prosper, taxes have to be further rationalised, more lands have to be allotted and law and order must be maintained. However, even with all the help and understanding from the Government, the industry will not be able to hold its own in the new climate of free market economy and globalization, unless its productivity improves most of which will have to come from the workers, through industry's efforts. Demanding productivity from workers as a quid pro quo for increase in wages does not work. It is industry's responsibility to ensure that workers are trained and motivated to use this training in the overall interests of all concerned.

PART V
CASE STUDIES ON TEA INDUSTRY

This part includes three Chapters 20 to 22. Chapter 20 throws light on the Economics of Tea cultivation in Kangra and its Problems of marketing; Effect of Growing Common Turmeric in the Periphery of Tea Area in some parts of West Bengal; Weaknesses and Opportunities of Tea Industry; Himachal Pradesh Tea Industry A Revival Package; Small Tea Growers in Assam and North Bengal. Chapter 20 aims at working out economics of tea cultivation in Kangra Valley with primary data. Endeavours have been exercised to: *(i)* outline the back ground of the valley, *(ii)* trace the research efforts *(iii)* estimate cost, gross income and returns per farm and per hectare, *(iv)* calculate break-even analysis. The marketing of Kangra tea is beset with problems like absence of product diversification, fall in tea output, poor quality of green leaf. Attention has been drawn on the weakness of the industry with probable opportunities like use of tea waste and development of product from such waste, eco-friendly or organic tea, health aspects of tea. Chapter 21 evolves the revival strategy of Himachal Pradesh Tea Industry. While mapping such strategy all probable aspects have been dwelt upon. These are replacement planting, filling up of vacancy, cultural practices, development initiatives like launching of business development cells, formation of farmers' club, commencement of rural entrepreneurship development programme (REDP), establishment of self help groups (SHGs). Further, future policies of state government such as introduction of latest technologies, optimum utilization of land resources to encourage value addition, increase in employment opportunities in tea through further commissioning of processing units, and extending green cover of on barren or fallow lands. Management of tea gardens, quality upgradation, weedding out substandard tea, shortening of pruning cycle, are some of the policy prescription suggested in this chapter. Chapter 22 intends to mention problems and prospects of small tea growers in Assam and North Bengal. Concept of small tea cultivation, socio-economic profile of selected borrowers of Assam, field practices and cultural operations of sample tea estates like variety, land preparation, manuring, fertilizing, pruning, weed and pest control, irrigation, drainage, harvesting and post harvesting have been discussed. Infrastructure support, credit flow, inputs, cost of cultivation, marketing, role of tea planters in development of Assam tea, rationale for bitter taste of Assam tea are some of the aspects, which have been mentioned in this chapter. Besides, some of weaknesses of the industry have been analysed with reference to sample studies. Based on the findings of these primary data recommendations and policy prescription have been suggested.

20

Economics and Marketing of Kangra Tea, Farm Business Analysis, Break Even Analysis etc.

SECTIONR I

Economics of Tea Cultivation in Kangra—A Study

Backdrop

Tea cultivation in Kangra valley had started when Britishers acquired land for the purpose in 1860, its cultivation went satisfactorily until 1905 when the area was rocked by the earthquake. After the earthquake the English planters sold away their estates to the local farmers of that area. They could not pay much attention to the industry because of their long absence from the area. However, the climatic condition of this area provide a good scope for cultivation of highly rainfall sensitive crop-tea. The tea gardens in the state are old and the tea bushes have mostly degenerated. Most of the gardens have been denuded of fertile soils. Tea gardens in the state are mainly maintained on individual holding with an average size of about 2.5 hectares. The tea industry popularly called India's finest agro-assets need to be exploited for the maximum benefits to the national economy. The state Govt. is also keen to develop this industry at a rapid pace due to its importance. Special steps have been taken by tea boards to assist the planters and cooperative factories to increase the profits from their enterprise. It is expected that these steps will results in improving the condition and boost the production of tea industry.

Kangra Tea Industry has China hybrid type of planting material. The total area under tea is approximately 2350 hectares with an annual production of 0.11 million kg. The yield is very low, i.e., 450 kg. per hectare as against the national average of 1650 kg per hectare With the establishment of Cooperative tea factories in the region for manufacture of green leaf, the quality of tea has regained its lost glory. Kangra tea is fetching the better price in Kolkata and international market. But the production still appears to be stagnant. Although the existing tea plantation has proved to be the most promising as regards its quality, survival and drought resistant, yet it is moderate in yield. Many of the introduced jats and clones from other tea growing areas of India did not do well under the prevailing climatic conditions. Almost all the gardens are rainfed. The keen interest of planters for increasing their productivity has necessitated the undertaking of the mass selection work from existing tea plantation for high yielding clones.

Research Efforts

Research efforts have been going on since late seventies. After series of preliminary investigations from existing plantations, fortunately, success has been met in identifying two clones which were found to excel both in yield as well as in quality. These two clones namely Kangra Asha (KVK-1) and Kangra Jwala (KVK–3) were released by the Adhoc Tea Research Advisory Committee comprising of experts from all tea development agencies and leading tea growers of the region. Those clones were recommended for the tea grower of Himachal Pradesh for extension plantation, so that production of this area reaches to almost about the level of national average. The names of those clones were suggested after the names of Goddesses of the Kangra region.

Kangra Asha and Kangra Jwala have unique characters. Kangra Asha is vigorous having uniform growth, orthotropic with good branching habit, excellent rooter. Leaf pose is semi erect and dark green in colour and resistant to drought, frost and hails. It has capacity to yield 1264 kgs per hectare at the 5th year of establishment. Kangra Jwala is uniform and has vigorous growth, semi orthotropic with profuse branching habit, leaf pose semi-erect, light green in colour, shoot large and pubescent and resistant to drought, frost and hails. It has a capacity to yield 1484 kgs per hectare at the 5th year of establishment. Both the clones are excellent in quality.

Availability of Clones

With the availability of those two clones in the area now the planters have planted tea with narrow spacing. Actually most of tea gardens of the area are under wider spacing, i.e. 1.5 m X 1.5 m having 4350 plants per hectare. The bushes take longer time to give maximum production per hectare besides weed problems, which may be due to low density population. The only way to get maximum production per unit area is to go for high density population and with improved high yielding clones. The only bottle neck in replanting or extension planting was non-availability of high yielding clones suitable to agroclimatic conditions of this area. Since planters prefer to go for China hybrid type of material, the bottleneck has been removed with the release of these two clones. Kangra tea Industry is fortunate enough that Tea Board has various subsidy schemes for replanting of existing tea plantations. Therefore ample scope is there for increasing productivity per unit area in this region by adopting these two clones. The commercialization of these clones in the region again revived the lost glory of Kangra tea. This not only helped to increase the production of Kangra, but its name and fame has figured in international market. Thus Kangra tea regained its lost reputation.

Objective

Tea, a perennial crop, requires high initial investment and long gestation period. This stress the need to understand the behaviour of profits in relation to the value of output.

Therefore, present study is an attempt to work out the: *(i)* Economics of tea cultivation, and *(ii)* Break Even Analysis.

Economics of Tea Cultivation

As an important plantation industry tea plays a vital role in the development of the national economy. Being labour intensive industry, it provides sizeable employment and contributes to 2.4 per cent of the gross value of agricultural output of the country. The ecological balance in the country, preventing the soil erosion, is being considerably maintained by tea gardens. In the map of commercial crops of HP, tea occupies large portion. Kangra valley of the state is the main centre of tea cultivation which are old and tea bushes have mostly degenerated. Keeping in view of the importance of tea in economy the Central Government has now making attempt to develop this industry with the opening of regional CSIR complex at Palampur, the emphasis being on research on tea. Special steps have been taken by the Tea Board to assist the planters enhancing revenue from tea industry. It is expected that these steps will boost tea production. Therefore, it was felt imperative to workout the economics of tea cultivation in the present study.

Methodology

For reasons of importance in respect of tea cultivation in the Himachal Pradesh, Tehsil Palampur of District Kangra was selected for the study. The present sample of five per cent tea planters (category wise) was selected with proportional allocation following a simple random sampling. Required data were collected from the farmers and related agencies respectively and therefore period is 2005-06.

Estimation of Cost and Returns of Tea Cultivation

The cost of cultivation of tea has been worked out on the basis of standard cost concepts i.e. Cost A, Cost B, Cost C. Net returns over different cost were estimated by subtracting the cost of cultivation from gross returns. The various components of returns have been computed as follows:

Net *Income=Gross Income–Total Expenses (i.e. Cost C)*
Family Labour Income=Gross Income–Cost B
Farm Business Income=Gross Income–Cost A (i.e. operational cost)–Interest on Working Capital

$$\text{Per Cent Return on Capital} = \frac{\text{Net Income} - \text{Imputed Value of Family Labour}}{\text{Average Capital Investment}} \times 100$$

The net return is based on per hectare and per farm.

Results and Discussions

Table 1. Cost of Cultivation of Tea for Different Sizes of Farms

(in Rs.)

Size of Farm	*Per Hectare*			*Per Farm*		
	Cost A	*Cost B*	*Cost C*	*Cost A*	*Cost B*	*Cost C*
Small	1,585	1,760	3,328	2,232	2,470	2,884
Medium	3,680	3,870	4,865	22,335	20,580	2,628
Large	2,905	3,107	3,705	1,14,504	1,22,490	1,80,190
Overall	2,715	2,870	3,833	22,683	24,230	26,653

The Table indicates that operational cost represented by cost A were Rs. 1585 Rs. 3680 and Rs. 2905 for small, medium and large farms respectively. The cost B noted to be Rs. 1760, Rs. 3870 and Rs. 3107. The cost C was found to be Rs. 3328, Rs. 4865 and Rs. 3705 on different categories of tea plants. The cost of cultivation is highest in case of medium tea planters because of greater use of fertilizers and chemicals on these tea gardens and increased investment on better management practices.

The net returns from tea for different categories have been worked out over cost A, cost B and cost C, Net returns over cost A shows the profit is taking care operational cost only. It can be seen from Table 2 that the net returns for tea over cost C worked out to be Rs.2,320, Rs.3,290 and Rs.2,772 per hectare for small, medium and large categories respectively. The net returns were noted to be highest in case of medium tea planters followed by large and small tea farms. This indicates that medium size planters are adopting better management practices than small and large farms. It is observed from the Table that net returns also increase with increase in the size of farms.

Table 2: Net Returns on Different Categories of Tea Farms

Size of Farm	*Gross Returns*		*Net return Over*					
			Cost A		*Cost B*		*Cost C*	
	Per ha Farm	*Per*	*Per ha Farm*	*Per ha*	*Per Farm*	*Per ha*	*Per Farm*	*Per*
Small	5643	7936	4056	5704	3885	5850	2320	3264
Medium	8235	43768	4576	24338	4625	23200	3290	17506
Large	6745	255264	3570	140800	3668	132801	2772	19275
Overall	6685	54576	3990	35725	3806	32054	2850	24005

Source: Field investigation.

Measures of efficiency have been presented in Table 3.

Table 3: Measures of Farm Business Analysis

(Rupees/ha)

Farm Business Measure	*Farm Size*			
	Small	*Medium*	*Large*	*Overall*
(a) Farm Business Income	3655	4025	3110	3620
(b) Net Income	2320	3295	2770	2850
(c) Family Labour Income	3885	4380	3360	3790
(d) Per cent Return on Capital (%)	9.58	16.57	14.01	15.50

Note: The figures have been rounded off to the nearest rupee.

Source: Field Investigation.

Farm business income, taken as return to farmers for investment on capital was estimated for small, medium and large tea planters at about Rs. 3655, Rs. 4025 and Rs. 3110 respectively (Table 3). Family labour income which is the income to the operator and his family was estimated at Rs.3885, Rs.4380 and Rs.3360 per hectare of small, medium and large farms respectively. Overall family labour income for the planters irrespective of size of holding was estimated as Rs. 3790 per hectare. Family labour income was found to be highest in case of medium planters followed by small and large planters. Percentage return on capital investment in small, medium and large tea farms are 9.58, 16.57 and 14.01 respectively. Figure in medium farms reflects better management practices. On an average, per cent return on capital investment was found to be 15.50.

In precise, more emphasis should be placed on proper management of tea gardens. And wherever attention to better management practices have been given the results found encouraging, particularly in medium farms.

Break Even Analysis

For the present study a sample of five percent tea planters (Category wise) was selected with proportional allocation following a simple random sampling from Tehsil Palampur. Required primary and secondary data were collected from the farmers and related agencies for the year 2005-064. Break even analysis was attempted to understand the behaviour of practices in relation to the value of outputs. The formula used to determine the break even amount of total revenue and total cost is as follows:

TR (Total Revenue) = F(X)

TC (Total Cost) = TFC + TVC

TVC = F(X)

Where x = output in kg

Break even point is that point where TR = TC

The TR and TVC were obtained through simple analysis using the form Y = bx

Results and Discussions

The break even points for different categories of tea planters have been worked out and the results of the same have been presented in table 4 to 6. The break even output for small tea planters at different levels of technology use has been estimated to be 676 kgs. In this case the total revenue and total cost are equal (Rs. 2068).

Table 4: Break-even Output of Tea on Different Sizes of Tea Farms in Palampur Tehsil, District Kangra

(Per farm)

Particulars (Kg)	*Break-Even Output (Rs.)*	*Total Revenue (Rs.)*	*Total Cost*
Small	676	2,068	2,068
Medium	2,600	8,006	8,006
Large	17,030	42,180	42,180
Overall	9,590	9,592	9,592

Table 5: Break-even Output of Tea on Different Sizes of Tea Farms in Palampur Tehsil, District Kangra

(Per farm)

Particulars	*Small*	*Medium*	*Large*	*Overall*
(a) Break-even Point (Kgs)	676	2,600	17,030	9,590
(b) Average output (Kgs)	2,592	13,433	82,622	18,150
(c) Per cent greater than break-even output	283	417	505	487

Table 6: Break-even Output of Tea on Different Sizes of Tea Farms in Palampur Tehsil, District Kangra

(Per hectare)

Particulars (Kg)	*Break-Even Output (Rs.)*	*Total Revenue (Rs.)*	*Total Cost*
Small	238	1,140	1,140
Medium	479	1,466	1,466
Large	489	1,563	1,563
Overall	348	1,070	1,070

The break-even output for medium farms have been estimated at 2600 kgs with total revenue and total cost are Rs. 8,066 per farm. Similarly, the break even output for large farms have been estimated at 17,030 kgs and total revenue and total cost in this case is Rs. 32,445. The break even out put in overall situation have been estimated at 9,590 kgs and total revenue and total cost in this case is Rs. 9,592. Details are shown in Table 4.

Break-even output has been compared with average output to tea farms of different sizes and given in Table 5. It is interesting to note from the table that all the farms are producing much higher quantity of tea as compared to the break even output. In other words small, medium and large tea farms are growing 283 per cent, 317 per cent and 505 per cent more than the break-even point. The break even output has also been worked out on per hectare basis and given in table 6. Such an analysis helps in visualizing the position of the farm more clearly and also is forwarding suitable suggestions.

SECTION II

Marketing of Kangra Valley Tea—A Study

Origin of Kangra Tea—Area, Production and Sale Price

Tea cultivation in Himachal Pradesh (HP) dates back to 1849 when Dr. Jameron the Superintendent of Botanical Garden, Peshawar, visited Kangra district and recommended the lower slopes of Dhauladhar range lying between 900 to 1400 m.s.l. with an average rainfall of 1520 mm to cultivate tea. The first commercial plantation with chinary type was established as Hailey Nager Tea Estate at Holta in 1852. Tea quality appeared excellent as evidenced by gold and silver medals won in Amsterdam and London market from 1886-95. The great earthquake of 1905 ruined the flourishing industry. The panic stricken Britishers sold their estates to local buyers. Total production has crossed 1022248 kgs in 2001 as against 550000 kgs during 1980. The highest premium price of Rs. 61.00 per kg at kolkata market is an indication of quality product. This industry is earning revenue of about Rs. 9.41 crore per annum, besides providing employment to 6000 workers directly or indirectly. The marketing pattern in the state is by and large dependent on auction system which has not favoured good prices for tea. The situation can not be retrieved unless adequate measures are taken for the upliftment of every sector of the industry especially marketing. The Kangra Tea, which swings between black and green tea, is sold through auction centres at Amritsar and Kolkata and the marketing agency of "The Kangra Tea Planters Marketing and Industrial Society" plays a vital role for the sale. But it is found that on one hand the poor quality of the made tea and on the other the exploitation of the seller in the hands of middlemen are responsible for the low realization as well as lower sales. Rentals for unsold stocks kept at auction centres only aggravate producers' misery.

Research Methodology

In order to study the problems of the tea industry and the planters, a complete list of planters was prepared with the help of the records obtained from the Tea Board office and from planters. The total number of gardens were classified as small, medium and large on the basis of their area under plantation. The data relating to average price, production, quantum of sale etc. for the study was collected from the secondary sourceTo examine the growth rate the following formula is used:

GR = (C y/B y)i/n-1
Where GR stands for growth rate
Cy stands for current year
By stands for base year
n for total no. of years.

Marketing of Kangra Tea

Product diversification is an important and progressive aspect of any industry. In order to keep pace with the market forces the production of tea in Kangra swings between green and black tea but with changing taste the production of black tea has increased in the last few years. From the beginning the green tea was specialized in Himachal Pradesh and before partition nearly 75 per cent of the green tea produced found its way to Afghanistan via Karachi harbour. However, after partition the borders being closed for trading.

At present the Kangra tea is sold at two auction centres in India. Green tea is sold through the industrial society at Amritsar auction and black tea through Kolkata Tea Trading Corporation. Tea is first sent to warehouses and here the auction is done on the basis of samples drawn. The Kangra Cooperative Marketing Society charges 5 per cent whereas the Kolkata society charges 1 per cent on the total amount of sales. The analysis of the sale of tea produced in Himachal Pradesh is based on the sale made by the industrial society, Palampur, Bir, Baijnath and Dharamsala which has been compiled and discussed here.

Production of Tea from Coopertive Tea Factories during 1992-93 to 2003-04

The production of tea has been reported in Table 1. Data was collected from the four cooperative factories. The data reveal that the production of Palampur tea factory increased by 25.78 per cent during last ten years (1992-2002) with an annual increase of 2.32 per cent in real terms.

Table 1: Production of Tea from Cooperative Tea Factories

(Qty. in kg.)

Year	*Palampur*	*Baijnath*	*Bir*	*Dharamsala*	*Total*
1992-93	348786	61002	73958	101717	585463
1993-94	408326	58458	98059	69580	634423
1994-95	381794	83488	91461	166880	723603
1995-96	441069	78062	90757	165031	774915
1996-97	437256	88815	83170	171991	781232
1997-98	396267	131133	74989	194467	796856
1998-99	419451	110753	101453	252574	884231
1999-2000	410423	75765	69278	191380	746946
2000-2001	500254	73946	69278	223050	866528
2001-2002	438712	79017	66108	110480	694407
2002-03					41000*
2003-04					43000*
Increase/Decrease over 1992-93 (per cent)	25.78	29.53	-10.61	8.62	18.60
Annual Growth rate (per cent)	2.32	2.62	-2.0	0.8	1.80

Source: Technical Office Tea, * Break-up not available.

In case of Bir cooperative tea factory it is evident that production has gone down by 10.61 per cent with an annual decrease of 2.0 per cent during the period, whereas production of Baijnath factory increased by 29.53 per cent with an annual growth of 2.62 per cent. Similarly the production from Sidbari tea factory i.e. Dharamsala reported 8.62 per cent and 0.8 growth annually over 1992-93.

Production of Black and Green Tea during 1992-93 to 2004-05

Table 2 revealed the production of black and green tea. The data reflect the shifting of product mix from green to black tea production. The total production of Kangra tea is reflected in Table 2.

Table 2: Production of Black and Green Tea in Kangra Tea Gardens

(Qty. in kgs.)

Year	*Total Production*	*Black Tea*	*Green Tea*
1992-93	1189663	481552	708111
1993-94	1300230	542575	757655
1994-95	1314405	631934	682471
1995-96	1359183	681522	677661
1996-97	1423414	755753	667661
1997-98	1442310	657081	785229
1998-99	1711242	909697	801545
1999-2000	1221624	696122	525502
2000-2001	1483452	871400	612052
2001-2002	1022298	654692	367606
2002-2003	1261000	996300	268000
2003-2004	1230000	952000	278000
2004-2005	1252300	945300	307000
Increase/decrease over 1992-93 (per cent)	-5.26	96.30	-95.66
Annual Growth rate (Per cent)	-0.40	7.40	-7.36

Source: Technical Office Tea.

The production of tea showed that there is a 24.69 per cent increase in the total production of tea by 2000-2001 over 1992-93 with the annual growth rate of 2.23 per cent but there is a decline in 2001-02 to the tune of 14.08 per cent and a negative growth rate of 1.5 per cent was observed over 1992-93. The data of black tea show that there is an increase of 96.30 per cent in 2004-05 in terms of growth rate calculated by taking 1992-93 as base year. The average annual growth displayed was 7.40 per cent in 2004-2005. The production figures of green tea exhibited somewhat different picture as reflecting a significant shift towards the production of black tea due to change in market demand. In 2004-05 the green tea production falls by 95.66 per cent for 1992-93 with a net negative growth rate of 7.36 per cent. The year 1998-99 registered the highest production so far and reported a production of 1711242 kg.

Prices of Black and Green Tea during 1971 to 2003

In comparison to the rising trend in sale the average price of tea is more or less fluctuating as evident from Table 3. The main reason of price fluctuation at auction is the poor quality of tea, which warrants quality improvement for better realization of prices.

Table 3: Average Prices of Green and Black Tea

(Rs./kg.)

Year	*Green Tea*	*Black Tea*	*Average price*
1971	5.06	14.85	10.43
1975	4.65	16.72	10.68
1980	6.52	15.96	11.25
1985	17.50	15.11	16.30
1990	29.90	35.00	32.45
1993	33.74	42.57	38.16
1994	32.20	37.26	34.73
1995	26.40	54.49	44.45
1998	54.74	70.00	62.39
1999	47.29	65.00	56.15
2000	51.94	56.62	54.78
2001	44.13	54.46	49.30
2002	46.43	56.50	51.61
2003	48.45	59.50	53.98
Increase/decrease over 1971 (per cent)	857.09	334.69	448.89
Annual Growth Rate	25.2	9.82	13.20

Source: Technical Office Tea.

There is an overall increase in price of tea by 2004 over 1971 to the tune of 448.89 per cent with an annual growth of 3.2. per cent. Black tea registered an increase of 334.69 per cent in 34 years at an annual growth rate of 9.82 per cent. While green tea exhibited a growth rate of 859.09 per cent with annual growth rate of 25.52 per cent. In 2004, green tea was 46.65 per cent dearer over 1994 at annual growth rate of 4.65 per cent.

Sales of Black and Green Tea

The initiative of the Palampur cooperative tea factory to switch over towards packet tea and labeling a few good varieties through Brand names like Bageshwari, Kailash is a step to value addition.

Table 4: Sales of Green and Black Tea in Rupees

(Qty. in thousand kgs.)

Year	*Green Tea*	*Black Tea*	*Total Sales*
1992	211.72	168.54	380.26
1993	238.20	230.97	481.73
1994	181.53	235.45	419.68
1995	198.08	371.36	569.44
1996	196.52	374.83	571.35
1997	338.83	492.36	826.13
1998	442.77	636.78	1079.55
1999	283.77	455.40	739.17
2000	321.02	449.81	770.83
2001	155.95	356.54	512.46
Increase/decrease over 1992 (percentage)	-26.36	111.55	34.75
Annual Growth Rate 1992	-3.01	7.78	3.03

Source: Technical Office Tea.

It is observed from the Table 4 that there is an increase in the total sales of tea by 2001 over 1992 by 34.75 per cent with an annual growth rate of 3.03 per cent. Black tea increased by 111.55 per cent in this period with an annual growth of 7.78 per cent. In 2001 the green tea sales declined by 26.36 per cent with an annual decline of 3.01 per cent. The year 1998 registered highest sale.

Conclusion

At the end, however, it may be mentioned that new areas should be brought under tea along with infilling the existing vacant areas. The profitability of the factories is continuously at stake and they are not in a position to retain sufficient surplus to plough back. It is a necessity, therefore, that Tea Board should have a plantation finance corporation to keep a close look on the financial need of the planters and factories. In improving the financial position of the factories the manufacturing subsidy as well as development allowances should be increased also.

SECTION III
Effect of Growing Common Turmeric in the Periphery of Tea Area

Common Turmeric (Circumalonga) is a valuable spice and condiment. It contains various medicinal and properties that have repellent effect to soil-borne insects, and animals. Turmeric helps wealth generation also. The main active ingredients include Curcuminoides (5 per cent), essential oil (6 per cent), volatile oil, Curcuminl (diferuloylmethane) (cr-II_ dicaffeoyl–methane, (coumarin–III). A research project on "Production and Processing of Tea in Non-conventional Area for Poverty Alleviation", undertaken by the Department of Agriculture and Food Technology, IIT, Kharagpur, inferred that growing of turmeric in the periphery of tea area may be considered for some benefits.

Research Methodology; In the Gopali site, Midnapore, West Bengal, a thick layer of common cultivated turmeric was raised as peripheral planting under the said project. To generate additional wealth in tea area, the four Blocks were planted with turmeric along with some evergreen horticultural plant (Area approx. 3.5 acre). The tea plants grown there were mainly of drought resistant varieties like TV – 26, TV – 22 etc. along with dense green crop/Dhencha *(Cesbania rostrate)*. The soil in these sites is poor, acid, lateritic in character. However, the soil was well prepared by sub-soiling, hoeing etc. Required amount of cowdung was applied to enrich the soil and Neem Khoal @ 10 gm/plant (approx) to protect it from the soil-borne insect. Since it is absolutely a bio-garden no chemical product was in application for any purpose. Three-storied system of plantation was adopted here. At the lower tier, the turmeric was planted, at the middle storey, the tea bushes and at upper storey, the well-trimmed horticultural and other common shed plants were raised to get maximum benefit from the soil. The area is dry and very prone to various soil-borne insects, chiefly termite (microceroterms sp. and, some odontoterms sp.).

Result and Discussion: The observation was made over a year. Findings of the effect of turmeric plantation on soil-borne insects are shown here:

Termite

Block	*I*	*II*	*III*	*IV*	*Remarks*
	6	8	6	9	Death per cent of plant without Turmeric planting
	Nil (affected)	2	1 (affected)	Nil	Death per cent of plant with Turmeric planting

It was found, however, some patches outside were badly attacked by this pest. The result indicates the potency of turmeric against soil-borne insect.

Cockchafer Grub: The cockchafer grub attack at the site is very rare due to poor soil. After planting of turmeric no case was recorded instead of giving huge organic matter to the field.

Mite (Oligonychus coffee): The major pest, particularly mite, attacks the tea bushes. Nevertheless, their population was not noticed in the peripheral planting of turmeric. In tea estates, insects like mite etc. harbour on this peripheral planting during lean time of spraying or dormancy and again attack the tea bushes from there. Thus, the peripheral planting of other plants acts like a "Trojan horse" to the estates, which is not found in the case of turmeric. Comparison of Mite Population between Tea plant and Turmeric is shown here.

Mite Population in %	*Block-I*	*II*	*III*	*IV*
Tea Bushes	20%	15%	20%	18%
Turmeric	Nil	Nil	Nil	Nil

Excellent repellent effect of turmeric over the animal pests like goat, cow, etc. was also observed. The pungent smell of turmeric due to volatile and essential oil also repels the Helopelties and other flies to enter the field. Mimosa (*Mimosa spp.*) is meant for this purpose. Vasak is a good repellent to animal but it creates hindrance to the normal flow of air and sunlight in tea bushes. In addition, due to that reason the plants are removed each year from the area. Thorny mimosa has some problem as well. On the other hand, turmeric generates some wealth and is devoid of any type of obstruction activities. Turmeric should be planted in combination with evergreen horticultural plant or other quick growing leafy species (like Fern, Kadam). It protects the tea plants at the time of drought and supports the fencing of the garden. However, there are various non-cultivated turmeric species of ethno-botanical interest also. Their potency against pest should be studied further.

SECTION IV
Weaknesses and Opportunities of Tea Industry

Backdrop

The British in India recognized the tea as a commercial crop. The growth of the industry was not satisfactory in terms of cultivation and manufacturing up to Pre-independence period. The phenomenal increase in yield and quality, started during independence period. Big tea institutes like Tocklai in Assam and UPASI in South India did pioneering research on both yield and quality of tea and the reward came out with manifold increase in yield and quality of tea. Other scientific institutes, namely the CSKKV Palampur and CSIR in North-West India have contributed significantly for undertaking much research on many aspects of tea.

Nutritional, Stimulating and Flavoured Beverage

Tea is a nutritional, stimulating and flavoured beverage. According to the published information, there are twelve kinds of functional components. These components prevent: *(i)* decay and crumbling of tooth, *(ii)* depression of blood pressure, and *(iii)* glucose. They also serve in the *(a)* prevention of artherosclerosis and *(b)* thrombus formation, *(c)* corpulence sensescence, *(d)* and radiation damage. Some components are anti-oxidative, immune function improving, deodorizing, detoxicating, germicidal and anti-viral, diuretic, liver protecting, anti-ulceric, anti-mutagenic and anti-carcinogenic.

Weaknesses

Revision of Camellia by Modern Concepts: Tea systematics are based mostly on subjective criteria, given little or no consideration to the application of modern techniques like numerical taxonomy, biological series or biosystematic classification system. There is, therefore, an urgent need for the revision of the genus Camellia by the Application of modern concepts. A study by Owour *et al* (1987), for example, suggested Terpene Index (TI) could be a reliable chemotaxonomic statistic for differentiating various taxa of tea. The Assam types have a TI close to one while in China types the TI is near zero. Studies of this nature are useful in establishing affinities of hybrids to major taxonomic categories. The array of tea hybrids suggests unrestricted introgression of many species of *Camellia* into the tea gene pool. Nevertheless, taxonomic affinities of most inter-specific and intra-specific hybrids are unknown; otherwise, they could have provided clues to the evolutionary organization of the gene pool. However, conventional breeding programmes, including earlier production of improved seed varieties, superior clones and clonal seeds, improved tea yields. A little progress has been made in increasing the relatively low harvest index of tea.

Effects of Climate and Weather on Potential and Actual Yields: Climate and weather influence the yield of tea. Attempts have been made to model the effects of these variables on the principal growth processes. This helps to predict potential and actual yields in different locations, and yield distribution during the year. A predictable interpretation of the effects of weather on yields would also help the next generation of clones. This will be selected against established criteria. These are capacity to grow at low temperatures, to tolerate dry air conditions, or to withstand drought with minimum damage. Removing the tea bush from its natural habitat and exporting it around the world has provided producers and scientists with many challenges. Fortunately, there is a great deal of genetic variability, which remains to be exploited. This is required for the sake of a 'nice cup of tea'.

Foliar Analysis for Assessment of Fertilizers Requirements: Tea further requires exploration of tea nutrition. If tea can grow in soil with over 0.5 per cent (5000 ppm) Calcium, is it correct to refer it as Calcifuges? On the other hand, is a trace of lime as Calcium carbonate is almost fatal? However, lime as Calcium carbonate is being used in cultivation in South and North-West India. Based on soil test, crop correlation studies have not been found to give authentic results on deficiency or sufficiency of nutrients. These questions need answer prior to understanding clearly the indication of tea nutrition and soil acidity. Extensive research is needed on the dormancy related factors of tea bushes. The bushes remain dormant for 2-5 months in North-west and North-east India. This is considered a lean period in terms of yield of crop. Use of foliar analysis for assessment of fertilizer requirements in tea is not well established.

Economic Threshold Levels—A Function of Several Factors: In Asia, tea sustains 8 per cent loss through pests. Nevertheless, there is a big lacuna in our understanding of the ecology of most of the pest species, despite the knowledge of their life histories. Population dynamics of the natural enemies of many of these noxious species is not understood in detail. Crop loss appraisals and establishment of economic threshold levels for different pest species of tea are amazingly poor. However, the establishment of economic threshold levels as a function of several factors such as weather, vigour and maturity of the crop, time of pest infestation, age structure of pest population, size of the population of beneficial organisms etc. requires a large number of filed experiments. The effect of pesticides on non-target organisms in this eco system is poorly understood and the possibilities of non-chemical means of control need details study. Mathematical modes can greatly help us to understand the ways in which the different factors interact to affect the yield and on the success of different control strategies. Tea plants suffer due to moisture stress since tea is grown as a rain-fed crop under South Indian conditions.

Other Factors: On contrary, tea plants suffer due to water stagnation in North-east India that limits crop productivity. Lack of awareness on quality tea plucking, existence of extended pruning cycles, dearth of financial assistance for adopting medium prune, shortage of labour, practice of accepting any standard of leaf by the factories, inadequate finance for development of infrastructure in the factories and poor adoption of scientific methods both in field and factory are also our weaknesses.

Opportunities

Some crops can be grown in association with tea, within or around the tea areas. It can be an important facet of tea cultivation. Multiple cropping system should be thoroughly studied to enable growers achieve the maximum benefit. There are markets for by-products of leaf and products other than leaf. Currently tea waste is either returned to the field as fertilizer or sold at a very low price.

Various Products from Tea Waste: Products that can be produced from tea waste are: Caffeine (stimulant), polyphenols (antixodant), pigments (edible colour), polymer, animal feeds, tobacco and its substitutes, foaming agent, plant growth regulator, vinegar, tea seed oil for cooking, cosmetics and pharmaceuticals, saponins (plant growth stimulants) and furfural (versatile chemical) produced from tea seed husk. Instant tea, herbal teas, blended tea, blended tea with flavour and organically grown tea could also be produced.

Eco-Friendly/Organic Tea or Green Movement: One of the trends since 1980s is desire on the part of consumers to buy products that are 'friendly' to the environment. The 'green' movement is set and organic tea is of great demand. This is growing fast in the near future. However, the average transition period from conventional to organic culture is three years allowing time for chemicals to disperse. Such teas will definitely find the ready market of Indian tea abroad, which would harness our export potential. The future of speciality/herbal may be a significant one.

Health Aspects of Tea: Despite considerable evidence demonstrating the anti cancer properties of tea and its components from experimental studies, it is not adequate to fully project their protective role against cancer. It is mainly die tc wide variability in the methods of processing, preparation and consumption of tea among different populations. The experimental studies provide support to the cancer chemo-preventive effect of tea using its extracts or purified components, it needs to be clarified how much of these agents are available to humans through their daily consumption of tea. Moreover, the ideal quantity of tea or its active compounds are yet to be determined that may be considered sufficient for exerting desired anti-cancer effect in humans. (Global Advances in Tea Science, 1999). Hybridization studies revealed (Yamaguchi et al., 1999) possible lines of evolution of tea varieties. However, these studies are not sufficient to explain the existence of extremely heterogeneous tea population in cultivation. The need is to correct all these germ plasma before they become extinct because of clonal predominance.

Conclusion

There are some threats to our industry, however, wake of alternative drinks and their presence may cause a decline in tea consumption. So, it is imperative that all connected with the country's tea industry should adopt suitable measure to stop the aggression of alternative drinks to beverage market. Moreover, the per capita consumption of tea in the country has to be increased also in view of growing production. Threat from other tea producing and exporting countries, namely Sri Lanka, Kenya, China, Vietnam, Bangladesh, is also very much present to our exports. They are coming with quality produce at a low price. Not only that, the government of those countries is also pushing the exports of the producers with various economic and political measures. The tea industry and the government should attend the said fact to help the tea units flourish with vigour.

Source: The Assam Review and Tea News, March 2002.

21

Himachal Pradesh Tea Industry: A Revival Package

Small Tea Growers in Himachal Pradesh

Introduction

The quality and yield of tea in Himachal Pradesh could not be maintained for a pretty long time because the people engaged in the industry followed the traditional old practices. The tea gardens in Himachal Pradesh are mainly concentrated in Baijnath, Kangra and Dharamsala tehsils of Kangara district, Bhat Tehsil of Chamba district and Jogindernagar Tehsil of Mandi district. Based on the statistics available with Tea Board, there are 3,679 tea estates covering an area of 2325 ha. with an annual production of 1,247 thousand kg. in 2004. All the estate fall in the size group "upto 10.12 ha." and they are small ones.

Salient Features of Small Tea Gardens in Himachal Pradesh

The salient features of small tea gardens are discussed with reference to various parameters as given below:-

a. Area, Production and Yield of Small Tea Estates/Gardens

Area under tea plantation in the state reduced from 4317 ha. in 1951 to 2328 ha. in 2005 accounting for a fall of

46 per cent. Average size of the plantation is 0.63 ha. compared to North Indian average of 1.62 ha., South Indian average of 0.67 ha. and all India average of 0.85 ha. Tea production in 1951 was 1125 thousand kgs., which was slightly increased to 1252 thousand kgs. in 2005. Majority of the estates are smallholdings and the average yield of small estates is 517 kg. per ha., as against the North Indian average of 1,587 kg./ha., South Indian average of 1,634 kgs./ha. and all India average of 1,610 kgs./ha.

Only Chinese varieties of tea plants were prevalent in the area. Majority of estates are dependent on rainfed irrigation

b. Share of Area, Production and Yield of Himachal Pradesh Estates Compared to North India, South India and All India

Small tea estates in Himachal Pradesh accounts for 10.32 per cent of small estates in North India, 5.97 per cent in South India and 3.78 per cent in all India. Area-wise Himachal Pradesh represents 5.45 per cent of North India, 5.37 per cent in South India and 2.70 per cent in all India. Himachal Pradesh constitutes 1.77 per cent of North Indian tea produced by small growers 1.70 per cent in South India and 0.87 per cent in all India.

c. Green Tea–Himachal Pradesh and All India

Himachal Pradesh produced 954 thousand kg. of green tea representing 16.79 per cent of all India green tea in 1961. The share was, however, reduced to 11.13 per cent in 2004. Of the total production, Himachal Pradesh produced 75 per cent of green tea in 1961 and 60 per cent in 2004. Average production of green leaf ranged between 800–2000 kg./season as against 8000 kg/ha. in well managed estates.

d. Age Group of Bushes

About 90 per cent of the existing tea plantation has already attained the age of more than 100 years as against the economic life of 50 years. Average bush population was around 8000–10000/ha. as against the normal limit of 15000/ha. The farmers were not resorting to mulching.

e. Tea Factories

There were four major tea-processing factories in co-operative sector operating in the district. These factories were operating at 70–75 per cent level of capacity utilization.

Findings of Selected Tea estates

Major findings of the surveyed estates are given below:

i. Tea Estates at a Glance

- About 60 per cent of the units are lying unattended or abandoned due to small holding.
- About 20 per cent of the farmers had leased out their tea estates to other farmers.
- About 1024 gardens covering an area of 464.4 ha. have been declared as neglected area because of absentee landlord, lack of economic resources and production of green leaves below 2000 kg./ha/season.

Although the Department of Agriculture has been providing extension services to the tea estate owners regarding cultivation and cultural practices, the majority of them are not following properly.

- The tea farmers are not resorting to mulching.
- Tea plantation was a better vocation earning of about Rs. 12000–15000 per acre as compared to earning of Rs. 5000–8000 per acre from other traditional crops viz., wheat, maize, paddy, etc.
- Tea planters had utilised about 40 per cent of the their land for tea cultivation (cash crop) and the remaining 60 per cent for other traditional crops such as wheat, maize, paddy, fodder mainly for domestic consumption only.
- There were about 150 tea growers (4 per cent of the total tea planters) having 445 ha. land was fully dependent on tea plantation for livelihood.

ii. Tea Financing–Major Issues

It was observed during the field investigation that tea

industry requires huge funds to carry out day-to-day field and factory operations. However, discussions with the planters revealed they are facing major problems in tea financing. It was brought to our notice that loan was provided only for rejuvenation of tea farms in earlier years and loan facility was availed by 5–7 per cent of the farmers. About 20 per cent of the farmers expressed their ignorance about the facilities available from bank to the tea planters and some planters are shy of bank loan.

Tea plantation was the major activity in the area. The poor off take of bank credit in this activity were not discussed in BLBC/DCC/DLRC meetings. The district level task force had not fixed the scale of finance for maintenance of tea gardens after 3 – 4 years of plantation. This may be fixed accordingly for providing working capital to tea planters. Unit cost of new tea plantation was fixed at a very low level. The same needs to be revised immediately.

About 5–10 per cent of the land under tea plantation was leased out to planters by the state government on which bankers are not providing credit because title of the land was not in favour of the planters. On perusal of loan account of tea planters, it was observed that heavy drawal was resorted during off-season. These funds of tea plantation were diverted to other purposes.

Only Palampur branch of KPARDB provided term loan for rejuvenation purpose. KCCB provided cash credit limit to the Co-operative Marketing cum Industrial Society for produce and fertilizer loans to the farmers. ADB branch of SBI sanctioned cash credit for tea plantation. Recovery performance under tea plantation was very satisfactory (90 per cent).

iii. Low Productivity–Areas of Concern

Low productivity is the major problems of Himachal tea industry. There are innumerable reasons, which are attributed to low productivity. It transpired from the sample estates that skilled labour for plucking of the leaves was not easily available. Such skilled labour was also costly. Cost of production/cultivation of tea plantation is very high and plucking accounts for 70–80% of the total cost of leaf production.

Due to urbanizing, cost of land around town has spurted. Tea planters preferred the land use for purposes other than tea plantation for immediate gains. Further the rates of green leaf have not increased over the years. Gap in the gardens were not being filled up with new plantation. Shade trees were not being planted in gardens resulting in low productivity. Majority of the tea plantation was more than 100 years old

Strategy for Revival of Tea Industry in Himachal Pradesh

a. Replacement Planting, Filling up of Vacancy, Cultural Practice, etc.

There are urgent requirement for replacement of old plantation and arrangements for irrigation facilities. Adequate number of shade trees is to be planted and unwanted weeds in the field are to be weeded out. Further proper and timely pruning of the plants as per the recommended practices are need of the hour. Proper cultural practices as per research and extension agencies norms are require to be adopted. Appropriate plucking practices, filling up the vacancy and encouragement of production of more green tea for fetching higher price realization are some of the areas, which require attentions.

b. Development Initiatives–Business Development Cell, Farmers' Club, REDP, SHGs, etc.

Some of the development initiatives are required for survival of tea industry in Himachal Pradesh. These are: *(i)* setting up Business Development Cell, *(ii)* Formation of Farmers Clubs of tea planters, *(iii)* conduct of Rural Entrepreneurship Development Programme (REDP) for adoption of better agricultural practices to be followed by the tea planters/processors at the household levels, *(iv)* Strengthening of co-operative structures in the districts, *(v)* setting up of co-operative tea societies of the planters, *(vi)* formation of SHG for small planters, and *(vii)* pooling of small holdings for joint farming, *(viii)* co-ordination among various agencies of the tea plantation, *(ix)* mechanical plucking (motorized plucking) may be adhered to wherever possible,

Future Potentials

Himachal tea industry has future potentials. The Govt. of Himachal Pradesh in consultation with the Council for Scientific and Industrial Research (CSIR), Himachal Pradesh Krishi Vishwa Vidyalaya and Institute of Himalayan Bio-resource Technology (IHBT) has identified 7700 ha. land in Chamba, Mandi and Kangra for propagating tea cultivation in new areas (traditional and non-traditional). About three parties from Assam have been short listed for allotting 1800 ha. of land to cultivate tea on modern lines for demonstrative effect on the other tea planters in the district. The modalities of the scheme are worked out by the Agricultural Department. The parties will be advised to set up their own processing factories in the area. IHBT and HPKVV are working out strategies to increase the production and productivity with latest research and development techniques. The Government of Himachal Pradesh has mooted the idea of tea tourism to construct guesthouses in the tea gardens to attract more guests in the area for increasing the tourist flow, which shall enhance the returns from the gardens. State Agricultural Department and HPKVV are increasing the number of demonstrative plots for providing necessary training exposure, education to the tea planters.

The Future Policy of the State Government

The future policies of the state governments must address the issues like: *(i)* induction of latest technologies, *(ii)* optimum utilization of land resources to encourage value addition, *(iii)* increase in employment opportunities in the tea production and processing sector and *(iv)* Extension of green cover on barren/fallow lands.

For popularizing tea in the market the State Government proposes better marketing techniques, attractive packing and sale through cooperative societies etc.

Policy Prescriptions

The following policy prescription have been suggested:

- Government has to take measures, which aim at reinstating the lost glory of this industry.
- One of the important initiatives that government has already taken is setting up of price stabilization fund of Rs. 500 crores for plantation sector; the fund will be focused to small growers.
- The sustenance and survival of tea industry is of critical importance for the nation. Therefore, multi-pronged strategy is required for rejuvenating the tea industry.
- Management of tea gardens is another area that needs to be looked into. For this there is need for quality up-gradation with ample vigor.
- Efforts of weeding out sub-standard tea from the system, caused a major over supply situation in the plain categories.
- In the North-Eastern region, plucking should be stopped in the first week of December to eliminate end-season-poor teas, while in South India, pruning cycle should be shortened to three years in mid-elevation estates and four years in high-elevation ones to ensure harvest of softer flushes.

It is advisable to complete the pruning work early in the season to keep May/June production under control when comparatively plainer teas are produced. In the small grower sector, plucking standard will have to improve drastically. Shear plucking may be the answer because judicious shearing during the cropping months will ensure a more acceptable standard of leaf than the longer plucking rounds.

Further auctioning companies should focus totally on servicing their clients instead of being competitor-oriented and they must set up their dialogue with the planters on market requirements.

There have been allegations of formation of cartels of multi-national companies keeping the price at low level. With the collapse of Soviet Union, India has to eye to other markets. Iraq has emerged as the faster growing market for Indian tea. The recent peace initiatives between India and Pakistan may help in Indian tea industry. Industry is looking forward for commercial exploitation of the same.

The more respectable and well established merchants-exporters have to play a significant role in servicing the buyers in various parts of the world and they should seek active support from the government for export promotion to select destination, i.e. CIS, West Asia, the U.K., Germany, Japan, etc. There is a limit to how much one can expand in the export market. Further the changes in the export market did not take place in one night. One must explore the new markets in this regard.

In the short-term the Tea Board needs to aggressively promote tea in the domestic market. The slight change in the promotion theme from health to fitness (e.g., 'Drink Tea and be Fit', 'Anytime is Tea Time' and so on) will appeal more to the younger generation. If domestic per capita consumption can be increased to 800/1000 gms., the tea will regain its glory. There is scope for increasing the intake of tea in other parts of the country as well. Uttar Pradesh, Madhya Pradesh, Bihar, Jharkhand and Andhra Pradesh, where per capita consumption is very low, could be targeted first.

The government wants the industry to take up the replanting of old tea gardens. Since this exercise has long gestation period and is very costly, the replanting work is going on at a very slow rate. It is estimated that by replanting, the average yield raised from 1,696 kgs per ha. at present to 2,881 kgs per ha. in West Bengal and from 1,522 kg to 2,228 kgs per ha. in Assam.

Conclusion

In the last few years there has been remarkable increase in the demand for organic tea. The organic tea commands a very hefty premium in the overseas market. This is one area where India can make a significant headway. The tea plantations in South India have already jumped on the bandwagon, contributing about 1 million tonne of organic tea of the total 3 million tonne per annum that is produced globally. The trend of producing organic tea has got a boost with the FAO taking initiative in providing financial assistance to the tea growers for converting chemical tea into organic tea. The Nilgiris Planters Association, Tamil Nadu has set the target to triple its organic tea production in the next two years. More and more plantations are converting to organic tea purely because of high price. The price difference between the normal tea and the organic tea is anywhere between 100 to 150 per cent. The price, which the grower can get for organic tea, ranges between Rs.200 and Rs.250 per kg of tea as against Rs.80 per kg for normal tea.

All this would require huge investment and the co-ordination among the government, Tea Board, tea growers, buyers and sellers. Tea Board has taken commendable initiatives towards marketing of Indian tea. Besides the national tea campaign 'Piyo More Chai', it is now eyeing to foreign market. Tea Board has planned to set up more than 20 Chai Bazars in different parts of the world. The first such Chai Bazar has already come up at London.

Recently a workshop on 12 November 2003 was organized at Dharamsala, Dist. Kangra for development of tea industry in the State and the then Hon'ble Agricultural Minister, Government of Himachal Pradesh kindly presided over the workshop. The workshop drew the comprehensive package. It is believed this will go a long way in accelerating the development of tea industry.

22

Small Tea Growers in Assam and North Bengal

SECTION I
Small Tea Growers in Assam

Small Tea Growers in Assam

Introduction

India is the world's largest producer, consumer and exporter of tea accounting for 30 per cent, 20 per cent and 11 per cent of global production, consumption and exports respectively. India has 112 thousand registered tea estates covering an area of 5,07,196 ha with estimated annual production of 840 million kgs in 2004. Small gardens (up to 10.12 ha) constitute 98.38 per cent of total tea estate, 16.92 per cent of total area and 16.21 per cent of total production.

Assam has 39390 registered tea gardens occupying an area of 2.67 lakh ha (53 per cent of area) with an annual production of 452 million kgs (55 per cent of total). Amongst them there are 30,174 small estates (84.64 per cent of the entire North Indian estates) cultivating 30,717 ha (74.13 per cent) and producing 49,487 kgs (75.26 per cent). Besides, tea industry provides employment to nearly 5.55 lakh work force. Though tea cultivation is spread throughout the estate, the major districts are Dibrugarh, Tinsukia, Jorhat, Golaghat,

Sibsagar, Darrang, Sonitpur and Cachar Valley. The average productivity of the estate is 1,850 kgs per ha and is at par with all India productivity at 1,865 kgs per ha. The highest productivity is observed in Darrang (1,984 kg per ha.) and lowest in Karbi Anglong (866 kg per ha). Tea cultivation in small holdings in Assam ranges from 0.13 to 3.0 ha or more are spread over almost all the districts. However, the highest concentration is in the 5 districts viz. Dibrugarh, Tinsukia, Sivsagar, Jorhat and Golaghat.

Concept of Small Tea Cultivation

The concept of small tea cultivation in home stead gardens and unutilised land along with other crops to sell the green leaf to the existing big factories for enhancing farm income was initiated during the seventies by the then Janata Government in Assam. Encouraged by the Government

Patronage a few farmers of erstwhile Sibsagar district initiated tea cultivation in their high land ranging from 0.13 hectare to 3 hectare. During the end of eighties the Department of Tea Husbandry of Assam Agriculture Industry surveyed the possibility of growing tea in small scale and Advisory Cell was established to promote small scale tea cultivation by providing technical know-how. In the meanwhile, the formation of all Assam Small Tea Growers Association during 1987 was another landmark for extension of Small Tea Cultivation in Assam. In 1991, the Tea Board of India approved the proposal of the Agriculture University to provide financial support to the Advisory Cell of the Department of Tea Husbandry and Technology and the Cell was reconstituted as "Small Tea Growers Advisory Programme" to the broad mandate. Apart from Self Employment the cultivation of tea has opened a wide vista of business opportunities by providing not only indirect employment but also creating a sound base for farm income. In a nutshell tea cultivation could act as a catalyst for the overall economic changes in the rural scenario of Assam especially in tea growing districts. There are 38,393 small tea growers in the State. The Small holdings are spread over all the districts , however concentration is in the five upper Assam districts viz. Dibrugarh, Tinsukia, Sibsagar, Jorhat and Golaghat.

Socio-economic Profile of the Selected Borrowers

Small Tea Growers of Assam have been categorised into 6 socio-economic background viz. *(i)* Sedimentary cultivators, *(ii)* Educated rural youth, *(iii)* Educated urban youth, *(iv)* In service personnel, *(v)* Tea garden workers/supervisors, and *(vi)* Sleeping growers.

Field Practices and Cultural Operations

(i) *Climate and Soil*—In Brahmaputra valley, tea is cultivated on flat lands at an alleviation of 50-120 msl. In Barack valley, tea is grown in small hillocks and to some extent plains adjoining the hillocks. The alluvial soils are generally deep fertile, have good water logging capacity and respond well to manure. The annual rainfall of the State varies from 210-290 cm.

(ii) *Variety*—The small tea growers are generally using a mixture of clonal plants and seedlings of seed origin. They also use approved planting materials recommended by the Tea Board.

(iii) *Land preparation and planting*—Deep Cross Ploughing followed by harrowing and levelling is done and small drains are dug as per specification (45 cm x 30 cm) at 105 cm spacing between drains. The rehabilitation crops are also sown with same spacing as that of tea after 18-24 months. The planting density varies from 14,000 to 17,000 bushes per hectare. About 2 kg of farm yard manure, 30 gm SSP, 30 gm rock phosphate and 2 gm thymate are mixed with excavated soil and the pits are refilled with natural compaction.

(iv) *Manuring and Fertiliser*—The young tea is manured with 10:5:15 NPK mixture. The matured tea crops of more than 5 years of age is given fertiliser in the ratio of 110 to 140 kg: 30 to 35: 110 to 140 kg per

hectare of NPK. Generally, ring method is adopted for manuring and fertiliser. However, in some cases broadcasting method is also applied.

(v) *Shade*—Conventionally, tea is grown under shade. These shade trees help in regulating the temperature and humidity at the bush level and minimising the loss of water through evaporation and transpiration.

(vi) *Pruning*—The bushes are pruned to maintain the desired shape and height in the plantation, revitalise the vegetative vigour and attain good yield of crops. Pruning is carried out in pre-monsoon or post monsoon period since adequate soil moisture is pre requisite. Generally, 4 year pruning cycle is followed in Assam. The pruning cycle followed by small tea growers is as follows: *(a)* 1st year : Prune at 30 cm and centre, *(b)* 2nd year: Cut across at 75 cm and recentre, *(c)* 3rd year: Prune 28-40 cm/level skiff at 60 cm, *(d)* 4th year: Prune at 50 cm, *(e)* 5th year: Deep prune/top prune at 35 cm, and *(f)* 6th year: Unprune

(vii) *Weed control*—Weeds are responsible for considerable loss to the crop. It is estimated that dicot weeds can cause 12per cent loss in the crop while grasses are responsible for 20per cent crop loss. Weed control is achieved by use of paraquat dichloride, 2,4 - D and glyphosphate. Application of weedicides in different doses during 3-5 years and hand weeding for 2 years are also made to control weeds.

(viii) *Pest control*—Tea is prone to attack by various pests like mites, caterpillars, thrips, etc. Mites are controlled by spraying Acaricite with water and other pests are controlled by spraying thiodan or ekalux, etc. Fungal and bacterial diseases are controlled by spraying fungicides.

(ix) *Irrigation*—There is definite increase in crop yield due to irrigation either by sprinklers or by drip system. Some small tea growers are nowadays adopting sprinkler irrigation to increase the green leaf yield during the dry period. It is done in the morning or night.

(x) *Drainage*—The drains of 2 ft wide and 3 ft deep are sprayed over the area of 40 ft intervals along with the slope of the land.

(xi) *Harvesting and post harvest management*—Harvesting of tea involves regular removal of young shoots comprising an apical bud and two or three leaves immediately below it. The shoots arising out of the sticks (frame) of pruned bushes are called primaries. Tea shoots are plucked in the months of mid February to mid December and plucking round (the number of days between two successive plucking) of 4-14 days is followed by small tea growers and 7 day plucking round is most common. Harvesting is carried out when the shoots attain maximum weight without compromising the quality.

Infrastructure Support

The Small Tea Growers Advisory Programme in the Assam Agriculture University, funded by Tea Board, impart required training and provide technical inputs free of cost. Tea Board has recently sanctioned another small Tea Advisory Cell at Tocklai Experimental Station for the benefit of small tea growers. Further, small tea growers have informal access of information from the big gardens in the organised sector, located nearer to them. For processing green leaf there are sufficient number of bought leaf factories operating in the district. Besides, most of the gardens in the organised sectors have their own factory.

Credit flow

Out of the farmers visited only a few small tea growers had availed of loan from banks. All others raised plantation with their own funds or borrowed from relatives. Many of them did not approach bank for loan with the apprehension that they will have to waste their time running after bank officials without any effective results. It was learnt that most of the tea growers did not have patta land. Further, in many cases title was not clear which was a handicap in obtaining loan. The growth of small tea sector has slowed down on account of limited availability of further suitable land as major portion of the land has already been put under cultivation. Further, as most of the plantations are 8 to 10 years old, there is hardly any possibility of rejuvenation or replantation. Requirement of loans for such operations may arise after another 5-6 years. A field study reveals that farmers expressed their requirement for working capital for purchase of fertiliser , pesticides and payment of wages including advance during puja season.

Inputs (Raw materials) and Output (Production)

Input like planting materials, fertilisers, pesticides, insecticides, etc. are locally available. Generally, small growers purchase fertilisers, etc. from the wholesalers in nearby towns and also purchase clones from big estates or private nurseries because of low requirement. Average yield reported by the farmers ranged from 1200 kg to 2000 kg green leaf per bigha which is equivalent to 1850 to 3000 kg made tea per hectare.

Cost of Cultivation

The farmers have reported that average cost of plantation up to 4 year is Rs 76,750 while it was Rs.45,000 per acre in the first year.

Marketing

All the small tea growers sell their green leaf either to nearby big gardens or to bought leaf factories and average price varies from Rs. 6.70 to Rs. 9.35 for depending upon the quality. It was learnt that during 1998-99, the green leaf was maximum at Rs. 11.50 to Rs. 12.00 per kg. and in some cases it was Rs. 13.00 per kg.

The major problems in marketing of green leaf is the poor handling in transportation, etc. The factory owners buy on 'first come first served' basis or at competitive price and growers had to be at the receiving end.

The situation has now been solved through the price sharing scheme of Tea Board. The scheme states that the growers must be paid minimum @ 60per cent of the average auction price upto Rs. 70 per kg of made tea. Beyond this, if auction price is more, then the amount should be shared @ 50:50 basis.

Problems of Small Tea Growers

(i) *Unorganised Growth*—The production of green leaf from small tea growers is not matched with the demand for tea market. Further, the production of green leaf is not properly channelised to tea processing facilities. In many cases, unsuitable land and marginal lands were utilised for cultivation of tea affecting the quality as well the productivity of the plantations.

(ii) *Land Patta and Title*—Most of the small tea gardens established on government land, ceiling surplus land, grazing land or annual patta land are deprived of being registered with tea board. As a result they could not avail the benefit of plantation subsidy scheme and the bank loan. Although, there is a provision for issuing provisional registration to the growers with annual patta, normal land, etc. on the basis of certificate of enjoyment of holding for tea plantation ,the revenue authorities are making in ordinate delay in this regard.

(iii) *Technical Backup*—There is a vide technological gap between the trained and untrained small tea growers. Small tea growers may be imparted training in certain areas like drainage, manuring, weed/pest control, pruning, etc. This may help in enhancing the productivity of tea crop.

(iv) *Ecological Imbalance*—The mushrooming growth of tea plantation has reported a large scale ecological problem by way of clearing village wood lots. The commercial forestry (bamboo plantation, etc.) has vanished and crops like orange, pineapple, sugarcane, citronella have been replaced by tea. The indiscriminate use of pesticides and agro chemicals have brought in havoc to river and waterline population.

(v) *Finance*—About 98per cent of small tea cultivation has been developed through self finance or finance arranged by growers themselves from informal sources. In absence of financial back up most of the plantation could not be developed on scientific lines.

(vi) *Marketing*—In the absence of well knit marketing channel for the produce of small tea growers, the term is ,many a time, dictated by factory owners and growers are at the receiving end. The problem is aggravated due to the fact that some growers tend to supply inferior leaf.

(vii) *Uncareful handling*—The growers and the transport agents do not appreciate the utmost need of maintaining the ultimate product quality to realise better option market and take little care to maintain high standard in parking and avoid damage in handling and transport.

Observations and Recommendations

(a) Observations

The following observations based on the data collected from the sample estates are given below:

- The small tea sector has come up in the districts of Assam since the last 15-20 years and presently contributes 25-30per cent of the State Tea production. The sector suffered due to recession in green leaf price during the last four years commencing from 2000.
- The scientists in the Tea Husbandry department of Assam Agriculture University opined that the operational cost of production in a matured plantation would not be more than Rs. 5.00 per kg.
- Due to unscientific cultivation, price fluctuations, etc. small tea growers are facing difficulty in repayment of loans.

- Mushrooming growth of tea plantation has brought in large scale ecological problem.
- Although, a Small Tea Growers Advisory Programme has been set up in Assam Agriculture University at the instance of Tea Board, it can hardly meet the requirements of large number of growers, primarily due to inadequate staff strength.
- The benefits of Tea Board Plantation Subsidy Scheme, Price Stabilisation Scheme of Government of India etc. have hardly been gone to the growers due to defect in the prevailing system of land ownership and timely inaction of Government.
- At present, agents are involved in transporting of green leaf from farmers to bought leaf factories in many areas. This has resulted in reduction of net gain to the growers and quality of made tea is also not maintained.

(b) Recommendations

The following recommendations are listed below:

- The integration of small tea growers areawise under a single management to synchronise farm activities to the tune of market requirement.
- Setting up of multi-point advisory centres at different locations is essential to encourage small tea growers with proper scientific and technical back up.
- Arrangements for training on scientific and cultural operations as well as organisation of awareness camps
- Maintenance of ecological balance through utilising high lands for tea plantation and not destroying village woodlots.
- Developing viable mixed cropping system to be adopted by small growers.
- Carrying out research on developing a prototype processing unit capable of manufacturing small quantity of green leaf.
- Streamlining the marketing system and developing market linkages in a scientific and systematic manner.

- Allowing only registered agents to transport and supply green leaves to factory and implementation of price sharing scheme during slumps in the market.

Integration of small farming units and its attachment to a single processing unit for sale of green leaf.

- Marketing of small tea growers production under a separate logo or brand as in case of Amul or NOGA (Nagpur Orange Growers Association).
- Strict watch on bought leaf factories for improving the quality of made tea.
- Facilitating term loan/working capital loan for expanding existing gardens.
- Creating better awareness among small tea growers about the credit facilities, subsidies and other functional schemes of the Tea Board.
- Before sanctioning any fresh loans, adequate care to be taken to verify land records, technical feasibility of the land, marketing facility, tie up arrangement with leaf factories and proper verification of the application.

Policy Issues

- There is a need to frame Government policies for allotment of land pattas to those farmers taking up tree plantation on government/quasi-government lands to enable the farmers to register with the Tea Board.
- Government may issue land holding certificates to the effect that the farmer is a small tea grower having holding with government land/annual patta land under his possession so as to enable him to get provisional registration with the Tea Board. All these will help farmers to avail of benefits of the price subsidy scheme.
- Government may strengthen the mechanism for price fixation for the small tea growers .
- For ensuring quality tea from the small tea growers sector, an effective co-ordination mechanism amongst small tea growers, green leaf transporter and bought leaf factory may be evolved.

- The existing Directorate of Tea, Government of Assam may be entrusted with the task of co-ordinating the entire activities of the small tea sector in Assam.
- The Small Tea Growers may take up organic tea cultivation in a later stage after gaining experience in tea cultivation for few years.
- Setting up of tea nurseries with technical support from Assam Agricultural University (AAU) and financial support from banks may be considered at different places in the district. Further, streamlining of small tea growers advisory programme by AAU may be strengthened.
- Tea Board may redesign its schemes to make it accessible to the farmer.
- Improve co-ordination among various segments of industry, Government (Central & State), University/ Research Organisations, Financial Institutions, Tea Associations/Tea Factories, etc. for better quality tea and stabilisation of falling prices.

SECTION II
Factors to The Bitter Taste of Tea Brew

Over the last few years, the tea industry of our country has been passing through a bad phase in terms of very poor price realization in the domestic market and drastic fall of export quantum. In effect, many medium and small-sized tea plantation units in the corporate and proprietory sector have become financially crippled, reached at shut down point. But this situation has not occurred suddenly, nor caused by any isolated factor. An attempt, however, has been made to diagnose in brief the contributing factors to the bitter taste of our brew with special reference to that of Assam. The factors include: *(i)* The Market, *(ii)* The Plantation Working : human element and its contribution—the weather/climate, the infrastructure at grass root level, *(iii)* The ethos of an 100-year old industry, *(iv)* Exploitation by surrounding populace of garden residents and *(v)* Barriers/mindsets to improving the lot of garden residents.

The Market: A recent study of FMCG in the rural area

reveals that there has been an increase in the tea consumption. Also there are pointers that speciality teas are increasingly in demand in US, UK, and some other countries. Quality is what the consumer desires and at a price he is willing to afford. The problem which lies here is not that our teas/Assam teas are poor but they are relatively high priced – because of the inbuilt high costs at which they are produced. The buyers of our teas are moving away as teas commensurate with prices is available elsewhere. For, our teas to compete with others in the market means that all those in the industry have to compete with those at people level too in order to finalise a good product acceptable.

At Plantation: Now what is stopping us from producing such teas that sell well? The path travelled has shaped the current position. Hence, it would be in place to admit that there has been imperfect congruence in activities leading to finished product.

a) Under the present and as it ought to have never been that tea is an industry. An indepth look will reveal that all estates function at varying level of costs, yields, employment, productivity, etc. which in turn is based on an individual estate's efficiency or inefficiency. Thus, the working becomes different though all input costs remain same is now being seen as producing the results.

b) The cost of wages, salaries at the garden level should be at the unit's performance levels with an inbuilt mechanism of being linked to productivity/ marketability of the final product.

c) *The Worker:* Not enough to talk about quality when absenteeism takes a heavy toll on harvest, also on other timebound agricultural practices—like planting, manuring, application of weedicides etc. Tea is an agriculture and time bound product but most gardens fail to conform without at additional costs. Unfortunately vested interests have made it so that as it they are concerned about the worker and foisted on them negativities which have become a boomerang.

d) *The Staff*: They are far from exploited category and could do with soul searching and come out with positive and constructive ideas suited to their individual dilemma or may even highlight methods and means to improve couple of properties which are now awaiting change of hands.

e) The Management: Highest degree of dedication and integrity is necessary not only for the property but all round. In challenges they should look for opportunities as we find ourselves in a moment of history where we can do our bit too.

The worker, staff and management have to work in tandem and not confront each other. These are the valuable intangible assets that must be seen as they are and understood before one strategises. Could we possibly bet on these assets to deliver even at the cost of disregarding the golden rules—with training anyone can do it or know that there is a limit to helping those who do not help themselves.

The Climate: Whilst we suffer the adverse weather conditions which has also, to some extent, been brought about by man himself, it is a paradox that the rest of the country farmers get relief and succour while the tea industry has still to fulfil obligations in respect of employment.

Infrastructure at Ground Level: At the local level each property is operating in economies with salient institutional and infrastructural deficiencies. Assam State Electricity Board (ASEB) has to be paid their pound of flesh (and that pound is the heaviest in the whole country) whilst gardens are to procure HSD etc. for generators to run the factory. A lot of gardens continue to pay for natural gas while having to use TDO. There are many such hurdles. Even petty nuisances and thefts and land encroachments etc., because of their magnitude, are no longer to be looked away from unless at a cost of the gardens.

Ethos: One should seriously think that this is an industry over 100 years old. The sense of urgency displayed at present is an illustration, albeit painful as one waits and wishes for the dark clouds to part or that somebody else will do something to alleviate our miseries. Human relations are sadly not what is generally assumed to be.

Exploitation: Exploitation of garden residents and garden areas is very common today as one sees many money lenders on pay-days touts even collect a/c payee cheques of workers, their paddy-lands are virtually taken over and they are the single largest consumer of neighbouring bootleggers. Cattle from the neighbouring areas are put into tea areas frequently. Of course, there is no limit to number of bushes and shade trees that stolen each day. Local quacks flourish, illegal abortions are performed on women and under-age girls.

Barriers/Mindsets: These cause an immense hardship to those who live in and by the garden. Each body wants something without an obligation to reciprocate. Education is seemingly more of a farce as it hardly brings forth positive attributes in individual. Various government schemes in the area make use of the garden residents to suit others' interests. It has been observed that many a politician raises aspirations sky-high without asking for contributory efforts and promises all kinds of freebies at election times when they distribute spurious alcohol and then talk about health etc. Large families and minor marriages are encouraged. Such seemingly small things are only hardening an already outdated and injurious mind-set.

SECTION III
Why Fortunes of Tea Industry Have Plummeted?

In recent years whenever a section of the tea producing fraternity meets, all discussions centre around the deplorable plight of the tea industry and the incidence of fiscal levies imposed by the Government. The question, therefore, arises "who is responsible for bringing about this state of affairs". The answer is the tea producers themselves aided by faulty planning of inefficient, and indifferent Government in place from time to time whose objects are given shape through the Tea Board. The major buyers are neither free from blame.

Tea Industry does not have Direct Relationship: The tea industry which started operating on a more organized scale after 1860s, has been easy-going from inception. Even today, a sizeable number of tea produces ignore the threat posed by competitive beverages—supported by aggressive publicity to wean away consumers. Auctions were considered to be the most suitable mechanism for disposal of a large volume of tea. As a result, the tea industry did not have direct relationship with the consumer and remained ignorant of the latter's drinking habits and attitudes. Disposal of the orthodox varieties, which formed the entire production in the early years, was not much of hassle as buyers were less quality-conscious. The advent of Legg-Cut and then its improvised version, CTC (crush, tear, curl) manufacture in the post-war period prompted the producers to gradually switch to the latter varieties to increase harvest (CTC tea gives more cups) and attendant higher returns to abort the rising cost of production. Manufacture of orthodox teas started dwindling from 1960 onwards.

Emergence of Other Countries as Major Suppliers and Improper Use of Funds for Development of Tea Industry: The emergence of Sri Lanka as a major supplier of tea (with lower cost of production) to the global market in 1965 found India's share of world consumption declining from 45 per cent in 1958 to 18 per cent in 2006. In subsequent period, Kenya became a sizeable exporter followed by other East African and Asian countries including China. This situation limited prospects of common tea from India which account for over 60 per cent of country's production. The situation was compounded in 1990s by the uncertainty of the Indian tea's over-dependent Russian market following disintegration of the USSR. What went wrong on the Indian scene? Various reasons are cited and it would be prudent to highlight one of the aspects. A spokesman of the Kolkata-based United Bank of India which has fairly large accounts of tea producers in North-East India indicated that the funds allotted to the borrowers against hypothecation of tea crop were not being properly utilized towards development (not applicable to all) of the respective tea estates. In course of time, the lended sum turned out to be unproductive or became non-performing assets, as known in banking parlance. When the cumulative liabilities of the producers mounted, the banks exerted pressure on the former to sell the properties to clear the dues which ran into crores of rupees.

Lack of Professionalism, Govt. Policies etc.: A number of these tea estate owners who inherited the properties from their ancestors were neither professionals nor made any effort to pay the debts even during the 'tea boom'. Their tea estates lacked proper supervision in field as well as in factory, thefts were common, yields declined and the trend was more or less in evidence in large number of tea estates in North East India. Unfortunately the Tea Board and other Tea Industry bodies have no authority to prevent the majority of weak estates from passing into incompetent hands since the law of the land does not permit. The buyers or precisely the fly-by-night operators tended to maximize and quicken returns on investments and spurted increase in crop by whatsoever means without improvement in quality. A glut in supply resulted—making the prospective buyers selective. On the other hand, the Government of India's policy of allowing cheap imports from Indonesia, Taiwan and other countries for use in blends to bolster exports spell disaster for the common and medium Indian tea producer. The landed costs of imported tea (after paying relative duty of 100 per cent) worked out to Rs.46/47 per kg.

Mushrooming of Tea Factories: To combat the spiraling costs of production, a few tea estate owners and some newcomers set up bought leaf factories which mushroomed all over the tea producing regions in India. With lower overheads/expenses and little statutory commitments, owners of bought leaf factories were able to sell 'made tea' below Rs. 40 per kg which is below cost of production of over 95 per cent of the established tea estates in India. These teas despite being devoid of quality attracted the price-conscious Indian consumer to the detriment of common and medium tea estates. Although official figures of production from bought tea leaf factories are not available, reliable sources indicate this to be in excess of 100 million kgs.

Equation of Supply and Demand of Tea: The equation of supply and demand plays a role in determination of prices but when a buyer gets tea @ Rs. 40 per kg., he would be wary of raising the value for a lot bereft of quality unless a state of urgency forces him to make purchases at higher prices. In the process, the established tea producer suffered—as the value of all categories of tea tumbled due to presence of sizeable quantity of common and medium varieties throughout the year.

SECTION IV

Indian Tea Planters for Development of Assam Tea Industry

Most of the tea production in Assam is done by large companies, which were originally British owned. Since promulgation of the Foreign Exchange Management Act, all foreign companies have had to become Indianised, with the foreign company being allotted shares in the converted Indian company. However, although their production base was small many local Indian tea planters have made significant contributions to the growth of the tea industry in Assam in particular and to Assamese society in general. The scions of many planting families such as Jyoti Prasad Agarwala and Parvati Prasad Barua enriched the cultural life of Assam with their songs and writings. Others like Karmavir Nabin Chandra Bordoloi, Bishnuram Medhi, Kuladhar Chaliha, Jadav Prasad Chaliha, Bimala Prasad Chaliha and Prafulla Chandra Borooah jumped into the freedom struggle and suffered imprisonment and contributed their mite to the cause. Still other like Hanumanbux Kanoi and Murlidhar Jalan donated large sums for noble causes. Nilambar Dutta and Rohini Baruah of Dibrugarh and Bishnu Ram Barooah, Prasanna Baruah of Jorhat, Ghanashyam Barua of Golaghat and Someswar Baruah of Tinsukia were all philanthropic gentlemen who gave freely and worked for the benefit of the people.

Role of Producers' Associations and Trade Unions: All tea estates are members of one or other of the five Producers' Associations namely Indian Tea Associations, Tea Association of India, Assam Tea Planters' Association, Bharatiya Cha Parishad and North East Tea Association. They are all members of the Consultative Committee of Plantation Associations (CCPA) which is an umbrella organization. The responsibility of the CCPA is to represent the problems of the tea industry before the Assam and Central Govts. The CCPA also will participate in negotiations with workers' unions in respect of wage fixations and other demands. There are three major trade unions in the tea industry in Assam and they are all affiliated to the INTUC. These are Assam Cha Karmachari Sangha, Assam Cha mazdoor Sangha and Cachar Shramic Union. There are also other unions affiliated to AITUC and

Hind Mazdoor Sabha but their membership is very small. Now a days a few number of trade unions have also emerged. CCPA therefore sits at the negotiating table only with the INTUC affiliated unions for discussions on industry wise issues. Over decades of having worked together for the common good of the industry, a harmonious relationship based on mutual trust and respect for one another has grown between the producers' associations and trade unions. Industrial unrest in Assam tea industry is very rare indeed.

Workers are paid their wages or salaries in cash and kinds. Wages in kind include among others subsidized rations, cooking fuel, dry tea, protective clothing, firewood, blankets and chappals. Wages and salaries are fixed and agreements are signed bilaterally for three year periods. Currently, in Assam Valley the daily cash wages on an average are Rs. 100 for both male and female workers. For the junior most clerk in the lowest rung of the scale working in a tea garden having less than 250 acres under tea the cash component of his remuneration is Rs. 4000 per month. This, however, is revised time to time.

Implementation of Various Acts and Their Impact on Tea Earnings

All tea estates over 5 hectares in area and employing over 15 workers come under the purview of the Plantation Labour Act, 1951, the provisions of which the estate managements are obliged to implement. It is the responsibility of the Chief Inspector of Plantation, under the Dept. of Labour to monitor and enforce these provisions. In addition, those tea estates having tea factories also come under the Factories Act, 1948. Some other important statutes governing the tea industry in Assam are: *(i)* Provident Fund and Pension Fund Scheme Act, 1955, *(ii)* Payment of Wages Act, 1948, *(iii)* Payment of Bonus Act, 1965, iv) Payment of Gratuity Act, 1972, *(iv)* Workmen's Compensation Act, 1923, *(v)* The Assam Taxation (on Specified Lands) Act, 1990, vi) Industrial Disputes Act, 1947, *(vii)* Assam Land Ceiling Act, 1972, *(viii)* Equal Remuneration Act, 1976, *(ix)* Minimum Wages Act, 1948.

Earnings of Tea Industry Taxed by Central and State Governments: The earnings of the tea industry is taxed both by the Central and State Govts. sixty per cent of the income is considered as Agricultural income and it is taxed by the State Govt.'s Agricultural income Tax Act. The balance 40 per cent is considered to be Business Income and it is taxed under the Central Income Tax Act, 1939, Currently, for companies, the rate of tax under Assam Agricultural Income Tax Act is 60 per cent and that under the Central Income Tax Act is 46 per cent. Thus a tea company in Assam has to bear a total tax burden of 54.4 per cent. For all other industries in India the tax burden is only 46 per cent i.e. 8.4 per cent lower. Considering all taxes and levies in Assam, tea company has to pay 65.70 per cent whereas other industries pay only 51.75 per cent i.e. the tea company pays nearly 14 per cent more.

Bypassing the Auction System: The teas produced in the estates have been traditionally sold in one or other of the 8 auction centres in India or in London. However, lately many producers are bypassing the auction system and selling their produce directly to buyers all over the country, either in bulk or in pockets. In order to limit these so called "private sales", Govt. has promulgated the Tea (Marketing) Control order, 1984, which required that 75 per cent of the tea produced, must be sold in one of the auction centres. Concessions were made for teas exported and/or sold in packets in the domestic market and instant tea. The tea auction system has been honed to perfection over decades of operation. The Guwahati Auction Centre was started at the initiative of late Bimala Prasad Chaliha, the then Chief Minister and himself a tea planter, in the face of strong and determined opposition from the Kolkata lobby. It has brought immense benefit to the State by generating direct and indirect employment for thousands of people and also by ensuring safe and quick disposal of Assam teas thereby improving the cash flow position of the planters. Also arrival of teas at destinations outside the State was much quicker since it was no longer necessary to go via Kolkata. Guwahati is the only auction centre in the country that was started by the State Govt. All the other centres were started by the traders. It is a matter of great pride that in short span of three decades Guwahati has managed to become the largest auction centre in the world for CTC teas, handling over 200 million kgs.

SECTION V
Problems of Tea Industry

Refusal of Local People to Work in the Tea Plantation as Wage Earners: When the British first started tea cultivation in Assam, the local people refused to work in the plantations as daily wage earners. They were too proud to work as coolies and in any case there was enough for them to do to look after their own cultivations and properties. Indentured labour, therefore, had to be brought from the states of Orissa, Bihar and Madhya Pradesh and Andhra Pradesh. Although it was intended that these labourers would be sent back to their homes after they had served their terms, many stayed back in Assam and settled here. Their descendants now form a sizeable segment of the State's population. They are collectively known as Tea Tribes. Although these people still live mainly in or around tea estates where they work, many of them have assimilated into Assamese society. A past Chief Secretary of Assam was from this community. So is Shri Pawan Singh Ghatowar, who was the then Minister of State for Health, Government of India. They have become a politically powerful force and no State Govt. can afford to ignore them. For decades, in every Govt. in Assam the Labour Minister has been from this community.

High Cost of Production, Low Productivity and Labour etc.: As regards the problems of the tea industry in Assam, the biggest one is the high cost of production. This is due to various factors such as low productivity of land and labour, high cost of labour and inputs, unremunerative prices and high taxation. All these resulted in low retention of profits and thereby ploughing back of funds to the desired extent for modernization, extension and improvement of the properties is difficult. Without improvements, returns are not remunerative. So it is a vicious circle.

Blocking of Natural Water Courses: Silting up of the bed of the Brahmaputra and other major rivers coupled with blocking of natural watercourse by human habitation is creating problems in drainage of water from the tea fields during the rains. The tea plant cannot tolerate water logging for long periods. So any factor which hinders quick drainage of water will result first in loss in productivity and if uncorrected, in due course, death and abandonment.

Insecurity and Helplessness: The major problem of the tea industry is the feeling of insecurity and helplessness in the face of terrorism, which the workers and executives in the remote areas have to face. With improvement of the law and order position and formation of the Tea Security Force situation is improving. Not very long time ago, every single day in the tea gardens was a nightmare.

Poor Infrastructure: Poor infrastructure in the tea areas is another major problem. Maintenance of roads and bridges and all other public utilities such as power and telecommunications, where this exist, is abysmally poor. Load shedding, low voltage and line tripping are regular features. The gardens have to run their stand-by gensets for long periods and this adds to costs. All these points stated are a direct result of the total apathy towards the fate of this industry and a mistaken belief in Govt. circles is that it is rich or capable enough to look after itself. May be this state of affairs has been brought on by the insular and highbrow attitude of the earlier British and Indian planters. That is the situation today.

However, unless some thing drastic happens, in spite of the various problems with which the industry in Assam is besotted, future prospects in the short and medium terms appear to be good. This is because of mainly three reasons. Firstly, demand for high quality Assam tea will always remain both inside and outside the country. Secondly, internal demand for the commodity is rising @ approx. 5 per cent whereas increase in production is only to the extent of 3 per cent. Demand is outstripping supply and all indications are that this will continue. Thirdly, tea is the cheapest drink next to water. It is the poor man's drink. India being a developing country with bulk of its population having low purchasing power, there is no fear that people will divert to other beverages, such as coffee, soft drinks or beer, as is happening in many countries. There is no threat of competition. At present in true sense of the term, tea is facing competition with other soft drinks like Thumps-up, etc.

SECTION VI
Welcome Phenomenon

Unemployed Youth Growing Teas: One would like to mention a most welcome phenomenon of the recent past. Within the past thirty years many unemployed educated youths have taken to cultivate tea on any suitable land they could occupy whether it belonged to their families or to the government. Vast tracks of vacant Govt. land in Pengari near Digboi, Sonari Sub-Division, Golaghat District, Tingkhong in Dibrugarh District were occupied by these people and tea plantations started. Although this may seem to be highly irregular, Assam will certainly stand to benefit in the following ways:

- By bringing into cultivation these lands which have been lying vacant for decades, they have been saved from degradation,
- There was every likelihood that these lands would eventually have fallen into the hands of aliens.
- A large number of young persons have found productive employment thereby easing, however slightly the unemployment problem and preventing onset of frustrations with its terrible repercussions, at least for these people.
- Their actions contributed to increase in the production of the State's wealth. The table below gives the details of Assam:

No. of Small Growers, Area, Production, Value of Tea during 2006

Sr.	*Parameter @*	*No.*
1	No. of small growers	35,600
2	Total grant Area in hectare (ha)	36,228
3	Area under tea cultivation in ha	1,78,000
4	Production during 2005-06 in Kgs 58,386 kgs of made tea	2,33,534 kgs of green leaf or
5	Value of Tea in Rs crore	5.83
6	Unit Price (Rs./Kg)	100.00

@ *Note:* Estimated on the basis of trend

Source: Tea Statistics various Issues, Tea Board, Kolkata.

It is observed from the above table that Assam constitutes 80.72 per cent and 32.26 per cent of small tea growers in North India and All India respectively. As regards production, Assam represents 71.38 per cent of area under tea of small growers in North India and 37.12 per cent of all India. A small tea grower of Assam plays a significant role in production of tea. They contribute 58,386 kgs of made tea against the estimated production of tea grown by small growers in North India 75,951 kgs (76.87 per cent) and all India 164213 kgs (35.53 per cent). Most interestingly, average yield of tea for small growers of Assam stood at 1611 kgs per ha where as it was 1450 kgs per ha in North India and 1713 kgs per ha in All India. Thus, the scope of small tea growers needs more focused attention. Although, GoI, Tea Board, TRA are taking active initiatives in this regard, all out efforts are to be strengthened so as to make the small tea growers as viable proposition by extension services, dissemination of information from lab to field etc.

Pioneer in Scientific Research

Assam is the pioneer in scientific research on all aspects of tea production. The first research station in the world exclusively devoted to tea research was set up in Tocklai near Jorhat in 1911. The large increase in productivity in tea gardens is because of the sincere and hard work put in under difficult conditions by countless scientists at Tocklai. The benefits of their early research have been enjoyed by tea industries not only in India but all over the world. Tocklai Experimental Station is forging ahead with more scientific research to enable planters to meet the challenge of the next century. The target set for production by the year 2010 was initially 1100 million kgs for meeting domestic requirements and to maintain our present share of the export market. It has now been scaled down to 1000 million kgs. Given the funds, facilities and impetus in the form of remunerative prices the industry should be in a position to some close, if not research the revised target. Many other areas such as the technical aspects of tea growing, manufacture and sale are to be relooked.

Table 1: Production, Export & Internal Retention of Indian Tea during 1993 to 2006

(Thousand Kgs.)

North India (Production)	*1993*	*2003*	*2006*
Assam Valley	354908	409076	428270
Cachar	48039	55607	51614
Total Assam	402947	464683	479884
West Bengal	168022	182200	192737
Tripura	5529	6729	7094
Others (Bihar, UP etc.)	22223	2602	3168
Total North India	**578721**	**656214**	**682883**
South India Production			
Tamil Nadu	108652	125702	140053
Kerala	66691	73935	78116
Karnataka	3999	4490	5400
Total South India	**179342**	**204127**	**223569**

The data presented in the table showed that production of tea increased from 758 m kgs in 1993 to 906 m kg in 2006 i.e. 19 per cent. The increase in production was mainly due to increase in yield from 1650 kg/ha to 1725 kg/ha. The exports are, however, hovering around 200 m kgs. Thus special efforts are to be strengthened to increase the exports either by evolving more and more markets, introducing new/further value added products and aggressive marketing. Duties and Taxes: The following duties and taxes are levied by the State government on tea industry: State Sale Tax - *(i)* 2 per cent Assam sale tax is levied on tea sold in Guwahati with effect from 28.03.1989, *(ii)* Tea bought for export in Guwahati Auction are exempted from this tax and *(iii)* 7 per cent Assam Sale tax is levied on private sales within Assam on purchase outside auction.

Assam Taxation (on specified lands), Amendment Act 1994—Taxation at the rate of 18 paise for every kilogram of green tea with effect from 15.5.1994 and 30 paise for every kilogram of green leaf produced on Assam valley is levied. This rate is 27 paise for every kilogram of green leaf produced in Cachar.

SECTION VII

Small Tea Growers in North Bengal

Tea is one of the major plantation crops of the world. In India, tea cultivation on a large scale started with lot of inputs like huge finance, large area, imported labour, big organization and management facilities etc. during the colonial period. However, small tea plantations (STPs) are of recent origin, because the large tea plantations already occupied whatever suitable land was available for tea cultivation. These can be called the traditional areas of the tea plantation whereas the STPs have emerged beyond the traditional tracts of tea cultivation. Small Growers with little finance have developed the STPs.

Definition of Small Tea Growers

Area and Crop Produced: The Tea Board of India defines "Small Grower' as having an area of plantation with 10.12 hectares or 25 acres of land. The West Bengal Land Reforms Office considers 9.79 hectares or 24.20 acres of land as smallholding and explains small tea growers as 'Tea Cultivator'. According to the Tea Board, there were only 37 Small Growers occupying an area of 155 hectares as on 31st December, 1995 in North Bengal. It may be mentioned that data do not represent the ground situation, since most of the STPs in North Bengal are not registered with the Tea Board. The number of such STPs is not incorporated in any record—both Government and other organizations. Such plantations have been increasing day by day in the region. Today, there are about 800 STPs occupying an area of 6600 hectares producing near about 90million kgs of green leaf every year (*Utttarbanga Sambad*, 22.02.2000:4) in North Bengal. According to other sources, there are about 600 Small Growers in the North Bengal region and a potential of 24000 hectares of land under small scale tea plantations (anonymous, 1999:39). These small gardens are mainly located in three localities, i.e. Islampur subdivision of Uttar Dinajpur District, Khoribari-Phansidewa Block of Darjeeling District and Rajganj Block of Jalpaiguri District.

Small Tea Growers were Originally Pineapple Growers

The emergence of STPs in the region has created many problems. All the small growers of today in the region were pineapple growers earlier. They resorted to tea cultivation due to non-availability of suitable market for pineapple. Since this is a perishable product once it is ripe, it cannot be kept for long. In the absence of market, the pineapple growers had to face lot of difficulties for selling their products. Price fluctuation was also common, for most of the products were sent outside the region. Thus, there were great uncertainties attached to pineapple cultivation in the region. These constraints led pineapple growers to look for an alternative occupation—the outcome is STPs of today.

Development of Tea Plantation in North Bengal

In the North Bengal region, the STPs started developing in the year 1988-89 (Sharma, 1999:16). The investment in this enterprise in the beginning was slow and small due to weak economic status of the pineapple growers. These plantations were often regarded as 'illegal plantations', since these were not registered with the Tea Board of India (*The Statesman*, 14.10.1994: 7). As a rule, before commencing tea cultivation, an intended planter has to take permission from the Tea Board of India. He has to apply to the Tea Board with the Deeds of the Land, Mutation Certificate of Land, Land Revenue Receipt, Soil Analysis Report and the Surveyed Map of the area to be planted etc. for obtaining registration of the farm. Before 1990, only a few followed the rules and registered their plantation with the Tea Board. Some of the registered tea plantations are Dhiramati Tea Estate, Hari Tea Estate. However, in majority of the cases, planters did not follow the norms and started cultivation of tea in their pineapple fields, i.e., a conversion from pineapple to tea cultivation. At the initial phase of the development of STPs in the region non-existence of drains in the lands, purchased through intermediary by big companies like Terai Land Project of Duncans, Longview Tea and Gangabari Tea Estates (Sharma 1999:18), created a problem.

Digging of Big Drains Affected the Surrounding Agricultural Lands

These companies dug big drains to keep their plantations free from being waterlogged. As a result, the surrounding agricultural lands were adversely affected and the long-practised wet-rice cultivation was disturbed. Because of this problem, people living in the surrounding areas of big plantations started selling their lands. Great fear developed among the people about their livelihood depending on the wet-rice cultivation. This triggered an agrarian movement in the region during the year 1989-90, demanding tea cultivation to be declared illegal which forced the West Bengal Government to come up with a land policy in early 1990. The new policy laid down the following conditions to establish tea plantation in the region of North Bengal : *(a)* It is not to be an agricultural land; *(b)* It is not to be tribal land; *(c)* It does not fall within the Teesta Command Area, and *(d)* It is not a forest land. From then onwards NOC (No Objection Certificate) from the State Government has been a necessity before going for tea cultivation.

Issuing of NOC

The issuing of NOC was unusually delayed for no specific reasons. However, on 21st August, 1998 the State Government made an order to issue NOC to the tea planters in the region of north for tea cultivation (*Uttarbanga Sambad*, 02.02.2000:5). Under this order, the owners of tea gardens up to 24.20 acres of land holding are termed as "Tea Cultivator" and the certificates issued to them called as "Certificate for Cultivation of Tea'. It is regrettable that to arrive at a clear-cut decision on unauthorized plantations, the State Government took long time. During this period, the small growers of North Bengal region never received any kind of financial assistance or any other help from institutions like commercial banks. In this way, the delayed action of the State Government actually retarded the development of the STPs in the region.

Conclusion

It is felt, this long years of vacuum cannot be filled even though the STPs are being recognized now. The delayed recognition of the STPs has adversely effected the growth of tea industry in the small-scale sector in general and the economic conditions of the Pineapple Growers-cum-Small Tea Growers in particular. Contextually, it maybe mentioned that the situation in West Bengal is in sharp contrast to that in South India where the small growers get financial support from the banks on regular basis right from their inception (anonymous, 1999:39). In the same way, the STPs in North Bengal need be supported. By providing employment opportunity to the people in the backward areas of North Bengal, such tea units could strengthen their economic condition and the economy of this region, which has no other big industry worth mentioning.

Annexures

i) Number of Tea Estates—a) North India

Districts/State	*1951 (+)*	*1961*	*1971*	*1990*	*1995*	*2000*	*2001*	*2004*
Darrang		98	94	93	116	829	829	1540
Goalpara		10	10	13	13	249	249	263
Kamrup		15	14	15	13	54	54	54
Lakhimpur		229	233	15	20	326	326	461
Dibrugarh		@	@	280	385	21388	22392	22855
Nowgong		22	23	24	34	213	213	364
Sibsagar (a)		254	262	264	471	15735	16375	17149
Cachar		116	114	121	115	206	206	206
North Cachar		-	-	9	9	8	8	8
Karbi Anglong		-	-	14	20	143	143	393
Total Assam	785	744	750	848	1196	39151	40795	43293
Darjeeling		99	97	102	83	85	85	85
Dooars		155	151	163	168	545	548	2985
Terai (b)		47	48	82	92	910	921	5693
Total West Bengal	296	301	296	347	343	1540	1554	8709
Tripura	55	55	53	58	57	292	292	1567
Bihar	9	3	3	1	17	244	244	981
Uttar Pradesh	45	33	30	8	11	11	11	80
Himachal Pradesh	1115	1385	1385	1660	3679	3679	3679	3719
Manipur		-	-	2	5	39	39	433
Sikkim		-	-	1	1	74	74	4
Arunachal Pradesh		-	-	6	21	50	50	63
Nagaland		-	-	1	8	94	94	1458
Orissa		-	-	1	2	1	1	1
Meghalaya		-	-	-	-	15	15	45
Mizoram		-	-	-	-	12	12	276
North India Total	2305	2521	2517	2933	5340	45202	46860	60629

(a) Including Karbi Anglong & North Cachar upto 1989, (b) Including West Dinajpur, (c) Including Cooch Behar, + Break up by district are not available

@ Figures prior to 1981 included with Lakhimpur, * Provisional.

ii) Number of Tea Estates- b) South India

Districts/State	*1951*	*1961*	*1971*	*1990*	*1995*	*2000*	*2001*	*2004*
Kanyakumari		6	7	7	7	7	7	7
Tirunelveli		3	3	4	4	4	4	4
Madurai		4	4	6	6	6	6	5
Coimbatore		34	31	40	45	52	52	52
Nilgiris		4942	6405	6760	25749	60549	62145	62145
Total Tamil Nadu	2772	4989	6450	6817	25811	60618	62214	62213
Cannanore		8	11	-	-	-	-	-
Palghat		5	5	32	33	33	33	33
Kozhikode		22	19	-	-	-	-	-
Malapuram (d)		-	1	1	1	1	1	1
Trichur		1	1	1	1	1	1	1
Trivandrum		6	6	6	6	6	6	6
Quilon		28	110	104	104	104	104	103
Ernakulam		4	16	2	2	2	2	2
Kottayam		1902	2863	3705	953	954	954	954
Idukki (e)		-	-	204	4978	4967	4967	4956
Wynaad (+)		-	-	34	53	85	85	97
Total Kerala	1125	1976	3032	4089	6133	6153	6153	6153
Chikmagalur		11	14	14	29	29	29	29
Coorg		1	1	6	7	7	7	2
Hassan		1	1	1	1	1	1	1
Total Karnataka	12	13	16	21	37	37	37	32
Total South India	3909	6978	9498	10927	31979	66808	68404	68398
Total All India	6214	9499	12015	13860	37319	112010	115264	129027

(d) New District formed since 1969 out of Kozhikode District., (e) New District formed since 1972 out of Kottayam & Ernakulam District., + Break up by district is not available

* Provisional.

Note: Since 1998 figures are inclusive of Small Growers operating in different tea producing District/States.

iii) Area under Tea in India- a) North India

Districts/State	*1951 (+)*	*1961*	*1971*	*1990*	*1995*	*2000*	*2001*	*2004*
Darrang	25320	26509	30897	39989	40284	41037	41233	41300
Goalpara	1467	1603	2098	3141	3176	3460	3454	3643
Kamrup	1881	2074	2713	3557	3013	3442	3436	3460
Lakhimpur	46926	50243	57297	4212	4494	4815	4727	4873
Dibrugarh	@	@	@	68207	68998	93076	94080	95118
Nowgong	5064	5577	6372	7780	7723	7994	8001	8137
Sibsagar (a)	44571	46433	51930	63348	62810	74807	75864	77135
Cachar	30445	29928	31018	35075	29969	32008	32272	32149
North Cachar	-	-	-	3696	4263	4004	4047	4032
Karbi Anglong	-	-	-	1358	1550	1869	1869	1923
Total Assam	155674	162367	182325	230363	226280	266512	268983	271768
Darjeeling	16569	18605	18245	20065	18932	17228	17318	17522
Dooars	54609	54756	59485	67760	69175	69703	70017	72883
Terai (b)	8402	9344	10769	13345	13083	20548	21467	23598
Total West Bengal	79580	82705	88499	101170	101190	107497	108802	1140033
Tripura	4773	5055	5444	5778	5952	6623	6700	8268
Bihar	1644	534	460	22	76	1350	1445	2000
Uttar Pradesh	2605	2084	1818	876	1068	1068	1068	1446
Himachal Pradesh	4317	4183	4183	2063	2312	2325	2325	2348
Manipur	-	-	-	140	347	907	950	1319
Sikkim	-	-	-	171	172	296	300	195
Arunachal Pradesh	-	-	-	195	1361	2176	2250	1729
Nagaland	-	-	-	13	256	1214	1270	1898
Orissa	-	-	-	213	219	214	214	214
Meghalaya	-	-	-	-	-	351	370	252
Mizoram	-	-	-	-	-	391	400	750
North India Total	248593	256928	282729	341004	339233	390906	395077	

(a) Including Karbi Anglong & North Cachar upto 1989, (b) Including West Dinajpur, (c) Including Cooch Behar, + Break up by district are not available.

@ Figures prior to 1981 included with Lakhimpur, * Provisional.

iv) Area under Tea in India - b) South India

Districts/State	*1951*	*1961*	*1971*	*1990*	*1995*	*2000*	*2001*	*2004*
Kanyakumari		451	484	434	434	434	434	433
Tirunelveli		449	509	800	800	800	800	800
Madurai		734	944	945	946	973	973	972
Coimbatore		10249	10058	10187	11241	11764	11784	11734
Nilgiris		20840	22651	26237	35537	60427	61634	62039
Total Tamil Nadu	33375	32723	34646	38603	48958	74398	75625	75978
Cannanore		1448	1505	-	-	-	-	-
Palghat		574	635	681	829	850	850	852
Kozhikode		4014	3874	-	-		-	-
Malapuram (d)		-	174	174	174	174	174	174
Trichur		401	459	466	496		530	529
Trivandrum		1082	1057	1023	965	965	965	965
Quilon		3006	2673	1362	1348	1348	1348	1348
Ernakulam		161	147	2	2	2	2	2
Kottayam		29098	26747	2019	776	840	840	840
Idukki (e)		-	-	23584	26710	26748	26748	26893
Wynaad (+)		-	-	5375	5475	5483	5483	55040
Total Kerala	33203	39784	37271	34686	36775	36940	36940	37107
Chikmagalur		1168	1222	1320	1414	1428	1434	1434
Coorg		178	205	261	290	299	299	299
Hassan		448	443	395	395	395	395	299
Total Karnataka	1669	1794	1870	1976	2099	2122	2128	2128
Total South India	68247	74301	73787	75265	87832	113460	114693	115213
Total All India	316840	331229	356516	41269	427065	504366	509770	521403

(d) New District formed since 1969 out of Kozhikode District., (e) New District formed since 1972 out of Kottayam & Ernakulam District.

+ Break up by district are not available, * Provisional

Note: Since 1998 figures are inclusive of Small Growers operating in different tea producing District/States.

v) Production of tea - a) North India

(in million kgs.)

Districts/State	*1951(+)*	*1961*	*1971*	*1990*	*1995*	*2000*	*2001*	*2004*
Darrang	26909	31194	41283	79632	80538	77030	78224	80474
Goalpara	1616	1717	2428	5027	5779	6297	6223	5665
Kamrup	1157	1668	2557	4702	4766	4302	4585	4304
Lakhimpur	5996	73339	91949	8257	8678	9068	9113	8280
Dibrugarh	*	*	*	140047	143931	163426	166504	178352
Nowgong	3691	5643	7423	11690	13846	11788	11793	10981
Sibsagar (a)	41174	48569	55289	92331	98186	119978	119626	102192
Cachar	19827	20181	22736	40174	40180	49206	50296	38755
North Cachar	-	-	-	4873	5115	6179	5643	4632
Karbi Anglong	-	-	-	1048	1598	1945	1929	2012
Total Assam	150370	182311	223665	388181	402617	449219	453936	435649
Darjeeling	7838	10107	10293	14499	11298	9281	9742	10065
Dooars	63944	66898	80840	114124	121420	128964	130739	135237
Terai (b)	6376	9253	12954	21130	24804	43291	46395	69237
Total West Bengal	78158	86258	104087	149753	157522	181536	186876	214541
Tripura	1873	2689	2960	5205	5679	6431	6506	7168
Bihar	1098	55	41	76	130	538	543	1023
Uttar Pradesh	901	804	690	534	341	264	327	246
Himachal Pradesh	1125	1188	888	1180	1359	1247	1022	616
Manipur	-	-	-	18	102	96	101	110
Sikkim	-	-	-	90	83	105	110	150
Arunachal Pradesh	-	-	-	38	707	993	1047	2219
Nagaland	-	-	-	-	74	43	45	190
Orissa	-	-	-	31	17	105	105	101
Meghalaya	-	-	-	-	-	140	148	99
Mizoram	-	-	-	-	-	39	41	72
North India Total	233525	273305	332331	545106	568631	640756	650807	662148

(a) Including Karbi Anglong & North Cachar upto 1989, (b) Including West Dinajpur, (c) Including Cooch Behar, + Break up by district are not available.

* Provisional.

vi) Production of tea- b) South India

(in million kgs.)

Districts/State	*1951*	*1961*	*1971*	*1990*	*1995*	*2000*	*2001*	*2004*
Kanyakumari		267	247	182	120	137	117	81
Tirunelveli		444	858	2262	2447	990	1779	1454
Madurai		1062	1738	3397	2906	2660	3152	2306
Coimbatore		13913	18434	28210	28168	32831	31261	29417
Nilgiris		24082	36254	76525	84274	95194	96092	129757
Total Tamil Nadu	25225	39768	57531	110576	117915	131812	132401	163014
Cannanore		1175	1441	-	-	-	-	-
Palghat		720	975	1697	1999	2267	1898	2206
Kozhikode		4827	6140	-	-	-	-	-
Malapuram (d)		-	138	97	NA	NA	NA	-
Trichur		669	674	1503	1553	1896	1668	1796
Trivandrum		1058	940	744	433	399	124	441
Quilon		1878	1648	423	438	364	364	237
Ernakulam		46	67	-	-	-	-	-
Kottayam		29172	30706	324	140	308	245	557
Idukki (e)		-	-	46697	49473	51406	46439	44861
Wynaad (+)		-	-	9180	10742	12307	14413	12075
Total Kerala	25775	39545	42729	60665	64778	68947	65151	62146
Chikmagalur		1157	2022	2701	2993	3521	3606	3755
Coorg		192	273	497	606	687	797	823
Hassan		430	582	793	1093	1199	1161	1042
Total Karnataka	874	1779	2877	3991	4692	5407	5564	5620
Total South India	51874	81092	103137	175232	187385	206166	203116	230781
Total All India	285399	354397	435468	720338	756016	846922	853923	892960

(d) New District formed since 1969 out of Kozhikode District., (e) New District formed since 1972 out of Kottayam & Ernakulam District., + Break up by district are not available

* Provisional

Note: Since 1998 figures are inclusive of Small Growers operating in different tea producing District/States.

vii) Average yield of tea - a) North India

(kgs. in ha.)

Districts/State	*1951(+)*	*1961*	*1971*	*1990*	*1995*	*2000*	*2001*	*2004*
Darrang	1063	1177	1336	1991	1999	1877	1897	1949
Goalpara	1102	1071	1157	1600	1820	1820	1802	1555
Kamrup	615	804	942	1322	1582	1250	1334	1244
Lakhimpur	1193	1460	1605	1960	1931	1883	1928	1699
Dibrugarh	-	-	-	2059	2086	1756	1770	1875
Nowgong	729	1012	1165	1503	1793	1475	1474	1350
Sibsagar (a)	924	1046	1065	1458	1563	1604	1577	1325
Cachar	651	674	733	1145	1341	1537	1559	1206
North Cachar	-	-	-	1318	1200	1543	1394	1149
Karbi Anglong	-	-	-	772	1031	1041	1032	1046
Total Assam	966	1123	1227	1685	1779	1686	1688	1603
Darjeeling	473	543	564	723	597	539	563	574
Dooars	1171	1222	1359	1684	1755	1850	1867	1856
Terai (b)	759	990	1203	1583	1896	2107	2161	2934
Total West Bengal	982	1043	1176	1480	1557	1689	1718	1882
Tripura	392	532	54489	901	954	971	971	867
Bihar	668	103	380	3455	1711	399	376	512
Uttar Pradesh	346	386	212	610	319	247	306	170
Himachal Pradesh	261	284		572	588	536	440	262
Manipur	-	-	-	129	294	106	106	83
Sikkim	-	-	-	526	483	355	367	769
Arunachal Pradesh	-	-	-	195	519	456	465	1283
Nagaland	-	-	-	0	289	35	35	100
Orissa	-	-	-	146	78	491	491	472
Meghalaya	-	-	-	-	-	399	400	393
Mizoram	-	-	-	-	-	100	103	96
North India Total	939	1064	1175	1599	1676	1639	1647	1630

(a) Including Karbi Anglong & North Cachar upto 1989, (b) Including West Dinajpur, (c) Including Cooch Behar, + Break up by district are not available, @ Figures prior to 1981 included with Lakhimpur

* Provisional

viii) Average Yield of Tea- b) South India

(kgs. in ha.)

Districts/State	*1951*	*1961*	*1971*	*1990*	*1995*	*2000*	*2001*	*2004*
Kanyakumari		592	510	419	276	316	270	187
Tirunelveli		989	1686	2828	3059	1238	2224	1818
Madurai		1447	1841	3595	3072	2734	3239	2372
Coimbatore		1357	1833	2769	2506	2791	2653	2507
Nilgiris		1156	1601	2917	2371	1575	1559	2092
Total Tamil Nadu	756	1215	1661	2864	2408	1772	1751	2147
Cannanore		811	957	-	-	-	-	-
Palghat		1254	1535	2492	2411	2667	2233	2589
Kozhikode		1203	1585	-	-	-	-	-
Malapuram (d)		-	793	557	-	-	-	-
Trichur		1668	1468	3225	3131	3577	3147	3344
Trivandrum		978	889	727	449	413	128	457
Quilon		625	617	311	325	270	270	176
Ernakulam		286	456	-	-	-	-	-
Kottayam		1003	1148	160	180	367	292	663
Idukki (e)		-	-	1980	1852	1922	1736	1668
Wynaad (+)		-	-	1708	1962	2245	2629	2194
Total Kerala	776	994	1146	1749	1761	1866	1764	1675
Chikmagalur		991	1655	2046	2117	2466	2515	2619
Coorg		1079	1332	1904	2090	2298	2666	2753
Hassan		960	1314	2008	2767	3035	2939	2638
Total Karnataka	524	992	1539	2020	2235	2548	2615	2641
Total South India	760	1091	1398	2328	2133	1817	1771	2003
Total All India	901	1070	1221	1730	17770	1679	1675	1713

(d) New District formed since 1969 out of Kozhikode District., (e) New District formed since 1972 out of Kottayam & Ernakulam District., + Break up by district are not available.

* Provisional.

Note: Since 1998 figures are inclusive of Small Growers operating in different tea producing District/States.

ANNEXURE II

Supply Sources

Country	Market Size	Sri Lanka	Kenya	China	India	Indonesia	Argentina	Malawi	Bangladesh	Tanzania	Vietnam	Uganda	Turkey	Zimbabwe
		[illegible]% Share in W. Exports	[illegible]% Share in W. Exports	[illegible]% Share in W. Exports	[illegible]% Share in W. Exports	[illegible]% Share in W. Exports	[illegible]% Share in W. Exports	[illegible]% Share in W. Exports	[illegible]% Share in W. Exports	[illegible]% Share in W. Exports	[illegible]% Share in W. Exports	[illegible]% Share in W. Exports	[illegible]% Share in W. Exports	[illegible]% Share in W. Exports
UK Data														
UK [illegible]% Share World Imports	[illegible]	[illegible]	[illegible]	[illegible]	[illegible]	[illegible]	[illegible]	[illegible]	[illegible]	[illegible]	[illegible]	[illegible]	[illegible]	[illegible]
Russian Federation Data														
Russian Federation [illegible]% Share in World Imports	[illegible]	[illegible]	[illegible]	[illegible]	[illegible]	[illegible]	[illegible]		[illegible]		[illegible]		[illegible]	
Pakistan Data														
Pakistan [illegible]% Share in World Imports	[illegible]	[illegible]	[illegible]	[illegible]	[illegible]	[illegible]	[illegible]	[illegible]	[illegible]	[illegible]	[illegible]	[illegible]		[illegible]
USA Data														
USA [illegible]% Share in World Imports	[illegible]	[illegible]	[illegible]	[illegible]	[illegible]	[illegible]	[illegible]	[illegible]		[illegible]	[illegible]			[illegible]

Supply Sources														
Country	Market Profile	Sri Lanka	Kenya	China	India	Indonesia	Argentina	Malawi	Bangladesh	Tanzania	Vietnam	Uganda	Turkey	Zimbabwe
		20.14% Share in W. Exports	18.07% Share in W. Exports	16.67% Share in W. Exports	15.12% Share in W. Exports	6.50% Share in W. Exports	3.90% Share in W. Exports	3.43% Share in W. Exports	2.22% Share in W. Exports	1.37% Share in W. Exports	1.62% Share in W. Exports	1.12% Share in W. Exports	1.30% Share in W. Exports	0.82% Share in W. Exports
Egypt Data														
Egypt 6.32% Share in World Imports	73.0[illegible] mkg (Large) ROG: [illegible]	20.54% Share 12.97 ROG 1.21 UVR Sri Lanka Data [illegible] Share [illegible] ROG 1.71 UVR	51.72% Share 33.52 ROG 1.48 UVR Kenya Data [illegible] Share [illegible] ROG 1.60 UVR	5.54% Share 1.36 UVR China Data 4.4[illegible] Share	6.37% Share [illegible] ROG 1.77 UVR India Data 3.47% Share 1.79 ROG 1.73 UVR	10.28% Share -26.44 ROG 1.42 UVR Indonesia Data 7.72% Share 25.47 ROG 1.14 UVR	Argentina Data	1.33% Share 1.39 UVR Malawi Data 0.94% Share 8.77 ROG 0.94 UVR	Bangladesh Data 2.10% Share	Tanzania Data	0.26% Share 1.12 UVR Vietnam Data	[illegible] Share 1.20 UVR Uganda Data 0.47% Share 0.56 UVR	Turkey Data	Zimbabwe Data
Japan Data														
Japan [illegible] Share in World Imports	42.91 mkg (Med. Medium) ROG: [illegible]	15.52% Share 7.01 ROG 2.98 UVR Sri Lanka Data 2.72% Share 6.50 ROG 2.70 UVR	3.52% Share [illegible] ROG [illegible] UVR Kenya Data 0.27% Share -1.20 ROG 1.51 UVR	15.25% Share 2.16 UVR China Data 1.63% Share 15.25 ROG	7.47% Share 1.26 ROG 6.5[illegible] UVR India Data 2.40% Share 2.14 ROG 4.05 UVR	2.15% Share 8.6[illegible] ROG 2.50 UVR Indonesia Data 0.84% Share 12.84 ROG [illegible] UVR	Argentina Data	0.34% Share 0.43 ROG 1.84 UVR Malawi Data	0.91% Share [illegible] ROG 1.21 UVR Bangladesh Data 0.51% Share 1.03 ROG 1.41 UVR	Tanzania Data	1.47% Share 26.10 ROG 2.00 UVR Vietnam Data	Uganda Data	Turkey Data	Zimbabwe Data
Iran Data														
Iran 3.85% Share in World Imports	41.12 mkg (Med. Medium) ROG: -6.84	23.15% Share -6.86 ROG Sri Lanka Data 6.16% Share -17.85 ROG 2.31 UVR	5.20% Share Kenya Data 1.56 UVR	1.17% Share China Data 4.58% Share	15.42% Share -2.58 ROG India Data 3.81% Share -30.29 ROG 2.09 UVR	3.22% Share 13.22 ROG Indonesia Data 1.01% Share 11.14 ROG 1.52 UVR	Argentina Data	Malawi Data	Bangladesh Data 7.39% Share	Tanzania Data	Vietnam Data	Uganda Data	Turkey Data 5.15% Share	Zimbabwe Data
Morocco Data														
Morocco 2.87% Share in World Imports	32.07 mkg (Med. Medium) ROG: 4.22	1.07% Share -17.46 ROG 3.21 UVR Sri Lanka Data	Kenya Data	71.00% Share [illegible] ROG 2.24 UVR China Data 1.08% Share -2.72 ROG	2.40% Share 3.70 UVR India Data 0.21% Share 2.07 UVR	2.75% Share -2.10 ROG 1.63 UVR Indonesia Data 0.87% Share 0.87 UVR	Argentina Data	Malawi Data	Bangladesh Data	Tanzania Data	Vietnam Data	Uganda Data	Turkey Data	Zimbabwe Data

ANNEXURE III

Importer	Rank	Exporter	Importer	Rank	Exporter
United Kingdom	1	Kenya (43.82%)	Poland	1	India (34.90%)
11.90% Share in World Imports	2	India (16.67%)	2.39% Share in World Imports	2	Bangladesh (22.26%)
	3	Indonesia (6.57%)		3	China (10.63%)
	4	Sri Lanka (4.98%)		4	Sri Lanka (6.99%)
	5	South Africa (2.75%)		5	Indonesia (5.48%)
Russian Red.	1	India (66.66%)	Germany	1	India (22.92%)
12.28% Share in World Imports	2	Sri Lanka (19.61%)	1.80% Share in World Imports	2	China (19.68%)
	3	China (4.66%)		3	Sri Lanka (13.33%)
	4	Georgia (3.33%)		4	Indonesia (11.56%)
	5	Indonesia (1.67%)		5	Vietnam (5.39%)
Pakistan	1	Kenya (58.44%)	Australia	1	Indonesia (31.22%)
8.45% Share in World Imports	2	Indonesia (14.60%)	1.29% Share in World Imports	2	Sri Lanka (19.32%)
	3	BFangladesh (5.21%)		3	Papua New Guinea (18.08%)
	4	Sri Lanka (4.12%)		4	Kenya (7.23%)
	5	Tanzania (3.75%)		5	India (6.76%)
USA	1	Argentina (37.44%)	Canada	1	UK (30.52%)
7.47% Share in World Imports	2	China (15.57%)	1.45% Share in WOrld Imports	2	Kenya (12.25%)
	3	Indonesia (10.22%)		3	Sri Lanka (9.96%)
	4	Kenya (4.87%)		4	USA (9.72%)
	5	Germany (3.61%)		5	India (5.80%)
Egypt	1	Kenya (69.16%)	Libya	1	Sri Lanka (71.78%)
5.99% Share in World Imports	2	Sri Lanka (12.30%)	1.16% Share in World Imports	2	India (16.65%)
	3	India (5.68%)		3	China (9.69%)
	4	Malawi (4.25%)			
	5	Indonesia (3.29%)			

(Contd...)

ANNEXURE III *(Contd...)*

Importer	*Rank*	*Exporter*	*Importer*	*Rank*	*Exporter*
Japan	1	China (60.14%)	France	1	Sri Lanka 15.40%)
4.06% Share in World Imports	2	Sri Lanka (15.91%)	1.14% Share in World Imports	2	UK (13.58%)
	3	India (8.52%)		3	China (11.96%)
	4	Indonesia (3.92%)		4	Belgium & Luxembourg (8.58%)
	5	Taiwan (2.93%)		5	Indonesia (1.96%)
Morocco	1	China (98.35%)	Ireland (Rep.)	1	Kenya (54.46%)
3.06% Share in World Imports	2	Indonesia (1.02%)	0.85% Share in World Imports	2	India (15.16%)
	3	UK (0.15%)		3	Indonesia (6.64%)
	4	Sri Lanka (0.12%)		4	Zimbabwe (5.91%)
				5	UK (5.49%)
Iran	1	Persian Gulf Staes (32.65%)	Netherlands	1	Indonesia (22.94%)
2.85% Share in World Imports			0.65% Share in World Imports		
	2	Sri Lanka (20.71%)		2	Sri Lanka (14.06%)
	3	Kenya (13.41%)		3	Malawi (9.99%)
	4	India (9.38%)		4	Turkey (7.28%)
	5	Indonesia (2.11%)		5	China (7.22%)

Source: Based on the basic data from various issues of ITC Bulletins, London.

ANNEXURE IV
Quantity and Value of Tea Exports from India (Excluding Instant Tea)

Year	Quantity Th.Kgs	Value Th.Rs	Unit Price Rs./Kg	Year	Quantity Th.Kgs	Value Th.Rs	Unit Price Rs./Kg
1954-55	208462	1482316	7.11	1954	203195	1307523	6.43
1955-56	183769	1096448	5.97	1955	166708	1136132	6.82
1956-57	233088	1451344	6.23	1956	237484	1428249	6.01
1957-58	191755	1436435	7.49	1957	200786	1233859	6.15
1958-59	217322	1296953	5.97	1958	229503	1365859	5.95
1959-60	215459	1290846	5.99	1959	213680	1260135	5.9
1960-61	196473	1222549	6.22	1960	193063	1199883	6.21
1961-62	205329	1221680	5.95	1961	206292	1242513	6.02
1962-63	220800	1296000	5.87	1962	211826	1235339	5.83
1963-64	209328	1231885	5.88	1963	223542	1323710	5.92
1964-65	212325	1246657	5.87	1964	210523	1249012	5.93
1965-66	197385	1148374	5.82	1965	199365	1149747	5.77
1966-67	190383	1562189	8.21	1966	179205	1565921	8.74
1967-68	203333	1801974	8.86	1967	213676	1890384	8.85
1968-69	200824	1565092	7.79	1968	208440	1664825	7.99
1969-70	174112	1245029	7.15	1969	168709	1205371	7.14
1970-71	199139	1842470	9.25	1970	202016	1487533	7.36
1971-72	214317	1609204	7.51	1971	202052	1536678	7.61
1972-73	193228	1472935	7.62	1972	198195	1511439	7.63
1973-74	190268	1448490	7.61	1973	188192	1427072	7.58
1974-75	225057	2235355	9.93	1974	210583	1927972	9.16
1975-76	211409	2382948	11.27	1975	218128	2446592	11.22
1976-77	242418	2954777	12.19	1976	233611	2731364	11.69
1977-78	221522	5637117	25.45	1977	229637	5416157	23.59
1978-79	177327	3591193	20.25	1978	176051	3628916	20.61
1979-80	208448	3768961	18.08	1979	199639	3618401	18.12
1980-81	231736	4352730	18.78	1980	224026	4290277	19.15
1981-82	224200	4068252	18.15	1981	241246	4342541	18
1982-83	194090	3694482	19.03	1982	189933	3555525	18.72
1983-84	202312	5575549	27.56	1983	208476	5168145	24.79
1984-85	217401	7713889	35.48	1984	217040	7404551	34.12

1985-86	214234	6479796	30.25	1985	214021	6952966	32.49
1986-87	196232	5794783	29.53	1986	203149	5808510	28.59
1987-88	201830	6277688	31.1	1987	201891	6392466	31.66
1988-89	204075	6352799	31.13	1988	200956	6126937	30.49
1989-90	210615	9047231	42.96	1989	211622	8400923	39.7
1990-91	198240	10620939	53.58	1990	209085	11041507	52.81
1991-92	215166	11964625	55.61	1991	201720	11203136	55.54
1992-93	178950	10316425	57.65	1992	173358	9717402	56.05
1993-94	153427	10398935	67.78	1993	173726	11325271	65.19
1994-95	150836	9635458	63.88	1994	149317	9652334	64.64
1995-96	166239	12184298	73.3	1995	167143	11908077	71.24
1996-97	167172	12568167	75.18	1996	160004	12070978	75.44
1997-98	208773	19453207	93.18	1997	200713	17218472	85.79
1998-99	203431	21288720	104.65	1998	207640	22383087	107.8
1999-00	189837	18672822	98.36	1999	189092	19024369	100.61
2000-01	200770	18066853	89.99	2000	204353	18270324	89.41
2001-02	187407	16215897	86.53	2001	179857	16022060	89.08

Source: Tea Statistics 2000-2001 issued by Tea Board of India.

Bibliography

PUBLICATIONS by Dr G.D. BANERJEE

A. Books

1. Banerjee, G.D. (1983), Structural Changes in Tea Industry since 1956 unpublished thesis submitted to Jadhavpur University, Kolkata.,1982
2. Banerjee, G.D. (1996), *Tea Plantation Industry in India between 1815 and 1992*, Lawyers Book Stall, Guwahati, Assam
3. Banerjee, G.D., Hundekar and Das, Edited, (1997), *Challenges before Small Scale Industries*, Horizontal Publishers, Darbhanga Castle, Allahbad, Uttar Pradesh, India.
4. Banerjee, G. D. and Karmakar, K.G., *The Tea Industry in India – A Survey,* (September 2005), Department of Economic Analysis and Research, NABARD, Mumbai.
5. Banerjee, G.D. and Banerjee, Sarda, *Sustainable Tea Plantation Management,* (2007) International Book Distributing Company, Lucknow, Uttar Pradesh, India.
6. Banerjee, G.D. and Banerjee, Sarda, *Agriculture and Rural Development Policy Agendas in the New Millennium,* (2007), International Book Distributing Company, Lucknow, Uttar Pradesh, India.
7. Banerjee, G.D. and Banerji, Srijeet, *Darjeeling Tea—The Golden Brew,* (2007), International Book Distributing Company, Lucknow, Uttar Pradesh, India.

B. Eight Reports

1. *Socio-Economic Implications of High Yielding Varieties of Food Grains in the EasternRegion of India,* UNDP Global Project, Agro-economic Research Centre, Santiniketan.
2. Efficiency of Small Farms Under Different Tenurial Conditions with Special Reference to North Bengal, ICAR, New Delhi - 1.
3. Techno-Economic Survey of Darjeeling Tea Industry, Tea Board, India, Kolkata, West Bengal.
4. Techno-Economic Survey of Tripura Tea Industry, Tea Board, India, Kolkata, West Bengal.
5. Techno-Economic Survey of Small Tea Gardens in Kottayam and Idukki (Kerala), Tea Board, India, Kolkata.
6. Techno-Economic Survey of SmallTea Gardens in Kangra (H.P.), Tea Board, India, Kolkata.
7. Techno-Economic Survey of Nilgiri Tea Industry, Tea Board, India, Kolkata, West Bengal.
8. Techno-Economic Survey of Cachar Tea Industry, Tea Board, India, Kolkata, West Bengal.
9. Evaluation Study Report on Inland Fisheries in Nadia district NABARD, Regional Office, West Bengal, Kolkata.
10. Evaluation Study Report on Inland Fisheries in West Tripura, Tripura, NABARD, Assam Regional Office, Guwahati.
11. Evaluation Study Report on Poultry Farming (Broiler) in Medinipur District, West Bengal, NABARD Regional Office, West Bengal, Kolkata.

C. About 170 Papers published by Dr. G.D. Banerjee

a. *Indian Journal of Agricultural Economics,* Indian Society of Agricultural Economics, Krishi Vikas Sadan, First Floor (Near Dr Antinio De si Technical High School), Veer Savkar Marg, Dadar (west) Mumbaito 400028; Tel—022 24374789, Fax—022 24374790; E. mail- isae@bom7. vsnl.net. in ; website www.isacindia.org

1. Changes Overtimes In the Levels of Income of the Weaker Section of Rural Community (WB), Annual Conference Issue, June to July 1972.
2. Impact of Agro Processing on Incomes of Primary Producers, Annual Conferences, Dec. 2003.

b. *TAI News Letter,* Published by Tea Association of India, Indian Exchange Palace, Kolkata 1, (West Bengal)

3. Problems and Prospects of Tarai Tea Industry, Feb. 1983, Vol.16, No.2.
4. Problems and Prospects of Indian Tea Exports, March 1983, Vol.16, No.3.
5. The Role of FAO, UNCTAD and ITPA for Development of World Tea, May 1983, Vol. 16, No. 5.
6. Export Prospects of Indian Tea in Tunisia, July 1983, Vol. 16, and No. 7.
7. Tea Plantation of India (North), September-October 1983, Vol. 16, Nos. 9 and 10.
8. Structural Development in Tea Industry, November 1983, Vol.16, No.11.
9. Evolution of Tea Industry in India (Part I), December 1983, Vol.16, No.12.
10. Evolution of Tea Industry in India (part II), February 1984, Vol. 17, No.2.
11. Ownership of Tea Estates, March 1984, Vol. 17, No.3.
12. Japan As A Base of Indian Tea, August 1984, Vol. 17, No. 3.
13. Changes in Pattern of Management, September 1984, Vol. 18, No. 9.
14. Area, Production and Yield of Tea in Different Excise Zones, December 1984, Vol. 17, No. 12.
15. Changes in the Pattern of Ownership, February 1985, Vol. 19, No. 2.
16. Market Research, Vol. 20, No. 3, March 1985.
17. The Role of Tea in Indian Economy, April 1985, Vol.21, No.4.
18. Export Prospects of Indian Tea in Nigeria, June 1985, Vol. 21, No. 6.
19. Export Prospects of Indian Tea in Singapore, November 1985, Vol. 21, and No. 11.
20. Tea Plantation in South India, October 1986, Vol.22, No. 10.
21. Impact of Area, Production of Tea in New Planting,Yield Rates, Exports and Quantity Retained for Domestic Consumption, November 1986, Vol. 22, No. 11.
22. Efficiency of Tea Estates, January 1987, Vol. 23, No. 1.

23. Role of Tea Plantation in North India, May 1987, Vol. 23.
24. Export Prospects of Indian tea in Iran, January 1988, Vol. 24, No. 1.
25. Structural Changes in Tea Exports in India, February 1988, Vol. 24, No. 1.
26. Export Possibility of Indian Tea in Arab Republic of Egypt, May 1988, Vol. 24, No. 5.
27. Export Prospects of Indian Tea in Canada, July 1988, Vol. 24, No. 7.
28. Export Prospects of Indian Tea in Poland, September 1988, Vol. 24, No. 9.
29. Export Prospects of Indian Tea in Syria, January 1989, Vol. 24, No. 1.
30. International Tea Promotion, March 1989, Vol. 25, No. 5.
31. Export Prospects of Indian Tea in Libya and Jordan, May 1989, Vol. 25.
32. Tea in South India, July 1989, Vol. 25, No. 7.
33. Production and Exports of Value Added Teas in India, October 1989, Vol. 25, No. 10.
34. Problems and Prospects of Coimbatore Tea Industry, July 1990, Vol. 26, No. 7.
35. Problems and Prospects of Wynaad Tea Industry, October 1990, Vol. 26, No. 10.
36. Tea Statistics, Tea Boards of India, various issues.
37. Tea Directory, Tea Boards of India, various issues.
38. FAO 1995, 1999: Impact of Uruguay round agreement on the World Economists position, 2005 and Current Situation and Short Term Outlook, paper presented to Inter Government Group on Tea Ottawa September, 2005.

c. *The Assam Review and Tea News* Published by Assam Review Publishing Company, 27A, Waterloo Street, Kolkata –69, Phone to 033 248251

39. World Markets of Tea and Its International Arrangements, January 1985, Vol. 73, No. 11.
40. Tea Economy in South India, February 1985, Vol. 73, No. 12.
41. Export Prospects of Tea in Singapore, July 1985, Vol. 74, No. 5.
42. Structure of Tea Industry, August 1985, Vol. 74, No. 6.

The Entire Thesis, namely, "Structural Changes in Tea

Plantation Industry since 1956", was published by the above publisher in 17 instalments, like,

43. October 1985, Vol. 74, No. 8.
44. November 1985, Vol. 74, No. 9.
45. December 1985, Vol. 74, No. 10.
46. January 1986, Vol. 74, No. 11.
47. February 1986, Vol. 74, No. 12.
48. March 1986, Vol. 75, No. 1.
49. April 1986, Vol. 75, No. 2.
50. May 1986, Vol. 75, No. 3.
51. June 1986, Vol. 75, No. 4.
52. July 1986, Vol. 75, No. 5.
53. August 1986, Vol. 75, No. 6.
54. September 1986, Vol. 75, No. 7.
55. October 1986, Vol. 75, No. 8.
56. November 1986, Vol. 75, No. 9.
57. December 1986, Vol. 75, No. 10.
58. January 1986, Vol. 75, No.11
59. February 1986, Vol. 75, No. 12.
60. Export Possibility of Indian Tea in Iraq, 1, January 1988, Vol. 77, No. 12.
61. Export Possibility of Indian Tea in Iraq, II, February 1988, Vol. 77, No. 13.
62. International Tea Promotion, May 1989, Vol. 78, No. 3.
63. Tea in South American Countries, July 1989, Vol. 78, No. 4.
64. Production and Export of Value added Tea in India, August 1989, Vol. 78, No. 6.
66. Export pospects of Indian Tea in Jordan, October 1989, Vol. 78, No. 8.
67. Export Prospects of Indian Tea in Iran in February 1990.
68. Export Prospects of Indian Tea Libya in June 1990.
69. Export Prospects of Indian Tea japan in August 1990.
70. Export Prospects of Indian Tea in Argentina, March 1991.
71. Export Pospects of Indian Tea in South America, November 1991.
72. Export Prospects of Indian Tea in Poland, September 1991.
73. Export Prospects of Indian Tea in Australia, June 1993.

74. Export Prospects of Indian Tea in Egypt, October 1993.
75. Export Prospects of Indian Tea in Germany, November 1993.
76. Export Prospects of Indian Tea in Nethereland, December 1993.
77. Export Prospects of Indian Tea in Srilanka, January 1994.
78. Export Prospects of Indian Tea in Indonesia, February 1994.
79. Export Prospects of Indian Tea in China, March 1994.
80. Export Prospects of Indian Tea in Peru, April 1994.
81. Export Prospects of Indian Tea in Pakistan, May 1994.
82. Export Prospects of Indian Tea in Canada, June 1994.
83. Export Prospects of Indian Tea in Ethiopia, September 1994.
84. Export Prospects of Indian Tea in Kenya, October 1994.
85. Export Prospects of Indian Tea in Tanzania, November 1994.
86. Export Prospects of Indian Tea in Uganda, December 1994.
87. Export Prospects of Indian Tea in Vietnam, January 1995.
88. Export Prospects of Indian Tea in South Africa, February 1995.
89. Export Prospects of Indian Tea in Zimbabwe, March 1995.
90. Export Prospects of Indian Tea in Mozambique, April 1995.
91. History of Darjeeling Tea, December, 1999,Vol. 88,No, 10.
92. Development Issues of Tea Industry, February, 2000, Vol. 88, No 12.
93. Development Issues of Tea Industry, March 2000, Vol 89, No 1 D.
94. Development Issues of Tea Industry, April 2000, Vol 90, No 1 D.
95. Structural Issues in Tea industry, May, 2000, Vol 90, No 1 D.

d. *Chai ki Bat* published by Bharatiya Chai Parishad, 25 Ballyganj, Circular Road, Kolkata 700 019.

96. Export Prospects of Tea in Canada, January 1988, Vol. 33, No. 1.
97. Export Prospects of Tea in Saudi Arabia, February 1988, Vol. 33, No. 2.
98. Export Prospects of Indian Tea in Iran, April 1988, Vol.33, No.4.

99. Export Prospects of Indian Tea in Poland, May 1988, Vol. 33, No. 5.

100. Structural Changes in the Tea Exports of India, August 1988, Vol. 33, No. 8.

101. Export Possibility of Indian Tea in Arab Republic of Egypt, January 1989, Vol. 34, No. 7.

102. Availability of Tea in Internal Market or Maximisation of Export Earnings, March 1989.

103. Export Prospect of Tea in Iraq, May 1989, Vol. 34, and No. 5.

104. Market Research on Tea Consumption, August 1989, Vol. 34, No. 9.

105. Market Research on Tea Consumption, October 1989, Vol. 34, No. 10.

106. Green Tea (Part I), March 1992, Vol.xxxvii, No.3.

107. Green Tea (Part II), April 1992, Vol.xxxviii, No.4.

e. *The Northeast Times*, G.L. Publications, MG Road, Guwahati.

108. Industrialisation Sets Back to Farm income, 21 January 1992.

109. Economics of Green Tea, 28 May 1992.

110. Indian Tea in Syria, 16 June 1992.

111. Indian Tea in Jordan, June 21, 1992.

112. Indian Tea in Libya, July 07, 1992.

113. National Bank's Role for Tea Development, July 12, 1992.

114. The Role of National Bank for Development of Tea Industry, July 15, 1992.

114. Dry Land and Rain fed Farming, November 18, 1992.

115. Potentials of Horticulture Crops, November 28, 1992.

116. Market Potential of Indian Tea in Syria, December 10, 1992.

117. Cashew Nut Plantation, December 19, 1992.

f. Financial Express, Mumbai.

118. Green Tea Peep Into the Past, 07 November 1992.

119. Rain Fed and Dry Land Farming A Balanced Agricultural Strategy Vital, 02 January 1993.

g. *Eastern Mirror,* Dimapur, Nagaland.

120. Economics of Organic Farming—A case for Banana Plantation (Dec. 27, 2005)

121. Dairy Industry in 21st Century, January 4, 2005.

122. Problems of Agricultural Marketing in Nagaland, February 26, 2005.
123. The Role of SHGs in Poverty Allivation, October 20, 2005.
124. The Development of Handicrafts and Handloom in Nagaland, November 16, 2005.
125. Economics of Tea cultivation in Kangra, December,18, 2005.
126. Himachal Pradesh Tea Industry—A Revival Package, 15 January, 2006.
127. Agricultural Economy of Nagaland—Opportunities and Challenges, 20, February, 2006.
128. Village Development Board as Financial Institution—Published in three instalments on 15, 16 and17 April, 2007.

h. *National Bank News Review*, NABARD, Mumbai.

129. A Fresh Insight Into the Problems of Rural Development in the North East Region, February 1992.
130. Brackish Water Fish Culture A Case Study, January- March Issue, 1995.
131. Agro Processing Sector—Some Issues, July- September, 2004.

i Financing Agriculture, Agriculture Finance Corporation, Dhanaraj Mahal, Ist Floor,Chatrapati Shivaji Marg, Mumbai 400001, Tel No. 2028924, Fax 022-2028966, *E mail: (i) afcl@bom vsnl.net.in, (ii) piplapure@afcmails.com*

132. Horticulture Strives Well in Food and Nutritional Security, April-June 2000, Vol. XXXII, No. 1.
133. Agricultural Extension Assessment of various Models, October-December 2000, Vol. XXXII, No. 2.
134. Bio-technology for Indian Farmers, July-September 2001, Vol. 33, No. 3.
135. Water Resources Management—A Long Term Planning and Judicious Use of Water and Food Security, October-December 2001, Vol. 33, No. 4.
136. Evaluation Studies of Self Help Groups, April–June 2002, Vol. 34, No. 2.
137. Economics of Medicinal Plants, July–September 2003, Vol. 34, No. 3.
138. Boosting of Agricultural Exports—Opportunities and Challenges, Janurary-March, 2005.
139. Dairy Development in the Context of Globalization, January–March, 2006.

J. Man and Development, Center for Research in Rural and

Industrial Development, Sector 19 A, Madhya Marg, Chandigarh 160019, E mail cridchd@sancharnet.in

140. Agricultural Extension: A Critical Analysis of Various Models, September 2001, Vol. XXXIII, No. 3.

k. *Indian Journal of Agricultural Marketing,* Indian Society of Agricultural Marketing, Nagpur, 57/ IV, Seminary Hills, Nagpur 440006, Email — kumar81@indianet,

141. Primary Marketing of India Tea, Annual Conference Issue, December 2000.

142. *Marketing of Indian Tea—A Review,* Sept. 2001, Vol. 33, No. 3.

l. *Afro-Asian Journal of Rural Development,* No. 2, State Guest houses Complex, Chanakyapuri,New Delhi- 110021, Phone (011) 4100475, 6877783, 61115936, Fax Noto (011) 4672045,6115937 ,E mail aardohq@nde.vsnl.net.in

143 Marketing of Mango processing under Institutional Finance—A case Study in Andhra Pradesh, July-December 2001,Vol. XXXIV, No 2.

m *Indian Association of Social Science Institutions (IASSI) Quarterly Journal,* Care of Institute of Applied Man Power Research, Indra Prasthousanda Estate, New Delhi, Gram Samaj Vidya, New Delhi, Tel 3315284, 3356834, E mail stiassi@ bol. net. in

144. Indian Tea No Longer A Fashionable Slogan, April- June 2002,Vol. 19, No. 4.

145. Agro Processing—A Link between Agriculture and Industry, Jan-March, 2004 (jointly with Dr. K.G. Karmakar).

146. Sustainable Tea Plantation Management, Jan-March 2004 (jointly with Sarda Banerjee)

147. China's P'ure Tea—Tea with Miraculous Function, Oct–Dec 2005.

n. *Times Agriculture Journal,* The Economic Times and NABARD, The Times of India Building, Dr. D. N. Road, Mumbaito 400001,Eto mailprittik@marwar.com (ii) b2bedit @ timegroup.com

148. All Hands on Deck, September-October Issue, 2002

149. Horticulture An Overview Poised for Golden Revolution, November-December Issue, 2002.

148. Financing Horticulture January-February Issue, 2003.

149. A Difficult Terrain, July-August Issue, 2003.

o. Waste Lands News Society for Promotion of Waste Lands Development, 14-A Vishnu Digamber Marg, New Delhi 110002, e mail: spwd@vsnl.com, Editor Sujata Kausik

150. Water Vision, Jointly with Dr. K. G. Karmakar and Sarda Banerjee, November, 2004 January, 2005.

p. Kurukshetra, A journal of Rural Development, Room Noto 655/661, Nirman Bhavan, A wing, (GateNo.5) Ministry of Rural Development, New Delhi to 110011, E mailto kurupage@ yahoo. co. in. Editor Anjani Bhushan, Assistant Editor Kalama.

151. Corporate Partnership for Agricultural Development Vol. 53, No. 6, April 2005.

152. Eco Labeling in Agriculture, January 2006.

q. *Yojana, Journal of Rural Development,* Room No. 655/ 661, Nirman Bhavan, A wing, (Gate No. 5), Ministry of Rural Development, New Delhi 110011.

153. Tea Industry at the Cross Roads, Independence Special Issue, 15 August, 2005.

r. Agriculture Today—The National Agriculture Magazine, Editor, MJ Khan, C 17, III Floor, Lajpat Nagar I, New Delhi, 110024, E amil: agricult@del3.vsnl.net.in and editor@agriculture-day.org

154. Economics of Organic Farming, October 2005 issue, Volume-VIII, No. 10.

155. Ecolabeling in Agricultural Products December issue, 2005.

D. Books by Other Authors

155. Sarkar, Gautam K. 1972, *The World Tea Economy,* New Delhi Oxford University Press.

156. V.N. Asopa, 2004, Competitiveness of Global Tea Trade Oxford and IBH Publishing Company Pvt Ltd., New Delhi.

157. Banerjee, Barundev (1993): *Tea Production and Processing,* New Delhi, Oxford, IBH and Publishing Company.

158. Arunachalam, K. (1995), *A Handbook of Indian Tea,* Coonoor, The Tamil Nadu Tea Plantation Corporation Ltd.

159. Dr. K.G. Karmakar (1995), *Agricultural Project & Management for Banks,* Popular Prakashan, Mumbai.

161. Dr. K.G. Karmakar (1999), *Rural Credit, Micro-Finance and SHGs,* Sage Publications, New Delhi.

162. Dr K.G. Karmakar (2002), The Silence Drums: A Review of Tribal Economics Development, Northern Book Center, New Delhi.

163. Dr. K.G. Karmakar, about 28 papers are published in the various fields viz. Agriculture, Rural Development, Management, Plantation & Horticulture etc. in the leading Journals of National and International repute.

164. Vijay Dudeja, Spot Light of Tea 65.

165. Culpin, Claude (1986): *Tractors—Use of Farming and Farm Machinery.*

168. Kamble, H.G. and Panwar, J.S. (1985), Pattern of Use and Maintenance of Tractors on A Mechanised, Farm–A Case Study, *Journal of Institution of Engineers, Agricultural Engineering* 67: 111–113.

169. Maheshwari, S. K. and Singh, B. (1987), Analysis of Repair Cost of Various Systems of Indigenous Agricultural tractors, Paper presented at Annual Convention of Indian Society of Agricultural engineers held at JNKVV, Jabalpur, 9-11 March.

170. Singh, B. and Singh, K. N., (1991) Utilization of Different Models of Tractors on Large Mechanized Farms. Proceedinkgs of Annual Convention of Indian Society of Agricultural Engineers held at IARI, New Delhi, India 9-11 October.

171. Shyam, M., (1992) Farm Tractor Utilization in Selected Districts of Madhya Pradesh, Indian Journal of Agricultural Engineering 2(1): 12-16 March.

172. Barua, D.N. (1989), Science and Practice in Tea Culture, Tae Research Association, Jorhat, Assam, India.

173. Shri D. Ganguly, CTC Segment Roller and its Reshaping at the Tea Factory, Director Vikram, Agro Tech Services Pvt. Ltd.

174. Shri C. E. Sooria Moorthousandi, Advanced and Microwave Technology, Dept. of Solar Energy Service, Madurai Kamraj University.

148. J.K. Bhavannani and S Sareen (1990). Standardisation in the field of Processed Foods. *Ind. Food Packer.* Mar–Apl.

149. B. Roy 1991. Safety of Tea Packaging in Plastic Films and Laminates. Seminar Flexible Packaging in Tea, IIP.

175. R.N. Chatterjee, Commercial Model of MC Tear Rotorvane Technical Manager, Andrew Yule Co. Ltd.

176. Rupai Tea Estate, James Waren Group, Annual Resports 1991, 1994, 1995, 1996, 1997

177. Tea Research Association, Jorhat, Assam, "Two Leaf and a Bud".

178. C. A. Harler, Tea Manufacture.

179. Surjeet Ghosh, CTC Roller Driver System, Group Engineer Warant Tea Company Ltd. and Member of Technical Committee of TRA, TOCKLAI, Jorhat.

180. Anonymous, (1999), Banks to assist West Bengal Small Tea Growers, *The Assam Review & Tea News*, 88(9) p. 38-39.

181. I. Sharma, Khemraj, (1999), *Tea industry in India: An Introduction,* N L Publishers, Dibrugarh, Assam.

182. Eden, T., *Tea,* Third Edition, London.

183. Eden, T., *World Crops.*

184. Forests Denys, *Tea for the British.*

181. Suchanti, R. (Ed) (2000), *Tea Market Annual Report and Statistics 1999,* J. Thousandomas & Company Private limited, Kolkata.

182. *The Statesman*, Where the Land under Tea is Disputed? 14.10.1994:7 (Pabitra Dey)

183. *Uttarbanga Sambad,* Naya Cha Bagan: Jatilata Door Hachhe, 03.02.2000:5

184. *Uttarbanga Sambad,* Chhoto Cha Bagan Niye Ashabadi Tripurar Mantry, 22.02.2000:4.